ANDERSON PUBLIC LIBRARY
ANDER
P9-CEG-308

2199

wrinkled pgs. 1/18 JH

50¢

lonely planet

Austria

Neal Bedford, Gemma Pitcher

WITHDRAWN

Contents

Lonely Planet books provide independent advice. Lonely Planet does not accept advertising in guidebooks, nor do we accept payment in exchange for listing or endorsing any place or business. Lonely Planet writers do not accept discounts or payments in exchange for positive coverage of any sort.

Lonely Planet Bücher geben unabhängige Ratschläge. Lonely Planet akzeptiert keine Werbung in seinen Reiseführern; ebenso werden für Erwähnung oder Empfehlung einzelner Orte oder Firmen keine Zahlungen entgegengenommen. Die Autoren von Lonely Planet akzeptieren weder Zahlungen noch Preisnachlässe als Gegenleistung für eine positive Berichterstattung.

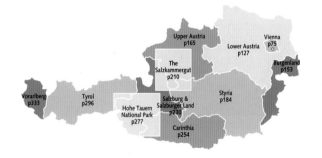

Destination Austria

With such an abundance of natural beauty and culture, the small realm of Austria (Öster-reich), in the heart of Central Europe, sure packs a punch.

Its dominating feature is the magnificent Eastern Alps, where ecstatic skiers and snow-boarders carve up the slopes during winter, and over summer walkers and hikers traverse its ridges and valleys under a rejuvenating sun. It may lack an ocean, but who cares when you have around 6000 cool alpine lakes to splash around in?

Complementing such splendour is human genius. Exquisite palaces, sublime baroque abbeys, powerful castles, soaring Gothic cathedrals and subtle Jugendstil houses all vie for your attention. Mozart, Beethoven, Haydn and Schubert are effortlessly reproduced by orchestras and street buskers alike, while unfathomable art collections make you wonder if *any* more art actually exists in the world.

Austria's enchantments don't stop there. Its cities are charmers, which seamlessly inter-weave tradition with the modern world: horse-drawn carriage rides, classical concerts, con-temporary art and progressive clubs sit comfortably side by side. Take to the countryside and all this transforms again; grizzled farmers sell wine in 2L bottles, children greet complete strangers on the street, and alpine culture, with its yodelling and thigh-slapping, is still primetime telly.

So leave any preconceived notions of Austria gained from the likes of *The Sound of Music* or *The Third Man* behind and experience possibly the best combination of nature and culture on the planet.

CHRIS MELLOR

ELEVATION

3000m
1500m
1000m
400m
0

Nuremberg

Danube

Regensburg

GERMANY

INNSBRUCK (p299)
The Austrian Alps capital with a
medieval heart and a modern soul

SALZBURG (p234)
Birthplace of Mozart and a city of
homogeneous baroque architecture

Braunau am Inn

MUNICH

SALZBURG

Hallein

*Bodensee
(Lake Constance)*

Hard   Bregenz

Lustenau   Dornbirn
Hohenems

Feldkirch

Bludenz   St Anton
am Arlberg

VORARLBERG   Landeck

A12   INNSBRUCK
Hall

TYROL   A13

Brenner Pass
(1374m)

Kufstein

Wörgl   Kitzbühel

Schwaz

Zell am See

Werfen

Saalfelden
Bischofshofen

SALZBURG
(SALZBURGER LAND)

Grossglockner
(3797m)

Bad Gastein

CENTRAL A

Hohe Tauern
National Park

LIECHTENSTEIN

SWITZERLAND

EAST TYROL
(OSTTIROL)

Lienz

HOHE TAUERN NATIONAL PARK (p277)
Europe's largest national park and
Austria's most spectacular alpine scenery

TYROL'S VALLEYS (p325)
Steep, narrow, awe-inspiring alpine valleys
once carved by unstoppable glaciers

GROSSGLOCKNER ROAD (p285)
Winding road through epic countryside,
climbing to Austria's highest peak

ITALY

Trento

50 km
30 miles

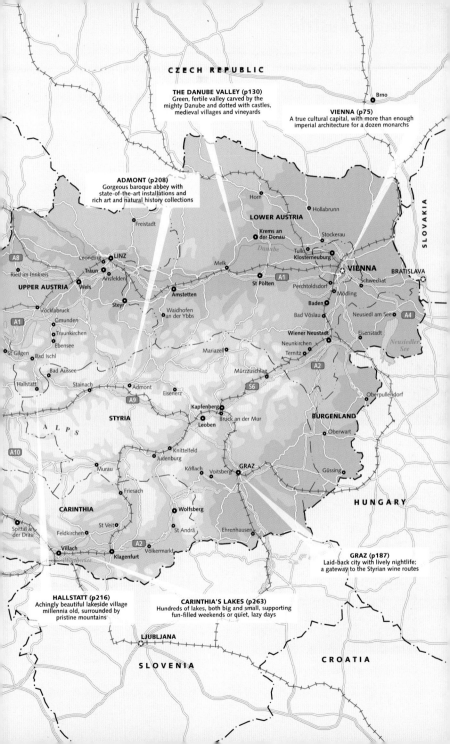

CZECH REPUBLIC

THE DANUBE VALLEY (p130)
Green, fertile valley carved by the
mighty Danube and dotted with castles,
medieval villages and vineyards

VIENNA (p75)
A true cultural capital, with more than enough
imperial architecture for a dozen monarchs

ADMONT (p208)
Gorgeous baroque abbey with
state-of-the-art installations and
rich art and natural history collections

Brno

Horn

Freistadt

LOWER AUSTRIA

Krems an
der Donau
Hollabrunn
Stockerau

Danube

A8
Leonding LINZ
Traun
Ansfelden
Ried im Innkreis

Melk
St Pölten
A1

Tulln
Klosterneuburg

VIENNA
Schwechat
BRATISLAVA

SLOVAKIA

UPPER AUSTRIA
Wels

Steyr

Amstetten

Perchtoldsdorf
Mödling

Vöcklabruck

Waidhofen
an der Ybbs

Baden
Bad Vöslau

Neusiedl am See
A4

A1
Gmunden
Traunkirchen
Ebensee
St Gilgen
Bad Ischl
Bad Aussee

Mariazell

Wiener Neustadt
Neunkirchen
Ternitz

Eisenstadt

*Neusiedler
See*

Hallstatt
Stainach
Admont
A9
Eisenerz

Mürzzuschlag
A2
S6

Oberpullendorf

A L P S

Kapfenberg
Bruck an der Mur
Leoben

STYRIA

BURGENLAND

A10

Knittelfeld
Judenburg

Oberwart

Murau

Köflach
Voitsberg
GRAZ

Güssing

Friesach

CARINTHIA

Wolfsberg

H U N G A R Y

Spittal an
der Drau
Feldkirchen
St Veit
St Andrä
Ehrenhausen

GRAZ (p187)
Laid-back city with lively nightlife;
a gateway to the Styrian wine routes

Villach
A2
Klagenfurt
Völkermarkt
Wörthersee

HALLSTATT (p216)
Achingly beautiful lakeside village
millennia old, surrounded by
pristine mountains

CARINTHIA'S LAKES (p263)
Hundreds of lakes, both big and small, supporting
fun-filled weekends or quiet, lazy days

LJUBLJANA

SLOVENIA

CROATIA

Austria's highlights dot the length and breadth of the country. Stunning baroque abbeys and palaces, picturesque historic towns, dominating castles, deep cool lakes and majestic mountain ranges all vie for your attention.

Admire Stephansdom (p89), Vienna's glorious Gothic cathedral and its beloved icon

Ski the awesome Austrian Alps (p58)

Gaze at Michaelerkirche and Steyr Bridge in the picture-perfect town of Steyr (p176)

Wander the halls and gardens of Schloss Schönbrunn (p100), the epitome of imperial grandeur

See baroque at its absolute best in St Florian's Augustiner Chorherrenstift (p174)

Drive or cycle the winding Grossglockner road (p285), with staggering views on all sides

Escape to the far reaches of Tyrol's
Ötztal (p325)

Meander through Stift Melk (p131), a
magnificent baroque monastery on the
banks of the Danube

See *haflinger* horses grazing in the Zillertal (p315)

Getting Started

Austria is a traveller-friendly destination with a world-class transport system, well-maintained roads and information offices in almost every village. Its social infrastructure leaves no gaps: banks, hospitals, doctors, police, supermarkets – you name it, it's all easy to find and readily available. Distances between sights aren't massive, so you needn't worry about your butt going numb before you arrive at your destination.

Although Austria requires a minimum of planning, a few nights mulling over what you'd like to see doesn't do any harm; this will allow your travels to become all that more fluid once you hit the road.

WHEN TO GO

Summer sightseeing and winter sports make Austria a year-round destination and when to go depends on what you want to do or see. Festivals occur year-round, although the majority of music festivals are held between May and October.

For warm weather, aim for the months between April and October, although it must be said that April and October can swing from cold to warm all too quickly. The summer high season is in July and August, when crowds will be bigger and prices higher. Just because it's the high season doesn't mean it's the best time to visit; temperatures in cities can rise to uncomfortable levels, Austrians take their summer break at this time and many famous institutions close down, including the opera, the Spanish Riding School and the Vienna Boys' Choir. Consequently, June and September are also busy months for tourism, and are quite often the best times for city trips and hiking in the Alps.

During winter you'll find the cities less crowded and the hotel prices lower (except over Christmas and Easter), but it can get bitterly cold. Winter sports are in full swing from mid-December to late March, with the high season over Christmas and New Year and in February. The length of the skiing season depends on the altitude of the resort – skiing is possible on glaciers nearly year-round. Alpine resorts are very quiet from late April to mid June, and in November and early December; at these times some bars, restaurants and hotels close down. School children have week-long breaks over Christmas and during February, making it a good time to avoid the pistes.

Austria lies within the Central European climatic zone, though the eastern part of the country has what is called a Continental Pannonian

See Climate Charts (p351) for average temperatures and precipitation in Austria's major cities.

DON'T LEAVE HOME WITHOUT ...

- Double-checking the visa situation and your passport expiry date (p360)
- Organising a good health-insurance policy (p355)
- A spattering of the language, or a phrase book – a little goes a long way (p379)
- A servitude of politeness; Austrians love their greetings, titles, pleases and thank yous (p381)
- A good relationship with dogs; in Vienna, owners take them everywhere, including bars and restaurants
- Good hiking boots and swimming trunks; this is the land of mountains and lakes
- Hair dye, socks and sandals so you'll fit right in

climate, characterised by low precipitation, hot summers and moderate winters. The Alps have high precipitation, short summers and long winters, and visitors need to be prepared for a range of temperatures depending on altitude. Seasons are distinct. Summer falls between June and August and has the highest temperatures, but also the highest levels of rainfall. Winter can bite hard, especially in December, January and February. Spring and autumn bring changeable weather, but quite often the most comfortable temperatures.

COSTS & MONEY

Vienna is averagely expensive for a European city – cheaper than London, Paris, Zürich or Rome, similar to Munich, more expensive than Prague or Budapest. With the exception of plush ski resorts such as Lech and Kitzbühel, most of the rest of Austria is noticeably cheaper than Vienna, particularly if you're visiting less-touristed regions. Overall, Britons and Americans will probably find things pretty affordable.

Accommodation will invariably be the most expensive item on your budget. Budget travellers will get away with €16 in a hostel, mid-range with €45 in a hotel or pension (at the low end of the price scale) and top-end travellers, well, the sky's the limit; add another third to these prices for Vienna. Public transport is not outrageously expensive, but if you're moving around a lot or taking cable cars in the mountains, it will soon add up. Food and drink is on the cheap side of Western European standards; sticking to breakfast at your hotel or pension, a midday menu at lunch and a meal at night (both with drinks) will set you back around €25. Of course there are savings to be made; a sandwich on the run or eating at food stalls only costs about €3 to €4. Museums and attractions average around €4 to €5 for entry, but some can be as high as €10 or as low as €1.

To sum up, staying at a hostel, eating cheap, using public transport, visiting a museum and having a couple of beers at night costs around €45 per day. Using moderately priced hotels or pensions, taking trains between cities, eating out twice a day, going for drinks and visiting a big-ticket attraction will be about €130 per day.

Note that children, students and senior citizens often pay lower prices.

TRAVEL LITERATURE

A great deal has been written about Austria, especially Vienna, but most authors have focused on Austria's rich historical context rather than personal travels through this mountainous land. There are, however, a few tales of trials, tribulations and thrills in Austria which provide a fine backdrop for your own journey.

A superb starting point is *A Time of Gifts*, the first volume of Patrick Leigh Fermor's trilogy detailing his epic and inspiring walk from the Hook of Holland to Constantinople in 1933–34. Written 40 years after his feet took him along the Danube Valley and through Vienna, this rich, evocative tale is an insight into Austria between the world wars.

In *Danube*, Claudio Magris passes an erudite, Italian eye over the length of the Danube in his travel journal from the mid-1980s, and naturally spends time in Austria. His sharp, individual style tackles topics like the source of the Danube (a leaky tap in a remote mountain farmhouse, according to one sedimentologist) and larger-than-life characters such as Wittgenstein and Kafka.

Edward Crankshaw combines travel literature and historical detail in *Vienna: The Image of a Culture in Decline*. This study of the golden city

HOW MUCH?

Lederhosen made from wild-pig leather €275

Achtel at a *Heurigen/ Buschenshank* €1 to €1.50

Wiener Schnitzel €8 to €12

Double room in pension from €45

Single ticket on public transport €1.50

LONELY PLANET INDEX

Litre of gas/petrol €0.95 to €1

Litre of bottled water from €0.35

Bottle of Steigl/Ottakring beer in a bar around €3

Souvenir T-shirt €15

Kasekrainer €3 to €3.50

TOP TENS
BEST READS

Immersing yourself in a good book is the perfect way to learn about contemporary issues and culture and grasp a sense of people and place. The following page-turners have won critical acclaim in Austria and abroad. See p43 for more on literature.

- *Death of Virgil* by Hermann Broch
- *Radetzky March* by Joseph Roth
- *Cutting Timber* by Thomas Bernhard
- *Setting Free the Bears* by John Irving
- *Burning Secret and Other Stories* by Stefan Zweig
- *Lust* by Elfriede Jelinek
- *Play of the Eyes* by Elias Canetti
- *Vienna Coffeehouse Wits, 1890–1938* by Harold B Segel (ed)
- *Night Games: And Other Stories and Novellas* by Arthur Schnitzler
- *Man Without Qualities, Vol 1* by Robert Musil

MUST-SEE FILMS

One of the best and most relaxing ways to do a bit of predeparture planning and dreaming is to curl up on a comfy sofa with a bowl of popcorn and press play on your remote. Head down to your local video store to pick up these flicks, which range from the best-known films about Austria to the cheesiest. See p44 for more details.

- *The Third Man* (1949) directed by Carol Reed
- *Indien* (1993) directed by Paul Harather
- *Funny Games* (1997) directed by Michael Haneke
- *Dog Days* (2001) directed by Ulrich Seidl
- *Lovely Rita* (2001) directed by Jessica Hausner
- *Amadeus* (1984) directed by Milos Forman
- *Foreigners Out!* (2002) directed by Paul Poet
- *Siegfried* (1924) directed by Fritz Lang
- *Der Bockerer* (1981) directed by Franz Antel and Rainer C Ecke
- *The Sissi Trilogy* (1955–1957) directed by Ernst Marischka

OUR FAVOURITE FESTIVALS & EVENTS

Austrians love festivals and you can always count on some kind of celebration going on around the country. The following list is our Top 10, but other festivities and events are listed in the Directory chapter (p353) and throughout this book.

- Graz Erzählt (Graz), May and June (p193)
- Wiener Festwochen (Vienna), May and June (p107)
- Musikwochen Millstatt (Millstatt), May to September (p275)
- Styriarte (Graz), June and July (p193)
- Milka Chocolate Festival (Bludenz), July (p343)
- Salzburger Festspiele (Salzburg), July and August (p241)
- Bregenz Festival (Bregenz), July and August (p338)
- Lange Nacht der Museen (countrywide), September (p105)
- Halleiner Stadtfestwoche (Hallein), September (p251)
- Viennale Film Festival (Vienna), October (p107)

in the early- and mid-1930s is certainly nostalgic but still manages to tell it like it is.

Arguably the best account of Jewish life in Vienna between the World Wars is *Last Waltz in Vienna: The Destruction of a Family 1842–1942*, by George Clare. This heartbreaking autobiography details one family's fate at the hands of the Nazis; it's a superb read and an insight into how the ordinary lives of so many were forever changed from one day to the next.

Stefan Zweig's *The World of Yesterday* is an extraordinary account of *fin de siécle* Vienna, a time when intellectual brotherhood tried to stop the destruction of Europe. It's all that more poignant considering Zweig, who had been forced into exile by the Nazis, committed suicide in 1942 on completion of the book.

For a tongue-in-cheek look at Austrians and their society, don't pass over Louis James' highly amusing *Xenophobe's Guide to the Austrians*. This book not only tells you about the locals' quirky traits but also reveals *why* Austrians are the way they are.

Want to stay in a castle? Then check out www .schlosshotels.co.at.

INTERNET RESOURCES

Austrian Federal Government (www.austria.gv.at) Gateway to various ministries of the Austrian government.

Austrian National Tourist Office (www.austria.info) The perfect introduction to Austria in a number of languages, with plenty of information and links.

Austrian Press & Information Service (www.austria.org) US-based site with current affairs and links to a range of topics.

Austro Search (www.austrosearch.at) Exhaustive online directory of Austrian businesses and organisations.

Lonely Planet (www.lonelyplanet.com) General facts on Austria, links to Austrian sites and reports from fellow travellers on the Thorn Tree.

Tiscover (www.tiscover.com) Useful site for information on the provinces; comes complete with online booking facilities.

Itineraries

CLASSIC ROUTES

VIENNA TO SALZBURG   Two weeks

Begin at the city without cultural equal, **Vienna** (p75). A good few days could easily be spent here, but leave time for excursions to the **Neusiedler See** (p159) and the **Wienerwald** (Vienna Woods; p144). Follow the Danube through **Klosterneuburg** (p126), **Tulln** (p137) and onto the **Wachau** (p132). Highlights abound in this area, including charming **Krems An Der Donau** (p134), medieval **Dürnstein** (p133) and abbey-dominated **Melk** (p130). Stick close to the Danube until you reach **Mauthausen** (p175), then head to **Steyr** (p176), an achingly pretty town at the confluence of the Enns and Steyr rivers. Backtrack north to Upper Austria's bustling hub, **Linz** (p167), and take time out for **St Florian's abbey** (p174).

Continue southwest to **Gmunden** (p222), the gateway to the Salzkammergut lakes. Not far south is **Bad Ischl** (p212), and only a little further south again is **Hallstatt** (p216). No trip to Austria would be complete without a cable car ride, so take a trip up the **Dachstein** (p218) before following the stream of pilgrims west to **St Wolfgang** (p226). The only thing left to do now is continue onto Mozart's birthplace, **Salzburg** (p234).

There is no better way to sample Austria's historical and natural wonders than to journey along the Danube between two of the country's most celebrated cities, Vienna and Salzburg.

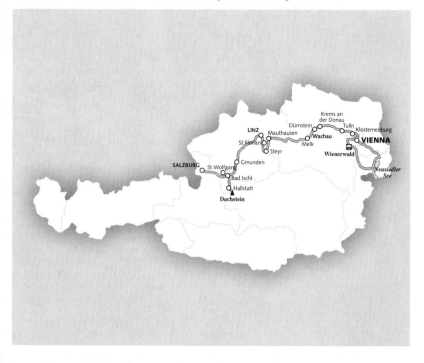

THE SOUTHERN ROUTE   Two Weeks

Wake up bright and early in **Vienna** (p75) and spend the next couple of days exploring as many nooks and crannies as time permits. Jump on the A2 autobahn heading south and call in at Burgenland's compact capital and favourite of Haydn, **Eisenstadt** (p156); while here don't miss the opportunity for a glass of Grüner Veltliner at **Rust** (p159) and a dip in the **Neusiedler See** (p159). Continue south, but veer west soon after **Wiener Neustadt** (p149) and take the **Semmering Pass** (p151) into the Murz valley until you reach **Bruck an der Mur** (p205). The trail once again turns south, following the cool, alpine Mur river right to the gates of **Graz** (p187), a city with a graceful charm and lively nightlife.

After Graz, Carinthia's lakeside capital **Klagenfurt** (p256) awaits, but call in on two destinations along the way. **Burg Hochosterwitz** (p271), perched high on a hill, is a true classic, and **Freisach's** (p268) medieval heart is as authentic as it gets. A dip in the thermally-warmed **Wörthersee** (p263) is next on the list, before moving onto bustling **Villach** (p264), a fine base for exploring the area's mountains and lakes. The next port of call is Millstatter See and its two attractive towns, **Millstatt** (p275) and **Spittal an der Drau** (p273).

The best however is saved for last; the **Hohe Tauern National Park** (p277), with its snow-capped peaks, cascading waterfalls, outdoor pursuits and hairpin corners is simply a mind-blowing experience. The highlight is the **Grossglockner road** (p285), a winding, scenic extravaganza that leads north, eventually connecting with roads to **Salzburg** (p234).

For a taste of culture, wine, lakes and the highest peaks in Austria, follow this route, which takes you through the southern reaches of the country.

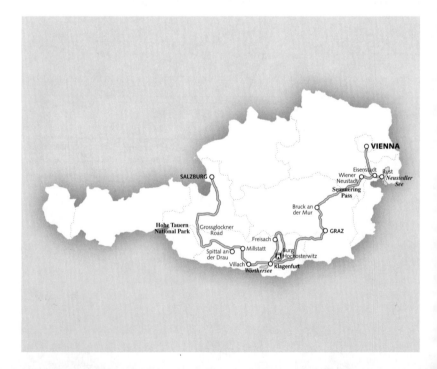

HAVE YOUR CAKE & EAT IT

One Month

What better place to start than the capital, **Vienna** (p75), with all its cultural delights. From here, head west following the **Danube Valley** (p130), taking in a few castles and wineries along the way. **Linz** (p167) and its museums is the next up, with a side trip to historical **Steyr** (p176), before the lakes of the **Salzkammergut** (p210) command your attention as far south as **Hallstätter See** (p216) and **Dachstein** (p218). **Salzburg** (p234), with its music, Mozart balls and baroque magnificence will enthral for a few days, but the Alps await further west.

From Salzburg, slowly wind your way west to the capital of the Austrian Alps, **Innsbruck** (p299), stopping in at the old silver mint towns of **Schwaz** (p312) and **Hall in Tirol** (p311). To truly appreciate the area's mountainous extravaganza, follow your nose down the narrow **Zillertal** (p315) and **Ötztal** (p325) valleys, and then skip further west to the green hills, stark mountains and wooden houses of the **Bregenzerwald** (p341). **Bregenz** (p336) and the graceful Bodensee are only a stone's throw from here, but the next destination, the glorious **Hohe Tauern National Park** (p277), is a long back-track east.

Continuing east from the park you reach Carinthia, a province famous for it's thermally-warmed lakes such as the **Wörthersee** (p263), after which the country's second-largest hub, **Graz** (p187) requires a minimum of two days' exploration. Make a quick detour to the sublime abbey of **Admont** (p208) and the opencast mine at **Eisenerz** (p207) before climbing over the **Semmering Pass** (p151) and down onto the wide, open Pannonian plains, finally coming to rest back at Vienna.

If you have plenty of time for exploration, why not take in the whole country? This suggested itinerary passes through the major highlights of Austria, plus a few of its minor ones.

ROADS LESS TRAVELLED

NOT A MOUNTAIN IN SIGHT

Start your trip in the middle of Burgenland at **Lockenhaus** (p163), a town once home to the Blood Countess Elizabeth Báthory, and featuring a bold castle. Before moving on, take time to sample the Blaufränkisch wine so famous in this region. The road then takes you west past another castle, **Bernstein** (p163), before heading south to the soothing spa waters of **Bad Tatzmannsdorf** (p163). If you'd rater bathe amongst Hundretwasser's unique architectural vision, skip Tazmannsdorf for **Rogner-Bad Blumau** (p202) in Styria. Crossing back into Burgenland once more, turn south and before long the arresting sight of **Güssing Castle** (p164) comes into view.

Next there is only one place to head: **Riegersburg** (p202) in Styria. Its castle is possibly the most impressive of its kind in Austria. **Schloss Kapfenstein** (p203), Riegersburg's more refined cousin, has excellent dining and accommodation. The countryside here is Austria's equivalent of Chianti in Tuscany: a wine-lovers paradise, crisscrossed by Styrian wine routes. Not far west of Kapfenstein is the small, rural spa **Bad Gleichenberg** (p202), while only 25km further south on the Slovenia border is the walled spa town **Bad Radkersberg** (p202). From here, the road veers west through the heart of the Styrian wine country, taking in pretty **Ehrenhausen** (p201) and Celtic-rich **Grossklein** (p201) before winding up at the gates of **Deutschlandsberg's Castle** (p201), surrounded by vineyard-covered hills.

A trip through Austria without spotting a snow-capped peak? Are you crazy, you ask? Certainly not; this suggested itinerary reveals that Austria is not only home to the Alps, but a rich array of castles, spas and vineyards too.

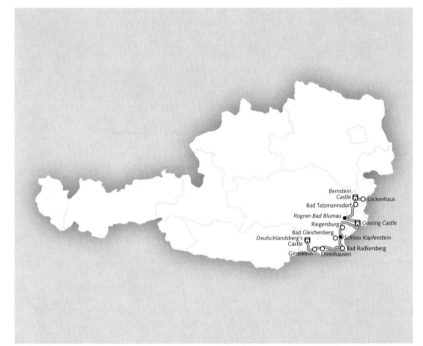

Bernstein Castle • Lockenhaus
Bad Tatzmannsdorf
Rogner-Bad Blumau • Güssing Castle
Riegersburg
Bad Gleichenberg
Deutschlandsberg's Castle • Schloss Kapfenstein
Grossklein • Bad Radkersberg
Ehrenhausen

TAILORED TRIPS

WORLD HERITAGE SITES

Vienna's **Innere Stadt** (p89), an open-air museum of epic proportions, is not the only Unesco site within the city; the opulent baroque palace and gardens of **Schloss Schönbrunn** (p100) also make the list. Not far from the city's border is **Neusiedler See** (p159), a vast expanse of water – Central Europe's largest steppe lake in fact – encircled by vineyards and historical towns. Only an hour further south is the Alps' seminal **Semmering Railway** (p151), a remarkable feat of civil engineering from the mid-1800s. The **Wachau** (p132), not far west of Vienna, is a region of unmatched beauty along the Danube, characterised by steep, forested slopes, vineyards, quaint wine villages and imposing fortresses at every river bend. Further west in the southern reaches of Salzkammergut is another of Austria's natural World Heritage sites, **Hallstatt-Dachstein** (p216). This breathtaking region of towering peaks and calm lakes has been home to social and economic activity since prehistoric times.

Rivalling Vienna's Innere Stadt for the best-preserved old town is **Salzburg's Historical Centre** (p238), a grand mix of flamboyant Gothic and baroque architecture. And not to be outdone is the old centre of **Graz** (p187), with is harmonious mix of architectural styles from the Middle Ages onwards.

THE SOUND OF MUSIC

Vienna has the lion's share of Austria's world-class music venues, performers and festivals, including the **Staatsoper** (p119), the home of opera, the **Musikverein** (p119), with its unequalled acoustics, the angelic **Vienna Boys' Choir** (p120), the **Wiener Festwochen** (p107) and the **OsterKlang Festival** (p106). This is not to say the rest of the country can't put on a musical show though. Vorarlberg's capital, Bregenz, hosts the **Bregenz Festival** (p338), while nearby Schwarzenberg is the site of the **Schubertiade** (p341), featuring works exclusively by Schubert. Tyrol's main city Innsbruck comes alive to the sound of music in July and August during its **Festival of Early Music** (p306), and pride of place on Salzburg's musical calendar is **Salzburger Festspiele** (p241), a celebration of music ranging from Mozart to modern works.

Upper Austria's capital Linz is home to the internationally renowned **Brucknerfest** (p171), and Millstatt in Carinthia is inundated during its **Musikwochen** (p275). Graz, Styria's capital, has the **Styriarte** (p193) festival, while Burgenland plays host to the **International Haydntage** (p158) in Eisenstadt, rock, jazz and pop concerts in **Wiesen** (p159) and one of the country's largest operetta events in Möbisch am See, the **Seefestspiele** (p161).

FOR THE LITTLE 'UNS

While you're digesting Vienna's sublime art collections, drop the kids off at **Zoom** (p104), an arts and crafts bonanza for children up to 14, or Schönbrunn's **Kindermuseum** (p104), which transforms them into royalty for a day. Otherwise get some fresh air at the **Prater** (p97), an enormous city park complete with funfair and playgrounds, the **Tiergarten** (p101), the oldest zoo in the world, or the **Donauinsel** (p97), an island perfect for swimming and mucking about. Nearby **Neusiedler See** (p159), with its shallow waters and water sports, is another spot for kids to enjoy the water.

Graz's **FriDa & FreD** (p192) is a children's museum in the same mould as Vienna's Zoom, while the city's **Schlossberg Cave Railway** (p192), with its fairytale scenes, is fun for kids of all ages.

Take them on a trip around the world's most famous architectural sites at **Minimundus miniature park** (p259) in Klagenfurt or inspire future puppet-

eers at the **puppet museums** (p267) near Villach. While in Linz, let the electronic wizardry of the **Ars Electronica** (p171) entertain them, or trundle them up the **Pöstlingberg** (p171) for views of the city and a ride on its grotto railway. If you're way out west, stop at Dornbirn's **Inatura** (p340) to explore nature up close and personal.

At Eisenerz in Styria, take 'em underground or for a ride on the world's largest taxi at **Erzberg mine** (p207), or have them shooting down wooden miners' slides and riding the subterranean railway of Hallstatt's **Salzbergwerk** (p217).

The Authors

NEAL BEDFORD   Coordinating Author, Vienna, Lower Austria, Burgenland, Upper Austria, Styria, Tyrol & Vorarlberg

When Neal first came to Austria in 1994, all he knew about it was that Falco and Mozart were locals and there were no kangaroos. Since then he's learnt a lot; *Wurscht* and *Schaas* are the two most important words in the German language, *Käserkrainer* taste *much* better after a night on the turps and helping people move house is part-and-parcel of living in Vienna. He's managed to live in Vienna three times, swim in Salzkammergut's lakes, cycle around the Neusiedler See, bust his knee on Vorarlberg's ski slopes, and adopt a Lower Austrian family. Neal also worked on Lonely Planet's *Vienna* guide.

My Favourite Trip

Austria is dotted with places I would happily take a detour to see, but if I was to knock off those on the top of my list, I would start with **Vienna** (p75), a city close to my heart. I'd then head south to **Graz** (p187) for its museums and laid-back atmosphere, before heading north to my *Lieblings* stretch of Austria, the **Nationalpark Gesäuse** (p208) and **Admont Abbey** (p208), which lie side by side in the Enns valley. There is no way I could complete this trip without a visit to the **Hohe Tauern National Park** (p277), after which the connecting valleys of **Paznauntal** (p329) and **Montafon** (p344) would draw me in. I'd end my journey with my feet up in a rural pension in the heart of the **Bregenzerwald** (p341), enjoying the grand vista.

GEMMA PITCHER   Salzkammergut, Salzburg & Salzburger Land, Carinthia & Hohe Tauern National Park

Gemma Pitcher spent her childhood in the UK then Buckinghamshire with her nose buried in dusty travel books. These prompted her to don her backpack for the first time at 17, travelling through most of Europe and a good slice of Africa before returning to the UK to read English at Exeter University. She followed this with a year ski bumming in the Alps and then began work as a freelance travel writer. She speaks French and German and loves hiking, skiing and snow blading.

LAST EDITION

Mark Honan wrote the 1st, 2nd and 3rd editions of this book.

Snapshot

Like the rest of the world, Austrians have closely observed the goings-on in the Middle East in recent times. Public opinion rejected the invasion of Iraq, but this didn't exactly equate to extensive protests; people certainly took to the streets in 2003 and 2004, but numbers were in the thousands rather than the tens of thousands. Austria, as a neutral country, played no part in the Iraq war.

On the home front, domestic politics makes front-page headlines all too frequently. November 2002 saw the Austrian People's Party (ÖVP) make sweeping gains in the general election, but they took power in 2003 thanks to a coalition with the far-right Freedom Party (FPÖ). The coalition partner's controversial former leader, Jörg Haider, seemed on the way out – until he defied all expectations and regained his job as governor of Carinthia in 2004. Sadly, the country's president, Thomas Klestil, died two days before the end of his term in office, and sent the country into mourning.

Pension reform has caused major ripples in Austria's normally calm domestic pond. Objections to the government's proposed changes (which included a proposal to increase the statutory retirement age to 65 for men and 60 for women) came from every corner of society; between 100,000 and 200,000 Viennese took to the streets in protest, opposition politicians screamed blue murder and the country experienced the worst strikes since WWII. Despite the protests the reforms went ahead, and looking at the figures, it may well prove a wise move; immigration is the only motor of growth for the country and by 2035, every third Austrian will be more than 60 years of age.

As Europe pushes open its doors a little further, Austria seems to be battening down the hatches. In late 2003 a new asylum law – one of the most restrictive in Europe – was introduced; asylum-seekers may now face deportation while up for appeal, and full statements must be given within 72 hours of a person's arrival in the country. Fears of mass immigration from the east after EU expansion have been to date unfounded.

The Catholic Church, such an important institution in Austria's society for hundreds of years, has recently been rocked by scandal, causing thousands to leave the faith. In 2004, a 27-year-old trainee priest was sentenced to six months' imprisonment for possession of child pornography. Eight others were under suspicion but a lack of evidence led to no further arrests. The country's congregation had only just recovered from a 1995 scandal, when Austria's top churchman, the late Cardinal Hans Hermann Groer, was ousted by the Vatican over molestation allegations.

Although Arnold Schwarzenegger left Austria more than 30 years ago, he still manages to invade conversations back home. His recent appointment as governor of California has raised his profile even further; Austrians wonder whether his meteoric political rise to fame will stop at the White House. For more information, see the boxed text 'The Terminator from Graz' (p193).

In 2004, provocative Austrian novelist and playwright Elfriede Jelinek won the Nobel prize for literature. Jelinek, whose work often belittles her home country, was both pleased and dismayed at receiving the award. At the time of writing she planned to boycott the December awards ceremony.

FAST FACTS

Population: 8,098,000

Number of mobile phones in Austria: 6,415,000

GDP: $224.3 billion

Inflation rate: 2.3%

Unemployment rate: 4%

Average monthly wage before tax: €1785

Number of dogs in Vienna: 65,000

History

Looking at the size of Austria, it's hard to believe that such a small country played such a grand role in the history of Europe; for centuries, its regal monarchies shaped the fortunes of untold burghers the length and breadth of the continent. But its history starts well before kings, queens and countries divided up Europe.

FROM THE BEGINNING

One of the earliest examples of human art, the 25,000-year-old *Venus of Willendorf*, was found in the Danube Valley, proving Austria has been inhabited since the Palaeolithic Age. The next major find – the body of a man – dates from the late Stone Age. Discovered frozen in a glacier in the Ötztaler Alpen (Ötztal Alps), Ötzi (his nickname) was perfectly preserved and a mere 5500 years old (see p326).

It wasn't until the Celts arrived from Gaul around 500 BC that civilisation truly took hold in Austria. They settled across the country, and made great use of the salt mines of Salzkammergut, particularly around Hallstatt (p216), and the north–south alpine trading routes. By the time the Romans rocked up around 15 BC, the Celts had extensive settlements in the Danube Valley, which soon became a central point for the new arrivals. This area, known as Pannonia, marked the northern border of the empire and served as a natural border between them and the advancing Germanic tribes from the north. Roman settlements centred on Carnuntum (p143) and Vindobona (the forerunner of Vienna), although *Limes* (fortifications) lined much of the Danube. Other important Roman centres around Austria include Brigantium (Bregenz; p336), Juvavum (Salzburg; p234), Flavia Solva (Leibnitz) and Virunum (north of Klagenfurt).

By the 5th century AD, the Roman Empire had collapsed and the Romans were beaten back by invading tribes. The importance of the Danube Valley as an east–west crossing meant successive waves of tribes and armies tried to gain control of the region; before and after the Roman withdrawal came the Teutons, Slavs, Huns, Goths, Franks, Bavarians and Avars. However, it was the Bavarians and Slavs that proved the most successful. Much of Austria was under the control of the Bavarians by the 7th century, but the Slavs, coming from the east, managed to move into what is now Carinthia and Styria.

AUSTRIA'S FIRST RULERS

The rise of Charlemagne, the king of the Franks, marked the end of the Dark Ages. Crowned Holy Roman Emperor (ruler of the German-speaking lands) in 800, he managed to brush aside all opposition in Central Europe and establish a territory in the Danube Valley known as the Ostmark (Eastern March) three short years later. Its borders were marked by the Rivers Enns, Raab and Drau. Upon his death in 814 the Carolingian empire was divided into three parts, and the Magyars had overrun Ostmark in determined invasions.

Learn more about iceman Ötzi (not to be confused with DJ Ötzi, who should remain frozen in ice) at www.archaeologie museum.it.

One of the few books to tackle the history of Austria from the Babenbergs through to the country's entry into the EU is *The Austrians: A Thousand Year Odyssey* by Gordon Brook-Shepard. It's a little light on detail but it's great for a general overview.

TIMELINE	976	996
	Babenburgs take control of Austrian lands	Ostarrichi, the forerunner of Österreich, is first mentioned in documents

The Magyars held sway over Ostmark till the arrival of Otto the Great, the controller of the eastern portion of Charlemagne's old empire. His defeat of the Hungarians at Augsburg in 955 passed the region back into Germanic hands. Seven years later Pope John XII crowned Otto as Holy Roman Emperor of the German princes, but in 976 Ostmark changed hands once again, landing in the lap of Leopold von Babenberg, a descendant of a noble Bavarian family. The Babenberg dynasty then proceeded to rule the territory for the next 270 years. However the region received no mention in imperial documents until 996, at the time referred to as 'Ostarrichi', the forerunner to modern-day Österreich.

The Babenbergs were a skilful bunch, and it wasn't long before their sphere of influence expanded: in the 11th century most of modern-day Lower Austria (including Vienna) was in their hands; a century later (1192) Styria and much of Upper Austria was safely garnered. Heinrich II 'Jasomirgott' (so called for his favourite exclamation 'Yes, so help me God') was the most successful of them all, convincing the Holy Roman Emperor to elevate the territory to a dukedom and moving his court to Vienna in 1156. This was a time of great prosperity for all of Austria.

In 1246 Duke Friedrich II died leaving no heirs in a battle with the Hungarians over the Austro-Hungarian border. This allowed the ambitious Bohemian king, Ottokar II, to move in and take control. He bolstered his claim to Austria by marrying Friedrich II's widow. Ottokar however refused to swear allegiance to the new Holy Roman Emperor, Rudolf of Habsburg, and his pride proved costly – Ottokar died in a battle against his powerful adversary at Marchfeld in 1278. Rudolf granted his two sons the fiefdoms of Austria and Styria in 1282, and thus began the rule of one of the most powerful dynasties in European history, a dynasty that would retain the reins of power right up to the 20th century.

THE EARLY HABSBURGS

The Habsburgs initially suffered a few setbacks (including some humiliating defeats by the Swiss) but managed to consolidate their position: Carinthia and Carniola were annexed in 1335, followed by Tyrol in 1363. These solid foundations allowed Rudolf IV to forge ahead with development; he founded the University of Vienna in 1356 and Gothic Stephansdom in 1359. He is more famous however for his forgery of the *Privilegium maius,* a document supposedly tracing the Habsburg lineage back to early Roman emperors.

In 1453 Friedrich III managed to genuinely acquire the status that was faked by Rudolf IV and was crowned Holy Roman Emperor. The crown remained in Habsburg hands until its cancellation by Napoleon in 1806. Friedrich also persuaded Pope Paul II to raise the status of Vienna to that of a bishopric in 1469. His ambition knew few bounds – his motto, *Austria Est Imperator Orbi Universo* (AEIOU), or *Alles Erdreich Ist Österreich Untertan,* expressed the view that the whole world was Austria's empire. To prove this he waged war against King Matthias Corvinus of Hungary (who famously quipped that the Holy Roman Empire was 'neither holy, Roman, nor an empire'), but he was not entirely successful; Corvinus managed to occupy Vienna from 1485 to 1490. He was also no friend of the archbishop of Salzburg, who sided with his opponents. Salzburg

Saint Leopold III of Babenberg (1096–1135) is the patron saint of Austria.

The Habsburgs ruled Austria and its extended lands from 1278 until 1918.

The distended lower jaw and lip, a family trait of the early Habsburgs, is discreetly played down in official portraits.

remained a powerful ecclesiastical principality until the 19th century when it finally fell into the hands of the Habsburgs.

What Friedrich could not achieve on the battlefield, his son, Maximillian I, acquired through marriage. Maximillian's marriage to Maria of Burgundy gained him Burgundy and the Netherlands, while his son Philip's marriage to Princess Juana of Castille gathered up Spain and its overseas lands. This prompted the proverb, adapted from the Ovid: 'Let others make war; you, fortunate Austria, marry!' The crowns of Bohemia and Hungary were obtained when the childless Hungarian King Lewis II died in the battle of Mohács in 1526.

After Philip's son Karl V took control of the thrown, the sun did not set on an empire that stretched from South America to the eastern reaches of Hungary. It was however too unwieldy for one person to rule, so in 1521 Karl abdicated and the territories were carved up; Austria, Bohemia and Hungary fell to his younger brother Ferdinand I and Spain and its colonies went to his (Karl's) son Philip II.

PROBLEMS WITH TURKS & RELIGION

Ferdinand became preoccupied with protecting his territories from the incursions of the Turks, who were rampant under the leadership of Süleyman the Magnificent, sultan of the Ottoman Empire. Styria and Burgenland were particularly vulnerable to attack. The Turks overran

Jews were a convenient scapegoat for Austria's rulers long before the Nazis came along; the first Jewish community was run out of Vienna in 1420.

Austria's greatest military hero, Prince Eugène of Savoy, was in fact French. Refused entry into the French Army by Louis XIV, Eugène went on to humiliate him on the battlefield.

THIRD TIME'S THE CHARM

The Ottoman Empire viewed Vienna as 'the city of the golden apple', but it wasn't *Apfelstrüdel* they were after in their two great sieges. The first, in 1529, was undertaken by Süleyman the Magnificent, but the 18-day endeavour was not sufficient to break the resolve of the city. The Turkish sultan subsequently died at the siege of Szigetvár, yet his death was kept secret for several days in an attempt to preserve the morale of his army. The subterfuge worked for a while. Messengers were led into the presence of the embalmed body which was placed in a seated position on the throne. They then unknowingly relayed their news to the corpse. The lack of the slightest acknowledgment of the sultan towards his minions was interpreted as regal impassiveness.

At the head of the Turkish siege of 1683 was the general and grand vizier Kara Mustapha. Amid the 25,000 tents of the Ottoman army that surrounded Vienna he installed his 1500 concubines, guarded by 700 Black eunuchs. Their luxurious quarters contained gushing fountains and regal baths, all set up in haste but with great opulence.

Again, it was all to no avail, even though Vienna was only lightly defended by 10,000 men. Mustapha's overconfidence was his downfall; failing to put garrisons on Kahlenberg, he and his army were surprised by a swift attack from Charles of Lorraine heading a German army and supported by a Polish army led by King Sobieski. Mustapha was pursued from the battlefield and defeated once again, at Gran. At Belgrade he was met by the emissary of the Sultan Mehmed IV. The price of failure was death, and Mustapha meekly accepted his fate. When the Austrian imperial army conquered Belgrade in 1718 the grand vizier's head was dug up and brought back to Vienna in triumph.

While the Turks aren't in control of Vienna today, they've certainly conquered parts of it. The city's 16th district is now home to a large percentage of the 40,000 or so Turks who have immigrated to the city. Its Brunnengasse is lined with Turkish food stalls and superb kebab houses, which not only cater to the large Turkish population, but also an ever-increasing amount of Austrians who have discovered the delights of Turkish coffee, sweets and shish kebabs.

1683	**1740**
Turks defeated at the gates of Vienna; the Turkish threat in Europe is once and forever crushed	Maria Theresia ascends the throne; start of the age of Reform

the Balkans and Hungary and by 1529 they were on Vienna's doorstep. The city managed to defend itself and the 18-day siege foundered with the onset of an early winter, but it highlighted glaring holes in Vienna's defences. The Turks withdrew but continued to be a powerful force, and it was this threat that prompted Ferdinand to move his court to Vienna in 1533, the first Habsburg to reside in the city permanently. This move increased the city's prestige, and also its defences.

For a short, succinct biography of every Habsburg ever born (including the current family), check out www.antiquesatoz.com /habsburg/.

In 1556 Karl abdicated as emperor and Ferdinand was crowned in his place. Aside from the Turks, he faced the problem of a depressingly low Catholic following; except in Tyrol, almost the entire population of Austria was Protestant. To solve this problem, he invited the Jesuits to Vienna. Ferdinand's successor, Maximillian II, eased the imperial stranglehold on religious practice, but this was reversed in 1576 by the next emperor, Rudolf II, who embraced the Counter-Reformation. Much of the country reverted to Catholicism, but not without a bit (or a lot) of coercion.

All this religious to-ing and fro-ing did nothing to calm the population, not only in Austria but also its neighbours. By the time the fanatically Catholic Ferdinand II took the throne in 1619, the Protestant nobles in Bohemia had had enough; their armed rebellion lead to the start of the Thirty Years' War, a war which would leave Europe devastated. In 1645 a Protestant Swedish army marched to within sight of Vienna but did not attack. Peace was finally achieved in 1648 and, through the Treaty of Westphalia, Austria lost some territory to France.

For much of the rest of the century, Austria was preoccupied with halting the advance of the Turks into Europe. Graz (p187) and Riegersburg (p202) proved effective strongholds against their armies, whose numbers in the end were too great and in 1683 Vienna found itself once again under Turkish threat (see p23). Vienna, already depleted by a severe epidemic of bubonic plague (between 75,000 and 150,000 died), managed to defend itself and combined forces subsequently swept the Turks to the southeastern edge of Europe. One of Austria's most celebrated military minds, Prince Eugène of Savoy, was successful against the Turks on a number of occasions, including the Battle of Zenta in 1697. The removal of the Turkish threat threw the then ruler Leopold I into a frenzy of cultural expansion; a proliferation of baroque building took place in many cities and Vienna became a magnet for musicians and composers. Leopold did however take time out from his toys to expel the Jews from the capital in 1670.

THE YEARS OF REFORM

The death of Charles II, the last of the Spanish line of the Habsburgs, saw Austria become involved in the War of the Spanish Succession (1701–14). At its conclusion Karl VI, the Austrian emperor, was left with only minor Spanish possessions (such as the Low Countries and parts of Italy). Having produced no male heirs, his biggest headache was ensuring his daughter, Maria Theresia, would succeed him. To this end he drew up the *Pragmatic Sanction,* cosigned by the main European powers. Of course, most who signed had no intention of honouring such an agreement, and as soon as Maria Theresia ascended to the Habsburg throne in 1740, she was fighting off would-be rulers in the War of the Austrian

1803, 1805 & 1809	1814–15
Austria is defeated on the battlefield by Napoleon	Congress of Vienna; Austria recovers much of its territory lost to Napoleon

---

MOTHER THERESIA

Maria Theresia (1717–80) was a hugely influential figure in Austrian history. Thrust into the limelight when her father died with no male heirs, she held onto power for 40 years, while also managing to give birth to 16 children – among them Marie Antoinette, future wife of Louis XVI, who has gone down in history for her failure to understand why the starving French peasants didn't eat cake. Maria Theresia's fourth child, Joseph II, weighed a daunting 7kg at birth.

Though Maria Theresia pushed through many enlightened reforms, she was also prudish and anti-Semitic (Jews had to keep behind a screen when in her presence). One of her less popular measures was the introduction of the short-lived Commission against Immoral Conduct in 1752, which raided private homes, trying to catch men entertaining women of supposed doubtful virtue – the commission tried to snare Casanova during his visit to Vienna.

Maria Theresia's attitude to philanderers was no doubt coloured by the conduct of her husband, Francis I, who was particularly adept in just that field. Yet despite his questionable conduct, Maria Theresia remained loyal to her spouse, and when he died suddenly in 1765 she stayed in mourning for the rest of her life. She retreated to Schloss Schönbrunn, left the running of the state in the hands of Joseph II, and kept a low-profile and chaste existence while she gradually ballooned in weight. Her achievements weren't fully appreciated during her lifetime; it was only after her death that she began to be acknowledged as the mother of the nation.

Succession (1740–48). Hardly had she caught her breath than the Seven Years' War (1756–63) was fought to retain Habsburg lands. Prussia took advantage of the Europe-wide conflict to wrest control of Silesia from Austria, which it retained in the ensuing peace.

Maria Theresia is widely regarded as the greatest of the Habsburg rulers, ringing in a golden era in which Austria developed as a modern state. In her 40 years as empress, she (and her wise advisers) centralised control, reformed the army and economy, introduced public schools, improved civil rights and numbered houses (initially for conscription purposes).

Maria Theresia's son, Joseph II, who ruled from 1780 to 1790 (he was also jointly in charge from 1765), was an even more zealous reformer. He issued an Edict of Tolerance (1781) for all faiths, secularised religious properties and abolished serfdom. Yet Joseph moved too fast for the general population and was ultimately forced to rescind some of his measures.

The latter half of the 18th century (and beginning of the 19th) witnessed a blossoming musical scene never before, and never again, seen in Vienna or Europe. During this time, Gluck, Haydn, Mozart, Beethoven and Schubert all lived and worked in Vienna, producing some of the most memorable music ever composed.

Robert A Kann's rather large tome *A History of the Habsburg Empire 1526–1918* is at times hard to struggle through, but it certainly delivers the goods on the Habsburgs and their far-reaching empire.

THE CRUMBLING EMPIRE

Napoleon's rise in the early 19th century spelt hard times for Austria and its rulers: his military genius inflicted major defeats on Austria in 1803, 1805 and 1809, and he occupied Vienna twice in 1805 and 1809. During the 1805 campaign, Austria lost its Italian lands, along with Tyrol and Vorarlberg; in 1809 it was forced to hand over Croatia. There was however an uprising in Tyrol in 1809 (see p299), led by innkeeper Andreas Hofer, but without sorely needed funding from the Habsburgs it collapsed later that same year.

1848	1918
Revolutions across the Empire; Franz Joseph I succeeds to the throne and overthrows the revolution	End of WWI and Habsburg reign; the First Republic is formed

A Nervous Splendour: Vienna 1888/1889 and Thunder at Twilight: Vienna 1913/14 by Frederic Morton are enthralling accounts of the Habsburg rule. The first deals with the Mayerling affair, the second with the assassination of Franz Ferdinand.

Due to the Frenchman's success, Franz II, the current Habsburg ruler and grandson of Maria Theresia, was forced into a bit of crown swapping; he took the title of Franz I of Austria in 1804 but had to relinquish the Holy Roman Emperor badge in 1806. In 1809 Klemens von Metternich (1773–1859) was appointed Austrian foreign minister, and in an attempt to buy peace, he arranged the marriage of Franz II's daughter, Marie Louise, to Napoleon in 1810. But the move came too late – the cost of the war caused state bankruptcy and a currency collapse in 1811.

With Napoleon's defeat at Leipzig in 1814, the conquering European powers celebrated with great gusto at the Congress of Vienna. The proceedings were dominated by the skilful Metternich, who restored some measure of pride to his homeland. Austria managed to win back Tyrol, Vorarlberg, Croatia and much of northern Italy, and in the process bring Salzburg into the fold for the first time.

On the home front, all was not well in post-Congress Vienna. Although the arts and culture, as pursued by the middle classes, flourished in this so-called Biedermeier period, the lower-class burghers were suffering. Metternich began to rule with an iron fist, first establishing a police state and then removing civil rights. Coupled with poor wages and housing, Austria was eventually ripe for revolution, which broke out in March 1848. The war minister was hanged from a lamppost, Metternich was ousted and Emperor Ferdinand I abdicated. The subsequent liberal interlude was brief, but it did bring about legislation for the emancipation of the peasant class. By the end of October that same year the traditional ruling parties were back in power; General Radetzky's defeat of rebels in northern Italy and General Windischgrätz's recapture of Prague and Vienna restored an absolute monarchy. The new emperor, Franz Josef I (1830–1916), a nephew of Ferdinand, was just 18 years old.

A highly readable account of the demise of the Habsburg empire is retold in AJP Taylor's The Habsburg Monarchy 1809–1918.

Franz Josef promptly quashed the last specks of opposition, executing many former revolutionaries. He soon eased off his harsh reproaches and in 1857 ordered the commencement of the massive Ringstrasse (p93) developments around Vienna's Innere Stadt (p89). The years 1866 to 1867 were telling on the empire's powers: not only did it suffer defeat at the hands of Prussia, but it was forced to create the dual Austro-Hungarian monarchy, known as the *Ausgleich* (compromise). Franz Josef was crowned king of Hungary and Hungary got its own parliament, with autonomy over defence, foreign and economic policies. Austria's economy improved with the help of technical innovations, and Vienna in particular received a plethora of advances, including electric trams, gasworks and fledgling health and social policies.

Carl E Schorske magically interlinks seven essays on the intellectual history of Vienna in his seminal work Fin-de-Siècle Vienna.

Everything was coming up roses until a huge stock market crash in 1873 sent the economy into a downward spiral. However it resiliently bounced back and the *fin de siècle* years of Austria – particularly Vienna – were a period of supreme artistic and intellectual creativity. Sigmund Freud coined the term 'psychoanalysis', Gustav Mahler composed and conducted, Otto Wagner and Adolf Loos took architecture to new levels and Gustav Klimt pushed the boundaries of art, paving the way for the likes of Egon Schiele and Oskar Kokoschka. Universal suffrage was introduced in Austro-Hungarian lands in 1906.

1934	1938
Civil War breaks out	Austria's Anschluss with Nazi Germany

The assassination of Franz Ferdinand, nephew of Franz Josef, in Sarajevo on 28 June 1914, put an end to all that. A month later Austria–Hungary declared war on Serbia and WWI began.

THE FIRST REPUBLIC

At first, the general populace was heavily patriotic towards the Habsburgs, believing the war would be over by Christmas. But the 'war to end all wars' dragged on and on, with no end in sight. In 1916 Franz Josef died and his successor, Karl I, secretly tried to negotiate a peace deal with the western allies. His attempts failed miserably, as did Austria's military efforts towards the end of the war. At the conclusion of the war Karl I abdicated, and on 12 November 1918 the Republic of Austria came into being. After 640 years of rule, the Habsburg monarchy finally came to an end.

Although the majority of citizens pushed for union with Germany (Vorarlberg wanted to join the Swiss), the victorious allies prohibited such an act. Austria was forced to recognise the independent states of Czechoslovakia, Poland, Hungary and Yugoslavia; previously, these countries, along with Transylvania (now in Romania), had been largely under the control of the Habsburgs. The loss of so much land caused severe economic difficulties in Austria – the new states declined to supply vital raw materials to their old ruler – and many urban families were soon on the verge of famine. By the mid-1920s, however, the federal government had stabilised the currency and established new trading relations.

After WWI, Vienna's socialist city government embarked on a programme of enlightened social policies. The period, known as *Rotes Wien,* or 'Red Vienna', created a mass of public housing that at the time the city severely lacked. The rest of the country, however, was firmly under the sway of the conservative federal government of the Christian Socialists, causing great tensions between the capital and the state.

These tensions were heightened on 15 July 1927, when a very dubious judgment acquitted right-wing extremists of an assassination charge. Demonstrators gathered outside the Palace of Justice in Vienna (the seat of the Supreme Court) and set fire to the building. The police responded by opening fire on the crowd, killing 86 people (including five of their own number). The rift between Vienna's Social Democrats and the federal Christian Socialists grew.

THE RISE OF FASCISM & WWII

Political and social tensions, coupled with a worldwide economic crisis, gave federal chancellor Engelbert Dollfuss the opportunity he was looking for, and in 1933 he dissolved parliament on a technicality. In February 1934 civil war erupted, with the *Schutzbund,* the Social Democrat's militias, up against the conservative's *Heimwehr.* The *Schutzbund* were soundly beaten, and the party outlawed. However, Dollfuss' reign was short-lived – in July of the same year the Nazis assassinated him in an attempted coup. His successor, Schuschnigg, buckled under increasing threats from Germany, including National Socialists (Nazis) in his government in 1938.

On 12 March 1938 German troops marched into Austria, encountering little resistance. Hitler, who had departed Vienna many years before as a failed and disgruntled artist, returned to the city in triumph, and

Steven Beller's *Vienna and the Jews, 1867–1938: A Cultural History* is an insightful look into the cultural contributions Vienna's Jewish community made to the city.

The Habsburgs may no longer rule Austria, but they're still around; otto.twschwarzer.de (in German) is the website of current family head, Otto von Habsburg.

When Otto von Habsburg was asked who he thought would win an Austria vs Hungary football match, he reputedly replied 'Who are we playing?'.

1945	1955
End of WWII and liberation of Austria by Allied troops	Austrian Staatsvertrag (State Treaty) signed

Vienna's population peaked at more than two million between 1910 and 1914. After WWI, Vienna was one of the world's five largest cities.

held a huge rally at Heldenplatz on 15 March in front of 200,000 ecstatic Viennese. Before entering Vienna, he passed through his birth place Braunau am Inn (p182) and his beloved Linz (p167). Austria was soon incorporated into the German Reich under the Anschluss, which was supported by a national referendum in April.

The arrival of the Nazis had a devastating effect on Austrian Jews, though many non-Jewish liberals and intellectuals also fled the Nazi regime. After May 1938, Germany's Nuremberg Racial Laws were applicable in Austria, leading to Jews being stripped of many rights. Excluded from some professions and universities, they were forced to wear the yellow Star of David and go by the name of 'Sara' or 'Israel'. Vienna's Jewish community, which comprised 95% of Austria's Jews, was rocked by racial violence on Reichskristallnacht (9 November 1938), when shops were looted and all but one of the temples was razed. Of the 180,000 Jews living in Vienna before the Anschluss, more than 100,000 managed to emigrate before the borders closed in May 1939, 65,000 died in ghettos or concentration camps and only 6000 survived to see liberation by Allied troops.

Hella Pick's *Guilty Victim: Austria from the Holocaust to Haider* is an excellent analysis of modern-day Austria.

Austria was part of Germany's war machine during WWII and its government just a puppet of the German Nazis. However, there were undercurrents of resistance to Germany: 100,000 Austrians were imprisoned for political reasons and 2700 resistance fighters were executed. Towards the end of the war, Vienna suffered a heavy toll from Allied bombing raids: most major public buildings, plus around 86,000 homes, were damaged or destroyed. On 11 April 1945 advancing Russian troops liberated the city.

POST-WWII

It wasn't long after liberation that Austria declared its independence from Germany. A provisional federal government was established under Socialist Karl Renner; the country was restored to its 1937 frontiers and occupied by the victorious Allies – the Americans, Russians, British and French. Austria was divided into four zones, one for each occupying power. Vienna, within the Soviet zone, was itself divided into four zones, with control of the city centre alternating between the four powers on a monthly basis. This was a time of 'four men in a jeep', so aptly depicted in Graham Greene's *The Third Man*. Austria's and Vienna's situation was very similar to that of Germany and Berlin; while the Soviet zones in the latter were eventually sealed off, Austria's remained united because its postwar communists failed to gain electoral support.

The findings of the Historical Commission's report into Austria during the Nazi era can be found on www.historikerkommission.gv.at.

Delays caused by frosty relations between the superpowers ensured that the Allied occupation dragged on for 10 years. It was a tough time for Austrians; the black market dominated the flow of goods and the rebuilding of national monuments was slow and expensive. On 15 May 1955 the Austrian Staatsvertrag (State Treaty) was ratified, with Austria proclaiming its permanent neutrality. The Allied forces withdrew, and in December 1955 Austria joined the United Nations (UN). As the capital of a neutral country on the edge of the Cold War frontline, Vienna attracted spies and diplomats: Kennedy and Khrushchev met here in 1961, Carter and Brezhnev in 1979; the International Atomic Energy Agency set up shop in 1957, as did the UN in 1983.

1995	1999
Austria enters the EU	Freedom Party (FPÖ) and Austrian People's Party (ÖVP) join forces

Austria's international image suffered following the election in 1986 of President Kurt Waldheim who, it was revealed, had served in a German *Wehrmacht* unit implicated in WWII war crimes. But a belated recognition of Austria's less-than-spotless WWII record was a long time in coming. In 1993 Chancellor Franz Vranitzky's finally admitted that Austrians were 'willing servants of Nazism'.

THE EUROPEAN UNION YEARS

With its inclusion into the European Union in 1995, Austria entered a new age of politics. The move was endorsed by the populace, which voted a resounding 66.4% in favour of EU membership in the June 1994 referendum. Since then however, people have been rather more ambivalent about the advantages of EU membership – the strict criteria required for a single European currency has placed doubt in the minds of many.

After the 1999 national elections, Austria suffered international criticism when the far-right Freedom Party (FPÖ) formed a new federal coalition government with the Austrian People's Party (ÖVP) under the leadership of Chancellor Schlüssel. The new administration, though democratically elected, was condemned before it even had the opportunity to put a foot wrong. The EU immediately imposed sanctions against Austria by freezing all high-level diplomatic contacts.

The problem arose from the then leader of the FPÖ, Jörg Haider, and his flippant and insensitive remarks towards foreign members of state, his comparison of Churchill's war record with that of Hitler, and his xenophobia. Many Austrians, irrespective of their views towards the FPÖ, were upset at the EU's pre-emptive move, believing that Austria would not have been targeted had it been a more important player in European affairs. In any event, sanctions proved not only futile but counterproductive, and they were withdrawn in September 2000.

As the dust settled on Austria's political woes, a new crisis thrust the country into world headlines. The Gletscherbahn underground railway in Kaprun caught fire halfway up the mountain in November 2000, killing 155 in the worst ever alpine disaster.

In the 2002 elections FPÖ's popularity took a nose dive, dropping to a mere 10.1% (from 26.9% in 1999). The ÖVP was the winner all-round, snatching 42% of the vote and ensuring another term in government. Haider instantly offered his resignation as head of the FPÖ, and soon after a second term of the ÖVP-FPÖ coalition began in earnest. In-fighting and scandal has dogged the FPÖ in the ensuing years, causing national support to plummet to even greater depths, yet Haider pulled another rabbit out of the hat, winning the election for Carinthian governor in early 2004.

The swearing in of Austria's new president Heinz Fischer in 2004 was a sad affair; the outgoing president, Thomas Klestil, died of a heart attack two days before finishing his second presidential term.

Hear and read stories of Holocaust victims on the United States Holocaust Memorial Museums' website www.ushmm.org.

For a lowdown on Austria's current political players, visit www.austria.gv.at.

The last Habsburg Emperor, Karl I, moved one step closer to sainthood after his beatification by the Pope in October 2004. The move was praised and criticised – Karl was a devout Christian but also authorised the use of poison gas in WWI.

2000	2004
Gletscherbahn railway catches fire, killing 155	President Heinz Fischer sworn in

The Culture

THE NATIONAL PSYCHE

Austrians in general are an intelligent, friendly bunch with a dollop of grumpiness thrown in. The younger generation are easy to engage in conversation (especially if you speak their own language) and are happy to talk about almost anything, including politics, religion and sex, but they are not known for their warmth – until you get to know them better. *Die Höflichkeit* (politeness) and formality are held in high regard, especially by the older generation; a hangover from the heady days of the Habsburg empire. Westerners are easily accepted and welcomed into the fold, but many Austrians are suspicious of folk from Eastern Europe, Africa and Asia and give them the cold shoulder.

Burgenlanders are normally the butt of Austrians' 'dumb' jokes.

The landscape is a major feature of Austria, and its effect on the country goes as deep at its psyche. In the east, where the land is flatter and neighbouring countries more accessible, people are less constricted in their thinking, and more open to new ideas. In the Alps, things are a little different; the mountains are high, the valleys deep and the thinking more narrow.

The Viennese are a law unto themselves; they can swing from grumpy, moody, morose, and downright mean to warm, friendly, witty and giving in the space of a conversation. This quagmire of emotions has in the past been a superb breeding ground for some of the world's greatest thinkers, including Sigmund Freud, Ludwig Wittgenstein, Sir Karl Popper, Ernst Mach and the Wiener Kreis (Vienna Circle). The Wiener Kreis, a group of philosophers in the '20s and '30s, coined the term logical positivism and formulated the verifiability principle as a yardstick for judging whether things are meaningful.

The Austrian Federal Government's official website www.austria.gv.at has plenty of information on the country's political situation in English.

LIFESTYLE

Comparing their lifestyle to the rest of the world, Austrians have it made. The country has an exceptional social system and an astounding outdoor

---

DOS & DON'TS

Austria is a society of politeness; to ignore the rules is the height of rudeness. Stick to the following dos and don'ts and you'll do just fine (for dos & don'ts during meal times, see p71):

- Do greet people with *Grüss Gott* or *Guten Tag,* whether it be in a social setting, shop, café, restaurant or information office. *Servus* is reserved for greetings between friends or the younger generation. When departing, *Auf Wiedersehen* or *Auf Wiederschauen* is appropriate.

- Do shake hands when introduced to someone, even in younger, informal company. Likewise, shake hands when you leave.

- Do dress up if going to the opera, theatre or a top restaurant. A jacket and tie for men is the norm.

- Do use full titles at the beginning of formal meetings; *Herr* for men and *Frau* for women is the minimum required. If you speak German, always use the *Sie* form with the older generation and on the telephone; it's not so common with the younger generation.

- Don't cross at the traffic lights when the figure is red, even when there is no traffic in sight. Austrians rarely do it, and the cops can instantly fine you for jaywalking.

- Don't strip off or go topless at every beach in Austria. Nude bathing is limited to areas with FKK signs and if no-one else is going topless at other beaches, you shouldn't either.

playground within its borders, and they make good use of both. Austrians love to go hiking, and most are literally born on skis.

Life in Vienna is like that of any other Western city, except at a slower pace. The Viennese like to enjoy themselves, preferring to spend balmy summer evenings with a beer in hand and a friend at their side rather than racking up overtime in order to leap-frog it up the career ladder. The average wage (€21,400 a year before tax) may not be high as other Western nations, but neither are the costs; even most students can afford their own apartment alongside plenty of partying. However, finding an *echte Wiener* (real Viennese) can sometimes prove hard – many of the city's burghers come from Austria's rural provinces. It would seem the bulk of its university students and 20- and 30-something professionals fall within this category, and are often able to have their cake and eat it too, by making the most of city life and then escaping home for Mama's cooking and fresh country air once a month.

National service is still compulsory for males in Austria, who can either serve their time in the military or perform civil service duties.

The people in alpine and rural areas often live up to the Austrian stereotype. The older country folk are often homebodies, not very well travelled and happy to tend their two cows, while their children head off on adventures. Women can still be seen in the *Dirndl,* a full, pleated skirt with tight bodice, worn with traditional apron, bonnet, and blouse with short, puffed sleeves. The men, meanwhile, are anything but self-conscious in collarless loden jackets, green hats, wide braces and shorts or knee breeches. Although such clothes are worn on a daily basis in some out-of-the-way places, as a tourist you're more likely to see them during celebrations and processions. In early summer, hardy herders climb to alpine pastures with their cattle and live in summer huts while tending their herds. Rural ritual retains a foothold in the consciousness of alpine village folk, and finds exuberant expression in the many festivals scattered throughout the year. These often act out ancient traditions, such as welcoming the spring with painted masks and the ringing of bells. Yodelling and playing the alphorn are also part of the tradition.

Lukas has been the most popular name for boys born since 1996; Sarah topped the list for girls in 2003, but had been in the running for top spot since the late 1990s.

Austria's social system works well for its citizens. The working week is restricted to 40 hours (sometimes 37½ hours). Workers receive a minimum of five weeks' holiday and can take up to 12 weeks sick leave a year. Part of a person's pay packet is automatically siphoned into pension and healthcare schemes; medical checkups and hospital care require no extra payment. Expectant mothers must leave work eight weeks before the baby is due, and parental leave, which can be split between the mother and father, is two years. During this time the mother receives a small benefit from the government and her job is kept open for her return. Pension can be taken at 65 by men, 60 by women.

www.wien.gv.at/english/ancestors/ is a good starting point for tracking down ancestors in Vienna.

Austrians are among the best educated in the world; 98% of the population (aged 15 and above) is literate. Universities are found countrywide.

POPULATION

Austria's population spread is rather lopsided; the country's two largest provinces – Vienna, followed by Lower Austria – are in the east of the country. Most of Austria's immigrants have also settled here (see p33).

On average, there are 96 inhabitants per sq km, but this figure is not a true representation of population density. Vienna's density is well above this figure, while the rest of Austria's provinces (aside from Vorarlberg) are well below this mark; Tyrol, with only 53 inhabitants per sq km, is the least populated.

More females than males reside in Austria; at last count, the population was divided: 51.5% females to 48.5% males. Females also win the life expectancy race, on average living to the ripe old age of 82. Men live to an average of 76.

SPORT

Austrians are not as crazy over sport as the English or the Australians, but they do take time out to watch big sporting events. Football is the number one spectator sport; also-rans include skiing and motor racing.

Summer is pretty much a dead time for spectator sports. With the arrival of autumn and winter however, things heat up, so to speak.

Football

Austria was the first European country to import football from England, just before WWI.

Austria may not be a football power today, but in the time between the two World Wars, it was a force to be reckoned with, losing narrowly to invincible England at Wembley in 1932 (4–3) and to Italy in the World Cup semifinal of 1934 (1–0).

The national football league, the Austrian Bundesliga, kicks off at the end of autumn and runs until the beginning of spring with a break during the severe winter months. The country's better teams are based in Vienna, Innsbruck, Salzburg and Graz; games are hardly ever sold out so it should prove no problem getting hold of a ticket.

Vienna will be in the world-football spotlight when it cohosts the European championships with Switzerland in 2008. Expect the city to put on quite a show.

Skiing

If a sport is played in Austria (such as mini-golf and skibobbing), then its governing body is listed on www.bso.or.at (in German), the Austria Sports Organisation website.

Football may be the most popular spectator sport, but skiing is Austria's national pastime. Conditions rank among the best worldwide (and will stay that way as long as global warming is kept at bay). Innsbruck has hosted the Winter Olympics twice, in 1964 and 1976. World Cup ski races are annually held in Kitzbühel (p319), St Anton am Arlberg (p329) and Schladming.

Stars of the Austrian skiing scene abound, but there are a handful of names which shine that much brighter than the rest. The current favourite is 'The Herminator', Hermann Maier (see opposite), a superhuman skier from Salzburg. Austria's first true superstar, Toni Sailer, is arguably the greatest skier the country has ever produced. At 17 he claimed the Tyrolean championships at downhill, slalom and giant slalom and four years later won gold medals in all three disciplines at the 1956 Winter Olympics in Cortina d'Ampezzo. Karl Schranz, from St Anton, was a giant among skiers in the late '50s and '60s and Franz Klammer dominated the ski scene in the mid-1970s, snatching eight downhill victories in the 1974–75 season and taking gold in the downhill at the 1976 Innsbruck Olympics.

Toni Sailer's clean sweep of gold in the downhill, slalom and giant slalom disciplines at the 1956 Winter Olympics has never been matched.

Motor Sports

Many Austrian's love their motor sports and will spend an entire weekend in front of the telly catching every second of the Formula One. Austria even hosted the Formula One Grand Prix from 1964 until 2003 at its A1-Ring in Spielberg, 70km north of Graz. Aside from Niki Lauda (see opposite), the only other Austrian to win the Formula One championship was Jochen Rindt in 1970; he died in a fatal crash the same year. Current favourite is Christian Klien, a native of Vorarlberg who drives for Jaguar.

Tennis

Association of Tennis Professionals (ATP) tennis events are held in Vienna, St Pölten and Kitzbühel. Austria's biggest star of the modern game of tennis is Thomas Muster (see opposite).

FEATS OF AUSTRIAN ENDURANCE

Austria has produced its share of determined sports persons, but three have gone that extra mile in the name of their chosen sport.

Niki Lauda, a household name and one of the most famous Austrian sportsmen of all time, is a Formula One legend, winning the racing championship three times, the first coming in 1975. Lauda suffered horrific burns in a high speed crash during the 1976 season, yet he was back in his car after missing only two races. That year he narrowly failed to retain the world championship, losing out to James Hunt by a single point on the last race of the season. Undeterred, he regained the title the following year, and proceeded to net his third championship win in 1984.

The somewhat bumbling side of skier Hermann Maier has led to him being likened to Superman's human alter ego, Clark Kent. However, in the 1998 Nagano Olympics, Maier showed the amazing toughness and resilience he had gained as a bricklayer and which characterises his all-or-nothing skiing style. During the men's downhill competition, he misjudged a difficult curve, got too close to a gate, somersaulted 30m through the air, bounced over a fence and crashed through two safety nets before finally coming to rest. Austria held its breath as the man known as 'The Herminator' got to his feet, dusted himself down and waved at the crowd. He went on to win two gold medals in the next six days.

But a more amazing feat was yet to come. In August 2001 Maier was involved in an horrific motorcycle crash that almost took his life. Doctors had an agonising decision to make: amputate a very damaged leg or try to save it. Fortunately the decision was made to save it, and Maier underwent some painful operations to insert a titanium rod into the leg to hold it together. His recovery was miraculous; in January 2003, only 18 months after the accident, he went on to win the super-g (super giant slalom) at Kitzbühel – his 42nd World Cup victory.

Thomas Muster, Austria's top tennis player during the 1990s, had his kneecap crushed by a drunk driver, just hours after a win at the 1989 Lipton Championship semifinal in Florida. The resulting damage to the joint made it doubtful he would play tennis again. Yet he showed massive courage in undertaking a gruelling rehabilitation programme, which entailed on-court training while strapped to an osteopathic bench. He went on to become world number one and in the process earned the nickname 'The Iron Man'.

MULTICULTURALISM

In general, Austria is not a particularly multicultural society; almost 89% of the country is of German origin. A tiny 1.5% of the population is made up of indigenous minorities, invariably from Eastern Europe. Most settled in Austria's eastern half between the 16th and 19th centuries and include Croatians, Slovenes, Hungarians, Czechs, Slovaks and Roma. A number of traditional languages have also managed to cross the border; Slovene is an official language in Carinthia – although Jörg Haider, at the time of writing the new governor of Carinthia (p29), isn't too happy about it. Croatian and Hungarian are spoken in Burgenland.

For exhaustive online information on all things Austrian, consult the Austrian Encyclopaedia website www.aeiou.at.

The remaining 10% comes from recent immigration. Serbians, Turks, Croatians and Bosnians make up the bulk of their number and once again, most have immigrated to the east of Austria, in particular Vienna. Some districts of the capital, such as the 16th, are more Turkish or Serbian than Austrian, which disturbs some locals and pleases others. Fears of being overrun by immigrants gained momentum in the early 1990s (thanks in part to a cynical antiforeigner campaign by the Freedom Party, the FPÖ), when the immigration figures stood at 600,000, and the federal government subsequently tightened immigration controls considerably. Austria still has a problem with illegal immigrants from Eastern Europe, but fears of the floodgate bursting once the EU opened its doors to the east have yet proved unfounded.

From the mid-1990s onwards, Vienna has experienced an influx of two other ethnic groups, one very new, the other almost as old as Austria itself. Africans are now more prominent on the streets of the capital, but this hasn't gone down well with everyone; some believe that every Black person is a drug dealer. Long residents and scapegoats of the small-minded Austrian rulers, Jews are slowly returning to the Leopoldstadt district. While numbers will never reach those of before WWII (currently 7000 live in Vienna; before the Anschluss (p27) 180,000 resided in the city), it is good to see the Jewish community once again comfortable in Austria.

MEDIA

Austria has a long history in media and press freedom. The *Wiener Zeitung* (www.wienerzeitung.at), first published in 1703, is the oldest newspaper in the world still regularly produced. With such long and solid journalistic background, it's no surprise that Austria receives a wide and varied view on political and social matters by its media.

Alongside a plethora of regional papers, eight national newspapers vie for Austria's readers. Of these eight, two follow tabloid-style reporting and the rest stick to quality over quantity, which results in fierce competition and generally good investigative journalism. At the time of writing newspapers received state grants, but this was under review.

With all this competition and high standards, it's hard to believe that the *Kronen Zeitung* (www.krone.at in German), a thoroughly tabloid spread, is easily Austria's most-read newspaper. Its influence on the nation is said to be so great that no national decision or project can go ahead without its consent. Of the weekly news magazines, *News,* owned by Germany's *Gruner und Jahr* publishers, is the largest of its kind per household readership in Europe.

One in every three news-papers sold in Austria is a *Krone Zeitung,* making it the widest-read newspaper per capita in the world.

Founded in 1957, Österreichischer Rundfunk (ÖRF; Austrian Broad-casting Corporation; www.orf.at in German) is the country's independent public broadcaster. For decades it held a monopoly on radio and TV until the government passed a law in January 2002 cancelling such rights. To date, however, ÖRF has received only minimal competition. It owns a grand total of 13 radio stations and the country's only two noncable and satellite TV channels, ÖRF1 and ÖRF2.

RELIGION

Religion plays an important part in the lives of many Austrians, and the country has been a stronghold of Catholicism for centuries – except during the Reformation of course (see p23). This can be seen everywhere; towns invariably have at least one church, and the countryside is dotted with small roadside shrines decorated with fresh flowers. In the latest census, 73.6% of the population classed themselves as Roman Catholic, 4.7% Protestant and 4.2% Muslim. Freedom of religion is guaranteed under the constitution.

ARTS
Music

Above all other artistic pursuits, Austria is known for music. As early as the 12th century, Vienna was known for its *Minnesänger* (troubadours) and strolling musicians and in 1498 Maximilian I relocated the court orchestra from Innsbruck to Vienna.

Composers throughout Europe were drawn to the country, and es-pecially to Vienna, in the 18th and 19th centuries by the willingness of

TOP 5 CDS

- Mozart: *The Magic Flute*
- Schubert: *The Trout Quintet*
- Falco: *Falco 3* (try to get the original LP with the full version of 'Rock Me, Amadeus', rather than the CD)
- Kruder & Dorfmeister: *The K&D Sessions*
- Arnold Schönberg: *Pierrot Lunaire*

the Habsburgs to patronise this creative medium. In fact many members of the royal family were themselves gifted musicians – Leopold I was a composer, and Charles VI (violin), Maria Theresia (double bass) and Joseph II (harpsichord and cello) were all players. The various forms of classical music – symphony, concerto, sonata, opera and operetta – were explored and developed by the most eminent exponents of the day. Among those who came in search of Habsburg readies were Mozart, Haydn, Schubert and Beethoven: between 1781 and 1828 they produced some of the world's greatest classical music. The Johann Strausses, father and son, kept the ball rolling when they introduced the waltz to Vienna.

The Austrian love affair with music has by no means waned since then. After WWI and WWII, when people were starving due to a lack of resources, money was still put aside to keep up performances at the Staatsoper (State Opera; p119).

Heurigen (wine taverns) in Vienna have a musical tradition all their own, with the songs often expressing very maudlin themes; the perfect accompaniment for drunkenness. Known as *Schrammelmusik,* it is usually played by musicians wielding a combination of violin, accordion, guitar and clarinet. In the Alpine regions, *Volksmusik* (folk music), based on traditional tunes, is popular.

In the field of rock and pop Austria has made little international impact (unless you count the striking but tragically short career of Falco), though both Vienna and Graz have a thriving jazz scene, the small local rock scene is alive and kicking. Particularly popular is Ostbahn Kurti (or Kurt Ostbahn, depending on how he feels at the time), who sings in a thick Viennese dialect.

Vienna is making small waves on the DJ and clubbing scene worldwide, and attracts well-known international acts. Local DJs Kruder & Dorfmeister (www.g-stoned.com) and the Sofa Surfers (www.sofasurfers.net) have both enjoyed international success and are slowly putting Vienna on the map of modern music.

Today, Austrian orchestras, such as the Vienna Philharmonic (p119), have a worldwide reputation, and institutions such as the Vienna Boys' Choir, the Staatsoper (p119), the Musikverein (p119) and the Konzerthaus (p119) are unrivalled. Salzburg and Graz are also major music centres and like Vienna, they host important annual music festivals. Linz has the international Brucknerfest (p171), Schwarzenberg in Vorarlberg hosts Schubertiade (Schubert Festival; p341), and Innsbruck its Festival of Early Music (p306). The Bregenz Festival (p338) is famous for productions performed on a floating stage on the Bodensee.

The major movers and shakers in Austria's classical music arena deserve special attention and are discussed next.

A gem of a thriller, *The Third Man* (1949) by Carol Reed tells the tale of postwar Vienna and underhanded dealings at the time of 'four men in a jeep'.

CHRISTOPH WILLIBALD VON GLUCK (1714–87)

Although hardly anyone has heard of Gluck, his marriage of operatic music and the dramatic format paved the way for the next generation of composers. His major works include *Orfeo* (1762) and *Alceste* (1767).

JOSEF HAYDN (1732–1809)

No other figure was more dominant in classical music in the 18th century than Haydn, and he has been credited with ushering in the classicist era.

His musical career began early; by the age of eight he was a chorister at Stephansdom in Vienna. When his voice broke at 17, he was forced to make a living as a freelance musician and study musical theory, of which at this stage he had no idea. His big break was his appointment as Kapellmeister (music director) to the Esterházys in Eisenstadt, Burgenland (p156).

During his lifetime Haydn composed 19 operas and operettas, 108 symphonies, 68 string quartets, 62 piano sonatas and 43 piano trios. His greatest works include the oratorios *The Creation* (1798) and *The Seasons* (1801) and Symphony No 102 in B-flat Major.

Haydn's wife, Maria Anna Keller, was no fan of his music and reputedly lined her pastry pans with his manuscripts.

WOLFGANG AMADEUS MOZART (1756–91)

No other name is as synonymous with classical music as Mozart's. Praise for his music came from many quarters – Haydn believed him to be the 'greatest composer' and Schubert effused that the 'magic of Mozart's music lights the darkness of our lives'.

Mozart was a child prodigy, learning to play the harpsichord at age three and violin at five. By six he was performing for royalty and at eight touring Europe with his incredible talents. In 1770, though only 14 years old, Mozart was appointed director of the archbishop of Salzburg's orchestra. After seven years he'd had enough of the job and finally settled in Vienna in 1781.

Mozart was only 35 when he died, yet he had composed some 626 pieces: 24 operas, 49 symphonies, more than 40 concertos, 26 string quartets, seven string quintets and numerous sonatas for piano and violin. He took opera to new heights, achieving a fusion of Germanic and Italianate styles (his librettos were first in Italian and later, innovatively, in German). Pundits consider Mozart's greatest Italian operas to be *The Marriage of Figaro* (1786), *Don Giovanni* (1787) and *Così fan Tutte* (1790). Mozart's *The Magic Flute* (1791) was a direct precursor of the German opera of the 19th century. The *Requiem Mass,* apocryphally written for his own death, remains one of the most powerful works of classical music.

Mozart was a bit of a womaniser and at 24 quipped, 'If I had married everyone I jested with, I would have well over 200 wives'.

LUDWIG VAN BEETHOVEN (1770–1827)

Beethoven may have been born in Bonn, Germany, but his musical genius blossomed in Vienna. The city provided him the best classical music teachers a student could possibly wish for, Mozart in 1787 and Haydn in 1792. From the age of 21 until his death he called Vienna home.

Beethoven began to lose his hearing at the age of 30, and was totally deaf by 32, but that didn't stop him composing. Many consider his final 10 years to have been his best period; during this time he wrote (among others) Symphony No 9 in D Minor and Symphony No 5.

In addition to the numerous symphonies, concertos, string quartets, piano sonatas, masses and overtures created by Beethoven, he wrote just one opera – *Fidelio* (1814).

Beethoven must have been picky with his dwelling; he lived in as many as 60 addresses during his time in Vienna.

FRANZ SCHUBERT (1797–1828)

Schubert was the last in the great line of composers from the Viennese School's Classical period (1740–1825). A native of Vienna, he was responsible for giving the ancient German *Lieder* (lyrical song) tradition a new lease of life, creating a craze for what became known as 'Schubertiade' musical evenings. His musical ability and output is quite staggering: nine symphonies, 11 overtures, seven masses, more than 80 smaller choral works, more than 30 chamber music works, 450 piano works and more than 600 *Lieder* (in excess of 960 works in total). All this before he died at the age of just 31 (of syphilis), 18 months after his hero Beethoven.

Probably Schubert's most famous piece, his 'Unfinished' Symphony, was written in 1822 when he was only 25. Like almost all of his works, it was first performed after his death; his musical genius was not fully recognised during his lifetime.

THE STRAUSSES & THE WALTZ

The waltz originated in Vienna at the beginning of the 19th century and went down a storm at the Congress of Vienna (1814–15). The early masters of this genre were Johann Strauss the Elder (1804–49), who also composed the *Radetzky March*, and Josef Lanner (1801–43). Both toured Europe, bringing the genre to wide prominence.

The man who really made this form his own was Johann Strauss the Younger (1825–99), composer of 400 waltzes. Young Strauss became a musician against the wishes of Strauss senior (who had experienced years of struggle) and set up a rival orchestra to his father's. He composed Austria's unofficial anthem, the *Blue Danube* (1867), and *Tales from the Vienna Woods* (1868).

The younger Strauss proved also to be a master of the operetta, especially with his eternally popular *Die Fledermaus* (1874) and *The Gypsy Baron* (1885). Strauss was very adept at marketing himself and his music, and was fêted both at home and abroad.

Museum after museum is listed on www.austrian museums.net; it's in German but it's pretty easy to navigate.

OTHER 19TH-CENTURY COMPOSERS

Anton Bruckner (1824–96) was raised in Upper Austria and was long associated with the abbey in St Florian (p174). He settled in Vienna on his appointment as organist to the court in 1868. Bruckner is known for dramatically intense symphonies (nine in all) and church music.

In the late 19th century Austria was still attracting musicians and composers from elsewhere in Europe. At the age of 29, Johannes Brahms (1833–97) moved to Vienna from Hamburg and spent 35 years in the Austrian capital. He greatly enjoyed Vienna's village atmosphere and said it had a positive effect on his work, which was of the classical-Romantic tradition. His best works include violin concertos, *Ein Deutsches Requiem* and Symphonies 1–4.

Hugo Wolf (1860–1903) rivalled Schubert in *Lieder* composition, and had spells of intense creativity. Born in what is now Slovenia, he moved to Vienna when he was 15 and died at the age of 43 in one of the city's lunatic asylums. Born in Germany the same year was Gustav Mahler (1860–1911), who is known mainly for his nine symphonies, and was director of the Vienna Court Opera from 1897 to 1907. Richard Strauss (1864–1949), from Munich, favoured Salzburg above Vienna, though he did have a spell as the conductor and director of the Staatsoper. Franz Lehár (1870–1948), originally from Hungary, was a notable operetta composer, renowned for *Die lustige Witwe* (The Merry Widow).

THE SECOND VIENNESE SCHOOL

Vienna's musical eminence continued in the 20th century with the innovative work of Arnold Schönberg (1874–1951), who founded what has been dubbed the 'New School' of Vienna. Schönberg developed theories on 12 tone composition, yet some of his earlier work (such as *Pieces for the Piano op. 11* composed in 1909) went completely beyond the bounds of tonality.

The most influential of his pupils were Alban Berg (1885–1935) and Anton von Webern (1883–1945), who both explored the 12 tone technique, and were also born in Vienna. At the first public performance of Berg's composition *Altenberg-Lieder,* the concert had to be cut short due to the audience's outraged reaction.

Architecture

Austrian architecture dates back to pre-Romanesque times, but unfortunately there is little left to study. The Romans, however, built things to last, and significant Roman ruins, dating from the 1st to the 5th centuries AD, still weather the storms at sites such as Carnuntum (p143), Michaelerplatz (p103) and Hoher Markt (p113) in Vienna. Singular Celtic ruins are few and far between, although a plethora of grave mounds can be viewed outside Grossklein (p201).

Learn more about Austrian architecture at the Architekturtage (Architectural Days) in June. For more information go to www .architekturtage.at.

ROMANESQUE

The Romanesque style in Austria, characterised by thick walls, closely spaced columns and heavy, rounded arches, along with the use of statues and reliefs on the portals and apses, was almost entirely religious in nature. It flourished under the Babenberg dynasty, which spent plenty of cash building cathedrals and abbeys across the country.

Pure Romanesque buildings are rare in Austria as many were extended and modified using more popular architectural styles through the ages. One exception is the Gurk Dom (p269) in Carinthia; it has not only retained its Romanesque shape, but also has fine Romanesque sculptures and frescoes. Schloss Porcia (p273) in Spittal an der Drau is another fine example.

GOTHIC

The Gothic style didn't really take hold in Austria until the accession of the Habsburgs, and stuck around until the 16th century. It was made possible by engineering advances that permitted thinner walls and (in churches) taller, more delicate columns and great expanses of stained glass. Distinctive features include pointed arches and ribbed ceiling vaults, external flying buttresses to support the walls, and elaborately carved doorway columns.

In the 15th century, Austria was the site of some of the grandest architectural experimentation, and the use of stained glass windows enhanced some of the finest sacred buildings ever constructed. The most impressive Gothic structure in Austria is Vienna's Stephansdom (p89); its three naves of equal height are typically Austrian Gothic. Secular Gothic buildings include the Goldenes Dachl (p305) in Innsbruck, the Kornmesserhaus (p205) in Bruck an der Mur and the Bummerlhaus (p176) in Steyr.

RENAISSANCE

By the 16th century, Gothic was old hat, and it was time for something new. A new enthusiasm for classical forms and an obsession with grace and symmetry coincided with the emergence of the Habsburgs as a major power, and Renaissance entered the Austrian architectural scene. Palaces, mansions and houses were built by Italian architects, who combined Italian and Austrian influences, though in general, Renaissance architecture had little impact in Austria except in Salzburg.

One of the hallmarks of the era was the arcade courtyard, and supreme examples of this can be seen at Schloss Schallaburg (p132) and at the

Landhaushof (p189) in Graz. Another typical trait of Renaissance was the creation of sgraffito façades; two layers of different colours are applied, onto which designs are scratched into the top layer to reveal the layer beneath. Houses in Gmünd in Carinthia (p272) perfectly display this technique.

BAROQUE & ROCOCO

With the end of the Thirty Years' War and the threat of the Turks gone once and for all, Austria's monarchy had plenty of money and energy previously spent on defence. It was channelled into urban development, right at the time baroque was making huge ground in architecture. This resplendent, triumphal style featured marble columns, emotive sculpture and painting, and rich, gilded ornamentation; it added up to extravagant and awe-inspiring interiors designed to impress. The church also chipped in with a profusion of churches and abbeys in this style.

Learning from the Italian model, Graz-born architect Johann Bernhard Fischer von Erlach (1656–1723) developed a national style called Austrian baroque, which was prominent from 1690 to 1730. This mirrored the exuberant ornamentation of Italian baroque but gave it a specifically Austrian treatment through dynamic combinations of colour coupled with irregular or undulating outlines. Among the many outstanding examples of baroque in Austria are Fischer von Erlach's Kollegienkirche (p240) in Salzburg and his Karlskirche (p99) in Vienna, Johann Lukas von Hildebrandt's Schloss Belvedere (p97), also in Vienna, and Stift Melk (p131) and Augustiner Chorherrenstift (p174) by Jakob Prandtauer (1660–1726).

Rococo, the extreme version of baroque, is florid, elaborate and 'lightweight'. It was a great favourite of the empress Maria Theresia, who chose this fussy style for most of the rooms of Schloss Schönbrunn (p100) when she commissioned Nicolas Pacassi to renovate it in 1744. Austrian rococo is sometimes referred to as late-baroque Theresien style.

Viennese architects aren't always the most mentally stable; one of the Staatsoper's architects committed suicide because of intense public criticism, while the Rossauer Kaserne's designer reputedly topped himself after forgetting to include toilets.

NEOCLASSICISM

All this baroque and rococo extravagance became too much after a while, and a change was in the wind. From the 18th century (but culminating in the 19th), the revival of old architectural styles, known as neoclassicism, took hold. In architecture, this meant cleaner lines, squarer, bulkier buildings and a preponderance of columns. The TU Wien in Vienna (Vienna University of Technology; p89) is a good example of this.

OTTO WAGNER

Otto Wagner (1841–1918) was one of the most influential *fin de siècle* Viennese architects. He was trained in the classical tradition, and became a professor at the Akademie der bildenden Künste (Academy of Fine Arts; p95). His early work was in keeping with his education, and he was responsible for some neo-Renaissance buildings along the Ringstrasse. But as the 20th century dawned he developed an Art Nouveau style, with flowing lines and decorative motifs. Wagner joined the Secession in 1899 and attracted public criticism in the process, one of the reasons why his creative designs for Vienna's Historical Museum were never adopted. In 1905, Wagner, Gustav Klimt and others split from the Secession. Wagner began to discard the more decorative aspects of his designs, concentrating instead on presenting the functional features of buildings in a creative way. His greatest works include the Postsparkasse (Post Office Savings Bank; p95), the Kirche am Steinhof (p101) and the Majolikahaus (p97), but his work can be seen everywhere in the capital; he designed some 35 stations of the current U-Bahn system.

When Emperor Franz Josef I took the Austro-Hungarian throne in 1848, the building boom reached a whole new level. Austria's showcase from this time is Vienna's Ringstrasse (p93), which was developed on the site of the old city walls from 1857 onwards. The Ringstrasse demonstrates a great diversity of retrograde styles, including French Gothic (Votivkirche), Flemish Gothic (Rathaus; p93), Grecian (Parlament; p93), French Renaissance (Staatsoper; p119) and Florentine Renaissance (Museum für angewandte Kunst; p96). If you're a fan of neoclassicism (or just a fan of architecture), this is the best Europe has to offer.

MODERN

The end of the 19th century saw the emergence of Jugendstil (Art Nouveau), a sensuous and decorative style of art and architecture that spread through much of Europe. In Vienna the style flowered with the founding of the Secession (p95) movement in 1897. Otto Wagner (1841–1918; see the boxed text 'Otto Wagner' p39) was one of the leading architects in the field, alongside Adolf Loos (1870–1933). Loos was even more important in moving towards a new functionalism; a bitter critic of the Ringstrasse buildings, he also became quickly disillusioned with the ornamentation in Secessionist buildings. His work can be seen in the Loos Haus (p103) and American Bar (p118) in Vienna.

The dominance of the Social Democrats in the Vienna city government of the new republic (from 1918) gave rise to a number of municipal building projects, not least the massive Karl-Marx-Hof apartment complex. Postwar architecture was mostly utilitarian. More recently, some multicoloured, haphazard-looking structures that some may see as downright strange have been erected in Vienna; they're the work of the maverick artist and architect Friedensreich Hundertwasser (see below).

Austria's premier postmodern architect is Hans Hollein, designer of the Haas Haus in Vienna.

Painting

Medieval Viennese artists were not a prolific bunch, but if you're interested in what they were producing, the Orangery in Unteres Belvedere (p98) has a collection of Gothic religious art from the period. Once the Renaissance hit the scene, the Viennese shifted their focus from Biblical

THE STRAIGHT LINE IS GODLESS

Friedensreich Hundertwasser is one of Austria's most celebrated architects/artists of Austria's modern era. Starting a career in art with three months at the Akademie der bildenden Künste (Academy of Fine Arts) in 1948, he soon drew away from conventional ideas and started on his own path. His path wasn't exactly straight; he felt that 'the straight line is Godless', and faithfully adhered to this principle in all his building projects, proclaiming that his uneven floors 'become a symphony, a melody for the feet, and bring back natural vibrations to man'. He believed that cities should be more harmonious with their surrounding (natural) environment: buildings should be semisubmerged under undulating meadows, homes should have 'tree tenants' that pay rent in environmental currency.

Hundertwasser was always something of an oddity to the Viennese establishment, and he complained that his more radical building projects were quashed by the authorities. Nevertheless, he was commissioned to re-create the façade of the Spittelau incinerator in Vienna. This was opened in 1992 and is the most unindustrial-looking heating plant you'll ever see. Other Hundertwasser creations include the KunsthausWien and Hundertwasserhaus in Vienna (p99), the church of Bärnbach, St Barbara Kirche, (p200) and Bad Blumau's spa resort (p202).

GUSTAV KLIMT

Born in Baugarten, near Vienna, in 1862 Gustav Klimt was the leader and best-known member of the Secession movement founded in 1897. Secession was born when a group of young artists revolted against the traditional art establishment and established their own journal *(Ver Sacrum)*, exhibition forum (The Secession) and unique modern style. The Secession (p95) artists worked in a highly decorative style. Klimt's famous painting *The Kiss* is typical of the rich ornamentation, vivid colour and floral motifs favoured by the Secession artists. His later pictures (such as the two portraits of Adele Bloch-Bauer) employ a harmonious but ostentatious use of background colour with much metallic gold and silver to evoke or symbolise the emotions of the main figures.

Klimt became the most celebrated artist in Vienna at the turn of the century. His works were renowned then, as now, for their sexuality and decadence. However, his *femmes fatales* exuded an eroticism and power too explicit for their time. Klimt was accused of ugliness, pornography and perverted excess. His response was typical: a work entitled *Goldfish* or *To My Critics*, portraying a voluptuous flame-haired maiden baring her bottom to the world.

to natural. The Danube School combined landscapes and religious motifs; a few of the notable exponents were Rueland Frueauf the Younger, Wolf Huber, Max Reichlich and Lukas Cranach the Elder.

While Austria didn't produce the same calibre of baroque artists as other Central European countries, some striking church frescoes were painted by Johann Michael Rottmayr and Daniel Gran. Franz Anton Maulbertsch, working on canvas, was well known for his mastery of colour and light and his intensity of expression and Paul Troger (1698–1762), who was particularly active in Lower Austria.

The mid-19th century was known as the Biedermeier period; leading artists of the time included Georg Ferdinand Waldmüller (1793–1865) and Friedrich Gauermann (1807–62), who captured the age in portraits, landscapes and period scenes. Some of Waldmüller's evocative if idealised peasant scenes can be seen in the Historisches Museum der Stadt Wien (p99) and the Oberes Belvedere (p98), both in Vienna. Rudolf von Alt, an exponent of watercolour, and Moritz Michael Daffinger were other well-known Biedermeier artists.

While the neoclassical period certainly had its prominent artists, including August von Pettenkofen and Hans Makart (1840–84), Austria's golden age was still just around the corner. The turn of the century marked the Jugendstil period, which featured organic motifs such as flowing hair, tendrils of plants, flames and waves. No-one embraced the sensualism more than Gustav Klimt (1862–1918; above), perhaps Austria's most famous.

A contemporary of Klimt, Egon Schiele (1890–1918) created work that was far more gritty and confrontational. Schiele worked largely with the human figure, and many of his works are brilliantly executed minimalist line drawings splashed with patches of bright colour and usually featuring women in pornographic poses. He also produced many self-portraits and a few large, breathtaking painted canvases, most of which can be seen in the Leopold (see p95). For more on Schiele's life and work, see Oberes Belvedere (p98) and Tulln (p137). The other major exponent of Viennese Expressionism was playwright, poet and painter Oskar Kokoschka (1886–1980), whose sometimes turbulent works show his interest in psychoanalytic imagery and baroque-era religious symbolism. Kokoschka's work is also collected by the Leopold.

Painting took a bit of a backseat between the two World Wars, but came back with a vengeance after WWII. In the 1950s HC Artmann founded

VIENNESE ACTIONISM *Dr Ed Baxter*

Viennese Actionism spanned the years 1957–68 and was one of the most extreme of all the modern art movements. It was linked to the Wiener Gruppe (Vienna Group) and had its roots in abstract expressionism. Actionism sought access to the unconscious through the frenzy of an extreme and very direct art: the Actionists quickly moved from pouring paint over the canvas, which was then slashed with knives, to using bodies (live people, dead animals) as 'brushes', and using blood, excrement, eggs, mud and whatever else came to hand as 'paint'. The traditional canvas was soon dispensed with altogether. The artist's body became the canvas, the site of art became a deliberated event (the scripted action, staged both privately and publicly) and even merged with reality.

It was a short step from self-painting to inflicting wounds upon the body, and engaging in physical and psychological endurance tests. For 10 years the Actionists scandalised the press and public and incited violence and panic – and got plenty of publicity. Often poetic, humorous and aggressive, the actions became increasingly politicised, addressing the sexual and social repression that pervaded the Austrian state. Art in Revolution (1968), the last Action to be realised in Vienna, resulted in six months hard labour all round.

the Wiener Gruppe (Vienna Group); its members incorporated surrealism and Dadaism in their sound compositions, textual montages, and Actionist happenings (above). Public outrage and police intervention were a regular accompaniment to their meetings. The group's activities came to an end in 1964 when Konrad Bayer, its most influential member, committed suicide; many Actionism works can be seen in the MUMOK (p96).

Big names in Austria's contemporary art scene include Gunter Brus and Hermann Nitsch, both former members of the Actionism group, Arnulf Rainer, also associated with Actionism but more recently involved in photographing and reworking classic pieces by Schiele, van Gogh and Rembrandt, and Eva Schlegel, who works with a number of media. All are collected by the Essl Collection (see p126).

Hermann Nitsch still practices Viennese Actionism; decide for yourself if it's your cup of tea at www.nitsch .org (in German).

Sculpture

Sculpture is one of the earliest forms of expression in Austria; the 25,000-year-old *Venus of Willendorf*, discovered in the Danube Valley (opposite), is a classic example of man's desire to artistically capture what he sees around him.

Quite a few thousand years later, sculpture began to develop through the changes in architectural styles. Romanesque sculpture is rare; the *Verdun Altar* in Klosterneuburg abbey (p126) is certainly one of the period's finest pieces. Austria has some beautiful Gothic altars carved using limewood: the best known can be seen in St Wolfgang, and was the work of Michael Pacher (1440–98), a seminal figure in religious art in the 15th century. The tomb of Maximilian I in Innsbruck's Hofkirche (p302) is the best of Renaissance. The same church has impressive statues in bronze, including several by that master of all trades, Albrecht Dürer (1471–1528).

Take a peak at the sublime works of the Wiener Werkstätte and learn something of the organisation's history at www .wiener-werkstaette.at.

Moving onto baroque, which seems to be everywhere you look in Austria, the fountain by George Raphael Donner in Vienna's Neuer Markt p98), and Balthasar Permoser's statue of Prince Eugène in the Unteres Belvedere (p98) are fine examples of the period. Baroque even extended to funeral caskets, as created by Balthasar Moll for Maria Theresia and Francis I.

Neoclassical sculpture is typified by the equestrian statue of Emperor Joseph II in Josefsplatz in Vienna's Hofburg. Salzburg has several distinctive equine fountains in its old town centre.

The Biedermeier period was strongly represented in furniture, examples of which can be seen in Vienna's Museum für angewandte Kunst (Museum of Applied Art; p96). After Biedermeier, the technique of bending wood in furniture, particularly in the backs of chairs, became popular; the bentwood chair has since became known as the Viennese chair.

The Secessionist movement not only had a hand in painting and architecture, but also sculpture. This offshoot was known as the Wiener Werkstätte (Vienna Workshops), which was deadset on changing the face of domestic design. Wallpaper, curtains, furniture, tiles, vases, trays, cutlery, bowls and jewellery were all targets for design; aesthetic considerations were given priority over practicality, resulting in some highly distinctive styles. Josef Hoffmann was a prominent figure in the Werkstätte, as was Kolo Moser; many of their works, along with other members, can be seen at the Museum für angewandte Kunst (p96) and Leopold Museum (p95).

Set in 1932, The Radetzky March by Joseph Roth is the study of one family affected by the end of empire. The themes of The Radetzky March are applicable to any society emerging from a long-hated, but at least understood, regime.

Literature

The outstanding Austrian work produced in the Middle Ages was the *Nibelungenlied* (Song of the Nibelungs), written around 1200 by an unknown hand. This epic poem told a tale of passion, faithfulness and revenge in the Burgundian court at Worms. Its themes were adapted by Richard Wagner in his *The Ring of the Nibelungen* operatic series. However the *Nibelungenlied* does not mark the beginning of literature in Austria; the Vorau abbey in Styria houses a collection of poems dating from 1150.

Aside from Franz Grillparzer (see p45), Austria's literary tradition didn't really take off until around the turn of the twentieth century, when the Vienna Secessionists and Sigmund Freud were creating waves. Influential writers who emerged at this time included Arthur Schnitzler, Hugo von Hofmannsthal, Karl Kraus and the poet Georg Trakl. Kraus' apocalyptic drama *Die letzten Tage der Menschheit* (The Last Days of Mankind) employed a combination of reports, interviews and press extracts to tell its tale – a very innovative style for its time. Peter Altenberg was a drug addict, an alcoholic, a fan of young girls and – even more importantly – a poet who depicted the

Thomas Bernhard's one-sentence prose poem On the Mountain is the story of a man about to die of lung disease. The first book Bernhard wrote and the last he published, it is bleak and bitter. Also try Cutting Timber and Wittgenstein's Nephew.

THE VENUS OF WILLENDORF *Lisa Ball*

The 25,000-year-old *Venus of Willendorf* is one of the most famous prehistoric sculptures of the human form. Discovered by archaeologist Josef Szombathy in 1908, it has since become an icon of the original 'Earth Mother'. There is much debate about what clues the 5cm-tall sandstone figure can reveal about life in 23,000 BC. Some believe the sculpture shows the esteemed role of women in prehistoric society and that mankind worshipped a female deity or Earth Mother.

Others reject Venus' status as goddess, arguing that the attention to detail, from her plaited hair to her dimpled arms, suggests that the artist used a living model, although a lack of face and feet would seem to refute this. If, however, the figure was modelled on that of a real woman, her generous body reveals clues about that woman's status. In a hunter-gatherer society, such a body would equate with an unusually sedate lifestyle, implying a special social status.

The tiny figurine may have served as a good-luck charm, carried on hunting missions to ensure a fruitful catch. The red ochre staining could represent blood spilt while foraging, or menstrual blood, indicating that Venus was a symbol used to promote fertility.

Whatever the *Venus of Willendorf* signified in prehistoric times, today her great age and voluptuous form make her a symbol of fertility, procreativity and nurturing, as well as a modern-day commodity in reproduction art. The statue is on show in the Naturhistorisches Museum (Natural History Museum; p95) in Vienna.

MARTIN HARRIS

bohemian lifestyle of Vienna. Hermann Broch (1886–1951) was very much part of Viennese café society. A scientist at heart, Broch believed literature had the metaphysical answers to complement new scientific discoveries. His masterwork was *Der Tod des Vergil* (The Death of Virgil) written in a Nazi concentration camp and after his emigration to the USA.

Robert Musil (1880–1942) was one of the most important 20th-century writers, but he only achieved international recognition after his death, when his major literary achievement, *Der Mann ohne Eigenschaften* (The Man without Qualities), was – at seven volumes – still unfinished. It's a fascinating portrait of the collapsing Austro-Hungarian monarchy. Heimito von Doderer (1896–1966) grew up in Vienna: his magnum opus was *Die Dämonen* (The Demons), an epic fictional depiction of the end of the monarchy and the first years of the Austrian Republic. A friend of Freud, a librettist for Strauss and a victim of Nazi book burnings, Stefan Zweig (1881–1942) had a rich social pedigree. A poet, playwright, translator, paranoiac and pacifist, Zweig believed Nazism had been conceived specifically with him in mind and when he became convinced in 1942 that Hitler would take over the world, he killed himself. Joseph Roth (1894–1939), primarily a journalist, wrote about the concerns of Jews in exile and of Austrians uncertain of their identity at the end of empire. His recently re-released *What I Saw: Reports from Berlin* is part of an resurgence of interest in this fascinating writer.

Perhaps it's something in the water, but the majority of contemporary Viennese authors (at least, those translated into English) are grim, guilt-ridden, angry and sometimes incomprehensibly avant-garde. Thomas Bernhard (1931–89) was born in Holland but grew up and lived in Austria. In true Viennese fashion, he was obsessed with disintegration and death, and in later works like *Holzfällen* (Cutting Timber) turned to controversial attacks against social conventions and institutions. His novels are seamless (no chapters or paragraphs, few full stops) and seemingly repetitive, but surprisingly readable once you get into them.

The best-known contemporary writer is Peter Handke (born 1942). His postmodern, abstract output encompasses innovative and introspective prose works *(The Left-Handed Woman)* and stylistic plays *(The Hour When We Knew Nothing of Each Other).* The provocative novelist and 2004 Nobel Laureate Elfriede Jelinek dispenses with direct speech, indulges in strange flights of fancy and takes a very dim view of humanity, but she is worth persevering with. Translations of her novels *The Piano Teacher, Lust, Women as Lovers* and *Wonderful, Wonderful Times* have been successfully published in paperback; *The Piano Teacher* has also been turned into a film (opposite). Friederike Mayröcker, a prominent contemporary poet and author of *Phantom Fan* and *Farewells,* has been described as 'the avant-garde's bird of paradise'. Elisabeth Reichart is considered an important – if obscure and ferocious – new writer, producing novels and essays concerned with criticism of the patriarchy and investigations of Nazi-related Austrian guilt, both during WWII and more recently.

Cinema & TV

Austria may have a long history in film (1908 marked the country's first feature film, *Von Stufe zu Stufe;* From Stage to Stage), but its endeavours have generally gone unnoticed outside the German-speaking world. As a backdrop for film, the story is quite different; two of the most famous films in cinematic history, *The Third Man* and *The Sound of Music,* are set in Vienna and Salzburg respectively. Both flopped on release in the country, and while most Austrians still haven't a clue about 'Do, a deer,

Not just a novel, but a complete overhaul of what a novel can be, *The Death of Virgil* by Hermann Broch is as stylistically groundbreaking as Joyce's *Ulysses.* Covering the last day of the poet's life, this book is hard, hard work.

Witty and clever, Elfriede Jelinek hates all her characters. Her novel *Lust* is the story of a rural woman preyed on by her husband and lover, told without a gram of sympathy for the filthy habits of humans.

For a complete rundown of Austrian films in English, consult the archives of www.afc.at, the Austrian Film Commission's website.

a female deer', opinions on Harry Lime and his penicillin racquet have turned 180 degrees since then. There are literally hundreds of other films and TV programmes filmed in Austria; *Before Sunrise, The Living Daylights* and *Where Eagles Dare* are three of the most famous.

Many of Austria's early big names had to travel to Hollywood to cultivate any semblance of success. Director Fritz Lang made the legendary *Metropolis* (1926), the story of a society enslaved by technology, and *The Last Will of Dr Mabuse* (1932), during which an incarcerated madman spouts Nazi doctrine. Billy Wilder, writer and director of massive hits like *Some Like It Hot, The Apartment* and *Sunset Boulevard,* was Viennese, though he moved to the US early in his career. Hollywood glamour girl Hedy Lamarr (not to be confused with Hedley Lamarr of *Blazing Saddles* fame) was also born in Vienna. Fred Zinnemann *(From Here to Eternity* and *High Noon)* was Austrian born, as is Klaus Maria Brandauer, star of *Out of Africa* and *Mephisto*. And who could forget Arnold Schwarzenegger, a major Hollywood star and now Governor of California (p193).

Modern Austrian cinema churns out around 15 films per year and the country's film commission, the AFC, was founded in 1986 to support local efforts and strongly promote them around the world. Themes are often realistic, bleak and harsh, with plenty of violence, cruelty and venal characters. Names of the moment include Michael Haneke, whose films tend to feature large doses of sadism and masochism. His first film, *Funny Games,* played at Cannes, and his *The Piano Teacher,* based on the novel by Viennese writer Elfriede Jelinek (opposite) went one step better, winning three Cannes awards. Documentary-maker Ulrich Seidl has made *Jesus, You Know,* following six Viennese Catholics as they visit their church for prayer, and *Animal Lovers,* an investigation of Viennese suburbanites who have abandoned human company for that of pets. Lately he has branched into features with *Dog Days*. Jessica Hausner has made several short films and recently released her first feature, *Lovely Rita,* the story of a suburban girl who kills her parents in cold blood.

Compared to film, Austrian TV is thoroughly bland. Locally produced content is low and much of the programming is dominated by foreign shows dubbed into German, though you can also catch interminable broadcasts of parliament, Austrian talk shows, local variants on reality TV or specials on folk music (that said, the news coverage is excellent). One local hit show that has made it overseas (to Australia at least) is *Komissar Rex,* the bizarrely genre-fluid, violent crime series with a dash of slapstick featuring a ham roll–stealing Alsatian dog and plenty of local scenery.

Theatre & Dance

Vienna's tradition in the theatre was – and still is – bolstered by the quality of the operas and operettas produced in the golden age of music. In addition to these forms, Greek drama, avant-garde, mime, comedy, cabaret, farce and other theatrical genres are regularly performed. Vienna is home to the four federal theatres and opera houses – the Staatsoper (p119), Volksoper (p120), Akademietheater and Burgtheater (p120). The Burgtheater is one of the premier theatre and opera venues in the German-speaking world. The Theater in der Josefstadt is known for the modern style of acting evolved by Max Reinhardt while the Theater an der Wien (p120) favours musicals. All provincial capital cities are blessed with major theatres.

The first great figure in the modern era was the playwright Franz Grillparzer (1791–1872), who anticipated Freudian themes in his plays.

A slice of Viennese life in the late '60s from popular US author John Irving, *Setting Free the Bears* tells a charming, sad and amusing story about a plan to release the animals from the zoo at Schönbrunn.

Viennese *enfant terrible* Haneke's first world-renowned work, *Funny Games* (1997) is a disturbing study of sadism and destruction. A family on holiday is taken hostage by two well-educated young men who want to push some boundaries.

So it's kitsch, tacky and full of cheesy songs, but there's no denying the popularity of *The Sound of Music* (1965) by Robert Wise, the story of the multitalented Von Trapp family and their too-good-to-be-true nanny.

Other influential playwrights who still regularly get an airing are Johann Nestroy, known for his satirical farces, and Ferdinand Raimaund, the 19th-century author of *Der Alpenkönig und der Menschenfeind* (The King of the Alps and the Misanthrope). Adalbert Stifter (1805–68) is credited as being the seminal influence in the development of an Austrian prose style.

Many Viennese authors are also playwrights – perhaps the Viennese fondness for the avant-garde encourages crossing artistic boundaries. Arthur Schnitzler, Thomas Bernhard, Elfriede Jelinek and Peter Handke (p43) have all had their plays performed at the Burgtheater.

Dance is by no means as popular as the other arts, but it does have a world-class venue in the TanzQuartier Wien (p120).

Environment

Austria is a country of incredible natural beauty; this is a land where the flat, open Pannonian plains collide with the mighty Eastern Alps. Here deep valleys and cold alpine streams snake their way between the tall mountain ranges that cut a rugged path across the skyline, and gentle, undulating hills are a patchwork quilt of forest, cultivated fields and vineyards.

THE LAND

Think of Austria and invariably the first thing to pop into your head is mountains. Of the 83,858 sq km of land that lies within Austria's borders (which stretch 560km east to west and 280km north to south at its widest point) almost two-thirds are mountainous. Glaciers, which began carving up the landscape with ease some 2½ million years ago, played a big hand in creating the country's current alpine shape of not only mountains, but also valleys and lakes.

The Alps of Austria can be grouped into three mountain ranges, all of which basically run in a west–east direction. The Northern Limestone Alps, on the border of Germany, reach nearly 3000m and extend almost as far east as the Wienerwald (Vienna Woods). The valley of the Inn River separates them from the High or Central Alps, which form the highest peaks in Austria including the king of Austrian mountains, the Grossglockner (3797m). Many ridges found here are topped by glaciers and most peaks surpass the 3000m mark. The Southern Limestone Alps, which include the Karawanken Range, form a natural barrier along the border with Italy and Slovenia.

The rest of the country is a mixed bag of alpine foothills, Pannonian lowlands, and granite highlands. Most of the country's population is within these geographical areas, due mainly to the fertile and farmable land found there. By far the most fertile land is in and around the Danube Valley; cultivation is intensive and 90% of Austria's food is grown here. In the northeast the landscape is noted for its rolling hills and clumps of forest, while the east is quite often dead flat; a direct influence of the Pannonian plains. What these regions lack in majestic scenery they make up for with vineyard after vineyard. The southeast of the country is also known for its undulating landscape and wine, and is reminiscent of Tuscany in Italy.

Austria's greatest feature outside the Alps is the thoroughly un-blue Danube (Donau), which flows west–east from Germany through the Danube Valley and Vienna, and eventually exits in Slovakia. Joining the Danube as it enters Austria is another of the country's important waterways, the Inn River. To the southeast, the main rivers are the Mur and the Drau.

Aside from rivers, Austria is covered in lakes; it's hard to move without toppling into one in the Salzkammergut region and Carinthia. The country's most unusual lake though is in the eastern fringes of the country, in the province of Burgenland. This, the Neusiedler See, is Central Europe's only steppe lake and Austria's lowest point (115m). It's a haven for bird lovers, water-sport fanatics and cyclists alike.

WILDLIFE

Austria has its fair share of wildlife, but outdoor enthusiasts who visit the country are generally far more interested in exercising their legs and

www.naturschutz.at is a one-stop shop for info on Austria's landscape, flora and fauna. It's in German, but there are a few links to English sites too.

Austria is about one third the size of the UK, or slightly smaller than Maine in the US.

Cascading over rocks for 380m, the Krimml Falls in the Hohe Tauern National Park are the longest in Europe.

expanding their lungs than sitting around trying to catch a glimpse of an elusive lynx or golden eagle. Ornithologist aficionados, however, flock to the Neusiedler See to see the 150 different species of birds that breed in the area. During the Europe–Africa migration period, the same number of species once again drop in on the Neusiedler See during their flight south.

Animals

The fauna of Austria's alpine regions is often the most intriguing for visitors. There you'll find the ibex, a mountain goat with huge curved horns, which was at one stage under threat but fortunately is now breeding again. It's the master of mountain climbing and migrates to an elevation of 3000m or more come July. The chamois, a small antelope more common than the ibex, doesn't climb quite as high but is equally at home scampering around on mountain sides. It can leap an astounding 4m vertically and its hooves have rubbery soles and rigid outer rims – ideal for maintaining a good grip on loose rocks.

The marmot, a chunky rodent related to the squirrel, is also indigenous to the Alps. It's a sociable animal that lives in colonies of about two dozen members. Like meerkats, marmots regularly post sentries, which stand around on their hind legs looking apprehensive and alert. When a predator (such as a fox) is spotted, a warning cry is sounded and the whole tribe will scurry to safety down a complex network of burrows. Winged fauna in the Alps include golden eagles, vultures – both bearded and griffin – and a multitude of colourful butterflies.

In the far east the picture is completely different. The Neusiedler See, a large steppe lake, is a unique sanctuary for numerous species of bird. Commonly spotted are avocets, Eurasian curlews, yellow wagtails, short-eared owls, great bustards and white storks.

ENDANGERED SPECIES

Like every country, Austria has its fair share of endangered species. The species below are the country's 'flagship' species – those that stand out in a list that's far too long. For more information, consult the online *Rote Liste* (red list; www.roteliste.at), a comprehensive list of endangered species collated by the knowledgeable Umweltbundesamt (Federal Environment Agency).

Austria's most endangered species is the *Bayerische Kurzohrmaus* (Bavarian pine vole), which is endemic to Tyrol and found only in six localities. Following close behind is the *Kaiseradler* (imperial eagle), at one time extinct in Austria but fortunately making a comeback through reimmigration. The *Triel* (stone curlew), a rare bird found only in eastern Austria, is also under threat, as is the *Europäische Sumpfschildkröte* (European pond terrapin), which inhabits the Danube floodplains. The *Europäische Hornotter* (long-nosed viper) may be a venomous snake at home in Carinthia, but humans are a far greater threat to its survival than its bite will ever be to our survival.

The *Grosse Sägeschrecke* (saw-legged grasshopper) may be the largest of Austria's grasshopper species, but it's also one of the most endangered, while the *Berghexe* (the hermit), a brown-flecked butterfly that flutters around open dry grassland, is now only found in three localities in Austria.

Plants

An incredible 47% of Austria is forested, making it one of the most wooded countries in Europe. At low altitudes expect to find a plethora

---

For such a small country, Austria shares its borders with eight countries: Germany, the Czech Republic, Slovakia, Hungary, Slovenia, Italy, Switzerland and Liechtenstein.

Collins Bird Guide, by Lars Svensson et al, is reputedly one of the best bird-watching guides for Europe.

For those wishing to spend time around Neusiedler See bird-watching, pick up a copy of *Finding Birds in Eastern Austria*, by Dave Gosney.

of oak and beech; at higher elevations conifers, such as pine, spruce and larch, take over. At around 2200m trees yield to alpine meadows and beyond 3000m, only mosses and lichens cling to the stark crags.

A highlight of the Alps is its flowers, which add a palette of colour to the high pastures from about June to September. The flowers here are built to cope with harsh conditions: long roots counter strong winds, bright colours (a result of strong ultraviolet light) attract few insects, and hairs and specially developed leaves protect against frost and dehydration. By far the most popular is the edelweiss, which is a white, star-shaped flower found on rocky crags and crevices. Although most alpine flowers are protected and should not be picked, many young, love-struck men have risked life and limb to bring such a flower to the lady of their choice. Aside from the beloved edelweiss, you'll notice delicate orchids, dandelions and poppies growing at higher altitudes.

Of particular note once again is the Neusiedler See, whose western shores are lined with a vast, almost impenetrable belt of reeds.

If you're heading to Austria for a bit of bird-watching, www.birdlife .at should be your first port of call.

Want to know more about Austria's national parks? www.national parks.or.at has links to all six and a brochure in English to download.

NATIONAL PARKS

For a country of such stunning natural beauty, it may come as a surprise to learn that only 2.8% of Austria falls within the boundaries of national parks. And even within this 2.8%, commercial operations such as traditional farming and hunting, are still ongoing. However, the national park authorities have managed to strike a good balance between preserving the

AUSTRIA'S NATIONAL PARKS

Park (area)	Features	Activities	Best Time to Visit	Page
Donau-Auen (93 sq km)	floodplains, meadows, still rivers; beavers, turtles, catfish	walking, cycling, boating	summer	p144
Gesäuse (110 sq km)	mountains, gorges, meadows & forests; owls, eagles, falcons, woodpeckers	rock climbing, hiking, rafting, caving, mountain biking	spring, summer, autumn	p208
Hohe Tauern (1787 sq km)	mountains; ibex, marmots, bearded vultures, golden eagles	hiking, rock & mountain climbing, skiing, canyoning, kayaking, paragliding	year-round	p277
Kalkalpen (210 sq km)	forests, gorges, mountains; lynx, golden eagles, owls, woodpeckers	cycling, hiking, rock climbing, cross-country skiing	year-round	p179
Neusiedler See-Seewinkel (97 sq km)	saline steppe lake, salt marshes; storks, great bustards, avocets, owls	sailing, swimming, cycling, walking, bird-watching	summer	p162
Thayatal (13 sq km)	rocky outcrops, virgin forest; otters, eagles, storks, bats	walking	spring, summer, autumn	p143

natural wildlife and keeping local economic endeavours alive; the natural habitat thrives while humans can eke out a living.

Of Austria's national parks, Hohe Tauern National Park is the most spectacular and frequented hands down. Neusiedler See–Seewinkel takes second place, due to its closeness to Vienna and the plethora of water-sports activities available there.

Aside from the 2300 sq km covered by the country's national parks, 37 *Naturparke* (nature parks; areas of particular natural importance) are dotted across Austria and add an extra 305 sq km to Austria's protected areas tally.

The Austrian Federal Ministry of Agriculture, Forestry, Environment & Water Management (BMLFUW) website – www.lebensministerium .at/en/home/– has a bunch of useful environmental information.

ENVIRONMENTAL ISSUES

On the whole, Austrians are an environmentally friendly bunch who treat their backyard better than most nations. They're well informed about environmental issues and the government, which spends 3% of its Gross Domestic Product (GDP) on environmental measures, has been more than happy to sign various international agreements intended to reduce pollution and preserve natural resources.

A gorgeous picture book covering all aspects of Austria's landscape and wildlife is Ewald Neffe's *Naturerlebnis Österreich*.

Recycling is big in this country; Austrians are diligent and forthright about separating recycling material from other waste, and the practice is very much ingrained in society. It's also against the law not to recycle, but it's hardly ever enforced. You'll see recycling bins for metal, paper, plastics and glass on many street corners, and most neighbourhoods have stations for hazardous materials. Some glass containers, in particular beer bottles, have a return value that can be claimed at supermarkets; look for *Flaschen Rücknahme* (bottle-return) machines.

Measures have been in place for years to protect the fragile ecosystem of Austria's alpine regions, yet some forest degradation has taken place. This is due to air and soil pollution caused by emissions from industrial plants, exhaust fumes from traffic in the Alps and the use of agricultural chemicals. The government has moved to minimise such pollutants by banning leaded petrol, assisting businesses in waste avoidance and promoting natural forms of energy, such as wind and solar power. Wind farms are prevalent in the flat plains in the east of the country and home owners are encouraged through tax breaks to install solar panels. Some buses are gas powered and environmentally friendly trams are a feature of many cities.

Austria's water resources are extensive and their protection is of para-mount importance to the Austrian government. Nitrate from overfer-tilisation is the main threat to ground water, along with pesticides and atrazine. Since 1995 however, atrazine has become a banned substance, so water pollution levels are decreasing. Around 75% of the country's waste water is biologically purified.

Two of Austria's biggest environmental concerns are in many ways not within the country's sphere of control. In a 1978 referendum, Austrians

---

RESPONSIBLE TOURISM

As a visitor, you have a responsibility to the local people and to the environment. When it comes to the environment, the key rules are to preserve natural resources and avoid degrading your surroundings. One way to achieve the former is to follow the local habit of recycling, which the Austrians should be awarded medals for. For pointers towards the latter, see p54 for pointers. Traffic congestion on the roads is a major problem, and visitors will do themselves and residents a favour if they forgo driving and use public transport.

voted against developing a nuclear power industry, prompting the federal Nuclear Prohibition Law later that year. The Czech Republic was of another viewpoint, and in October 2000 its Temelín nuclear reactor was brought online just 60km from the Austrian border. Many locals, environmentalists and politicians were appalled and angered at such a move. Their worries were not unfounded; 2002 saw a swathe of shutdowns due to faulty valves and sensors, and a pipe being welded on incorrectly (it was out by 180 degrees). While no radiation leaks have yet to be reported, environmental agencies believe it will only be a matter of time. Protests and blockades by Austrians at the Czech–Austrian border between Upper Austria and Bohemia are sporadic but ongoing.

With global warming on the increase, Austria's ski pistes are on the decrease. A UN environmental report published in late 2003 stated that if temperatures continue to rise at their current levels, some ski runs, and even ski resorts, will be without snow as early as 2030. The report estimated that temperatures are set to rise between 1.4°C and 5.8°C by 2100 if drastic action was not immediately taken. Austria's snow line would then move from 1200m to 1800m. If these predictions are correct, this would hit dozens of resorts where it hurts, including Kitzbühel (760m), one of Austria's most famous ski resorts, which would eventually be cut off from its slopes.

Outdoor Activities

Austria is a nature-lover's paradise, a country made up entirely of jagged mountain ranges, snow-capped peaks, glistening lakes, gentle rolling hills and pastures and glacier-carved valleys. Almost any outdoor activity can be pursued within its borders, and you don't have to travel far to find them. Seasons are certainly not a concern for those wishing to do *something* outside; skiers can seek out slopes to carve up during the heat of summer, walkers will find a mountain to climb or a valley to cross in the heart of winter, even in the Alps, and cyclists can locate a trail to zip along no matter what the time of year.

A great introduction to the plethora of outdoor activities on offer in Austria is the national tourist board's website www.austria.info.

WALKING & HIKING

If a walker is looking for earthly paradise, they will find it in Austria. Over 50,000km of (mostly) well-marked walking trails extend from Vienna to Bregenz, passing through a varied landscape of mountains, pastures, lakes and lazy hills. There is so much on offer that you could spend every weekend of your entire adult life out walking or *Wandern* (hiking) and never tramp along the same path twice.

Because Austrians are an organised lot, and many spend their summer weekends out walking, an ever-increasing number of paths are indicated by red-white-red stripes on a convenient tree trunk or rock, and regular signs direct the way. The practice of marking mountain trails according to their difficulty started in Tyrol and is becoming more widespread. Paths are colour-coded according to the skiing system: blue for easy, red for moderate (trails are fairly narrow and steep), and black for difficult (these trails are only for the physically fit; some climbing may be required).

It's badly laid out but www.publish.at/trekking (in German) does give extensive information on maps and books for Austria's most popular hiking regions.

The best time to tackle walks in Austria is from June to the end of September, but good walking, even in parts of the Alps, is possible in winter. The top trails are away from the towns and in the hills; if you can afford it, take a cable car to get you started. Alongside walking and hiking, the new sport of Nordic Walking is rapidly increasing in popularity due to its added health benefits. It's basically the practice of walking with ski poles; the upper body also gets a workout, posture is improved and the heart rate is increased without any perceived increase in exertion. Poles are available in sport stores countrywide and some tourist offices organise guided Nordic Walking.

Information

The website www.wanderdoerfer.at is a perfect place to start planning your walking holiday; it details the top 'hiking' villages in the country.

A great starting point for information on walks is tourist offices. Most stock brochures, booklets and maps on walking possibilities in their area, many of which are free (or cost only a couple of euros). For more specific and detailed information on the Alps, the **Österreichischer Alpenverein** (ÖAV; Austrian Alpine Club; ☎ 0512-59 547-0; www.alpenverein.at - in German; Wilhelm Greil Strasse 15, A-6010 Innsbruck) is an excellent source. Adult membership costs €48 per year, with substantial discounts for students and people aged under 25 or over 60; members pay half-price at alpine huts and get other benefits, including insurance. The club also organises walks, but you have to either join the club or be a member of an alpine club in your home country; there is an arm of the club in England, the **Austrian Alpine Club** (☎ 0044-1707 386 7402; www.aacuk.uk.com; Church Rd, Welwyn Garden City, Herts AL8 6PT).

Two further clubs worth contacting for information are the **Naturfreunde Österreich** (NFÖ; Friends of Nature Austria; ☎ 01-892 35 34-0; www.naturfreunde.at - in

German; 01, Viktoriagasse 6, Vienna) and **Österreichischer Touristenklub** (ÖTK; Austrian Tourist Club; ☎ 01-512 38 44, www.touristenklub.at - in German; 01, Bäckerstrasse 16, Vienna). The first concentrates on Austria's lowlands and the second has an excellent **library** (🕑 4-7pm Thu); the majority of books on the Alps are in German, but there is an extensive collection of maps, which can be photocopied, and staff are supremely knowledgeable.

Of the 1000-odd huts in the Austrian Alps, 535 are maintained by the ÖAV. Huts are at altitudes between 900m and 2700m and may be used by the general public. Meals or cooking facilities are often available and overnighting costs €24 to €30 for a bed in a dorm or €12 to €18 for a mattress on the floor. Members of the ÖAV or affiliated clubs pay half price.

Maps are widely available; see p355.

Mountain Safety & Emergencies

First, a sobering statistic: during some summers, fatalities involving walkers account for almost 50% of all deaths resulting from 'mountain recreation accidents'. The remainder lose their lives pursuing more obviously dangerous activities – mainly roped mountaineering, rock-climbing and paragliding. Unlike other mountain sports, however, where the objective risks are higher, most walker deaths are directly attributable to tiredness, carelessness and inadequate clothing or footwear. A fall resulting from sliding on grass, autumn leaves, scree or iced-over paths is a common hazard. Watch out for black ice. In high alpine routes avalanches and rockfall can be a problem. It's hard to get lost in Austria, where all paths are well signposted, but never leave the marked route. Study the weather forecast before you go and remember that in mountain regions weather patterns change dramatically, so take appropriate clothing and good walking shoes. Make sure you have enough carbohydrate-rich food for the day (including emergency rations) and at least 1L of water per person to avoid dehydration. Increase the length and altitude of your walks gradually, until you are acclimatised to the vast alpine scale.

Where possible don't walk in the mountains alone. Two is considered the minimum number for safe mountain-walking, and having at least one additional person in the party will mean someone can stay with an injured walker while the other seeks help. Properly inform a responsible person, such as a family member, hut warden or hotel receptionist, of your plans, and avoid altering your specified route. Under no circumstances should you leave the marked trails in foggy conditions. With some care, most walking routes can be followed in fog, but otherwise wait by the path until visibility is clear enough to proceed.

The standard alpine distress signal is six whistles, six calls, six smoke puffs – that is, six of whatever sign you can make – followed by a pause equalling the length of time taken by the calls before repeating the signal again. If you have a mobile phone, take it with you. **Mountain rescue** (☎ 140) in the Alps is very efficient but extremely expensive, so make sure you have insurance.

Mountaineering is a potentially dangerous activity, and you should never climb on your own or without proper equipment.

Walking Highlights

Ask an Austrian to name their top 10 walks, and invariably they'll puff, look skywards, tell you that's *impossible* – and then rattle off their top 30. They're not being arrogant; they're just telling the truth. So many regions have so many great walks, and all have their own merits.

As well as walks specific to a particular location, the country is crisscrossed by 10 *Weitwanderwege* (long-distance hiking trails). Each one of

A useful volume for walkers is *Mountain Walking in Austria* by Cecil Davies. It includes 98 single and multi-day tours in 25 of Austria's mountain groups but some descriptions are up to 20 years old.

RESPONSIBLE WALKING

The popularity of walking is placing great pressure on the natural environment. Please consider the following tips when walking and help preserve Austria's ecology and beauty.

Trail Etiquette

Of course, walking can be a very casual affair, but observing a few simple rules of etiquette will keep you in good stead with other walkers.

- On narrow paths, ascending walkers have right of way over those descending.
- Always leave farm gates as you find them. In summer low-voltage electric fences are set up to control livestock on the open alpine pastures; where an electric fence crosses a path, it usually has a hook that can be easily unfastened to allow walkers to pass through without getting zapped.
- Don't pick alpine wild flowers – they really do look lovelier on the mountainsides. Animal watchers should approach wildlife with discretion. Moving too close will unnerve wild animals, distracting them from their vital summer activity of putting on fat for the long winter.

Rubbish

- If you've carried it in you can carry it out. And don't overlook those easily forgotten items, such as silver paper (tin foil), orange peels, cigarette butts and plastic wrappers. Empty packaging weighs very little anyway, and should be stored as you go along in a dedicated rubbish bag. Make an effort to carry out rubbish left by others.
- Never bury your rubbish: digging disturbs soil and ground cover and encourages erosion. Buried rubbish will more than likely be dug up by animals, who may be injured or poisoned by it. It may also take years to decompose, especially at high altitudes.
- Minimise the waste you must carry out by taking minimal packaging and no more food than you will actually need. If you can't buy in bulk, unpack small-portion packages and combine their contents in one container before your trip. Take reusable containers or stuff sacks.
- Don't rely on bought water in plastic bottles. Disposal of these bottles is creating a major problem in the world. Use iodine drops or purification tablets instead.

Johnathan Hurdle's *Walking Austria's Alps, Hut to Hut* is a contemporary take on an old theme; it is based on tours completed by Austrian Alpine Club members and covers all the major alpine hut walks.

these trails showcases a different section of Austria's beautiful and diverse landscape: 01, 02 and 03 all take an east–west line, cutting through the north, central and southern Alps respectively; 04 also runs east–west, but through the alpine foothills from Vienna to Salzburg; the rest snake north–south – 05, 06 and 07 through Austria's flatter landscape to the east and 08, 09 and 10 up and over the Alps. Freytag & Berndt's *Österreichische Weitwanderwege* (1:800,000) is a good, overall introduction to all trails mentioned above.

The following is a selection of the country's more recognised walks, a brief sample of what's on offer. For detailed maps and further information on each of these and other walks, consult the national tourist office or local offices. But remember that this is not gospel, and the best idea is to pick the brains of locals.

ARNOWEG (SALZBURGERLAND)

Rother Wanderführer *Arnoweg Der Salzburger Rundwanderweg*

The Arnoweg (www.arnoweg.com) rates high among the best long-distance walks in the country. Named after the first Archbishop of Salzburg, this 1200km-long path makes a convoluted circuit around the province of Salzburgerland and takes approximately two months to

- Condoms, tampons and sanitary pads should also be carried out, despite the inconvenience. They burn and decompose poorly.

HUMAN WASTE DISPOSAL

- Contamination of water sources by human faeces can lead to the transmission of giardia, a human bacterial parasite. It can cause severe health risks to members of your party, to local residents and to wildlife.
- Where there is a toilet, please use it.
- Where there is none, bury your waste. Dig a small hole 15cm deep and at least 100m from any watercourse. Consider carrying a lightweight trowel for this purpose. Cover the waste with soil and a rock. Use toilet paper sparingly and bury that too. In snow, dig down beneath the soil; otherwise your waste will be exposed when the snow melts.

WASHING

- Don't use detergents or toothpaste in or near watercourses, even if they are biodegradable.
- For personal washing, use biodegradable soap and a water container (or even a lightweight basin) at least 50m away from the watercourse. Disperse the waste water widely to allow the soil to filter it.
- Wash cooking utensils 50m from watercourses using a scourer, sand or snow instead of detergent.

EROSION

- Mountain slopes and hillsides, especially at high altitudes, are prone to erosion. It is important to stick to existing tracks and avoid short cuts that bypass a switchback. If you blaze a new trail straight down a slope, it will turn into a watercourse with the next heavy rainfall and eventually cause soil loss and deep scarring.
- If a well-used track passes through a mud patch, walk through the mud: walking around the edge will increase the size of the patch.
- Avoid removing the plant life that keeps topsoils in place.

complete. The official start and finish point of this walk is at Salzburg (p234), but many walkers choose to follow only the southerly stretch of the walk, which takes you through the Dachstein Alpen Park (p218), the Schladminger Tauern Park and the Hohe Tauern National Park (p282). The path climbs to a high point of 3106m, so a decent level of fitness is required.

The *ÖAV Hut Book for Austria* (German with key words in English) is a comprehensive book on alpine huts; details include opening times, telephone, nearby peaks and walking times from the valley and between huts.

BERLINER HÖHENWEG (TYROL)
Kompass Wanderkarte 37, *Mayrhofen Tuxer Tal Zillergrund,* 1:25,000
This 42km hike through the Hochgebirgs-Naturpark Zillertaler Alpen (p318) is an intensive excursion into the Alps. Starting at Ginzling (p318) or Finkenberg, the trail quickly gains altitude and stays there; its lowest point is 1782m, its highest 3133m. Views of the Zillertaler mountains which tower over the trail are truly spectacular, as is the vista across Schleggeisspeicher lake well below. It should only be attempted by those in good condition and with mountaineering experience, as snow patches are not uncommon and there are a number of passes to contend with. Depending on your fitness, it takes three to four days to complete the Berliner trail, and it can only be tackled from the middle of June till the beginning of October.

BIELERHÖHE (VORARLBERG)
Kompass Wanderkarte 41, *Silvretta Verwallgruppe,* 1:50,000
Starting at the road-pass linking the Montafon and Paznaun Valleys via the Silvretta Hochalpenstrasse, the 13km Bielerhöhe (p344) walk passes lakes, deep pools and mountains. The best time to visit is early summer when carpets of alpine flowers flourish on the hills. The terrain is fairly gentle, although you will need good walking boots for this five- to six-hour walk. The first descent from Radsattel can be tricky and there may be patches of snow on the route, even in early summer.

GAMLITZ (STYRIA)
Kompass Wanderkarte 217, *Südsteirisches Weinland,* 1:35,000
Starting at Gamlitz, follow waymarked route 03. This 17km, five-hour walk allows you to explore the farm tracks, footpaths and country lanes snaking through this vineyard region. The gentle rolling hills make walking fairly easy going. Gamlitz is south of Graz, 2km from Ehrenhausen (p201).

HALLSTATT (UPPER AUSTRIA)
Kompass Wanderkarte 20, *Dachstein, Südliches Salzkammergut,* 1:50,000
Starting at the Steeg-Gosau railway station, most of this 16km walk alongside the Hallstätter See (p216) is easy going, although the ascent of a long flight of steps on leaving Hallstatt (p216) can be taxing. Hallstatt is one of the most beautiful and historic villages in Austria, so make sure you have time to explore the village before setting off on the return leg. If you're more ambitious, you can take on the 40km Soleweg (brine trail) from Hallstatt north to Ebensee (p225), following the course of the world's oldest pipeline (1607).

'Hallstatt is one of the most beautiful and historic villages in Austria, so make sure you have time to explore the village'

HERMAGOR (CARINTHIA)
Kompass Wanderkarte 60, *Gailtaler Alpen-Karnische Alpen,* 1:50,000
This 13km route is a good family walk that explores the water-carved gorge cut deep into the Karnische Alpen. Although the waterfalls and pools make for some stunning scenery, watch out for the gorge path, which can be slippery in places. Allow 5½ hours if you leave from Hermagor or 4½ hours if you park at the gorge entrance. Hermagor is about 45km west of Villach (p264), in Carinthia.

INNSBRUCK (TYROL)
Freytag & Berndt WK333, *Innsbruck und Umgebung,* 1:25,000
Starting at Maria Theresien Strasse in Innsbruck (p299), this 9km walk explores the best of the old town before climbing the vast Nordkette Mountains to expose magnificent views of the town below. Footpaths and minor roads make for easy walking, although there are some steep ascents. For fit walkers, the route should take three to four hours.

KATRIN (UPPER AUSTRIA)
Kompass Wanderkarte 20, *Dachstein, Südliches Salzkammergut,* 1:50,000
Take the cable car from the spa town of Bad Ischl (p212) to the Mt Katrin (p214) upper cable car station to reach the start of this 11.5km route. Some of the more precarious segments of this walk, where the vegetation gives way to bare rocky ridges, have fixed ropes to assist walkers, who will need a good head for heights. The tough descent is made more bearable by the excellent views of lakes and valleys below. Allow about 4½ hours for this walk.

MATREI IN OSTTIROL (EAST TYROL)
Kompass Wanderkarte 46, *Kals am Grossglockner,* 1:50,000
This 15km walk is good for exploring the region's beautiful valleys, especially when low cloud is obscuring the panoramic mountain views. The pathway walking is gentle, although the uphill forest track can be slightly arduous and sometimes overgrown. There is some interesting architecture along the route, including the delicate whitewashed chapel at Hinteregg and the Romanesque church of St Nikolaus. Leaving from Matrei, allow five hours for this stroll. There's a national park office in Matrei.

ÖTZTALER ALPEN (TYROL)
Kompass Wanderkarte 43, *Ötztaler Alpen,* 1:50,000
The stunning mountain scenery of the Ötztaler Alpen is among the best in Austria, making this 18km, two-day walk well worth the effort for fit and experienced hill walkers. Starting at the Gepatschhaus at the southern end of the Gepatsch reservoir in the Kaunertal, well-signed paths mark the route. Some rock hopping is involved on this route, and you will also have to overcome a steep snow slope from the Ölgrupen Joch. One of the best parts of this walk is the great view you're treated to after an overnight stay in an alpine hut. The Kaunertal can be reached from Landeck (p327).

'The stunning mountain scenery of the Ötztaler Alpen is among the best in Austria'

SCHLADMINGER TAUERN (STYRIA)
Kompass Wanderkarte 31, *Radstadt/Schladming,* 1:50,000
This circular two-day walk covering just over 20km starts 13km south of Schladming at Riesach, a lovely spot famed for its waterfall. The walk passes through a range of rocky peaks, narrow ridges and deep cirques before climbing to its highest point, the Greifenberg peak (2618m). A highlight of the walk is the traverse of the Klafferkessel, a vast, flat-bottomed cirque littered with dozens of alpine tarns and lakes. Aside from Schladming, the nearest town of any size is Radstadt (p253) in Salzburgerland.

SCHNEEBERG (LOWER AUSTRIA)
Kompass Wanderkarte 210, *Wiener Hausberge,* 1:35,000
This particular walk is a favourite of the Viennese, many of whom flock here on sunny summer weekends by train from the capital to get a taste of the Alps – and it's easy to see why. The four-hour walk (p152) starts from the top of the Schneebergbahn and heads for Klosterwappen (2075m), the highest peak in Lower Austria. It then completes a fairly easy circuit of the mountain; views across to the nearby Rax Alps and back over the beginning of the Pannonian Plains are beautiful extensive.

STUBAIER ALPEN (TYROL)
Kompass Wanderkarte 83, *Stubaier Alpen – Serleskamm,* 1:50,000
Starting at Neustift/Neder in the Stubaital (Stubai Valley), you will need at least seven to nine days and a good level of fitness to tread the well-marked 120km route of the Stubaier Höhenweg. The huts along the way are as varied as the stunning views, although all are warm and comfortable. Every section involves battling at least one pass, and many sections have fixed wire ropes to assist with difficult steps. Snow patches are possible even in late summer. Buses run along the Stubaital from Innsbruck (p313).

TENNENGEBIRGE (SALZBURGERLAND)
Tennengebirge Wanderkarte (available from the Werfen tourist office), *Werfen, Pfarrwerfen, Werfenweng*, 1:35,000
For fit walkers, this 21km walk covers the high pasture of the Tennengebirge, the area used for the famous opening sequence of *The Sound of Music*. The town of Werfen, overlooked by Burg Hohenwerfen (Werfen fortress), is the start of an idyllic seven- to eight-hour walk through beautiful meadows, forest and farmland. The Eisriesenwelt Caves, the largest ice caves in the world, are nearby. The best accommodation options are in Werfen (p251).

SKIING

With much of the country given over to mountainous splendour, it's no surprise to learn that snow sports are hugely popular in Austria. Almost every Austrian you meet has skied since they could walk, and the average child will literally ski circles around you on the slopes. The best skiing is in the western reaches of the country, though almost anywhere in the Alps has T-bars, lifts and cable cars.

There's a whole range of choice here for skiers. Austria has gentle nursery slopes in picturesque surroundings to inspire any first-timer, as well as world-class serious terrain at resorts such as St Anton am Arlberg (p329) and Kitzbühel (p319) to satisfy the slickest of professionals. Getting to the slopes is easy, with most of the main areas accessible from major towns, including Salzburg and Innsbruck. Many resorts, such as Sportwelt (p253) in Salzburg province or Skiwelt (p325) in Tyrol, offer regional passes that allow free access to hundreds of different pistes in the district.

While this book contains plenty of skiing information, it is not a skiing guide. Austria has hundreds of top-notch ski resorts and no attempt has been made to cover them exhaustively. Don't assume the skiing is not good in a resort if it is not mentioned here. Rather, ski resorts have been selected if good skiing is allied to renown, scenery and general attractions. For a detailed assessment of resorts based primarily on skiing criteria, consult a specialist book or magazine, such as the UK's *The Good Skiing & Snowboarding Guide* (Penguin UK). More information on ski resorts can be provided by Österreich Werbung (p359) and the resort tourist offices.

Information

The skiing season starts in December and lasts well into April in the higher resorts. The slopes get the biggest crowds at Christmas/New Year and in February when schools send kids to the slopes for a week at a time. Mid-April to June and late October to mid-December fall between the summer and winter seasons in mountain resorts. Some cable cars will be closed for maintenance and many hotels and restaurants will be shut, but you'll avoid the crowds and find prices at their lowest. Year-round skiing is possible at eight glaciers: Dachstein (p218), Mölltaler, Hintertuxer (p317), Pitztaler, Kaunertaler, Sölden (p325), Kitzsteinhorn-Kaprun (p280) and Stubaier (p313). However, most alpine glaciers are now retreating in the face of global warming, and snow coverage is less secure at lower elevations in the early and late season.

Skiing is certainly not a cheap pastime, but a week on the pistes won't break the bank. Austria is not the most expensive ski destination in Western Europe, but it's not as cheap as resorts in Eastern Europe, which are improving their facilities all the time and attracting skiers more than ever. In the future, this competition may force prices in Austria to drop.

Details of every ski resort in Austria can be found on www.bergfex.at /austria/; the site also lists summer activities.

Updated yearly, *ADAC PistenAtlas* is a great resource for skiers. It provides prices, maps, elevation and tourist office information for every region in the entire Alps. It's in German, but very easy to navigate.

AVALANCHE WARNING

Modern safety precautions mean that the days of villages being buried by snow have passed, but the dangers of avalanches should not be underestimated. Austria made world headlines in February 1999 when an avalanche smashed through Galtür in Tyrol, killing 31.

Problems usually originate on slopes high above the prepared ski runs. Accordingly, mountain resorts now have a series of crisscross metal barriers built high on the peaks to prevent snow slips. In addition, helicopter teams routinely drop explosive devices in the mountains to cause controlled slides and prevent the dangerous build-up of snow. Resorts also have a system involving flags or flashing lights to warn skiers of the likelihood of avalanches, and up-to-date reports on weather conditions are always available.

Despite these measures, skiers cannot afford to be complacent. Avalanche warnings should be heeded and local advice sought before detouring from prepared runs. If skiers are buried in an avalanche, chances of rescue are improved if they carry an avalanche transceiver, a radio that transmits and receives a 457kHz signal. These cost US$220 or more. A more expensive precaution (but of debatable value) is an ABS air balloon rucksack. Keeping a mobile phone with you is also a good idea. If you are unfortunate enough to end up buried in snow, dribbling a little spit will help you work out which way is up. If you can't dig your way out, some experts recommend that you urinate, as the smell will attract the tracker dogs.

Ski passes cover the cost of specified mountain transport, including ski buses between the ski areas. Pass prices for little-known places may be as little as half that charged in the jet-set resorts such as Kitzbühel (p319). Vorarlberg and especially Tyrol are the most popular areas, but there is also skiing in Salzburg Province, Upper Austria, Carinthia and even Lower Austria. Ski passes are available from ski lifts and usually from buses to the lifts, and also occasionally from tourist offices.

Ski coupons (passes based on usage rather than time) for ski lifts can sometimes be purchased, but you're usually better off buying half-day/full-day/multiple-day passes. Count on around €22 to €40 for a one-day ski pass, with substantial reductions for longer-term passes. At the beginning and end of the season, and sometimes in January (the low season), ski passes may be available at a reduced rate.

Rental prices for carving-skis, stocks and shoes are around €15 to €25 for one day for downhill and €8 to €13 for *Langlauf* (cross-country), with reduced rates offered over longer periods; snowboards are a couple of euros more than carving skis. Telemark skis can be hired but are not always easy to find. You may initially get some strange looks if you ask to buy ex-rental stock, but great bargains can be picked up this way.

Most ski resorts have one or more ski schools. Individual tuition and group lessons are available and will normally set you back around €170/40 per day respectively. The more days you take, the cheaper it gets.

Weather and avalanche reports in Austria's ski regions are updated daily on www.lawine.at.

Austrian Matthias Zdarsky wrote the first skiing manual in 1897, invented the first practical ski binding and organised the first slalom competition in skiing history in 1905.

Ski Regions

The following is a selection of some of Austria's varied skiing highlights. Week ski passes are quoted here at high season rates; check with local tourist offices or turn to the regional chapter for details on possible discounts.

ARLBERG (TYROL/VORARLBERG)
Altitude 1304m–2811m

Made up of the resorts Lech (p345) and Zürs (p345) in Vorarlberg and St Anton am Arlberg (p329) in Tyrol, Arlberg (www.lech-zuers.at, www .stantonamarlberg.at) is Austria's premier ski area where the rich, royal and famous hang out. Lech and Zürs consist of relatively gentle runs, although there is some trickier off-piste terrain. St Anton is less elitist, popular with advance skiers and has a vibrant après-ski scene. The resorts are connected by bus, the season runs from November to mid-April and a seven-day pass costs €230.

275 people lost their lives to avalanches in the Austrian Alps between 1994 and 2003 – in the same period 10,543 died on Austria's roads.

DACHSTEIN TAUERN (STYRIA)
Altitude 750m–2700m
Encompassing the resorts of Schladming-Rohrmoos, Haus im Ennstal and Pichl-Reiteralm, Dachstein Tauern (p218; www.dachstein-tauern.at – in German) is a massive region with 208km of runs and 97 lifts. All levels of skiing and snowboarding are covered here, and the season lasts from the end of November till the end of April (except for summer glacial skiing). A seven-day pass costs €184.

HEILIGENBLUT (CARINTHIA)
Altitude 1301m–2604m
Heiligenblut (p286; www.heiligenblut.at) is a small resort of 14 lifts and 55km of piste but makes the list because of its pretty location at the foot of Grossglockner (3798m). Its slopes are more suited to beginners and intermediates and the season runs from December to April; for €169, you can ski for seven days.

ISCHGL (TYROL)
Altitude 1400m–2872m
Ischgl (p329; www.ischgl.com) lies in the Paznauntal, and is hailed as one of Austria's best skiing areas. It's more remote than most resorts in the country, and usually enjoys plenty of snowfall. The Silvretta Pass (seven days €228) not only covers Ischgl, but the nearby resorts of Galtür, Kappl and Samnaun (in Switzerland). The season runs from December to April.

KITZBÜHEL/KIRCHBERG (TYROL)
Altitude 800m–2000m
The combined ski fields of Kitzbühel (p319; www.kitzbuehel.com) and Kirchberg (p323; www.kirchberg.at) are, after Arlberg, the best known in Austria. The town of Kitzbühel still retains its medieval heart and exudes plenty of wealth, while Kirchberg is more relaxed and less expensive. Both access excellent intermediate and advanced ski slopes from December to April. A one-week pass costs €186; for true enthusiasts, a pass covering this and nearby ski areas (including Wilde Kaiser; see opposite) is available for €176 for six days.

MAYRHOFEN (TYROL)
Altitude 1620m–2500m
Combining steep slopes with broad pistes perfect for carving and cruising, Mayrhofen (p317; www.mayrhofen.at) is a picturesque resort in the Zillertal with something for everyone. A one-week pass (€180) covers 147km of piste and 45 lifts in the surrounding area, and the season runs from early December to mid-April.

MONTAFON (VORARLBERG)
Altitude 654m–2400m
The Montafon ski region (p344; www.montafon.at) stretches along a long valley in the southeast corner of Vorarlberg. It's week pass (€189.50) covers seven resorts, including Schruns/Tschagguns, Gargellen and Gas-

churn, and the season runs from December to April. Beginner and intermediate slopes are the most common here, although there is some excellent ski-touring available for advanced skiers.

OBERGURGL-HOCHGURGL (TYROL)
Altitude 1800m–3080m

In the furthest reaches of the Ötztal is Obergurgl-Hochgurgl (p325; www .obergurgl.com), one of the highest resorts in the country. Its plethora of beginner and intermediate slopes (110km, 23 ski lifts) and quiet ambience make it popular with families. A week pass costs €183 and its season is one of the longest in Austria, running from November to May.

SEEFELD (TYROL)
Altitude 1200m–2100m

The prosperous, attractively situated town of Seefeld (p313; www.seefeld .at) is a perfect spot for beginners and intermediate skiers and snowboarders. It's also a popular with cross-country skiers, who can enjoy an extensive network of 250km of trails. The week pass (€173) covers not only Seefeld, but also Ehrwald, Reith and, in Germany, Garmisch-Partenkirchen. The season runs from December to April.

SKIWELT WILDE KAISER-BRIXENTAL (TYROL)
Altitude 720m–1892m

Skiwelt (www.skiwelt.at) is reputedly the largest inter-connected skiing area in Austria, with 250km of pistes (160km of which is boosted with artificial snow) connected by 90 cable cars and lifts. Of the handful of villages surrounding Skiwelt, Söll (p325) is the most well-known. From December to March (longer, depending on snow conditions) the slopes, which are suited to beginners and intermediates, are accessible to skiers. A week pass costs €176 and the region's only drawback is its piste map, which we've been told is highly confusing.

SPORTWELT AMADÉ (SALZBURG)
Altitude 750m–2150m

For size, nothing in Austria compares to Sportwelt Amadé (www.sport welt-amade.at), with Radstadt (p253) at its heart. This ski region consists of a massive 865km of pistes and 276 lifts, and there is certainly something for everyone. The region has both towns with good après-ski and villages focusing on families. A one-week ski pass costs €184 and the season runs from December to April.

ZELL AM SEE/KAPRUN (SALZBURG)
Altitude 758m–3029m

This lively twin resort (p280; www.kitzsteinhorn.at) just north of the Hohe Tauern mountain chain has excellent skiing for all standards, but particularly for adept intermediates. Fifty-six lifts take you to 130km of prepared runs, and good snow conditions last from December until the end of March. There is also summer glacial skiing and a seven-day pass costs €170.

CYCLING & MOUNTAIN BIKING

For many, there is no better way to explore Austria than with your bum on a seat, free-wheeling it through the pristine countryside. The place is basically made for it; designated cycle paths crisscross the length and breadth of Austria, passing through both lowlands to the east and

Austria has around 3300 transport facilities in steep alpine regions, compared with just 26 in 1945.

mountains to the south and west. With such varied landscapes, there is certainly something for everyone.

A good starting point for collating information on cycling is the local and regional tourist offices. Most have some literature on the subject, ranging from maps to entire brochures. Cycle clubs are another good source of information; **Argus** (Map pp83–5 ; ☎ 505 09 07; www.argus.or.at - in German; 04, Frankenberggasse 11, Vienna) is one of the bigger clubs, with offices throughout the country and books (also in English) on the subject. **Esterbauer's** (www.ester bauer.com) line of Bikeline books are the best on the market, covering all of Austria's major trails in some detail. They are in German but are reasonably easy to navigate. Maps come in all shapes and sizes, but many Freytag & Berndt and Kompass hiking maps are reliable sources for cycling; they invariably have cycle-trails marked. Free tourist-office maps can range from highly detailed references, with trails, distances and altitude profile clearly recorded, to vague drawings of little practical assistance.

Aside from the plethora of national trails, three of the **Euro Velo** (www .eurovelo.org), a series of Europe-wide cycle trails, pass through Austria. Route N6 follows the Danube path, entering Austria at Passau in Germany and exiting at Bratislava in Slovakia, Route N7 heads north–south through Tyrol, Salzburg and Upper Austria and Route N9 also takes a north–south line, passing through Graz and Vienna.

Bikes can be taken on Austrian trains (see p367); and destination chapters list places to hire bikes throughout the country.

Bike riding broadly breaks down into two categories – cycling and mountain biking. Cycling is by far the more popular pastime of the two, simply because it is accessible to all and sundry.

Cycling

Cycling trails generally stick to flat ground, with only a few hills to climb. Most circle lakes and follow the course of rivers; the biggest and best are briefly outlined below:

- **Bodensee (Lake Constance)** Famous Lake Constance (p337), touching base with Austria in Vorarlberg, is easily explored by bicycle; the 240km cycleway is quite flat and mainly follows the banks of the lake not only through Austria, but also Germany and Switzerland.
- **Danube Trail** Following the Danube (p130) for over 365km from Passau to Bratislava, this trail is Austria's most popular bike route. The path is flat, the scenery (especially in the Wachau) impressive and most towns and hotels cater well to cyclists. Free booklets are available along the way, but for something with more detail, pick up Esterbauer's *Danube Bike Trail*, which contains maps, instructions and a smattering of practical tourist information.
- **Drau Trail** The southernmost trail in Austria, the Drau trail shadows the Drau River (p264) for 360km from its entry point in East Tyrol until it exits the country at the eastern end of Carinthia. There is some legwork involved as the beginning of the trail winds its way through the southern reaches of the Alps.
- **Enns Trail** Like the Drau, the Enns trail (250km) requires more effort than most, as it follows the Enns River (p203) between some of the highest peaks in Styria. Starting near Radstadt in Salzburg, it's a stunning ride through alpine scenery down into the flat lands of Upper Austria, finishing up at the township of Enns.
- **Inn Trail** The Inn trail, which starts at Innsbruck and travels 302km to Schärding, sticks close to the course of the Inn River (p301). It's basi-

Austria has a number of lakes filled with drink-quality water, including Thiersee, Urisee and Plansee, all of which are in Tyrol.

RadFernWege Österreich by Esterbauer gives an overview of the best 21 cycling trails throughout the country. Once again, it's in German, but the maps and practical details are very straightforward.

cally downhill all the way, passing through Tyrol, Bavaria and Upper Austria; the trip takes about seven days.

- **Mur Trail** The Mur trail is a varied 350km path cutting along the Mur Valley (p205) in Styria until Bruck an der Mur, where it turns south and heads through Graz and Styria's wine country. Historical towns, mountain scenery and undulating hills are all features of this route.

- **Neusiedler See** Circling the largest steppe lake in Central Europe, this extremely flat 135km path (p159) passes through wine towns, vineyards, marshlands and, at the southern end of the lake, Hungary. The free *Neusiedler See Radtouren* map is sufficient to get you around.

- **Salzkammergut Trail** For 300km this circular trail explores the lakes of the Salzkammergut area, including Hallstätter See, Attersee, Traunsee and Wolfgangsee. It's anything but flat, but the trail is well marked and only a moderate condition is required. To truly explore the area, pick up Esterbauer's *Radatlas Salzkammergut* book.

- **Tauern Trail** The 310km Tauern trail is a combination of mountain biking and cycling; it begins at the Krimml Falls (p284) and snakes along the Salzach river past the Hohe Tauern range before turning north to Salzburg, and finally heading south along the Saalach river to Zell am See.

- **Wörthersee** This short, 27km trail circumnavigates the Wörthersee (p263) in Carinthia and takes in historic towns and castles. If you overheat, the thermally heated waters of the lake are always close at hand.

> The best places to get all dirty on your mountain bike and a bunch of hotels to get cleaned up afterwards are listed on www.bike-holidays.com.

Mountain Biking

Mountain biking in Austria has been on the increase for years, and has now reached a level of popularity where tourist offices directly market the activity. There are around 17,000km of mountain biking trails in the country, and while the true challenges lie in Vorarlberg, Tyrol, Salzburg and Carinthia, even such places as the Wienerwald (Vienna Woods) offer testing trails. Below is just a sample of areas which should only be tackled by the fit and determined:

- **Dachstein & Tauern** Over 1000km of trails crisscross this area (p218), which includes some of the highest country in Austria.

- **Ischgl-Galtür** A steep valley (p329) in the southwest of Tyrol bordering Switzerland with single, medium and difficult trails climbing to well over 2500m. It's possible to cycle onto the Montafon valley via the Bielerhöhe pass (2036m).

- **Kitzbühel-Kirchberg** While trails here don't climb to the dizzying heights of other regions, Kitzbühel-Kirchberg (p319) is rated among the best in the Austrian Alps. Over 30 trails of all grades criss-cross this compact area.

- **Lungau** Around an hour south of Salzburg is this new mountain biking region (p253), with around 600km of bikeable trails. It's more suited to beginners.

- **Montafon** In the southern reaches of Vorarlberg is the Montafon valley (p344), which has trails heading off in all directions. The highlight here is the circular ride over the Bielerhöhe pass (2036m; p344) into the Ischgl-Galtür valley and back via the Kopssee.

- **Nochberge** North of Millstätter See is Nochberge, a mountain-biking region with superb views of the lakes of Carinthia. Trails are suitable for all levels of experience.

- **Stubaital & Zillertal** These two valleys (p313 and p315 respectively) running south from the Inn in Tyrol are wide and flanked by high mountains. Like Nochberge, there is plenty to keep both beginners and the most experienced entertained.

PARAGLIDING

The website www
.flugschulen.at lists
flight schools offering
paragliding throughout
the country.

Wherever there is a high mountain accessible by cable car, a bit of flat ground and a constant wind, you'll find paragliding and hang-gliding in Austria. It's particularly popular on bright, warm, sunny days in the Alps, when the sky is dotted with people floating effortlessly on thermal drafts.

Of the two, paragliding wins the popularity race, simply because the equipment is more portable. Many resorts have places where you can hire the gear, get a lesson, or simply go as a passenger on a flight. Tyrol is traditionally a centre for paragliding, with narrow valleys and plenty of cable cars. Prices for flights start at around €75 and top out at around €160.

WATER SPORTS

Austria has more than 6000 lakes and a mammoth number of rivers coursing through its valleys, so there are more than enough places to enjoy water sports.

For a landlocked country,
Austria is pretty handy on
the waves; it won gold in
sailing at both the Sydney
and Athens Olympics.

Zipping across lakes by wind power is the most popular water sport in the country, and the locals aren't at all bad at it if the Olympic medals are anything to go by. Sailing, windsurfing and kite surfing are all here to be had; the **Österreichischer Segel-Verband** (Austrian Sailing Federation; ☎ 02167-40 243-0; www.segelverband.at; Seestrasse 17b, A-7100 Neusiedl am See) can provide a list of clubs and locations in the country. The Neusiedler See (p159) is the number one lake for such activities (probably because Vienna is so close), followed by the lakes of Carinthia and Salzkammergut. Tyrol has the Achensee (p319) and Vorarlberg the Bodensee (p337) .

Rafting, canoeing or kayaking the white waters of Austria's alpine rivers are other favourite pastimes. Big rivers which support such adrenaline sports include the Enns and Salza in Styria, the Inns, Sanna and Ötztaler Ache in Tyrol and the Isel in East Tyrol. The township of Imst (p327) is a well-known centre for rafting. **Absolute Outdoors** (☎ 03612-253 43; www.rafting .at; Ausseerstrasse 2-4, A-8940 Liezen), a company that has been in operation for over 15 years, offers trips on all the above rivers.

Angeln (fishing) enthusiasts have ample opportunities to hook a prized catch. Carp and trout are the most common species found in Austria's waterways; anglers should contact local tourist offices to obtain a fishing permit valid for lakes and rivers.

There's not a lot of it, but there is diving in Austria. Most of it is located in the Salzkammergut's lakes, including Hallstättersee (p216), Attersee (p225) and Traunsee (p222).

ROCK CLIMBING

Those wishing to
experience rock-
climbing without hanging
precariously from a rock
face should try one of the
climbing paths suggested
in Paul Werner's *Kletter-
steig – Scrambles in the
Northern Limestone Alps*.

It's impossible to have mountains without *Klettern* (rock climbing), therefore Austria is covered with rock-climbing opportunities. A good introduction point for any would-be Spiderman or woman out there is the **Österreichischer Alpenverein** (p52), which not only offers advice on places to go but also runs rock-climbing courses. Peilstein, in the Vienna Woods, and Hohe Wand, in the Süd-Alpin in Lower Austria, are often used for such weekend courses. Other centres for rock-climbing include Dachstein in Salzkammergut, Hochkönig near Salzburg, the Hohe Tauern National Park, Gesäuse National Park in Styria, Wilde Kaiser near Kufstein in Tyrol and, north of Innsbruck, Karwendel.

If your German is up to it, check out www.bergsteigen.at (in German) for loads of information on climbing not only in Austria, but around the world, and links to the country's rock-climbing clubs.

HORSE RIDING

Austria has a long association with horse riding, and one of the world's most famous breeds, the Lipizzaner, is bred within its borders (at Piber in Styria, p199). *Reiten* (horse riding) is a popular activity that can be enjoyed the length and breadth of the country, although options are limited in the Alps and more prominent in the lowlands of Upper and Lower Austria. The Mühlviertel (p180) in Upper Austria is a particular hotspot for organised rides through the wilderness, while Hausruck, just north of the Salzkammergut in the same province, specialises in horse riding for the whole family.

'The Mühl-viertel is a particular hotspot for organised rides'

If you're considering a riding holiday in Austria, consult **Reitarena Austria** (☎ 07282-5992; www.reitarena.at - in German; A-4121 Altenfelden), the country's association in charge of all hotels offering riding holidays.

Food & Drink

Austrians would not be the people they are without their home-cooked food. This strongly meat-based cuisine is an integral part of their lives, and it's hard to find an Austrian with less than a chef's knowledge of how to bread a Wiener schnitzel or boil a *Tafelspitz* (boiled beef with apple and horseradish sauce). Time is taken to enjoy mealtimes, and while this is more so in rural areas, it is still true in the larger cities; many banks still shut up shop at lunchtime and midday *menü* are as popular as ever.

For many, the best is left for last. Deliciously divine cakes and pastries, with an international reputation hard to beat, round off a meal perfectly. They will also round that belly, but who cares? You're on holiday, and that *Palatschinken* (crepes) drowned in cream or *Apfelstrüdel* (apple strudel) lightly dusted with powdered sugar is simply too good to pass over. Honestly.

There are certainly regional variations, but in general Austrian cuisine is the same across the country.

Ewald Plachutta and Christoph Wagner put together their favourite Austrian dishes in The 100 Classic Dishes of Austria, published by Deuticke.

STAPLES & SPECIALITIES

Traditional Austrian food has a big place in Austrian hearts, and is cooked, consumed and talked about on a daily basis in many homes. It is generally quite heavy and hearty, with meat strongly emphasised; pork, veal, chicken, beef and turkey dishes are ever-present, but lamb is often glaringly absent.

The big meal of the day is more often than not taken at *Mittag* (midday), and is known as *Mittagessen* (midday meal) – although in Austria's cosmopolitan centres this is commonly a sandwich on the run. If there is time however, locals will sit down to a *Tagesteller* (set dish) or *Mittagsmenü* (set lunch, including soup; around €5 to €8) which is invariably a very cheap way to fill the belly. *Frühstück* (breakfast) is not so important, and usually consists of coffee or tea with a *Semmel* (bread roll) and jam, ham or cheese, or all three. On weekends, particularly in Vienna, breakfast is a completely different creature; people lazily while away the hours over coffee, rolls, and occasionally a full English breakfast.

Traditionally, *Abendessen* (dinner) is bread, cheese, ham and a beer; something light on the stomach for a good night's slumber. Snacking between meals happens all too often, and is often referred to as *Jause*.

Three courses are standard. Clear soups are a particular favourite as a *Vorspeise* (starter), such as *Frittattensuppe*, a clear soup with shreds of crepelike pancake. *Markknödelsuppe* is a clear bone-marrow soup with dumplings, while *Leberknödelsuppe* is yet another clear soup with liver dumplings. *Gulaschsuppe* (Goulash), a rich beef-vegetable soup with plenty of paprika, can be taken as a starter or a main. If you're not a soup fan, then try *Bauernschmaus*, a platter of cold meats and bread.

Wiener schnitzel, a breaded escalope of veal (and occasionally pork or turkey), is Vienna's best-known culinary concoction, but is ubiquitous throughout Austria. Variations on the schnitzel theme include the *Cordon Bleu*, with ham and cheese, and the *Natur*, a schnitzel fried on its own.

Other than schnitzel, *Speisekarte* (menus) normally feature classic Austrian dishes, such as *Bachhuhn* (fried chicken; also known as *Bachhendl*), *Tafelspitz*, *Schweinsbraten* (slices of roast pork) and *Zweibelrostbraten* (slices of roast beef smothered in gravy and fried onions). A great variety of *Wurst* (sausage) is available, and not only at the takeaway stands. As

---

TRAVEL YOUR TASTEBUDS

Austrian food is basically straight up and down, but there are a handful of surprises on the menu. The locals are fond of eating bits of beasts that some other nations ignore, and have created the dish *Beuschel*. It consists of thin slices of calf's lungs and heart in a thick sauce, usually served with a bread dumpling and is actually quite tasty. *Aspik*, a roll of vegetables, meat or fish set in clear *Gelee* (jelly), is normally found in deli supermarkets and on the occasional menu.

The king of sausages is the *Käsekrainer*, a sausage infused with cheese. It's heavy, filling and can sometimes be a messy affair, but it's something you won't forget in a hurry. In their typically morose way, the Viennese have nicknamed a *Käsekrainer* served with the end of a bread loaf '*Eitrige mit an Buckl*', which loosely translates as 'a hunchback full of pus'.

---

stated above, meat is the basis of many *Hauptspeise* (main dishes), but you'll also find enough fish dishes to satisfy. Common fish include *Forelle* (trout), *Hecht* (pike), *Fogosch/Zander* (pike-perch) and *Karpfen* carp. *Saibling* is a local freshwater fish, similar to trout.

Main dishes commonly appear with *Beilagen* (side dishes) and extras, which come in a variety of shapes and forms. *Knödel* (dumplings) are an element of many meals, and can appear in soups and desserts as well as main courses. *Nockerln* (sometimes called *Spätzle*, especially in the west) is small home-made pasta with a similar taste to *Knödel*. *Nudeln* is normally flat pasta (like tagliatelle), except when it's the tiny noodles in a soup. Austrians love their potatoes, and are not satisfied with just boiling them to death like the English. They appear as *Pommes* (French fries), *Kartoffel* (boiled), *Bratkartoffel* (roasted), *Geröstete* (sliced small and sautéed) and *Erdapfelsalat Erdäpfe* (boiled potatoes with chopped chives in a watery dressing).

A treat for food aficionados is the regional cuisine. Most menus will feature a couple of dishes specific to the local area; meals with peasant-culture roots. Burgenland has strong ties to Hungarian cooking, with lashings of paprika, beans, potatoes and kraut, while in Styria it's hard to go anywhere without encountering *Kürbis-Kern Öl*, a rich, dark pumpkin-seed oil. The region's beef is reputedly the best in Austria. In Carinthia, look for *Käsnudeln*, pasta made into balls and combined with cheese. *Käsnocken*, *Kässpätzle* and *Käsnödel* are variations on a the theme (see p261). Tyrol specialities include *Tiroler Gröstl*, pan-fried onions, meat and potatoes, and *Tiroler Knödel*, dumplings hiding small pieces of ham.

No meal in Austria would be complete without *Nachspeise* (dessert). Beating all-comers in the popularity race is the *Apfelstrüdel*, although *Palatschinken* come a close second. A speciality for Salzburg is the *Salzburger Nockerl*, a fluffy baked pudding made from eggs, flour and sugar. *Germknödel* are sourdough dumplings, but more appetising are *Marillenknödel* (apricot dumplings). Look for *Mohr im Hemd,* a chocolate pudding with whipped cream and chocolate sauce, *Guglhupf*, a cake shaped like a volcano, the *Sacher Torte* in Vienna and the *Linzer Torte* in Linz. The ever-present *Mozart Kügeln* (Mozart Balls) are another favourite.

Legend has it that the origin of the humble bagel dates back to 1683, when a Viennese baker created a *Beugal* (stirrup) for Polish King Jan III Sobieski in celebration of his victory over the Turks.

DRINKS
Nonalcoholic Drinks

Coffee is the preferred hot beverage rather than tea, and the *Kaffeehaus* or *Café Konditoreien* (coffee house) is an established part of Austrian life, particularly in Vienna. People spend hours over one cup of coffee and free newspapers in such establishments. Strong Turkish coffee is a popular variation. Mineral or soda water is widely available and cheap, though tap water is fine to drink. *Almdudler*, a cross between ginger ale

MORE THAN JUST COFFEE

Legend has it that coffee beans were left behind by the fleeing Turks in 1683, and it was this happy accident that resulted in today's plethora of coffee establishments. However, the popularity of the Viennese *Kaffeehaus* didn't take a firm hold on the city until the end of the 19th century when their numbers reached a reputed 600 cafés.

When ordering a cup of the brown stuff, a 'coffee, please' will not suffice. The list to choose from is as long as your arm, so it's best to know what you're ordering before making a random choice. It will generally be served on a silver platter accompanied by a glass of water, and if you're lucky, with a small sweet.

Here's what you'll generally find on offer:

■ *Brauner* – black but served with a tiny splash of milk; comes in *Gross* (large) or *Klein* (small)

■ *Einspänner* – with whipped cream, served in a glass

■ *Fiaker* – Verlängerter with rum and whipped cream

■ *Kapuziner* – with a little milk and perhaps a sprinkling of grated chocolate

■ *Maria Theresia* – with orange liqueur and whipped cream

■ *Masagran* (or *Mazagran*) – cold coffee with ice and Maraschino liqueur

■ *Melange* – the Viennese classic; served with milk, and maybe whipped cream too, similar to the cappuccino

■ *Mocca* (sometimes spelled *Mokka*) or *Schwarzer* – black coffee

■ *Pharisäer* – strong *Mocca* topped with whipped cream, served with a glass of rum

■ *Türkische* – comes in a copper pot with coffee grounds and sugar

■ *Verlängerter* – *Brauner* weakened with hot water

■ *Wiener Eiskaffee* – cold coffee with vanilla ice cream and whipped cream

and lemonade, is one local soft drink found the country over and *Most*, fresh, unfermented grapejuice, is only available in wine regions come September.

Alcoholic Drinks

Although *bier* (beer) is by far the most popular drink in Austria, internationally, *weine* (wines) outshine the amber liquid. White wine is traditionally Austria's mainstay, but the world's taste for red is even having its effect here; soon around a third of the country's viniculture will be planted in red wine. Burgenland, Vienna, Styria and Lower Austria are the only producers of wine in Austria; Grüner Veltliner is the most common variety, while Sekt is a sparkling wine. Different varieties are produced in Burgenland (p160) and Southern Styria (p201).

Come autumn the whole country goes mad for Sturm – new wine in its semifermented state. It's highly drinkable, has a kick like a mule, and hangovers are like a porcupine waltzing inside your head, but it's an absolute must. Staubiger is new wine fully fermented and is more sour and cloudy than Sturm. Some of the young wines can be a little sharp, so it is common to mix them with 50% soda water, called a *Gespritzer* or *G'spritzer*.

The perfect place to sample wine and *Sturm* is a *Heurigen* or *Buschenschank*, Austria's wine taverns. Rustic and rural, these wonderful establishments have plenty of character and traditionally only sell their own wine, but quite often you'll find stock from outside. They're easy to spot; just look for the *Busch'n* (green wreath or branch) hanging over the front door.

The Ultimate Austrian Wine Guide, by Peter Moser and published by Falstaff, is your wine lover's bible to Austria wine. It features a rundown on wines from Austria, 200 leading wineries and is in English.

Austria loves its home-grown beer, which is no surprise considering its quality. It's usually a light, golden-coloured lager or pilsner (there are dark versions too), and is produced by a plethora of breweries across the country. Common brands include Ottakringer from Vienna, Gösser and Puntigmer from Graz and Stiegl from Salzburg. *Weizenbier* (wheat beer), also known as *Weissbier* (white beer) has a full-bodied, slightly sweet taste and can be light or dark, clear or cloudy, and is sometimes served with a slice of lemon straddling the glass rim. *Vom Fass* (draught beer) comes in a either a 0.5L or a 0.3L glass. In Vienna and some other parts of eastern Austria these are called respectively a *Krügerl* (sometimes spelled *Krügel*) and a *Seidel*. Elsewhere these will simply be *Grosse* (big) or *Kleine* (small). A small beer may also be called a *Glas* (glass). A *Pfiff* is just 0.125L, which will probably satisfy you for all of two seconds. *Radler* is a mix of beer and lemonade.

Austrians have a fond spot for *Schnapps*, made from a variety of fruits and sometimes known as *Obstler*. Some of the country's better drops can be bought at *Bauernmärkte* (farmers markets) across the country.

With some 7 sq km of vineyards within its borders, Vienna is the largest wine-growing city in the world.

CELEBRATIONS

Austrian cuisine very much follows the seasons. Game, an integral part of most menus throughout the year, really comes into its own in autumn when most of the hunting takes place. Expect to find *Hirsch* (venison), *Wildschwein* (wild boar), *Gems* (chamois) and *Reh* (roe deer) on menus around this time. Come early autumn, the hills and forests are crawling with Austrians, with their bums up and their heads down, searching for *Schwammerl/Pilze* (mushrooms). In May, it's hard to avoid *Spargel* (asparagus), but why would you want to miss this crisp, freshly picked stick of goodness? It's often served with a rich, creamy sauce.

St Martin's Day (November 11) is traditionally marked with the serving of *Gans* (goose), St Martin's symbol. The tasty dish is available the entire month of November. As in the rest of the world, *Weinnachten* (Christmas) is a time for the mass consumption of food in Austria. Fish, in particular *Lachs* (salmon), is served on the 24th, and seasonal celebrations are complemented with *Vanillekipferl*, crescent cookies which have a special place in the hearts of all Austrians.

WHERE TO EAT & DRINK

Restaurants are by far the most common place to eat. Quite often this term is exchanged for *Gasthöfe*, *Gästehaus* or *Gastwirt*, which denotes a restaurant with more traditional setting and decor. Restaurants usually open from 11.30am to midnight; some close the kitchen, or even the premises, during downtime from 2.30pm to 5pm or 6pm.

Heurigen are fairly inexpensive places to eat in wine areas and the capital. Food is usually buffet style and consists of hearty, Austrian cuisine, and is available from around 11am to 11pm. Don't pass over a café or *Kaffeehaus* for a meal just because of the name; they often have daily specials and a menu loaded with *Hauptspeise*. Traditionally aimed at men, these establishments now welcome all walks of life, offer a full stock of newspapers and serve beer and wine. For cakes and pastries, a *Café Konditorei* will do nicely. Expect a more womanly place, with rococo mouldings and painted glass. Cafés open their doors early, often between 7am and 8am, and close from anything between 7pm and 1am, depending on the market they're catering to.

In mountainous areas, *Hütte* or *Almhütte* (alpine huts) are atmospheric places for basic Austrian cuisine in stunning surroundings.

Quick Eats

If you need something in a hurry, a *Würstel Stand* (sausage stand) shouldn't be too far away in any city. Schnitzelhaus, Austria's version of a fast-food joint, is found throughout the country, but it doesn't offer much more than schnitzels. Deli shops sometimes offer hot food, such as spit-roasted chicken (an Austrian favourite). Supermarket delis will always have sandwiches for those on the run.

VEGETARIANS & VEGANS

www.pumpkinseedoil
.cc – More information
than you will ever need
to know about Southern
Styria's liquid gold.

Vegetarians will have a fine time of it in Vienna, and in Austria's other large, cosmopolitan areas there are at least a couple of vegetarian restaurants to choose from. In the countryside however, things will prove more difficult. Many places now offer at least one vegetarian dish, but don't count on it every time; you may have to rely on a combination of salads and side dishes to create a full meal. Note that most soups are made with meat stock.

WHINING & DINING

Feeding the little 'uns will prove no problem in Austria; in general, only finer restaurants turn up their noses at children. Some restaurants have children's menus but most will be willing to serve smaller portions if you ask nicely.

See p350 for more on travelling with children.

HABITS & CUSTOMS

Eating and drinking habits should raise no eyebrows or cause any problems. In general, Austrians are a polite, neat bunch at the table, and tend to take their time over meals. More often than not, the next course will not be served until everyone at the table has finished, so don't ramble on to your neighbour while the rest of the diners are waiting. Nonsmokers (and some smokers) may be annoyed with smoking habits in restaurants; many smokers won't batter an eyelid lighting up while you're still only half way through your Wiener schnitzel.

Austrian's certainly like a drink, and the country has its fair share of alcoholics, but they're not into binge drinking; they like to take their time getting sozzled. Every drink bought deserves a *Prost* (cheers) and eye contact with your fellow drinkers; not following this custom is thought of as rude.

VIENNA'S TOP FIVE

■ **Stomach** (Map pp80-2; ☎ 310 20 99; 09, Seegasse 26; mains €10-17; ⏰ 4pm-midnight Wed-Sat, 10am-10pm Sun) Seriously good Austrian food and a setting straight from the country.

■ **Expedit** (Map pp83-5; ☎ 512 33 13-0; 01, Wiesingerstrasse 6; mains €8-18; ⏰ noon-11pm Mon-Fri, 6-11pm Sat) Italian classics served in laid-back yet smart surroundings.

■ **Aida** (Map pp83-5; ☎ 512 29 77; 01, Stock-im-Eisen-Platz 2; cakes from €1.50; ⏰ 7am-8pm Mon-Sat, 9am-8pm Sun) Excellent coffee, divine cakes, kitsch décor and a doddering clientele; what more can you want from a Viennese *Kaffeehaus*?

■ **Würstel Stand am Hohen Markt** (Map pp83-5; 01, Hoher Markt; sausages from €3; ⏰ 7am-5am) No self-respecting list of the best of Vienna would be complete with out a *Würstel Stand* (sausage stand), and this is the best of 'em.

■ **Zu den Zwei Liesln** (Map p86; ☎ 523 32 82; 07, Burggasse 63; mains €4.40-8; ⏰ 10am-10pm Mon-Sat) An authentic *beisl* (small tavern) with a lovely courtyard and schnitzels too large to finish.

DOS & DON'TS

■ If invited to someone's house, bring a small gift; wine or flowers will suffice.

■ Always tip, unless the service or meal was a complete nightmare.

■ When toasting, call out a resounding '*Prost*', clink glasses and make eye contact with the *entire* table.

■ At lunchtime, a simple '*Mahlzeit*' before digging in is appropriate; at dinner, '*Guten Appetit*' is more appropriate.

■ Buying rounds is not common practice, but if someone buys you a drink, it's polite to return the favour.

COOKING COURSES

Places offering cooking courses are rather thin on the ground, but if you're keen to learn how to bread a schnitzel the Austrian way, or roll the perfect *Knödel*, there are a few places out there.

In Vienna, the restaurant **Steirereck** (Map pp83-5; 01-713 31 86; www.steirereck .at; 01, Stadtpark, Meierei) is highly regarded for its upmarket cuisine and cooking courses, while **Babettes** (☎ 585 51 65; www.babettes.at - in German; 04, Schleifmühlgasse 17; ☻ 10am-7pm Mon-Fri, 10am-5pm Sat) is a food-lovers dream, with a zillion cookbooks and spices, and cooking courses to boot.

In Styria, try the **Erste Steirische Kochschule** (☎ 03135-522 47; www.kochschule .at - in German; Hauptstrasse 168) in Kalsdorf, or **Gasthof Vitalpension Hubinger** (☎ 03861-81 14; www.hubinger.com; 8633 Etmissl 25) in Etmissl for traditional Austrian cooking courses.

www.austrianfood wine.com – Classic dishes and their recipes can be found on this English website.

EAT YOUR WORDS

Want to know your *Germknödel* from your *Grammelknödel*? Your *Wiener Bachhendl* from your Wiener schnitzel? Get behind the cuisine scene, by getting to know the language.

Useful Phrases

Can you recommend …?
Können Sie … empfehlen?   *ker*-nen zee … emp-*fay*-len
…a restaurant
…ein Restaurant   ain res-to-*rang*
…a bar/pub
…eine Kneipe   ai-ne *knai*-pe
A table for …, please.
Einen Tisch für …, bitte.   *ai*-nen tish für … *bi*-te
I'd like to reserve a table for …
Ich möchte einen Tisch für … reservieren.   ikh *merkh*-te *ai*-nen tish für … re-zer-*vee*-ren
…(two) people
…(zwei) Personen   (tsvai) per-*zaw*-nen
…(eight) o'clock
…(acht) Uhr   (akt) oor

Do you have …?
Haben Sie …?   *hah*-ben zee …?
…a menu in English
…eine englische Speisekarte   *ai*-ne *eng*-li-she *shpai*-ze-kar-te
…vegetarian food
…vegetarisches Essen   ve-ge-*tah*-ri-shes *e*-sen

What would you recommend?
Was empfehlen Sie? — vas emp-*fay*-len zee

I'd like a local speciality.
Ich möchte etwas Typisches aus der Region. — ikh *merkh*-te *et*-vas *ti*-pi-shes ows dair re-*gyawn*

I'd like the set menu, please.
Ich hätte gerne das Tagesmenü, bitte. — ikh *ha*-te *ger*-ne das *ta*-ges- me-noo *bi*-te

What are the daily specials?
Was sind die Tagesspezialitäten? — vas zind dee *ta*-gez-*spe*-tsya-lee-*te*-ten

I'm a vegetarian.
Ich bin Vegetarier(in) m/f. — ikh bin ve-ge-*tah*-ri-e-r/ve-ge-*tah*-ri-e-rin

Is it cooked in meat stock?
Ist es in Fleischbrühe? — ist es in flaish-*brü*-e

What's in that dish?
Was ist in diesem Gericht? — vas ist in *dee*-zem ge-*rikht*

I'd like …, please.
Ich möchte …, bitte. — ikh *merkh*-te … *bi*-te

Can I have some more … please.
Bitte noch ein … — *bi*-te nokh ain

That was delicious!
Das war sehr lecker! — das vahr zair le-ker

The bill, please.
Die Rechnung, bitte. — dee *rekh*-nung, *bi*-te

Bon appétit.
Güten Appetit. — *goo*-ten a-pe-*teet*

Cheers!
Prost! — *prawst!*

The Wiener schnitzel is not in fact from Vienna, it was brought back to the capital from Milan in 1848 by Field Marshal Radetzky's chief cook.

Menu Decoder

SOUPS & STARTERS

Frittattensuppe (free-*ta*-ten-*zu*-pe) – clear soup with chives and strips of pancake
Leberknödelsuppe (*lay*-ber-kner-del-*zu*-pe) – liver dumpling soup
Rindssuppe (*rind*-zu-pe) – clear beef soup

MAINS

Bachhendl (*bakh*-en-del) – fried breaded chicken
Bauernschmaus (*bow*-ern-shmows) – platter of cold meats
Grammelknödel (*gra*-mel-*kner*-del) – pork dumplings
Gulasch/Gulas (*goo*-lash/*goo*-las) – thick beef soup
Kaiserschmarrn (*kai*-zer-shmar-ren) – sweet pancake with raisins
Schinkenfleckerl (*shin*-ken-flek-erl) – ovenbaked ham and noodle casserole
Schweinsbraten (*shvains*-bra-ten) – roast pork
Semmelknödel (*ze*-mel-kner-del) – bread dumplings
Stelze (*shtel*-tse) – roast hock
Tafelspitz (*ta*-fel-spits) – boiled beef, potatoes and horseradish sauce
Tiroler Gröstl (tee-*ro*-ler grer-stel) – potatoes, onions and flecks of meat fried in a pan
Wiener schnitzel (*vee*-ner *shni*-tsel) – breaded veal cutlets (sometimes with pork or turkey)
Zwiebelrostbraten (*tswee*-bel-*rost*-bra-ten) – roast beef slices with gravy and fried onions

DESSERTS

Apfelstrüdel (*ap*-fel-stroo-del) – apple strudel
Germknödel (jairm-*kner*-del) – yeast dumplings with poppy seeds
Marillenknödel – apricot dumplings
Mohr im Hemd (*morr* im hemd) – chocolate pudding with whipped cream and chocolate sauce
Palatschinken (*pa*-lat-shing-ken) – crêpes
Topfenknödel (*top*-fen-kner-del) – cheese dumplings

Food Glossary
MEAT & FISH

bacon	*Speck*	shpek
beef	*Rindfleisch*	*rint*-flaish
brains	*Hirn*	heern
carp	*Karpfen*	*karp*-fen
chicken	*Huhn/Hendl*	hoon/*hen*-dl
duck	*Ente*	*en*-te
eel	*Aal*	ahl
fish	*Fisch*	fish
goose	*Gans*	gans
ham	*Schinken*	*shing*-ken
hare	*Hase*	*hah*-ze
lamb	*Lamm*	lam
liver	*Leber*	*lay*-ber
minced meat	*Hackfleisch*	*hak*-flaish
plaice	*Scholle*	*sho*-le
pork	*Schweinsfleisch*	*shvai*-ne-flaish
salmon	*Lachs*	laks
tongue	*Zunge*	*tsung*-e
trout	*Forelle*	fo-*re*-le
tuna	*Thunfisch*	*toon*-fish
turkey	*Puter*	*poo*-ter
veal	*Kalbfleisch*	*kalp*-flaish
venison	*Hirsch*	hirsh

Get Elisabeth Mayer-Browne's take on the Austrian kitchen in the *Best of Austrian Cuisine*, published by Hippocrene.

VEGETABLES & FRUIT

apple	*Apfel*	*ap*-fel
apricot	*Aprikose*	a-pri-*ko*-ze
apricot	*Marille*	ma-*ree*-le
asparagus	*Spargel*	*shpar*-gel
banana	*Banane*	ba-*nah*-ne
beans	*Bohnen*	*baw*-nen
beetroot	*Rote Rübe*	*raw*-te- *rü*-ben
cabbage	*Kohl*	hawl
carrots	*Karotten*	ka-*ro*-ten
cherries	*Kirschen*	*kir*-shen
corn	*Mais*	mais
cucumber, gherkin	*Gurke*	*gur*-ke
garlic	*Knoblauch*	*knawp*-lowkh
grapes	*Trauben*	*trow*-ben
green beans	*Fisolen*	fee-*zo*-len
mushrooms	*Champignons/*	sham-pee-*nyon/*
	Schwammerl/Pilze	*shva*-mer/*pil*-tse
onions	*Zwiebeln*	*tsvee*-beln
pear	*Birne*	*bir*-ne
peas	*Erbsen*	*erp*-sen
peppers	*Paprika*	*pap*-ri-kah
pineapple	*Ananas*	a-na-*nas*
plums	*Zwetschgen*	*tsvetsh*-gen
potatoes	*Erdäpfel/Kartoffeln*	*ert*-ep-fel/kar-*to*-feln
raspberries	*Himbeeren*	*him*-bair-re
spinach	*Spinat*	shpi-*naht*
strawberries	*Erdbeeren*	*ert*-bair-re
tomatoes	*Paradeiser/Tomaten*	pa-ra-dai-ser/to-*mah*-ten

OTHER ITEMS

bread	*Brot*	brawt
bread roll	*Semmel*	ze-mel
butter	*Butter*	bu-ter
cheese	*Käse*	kay-ze
chocolate	*Schokolade*	sho-ko-*lah*-de
coffee	*Kaffee*	ka-fay
cream	*Schlagobers/Rahm/Sahne*	shlag-o-berz/rahm/*zah*-ne
dumplings	*Knödel*	kner-del
eggs	*Eier*	ai-er
honey	*Honiq*	haw-nikh
jam	*Marmelade*	mar-me-*lah*-de
mustard	*Senf*	zenf
nut	*Nuss*	nus
oil	*Öl*	erl
pepper	*Pfeffer*	pfe-fer
rice	*Reis*	rais
salad	*Salat*	za-*laht*
salt	*Salz*	zalts
sugar	*Zucker*	tsu-ker

www.globalgourmet .com/destinations /austria/ – Food history, wine glossary and menu guide; it's all here under one website.

COOKING TERMS

baked	*gebacken*	ge-*ba*-ken
boiled	*gekocht*	ge-kokht
crispy	*knusprig*	k-*noo*-sprik
fresh	*frisch*	frish
fried	*gebraten*	ge-*brah*-ten
grilled	*gegrillte*	ge-*grilt*
home-made	*selbst gemacht*	selbst ge-*makht*
roasted	*braten*	bra-ten
steamed	*gedämpft*	ge-dempft
smoked	*geräuchert*	ge-*roy*-khert
sour	*sauer*	zow-er
sweet	*süss*	züs

UTENSILS

ashtray	*Aschenbecher*	a-shen-be-kher
cup	*Tasse*	ta-se
fork	*Gabel*	gah-bel
glass	*Glas*	glahs
knife	*Messer*	me-ser
plate	*Teller*	te-ler
spoon	*Löffel*	ler-fel
toothpick	*Zahnstocher*	tsahn-shto-kher

Vienna

CONTENTS

Think of Vienna and a gamut of images surge forward to flood the memory banks: angelic choirboys, proud white stallions strutting in measured sequence, grand imperial palaces and bombastic baroque architecture too beautiful to ignore, Art Nouveau masterpieces of depth and quality, art galleries with unfathomable collections and, of course, coffee, delicate pastries and divine cakes. Then there's the music. Just let it roll off your tongue – Mozart, Beethoven, Haydn, Schubert, Strauss, Brahms, Mahler, Schönberg – for lovers of classical music, it doesn't get *any* better than this.

But Vienna is so much more than its past. Thankfully the wise denizens of this golden city haven't settled on their laurels and let themselves sleepily sink into their impressive history. Like the rest of the Western world, they want a taste of what's out there, and they want it on their own turf. Asian sushi and kebab houses compete with, but don't overpower, the traditional *Beisl* (small taverns or restaurants) and *Heurigen* (wine taverns). The upwardly mobile while away the wee hours in hip, unpretentious bars alongside the creatures of the night, before moving onto pumping clubs where DJs work their magic with the latest sounds on the planet. Modern art houses host contemporary artists unafraid to push the boundaries of art to their thought-provoking limits.

Combine all this with the mass of green space within the confines of the city limits (almost half the city expanse is given over to parkland), the 'blue' Danube cutting a path just to the east of the historical centre and the Wienerwald (Vienna Woods) creating much of Vienna's western border and you have a capital inconceivably well suited for the pursuit of the great outdoors.

HIGHLIGHTS

- Admire **Stephansdom** (p89), Vienna's glorious Gothic cathedral and its beloved icon
- Wander the halls and gardens of **Schönbrunn palace** (p100), imperial grandeur at its bombastic best
- Breakfast on the run or while away the hours in the **Naschmarkt** (p116), the city's colourful market
- Roam the **MuseumsQuartier** (p95), an art space to rival anything Europe has to offer
- Stand in awe at the incredible art collection of the **Kunsthistorisches Museum** (p94)

MuseumsQuartier & Kunsthistorisches Museum ★   ★ Stephansdom
★ Naschmarkt
Schönbrunn Palace ★

■ POPULATION: 1,550,000　　■ AREA: 415 SQ KM　　■ HIGHEST ELEVATION: HERMANNSKOGEL 542M

HISTORY

Vienna, situated at a natural crossing of the Danube, was probably an important trading post for the Celts when the Romans arrived around 15 BC. They soon set up camp and named it Vindobona, after the Celtic tribe Vinid. Centred on what is now the Innere Stadt, the settlement had blossomed into a town by the 3rd and 4th centuries and vineyards were introduced to the surrounding area.

It wasn't until 881 that the town, then known as 'Wenia', was first documented – in the annals of the archbishopric of Salzburg. In the ensuing centuries control of Vienna changed hands a number of times, but it was the Babenburgs who finally gained the upper hand (see p21).

The last of the Babenburgs died in battle leaving no heir; after a brief but bloody power struggle, control of Vienna fell into the hands of the Habsburgs. It wasn't until 1533 that the first Habsburg, Ferdinand I, permanently resided in the city, not long after the city was heavily besieged by the Turks in 1529.

Vienna was a hotbed of revolt and religious bickering during the Reformation and Counter-Reformation and suffered terribly through plague and siege at the end of the 17th century. However, the beginning of the 18th century heralded a golden age for Vienna, with the introduction of baroque architecture, civil reform and a classical music revolution.

Things turned sour at the beginning of the 19th century; Napoleon occupied the city twice, in 1805 and 1809. His reign over Europe was brief, and in 1814 Vienna hosted the Congress of Vienna in celebration. The city soon picked itself up and began to grow once more, and in 1873 hosted its second international event, the World Fair. The advent of WWI stalled the city's architectural and cultural development that had been surging ahead at great pace; by the end of the war, the monarchy was no more and the Republic of Austria was born, with Vienna as its capital. The socialists (Social Democrats) gained an absolute majority in the city's first elections, and retained it in all free elections up until 1996. Their rein from 1919 till 1934, known as 'Red Vienna', was by far the most industrious.

Fascism began to raise its ugly head at the end of the 1920s, and by 1934 civil war broke out in the city streets. The socialists were defeated and Vienna's city council dissolved. Austria was ripe for the picking, and Hitler came a-harvesting; on 15 March 1938 he entered the city to the cries of 200,000 ecstatic Viennese.

Towards the end of the war Vienna suffered heavily under Allied bombing, and on 11 April 1945 advancing Russian troops liberated the city. The next 10 years saw control of Vienna fall to the Allied troops, but the city regained its independence in 1955. Since then, Vienna has enjoyed an illustrious and prosperous life, being on the former East–West border.

ORIENTATION

Vienna occupies 415 sq km in the Danube Valley, with the hills of the Wienerwald (Vienna Woods) forming a natural border to the north and west. The Danube (Donau) river flows in a northeast–southwest direction through the city, dividing it diagonally into two unequal parts. Vienna's heart, the Innere Stadt (inner city; 1st District), is south of the river on a diversion of the Danube, the Danube Canal (Donaukanal). It is encircled on three sides by the Ringstrasse, or Ring, a series of broad roads sporting an extravaganza of architectural delights. The Ring is in turn at a distance of between 1.75km and 3km from the Gürtel (literally, 'belt'), a larger traffic artery which is fed by the flow of vehicles from outlying autobahns.

Stephansdom (St Stephen's Cathedral), with its slender spire, is in the heart of the Innere Stadt and is Vienna's principal landmark. Leading south from Stephansplatz station is Kärntner Strasse, an important pedestrian street that terminates at Karlsplatz, a major public transport hub.

The Danube runs down a long, straight channel, built between 1870 and 1875 to eliminate flooding. This was supplemented 100 years later by the building of a parallel channel, the Neue Donau (New Danube), creating a long, thin island between the two. This is known as Donauinsel (Danube Island), and is now a recreation area. The Alte Donau (Old Danube), the remnant of the original course of the river, forms a loop to the north of the Neue Donau.

(Continued on page 87)

INFORMATION
Hanusch-Krankenhaus
(Hospital).........................**1** C4
Slovak Embassy....................**2** E1

SIGHTS & ACTIVITIES (pp89–105)
Austria Memphis
Franz-Horr-Stadion............**3** F5

Hermesvilla...........................**4** B5
Kirche am Steinhof................**5** C3
Rapid Vienna
Gerhard-Hanappi-Stadion.....**6** B4
Strandbad Gänsehäufel
(Swimming Complex)...........**7** G2
Thermalbad Oberlaa.............**8** F6

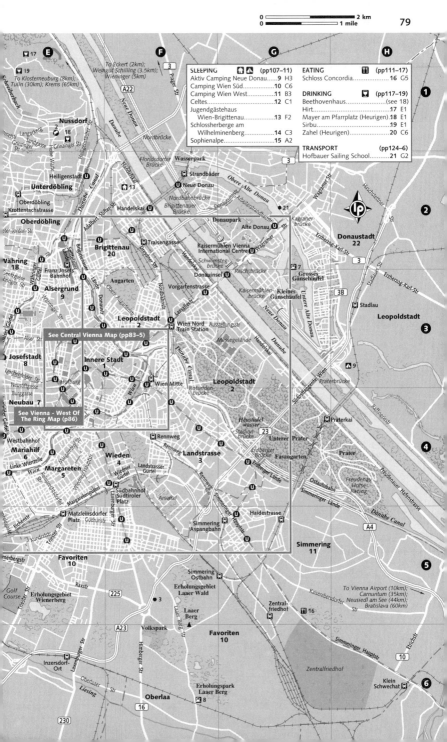

SLEEPING (pp107–11)
Aktiv Camping Neue Donau.....**9** H3
Camping Wien Süd.................**10** C6
Camping Wien West..............**11** B3
Celtes.................................**12** C1
Jugendgästehaus
  Wien-Brigittenau................**13** F2
Schlossherberge am
  Wilhelminenberg................**14** C3
Sophienalpe..........................**15** A2

EATING (pp111–17)
Schloss Concordia...................**16** G5

DRINKING (pp117–19)
Beethovenhaus......................(see 18)
Hirt......................................**17** E1
Mayer am Pfarrplatz (Heurigen)**18** E1
Sirbu...................................**19** E1
Zahel (Heurigen)....................**20** C6

TRANSPORT (pp124–6)
Hofbauer Sailing School..........**21** G2

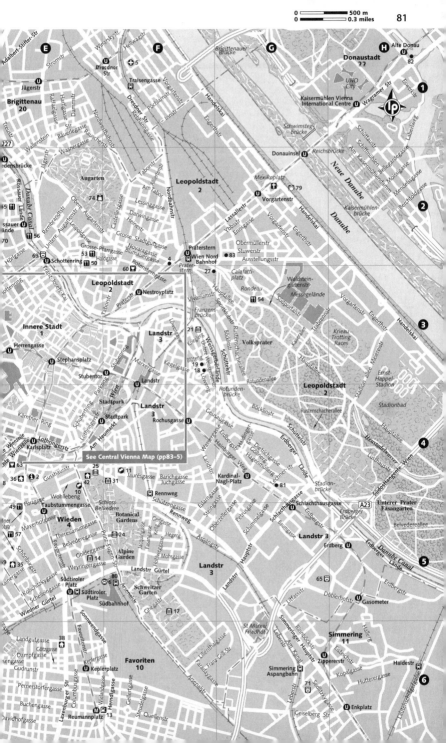

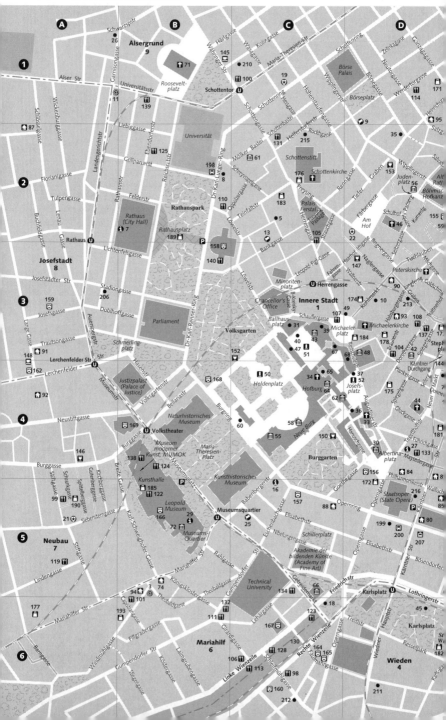

0   200 m
0   0.1 miles

Obere Donaustr

Karmelitergasse

Schmeltz gasse

Rotensteingasse

Praterstr

Majragasse

Czeningasse

Koretzgasse

Obere Donaustr

Holländstr

Zirkusgasse

Weintraubengasse

Komödiengasse

Große Mohrengasse

Nestroyplatz

Lichtenauergasse

Leopoldstadt
2

Lilienbrunngasse

Gredlerstr

Taborstr

Große Pratesrtr

Ferdinandstr

Czeningasse

Untere Donaustr

Canal

Franz-Josefs-Kai

Danube

Obere Donaustr

118

Canal

Aspernbrückengasse

Untere Donaustr

Dampfschiffstr

Obere Weissgerberstr

Löwengasse

Marzin-platz

Marien-brücke

Salztor-brücke

194

Sterig

Marc Aurel Str

Seitenstettengasse

161

24

Rabenstein

127

63

Schweden-platz

Schweden-platz

202

208

Schweden-brücke

203

203

Aspern-brücke

Franz-Josefs-Kai

Julius-Raab-Platz

Reichsr

Vordere Zollamtstr

Landstrasse
3

Radetzkystr

Kolonitzgasse

Radetzky-platz

141

udolfs-platz

186

Franz-Josefs-Kai

Griechengasse

Hafner-steig

Hoher 32

Markt

117

43

Griechengasse

135

120

6

Rosenbursenstr

115

G-Coch-Platz

Postparkasse

23

Kolinitzgasse

Hintere Zollamtstr

Bechardgasse

Kegelgasse

14

Hirsch-markt

Rotenturmstr

17

Wiesingerstr

Schauflergasse

Former
Kriegs-
ministerium
Oskar
Kokoschka
Platz

Obere Viaduktgasse

Viaduktgasse

Rabengasse

Kramergasse

154

79

83

102

Rosenbursenstr

Baumannstr

116

Grashofgasse

Wollzeile

Dr Karl Lueger

179

Schönlaterngasse

Barbarag

Predigerg

Fleischmarkt

77

Sonnenfelsgasse

Bäckerstr

Falkestr

idstr

142

195

Jasomirstr

Essiggasse

Akademie für
Angewandte
Kunst

Wien

Marxergasse

Gesaugasse

Crapka Gasse

76

112

Wollzeile

Schulerstr

86

Innere Stadt
1

109

126

Stubenring

ein

57

97

103

Stephans-20
platz

121

53

Schulerstr

Wien
Mitte

Wien

180

Bäckerstr

Blutgasse

187

492

82

196

Singer-str

Grünangergasse

151

73

Stubentor

Wollzeile

Weihburggasse

149

96

Jakoberg

Zedlitzgasse

Parking

54

201

Landstrasse

Invalidenstr

Untere

Sedlgasse

191

Franziskaner-platz

Ballgasse

Rauhen-steig

163

Wienerk

Cöbölgasse

Liebenberg

Schönbichlerstr

Landstrasser Hauptstr

Marxergasse

Rechte Bahngasse

4

hannegasse

4

Weihburggasse

Himmel gasse

28

Himmelpfortgasse

Gartenbau-
promenade

Parking

Ungargasse

129

Seilerstätte

Johannesgasse

38

Schwarzenberg-str

Fichtegasse

Akademiestr

Schellingasse

Himmelpfortgasse

Stadtpark

136

209

Johannesgasse

41

Kursalon

Beatrixgasse

Reisnerstr

15

Mahlerstr

205

Schubertring

204

Stadtpark

Fichtegasse

Beethoven-platz

75

81

Kärntner Ring

197

Schwarzen-bergplatz

Pestalozzigasse

Lothringergasse

Konzerthaus

Am Heumarkt

Wien

Lisztgasse

Lisztgasse

Am Heumarkt

Zaunergasse

Reisnerstr

Ungargasse

5

nstler-us

Musik-verein

Historisches
Museum der
Stadt Wien

2

Karlskirche

Lichtgasse

Marokkanergasse

Salesianergasse

Grimmelshausengasse

Am
Moderna-
park

Neulinggasse

Neuli

Gasshaus Str

Rennweg

Strohgasse

12

Schwindgasse

Traungasse

6

0   500 m
0   0.3 miles

INFORMATION
Allgemeines Krankenhaus (Hospital)..1 C3
Bücherei Wien................................2 B6
Post Office.....................................3 D2
Universität für Bodenkultur...............4 B1
US Embassy....................................5 D3
Wirtschaftsuniversität Wien...............6 D2

SIGHTS & ACTIVITIES   (pp89–105)
Josephinum (Museum of Medical
  History)......................................7 D3
Liechtenstein Museum......................8 D3
Pathologisch-Anatomisches
  Bundesmuseum.............................9 D4
Sigmund Freud Museum...................10 D4

SLEEPING   (pp107–11)
Academia......................................11 C5
Alla Lenz.......................................12 B6
Auer...13 C4
Hotel Am Schottenfeld....................14 C5
Hotel Atlanta.................................15 D3
Jugendherberge Myrthengasse.........16 C6
Pension Atrium..............................17 B6
Pension Carantania.........................18 B6
Theatre Hotel.................................19 C5
Thüringer Hof................................20 B4

EATING   (pp111–17)
Brunnenmarkt................................21 B5
Café Hummel.................................22 C5
Canetti......................................(see 2)
Gasthaus Wickerl...........................23 D3
Gaumenspiel..................................24 C6
Kent...25 B4
Kim Kocht.....................................26 C3
ON...27 C4
St Josef...28 C6
World Restaurant............................29 B5
Zu den Zwei Leisln.........................30 C6

DRINKING   (pp117–19)
Café Berg......................................31 D4
rhiz..32 B5

ENTERTAINMENT   (pp119–21)
Schauspielhaus...............................33 D3
Volksoper......................................34 C3
Votivkino......................................35 D4
WUK...36 C3

SHOPPING   (pp121–4)
Orator...37 C6

TRANSPORT   (pp124–6)
Train Ticket Office..........................38 D2

See Central Vienna Map (pp83–5)

(Continued from page 77)

This loop encloses the Donaupark, Vienna International Center (UNO City, home to the UN), beaches and water-sports centres. Squeezed between the Danube Canal and the Danube is the Prater, a large park and playground of the Viennese.

The majority of hotels, pensions, restaurants and bars are in the Innere Stadt or west of the centre between the Ringstrasse and the Gürtel.

Maps

For most purposes, the free Vienna map provided by the tourist office will be sufficient. It shows bus, tram and U-Bahn routes, has a separate U-Bahn plan, and lists major city-wide sights. It also has a blow-up of the Innere Stadt. For a street index, you'll need to buy a map; Freytag & Berndt's 1:25,000 fold-out map, available at most bookstores, is comprehensive enough.

INFORMATION
Bookshops

Amadeus (Map pp80-2; ☎ 595 45 50; 06, Mariahilfer Strasse 99; ⊙ 9.30am-7pm Mon-Fri, 9.30am-6pm Sat) Amadeus is one of the largest book stores in Vienna, with a wide range of travel books and a small amount of English fiction.

British Bookshop (Map pp83-5; ☎ 512 19 45; www .britishbookshop.at; 01, Weihburggasse 24; ☎ 522 67 30; 07, Mariahilfer Strasse 4) The largest selection of English reference and teaching books in Vienna, and its fair share of mainstream novels.

Freytag & Berndt (Map pp83-5; ☎ 533 86 85; www .freytagberndt.at; 01, Kohlmarkt 9; ⊙ 9am-7pm Mon-Fri, 9am-6pm Sat) The best place for maps and travel guides; stocks their own, plus competitors', maps.

Shakespeare & Co (Map pp83-5; ☎ 535 50 53; www.shakespeare.co.at; 01, Sterngasse 2; ⊙ 9am-7pm

---

ADDRESSES

Vienna is divided into 23 *Bezirke* (districts), fanning out in approximate numerical order clockwise around the Innere Stadt. Note that when reading addresses, the number of a building within a street *follows* the street name. Any number *before* the street name denotes the district. The middle two digits of postcodes correspond to the district. Thus a postcode of 1010 means the place is in district one, and 1230 refers to district 23.

Mon-Wed & Sat, 9am-9pm Thu & Fri) The Shakespeare is the place to go for literary and hard-to-find titles in English. Staff are incredibly friendly and only too eager to help.

Emergency

See Quick Reference on the inside front cover for nationwide emergency numbers for Ambulance, Doctor, Fire and Police.

Helpline (in English ☎ 713 33 74; ⊙ 9.30am-1pm & 6.30-10pm Mon-Fri, 6.30-10pm Sat)

Police Headquarters (Map pp83-5; ☎ 313 10; 01, Deutschmeisterplatz 3)

Women's Emergency Line *(Frauennotruf;* ☎ 71 719)

Internet Access

Vienna has dozens of places offering public access to online services. Free access is available at Amadeus branches (left), Flex (p120) and rhiz (p117; free after 9pm) but there aren't many terminals. Bücherei Wien (p88) also has free Internet access; just turn up with your passport and log on.

Internet cafés charging around €4 to €5 per hour include:

BigNet (Map pp83-5; ☎ 205 06 21; 06, Mariahilfer Strasse 27; ⊙ 8-2am) Branches at Kärntner Strasse 61 and Hoher Markt 8 in the Innere Stadt.

G-Zone (Map pp83-5; ☎ 407 81 66; 01, Universitätsstrasse 11; ⊙ 10am-11pm Mon-Fri, 2-11pm Sat & Sun)

Speednet Café (Map pp80-2; ☎ 892 56 66; 15, Europlatz, Westbahnhof; ⊙ 7am-midnight Mon-Sat, 8am-midnight Sun) Speednet Café is lurking at the back of Westbahnhof.

Internet Resources

About Vienna (www.aboutvienna.org) General website with cultural and sightseeing information.

City of Vienna (www.wien.gv.at) Comprehensive government-run website.

Falter (www.falter.at - in German) Online version of the ever-popular Falter magazine (p88).

Vienna Online (www.vienna.at - in German) Site with info on parties, festivals and news.

Vienna Tourist Board (www.wien.info) The first port of call for any visitor.

Left Luggage

Westbahnhof, Südbahnhof and Franz-Josef-Bahnhof have left-luggage lockers (24hr; €2 to €3.50).

Libraries

Bücherei Wien (Map p86; ☎ 4000 84500; www .buechereiwien.at; 07, Urban-Loritz-Platz; ⊙ 10am-7pm

VIENNA IN ...

Two Days

Start your day with a *melange* (coffee; specific to Austria) and *butter-semel* (butter-roll) at a traditional **Kaffeehaus** (café). Jump on tram 1 or 2 and circle the **Ringstrasse** (p93) for a brief but rewarding informal tour of the boulevard's buildings. Get out at **Kärntner Strasse** (p102) and wander towards the heart of the city where the glorious Gothic **Stephansdom** (opposite) awaits. Make your way to the **Hofburg** (p90) and its **Prunksaal** (p91) before crossing the Ringstrasse to the **Kunsthistorisches Museum** (p94), home to a breathtaking art collection. Recharge the batteries at one of the many **Innere Stadt restaurants** (p112) before attending a performance at the **Staatsoper** (p119).

Day two could begin with a visit to the imperial palace **Schönbrunn** (p100), before heading to the **MuseumsQuartier** (p95) and its **Leopold Museum** (p95), a treasure-chest of Austrian artists. Take an early dinner at Vienna's celebrated market, the **Naschmarkt** (p116), then cross the city for a ride on the **Riesenrad** (p97) in the **Prater** (p97). Finish the day with local wine and food at a **Heurigen** (p118).

Four Days

After fulfilling the two-day itinerary, start the third day with an exploration of the **Belvedere** (p97), an unequalled baroque palace, before lunching at **Zu den Zwei Leisln** (p115). Walk off that monstrous Wiener Schnitzel in the **Ringstrasse Gardens** (p93) before viewing Klimt's sumptuous *Beethoven Frieze* in the **Secession** (p95). If there's time, make for **Kahlenberg** to beat the setting sun. End the night in one of the **Gürtel's progressive bars** (p117) or the plethora of night spots in and around the Naschmarkt.

If you're still up for unfathomable art collections in regal surroundings, a visit to the newly renovated **Albertina** (p92) or recently opened **Palais Liechtenstein** (p98) is a must on the fourth day. This is a city where 'macabre' and 'imperial' comfortably exist in the same sentence, so an afternoon trip to the **Kaisergruft** (p92) should follow. Spend your last evening in one of the city's music houses, such as the **Konzerthaus** (p119) or **Musikverein** (p119), experiencing the music of Beethoven or Mozart where it was originally played.

Mon-Fri, 10am-2pm Sat) The new city library, straddling the U6 line.

British Council (Map pp83–5; ☎ 533 26 16-70; www .britishcouncil.at; 07, Siebensterngasse 21; ☺ 11am-7pm Tue-Fri) Newspapers, reference books, novels, films and English teaching aids in English.

Nationalbibliothek (Map pp83-5; ☎ 534 10 397; www.onb.ac.at; 01, Josefplatz 1; ☺ 10am-4pm, till 7pm Thu May-Oct, 10am-2pm, till 7pm Thu Nov-Apr) National library with huge reference and lending sections.

Media

Falter (www.falter.at - in German) Weekly magazine; best resource for political commentary and entertainment listings in every genre imaginable.

City (in German) Falter on a diet; weekly paper with entertainment listings.

For specific publications see p106.

Medical Services

The following *Krankenhäuser* (hospitals) have emergency rooms open 24 hours a day, seven days a week:

Allgemeines Krankenhaus (Map p86; ☎ 404 00; 09, Währinger Gürtel 18-20)

Hanusch-Krankenhaus (Map pp78-9; ☎ 910 21-0; 14, Heinrich-Collin-Strasse 30)

Lorenz Böhler Unfallkrankenhaus (Map pp78-9; ☎ 331 10; 20, Donaueschingenstrasse 13)

Unfallkrankenhaus Meidling (Map pp80-2; ☎ 601 50-0; 12, Kundratstrasse 37)

If you require a *Zahnarzt* (dentist) after hours call ☎ 512 20 78 (in German only); likewise if you need an *Apotheken* (pharmacy), dial ☎ 1550 (in German only).

Money

There are banks and currency exchange offices all over the city, but compare commission rates before changing money. *Bankomats* (ATMs) are everywhere, including all the main train stations and the airport.

The information offices in Westbahnhof and Südbahnhof exchange money. Money-changers at the airport tend to charge high commission, though the exchange rates are standard.

American Express (below) charges commission for cashing non-Amex travellers cheques; Amex cheques are cashed free of charge. Cash exchanges attract a small commission on a sliding scale.

Post

Franz-Josefs-Bahnhof Post Office (Map p86; 09, Althanstrasse 10; 6am-10pm)
Main post office (Map pp83-5; ☎ 515 09-0; www .post.at; 01, Fleischmarkt 19; 24 hr)
Südbahnhof post office (Map pp80-2; 10, Wiedner Gürtel 1b; 7am-10pm)
Westbahnhof post office (Map pp80-2; 15, Europlatz; 6am-11pm)

Tourist Information

Airport Information Office (8.30am-9pm) Located in the arrivals hall.
City Hall (Map pp83-5; ☎ 525 50; www.wien.gv.at; 01, Rathaus; 8am-6pm Mon-Fri) The City Hall provides information on social, cultural and practical matters, and is geared as much to residents as to tourists. There's an info-screen with useful information.
Jugendinfo (Map pp83-5; ☎ 1799; www.jugendinfo wien.at; 01, Babenbergerstrasse 1; noon-7pm Mon-Sat) Jugendinfo is tailored to those aged between 14 and 26, and has tickets for a variety of events at reduced rates for this age group.
Südbahnhof Information Office (Map pp83-5; 6.30am-midnight)
Tourist Info Wien (Map pp83-5; ☎ 211 14-555; www .wien.info; 01, Albertinaplatz; 9am-7pm) This is Vienna's main tourist office, with a ticket agency, hotel booking service, free maps, and every brochure under the sun.
Westbahnhof Information Office (Map pp80-2; 7am-10pm)
WienXtra-Kinderinfo (Map pp83-5; ☎ 4000 84 400; www.kinderinfowien.at; 07, Museumsplatz 1; 2-7pm Tue-Thu, 10am-5pm Fri & Sat) Marketed firstly at children (check out the knee-high display cases), *then* their parents, this child-friendly tourist office has loads of information on kids activities and a small indoor playground.

Travel Agencies

American Express (Map pp83-5; ☎ 515 40; 01, Kärntner Strasse 21-23; 9am-5pm Mon-Thu, 9am-4pm Fri) Travel section and financial services, and will hold mail (not parcels) free of charge for up to one month for customers who have American Express cards.
Österreichisches Verkehrsbüro (Map pp83-5; ☎ 588 00; www.verkehrsbuero.at; 04, Friedrichstrasse 7;

9am-5pm Mon-Fri) Major national agency organises everything under the sun.
STA Travel (Map pp83-5; ☎ 401 48; www.statravel .at; 09, Garnisongasse 7; 9am-5.30pm Mon-Fri) STA has discounted flights for students and helpful staff that speak English. There are five branches in the city.

Universities

Only the main universities are listed below:
TU Wien (Map pp83-5; ☎ 588 01-0; www.tuwien .ac.at; 04, Karlsplatz 13) Vienna's technical university.
Universität für Bodenkultur (BOKU; Map p86; ☎ 476 54; www.boku.ac.at; 18, Gregor-Mendel-Strasse 33) The agriculture and science university in the north of the city.
Universität Wien (Map pp83-5; ☎ 427 78 150; www .univie.ac.at; 01, Dr Karl Leuger-Ring 1) Vienna's main university; an Italian Renaissance building whose highlight is the Grosser Festaal, blessed with ceiling frescoes by Klimt.
Wirtschaftsuniversität Wien (Map p86; ☎ 313 36-740; www.wu-wien.ac.at; 09, Augasse 2-6) The Economics university of Vienna.

SIGHTS

The bulk of Vienna's top attractions are either inside the Innere Stadt or within 10 minutes' walk of its borders. The Innere Stadt is best tackled on foot as it's a maze of one-way cobblestone streets and pedestrian-only zones. The rest of the city is easily managed by public transport or, if you're feeling fit, by bicycle.

Innere Stadt

The Innere Stadt is a timeless and magical place, more an open-air museum than a city centre. It therefore should come as no surprise that the entire district has been designated a World Heritage site since 2001.

STEPHANSDOM

The most beloved and recognisable structure in all of Vienna is the Gothic masterpiece **Stephansdom** (Map pp83-5; ☎ 515 52-3520; www .stephanskirche.at; 01, Stephansplatz; admission free, guided tours adult/concession €4/1.50; 6am-10pm Mon-Sat, 7am-10pm Sun, tours in English 3.45pm Apr-Oct), or Steffl (litte Stephen), as the locals call it. It is the geographical and emotional heart of the city.

The cathedral was built on the site of a 12th-century church, of which the surviving Riesentor (Giant's Gate), main entrance and Heidentürme (Towers of the Heathens) are incorporated into the present building. Both are Romanesque in style; however, the church was rebuilt in Gothic style after 1359.

VIENNA

MORE FOR YOUR MONEY

If you're planning on doing a lot of sight-seeing in a short period, consider purchasing **Die Wien-Karte** (Vienna Card; €16.90), which provides 72 hours of unlimited travel plus discounts at selected museums, attractions, cafés and shops. It comes with an information brochure and is available from hotels and ticket offices.

The Kunsthistorisches Museum and its associated museums are covered by Gold, Silver and Bronze tickets. The **Gold ticket** (€23) allows entry to the Kunsthistorisches Museum, Schatzkammer, Neue Burg museums, Museum für Völkerkunde, Wagenburg in Schönbrunn and the Theatermuseum. The **Silver ticket** (€21) covers everything the Gold ticket does, minus the Wagenburg. Third place **Bronze** (€19) will get you into the Kunsthistorisches Museum, Schatzkammer, Neue Burg museums and the Museum für Völkerkunde.

The City of Vienna runs some 20 **municipal museums** (www.museum.vienna.at) scattered around the city, all of which are included in a free booklet available at the Rathaus. All are free Friday morning and all day Sunday.

The dominating feature is the skeletal **Südturm** (adult/concession €3/1; ☼ 9am-5.30pm). It stands 136.7m high and was completed in 1433 after 75 years of building work. Negotiating 343 steps will bring you to the cramped viewing platform for an impressive panorama. It was supposed to be matched on the north side by a **companion tower** (adult/concession €4/1.50; ☼ 9am-6pm Apr-Oct, 9am-6.30pm Jul & Aug, 8.30am-7pm Nov-Mar), accessible by lift, but the imperial purse withered and the Gothic style went out of fashion, so the incomplete tower was topped off with a Renaissance cupola in 1579. Austria's largest bell, weighing in at 21 tonnes, is the **Pummerin** (boomer bell), which was installed here in 1952.

Don't ignore the decorations and statues on the outside of the cathedral: at the rear the agony of the Crucifixion is well captured, although some irreverent souls attribute Christ's pained expression to toothache. A striking feature of the exterior is the glorious **tiled roof**, showing dazzling chevrons on one end and the Austrian eagle on the other.

Taking centre stage inside the rich interior is the magnificent Gothic **stone pulpit**, fashioned in 1515 by Anton Pilgram. The expressive faces of the four fathers of the church (the saints Augustine, Ambrose, Gregory and Jerome) are at the centre of the design, but the highlight is Pilgram himself peering out from a window below. He also appears at the base of the organ loft on the northern wall, seemingly holding up the entire organ on his own narrow shoulders. The baroque **high altar** in the main chancel depicts the stoning of St Stephen; the left chancel contains a winged altarpiece from Wiener Neustadt, dating from 1447; the right chancel houses the Renaissance-style red marble tomb of Friedrich III.

Last but by no means least is the cathedral's **Katoomba** (catacombs; adult/concession €4/1.50; guided tour every 15 or 30min 10-11.30am & 1.30-4.30pm Mon-Sat, 1.30-4.30pm Sun & holidays). The catacombs house the remains of countless plague victims, kept in a mass grave and a bone house. Also on display are rows of urns containing the internal organs of the Habsburgs. One of the many privileges of being a Habsburg was to be dismembered and dispersed after death: their hearts are in the Augustinerkirche in the Hofburg and the rest of their bits are in the Kaisergruft (p92).

HOFBURG

The **Hofburg** (Imperial Palace; Map pp83-5) is an impressive repository of culture and heritage. The Habsburgs were based here for over six centuries, from the first emperor (Rudolf I in 1279) to the last (Charles I in 1918). The Hofburg owes its size and architectural diversity to plain old one-upmanship; new sections were added by the new rulers, including the early baroque Leopold Wing (Map pp83-5), the 18th-century Imperial Chancery Wing (Map pp83-5), the 16th-century Amalia Wing (Map pp83-5) and the Burgkapelle (Royal Chapel; Map pp83-5).

The oldest section is the 13th-century **Schweizerhof** (Swiss Courtyard; Map pp83-5), named after the Swiss guards who used to protect its precincts. The Renaissance Swiss gate dates from 1553. The courtyard adjoins a much larger courtyard, **In der Burg** (Map pp83-5), with a monument to Emperor Franz at its centre. The palace now houses the offices of the Austrian president and a plethora of museums.

Kaiserappartements

The **Kaiserappartements** (Imperial Apartments; Map pp83-5; ☎ 533 75 70; 01, Innerer Burghof, Kaisertor; adult/concession/child €7.50/5.90/3.90, audio guide €2.50; 9am-7pm), once occupied by Franz Josef I and Empress Elisabeth, are as opulent as you might expect, with fine furniture, hanging tapestries and bulbous crystal chandeliers. However, they don't match those in Schloss Schönbrunn (p100). The adjoining **Hoftafel und Tafelkammer** (Court Tableware and Silver Depot), a collection of porcelain and tableware, is included in the entry price.

Mythos Sisi

Taking over the first six rooms of the Kaiserappartements is the museum, **Mythos Sisi** (Map pp83-5; ☎ 533 75 70; 01, Innerer Burghof, Kaisertor; adult/concession & child €7.50/3.90; 9am-5pm, 9am-5.30pm Jul & Aug), devoted to Austria's beloved Empress Elisabeth. A reconstruction of her luxurious coach which carried her on many a journey is impressive, but it's the small details which steal the show; a reconstruction of the dress she wore on the eve of her wedding, her sunshade, fans and gloves.

Schatzkammer

The **Schatzkammer** (Imperial Treasury; Map pp83-5; ☎ 533 79 31; 01, Schweizerhof; adult/concession & child/family €8/6/16; 10am-6pm Wed-Mon) is a mass of secular and ecclesiastical treasures of great value and splendour. The sheer wealth exhibited is staggering: Room 7 alone contains a 2860-carat Colombian emerald, a 416-carat balas ruby and a 492-carat aquamarine; Room 11 holds the highlight of the Treasury, the 10th century imperial crown with eight gold plates and precious gems; while Room 8 contains a 75cm-wide bowl carved from a single piece of agate, and a narwhal tusk, 243cm long and once claimed to have been a unicorn horn. The list goes on. The Sacred Treasury is just as impressive, with its rare, and hard to believe, religious relics, including fragments of the True Cross, one of the nails from the Crucifixion, and one of the thorns from Christ's crown.

Lipizzaner Museum

Expounding on the famous white stallions of the Spanische Hofreitschule (Spanish Riding School; see below) is the **Lipizzaner Museum** (Map pp83-5; ☎ 533 78 11; www.lipizzaner.at; 01, Reitschulestrasse 2; adult/concession & child/family €5/3.60/10; 9am-6pm). A cross-breed of Spanish, Arab and Berber horses, the Lipizzaner were first imported from Spain (hence 'Spanish') by Maximilian II in 1562, and in 1580 a stud was established at Lipizza (hence 'Lipizzaner'), now in Slovenia. There's English text, but the content is a little thin. Windows allow a view directly into the stallion stables, albeit obscured by thick glass and fine mesh.

Spanische Hofreitschule

For the real thing, cross the street to the **Spanische Hofreitschule** (Map pp83-5; ☎ 533 90 31; www.srs.at; 01, Michaelerplatz 1; adult/concession & child from €24/12; performances 6pm Fri, 11am Sat & Sun May, 11am Sat & Sun Apr, 11am & 6pm Fri & Sun Sep, 11am Sun Mar, Jun, Oct & Dec). These graceful stallions perform an equine ballet to a programme of classical music while the audience cranes to see from pillared balconies and chandeliers shimmer above. Reservations need to be booked months in advance: tickets can be ordered on the website. Otherwise, ask in the office about cancellations; unclaimed tickets are sold about two hours before performances. **Tickets** (adult/concession/child €11.50/8.50/5; 10am-noon Tue-Sat) to watch them train can be bought the same day at gate No 2, Josefsplatz in the Hofburg. Queues are very long early in the day, but if you try at around 11am most people have gone and you can get in fairly quickly – indicative of the fact that training is relatively dull except for a few isolated high points. If you only want to grab a few photos, you can try waiting to see them cross between the school and the *Stallburg* (stables), which usually happens on the half-hour.

Nationalbibliothek

The major reason to visit Vienna's largest **Nationalbibliothek** (National Library; Map pp83-5; ☎ 534 10 397; www.onb.ac.at; 01, Josefplatz 1; adult/concession & child/family €5/3/9; 10am-4pm, to 7pm Thu May-Oct, 10am-2pm, to 7pm Thu Nov-Apr) is to gaze on the **Prunksaal** (Grand Hall), a majestic baroque hall built between 1723 and 1726. Commissioned by Charles VI (whose statue is under the central dome), it holds some

200,000 volumes of leather-bound scholarly tomes. Rare ancient volumes (mostly 15th-century) are stored within glass cabinets, with pages opened to beautifully drawn sections of text. The central fresco, by Daniel Gran, depicts the emperor's apotheosis.

Neue Burg Museums

Taking up part of the **Neue Burg** (Map pp83-5; ☎ 525 24-484; 01, Heldenplatz; adult/concession & child/family €8/6/16, audio guide €2; ⏲ 10am-6pm Wed-Mon) are three museums in one. The **Sammlung Alter Musik Instrumente** (Collection of Ancient Musical Instruments) is the best of the bunch and contains a mass of instruments in all shapes and sizes which were invariably designed more for show than producing music. The **Ephesus Museum** features artefacts from Ephesus and Samothrace donated (some say 'lifted') by the Sultan in 1900 after a team of Austrian archaeologists excavated the famous site in Turkey. Last but not least is the **Hofjagd und Rüstkammer** (Arms and Armour), with fine examples of ancient armour dating mainly from the 15th and 16th centuries.

Museum für Völkerkunde

The **Museum für Völkerkunde** (Ethnological Museum; Map pp83-5; ☎ 534 30-0; www.ethno-museum.ac.at; 01, Heldenplatz; adult/concession & child/family €8/6/16; ⏲ 10am-6pm Wed-Mon) exhibits folk art from around the world; its highlight is an Aztec feather headdress once worn by Montezuma.

ALBERTINA

Once used to house imperial guests, the **Albertina** (Map pp83-5; ☎ 534 83-544; www.albertina.at; 01, Albertinaplatz 3; adult/concession & child €7.50/6.50/5.50; ⏲ 10am-6pm, to 9pm Wed) is now home to the greatest collection of graphic art in the world. It consists of an astonishing 1½ million prints and 50,000 drawings, including 145 Dürer drawings (the largest in the world), 43 by Raphael, 70 by Rembrandt and 150 by Schiele. There are loads more by Leonardo da Vinci, Michelangelo, Rubens, Bruegel, Cézanne, Picasso, Klimt, Matisse and Kokoschka.

Because of the sheer number of prints and drawings in the Albertina's archive, only a small percentage can be displayed at any one time. Exhibitions, which normally follow a theme or artist, are changed every three months and also feature works from other collections.

HAUS DER MUSIK

The well-presented **Haus der Musik** (House of Music; Map pp83-5; ☎ 516 48-0; www.hdm.at; 01, Seilerstätte 30; adult/concession & child €10/8.50, half-price 5-9pm Tue; ⏲ 10am-10pm) is a museum devoted to music, spread out over four floors. All descriptions are in English and German. The 1st floor pays homage, rather briefly, to the Vienna Philharmonic.

The 2nd floor is where the fun begins; rooms delve into the physics of sounds and use touch screens and loads of hands-on displays to explain the mechanics of sound. Here you can test the limits of your hearing and play around with sampled sounds and record your own CD (€7.30). The 3rd floor features the stars of Vienna's classical music – Haydn, Mozart, Beethoven, Schubert, Strauss and Mahler all receive a room apiece. Best of all though is the 'virtual conductor', where a video of the Vienna Philharmonic responds to a conducting baton and keeps time with your movements. Floor 4 has experimental and electronic music, which you can also modify yourself. Singing trees, sound sticks and beeping buttons are just some of the hands-on 'instruments' at your disposal.

KAISERGRUFT

The high-peaked **Kaisergruft** (Imperial Burial Vault; Map pp83-5; ☎ 512 68 53; www.kapuziner.at/wien - in German; 01 Neuer Markt; adult/concession/child €3.60/2.90/1; ⏲ 9.30am-4pm), beneath the Kapuzinerkirche (Church of the Capuchin Friars), was instigated by Empress Anna (1585–1618), and her body and that of her husband, Emperor Matthias (1557–1619), were the first to be placed here. Since then, all but three of the Habsburg dynasty members found their way here (in bits and pieces), the last being Empress Ziti in 1989. The only non-Habsburg to be buried here is the Countess Fuchs.

The royals' fashion extends even to tombs: those in the vault range from the unadorned to the ostentatious. By far the most elaborate caskets are those portraying 18th-century baroque pomp, such as the huge double sarcophagus containing Maria Theresia and Franz I. The tomb of Charles VI has been expertly restored. Both were the work of Balthasar Moll (p42).

JÜDISCHES MUSEUM

The **Jüdisches Museum** (Jewish Museum; Map pp83-5; ☎ 535 04 31; www.jmw.at; 01, Dorotheergasse 11; adult/concession & child €5/2.90; ☻ 10am-6pm Sun-Fri, 10am-8pm Thu), taking up three floors of Palais Eskeles, uses holograms and an assortment of objects to document the history of the Jews in Vienna, from the first settlements at Judenplatz in the 13th century up to the present. The ground floor is filled with the Max Berger collection – a rich compilation of Judaica mainly dating from the Habsburg era. Temporary exhibitions are presented on the 1st floor, with the 2nd floor dividing its space between more temporary exhibitions and 21 holograms depicting the history of the Jewish people in Vienna.

A combined ticket of €7/€4 allows entry to the **Stadttempel synagogue** (Map pp83-5; ☎ 535 04 31; www.jmw.at; 01, Seitenstettengasse 4; adult/concession & child €2/1; ☻ 11.30am-3pm Mon-Thu) and the Museum Judenplatz (below).

MUSEUM JUDENPLATZ

The **Museum Judenplatz** (Jewish museum; Map pp83-5; ☎ 535 04 31; www.jmw.at; 01, Judenplatz 8; adult/concession & child €3/1.50; ☻ 10am-6pm Sun-Thu, 10am-2pm Fri) focuses on excavated remains of a medieval synagogue (1420) that once took pride of place on Judenplatz. The basic outline of the synagogue can still be seen and a small model of the building helps to complete the picture. Documents and artefacts dating from 1200 to 1400 are on display, and spacey interactive screens explain Jewish culture. On Judenplatz is Austria's first Holocaust memorial, the 'Nameless Library'. This squat, box-like structure pays homage to the 65,000 Austrian Jews who were killed during the Anschluss.

ANKERUHR

The picturesque **Ankeruhr** (Art Nouveau clock; Map pp83-5; Hoher Markt 10-11) was created by Franz von Matsch in 1911 and commissioned by the Anker Insurance Co. Over a 12-hour period, figures such as Josef Haydn and Maria Theresia slowly pass across the clock face – details of who's who are outlined on a plaque on the wall below. Join the mass of tourists at noon when all the figures trundle past in turn, and organ music from the appropriate period is piped out.

Other sights worthy of note in the Innere Stadt include:

Figaro Haus (Map pp83-5; ☎ 535 62 94; 01, Domgasse 5; adult/concession & child €4/2; ☻ 9am-6pm Tue-Sun) Former resident Mozart penned The Marriage of Figaro here. More for Mozart fanatics.

Neidhart-Fresken (Map pp83-5; ☎ 535 90 65; 01, Tuchlauben 19; adult/child €2/1; ☻ 9am-noon Tue-Sun) The oldest extant secular murals in Vienna dating from 1398, retelling the story of the minstrel Neidhart von Reuental (1180–1240) in lively and jolly scenes.

Pasqualati House (Map pp83-5; ☎ 535 89 05; 01, Mölker Bastei 8; adult/child €2/1; ☻ 9am-12.15pm & 1-4.30pm Tue-Sun) Beethoven residence from 1804 to 1814 (he apparently occupied some 30 places in his 35 years in Vienna) where he composed Symphonies 4, 5 and 7 and the opera Fidelio, among other works. Two rooms are lightly filled with memorabilia.

Ruprechtskirche (St Rupert's Church; Map pp83-5; 01, Ruprechtsplatz) The oldest church in Vienna, first documented in 1137. Unfortunately rarely open to the public.

Ringstrasse

Emperor Franz Josef was largely responsible for the monumental architecture around the Ringstrasse (Ring). In 1857 he decided to tear down the redundant military fortifications and exercise grounds and replace them with grandiose public buildings in a variety of historical styles. Work began the following year and reached a peak in the 1870s. The stock market crash in 1873 put a major dampener on plans, and further grandiose plans were shelved due to lack of money and the beginning of WWI. The Ring is easily explored on foot or bicycle; if you've not the time, jump on tram No 1 or 2, both of which run the length of the boulevard and offer a snapshot of the impressive architecture.

PARLAMENT

The neoclassical façade and Greek pillars of **Parlament** (Map pp83-5; ☎ 40 110-2570; www.parlinkom.gv.at; 01, Dr Karl-Renner-Ring 3; tours €2; tours ☻ 9am, 10am, 11am, 1pm, 2pm & 3pm Mon-Fri mid-Jun–mid-Sep), designed by Theophil Hansen in 1883, are quite striking, as is the beautiful **Athena Fountain** directly in front of the building. Athena is flanked by statues of horse breaking (though some would say horse punching).

RATHAUS

The neo-Gothic **Rathaus** (City Hall; Map pp83-5; ☎ 525 50; www.wien.gv.at; 01, Rathausplatz; tours ☻ 1pm

Mon, Wed & Fri), which was modelled on Flemish city halls, steals the Ringstrasse show. Its main spire soars to 102m, if you include the pennant held by the knight at the top. You're free to wander through the seven inner courtyards but you must join a guided tour to catch a glimpse of the interior, with its red carpets, gigantic mirrors and frescoes.

KUNSTHISTORISCHES MUSEUM

The **Kunsthistorisches Museum** (Museum of Fine Arts; Map pp83-5; ☎ 525 24-403; www.khm.at; 01, Burgring 5; adult/concession & child/family €10/7.50/20, tours €2; ⏰ 10am-8pm Tue-Sun, to 9pm Thu, tours 11am Tue, 3pm Fri & Sat) ranks among the finest museums in Europe, if not the world, and should not be missed. The Habsburgs were great collectors, and the huge extent of lands under their control led to many important works of art being funnelled back to Vienna.

Rubens was appointed to the service of a Habsburg governor in Brussels, so it is not surprising that the museum has one of the best collections of his works. The collection of paintings by Pieter Bruegel the Elder is also unrivalled. The building itself has some delightful features and all the marble is genuine. The murals between the arches above the stairs were created by three artists, including a young Klimt (northern wall), painted before he broke with classical tradition.

It's impossible to see the whole museum in one visit; the best idea is to pick up the *Kunsthistorisches Museum Vienna* booklet in English for €1.50 and concentrate on specific areas.

Ground Floor

In the west wing is the Egyptian collection, including the burial chamber of Prince Kaninisut and mummified animal remains. The Greek and Roman collection here includes the Gemma Augusta cameo, made from onyx in AD 10.

The east wing contains sculpture and decorative arts covering a range of styles. There's some exquisite 17th-century glassware and ornaments, and unbelievably lavish clocks from the 16th and 17th centuries in Room XXXV and Room XXXVII. The prime item in this wing (in Room XXVII) is the gold salt cellar by Benvenuto Cellini, made for Francis I of France in 1543. It depicts two naked deities, the goddess of the earth and the god of the sea, and has tiny wheels within so it can be pushed easily around the table.

First Floor

The *Gemäldegalerie* (picture gallery) found on this floor is the most important part of the museum, featuring Bruegel, Dürer, Rubens, Rembrandt and many others. Some rooms provide information cards in English giving a critique of particular works.

The **East Wing** is devoted to German, Dutch and Flemish paintings. Room X is home to the Bruegel collection, amassed by Rudolf II. A recurrent theme in Bruegel the Elder's work is nature, as in *The Hunters in the Snow* (1565). The next gallery (Room XI) displays the warm, larger-than-life scenes of Flemish baroque. The motto in *The King Drinks* by Jacob Jordaens (1593–1678), to which the revellers are raising their glasses, translates as 'None resembles a fool more than the drunkard'. Works by Albrecht Dürer (1471–1528) are displayed in Rooms 16 and 17. His brilliant mastery of colour is shown in *The Holy Trinity Surrounded by All Saints*, originally an altarpiece.

The paintings by the mannerist Giuseppe Arcimboldo (1527–93) in Room 19 use a device well explored by Salvador Dalí – familiar objects arranged to appear as something else – the difference being that Arcimboldo did it nearly 400 years earlier. Room XIII, Room XIV and Room 20 feature the dramatic baroque scenes of Peter Paul Rubens (1577–1640), who synthesised northern European and Italian traditions. Several self-portraits by Rembrandt can be found in Room XV.

The **West Wing** starts with evocative works by Titian, a member of the Venetian school, in Room I. In Room 2 hangs *The Three Philosophers* (1508), which is one of the few properly authenticated works by Giorgione. Room 4 contains Raphael's harmonious and idealised *Madonna in the Meadow* (1505) – the triangular composition and the complementary colours are typical features of the Florentine high Renaissance. Compare this with Caravaggio's *Madonna of the Rosary* (1606) in Room V, in which the supplicants' dirty feet are an example of the new realism of early baroque. Tintoretto's *Susanna at her Bath* (1555) can be found in Room III. It re-creates the Old Testament tale and successfully portrays both serenity and implicit menace. Room VII contains paintings by Bernardo Bellotto (1721–80), Canaletto's nephew. He was commissioned by Maria Theresia to paint scenes of Vienna. Several are shown here, though some landscapes, such as the view from the Belvedere, are not faithful representations but have been creatively recomposed.

NATURHISTORISCHES MUSEUM

The **Naturhistorisches Museum** (Museum of Natural History; Map pp83–5; ☎ 521 77-0; www.nhm-wien .ac.at; 01, Burg Ring 7; adult/senior/student & child €8/6/3.50; ⊙ 9am-6.30pm Thu-Mon, 9am-9pm Wed) is the scientific counterpart of the Kunsthistorisches Museum. The building is just as grand but the exhibits aren't quite in the same league. Minerals, meteorites and animal remains are displayed in jars; zoology and anthropology are covered in detail and there's a children's corner. The 25,000-year-old *Venus of Willendorf* statuette is on display, though she's a mere youngster compared to the 32,000 BC statuette *Fanny from Stratzing* (the oldest figurative sculpture in the world).

AKADEMIE DER BILDENDEN KÜNSTE

The **Akademie der bildenden Künste** (Academy of Fine Arts; Map pp83–5; ☎ 588 16-0; www.akademie galerie.at; 01, Schillerplatz 3; adult/concession/child under 10 €5/3/free, audio guide €2; ⊙ 10am-4pm Tue-Sun) has a small picture gallery, the highlight of which is Hieronymus Bosch's *The Last Judgement* altarpiece. Flemish painters are well represented and the building itself has an attractive façade. It was this academy that turned down would-be artist Adolf Hitler. A statue of Schiller takes centre stage in front of the academy.

SECESSION

In 1897 the Vienna Secession movement was formed when 19 progressive artists broke away from the conservative artistic establishment that met in the Künstlerhaus art gallery. Their aim was to present current trends in contemporary art and leave behind the historicism then in vogue. Among their number were Gustav Klimt, Josef Hoffman, Kolo Moser and Josef M Olbrich, a former student of Otto Wagner.

In 1898, Olbrich designed the movement's **Secession Building** (Map pp83–5; ☎ 587 53 07; www .secession.at; 01, Friedrichstrasse 12; admission exhibition & frieze €5.50, exhibition only €4; ⊙ 10am-6pm Tue-Sun, till 8pm Thu); its most striking feature is the enormous golden sphere (prosaically described as a 'golden cabbage' by some Viennese) rising from a turret on the roof. Above the door are highly distinctive mask-like faces with dangling serpents instead of earlobes. The motto above the entrance asserts: 'Der Zeit ihre Kunst, der Kunst ihre Freiheit' (To each time its art, to art its freedom).

The 14th exhibition held in the building, in 1902, featured the famous *Beethoven Frieze* by Klimt. This 34m-long work was only supposed to be a temporary display, but has been painstakingly restored and is on view in the basement. The frieze, combining both dense and sparse images, shows willowy women with bounteous hair jostling for attention with a large gorilla, while slender figures float and a choir sings. The ground floor is still used as it was originally intended, presenting temporary exhibitions of contemporary art.

MUSEUMSQUARTIER

This excellent **MuseumsQuartier** (Museums Quarter; Map pp83–5; ☎ 523 58 81-1730, within Austria 0820-600 600; www.mqw.at; 07, Museumsplatz 1; tours €3; information & ticket centre ⊙ 10am-7pm, tours noon weekends), lying within the confines of the former imperial stables designed by Fischer von Erlach, is blessed with superb museums, grand cafés and warm public spaces (a perfect place to people-watch in summer). With over 60,000 sq metres of exhibition space, it's the eighth-largest cultural complex in the world.

Of the combi tickets on offer, the **MQ Kombi Ticket** (€25) includes entry into every museum (Zoom only has a reduction) and a 30% discount on performances in the TanzQuartier Wien (p120); **MQ Art Ticket** (€18) allows admission into the Leopold Museum, MUMOK, Kunsthalle and reduced entry into Zoom, plus 30% discount at the TanzQuartier Wien; **MQ Duo Ticket** (€12) covers everything the Art ticket does, minus the Kunsthalle.

Leopold Museum

In 1994 the Austrian government acquired the enormous private collection of 19th-century and modern Austrian paintings amassed by Rudolf Leopold – €160 million for 5266 paintings (sold individually, the paintings would have made him €574 million). It then went about building a museum suitable to display such a collection, and the **Leopold Museum** (Map pp83-5; ☎ 525 70-0; www.leopoldmuseum.org; 07, Museumsplatz 1; adult/concession €9/5.50, audio guide €2; ☺ 10am-7pm Wed-Sun, 10m-9pm Fri) was born.

Leopold began his art collection in 1950 with the purchase of his first Egon Schiele, so it comes as no surprise that the museum contains the largest collection of the painter's work in the world. Most are on the top floor; look for *Selbstportrait mit Judenkirschen* (Self-Portrait with Winter-Cherries) and *Kardinale und Nüne* (Cardinal und Nun), two masterpieces of the expressive artist. Klimt is also represented; his *Tod und Leben* (Death and Life) on the ground floor is by far the most impressive. Simple yet highly emotional sketches from both artists are displayed in the basement.

Other well-represented artists include Albin Egger-Lienz (1868–1922), Richard Gerstl (1883–1908) and, arguably Austria's third-greatest painter (after Klimt and Schiele), Oskar Kokoschka (1886–1980). Egger-Lienz had a knack for capturing the essence of rural life; this is seen in his stark *Pietá*, considered by Leopold as his greatest work. Kokoschka had a long life in the painting arena, but his earlier works steal the show; his *Selbstportrait mit ein Hand* (Self-Portrait with One Hand) from 1918 is his most substantial piece. Works by Hoffmann, Loos, (Otto) Wagner, Waldmüller and Romako are also on display.

MUMOK

The dark basalt rock edifice that houses the **Museum moderner Kunst** (MUMOK, Museum of Modern Art; Map pp83-5; ☎ 525 00-0; www.mumok.at; 07, Museumsplatz 1; adult/concession €8/6.50; ☺ 10am-6pm Tue-Sun, 10am-9pm Thu) is filled with Vienna's premier collection of 20th-century art, centred around fluxus and nouveau realism and pop art and photo-realism. Expressionism, cubism, minimal art, and Viennese Actionism (p42) are also represented. The best of the bunch is an extensive collection of Pop Art featuring the likes of Warhol, Jasper Johns and Rauschenberg. If you've never seen Viennese Actionism, this is your chance as MUMOK holds the largest collection of such art in the basement. Be prepared, though; Actionism is a confronting melting pot of animal sacrifice, bloody canvases, self-mutilation and defecation.

Kunsthalle

The **Kunsthalle** (Arts hall; Map pp83-5; ☎ 521 89 33; www.kunsthallewien.at; 07, Museumsplatz 1; Hall 1 adult/concession €6.50/5, Hall 2 €5/3.50, combined ticket €8/6.50; ☺ 10am-7pm, to 10pm Thu) is used to showcase local and international contemporary art. Programmes, which run for three to six months, tend to focus mainly on photography, video, film, installation and new media.

MUSEUM FÜR ANGEWANDTE KUNST

The **Museum für angewandte Kunst** (MAK, Museum of Applied Art; Map pp83-5; ☎ 711 36-0; www.mak.at; 01, Stubenring 5; adult/concession €7.90/4, free Sat; ☺ 10am-6pm Wed-Sun, 10am-midnight Tue) is devoted to practical, everyday items transformed into art forms. Each exhibition room is devoted to a different style, eg Renaissance, baroque, orientalism, historicism, empire, Art Deco, and the distinctive metalwork of the Wiener Werkstätte. Contemporary artists were invited to present the rooms in ways they felt were appropriate, the effect of which has created eye-catching and unique displays. The 20th-century design and architecture room is impressive; Frank Gehry's cardboard chair is a gem. The museum collection encompass tapestries, lace, furniture, glassware and ornaments, and Klimt's *Stoclet Frieze* is upstairs.

In the basement is the Study Collection, which groups exhibits according to the type of materials used: glass and ceramics, metal, wood and textiles. Actual objects range from ancient oriental statues to sofas (note the red-lips sofa).

Also of particular note on the Ring are:

Votivkirche (Map pp83-5; 09, Rooseveltplatz; ☺ 9am-1pm & 4-6.30pm Tue-Sat, 9am-1pm Sun) Commissioned by Franz Josef after he survived an assassination attempt, this neo-Gothic church has an impressive façade but its interior is too bleak and spacious to be welcoming.

Parks Take a rest in one of the Ring's three parks; Stadtpark (Map pp83-5; note the gold statue of Johann Strauss), Burggarten (Map pp83-5) and Volksgarten (Map pp83-5).

Postsparkasse (Map pp83-5; www.postsparkasse.at; 01, Georg Coch Platz; admission free; ☺ 8am-3pm Mon-Fri, 8am-5.30pm Thu) Celebrated Post Office Savings Bank designed by Otto Wagner using innovative materials.

Across the Danube Canal

The districts across the Danube Canal from the Innere Stadt are predominantly residential neighbourhoods, largely bereft of individual sights of interest to the average

THE THIRD MAN

'I had paid my last farewell to Harry a week ago, when his coffin was lowered into the frozen February ground, so that it was with incredulity that I saw him pass by, without a sign of recognition, among the host of strangers in the Strand.' Thus wrote Graham Greene on the back of an envelope. There it stayed, for many years, an idea without a context. Then Alexander Korda asked him to write a film about the occupation of postwar Vienna. The film was to be directed by Carol Reed, who had worked with Greene on an earlier film, *The Fallen Idol*.

So Greene now had an opening scene and a framework. He still needed a plot. He flew to Vienna in 1948 and roamed the bomb-damaged streets, searching in increasing desperation for inspiration. Nothing came to mind until, with his departure imminent, Greene had lunch with a British intelligence officer. The conversation proved more nourishing than the meal. The officer told him about the underground police who patrolled the huge network of sewers beneath the city. He also waxed lyrical on the subject of the black-market trade in penicillin, which the racketeers exploited with no regard for the consequences. Greene put the two ideas together and created his story.

Another chance encounter completed the picture. After filming one night, Carol Reed went drinking in the *Heurigen* area of Sievering. There he discovered Anton Karas playing a zither and was mesmerised by the hypnotic rhythms the instrument produced. Although Karas could neither read nor write music, Reed flew him to London where he recorded the soundtrack. The bouncing, staggering refrain that became Harry Lime's theme dominated the film, became a hit and earned Karas a fortune.

As a final twist of serendipity, the most memorable lines of dialogue came not from the measured pen of Greene but from the improvising tongue of Orson Welles as Harry Lime. They were delivered in front of the camera in the Prater, under the towering stanchions of the Ferris wheel: 'In Italy for 30 years under the Borgias they had warfare, terror, murder, bloodshed – they produced Michelangelo, Leonardo da Vinci and the Renaissance. In Switzerland they had brotherly love, 500 years of democracy and peace, and what did that produce? The cuckoo clock. So long Holly.'

visitor. But this area is also Vienna's outdoor playground.

PRATER

This large park encompasses grassy meadows, woodlands, an amusement park known as the **Wurstelparter** and one of the city's icons, the **Riesenrad** (Ferris wheel; Map pp80-2; ☎ 729 54 30; www.wienerriesenrad.com; 02, Prater 90; adult/child/family €7.50/3/19; ☺ 9am-midnight May-Sep, 10am-10pm Mar, Apr, Oct, 10am-8pm Nov-Feb). Built in 1897, the wheel rises to 65m and takes about 20 minutes to rotate its 430-tonne weight one complete circle, offering great views of Vienna. It achieved celluloid fame in *The Third Man* in the scene where Holly Martins confronts Harry Lime.

DONAUINSEL & ALTE DONAU

Dividing the Danube from the Neue Donau is the svelte **Donauinsel**, which stretches some 21½km from opposite Klosterneuburg in the north to the Nationalpark Donau-Auen in the south. The island features long sections of swimming areas, concrete paths for walking and cycling, and restaurants and snack bars. The **Alte Donau** is a landlocked arm of the Danube, a favourite of sailing and boating enthusiasts, swimmers, walkers, fishermen and, in winter (when it's cold enough), ice skaters.

Inside the Gürtel

The districts that lie inside the Gürtel are a dense concentration of apartment blocks pocketed by leafy parks, with a couple of grand baroque palaces thrown in for good measure.

SCHLOSS BELVEDERE

Belvedere is considered one of the finest baroque palaces in the world. Designed by Johann Lukas von Hildebrandt, it was built for the brilliant military strategist, Prince Eugene of Savoy, conqueror of the Turks in 1718. The Unteres (Lower) Belvedere was built first (1714–16), with an orangery attached, and was the prince's summer residence. Connected to it by a long, landscaped garden is the Oberes (Upper) Belvedere (1721–23), the

VIENNA

venue for the prince's banquets and other big bashes.

The palace is now home to **Österreichische Galerie** (Austrian Gallery; Map pp80-2; adult/concession €7.50/5; valid more than 1 day), split between the Unteres Belvedere which houses the baroque section, and the Oberes Belvedere, showcasing 19th- and 20th-century art.

Oberes Belvedere

The **Oberes Belvedere** (Map pp80-2; ☎ 795 57 134; www.belvedere.at; 03, Prinz Eugen-Strasse 27; adult/concession/child/family €7.50/5/3/15, audio guide €4; ✆ 10am-6pm Tue-Sun) houses the palace's most important collection but the building alone is worth the entrance fee; grand baroque fixtures include Herculean figures and a fresco depicting the apotheosis of Prince Eugene.

The 1st floor has paintings from the turn of the 19th century, particularly the work of Hans Makart (1840–84) and Anton Romakos (1832–89). However, the 20th-century section of this floor has the gallery's best exhibits. Two most noteworthy artists are Gustav Klimt (1862–1918) and Egon Schiele (1890–1918). Klimt's best known and most intriguing work, *The Kiss* (1908), is displayed here. Pundits disagree as to whether the kiss in question is proffered willingly or conceded under coercion. Some of Klimt's impressionistic landscapes are also here.

Schiele produced intense, melancholic work, typified by the hypnotic and bulging eyes on the portrait of his friend, *Eduard Kosmack* (1910). Schiele's bold, brooding colours and unforgiving outlines are a contrast to Klimt's golden tapestries and idealised forms.

Other Austrian artists represented include Herbert Boeckl, Anton Hanak, Arnulf Rainer and Fritz Wotruba. There are several examples of the work of the influential expressionist, Oskar Kokoschka. A smattering of international artists is also on display, including such greats as Munch, Monet, Van Gogh, Renoir and Cézanne.

The top floor has a concentration of 19th-century paintings from the Romantic, Classical and Biedermeier periods.

Unteres Belvedere

The **Unteres Belvedere** (Map pp80-2; ☎ 795 57 134; www.belvedere.at; 03, Rennweg 6; adult/concession €6/3; ✆ 10am-6pm Tue-Sun) is home to the baroque

section of the collection. It offers some good statuary, such as the originals from Donner's Neuer Markt fountain (1738–39), and *The Apotheosis of Prince Eugene* (again!), this time fashioned in marble in 1721 by the baroque sculptor Balthasar Permoser (p42). Paintings include portraits of Maria Theresia and Franz I, and a whole room is devoted to the vibrant work of Franz Anton Maulbertsch (1724–96).

The **Orangery** (Map pp80–2) houses a collection of Austrian medieval art comprising religious scenes, altarpieces and statues. There are several impressive works by Michael Pacher, who was influenced both by early art from the Low Countries and the early Renaissance of northern Italy.

Gardens

The long garden between the two Belvederes was laid out in classical French style and has sphinxes and other mythical beasts along its borders. South of the Oberes Belvedere is a small **Alpine Garden** (adult/concession €4/3; ✆ 10am-6pm Apr-Jul) which has 3500 plant species and a bonsai section. North from here is the much larger **Botanischgärten** (Botanical Gardens; admission free; ✆ 9am-1hr before dusk) belonging to the Vienna University.

PALAIS LIECHTENSTEIN

After many years collecting dust in depot vaults, this private collection of one Prince Hans-Adam II of Liechtenstein is on display in the magnificent **Palais Liechtenstein** (Liechtenstein Museum; Map pp80-2; ☎ 319 57 67-0; www.liechtensteinmuseum.at; 09, Fürstengasse 1; adult/concession/child €10/8/5, audio guide & tour €4; ✆ 9am-8pm). It's one of the largest private collections in the world and consists of some 200 paintings and 50 sculptures, dating from 1500 to 1700.

Built between 1690 and 1712, the palace is a supreme example of audacious and extravagant baroque architecture. Frescoes and ceiling paintings by the likes of Johann Michael Rottmayer and Marcantonio Franceschini decorate the halls and corridors of this sumptuous palace. Its **Herkulessaal** (Hercules Hall) – so named for the Hercules motifs within its ceiling frescoes by renowned Roman painter Andrea Pozzo – is an absolute highlight which extends over two storeys. The neoclassical **Gentlemen's Apartment Library**, on the ground floor, is not to be missed. It contains an astounding 100,000 volumes and just breathing the air in this room will raise your IQ by 10 points.

The collection is displayed over two of the palace's three floors and includes the likes of Rubens, Raphael, van Dyck and Rembrandt. Four galleries – one devoted to sculpture and the others to paintings – are located on the ground floor. Gallery III contains celebrated Biedermeier works and the lion's share of highlights on this floor; Friedrich von Amerling's *Portrait of Maria Franziska of Lichtenstein at Age Two* (1836) is a sublime piece of art capturing the peaceful princess.

The big guns, however, are on the upper floor. Seven galleries intertwine to provide a trip through 200 years of art history, starting in 1500 with early Italian religious paintings in Gallery IV. Gallery V is dedicated to Renaissance portraits; Raphael's *Portrait of a Man* (1503) takes first prize for the intensity and depth of the subject's stare. The focal point of the upper floor is Gallery VII, which is home to Peter Paul Rubens' *Decius Mus* cycle (1618). Consisting of eight almost life-size paintings, the cycle depicts the life and death of Decius Mus, a Roman leader who sacrificed himself so that his army would be victorious on the battlefield. Gallery VIII is totally devoted to Rubens, with over 30 of his Flemish baroque paintings, and even more Rubens are on display in Gallery IX – this time his portraits – alongside Van Dyck and Fran Hals. The sheer exuberance and life captured by Rubens in his *Portrait of Clara Serena Rubens* (1616) is testament to the great artist's talent. Gallery X is lined with Dutch still lifes and landscapes.

HEERESGESCHICHTLICHES MUSEUM

The superb **Heeresgeschichtliches Museum** (Museum of Military History; Map pp80–2; ☎ 795 61-60420; www.bundesheer.at/hgm; 03, Arsenal; adult/concession/child under 11/family €5.10/3.30/free/7.30; ☽ 9am-5pm Sat-Thu) is housed in the Arsenal, a large neo-Byzantine barracks and munitions depot.

Spread over two floors, the museum works its way from the Thirty Years' War (1618–48) to WWII, taking in the Hungarian Uprising and the Austro-Prussian War (ending in 1866), the Napoleonic and Turkish Wars, and WWI. Highlights on the 1st floor include the Great Seal of Mustafa Pasha, which fell to Prince Eugene of Savoy in the Battle of Zenta in 1697 (p23).

On the ground floor, the room on the assassination of Archduke Franz Ferdinand in Sarajevo in 1914 – which set off a chain of events culminating in the start of WWI – steals the show. The car he was shot in (complete with bullet holes), the sofa he bled to death on and his rather grizzly blood-stained coat are on show. The eastern wing covers the Republic years after WWI up until the Anschluss in 1938; the excellent displays include propaganda posters and Nazi paraphernalia, plus video footage of Hitler hypnotising the masses.

HISTORISCHES MUSEUM DER STADT WIEN

The **Historisches Museum der Stadt Wien** (Map pp83–5; ☎ 505 87 47-0; www.museum.vienna.at - in German; 04, Karlsplatz 5; adult/concession & child €4/2; ☽ 9am-6pm Tue-Sun) gives a detailed rundown on the development of Vienna from prehistory to the present day, and does a pretty good job of putting the city and its personalities in context, without needing words. Exhibits include maps and plans, artefacts and many paintings; works by Klimt, Schiele, and Biedermeier painters like Waldmüller (p41) are worth the entrance fee alone.

KARLSKIRCHE

Southeast of Ressel Park, **Karlskirche** (St Charles' Church; Map pp83–5; ☎ 712 44 56; www.karlskirche.at; 04, Karlsplatz; adult/concession/child under 10 €4/2/free; ☽ 9am-12.30pm & 1-6pm Mon-Sat, 1-6pm Sun), was built between 1716 and 1739 in fulfilment of a vow made by Charles VI at the end of the 1713 plague. Although predominantly baroque, it combines several architectural styles. The twin columns are modelled on Trajan's Column in Rome and show scenes from the life of St Charles Borromeo (who succoured plague victims in Italy), to whom the church is dedicated. The huge oval dome is 72m high and its interior is graced by cloud-bound celestial beings painted by Johann Michael Rottmayr; while the frescoes are being touched up, it's possible to take a lift to the dome for a close-up view (€2).

KUNSTHAUSWIEN

This **art gallery** (Map pp80–2; ☎ 712 04 91; www.kunsthauswien.at - in German; 03, Untere Weissgerberstrasse 13; adult/concession €8/6, incl temporary exhibitions €14/10, half-price Mon; ☽ 10am-7pm) looks like something out of a toy shop. It was designed by Friedensreich Hundertwasser, whose highly innovative buildings feature uneven floors, coloured ceramics, patchwork decoration, irregular corners and grass and trees on the roof. The permanent contents of the KunstHausWien are something of a tribute to Hundertwasser, presenting his paintings, graphics, tapestry, philosophy, ecology and architecture.

While you are in the area, walk down the road to see the **Hundertwasserhaus** (Map pp80-2; cnr Löwengasse & Kegelgasse), a block of residential flats designed by Hundertwasser. It's not possible to wander inside, but the unusual façade should satisfy most. Opposite is the **Kalke Village** (Map pp80-2; 9am-5pm, 9am-7pm summer), also the handiwork of Hundertwasser, containing cafés and souvenir and art shops.

Other attractions worth popping your nose into include:

Haydn Museum (Map pp80-2; ☎ 596 13 07; 06, Haydngasse 19; adult/concession & child €2/1; 9am-12.15pm & 1-4.30pm Tue-Sun) Features a smattering of period furniture and memorabilia from Haydn, who lived here from 1796 till 1809; he composed The Creation and The Seasons under its roof. There are also rooms devoted to Brahms.

Majolikahaus (Map pp80-2; 06, Linke Wienzeile 40) Art Nouveau masterpiece by Otto Wagner, so named for the majolica tiles used to create the flowing floral motifs on the façade.

Sigmund Freud Museum (Map p86; ☎ 319 15 96; www.freud-museum.at; 09, Berggasse 19; adult/concession/child €5/3/2; 9am-6pm Jul-Sep, 9am-5pm Oct-Jun) Former house of the famous psychologist, now housing a small museum featuring some of his personal belongings.

Stadt Pavillions (Map pp83-5; ☎ 505 87 47-84 059; 04, Karlsplatz; adult/concession & child €2/1; 1.30-4.30pm Tue-Sun) Jugendstil pavilions designed by Otto Wagner for Vienna's first public transport system.

Outside the Gürtel

The districts that fall outside the Gürtel are quite a mix. Parts are rather dull and forbidding (by Viennese standards) – in particular towards the south – while others are beautiful beyond belief and home to some of Vienna's greatest treasures. Apart from a few well-trodden routes, tourists rarely venture into these mostly residential outskirts.

SCHLOSS SCHÖNBRUNN

The regal rooms of **Schloss Schönbrunn** (Map pp80-2; ☎ 811 13-0; www.schoenbrunn.at; 13 Schloss Schönbrunn; Imperial tour adult/concession/child €8/5.40/ 4.30, grand tour €10.50/6.80/5.40; 8.30am-6pm Jul-Aug, 8.30am-5pm Apr-Jun & Sep-Oct, 8.30am-4.30pm Nov-Mar) are in a league of their own in Vienna; the interior is a majestic mix of frescoed ceilings, crystal chandeliers and gilded ornaments.

Commissioned by Leopold I, the palace was completed by Johann Bernhard Fischer von Erlach in 1700 but never reached the grandeur originally envisaged; it still has 1441 rooms, of which only 40 are open to the public. The full quota is viewed in the Grand Tour, which takes in the apartments of Franz Joseph I and Empress Elisabeth, the ceremonial and state rooms and the audience chambers of Maria Theresia and her husband Franz Stephan. The Imperial Tour excludes the chambers of Maria Theresia and Franz Stephan and only visits 22 rooms. Both include an audio guide in English if there are no tour guides available. It may be worth opting for an audio guide either way, as you can set your own pace and won't be dragged along on someone else's schedule. Because of the popularity of the palace, tickets are stamped with a departure time, and there may be a time-lag before you're allowed to set off in summer, so buy your ticket straight away and then explore the gardens.

Both tours start in the west wing at the bottom of the **Blauerstiege** (Blue Staircase) and climb to the private rooms of Franz Joseph I and Sisi. The ceremonial and state rooms start with the **Spiegelsaal** (Hall of Mirrors) where Mozart (then six) played his first royal concert in the presence of Maria Theresia in 1762. The pinnacle of finery is reached in the **Grosse Galerie** (Great Gallery), where gilded scrolls, ceiling frescoes, chandeliers and huge crystal mirrors create the effect. Numerous sumptuous balls were held here, including one for the delegates at the Congress of Vienna (1814–15).

Near the Great Gallery is the **Round Chinese Room**, which features a hidden doorway and table which can be drawn up through the floor. The Imperial Tour ends with the **Ceremonial Hall**, while the Grand Tour continues onto the **Blue Chinese Room,** where Charles I abdicated in 1918, and the **Million Room**, named after the sum that Maria Theresia paid for the decorations, which are comprised of Persian miniatures set on rosewood panels and framed with gilded rocaille frames. While not joined to the main

VIENNA

set of rooms, the **Bergl Rooms** are worth visiting for the paintings of Johann Wenzl Bergl (1718–89); his exotic depictions of flora and fauna attempt to bring the ambience of the gardens inside, with some success.

Gardens

The beautifully tended formal gardens (admission free; ⏰ 6am-dusk) of the palace, arranged in the French style, are a symphony of colour in the summer and a combination of greys and browns in winter; both are appealing in their own right. The extensive grounds hide a number of attractions in the tree-lined avenues, including fake **Roman Ruins**, the **Neptunbrunnen** (Neptune Fountain) and the **Gloriette**. The original **Schöner Brunnen**, from which the palace gained its name, now pours through the stone pitcher of a nymph near the Roman ruins.

The **Palmenhaus** (Map pp80-2; ☎ 877 50 87-406; adult/senior/student/child 3-5 €4/3/2.50/2; ⏰ 9.30am-6pm May-Sep, 9.30am-5pm Oct-Apr) is a glorious glass and iron construction still housing palms and hot-house plants from around the world. Close by is the **Wüstenhaus** (Desert House; Map pp80-2; ☎ 877 50 87; adult/senior/student/child 3-5 €4/3/2.50/2; ⏰ 9am-6pm May-Sep, 9am-5pm Oct-Apr), which makes good use of the Sonnenuhrhaus (Sun Dial House) to recreate arid desert scenes.

Behind both is the world's oldest zoo, the **Tiergarten** (Map pp80-2; ☎ 877 92 94; www.zoo vienna.at; 13, Maxingstrasse 13b; adult/senior/student/child €12/10/5/4; ⏰ 9am-6.30pm May-Sep, 9am-5.30pm Mar & Oct, 9am-5pm Feb, 9am-4.30pm Nov-Jan). Founded in 1752 as a menagerie by Franz Stephan, the zoo now houses some 750 animals of all shapes and sizes; thankfully most of the original cramped cages have been updated and improved but the odd one still remains untouched.

Wagenburg

The **Wagenburg** (Imperial Coach Collection; Map pp80-2; ☎ 877 32 44; 13; Schloss Schönbrunn; adult/concession & child/family €4.50/3/9, audio guide €2; ⏰ 9am-6pm Apr-Oct, 10am-4pm Tue-Sun Nov-Mar) displays carriages ranging from tiny children's wagons up to great vehicles of state, but nothing can compete with Emperor Franz Stephen's coronation carriage. Weighing in at 4000kg, it is literally dripping in ornate gold plating and has Venetian glass panes and painted cherubs.

ZENTRALFRIEDHOF

Opened in 1874, the **Zentralfriedhof** (Central Cemetery; Map pp78-9; ☎ 760 41-0; 11, Simmeringer Hauptstrasse 232-244; admission free; information office ⏰ 8am-3pm Mon-Sat, cemetery 7am-7pm May-Aug, 7am-6pm Mar, Apr, Sep & Oct, 8am-5pm Nov-Feb) has grown to become one of Europe's biggest cemeteries – larger than the Innere Stadt and, with 2½ million graves, far exceeding the population of Vienna itself.

It contains the lion's share of tombs of Vienna's Greats, including numerous famous composers; Gluck, Beethoven, Schubert, Brahms, Schönberg and the whole Strauss clan are buried here. A monument to Mozart has also been erected, but he was actually buried in an unmarked mass grave in the **St Marxer Friedhof** (Map pp80-2; 03, Leberstrasse 6-8; ⏰ 7am-7pm Jun-Aug, 7am-6pm May & Sep, 7am-5pm Apr & Oct, 7am-dusk Nov-Mar). The Ehrengräber (Tombs of Honour) are just beyond Gate Two and, besides the clump of famous composers, include Hans Makart, sculptor Fritz Wotruba, architects Theophil Hansen and Adolf Loos and *the* man of Austrian Pop, Falco (Hans Hölzel; p35).

Most graves are neat and well tended, in stark contrast to the old Jewish section, with its tangle of broken headstones and unfettered undergrowth; a reminder that few relatives are around to maintain these graves.

KIRCHE AM STEINHOF

The distinctive **Kirche am Steinhof** (Art Nouveau church; Map pp78-9; ☎ 910 60-11 204; 14, Baumgartner Höhe 1; tours €4; ⏰ 3-4pm Sat) was the work of Otto Wagner from 1904 to 1907. Kolo Moser chipped in with the mosaic windows. The roof is topped by a copper-covered dome that earned the nickname *Limoniberg* (lemon mountain) from its original golden colour. The design illustrates the victory of function over ornamentation prevalent in much of Wagner's work, even down to the sloping floor to allow good drainage. The church is on the grounds of the Psychiatric Hospital of the City of Vienna.

ACTIVITIES

With its abundance of parks, waterways and woodlands, Vienna is a great city for a bit of exercise and some fresh air, and the main culprits are covered below. For more contacts and locations check the *Gelben Seiten* (yellow pages) or pick up a copy of 'Sports &

VIENNA

Nature in Vienna', a brochure produced by the Vienna tourist board. It can also be downloaded from the website www.wien.info.

Boating

The Alte Donau is the main boating and sailing centre in Vienna, but the Neue Donau also provides opportunities for boating, windsurfing and water skiing. Places to rent boats include **Hofbauer** (Map pp80-2; ☎ 203 86 80; www.hofbauer.at - in German; 22, Wagramerstrasse 49; ✆ May–mid-Oct), which has electric boats for €12.60 for a full day or €14 after 8pm, rudder boats (basically dinghies) for €6.40/7, and paddle boats €9.40/10.50. The **sailing school** (Map pp78-9; ☎ 204 34 35; www.hofbauer .at; 22, An der Obere Alte Donau 191; ✆ Apr-Oct) is on the eastern bank of the Alte Donau and has sailing boats and windsurfers for hire, along with lessons for both in English.

Cycling

Vienna's layout and well-marked cycle lanes make cycling a pleasant and popular activity, especially along the banks of the Danube, in the Prater and around the Ringstrasse. The Wienerwald is also popular for mountain biking; check the websites www .mbike.at (in German) and www.mtbwiener wald.at (in German) for ideas and trails. For bike hire, see p125.

Swimming

The Donauinsel, Alte Donau and Lobau (all free bathing) are hugely popular places for taking a dip on steamy hot summer days. Topless sunbathing is quite the norm, as is nude sunbathing but only in designated areas; much of Lobau and both tips of the Donauinsel are *Frei Körper Kultur* (FKK, nude-bathing areas).

Alongside natural swimming areas are a large number of swimming pools owned and run by the city. In general, entry to these pools costs about €4/2 for adults/children, €3.50/2.50 after noon and €2.50 after 4pm. Some of the better baths include **Amalienbad** (Map pp80-2; ☎ 607 47 47; 10, Reumannplatz 23), a stunning *Jugendstil* bath, **Strandbad Gänsehäufel** (Map pp78-9; ☎ 269 90 16; 22, Moissigasse 21), occupying a section of island in the Alte Donau and the lovely **Thermalbad Oberlaa** (Map pp78-9; ☎ 6800 99600; 10, Kurbadstrasse 14), a large thermal complex with both indoor and outdoor pools.

For a full list of pools call ☎ 60112 8044 between 7.30am and 3.30pm Monday to Friday or log on to www.wien.at/baeder (in German).

Walking

To the west of the city, the rolling hills and marked trails of the Wienerwald are perfect for walkers. A good trail heading in the woods to the north of Vienna starts in Nussdorf (take tram D from the Ring) and climbs Kahlenberg (484m), a hill that offers great views of the city. On your return to Nussdorf you can undo all that exercise by imbibing a few at a *Heurigen*. The round trip is around 11km, or you can save your legs by taking the Nussdorf–Kahlenberg 38A bus in one or both directions.

The Prater (p97) also has a wood with walking trails and the thickly wooded Lainzer Tiergarten (Map pp78-9) animal reserve, a wild park in the west of Vienna, is perfect for roaming around.

WALKING TOUR

This 1½ to two hour walk takes you through some of the most well-trodden tourist trails in Vienna; instantly recognisable sights – Stephansdom and the Hofburg, the Habsburg's winter palace – dominate this quarter of the Innere Stadt while Kärntner Strasse, Graben and Kohlmarkt attract shoppers by the busloads. And the beauty of it all is that if you duck down a cobblestone side street you'll feel as though you have the city to yourself. The walk covers about 2½km.

Start your walk heading north from the southern end of pedestrian-only Kärntner Strasse, a walkway of plush shops, trees, cafés and street entertainers. Detour left down the short Donnergasse to take a peek at the **Donnerbrunnen (1)** in Neuer Markt, a fountain with four naked figures representing the main tributaries of the Danube: the Enns, March, Traun and Ybbs. Across the square is the **Kaisergruft (2**; p92). Back on Kärntner Strasse, detour left again down Kärntner Durchgang. Here you'll find the **American Bar (3**; p118), designed in 1908 by Adolf Loos, one of the prime exponents of a functional Art Nouveau style.

From Kärntner Strasse, the street opens out into Stock im Eisen Platz. Note the **nail-studded stump (4)**, flush against the building on your left, said to have acquired its

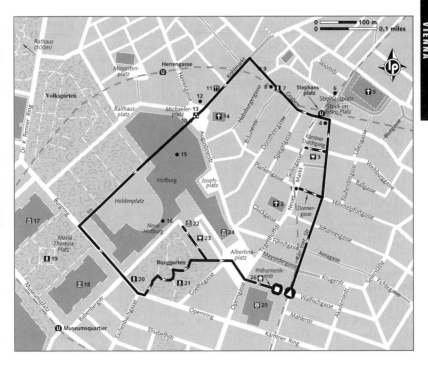

crude metal jacket in the 16th century from blacksmiths banging in a nail for luck when they left the city. Directly ahead is Vienna's prime landmark, Gothic **Stephansdom (5**; p89), offset by the unashamedly modern **Haas Haus (6)**. Many Viennese were rather unhappy about this curving silver structure crowding their beloved cathedral, but tourists seem happy enough to snap the spindly reflections of Stephansdom's spire in its rectangular windows.

Leading northwest from Stock im Eisen Platz is the broad pedestrian thoroughfare of **Graben**, another plush shopping street. It's dominated by the knobbly outline of the **Pestsäule (7)**, completed in 1693 to commemorate the 75,000 victims of the Black Death. Adolf Loos had a hand in the Graben's appearance, creating the **Schneidersalon Knize (8)** and the nearby **toilets (9)**. Turning left into Kohlmarkt, so named because charcoal was once sold here, the arresting sight of **Michaelertor (10)**, the Hofburg's northeastern gate on Michaelerplatz, comes into view. Towards the end of Kohlmarkt, on the right-hand side, is one of the most famous of the Konditorei-style cafés in Vienna, **Demel (11)**.

Reaching Michaelerplatz, keep an eye out for the **Loos Haus (12)**, a perfect example of the clean lines of Loos' work. Franz Josef hated it and described the windows, which lack lintels, as 'windows without eyebrows'. The **excavations (13)** in the middle of the square are of Roman origin. **Michaelerkirche (14)** on the square portrays five centuries of architectural styles, ranging from 1327 (Romanesque chancel) to 1792 (baroque doorway angels).

Cross Michaelerplatz and pass through the imposing Michaelertor and past the **Schweizertor (15)** to Heldenplatz and the impressive **Neue Burg (16**; p92), built between 1881 and 1908. Continue on past the line of *Fiakers* (fiacres), noting the Gothic spire of the **Rathaus** (p93) rising above the trees to the right. Ahead, on the far side of the Ring, stand the rival identical twins, the **Naturhistorisches Museum (17**; p95) and the **Kunsthistorisches Museum (18**; p94); between them is a proud **statue of Maria Theresia (19)**, surrounded by key figures of her reign.

Turn left onto the Ring and, once past the Neue Burg, turn left again into the peaceful **Burggarten**, formerly reserved for the pleasure of the imperial family and high-ranking officials. It now contains **statues of Mozart (20)** and **Franz Josef (21)**, the **Schmetterlinghaus (22**; Butterfly House; ☎ 533 85 70; adult/senior/student/child 3-6 €4.70/4/3.30/2.20; ☷ 10am-4.45pm Mon-Fri, 10am-6.15pm Sat & Sun Apr-Oct, 10am-3.45pm Nov-Mar) and the **Palmenhaus (23**; p101).

Only a hop, skip and a jump from the Burggarten is the newly renovated **Albertina (24**; p92) on Albertinaplatz. The square is home to a troubling work by sculptor and graphic artist Alfred Hrdlicka (1928–), created in 1988. This series of pale block-like sculptures commemorates Jews and other victims of war and fascism.

From here it's not far down Philharmoniker-strasse to the starting point of this walk. On your way you'll pass the rear of the grand **Staatsoper (25**; p119) and the frontage of **Hotel Sacher (26**; p109), a perfect spot to rest those weary legs.

VIENNA FOR CHILDREN

It was once said the Viennese love dogs more than they love children, and while this is true for some of the populace, attitudes, especially from the establishment, have changed in recent years. Vienna's museums, attractions and theatres, such as the Kunsthistorisches Museum and the Albertina, are cottoning on to the idea that kids need entertaining, and often arrange children's programmes over the summer months.

The **Prater** (p97), with its wide open playing fields, playgrounds and funfair, is ideal for children. **Lainzer Tiergarten** (Map pp78–9) and the **Donauinsel** (Map pp78–9) are just two more examples where kids can be let loose and run off all their energy. Swimming pools are dotted across the length and breadth of the city and are free to children under 15 over the summer school holidays.

Aside from summer programmes and parks, two museums are aimed directly at kids. **Zoom** (Map pp83-5; ☎ 524 79 08; www.kinder museum.at; 07, Museumsplatz 1; child €5; ☷ 8.30am-4pm), next door to the **WienXtra-Kinderinfo** (p89) in the MuseumsQuartier, is an arts and crafts bonanza aimed at kids between the ages of zero and 14. Programmes on various themes throughout the year begin every 1½ to two hours; it's advisable to

book ahead. Schönbrunn's **Kindermuseum** (Map pp80-2; ☎ 811 13-239; www.schoenbrunn.at; 13 Schloss Schönbrunn; adult/child/family €6.50/4.50/17; ☷ 10am-5pm Sat & Sun, 10am-5pm during school holidays) focuses on imperialism; activities and displays help kids discover the day-to-day life of the Habsburg court.

If you speak German, Falter's *Kinder in Wien* book is the only resource you'll ever need for any aspect of your child's life in Vienna. It's available from book stores.

QUIRKY VIENNA

It is said that nowhere are people so obsessed with death than in Vienna. The city seems to have more than its fair share of cemeteries and crypts, and some of the elderly populace still saves for a lavish funeral and a *Schöne Leiche* (beautiful corpse).

This may not be all that different to other Central European cities, but what Vienna has over its counterparts is its museums dealing with death. The **Pathologisch-Anatomische Bundesmuseum** (Pathological-Anatomy Museum; Map p86; ☎ 406 86 72; www.pathomus.or.at; 09, Spittalgasse 2; admission free; ☷ 3-6pm Wed, 8-11am Thu), housed in the Narrenturm (Fool's Tower), a former insane asylum, is possibly the most bizarre of all. It's filled with medical oddities and abnormalities preserved in jars of formaldehyde, and the odd wax model with one grisly disease or another; not a place for those with a weak stomach. Also known as the Geschichte der Medizin (Museum of Medical History), the **Josephinum** (Map p86; ☎ 4277 63 401; 09, Währinger Strasse 25; adult/concession €2/1; ☷ 9am-3pm Mon-Fri, 10am-2pm 1st Sat every month) features ceroplastic and wax specimen models of the human frame, created over 200 years ago for the Academy of Medico-Surgery to improve the skills of army surgeons who lacked medical qualifications. Three rooms of models, showing the make-up of the body under the skin, make you feel like you've wandered onto the set of a tacky horror movie, but if you can dismiss your queasiness, the models are in fact quite intriguing and the level of detail is a compliment to their creators. The **Bestattungsmuseum** (Undertaker's Museum; Map pp80-2; ☎ 501 95-4227; 04, Goldeggasse 19; admission free; ☷ by prior arrangement noon-3pm Mon-Fri) isn't quite in the same league as the Pathologisch-Anatomische Bundesmuseum or the Josephinum, but what you'll see is photos,

RICHARD NEBESKY

Flea market at Naschmarkt (p116), Vienna

RICHARD NEBESKY

Kunsthistorisches Museum (Museum of Fine Arts; p94), Vienna

Examples of children's work at Zoom (p104), MuseumsQuartier, Vienna

RICHARD NEBESKY

Example of a cogwheel steam train that runs up Schneeberg (p152), Lower Austria

PATRICK HORTON

MARK HONAN

Grape vines near Dürnstein (p133),
Lower Austria

Danube Valley (p130), Lower Austria, with ruins of Burg Aggstein (p132) in the foreground

DIANA MAYFI

documents and paraphernalia retelling the history of undertaking in the city.

Vienna's quirky side isn't all about death though; take, for example, the original snow globe, produced by Erwin Perzy I back in 1900. The company is still going strong and still in family hands (run by Erwin Perzy III, grandson of Perzy I); the factory even contains a small **museum** (Map pp80-2; ☎ 486 43 41; www.viennasnowglobe.at; 17, Schumanngasse 87; ☒ 8am-noon & 1-3pm Mon-Thu) which stocks their snow globes, and can be visited by appointment.

TOURS

Vienna has everything from bus tours to horse-drawn carriage rides, so if you're looking for a guided tour of the city you'll find something to suit. Bus tours are good if you're very short on time and want to pack in as much as possible, while the walking tours are perfect if you're interested in learning more on a specific topic.

Cityrama (☎ 534 13; www.cityrama.at; 01, Börsegasse 1; adult €33-109, child €15-45) Half- and full-day bus tours of Vienna and attractions within a day's striking distance of the city, including Salzburg, Budapest and Prague. Some tours require an extra fee for admission into sights, such as training at the Spanish Riding School.

DDSG Blue Danube (☎ 588 80; www.ddsg-blue-danube .at; 01, Schwedenbrücke; full-tour adult/child €14/7, half-tour €10/5, children under 10 free; ☒ 11am & 3pm May-Sep) Boat trips circumnavigating the districts of Leopoldstadt and Brigittenau via the Danube and Danube Canal.

Fiaker (20min/40min/1hr tour €40/65/75) More of a tourist novelty than anything else, a *Fiaker* is a traditional-style open carriage drawn by a pair of horses. Drivers generally speak English and point out places of interest en route. Lines of horses, carriages and bowler-hatted drivers can be found at Stephansplatz, Albertinaplatz and Heldenplatz at the Hofburg.

Hop On–Hop Off Vienna Line (☎ 712 46 83; www .viennasightseeingtours.com; 01, Opernring; 1hr/2hr/all-day tickets adult €12/15/20, all tickets child €7; ☒ 10am-5pm) Bus tour passing 13 major sights. Tickets range from one hour to all day, and you can hop on and off the buses as many times as you wish in that time. The main bus stop is outside the Staatsoper.

Music Mile Vienna (3hr-tour €5, extra hr €1.50) Audio-guided walking tour from Stephansdom to Theater an der Wien past some 70 stars embedded in the footpath commemorating musical geniuses related to Vienna in one way or another. Audio guide and booklet available between 10am and 7pm from **Musikmeile Wien Servicestelle** (Map pp83–5; 01, Stephansplatz), **Wien-Ticket Pavillon** (Map pp83–5; 01, Herbert-von-Karajan-Platz) and **Theater an der Wien** (Map pp83–5; 01, Linke Wienzeile 6).

Old Timer Trams (☎ 7909-105; www.wiener-tramway museum.org; adult/child €15/5) On weekends and holidays from May to October streetcars from 1929 trundle through Vienna on one-hour tours of the city. Departures from **Karlsplatz Stadt Pavilions** (Map pp83–5).

Pedal Power (Map pp80-2; ☎ 729 72 34; www.pedal power.at; 02, Ausstellungsstrasse 3; tour with own bike adult/ student/child €16/14/12, incl hired bike €23/19/12) Half-day bicycle tours in and around Vienna from May to September, starting at 10am. Five tours are offered: Innere Stadt and the Prater, Donau Park and Lobau, Donauinsel and Klosterneuburg, Donauinsel and the *Heurigens* of Stammersdorf, and Classical Music Memorials and the Zentralfriedhof.

Reisebuchladen (Map pp83-5; ☎ 317 33 84; reisebuchladen@aon.at; 09, Kolingasse 6; tour €27; ☒ 10am-6pm Mon-Fri, 9.30am-12.30pm Sat) This travel agency conducts alternative bus tours, including tours of Red Vienna, *Jugendstil* architecture and Hundertwasser creations.

Vienna Sightseeing Tours (☎ 712 46 83; www.vienna sightseeingtours.com; tour €32) Run by the same company that organises the Hop On–Hop Off tours, Vienna Sightseeing Tours offers a wide variety of half- and full-day bus tours in English with free hotel pick-up.

Vienna Tour Guides (☎ 876 71 11; www.wienguide.at; adult/child €11/6) Group of highly knowledgeable guides who conduct 40 different guided walking tours, 11 of which are in English. Everything from Art Nouveau architecture to Jewish traditions in Vienna is covered; one of the most popular is the Third Man Tour. The monthly *Wiener Spaziergänge* leaflet from the tourist office provides details of all the walks.

FESTIVALS & EVENTS

No matter what time of year you visit Vienna, there will be something special happening; pick up a copy of the monthly booklet of events from the tourist office. Tickets for many events are available to personal callers at Wien-Ticket Pavillion (Map pp83–5) in the hut by the Staatsoper.

Christkindlmärkte Vienna's much-loved Christmas market season runs from mid-November to Christmas Day.

Donauinselfest Free three-day festival of rock, pop, hardcore, folk and country music on the Donauinsel in June.

ImPuls Tanz (☎ 523 55 58; www.impulstanz.com; 07, Museumstrasse 5/21) Vienna's premier avant-garde dance festival attracts an array of internationally renowned troupes and newcomers between mid-July and mid-August.

Lange Nacht der Museen (langenacht.orf.at) On one late-September evening some 370 museums nationwide open their doors to visitors between 6pm and 1am. One ticket (adult/child €12/10; available at museums) allows entry to all of them.

Musikfilm Festival (01, Rathausplatz) Screenings of operas, operettas and concerts outside the Rathaus in July and August.

Opernball (☎ 514 44-7880; 01, Staatsoper) Of the 300 or so balls held in January and February, the Opernball (Opera Ball) is the ultimate. It's a supremely lavish affair, with the men in tails and women in shining white gowns.

OsterKlang Festival (☎ 427 17; www.osterklang.at; 01, Stadiongasse 9) Orchestral and chamber music recitals in some of Vienna's best music halls, the highlight of which is the opening concert, featuring the Vienna Philharmonic. Held at the beginning of April.

Silvester The Innere Stadt becomes one big party zone for Silvester (New Year's Eve), which features loads of alcohol and far too many fireworks in crowded streets.

GAY & LESBIAN VIENNA

Vienna is reasonably tolerant towards gays and lesbians, and things get better each year. Even the Vienna Tourist Board does their bit; their *Queer Guide* booklet has listings of bars, restaurants, hotels and festivals, while their *Vienna Gay Guide* is a city map with gay locations marked up. *Xtra* and *Night Life* (www.nightlifeonline.at - in German), two free monthly publications, are additional supplements packed with news, views and listings (in German only).

The best organisation in town is the **Rosa Lila Villa** (Map pp80-2; www.villa.at; 06, Linke Wienzeile 102), an unmissable pink house by the Wien river. Its **Lesbian Centre** (☎ 586 81 50; lesbenberatung@villa.at; ✆ 5-8pm Mon-Fri) is on the ground floor, while its **Gay Men's Centre** (☎ 585 43 43; schwulenberatung@ villa.at; ✆ 5-8pm Mon-Thu) is on the 1st floor. **Homosexualle Initiative Wien** (HOSI; Map pp80-2; ☎ 216 66 04; www.hosiwien.at; 02, Novaragasse 40; ✆ 5-10pm Tue-Thu, telephone counselling 6-8pm Tue, 7-9pm Wed & Thu), another helpful organisation, is politically minded and holds regular events.

Events to look out for on the gay and lesbian calendar include the **Regenbogen Parade** (Rainbow Parade), a colourful parade that takes over the Ring and MuseumsQuartier at the end of June, the **Life Ball** (www.lifeball.org), an AIDS-charity event around the middle of May, **Wien ist andersrum** (www.andersrum.at), a month-long extravaganza of gay and lesbian art in June, and **Identities – Queer Film Festival** (www.identities.at), a film festival showcasing queer movies, also in June.

Unfortunately there isn't much in the way of accommodation aimed at gay and lesbians; **Pension Wild** (Map pp83-5; ☎ 406 51 74; www.pension-wild.com; 08, Langegasse 10; s/d from €37/45) is an exception. It's a super-friendly pension welcoming both gays and straights. Note 'Wild' is the family name, not a description of the atmosphere.

The Scene

Vienna has enough bars and clubs to entertain its gay and lesbian community, and some straight clubs, for instance U4 (p121), feature gay nights on a weekly basis.

Café Berg (Map p86; ☎ 319 57 20; 09, Berggasse 8; ✆ 10am-1am) With some of the nicest staff in Vienna, a lovely, open layout and all-round friendly vibe, it's no wonder Café Berg is often full with a gay and straight crowd. Its bookshop, **Löwenherz** (✆ 10am-7pm Mon-Fri, 10am-5pm Sat), stocks a grand collection of gay magazines and books.

Café Savoy (Map pp80-2; ☎ 586 73 48; 06, Linke Wienzeile 36; ✆ 5pm-2am Mon-Fri, 9pm-2am Sat) This old haunt has a more traditional feel to it, except for the feathers everywhere. The clientele is generally very mixed on a Saturday – mainly due to the proximity of the Naschmarkt – but at other times it's full with men of all ages.

Café Willendorf (Map pp80-2; ☎ 587 17 89; 06, Linke Wienzeile 102; ✆ 6pm-2am) This is one of Vienna's seminal gay and lesbian bars in Vienna, housed in the pink Rosa Lila Villa.

Frauencafé (Map pp83-5; ☎ 406 37 54; 05, Lange Gasse 8; ✆ 6.30pm-2am Tue-Sat) A long established strictly women-only café/bar.

Orlando (Map pp80-2; ☎ 967 35 50; 06, Mollardgasse 3; ✆ 5pm-1am Sun-Thu, 6pm-2am Fri & Sat) This lesbian-owned and run bar/restaurant is a great little place that welcomes all walks of life.

Why Not? (Map pp83-5; ☎ 535 11 58; www.why-not.at; 01, Tiefer Graben 22; ✆ 10pm-6am Fri & Sat) Why Not? is one of the few clubs that focuses its attention on the gay scene. The small club quickly fills up with mainly young guys.

Santo Spirito (Map pp83-5; ☎ 512 99 98; 01, Kumpfgasse 7; ✆ 6pm-2am Mon-Thu, 6pm-3am Fri, 11am-3am Sat, 10am-2am Sun) Attracting both a gay and straight crowd, Santo Spirito specialises in classical music at high decibels. In summer, customers spill out onto the cobblestone street to take a break from the noise.

Viennale Film Festival (☎ 0800 664 003; www .viennale.at) The country's biggest and best film festival, featuring fringe and independent films from around the world in October.

Volksstimmefest (☎ 0676-69 69 002; www.kpoe.at - in German) Communist festival over a weekend around the end of August/beginning of September in the Prater (p97); features some 30 live acts and attracts a bizarre mix of hippies and staunch party supporters.

Wiener Festwochen (☎ 589 22-22; www.festwochen .or.at; 06, Lehárgasse 11) Wide-ranging programme of arts from around the world, from May to mid-June.

SLEEPING

Vienna's sleeping options cover the full spectrum, from basic youth hostels and student residences to hotels where chandeliers, antique furniture and original 19th-century oil paintings are the norm rather than the exception. In between are homey pensions and less ostentatious hotels, plus a small but smart range of apartments for long-term rentals.

Standards remain high, and so do prices. High season – June to September and over the Christmas and New Year period – means high prices and often a lack of availability at popular choices. At this time it's best to book ahead. Over winter rates can drop substantially and many places offer discounts and specials for longer stays. Some, especially the five-star hotels, offer special weekend rates, or 'two nights for the price of one' packages. It's definitely worth enquiring about cheaper rates before signing on the dotted line.

As a general guideline, breakfast is included in the price at hostels, pensions and hotels. It usually consists of a continental buffet but often the more the room costs, the more substantial the breakfast will be.

There are a handful of campsites on the outskirts of Vienna; all are listed online at www.wiencamping.at. Another cheap option is student residences, which are converted to seasonal hotels between July and September. They give a much-needed boost to the number of beds at the lower end of the market.

Accommodation Agencies

The tourist office (p89) can arrange accommodation, but charges a small commission per reservation irrespective of the number of rooms being booked. The staff can help to find private rooms but don't provide lists. What they can hand out is a

THE AUTHOR'S CHOICE

Hotel Im Palais Schwarzenberg (Map pp80-2; ☎ 798 45 15, www.palais-schwarzenberg .com; 03, Schwarzenbergplatz 9; s/d from €255/330; P ⊠ ⊠ ⊠) Combining history, luxury and decorum, Im Palais Schwarzenberg is arguably the best address to stay at in Vienna. While this exclusive B&B opened its doors in the early 60s, the baroque palace's history dates back to the 17th century when Prince Heinrich commissioned its construction. The rooms here are all about opulence and style, but it's the extras that are truly enviable; the 18 acres of private grounds, which sidle up to Belvedere, include a swimming pool and five clay tennis courts which are out of bounds to the general public. And just to top it all off, the hotel bar and restaurant (p114) are of the utmost sophistication.

Jugendherbergen pamphlet detailing youth hostels and campsites, and a booklet of hotels and pensions, revised annually.

Viennese looking for apartments rely on word-of-mouth or turn to *Bazar* magazine. It's *the* paper if you're looking to buy, sell or rent anything, including flats or rooms. The time scale of places on offer may range from indefinite rental to occupation of a flat for a month or so while the resident is on holiday. *Falter*, *Kurier* and *Der Standard* also carry accommodation ads.

A couple of short-term apartment rentals include:

Appartement Pension Riemergasse (Map pp83-5; ☎ 512 72 200; www.riemergasse.at; 01, Riemergasse 8; apartments per night/month from €91/2355) Apartments (five minutes walk from Stephansdom) all come with a kitchenette, telephone, cable TV, toilet and bath or shower.

Laudon Court (Map pp83-5; ☎ 407 13 70; 08, Laudongasse 8; apartments per day/month from €69/1350) Small array of variously sized fully furnished apartments with washing machines and dryers in the basement and a daily cleaner.

Singerstrasse Apartments (Map pp83-5; ☎ 514 49-0; www.singerstrasse2125.at; 01, Singerstrasse 21-25; weekly/monthly apartments from €616/2161) Apartments range in size from studios to large 1-bed apartments and come complete with telephone, satellite TV, Internet facilities for laptops, a kitchenette and the all-important cleaning service.

Choosing a Location

Staying within the Innere Stadt is convenient for sightseeing but invariably the most expensive option. Many hotels and pensions between the Ring and the Gürtel can often be a better deal; prices are lower and the Innere Stadt is within easy striking distance. Further out, prices tend to drop, but so does ease of accessibility.

If you have a car, parking costs in the city centre can be high (anything from €6 to €26). A better option might be to find somewhere further out where you can safely leave your car, and then rely on public transport. Even if you stay out late and have to take a taxi home, the taxi fare will still be less than a day's garage fees. Street parking is no problem in the suburbs.

Innere Stadt

BUDGET

Schweizer Pension (Map pp83-5; ☎ 533 81 56; www .schweizerpension.com; 01, Heinrichsgasse 2; s/d without bathroom from €40/60) This super-clean pension has bright, modern rooms with homey touches such as ornamental ceramic stoves. With only 11 rooms, a central location and low prices it's advisable to reserve well in advance.

Hotel Post (Map pp83-5; ☎ 515 83-0; www.hotel -post-wien.at; 01, Fleischmarkt 24; s/d without bathroom from €36/62) Gaining its name from Vienna's main post office which is directly across the street, the rooms are bright, spartan and a great deal for the Innere Stadt. Expect to pay a third extra for rooms with shower and toilet.

MID-RANGE

König von Hungarn (Map pp83-5; ☎ 515 84-0; www .kvu.at; 01, Schulerstrasse 10; s/d €133/153) The 'King of Hungary' pulls off a hard task – balancing class with informality. Its inner atrium has a wonderful quiet ambience and the rooms, individually decorated in antique furniture and displaying plenty of stripped wood, still manage to convey a homey appeal.

Pertschy Pension (Map pp83-5; ☎ 534 49-0; www .pertschy.com; 01, Habsburgergasse 5; s/d €77/122) This gem of a pension has a peaceful inner courtyard, expansive rooms and toys for the toddlers. Room furnishings are a little dated but that only adds to Pertschy's charm.

Hotel-Pension Suzanne (Map pp83-5; ☎ 513 25 07; www.pension-suzanne.at; 01, Walfischgasse 4; s/d €72/90) The name may say 'hotel', but Suzanne's look and feel easily puts it in the pension

category. Antique furniture distracts you from the smallish size of the rooms (many with kitchenettes) and adds a noble touch, while family-management makes you feel relaxed and quite at home.

Hotel Amadeus (Map pp83-5; ☎ 533 87 38; www .hotel-amadeus.at; 01, Wildpretmarkt 5; s/d from €80/142) The first indication that this hotel is something special is the completely carpeted lift. The second is the rooms; colourful and warm, they are filled with period furniture, except for the bathrooms, which are thankfully modern.

Pension Nossek (Map pp83-5; ☎ 533 70 41-0; www .pension-nossek.at - in German; 01, Graben 17; s without bathroom €54, d with bathroom €105) With a front door facing grand Graben and Stephansdom within sight, plus spotless baroque-style rooms, it's no wonder you need to book this fine pension weeks in advance during high season.

Pension am Operneck (Map pp83-5; ☎ 512 93 10; fax 512 93 10-20; 01 Kärntner Strasse 47; s/d €53/75) Am Operneck's massive drawing card is its proximity to the heart of Vienna. Rooms are large, basic and comfy and since there are only six of them, you'll usually need to reserve at least a month ahead.

Hotel Kaiserin Elisabeth (Map pp83-5; ☎ 515 26; www.kaiserinelisabeth.at; 01, Weihburggasse 3; s/d €75/200) The relatively plain frontage of the Hotel Kaiserin Elisabeth belies its pleasant interior and long history; the likes of Mozart, Wagner and Liszt graced the hotel with their presence. Rooms have a turn-of-the-century (that's the 1899–1900 turn) look and feel which comes across as demure yet highly appealing.

Hotel Austria (Map pp83-5; ☎ 515 23; office@ hotelaustria-wien.at; 01, Am Fleischmarkt 20; s/d €63/90) This three-star hotel has the advantage of close proximity to the Innere Stadt's action while maintaining a quiet, genteel atmosphere due to its hidden location on a quiet, cobblestone cul-de-sac. Accommodating staff and finely furnished rooms add to Austria's charm.

Hotel am Stephansplatz (Map pp83-5; ☎ 53 405-0; www.hotelamstephansplatz.at; 01, Stephansplatz 9; s/d from €105/130) Want to wake up with Stephansdom's glorious Gothicness towering above you every morning? Then this is your place, situated directly opposite the cathedral. Rooms are genuinely comfy and sizable and, of course, those fronting Stephansplatz are the most sought after.

TOP END

Hotel Sacher (Map pp83-5; ☎ 51 456-0; www.sacher
.com; 01, Philharmonikerstrasse 4; s/d from €215/312)
Opened in 1876, the elegant Sacher is not
only home to the world-famous *Sacher Torte*
but also baroque rooms that are perfectly
complimented by genuine 19th-century oil
paintings.

Hotel Ambassador (Map pp83-5; ☎ 961 610; www
.ambassador.at; 01, Kärntner Strasse 22/Neuer Markt 5; s/d
from €218/277) Recently re-opened, this lavish
hotel feels more like a palace; rooms still
manage to capture the Ambassador's century-old history while meeting every requirement of a thoroughly modern hotel.

Ringstrasse
MID-RANGE

Hotel am Schubertring (Map pp83-5; ☎ 717 02-0;
www.schubertring.at; 01, Schubertring 11; s/d from €106/
135) Of the highly sought after hotels on the
Ringstrasse, this is one of the cheaper options. Maze-like corridors, Biedermeier or
Art Nouveau furnished rooms (some with
rooftop views) and a welcoming atmosphere
top the list of attractions here.

TOP END

Le Meridien (Map pp83-5; ☎ 0800-295 390; www
.lemeridien.com; 01, Opernring 13; r from €305) The
newly built Le Meridien is as modern as you
can get; its impeccably furnished rooms include power showers, mammoth flat-screen
plasma TVs and Vienna-motif glass head
boards. The small touches, like real coffee
and an ironing board and iron, make you
feel right at home.

Hotel Imperial (Map pp83-5; ☎ 501 10-333; www
.luxurycollection.com/imperial; 01 Kärntner Ring 16; s/d from
€446/535) Originally the palace of the Prince
of Württemberg, the Imperial re-invented
itself as a hotel for the World Fair in 1873
but retained all the glory and majesty of the
former residence. It is a truly remarkable
hotel; marble bathrooms, precious antiques,
original paintings and silver service all help
to re-create 19th-century Vienna.

Hotel Bristol (Map pp83-5; ☎ 515 16-536; www
.westin.com/bristol; 01, Kärntner Ring 1; r from €385) The
Bristol is a Vienna landmark with impres-
sive views of the Staatsoper. It's saturated
with Art Nouveau furnishings – deep armchairs, sumptuously brocaded beds ·and
marble-lined bathrooms – and has every
conceivable service and modern amenity.

Across the Danube Canal
BUDGET

Jugendgästhaus Wien-Brigittenau (Map pp78-9;
☎ 332 82 94; jgh1200@chello.at; 20, Friedrich Engels Platz
24; dm from €14.50) This is one of five HI hostels
in Vienna and, with 410 beds, is by far the
largest. It's modern, multi-storeyed and just
a couple of minutes' walk from the Danube
and Donauinsel but not particularly handy
to the Innere Stadt.

Aktiv Camping Neue Donau (Map pp78-9; ☎ 202
40 10; 22, Am Kleehäufel; campsites per adult/tent €6.50/5;
☺ mid-May–Sep; ℗ 🖵) The closest camping
ground to the city centre and very handy to
the popular swimming areas of Alte Donau
and Donauinsel (p102). Rates drop outside
July and August.

Inside the Gürtel
BUDGET

Auer (Map p86; ☎ 406 21 21; auer.pension@chello.at; 09,
Lazarettgasse 3; s/d without bathroom €29/44) Homey,
personable, friendly, cluttered – if that
sounds good to you then you'll love Auer.
The rooms aren't modern but there is something wonderfully eclectic and very Viennese
about them. Some rooms have private facilities (an extra €6); reception is on the 1st floor
and there's no lift.

Pension Kraml (Map pp80-2; ☎ 587 85 88; www
.pensionkraml.at; 06, Brauergasse 5; s/d without bathroom
€28/48, apt without bathroom from €85) This little gem
is small, friendly and family run. Rooms are
indeed cosy, but private facilities will cost a
little extra than the rates quoted above.

Jugendherberge Myrthengasse (Map p86; ☎ 523
63 16; hostel@chello.at; 07, Myrthengasse 7; dm €15.50, tw
€35) This well-organised HI hostel on a quiet
side street has all the trappings you'd expect.
Based in two buildings, it's convenient, busy
and offers daytime check-in. Telephone reservations are accepted and strongly advised.

Hotel Fürstenhof (Map pp80-2; ☎ 523 32 67; www
.hotel-fuerstenhof.com; 07, Neubaugürtel 4; s/d without bathroom from €44/62) Fürstenhof is a family-run hotel
that's more than handy to Westbahnhof and
only five U-Bahn stops from Stephansplatz.
The decent-size rooms have a homey feel and
the bathrooms have been refurbished.

Westend city hostel (Map pp80-2; ☎ 597 67 29;
www.westendhostel.at; 06, Fügergasse 3; s/d €40.50/44.40,
dm in 12-/6–8-/4-bed room €17.80/16.80/19; 🖵) Handy
to Westbahnhof and catering to backpackers,
Westend is a cheap option in the suburbs. By
no stretch of the imagination is this a party

hostel, but it's very well organised and has a 24-hour reception, lockers, bathrooms and toilets in every room and a complete laundry service (€6).

Academia (Map p86; ☎ 401 76 55; www.academia -hotels.co.at; 08, Pfeilgasse 3A; s/d €48/64) Academia is a massive student residence (lift installed, thankfully) with two beds short of 500; it opens its doors to visitors over the summer months. Rooms are quite spacious. A buffet breakfast is included in the price and there's a coffee bar on site.

Quisisana (Map pp83-5; ☎ 587 71 55; www.quisi sana-wien.co.at; 06, Windmühlgasse 6; s/d without bathroom from €30/44) Quisisana's drawcard is its proximity to museums, shopping and eating options. Rooms, with both shared and private bathrooms, are small and simple, but perfectly adequate.

MID-RANGE

Pension Carantania (Map p86; ☎ 526 73 40; www .carantania.at; 07, Kandlgasse 35; s/d €55/80) It's easy to tell this is a family-run pension; convivial staff, old-style furnishings and characterful rooms are dead give-aways. The breakfast room, with a big bay window overlooking Kandlgasse, is bright and welcoming. Book ahead as Carantania only has six rooms.

Das Tyrol (Map pp83-5; ☎ 587 54 15; www.das tyrol.at; 06, Mariahilfer Strasse 15; s/d from €110/140) This intimate hotel has smallish, cosy rooms and is staffed by a friendly bunch. The greatest advantage here though is its proximity to Mariahilfer Strasse, Naschmarkt, Spittalberg and the MuseumsQuartier. The entrance is around the side on Königsklostergasse.

Theater-Hotel (Map p86; ☎ 405 36 48; chwien@ cordial.at; 08, Josefstädter Strasse 22; s/d €140/183) Art Nouveau touches and friendly staff make this hotel one of the better 8th-district choices. Rooms are small but have an attached kitchen unit.

Pension Atrium (Map p86; ☎ 523 31 14; pension .atrium@chello.at; 07, Burggasse 118; s/d €51/73) You won't be blown away by the plush interior at the Atrium but rooms are clean, roomy and come complete with balcony. Plus breakfast can be enjoyed in the privacy of your room. Burggasse is a main thoroughfare so ask for something at the back.

Hotel Atlanta (Map p86; ☎ 405 12 30; www.hirners .com/atlanta; 09, Währinger Strasse 33; s/d €91/128) Built in 1895, the Atlanta has lost its sparkle of grandeur, but it still exudes an air of nobility.

Chandeliers, creaky floors, ornate stained-glass windows and spacious rooms all add up to a charming, albeit over-the-hill, hotel.

Hotel Am Schottenfeld (Map p86; ☎ 526 51 81; www.falkensteiner.com; 07, Schottenfeldgasse 74; s/d €129/164) Don't let the garish reception and bar put you off; the highly modern rooms at the Schottenfeld are more than fine. Purposely built in 2003, this hotel is definitely slanted towards a business clientele but caters well to individual travellers and has a fitness room with sauna, steam room and solarium add-ons.

Attaché (Map pp80-2; ☎ 505 18 18; www.bestvien nahotels.at; 04, Wiedner Hauptstrasse 71; s/d from €72/102) This clean, neat pension is small and homey, and many of its 26 rooms are furnished with period or antique fittings, including some in the celebrated Art Nouveau style.

Alla Lenz (Map p86; ☎ 523 69 89-0; www.allalenz .com; 07, Halbgasse 3-5; s/d from €60/72; P ⚹ ⚹) This fine pension has the novelty of a rooftop swimming pool, which comes in very handy on scorching summer days. The rooms are quite sizable.

TOP END

Das Triest (Map pp80-2; ☎ 589 18-0; www.dastriest .at; 04, Wiedner Hauptstrasse 12; s/d €190/245) Das Triest is a refreshing change from the luxury and regality many of Vienna's top hotels so adamantly love to flaunt. Stylish in its simplicity and bathed in pastel warmth, it's an interior designer's dream; everything, from the rooms to the lobby to the stairwells, seems to fit effortlessly together in a mix of modern Italian and Viennese.

Outside the Gürtel

BUDGET

Do Step Inn (Map pp80-2; ☎ 923 27 69; www.dostepinn .at; 15, Felberstrasse 22/6; s/d €29/35) Newly opened Do Step Inn, a hop, step and a jump from Westbahnhof, has bright, colourful rooms decked out in Ikea-like simplicity. Facilities, which include a better-than-average kitchen, are shared with other guests. Helpful staff give the place a decidedly relaxed air.

Schlossherberge am Wilhelminenberg (Map pp78-9; ☎ 485 85 03-700; shb@verkehrsbuero.at; 16, Savoyenstrasse 2; dm €18; P) This HI Hostel, in the grounds of Schloss Wilhelminenberg, may be a long way from the Innere Stadt but it has glorious views of the city and easy access to the Wienerwald. Plus it's only a quick stroll downhill to a concentration of *Heurigen* near the Ottakringer cemetery.

Wombat's (Map pp80-2; ☎ 897 23 36; www.wombats.at; 15, Grangasse 6; dm from €16, rooms €42; 🖥 🔊) It's hard to find a more relaxed hostel than Wombat's in Vienna – the atmosphere is more Gold Coast Australia than the Capital of Culture. The staff are friendly, there's Internet access, bike rental, a pub, a pool and garden and it's about a 10-minute walk from Westbahnhof.

Hostel Ruthensteiner (Map pp80-2; ☎ 893 42 02; www.hostelruthensteiner.com; 15, Robert Hamerling Gasse 24; dm from €11.50; 🖥) Facilities at this enjoyable hostel include a kitchen, laundry and a shady rear courtyard. Dorms range from two- to 10-bed rooms. The hostel is near Westbahnhof, one block south of Mariahilfer Strasse.

Sophienalpe (Map pp78-9; ☎ 486 24 32; www.sophienalpe.at; 14, Sophienalpestrasse 13; s/d €41/60; 🏵 Apr-Oct; 🅿 🔊) The address may officially be within Vienna's borders, but Sophienalpe's location is in reality outside of the city's urban development and in the middle of the Wienerwald. Walks abound in all directions, there's a popular restaurant onsite and rooms are comfy. You really need a car to get here.

Fünfhaus (Map pp80-2; ☎ 892 35 45; 15, Sperrgasse 12; s/d without bathroom from €30/44; 🏵 Mar–mid-Nov) Fünfhaus is finely situated in a quiet residential area so there's no threat of excessive road noise. Rooms come with a range of amenities and in various sizes but all are clean and fresh.

Camping Wien West (Map pp78-9; ☎ 914 23 14; 14, Hüttelbergstrasse 80; campsites per adult/tent €6.50/5, 2-/4-person bungalows €27/37; 🏵 Mar-Jan; 🅿 🖥) Wien West is at the western edge of the city and handy to the Wienerwald. There are cooking facilities and convenient transport from the Innere Stadt; take the U4 to Hütteldorf, then bus No 148 or 152. Prices drop in July and August.

Camping Wien Süd (Map pp78-9; ☎ 867 36 49; 23, Breitenfurter Straße 269; campsites per adult/tent €6.50/5; 🏵 May-Sep; 🅿) In among the suburbs of Vienna's southwest corner is Wien Süd, a flat campsite with tree shade. Bus 62A (from U6 Station Meidling/Philadelphiabrücke) stops right outside its doors.

MID-RANGE

Altwienerhof (Map pp80-2; ☎ 892 60 00; www.altwienerhof.at; 15, Herklotzgasse 6; s/d €57/90) Altwien-

erhof, a small, family-run three-star hotel only a stone's throw from the Gürtel, offers an air of sophistication without the price tag. Rooms aren't overly plush but they're stylish and well-cared for by friendly and welcoming staff.

Celtes (Map pp78-9; ☎ 440 41 51; www.hotelceltes.at; 19, Celtesgasse 1; s/d €70/109) Celtes is perfectly located if you're into wine and walks; it's in the heart of the Neustift am Walde *Heurigen* and vineyard area and convenient to the Wienerwald. There's also a bar and a garden on the premises.

Favorita (Map pp80-2; ☎ 601 46-0; www.austria-trend.at/fav; 10, Laxenburger Strasse 8-10; s/d €112/138) The first thing you notice about Favorita is its striking yet simple façade, in almost *Jugendstil* style. Rooms are modern and bright and there's a sauna and steam bath free for guests to relax those weary bones in.

Thüringer Hof (Map p86; ☎ 401 79-0; www.thueringerhof.at; 18, Jörgerstrasse 4-8; s/d €75.60/99.60; 🅿) While Thüringer Hof's rooms could do with an update, they have the advantage of being particularly spacious (those facing the inner courtyard are quietest). Children aged six to 12 gain a 50% discount and those under six stay for free.

TOP END

Parkhotel Schönbrunn (Map pp80-2; ☎ 87 804-0; parkhotel.schoenbrunn@austria-trend.at; 13, Hietzinger Hauptstrasse 10-20; s/d from €125/170; 🔊) Partially built with money from Emperor Franz Josef, who considered it his guesthouse, Parkhotel Schönbrunn still exudes an air of regality. The façade is, of course, painted Schönbrunn yellow, the lobby and grand ballroom all have the majesty of a five-star place, and many rooms surround a large garden with sun lounges, trees and grass.

EATING

Vienna has thousands of restaurants covering all budgets and styles of cuisine, but the dining experience is not limited to them. *Kaffeehäuser* (coffee houses) and *Heurigen* (p118) are almost defining elements of the city, and just as fine for a good meal. The humble *Beisl*, Vienna's equivalent of a beer house or tavern, is normally a simple restaurant serving the best of Viennese cuisine in unhealthy portions.

If you've no time to sit around and wait, a *Würstel Stand* will suffice; sausage stands

VIENNA

THE AUTHOR'S CHOICE

Stomach (Map pp80-2; ☎ 310 20 99; 09, Seegasse 26; mains €10-17; ☽ 4pm-midnight Wed-Sat, 10am-10pm Sun) Stomach has been serving seriously good food for years, and it only seems to get better with age. The menu is a healthy mix of meat and vegetarian dishes and features plenty of game when it's in season. The interior is straight out of rural Austria and its garden, with its overgrown look and uneven cobblestones, has more character than some districts. The name comes from the re-arrangement of the word Tomaschek, the butcher shop originally located here. Reservations are highly recommended.

---

are conveniently located on street corners and squares, ready with sausages, bread and beer. Otherwise you could try the ubiquitous Schnitzelhaus chain which serves up fast food, Viennese style.

Self-caterers will have no problem stocking up on provisions; Hofer, Zielpunkt, Billa, Spar and Merkur supermarkets are commonplace throughout the city. Some have well-stocked delis which make sandwiches to order, the perfect cheap lunch on the run. The city is also dotted with markets (p123).

Innere Stadt
RESTAURANTS

En (Map pp83-5; ☎ 532 44 90; 01, Werdertorgasse 8; lunch menu €7.50-9.50, full meal €20; ☽ lunch & dinner) Shuffling Kimono-clad waitresses, authentic décor and great sushi create a small slice of Japan in the back streets of the Innere Stadt. En's menu also offers a whole gamut of Japanese specialities.

Expedit (Map pp83-5; ☎ 512 33 13-0; 01, Wiesingerstrasse 6; mains €8-18; ☽ noon-11pm Mon-Fri, 6-11pm Sat) With warehouse shelves, simple furniture and an open kitchen, the owners of Expedit have succeeded in creating a laid-back yet smart look. The ever-changing menu offers a mix of Italian classics and creations from whatever is in season, and is divinely prepared.

Griechenbeisl (Map pp83-5; ☎ 533 19 77; 01, Fleischmarkt 11; mains €14-18; ☽ 11am-1am) Griechenbeisl is almost more of a tourist attraction than a restaurant, and rightly so; it's been around since 1447 and was once frequented by musical greats Beethoven, Schubert and

Brahms. Choose to dine on Viennese standards in one of the vaulted rooms or in the plant-fringed front garden.

Wrenkh (Map pp83-5; ☎ 533 15 26; 01, Bauernmarkt 10; lunch menu from €7.70, mains €8-15; ☽ lunch & dinner) Creative vegetarian dishes from around the world are the order of the day for this upmarket restaurant. The front section is a thoroughly modern affair with a vibrant feel; the rear a quiet, intimate room with booths.

DO & CO (Map pp83-5; ☎ 535 39 69; 01, Stephansplatz 12, Haas-Haus; mains around €20; ☽ lunch & dinner) DO & CO is one of Vienna's finest restaurants, directly opposite Stephansdom, offering Asian creations and plenty of fish. The same people also run a luxurious museum-café in the Albertina.

Figlmüller (Map pp83-5; ☎ 512 61 77; 01, Wollzeile 5; mains €6.50-14; ☽ 11am-10.30pm, closed Aug) Figlmüller may be firmly on the tourist trail but that doesn't take anything away from the huge schnitzels which dwarf the plates they're served on. The interior has the look and feel of a rural *Heurigen*.

Beim Czaak (Map pp83-5; ☎ 513 72 15; 01, Postgasse 15; lunch menu €6.40, mains €5.50-12.50; ☽ 11am-midnight Mon-Sat) Beim Czaak is a proper locals' *Beisl*, albeit more upmarket than average. Wood panels, boisterous bar-leaners and a hearty welcome greet you upon entering.

Nudel & Strudel (Map pp83-5; ☎ 533 61 28; 01, Schottenbastei 4; lunch menu €6-10, mains €6-11; ☽ 9am-midnight Mon-Fri) A dark wood interior, rustic décor and solid Austrian fare with cheap student meals make this place a popular choice in the Innere Stadt.

Rosenberger Markt Restaurant (Map pp83-5; ☎ 512 34 58; 01, Maysedergasse 2; meals about €10; ☽ 6am-11pm) This downstairs buffet place has a fine array of meats, drinks and desserts which enables you to compile a meal. Watch out for extras (like bread and butter) that can be pricey.

CAFES

Aida (Map pp83-5; ☎ 512 29 77; 01, Stock-im-Eisen-Platz 2; cakes from €1.50; ☽ 7am-8pm Mon-Sat, 9am-8pm Sun) The 26 Aida cafés in Vienna are an absolute city icon and a rival to the traditional *Kaffeehäuser*. While their pink and brown colour scheme is a rather strange choice, the décor dated but fantastically retro and the majority of the clientele well into retirement, they're a superb place for cakes, pastries and coffee.

Café Bräunerhof (Map pp83–5; ☎ 512 38 93; 01, Stallburggasse 2; snacks €3-6; ☯ 8am-9pm Mon-Fri, 8am-7pm Sat, 10am-7pm Sun) Not much has changed in this fine Viennese *Kaffeehaus* since the late great Thomas Bernhard once called it his *Stammlocal* (regular watering hole). There's classical music on weekends and holidays from 3pm to 6pm, and British newspapers alongside Vienna's tabloids.

Haas & Haas (Map pp83–5; ☎ 512 26 66; 01, Stephansplatz 4; cakes €3-15, breakfast €6-11; ☯ 8am-8pm Mon-Fri, 8am-6.30pm Sat) This tea house has the attraction of hefty breakfasts (served 8am to 11.30am) and a location that ain't bad; Stephansdom to your left, quiet inner courtyard to your right.

Café Hawelka (Map pp83–5; ☎ 512 82 30; 01, Dorotheergasse 6; snacks €3-6; ☯ 8am-2am Mon & Wed-Sat, 4pm-2am Sun) This is the perfect spot to people-watch and to chat to complete strangers. It's also a traditional haunt for artists and writers and attracts the gamut of Viennese society; expect to be constantly shunted along to accommodate new arrivals at your table.

Café Central (Map pp83–5; ☎ 533 37 64-26; 01, Herrengasse 14; snacks €3-6; ☯ 8am-10pm Mon-Sat, 8am-7pm Sun) With its marble pillars, arched ceilings, glittering chandeliers, indifferent waiters, live classical music from 4pm to 7pm, Central is the atypical Viennese café. Trotsky even came here to play chess.

Café Sacher (Map pp83–5; ☎ 541 56-661; 01, Philharmonikerstrasse 4; sacher torte about €3; ☯ 8am-11.30pm) Sacher is the most celebrated café in all of Vienna and almost every visitor to the city wants a slice of the action here – a slice of *Sacher Torte* that is. The café does have other redeeming features, such as opulent furnishings and a battalion of waiters.

Demel (Map pp83–5; ☎ 535 17 17; 01, Kohlmarkt 14; mains €10-15; ☯ 10am-7pm) Demel is Sacher's *torte* rival. Naturally it's not the cheapest café in town, but you're paying for quality, location and an elegance. The *Créme schnitte* here is to die for.

Café Griensteidl (Map pp83–5; ☎ 535 26 92; 01, Michaelerplatz 2; mains €6.60-17; ☯ 8am-11.30pm) Griensteidl holds a prestigious position between the splendour of the Hofburg and the eyebrow-less windows of the Loos Haus (p102). It's a great place to people-watch and flick through the large selection of international newspapers.

QUICK EATS

Würstelstand am Hohen Markt (Map pp83–5; 01, Hoher Markt; sausages from €3; ☯ 7am-5am) Possibly *the Würstel Stand* in all of Vienna (which is truly saying something), am Hohen Markt attracts people from all walks of life. It's the consistent quality of the sausages, the location and its incredible opening hours that maintain its top-dog status year after year.

Maschu Maschu (Map pp83–5; ☎ 533 29 04; 01, Rabensteig 8; mains €3-8; ☯ 11.30am-midnight Sun-Tue, to 2am Wed, to 3am Thu-Sat) Maschu is basically a take-away place with a few seating options, and has the freshest falafels and humus in the Innere Stadt.

Trzesniewski (Map pp83–5; ☎ 512 32 91; 01, Dorotheergasse 1; breads from €3; ☯ 8.30am-7.30pm Mon-Fri, 8am-5pm Sat) This deli bar is a Viennese institution and has had more than its fair share of famous patrons (Kafka was a regular here). Choose your bread, then select your spread, or pick from the ready-made sandwiches. They're quite tiny (two bites and they're gone).

Gelateria Hoher Markt (Map pp83–5; ☎ 533 32 97-1; 01, Hoher Markt 4; ice cream €1.50; ☯ 9am-11.30pm) Forget Zanoni on Rotenturmstrasse and wander a few steps west to this supremely better ice cream shop on Hoher Markt. Thirty sorts, a concoction of elaborate sundaes, outdoor seating, and peaceful surroundings – need we say more?

If you're on a tight budget look no further than the various university *Mensas* (cafeterias) in the Innere Stadt, which include the **Universität Mensa** (Map pp83–5; ☎ 406 45 94; 01, Universitätsstrasse 7; meals €8; ☯ lunch Mon-Fri) – take the doorless, continuous lift to the 6th floor (which is worth the trip itself); **Katholisches Studenthaus Mensa** (Map pp83–5; ☎ 408 35 85; 01, Ebendorferstrasse 8; mains €3-5.20; ☯ lunch Mon-Fri, closed Aug–mid Sep); and **Music Academy Mensa** (Map pp83–5; ☎ 512 94 70; 01, Johannesgasse 8; mains €3.80-4.80; ☯ lunch Mon-Fri, to 1.30pm during summer holidays).

SELF-CATERING

There is an Interspar (Map pp83–5) on the 1st floor on the corner of Rotenturmstrasse and Fleischmarkt, and a Billa (Map pp83–5) on Singerstrasse.

Freyung (Map pp83–5; 01, Freyung; ☯ 8am-7.30pm Fri & Sat; U2 Schottentor) Freyung market exclusively sells fresh organic produce from farmers.

Ringstrasse

RESTAURANTS

Halle (Map pp83-5; ☎ 523 70 01; 07, Museumsplatz 1; lunch menu €7, mains from €7; ☉ 10am-2am) With excellent food, handsome waiters and a warm, gay-friendly atmosphere, it's no surprise that Halle, the Kunsthalle's restaurant, is a popular hang-out. Antipasti, salads and pastas from the Italian kitchen are the mainstay of the menu but there are other choices if that's not to your taste.

Vestibül (Map pp83-5; ☎ 532 49 99; 01, Dr Karl Leuger-Ring 2; evening menu €40, mains €20; ☉ 11am-midnight Mon-Fri, 6pm-midnight Sat) Vestibül has an equally rich menu – the finest from around the world – and interior – marble columns, chandeliers and sparkling mirrored bar. It's situated in the southern wing of the Burgtheater (p120).

CAFES

Café Prückel (Map pp83-5; ☎ 512 61 15; 01, Stubenring 24; coffee €1.80-3.60, mains €6-11; ☉ 8.30am-10pm) Prückel's original mould is a little different to other Viennese cafés; instead of a sumptuous interior, you'll find a café where the 1950s still prevail. The coffee is superb, the cakes irresistible and the service as aloof, but somehow friendly, as ever.

Una (Map pp83-5; ☎ 523 65 66; 07, Museumsplatz 1; mains €6.20-15; ☉ 9am-midnight Mon-Fri, 10am-midnight Sat, 10am-6pm Sun) Striking tiled walls, arched ceilings and massive windows, along with an unpretentious atmosphere, compliment an uncomplicated menu heavy on pasta and season specialities.

Kantine (Map pp83-5; ☎ 523 82 39; 07, Museumsplatz 1; daily menu €5.50-6.50, pita breads €4.50-9; ☉ 10am-midnight Sun-Wed, 10am-2am Thu-Sat) This upbeat café/bar, complete with disco ball, is housed in the former stables of the Emperor's personal horses. If the fresh daily menu, typically an Asian or Viennese dish with a vegetarian or fish choice thrown in, is sold out, you'll have to settle for salad-filled pita bread.

MAK Café (Map pp83-5; ☎ 714 01 21; 01, Stubenring 3-5; lunch menu €6.50-8, mains €7-18; ☉ 10am-2am Tue-Sun) Viennese and international cuisine is served under a 19th-century ornamental ceiling in this, the café of Museum für angewandte Kunst (p96). The garden is a must in summer.

Café Restaurant Landtmann (Map pp83-5; ☎ 241 00; 01, Dr Karl-Lueger-Ring 4; lunch menu €9.60, mains €7.80-19; ☉ 7.30am-midnight) This elegant old dame has sidelong views of the Burgtheater from its lovely covered outdoor area, which could quite easily be the largest of any Viennese café.

Across the Danube Canal

RESTAURANTS

Schweizerhaus (Map pp80-2; ☎ 728 01 52; 02, Strasse des Ersten Mai 116; mains €10-15; ☉ 11am-11pm Mon-Fri, 10am-11pm Sat & Sun mid-Mar–Oct) Every Viennese knows Schweizerhaus, and probably every Viennese has eaten here at least once in their life. It's famous for its massive, tree-shaded garden, roasted *Hintere Schweinsstelze* (pork hocks) and draught Budweiser (the Czech stuff) direct from the barrel.

Schöne Perle (Map pp80-2; ☎ 243 35 93; 02, Grosse Pfarrgasse 2; lunch menu €7, mains €5-12; ☉ noon-11pm Mon-Sat, noon-10pm Sun) Schöne Perle has the look and feel of a student cafeteria but the food is by no means as basic or bland. Classic Austrian dishes are created with organic produce only and complimented with a fine list of Austrian wines and juices.

QUICK EATS

Gesundes (Map pp83-5; ☎ 219 53 22; 02, Lilienbrunngasse 3; lunch menu €6.90-8; ☉ 9am-6pm Mon-Tue & Thu-Fri, 9am-5.30pm Wed, 10am-2pm Sat) Gesundes is the kind of place where just walking through the door makes you feel a whole lot healthier. Only vegetarian/vegan organic dishes are on the menu and it doubles as a shop for organic produce.

SELF-CATERING

Karmelitermarkt (Map pp80-2; 02, Im Werd; ☉ 6am-6.30pm Mon-Fri, 6am-2pm Sat) Karmelitermarkt has fruit and vegetables stalls and butchers selling kosher and halal meats. On Saturday the square features a *Bauernmarkt* (farmer's market).

Inside the Gürtel

RESTAURANTS

Palais Schwarzenberg (Map pp80-2; ☎ 798 45 15-600; 03, Schwarzenbergplatz 9; breakfast €25.50, lunch menu €33, dinner menu €55; ☉ 6.30-10.30am, noon-2pm, dinner) A grand baroque dining room and terrace with sweeping views of an 18-acre garden are the opulent settings for this wonderful restaurant. The cuisine – Austrian with a splash of Mediterranean flair – is a fitting match to such rich surroundings.

Wild (Map pp83-5; ☎ 920 94 77; 03, Radetzkyplatz 1; lunch menu €7, mains €7-15; ❤ 10am-1am Tue-Sun) The dark wood-panelled interior is the first sign of class when you walk through the doors of Wild; the quiet ambience the second. The menu is Viennese through and through, ranging from *goulasch* to the ever-present *schnitzel mit erdäpfelsalat*.

Aromat (Map pp80-2; ☎ 913 24 53; 04, Margaretenstrasse 52; menus €5-7, mains about €5; ❤ 11am-midnight Mon-Sat) This supremely relaxed restaurant features an ever-changing menu, concocted from whatever the cooks find fresh at the Naschmarkt. They don't take reservations so its first come first served, and with seating for around 30 people, don't be surprised to find it full.

Motto (Map pp80-2; ☎ 587 06 72; 05, Schönbrunner Strasse 30; mains €8-19; ❤ 6pm-4am) Motto's fusion of Asian, Austrian and Italian food is superb, the wine list selective and the décor, well, caters to a gay clientele. Dressed in her house-cleaning frock, Frau Helena is the Yin to the young, handsome, well-groomed male waiters Yang, but her steaks are legendary (Mondays, Tuesdays and Thursdays only). Entrance is through the forbidding chrome door on Rüdigergasse.

Tancredi (Map pp80-2; ☎ 941 00 48; 04, Grosse Neugasse 5; lunch menu €7, mains €7-16; ❤ lunch & dinner Tue-Fri, dinner Sat) This ex-*Beisl*, with stripped-back wooden floors, warm, pastel-yellow walls, and fittings from yester-year, attracts a more affluent clientele with lovingly prepared regional and fish specialities, bio-products and an extensive range of Austrian wines. Its tree-shaded garden fills up quickly in summer.

Zu den Zwei Liesln (Map p86; ☎ 523 32 82; 07, Burggasse 63; mains €4.40-8; ❤ 10am-10pm Mon-Sat) This thoroughly authentic *Beisl* is among the best in the business and its courtyard is a popular spot on warm summer days and evenings. Legend has it that some customers have been consumed by their Wiener schnitzels and when you receive the *riesige* (huge) portions it's half-believable.

Gaumenspiel (Map p86; ☎ 526 11 08; 07, Zieglergasse 54; lunch menu €7, mains €8-15; ❤ lunch & dinner Tue-Fri, dinner Sat, lunch Sun) Gaumenspiel keeps its regulars coming back time after time with an international mix with heavy Mediterranean influence, attentive and friendly service and an atmosphere of calm and informality. The menu is written on chalk boards, the décor is light in detail and in summer there are a handful of street-side tables.

Zum Alten Fassl (Map pp80-2; ☎ 544 42 98; 05, Ziegelofengasse 37; lunch menu €5.70-6.40, mains €6.20-14.50; ❤ lunch & dinner Sun-Fri, dinner Sat) An unassuming façade on a residential street hides this esteemed *Beisl* from many casual passers-by. Try the desserts – any of them – they're worth crossing town for. The rear garden is an absolute joy; overgrown with vines, it provides a sample of the hidden gardens of residential Vienna.

St Josef (Map p86; ☎ 526 68 18; 07, Mondscheingasse 10; small/large menu €4.80/5.80; ❤ 8am-6pm Mon-Wed & Fri, 8am-11.30pm Thu, 8am-4pm Sat) It's hard to find a more laid-back, relaxed and welcoming eatery than St Josef in all of Vienna. The creative menus which roll out of the open kitchen all day are 100% vegetarian and made from wholly organic produce. Take a seat upstairs or downstairs or get something to go.

ON (Map p86; ☎ 402 63 33; 08, Lederergasse 16; lunch menu €5.80, mains from €5; ❤ lunch & dinner Wed-Fri, 5.30-11pm Sat & Sun) ON is another in a long list of spartan Asian restaurants to grace the Viennese restaurant scene in recent years. But what makes ON stand out from the crowd is a combination of creative, gluten-free Chinese, Thai and Malaysian dishes, superb spices, an open kitchen and a friendly, convivial atmosphere.

Amacord (Map pp83-5; ☎ 587 47 09; 05, Rechte Wienzeile 15; breakfast €4.60-6, mains €6.40-10.80; ❤ 10am-2am) Shoppers on a Saturday morning fill Amacord to bursting point, all fighting for a table and a chance to enjoy breakfast. Outside Saturday morning, the pace is more sedate, but the food – a mix of Viennese classics and Italian pastas – is still of the highest quality and the atmosphere is convivial and local.

Chang (Map pp80-2; ☎ 961 92 12; 04, Waaggasse 1; mains €5.70-6.90; ❤ lunch & dinner Mon-Sat) If you've a craving for Asian noodles, Chang is for you. The selection is simply great, the noodles are cooked with expertise and flair and everything on the menu is also to take away. The place is bright, uncomplicated, open and highly relaxed.

Gasthaus Wickerl (Map pp80-2; ☎ 317 74 89; 09, Porzellangasse 24a; mains €6-12; ❤ 9am-midnight Mon-Fri, 10am-midnight Sat) Wickerl features excellent Viennese home cooking, bare wooden floors, simple furniture, summer street-side seating and a relaxed, warm environment.

Ra'mien (Map pp83-5; ☎ 585 47 98; 06, Gumpendorferstrasse 9; mains €6-15; ⏰ 11am-midnight Tue-Sun) Picture a grey-white room, with an open, simple look, full of bright, young, hip things bent over bowls of piping hot noodles, and you have Ra'mien. The menu not only consists of noodles, but covers the spectrum of Asian delights, from Thai to Japanese.

Kim Kocht (Map p86; ☎ 319 02 42; 09, Lustkandlgasse 6; mains €10.50-27; ⏰ dinner Mon-Fri) This wholesome, upmarket Asian restaurant hidden behind the Volksoper, has a selective menu which thankfully doesn't offer every Asian dish under the sun. It does, however, have a heavy Japanese slant (despite being Korean-owned and run).

Govinda (Map pp83-5; ☎ 522 28 17; 07, Lindengasse 2a; all-day menu €5; ⏰ 10am-6.30pm Mon-Fri, 10am-2pm Sat) Discuss the meaning of life and the existence of God at Govinda, a Hare Krishna–run restaurant-cum-esoteric shop. It specialises in heavenly meatless Indian curries just right for the Viennese palate; not too spicy, not too bland.

Saigon (Map pp83-5; ☎ 585 63 95; 06, Getreidmarkt 7; lunch menu €5.30-6.80, mains €7.30-16; ⏰ 11.30am-10.30pm Tue-Sun) Bamboo screens, Asian art and an incredible selection of dishes (the soups are the highlight) are all inviting touches to this popular Vietnamese restaurant.

Summer Stage (Map pp80-2; ☎ 315 52 02; 09, Rossauer Lände; mains €5-20; ⏰ 5pm-1am Mon-Sat, 2pm-1am Sun May-Sep) A diverse range of restaurants set up shop over the summer months at Summer Stage, a covered area overlooking the Danube Canal near the Rossauer Lände U4 stop.

Amerlingbeisl (Map pp83-5; ☎ 526 16 60; 07, Stiftgasse 8; lunch menu from €5, mains €4.50-8; ⏰ 9am-2am) Amerlingbeisl is one of the better restaurants in cobblestone Spittalberg. It attracts a young crowd, eager to take advantage of the cheap menu and relatively cheap beer. On balmy nights the roof slides back for those who are able to cram into the rear courtyard.

Ubl (Map pp83-5; ☎ 587 64 37; 04, Pressgasse 26; mains €8-12; ⏰ lunch & dinner) *Riesige* schnitzels are the standard at this Viennese *Beisl*. Fortunately though, the quiet, relaxed atmosphere and tree-shaded summer terrace help to appease your groaning stomach.

The **Naschmarkt** (Map pp83-5; 06, Linke & Rechte Wienzeile; ⏰ 6am-6.30pm Mon-Fri, 6am-5pm Sat), Vienna's biggest and boldest market, is a food-lovers dream come true. Not only are there food stalls selling meats, fruits, vegetables, cheeses and spices, but there's also a wide variety of restaurants. Some of the better places include:

Do-An (Map pp83-5; ☎ 585 82 53; 04, Naschmarkt 412; breakfast €4-6, salads €4.60-6.60; ⏰ 8am-10pm) A fish bowl with huge windows and an extensive range of breakfasts.

Naschmarkt Deli (Map pp83-5; ☎ 585 08 23; 04, Naschmarkt 421; sandwiches €4-7, mains €6-9; ⏰ 7am-10pm Mon-Fri, 7am-midnight Sat) Wraps, baguettes, sandwiches and breakfasts and the perfect place to people-watch; don't turn up at 10am Saturday expecting to find a seat.

Indian Pavillon (Map pp83-5; ☎ 587 85 61; 04, Naschmarkt 74-75; mains €7-10; ⏰ 11am-6.30pm Mon-Fri, 11am-5pm Sat) Serves dishes laden with spices from the subcontinent, including kebabs, samosas and rogan josh.

Mr Lee (Map pp83-5; ☎ 581 45 60; 04, Naschmarkt 278; mains €6-10; ⏰ 10.30am-10pm Mon-Sat) Asian eatery with top quality dishes (many with a little extra spice), service so friendly it almost seems fake and an open kitchen that hides no secrets.

CAFES

Café Sperl (Map pp83-5; ☎ 586 41 58; 06, Gumpendorfer Strasse 11; mains €5-10; ⏰ 7am-11pm Mon-Sat, 11am-8pm Sun, closed Sun in summer) *Jugendstil* fittings, a cosy appearance and a reputable menu (the highlight of which is the *Sperl Torte*) make this one of the finest cafés in Vienna, and overshadow the fact that it was once Hitler's regular haunt.

Canetti (Map p86; ☎ 522 06 88; 07, Urban-Loritz-Platz 2A; lunch menu €6, mains €7-18; ⏰ 9am-midnight) Canetti is one of only a handful of eateries in Vienna with rooftop views. Perched on top of the Bücherei Wien (p88), its vantage point provides a sweeping vista of Vienna to the south and is a better place for a coffee than a meal.

Café Hummel (Map p86; ☎ 405 53 14; 08, Josefstädter Strasse 66; lunch menu €5.20, mains from €5.20; ⏰ 7am-2am Mon-Sat, 8am-2am Sun) Unpretentious Hummel is a true locals' *Kaffeehaus*, with aloof waiters, outdoor seating, a huge range of Viennese dishes, top coffee and homemade cakes.

Café Drechsler (Map pp83-5; ☎ 587 85 80; 06, Linke Wienzeile 22; mains €4.70-5.50; ⏰ 3am-8pm Mon-Fri, 3am-6pm Sat) After a hard night drinking or dancing, greet the dawn at Café Drechsler where you'll rub shoulders with traders at the Naschmarkt. It's no surprise the breakfasts here are among the best in the business, but the *goulasch* gives them a run for their money.

QUICK EATS

Bagel Station (Map pp83-5; ☎ 208 08 94; 06, Capistrangasse 10; bagels €1.50-3.80; ☯ 7am-9pm Mon-Fri, 9am-9pm Sat, 10am-6pm Sun) It's been a long time coming but finally the bagel has made a comeback in Vienna (it was invented here in 1683 after the second Turkish siege). This bright, bold bagel station deal in bagels and coffee combos to go, and has plenty of weekly specials. Another station can be found at Währinger Strasse 2-4.

Outside the Gürtel
RESTAURANTS

Schloss Concordia (Map pp78-9; ☎ 769 88 88; 11, Simmeringer Hauptstrasse 283; mains around €10; ☯ 10am-1am) Concordia's overgrown garden, bare wooden floors, gargantuan mirrors and stained-glass roof create a strange but highly appealing interior, and the large stone Jesus statue which greets prospective diners only adds to its ambience. Its schnitzel menu reads like a list from the abattoir, but there is also a smattering of enticing vegetarian options.

Kent (Map p86; ☎ 405 91 73; 16, Brunnengasse 67; mains €3-9; ☯ 6am-2am) With a huge summer garden, excellent kebabs, pizzas and breakfasts Turkish-style, Kent leads the pack of Turkish restaurants in Vienna. On a Friday night you'd think half of Vienna's Turkish population comes to play cards in the back room.

World Restaurant (Map p86; ☎ 06991-130 28 07; 16, Hofferplatz 5; lunch menu from €4.40, mains €5-12; ☯ lunch & dinner Mon-Fri, dinner Sat) Tucked away in an unassuming, residential area of the 16th District is this superb restaurant, with a menu of Sri Lankan and Caribbean cuisines: curries, fish specialities and plenty of vegetarian choices.

CAFES

Café Gloriette (Map pp80-2; ☎ 879 13 11; 13, Gloriette; snacks €6-8; ☯ 9am-1am) Occupying the Gloriette, a neo-classical construction high on a hill behind Schloss Schönbrunn, is this noble café. Its sweeping views of the Schloss, magnificent gardens and the districts to the north is arguably one of the best vistas in all of Vienna.

SELF-CATERING

Brunnenmarkt (Map p86; 16, Brunnengasse; ☯ 6am-6.30pm Mon-Fri, 6am-2pm Sat) Brunnenmarkt is Vienna's largest street-market and totally

reflects its ethnic neighbourhood; most stall-holders are of Turkish/Balkan decent. On Saturday nearby Yppenplatz features the best *Bauernmarkt* in the city.

DRINKING
Bars

Vienna is riddled with late-night drinking establishments, but you'll find a concentration of trend-setting bars north and south of the Naschmarkt, around Spittalberg (many of these double as restaurants) and along the Gürtel (mainly around the U6 stops of Josefstädter Strasse and Nussdorfer Strasse). The Bermuda Dreieck (Bermuda Triangle), near the Danube Canal in the Innere Stadt, also has many bars, but they normally cater more for tourists than locals.

During the summer months, party-goers tend to congregate at Copa Kagrana and Sunken City, an area around the U1 Donauinsel U-Bahn station. It's quite a tacky affair, but it can be a lot of fun. Summer Stage (opposite) and the **Alte AKH** (cnr Alser Strasse & Spitalgasse) also wage war against the threat of melting indoors.

Palmenhaus (Map pp83-5; ☎ 533 10 33; Burggarten; ☯ 10am-2am, closed Mon & Tue Nov-Mar) Housed in a beautifully renovated palmhouse, complete with high, arched ceilings, glass walls and steel beams, this is one of the better locations in town. The crowd is generally well-to-do, but the ambience is often relaxed and welcoming to all walks of life. The outdoor seating in summer is fantastic.

Kleines Café (Map pp83-5; 01, Franziskanerplatz 3; ☯ 10am-2am Mon-Sat, 1pm-2am Sun) What this small café lacks in size it makes up for in oodles of bohemian atmosphere, excellent lunch menus and wonderful summer outdoor seating on Franziskanerplatz.

rhiz (Map p86; ☎ 409 25 05; www.rhiz.org; 08, Lerchenfelder Gürtel 37-38; ☯ 6pm-4am Mon-Sat, 6pm-2am Sun) The best of the Gürtel's bunch of bars due to its friendly staff, large outdoor seating area, relaxed atmosphere and brick-and-glass walls. The music is electronic and guest DJs are a regular event.

Das Möbel (Map pp83-5; ☎ 524 94 97; 08, Burggasse 10; ☯ 10am-1am) Das Möbel is the place to pick up something a little unusual for the lounge or kitchen; it stocks furniture produced by local designers and it's all for sale (check out their funky bags near the door, too). It has a relaxed crowd which

VIENNA

tends to spend the evening chatting over a couple of drinks.

A Bar Shabu (Map pp80-2; ☎ 0664-460 24 41; 02, Rotensterngasse 8; ☒ 9pm-late Tue-Sat, 1-11pm Sun) A Bar Shabu is a laid-back bar outfitted in '70s retro. Regular DJs provide an excellent backdrop of calming tunes and the absinthe selection from around Europe is extensive. Don't miss the Japanese room, or should we say, closet.

Schikaneder (Map pp80-2; ☎ 585 58 88; 05, Margareten Strasse 22-24; ☒ 6pm-4am) Grungy Schikaneder attracts a mix of students and arty types with its bottomless energy that runs well into the small hours of the morning. Schikaneder also hosts movies most nights.

Futuregarden Bar & Art Club (Map pp80-2; ☎ 585 26 13; 06, Schadekgasse 6; ☒ 7pm-2am Mon-Sat, 9pm-2am Sun) Futuregarden attracts a 30s to 40s crowd eager to soak up the buzzing atmosphere and listen to DJs spin soothing sounds. This basic bar's one piece of luxury – apart from the occasional art exhibition by local artists – is its rectangular disco 'ball' which swings from the ceiling.

Tanzcafé Jenseits (Map pp80-2; ☎ 587 12 33; 06, Nelkengasse 3; ☒ 9pm-4am Mon-Sat) Rumour has it that Jenseits was formally a brothel, which is highly plausible considering the kitschy red velvet interior. DJs perform most nights and the place attracts a mainly alternative and arty crowd which quickly fills the tiny dance floor.

Club U (Map pp83-5; ☎ 505 99 04; 04, Künstlerhauspassage; ☒ 10pm-2am Thu & Sun, 10pm-4am Fri & Sat) Club U occupies one of Otto Wagner's Stadt Pavillions on Karlsplatz. It's a small student-infested place with top DJs and a wonderful outdoor seating area in the summer months.

Volksgarten Pavillon (Map pp83-5; ☎ 532 09 07; 01, Burgring 1; ☒ 11am-4am Jun-Sep, 10pm-2am Mar-May & Oct) The larger garden of this 1950s-style pavilion is incredibly popular on warm evenings, due to views of the Hofburg and DJs providing a chilled-out atmosphere.

American Bar (Map pp83-5; ☎ 512 32 83; 01, Kärntner Durchgang 10; ☒ noon-4am summer, noon-4am Sun-Wed, noon-5am Thu-Sat winter) Designed by Adolf Loos in 1908, the American Bar also goes by the name Loos-Bar. It's basically a small box with enough room to fit about 20 people comfortably, but the mirrored walls help to trick you into thinking it's much larger.

The cocktails on offer are some of the city's best.

Café Stein (Map pp83-5; ☎ 319 72 41; 09, Währinger Strasse 6-8; ☒ 7am-1am Mon-Sat, 9am-1am Sun) During the day this three-levelled café is a popular haunt of students from the nearby university, but come evening the clientele metamorphoses into city workers with a lot more money to spend. DJs control the decks in the evenings and the all-day menu is tasty and extensive.

Heurigen

Vienna's version of a wine tavern, *Heurigen*, date back to the Middle Ages. Identified by a *Busch'n* (green wreath or branch) hanging over the door, many have outside tables in large gardens or courtyards and are fairly rustic and simple inside. *Heurigen* almost invariably serve food, which comes in the form of hot and cold buffet counters.

Heurigen usually have a relaxed atmosphere which gets livelier as the mugs of wine – and customers – get drunk. Many feature traditional live music, perhaps ranging from a solo accordion player to a fully fledged oompah band; these can be a bit touristy but great fun nonetheless.

Concentrations of *Heurigen* can be found in the wine-growing suburbs to the north, southwest, west and northwest of the city. Grinzing, in the northwest, is the most well-known *Heurigen* area, but it is also the most touristy. It's generally avoided by the Viennese but if you like loud music and bus loads of rowdy tourists, then it's the place for you.

Eckert (Map pp78-9; ☎ 292 25 96; 21, Strebersdorfer Strasse 158; ☒ from 10am every odd month) Located in the very northern outskirts of Vienna, Eckert is a *Heurigen* with a difference. Paintings by local artists are regularly featured and there's live music once a month (anything from jazz to rock 'n' roll).

Esterházykeller (Map pp83-5; ☎ 533 34 82; 01, Haarhof 1; ☒ 11am-11pm Mon-Fri, 4-11pm Sat & Sun) Esterházykeller is one of the few city *Heurigen* to grace the Innere Stadt. Low ceilings and rural decorations create a beautiful interior, and the wine, from the Esterházy Palace cellar in Eisenstadt, is above par.

Hirt (Map pp78-9; ☎ 318 96 41; 19, Eisernenhandgasse 165; ☒ 3pm-late Wed-Fri, noon-late Sat & Sun Apr-Oct, noon-late Fri, Sat & Sun) Hirt is a fantastic little *Heurigen* well hidden among the vineyards of Kahlenberg. It has everything going for it

– superb views, great food, friendly service and plenty of wine.

Mayer am Pfarrplatz (Map pp78-9; ☎ 370 12 87; 19, Pfarrplatz 2; ☿ 4pm-midnight Mon-Sat, 11am-midnight Sun) Mayer is one of the few gems in Grinzing and also has a place in the history annals – in 1817 Beethoven called it home. Its large garden is particularly pleasant and there's live music from 7pm to midnight daily.

Sirbu (☎ 320 59 28; 19, Kahlenberger Strasse 210; ☿ 3pm-midnight Mon-Sat Apr–mid-Oct) Sirbu has far-reaching views across Vienna's urban expanse and a quiet spot in among the vineyards of Kahlenberg. Its wines have reached the pinnacle of Austrian success in recent years and its garden is the perfect place to while away a sunny afternoon.

Weingut Schilling (Map pp78-9; ☎ 292 41 89; 21, Langenzersdorferstrasse 54; ☿ 4pm-midnight Mon-Fri, 3pm-midnight Sat & Sun every even month) Wiengut Schilling is located in the neighbourhood of Strebersdorf on the eastern side of the Danube. It has a good reputation for wine and an exceptionally large garden which backs onto its vineyard on the slopes of Bisberg hill.

Wieninger (Map pp78-9; ☎ 292 41 06; 21, Stammersdorfer Strasse 78; ☿ 3pm-midnight Wed-Fri, noon-midnight Sat & Sun Mar–mid-Jul & mid-Aug–Dec) Of the many *Heurigen* in the Stammersdorf area east of the Danube, Wieninger is classed as one of the finest, with a lovely, rustic setting, consistently great food, and Weingut Wieninger, its own wine label which is considered among Austria's best.

Zahel (Map pp78-9; ☎ 889 13 18; 23, Maurer Hauptplatz 9; ☿ 3pm-midnight Tue-Sun) Zahel, housed in 250-year-old premises, is classed as one of the oldest *Heurigen* in Vienna and rates among the best the Mauer area (in the southwest of Vienna) has to offer.

Zwölf Apostelkeller (Map pp78-9; ☎ 512 67 77; 01, Sonnenfelsgasse 3; ☿ 4.30pm-midnight) Even though Zwölf Apostelkeller plays it up large to the tourists, it still retains plenty of charm, dignity and authenticity. This is mostly due to the premises themselves – a vast, dimly lit, multilevel cellar.

ENTERTAINMENT

Vienna is still, and probably will be till the end of time, the capital of opera and classical music. The programme of music events is never-ending, and as a visitor in the centre you'll continually be accosted by people in Mozart-era costume trying to sell you tickets

for concerts or ballets. Even the city's buskers are often classically trained musicians.

The city also sports a number of great clubs, jazz bars and live-music venues. The tourist office produces a handy monthly listing of concerts and other events.

Opera & Classical Music

The list of venues below is certainly not complete, and many churches and cafés are fine places to catch a classical concert.

Tickets for the Akademietheater, Burgtheater, Schauspielhaus, Staatsoper and Volksoper can be purchased from the state ticket office **Bundestheaterkassen** (Map pp83-5; ☎ 514 44-7880; www.bundestheater.at; 01, Hanuschgasse 3; ☿ 8am-6pm Mon-Fri, 9am-noon Sat & Sun). The office charges no commission and tickets for the Staatsoper and Volksoper are available here one month prior to the performance. Credit cards are accepted and credit card sales can be made by telephone (☎ 513 15 13 English spoken; ☿ 10am-9pm). Alternatively, tickets can be booked over the Internet. Other ticket offices dotted around town include the **Wien-Ticket Pavillon** (Map pp83-5; 01, Herbert-von-Karajan-Platz; ☿ 10am-7pm) and **Jirsa Theater Karten Büro** (Map pp83-5; ☎ 400 600; http://viennaticket.at; 08, Lerchenfelder Strasse 12; ☿ 9.30am-5.30pm Mon-Fri).

Staatsoper (Map pp83-5; ☎ 514 44 7880; www .wiener-staatsoper.at; 01, Opernring 2; tours adult/child €4.50/1.50; box office ☿ 9am-until 2hr before performance Mon-Fri, 9am-noon Sat, closed Jul & Aug) This is the premier opera and classical music venue in Vienna, and possibly the world. Productions are lavish affairs and the Viennese take them very seriously and dress up accordingly. Standing-room tickets (€2 to €3.50) can only be purchased 80 minutes before the beginning of performances and any unsold tickets are available for €30 one day before a performance (call ☎ 514 44 2950 for more information).

Musikverein (Map pp83-5; ☎ 505 81 90; www .musikverein.at; 01, Bösendorferstrasse 12; box office ☿ 9am-7.30pm Mon-Fri, 9am-5pm Sat, closed Jul & Aug) The Musikverein, home to the Vienna Philharmonic Orchestra, is said to have the best acoustics of any concert hall in Austria. The interior is suitably lavish and can be visited on the occasional guided tour. Standing-room tickets in the main hall cost €5 to €7; there are no student tickets.

Konzerthaus (Map pp83-5; ☎ 242 002; www.konzerthaus.at; 03, Lothringerstrasse 20; box office ☿ 9am-7.45pm

Mon-Fri, 9am-1pm Sat, closed Jul & Aug) This is a major venue in classical music circles, but throughout the year ethnic music, rock, pop or jazz can also be heard in its hallowed halls. Student tickets are half-price.

Dating back to 1498, the Wiener Sänger-knaben (Vienna Boys' Choir) is an institution of the city. The choir sings every Sunday (except during July and August) at 9.15am in the Burgkapelle (Royal Chapel; Map pp83-5) in the Hofburg. Tickets (€5 to €29) should be booked around eight weeks in advance (☎ 533 99 27; www.bmbwk.gv.at/hmk), oth-erwise try your luck for a last-minute ticket at the **Burgkapelle box office** (11am-1pm, 3-5pm Fri) for the following Sunday or immediately before mass between 8.15am and 8.45am. Standing room is free and you need to queue by 8.30am to find a place inside the open doors, but you can get a flavour of what's going on from the TV in the foyer. The choir also sings a mixed programme of music in the Musikverein at 4pm on Friday in May, June, September and October. Tickets range from €35 to €48, and can be purchased from **Reise-büro Mondial** (Map pp83-5; ☎ 588 04 141; www.mondial .at; 04, Faulmanngasse 4) and hotels in Vienna.

Theater an der Wien (Map pp83-5; ☎ 588 30 265; www.musicalvienna.at; 06, Linke Wienzeile 6; box office 10am-7pm) Once the host of some monu-mental premier performances, such as Beet-hoven's *Fidelio*, Mozart's *Die Zauberflöte* and Strauss Jnr's *Die Feldermaus*, Theater an der Wien now features musicals.

Volksoper (Map p86; ☎ 514 44 3670; www.volks oper.at; 09, Währinger Strasse 78; box office 8am-6pm Mon-Fri, 9am-noon Sat) This is Vienna's second opera house and features operettas, dance performances and musicals. Standing tickets go for as little as €1, and there is a plethora of discounts and reduced tickets 30 minutes before performances.

Theatre & Dance

Theatrical performances in English can be seen at the **English Theatre** (Map pp83-5; ☎ 402 12 60; www.englishtheatre.at; 08, Josefsgasse 12; box office 10am-5pm Mon-Fri) or the smaller **International Theatre** (Map pp80-2; ☎ 319 62 72; www.international theatre.at; 09, Porzellangasse 8; box office 11am-3pm Mon-Fri, 6-7.30pm on performance days).

Of the German theatres around town, the best to visit is the **Burgtheater** (Map pp83-5; ☎ 514 44-4140; www.burgtheater.at; 01 Dr Karl-Leuger-Ring; box office 8am-6pm Mon-Fri, 9am-noon Sat &

Sun), which has standing tickets for €1.50 and other discounts. Other theatres include **Schauspielhaus** (Map pp80-2; ☎ 317 01 01-18; www .schauspielhaus.at; 09, Porzellangasse 19; box office 3-6pm Mon-Fri, 2 hr before performances) and **Volkstheater** (Map pp83-5; ☎ 524 72 63/4; www.volkstheater.at - in German; 07, Neustiftgasse 1; box office 10am-6pm Mon-Fri Jul & Aug, 10am-performance start Mon-Sat Sep-Jun).

In 2001 Vienna opened its first Dance in-stitution, the **TanzQuartier Wien** (Map pp83-5; ☎ 581 35 91; www.tqw.at; 07, Museumsplatz 1; box office 10am-7pm Mon-Sat). Located in the newly completed MuseumsQuartier, it hosts an array of local and international performances with a strong experimental nature.

Nightclubs

Goodmann (Map pp83-5; ☎ 967 44 15; www.good mann.at; 04, Rechte Wienzeile 23; 4am-10am Mon-Sat) Goodmann must keep the strangest opening hours of any establishment in Vienna, but no one seems to care. This is where clubbers go when the clubs close; most come for a snack (food is served till 8am) before head-ing downstairs to dance till closing.

Roxy (Map pp83-5; ☎ 961 88 00; www.sunshine .at; 04, Operngasse 24; 10pm-late Tue-Sat) Roxy manages to keep pace with Vienna's pro-gressive clubbing scene, and often leads the way. Its tiny dance floor is therefore regu-larly bursting at the seams and the sounds can be a bit of a lucky dip (ranging from garage to jazz and Brazilian).

Volksgarten (Map pp83-5; ☎ 532 42 41; 01, Burgring 1; 8pm-5am) This club attracts a well-dressed crowd, keen to strut their stuff and scan for

---

THE AUTHOR'S CHOICE

Flex (Map pp80-2; ☎ 533 75 25; www.flex.at; 01, Donaukanal, Augartenbrücke; 6pm-4am) So it looks like a complete dive, the stairwell leading from the U-bahn stop to its doors constantly reeks of urine, and the circling dealers are an annoyance, but Flex is still the finest club in town. Time after time this uninhibited shrine to music with one of the best sound systems in Europe puts on great shows and features the top DJs from Vienna and abroad. Each night is a different theme, with Dub Club on Monday and London Call-ing (alternative and indie) on Wednesday among the most popular. Live bands also commonly take the stage.

talent from the long bar. The quality sound system pumps out an array of music styles, which changes from night to night.

U4 (Map pp80-2; ☎ 815 83 07; www.u4club.at; 12, Schönbrunner Strasse 222; ☼ 10pm-late) U4 set the club standard in Vienna for decades, and while it's fallen behind the likes of Flex and Roxy, it still manages to pull loads of eager club-goers.

Live Music

Porgy & Bess (Map pp83-5; ☎ 512 88 11; www.porgy .at; 01, Riemergasse 11; ☼ 8pm-4am Mon-Sat, 7pm-4am Sun) This is the prime location for modern local and international jazz acts, with an atmosphere and interior relaxed and grown up. DJs are a regular feature on weekends and Wednesday nights sees impromptu jam sessions.

WUK (Map p86; ☎ 40 121-0; www.wuk.at; 09, Währinger Strasse 59) WUK is many things to many people. It's basically a space for art and hosts a huge array of events in its concert hall. International and local rock acts vie with clubbing nights, classical concerts, film evenings, theatre and even children's shows.

Szene Wien (Map pp80-2; ☎ 749 33 41; www .szenewien.at; 11, Hauffgasse 26) This intimate venue allows you to get up close and personal with whoever's on stage. Concerts cover a broad spectrum of musical tastes, including rock, reggae, funk, jazz and world music.

Arena (Map pp80-2; ☎ 798 85 95; www.arena.co.at; 03, Baumgasse 80; ☼ 2pm-late summer, 4pm-late winter) Arena normally hosts hard rock, metal and rock, which is well suited to the industrial zone it's located in. This former slaughterhouse also often plays films or holds once-a-month all-night parties; 'Iceberg', a German/British 1970s new wave bash, is particularly popular.

Jazzland (Map pp83-5; ☎ 533 25 75; www.jazz land.at; 01, Franz-Josefs-Kai 29; ☼ 7pm-2am Mon-Sat) Jazzland has been an institution of Vienna's jazz scene for the past 30 years. The music covers the whole jazz spectrum and the brick venue features a grand mixture of local and international acts.

Cinemas

Vienna has a fine mix of cinemas, featuring Hollywood blockbusters to arthouse films and everything in between, in both German and English. *Falter*, *City* and *Der Standard* (daily newspaper) all contain film listings.

Monday is *Kinomontag*, when all seats are discounted.

Artis International (Map p83-5; ☎ 535 65 70; www .cineplexx.at; 01, Schultergasse 5) Mainstream films in English.

Breitenseer Lichtspiele (Map pp80-2; ☎ 982 21 73; 14, Breitenseer Strasse 21) Opened in 1909; still contains the original fittings and plays old black-and-white classics and independent films.

Burg Kino (Map pp83-5; ☎ 587 84 06; www.burg kino.at; 01, Opernring 19) English films; has regular screenings of *The Third Man*.

English Cinema Haydn (Map pp80-2; ☎ 587 22 62; www.haydnkino.at; 06, Mariahilfer Strasse 57) Features mainstream Hollywood-style films in their original language.

Film Casino (Map pp80-2; ☎ 587 90 62; www.film casino.at; 05, Margaretenstrasse 78) Arthouse cinema with a mix of Asian and European independent films.

Österreichische Filmmuseum (Map pp83-5; ☎ 533 70 54; www.filmmuseum.at; 01, Augustinerstrasse 1; ☼ Oct-Jun) Monthly retrospectives on directors or genres.

Votivkino (Map pp83-5; ☎ 317 35 71; www.votiv kino.at; 09, Währinger Strasse 12) Hollywood and art house films in their original language.

Sport

Football is easily the largest spectator sport in Vienna. Catch Rapid and Austria Memphis, Vienna's local teams, at the **Austria Memphis Franz-Horr-Stadion** (Map pp78-9; ☎ 688 01 50; 10, Fischhofgasse 12) and the **Rapid Vienna Gerhard-Hanappi-Stadion** (Map pp78-9; ☎ 914 55 19; 14, Keisslergasse 6). International games are normally played at the **Ernst Happel Stadion** (Map pp80-2; ☎ 728 08 54; 02, Meiereistrasse 7).

Stadthalle (Map p86; ☎ 98 100-0; 15, Vogelweidplatz) hosts a diverse array of events, including tennis, horse shows and ice hockey.

SHOPPING

Vienna is not a place for cheap shopping, but it does offer numerous elegant shops and quality products. Local specialities include porcelain, ceramics, handmade dolls, wrought-iron work and leather goods, and there are many shops selling *Briefmarken* (stamps), *Münze* (coins) and *Altwaren* (second-hand odds and ends).

The city's main shopping street is Mariahilfer Strasse, which features plenty of High St names and masses of people. Kärntner Strasse, the Innere Stadt's main shopping street and a real crowd-puller, is more expensive but the quality of goods is generally better. Other streets worth a look include Josefstädter Strasse, an old-fashioned shopping street filled with quaint shops selling anything from flowers to tea, and Neubaugasse, a second-hand hunter's paradise lined with unusual shops. Shopping City Süd (SCS), to the south of the city, is Vienna's equivalent of a mall.

Antiques

Dorotheum (Map pp83-5; ☎ 515 60-0; www.doro theum.com; 01, Dorotheergasse 17) Founded in 1707 by Joseph I, the Dorotheum ranks among the largest auction houses in Europe. The range of objects up for sale is quite extraordinary, but stick to the categories of art, antiques and collectibles. Expect to find glass, porcelain, contemporary art, furniture, photography, jewellery, coins, posters ... the list goes on. Not everything is priced out of most people's budgets, there are also affordable household ornaments up for grabs.

Glasfabrik (Map pp83-5; ☎ 533 60 26; 01, Habsburgergasse 9; ⏰ 10am-6.30pm Mon-Fri, 10am-5pm Sat) Glasfabrik specialises in antiques dating from 1670 to 1970, so the range on offer is eclectic to say the least.

Ceramics, Glass & Crystal

Woka (Map pp83-5; ☎ 513 29 12; www.woka.at; 01, Singerstrasse 16) Accurate re-creations of Wiener Werkstätte lamps are the hallmark of Woka. In operation since 1977, the firm has faithfully stuck to designs by the likes of Adolf Loos, Koloman Moser and Josef Hoffmann.

J & L Lobmeyr (Map pp83-5; ☎ 512 05 08; www .lobmeyr.com; 01, Kärntner Strasse 26) In business since the beginning of the 19th century supplying the imperial court with glassware, Lobmeyr now focuses on Werkstätten pieces, but the quality still remains.

Österreichische Werkstätten (Map pp83-5; ☎ 512 24 18; www.oew.at; 01, Kärntner Strasse 6) The result of a collaboration of art groups in 1948, the Österreichische Werkstätten supports and creates the production of quality handmade craftwork, including jewellery, glassware and ornaments.

Swarovski (Map pp83-5; ☎ 512 90 32-33; www .swarovski.com; 01, Karntner Strasse 8) Named after the inventor of the unique machine used to cut the beautiful crystal, Swarovski showcases some of the finest crystal jewellery and ornaments.

Porzellan Manufacturer Augarten (Map pp80-2; ☎ 211 24-0; www.augarten.at; 02, Obere Augartenstrasse 1,

Schloss Augarten) Exquisite, albeit very traditional, porcelain ornaments and gifts are produced at this well-established factory. Prices start at around €35 and just keep on going up.

Clothes & Jewellery

Kaufhaus Schiepek (Map pp83-5; ☎ 533 15 75; 01, Teinfaltstrasse 3) If you're looking for cheap, colourful jewellery or beads to create your own, look no further than Kaufhaus Schiepek. The range is extensive and includes glittering bags and purses.

Braun & Co (Map pp83-5; ☎ 512 55 05-0; 01, Graben 8) Braun & Co is possibly the noblest of all the fashion and designer shops in this fair city; in 1911 Franz Josef himself granted the shop the famous k.u.k. (*Kaiserlich und Königlich*; Emperor and Kingly) seal of royal approval.

Helmut Lang (Map pp83-5; ☎ 586 07 73; 01, Seilergasse 6) The premier store of Austria's top designer (there are only six stores worldwide), Helmut Lang stocks fantastic clothes which will empty your wallet.

Loden-Plankl (Map pp83-5; ☎ 533 80 32; 01, Michaelerplatz 6) Loden-Plankl is a specialist in *Trachten*, traditional Austrian wear. It's been in operation for over 170 years, and its *Lederhosen* (leather trousers) and *Dirndl* (traditional women's dress) don't exactly fall within the 'budget' range.

Confectionary

Altmann & Kühne (Map pp83-5; ☎ 533 09 27; 01, Graben 30) Altmann & Kühne have been producing their hand-made bonbons for over 100 years using a well-kept secret recipe. The packaging is designed by Wiener Werkstätten.

Café Sacher (Map pp83-5; ☎ 541 56-661; www .sacher.com; 01, Philharmonikerstrasse 4) The legendary *Sacher Torte* can only be purchased at Café Sacher, or over the Internet if you'd like it delivered to your door.

Demel (Map pp83-5; ☎ 535 17 17; www.demel .at; 01, Kohlmarkt 14) Demel is Sacher's biggest rival, and produces stunning cakes, which are lovingly prepared – and lovingly devoured. Cakes can also be ordered over the Internet.

Manner Fabriksverkauf (Map pp80-2; ☎ 488 22; 17, Wilhelminenstrasse 6) If you only try one sweet or confectionary while in Vienna, then it *has* to be *Manner Schnitten*. This glorious collaboration of wafers and hazelnut cream has been around since 1898 and just gets better with time. The Manner factory shop sells the whole Manner confectionary range, and piles and piles of seconds.

Department Stores

Gerngoss (Map pp83-5; ☎ 521 80; 07, Mariahilfer Strasse 38-40) Five floors of shops at Gerngoss cover most shopping genres although the selection is very mainstream.

Steffl (Map pp83-5; ☎ 514 31; 01, Kärntner Strasse 19) Steffl is the most upmarket of Vienna's department stores, filled with designer labels and cosmetics.

Lingerie

Palmers (Map pp83-5; ☎ 512 57 72; 01, Kärntner Strasse 53-55) Palmers is easily the Queen of Lingerie in Austria. This home-grown industry leader seems to have a store (or two or three) on every major shopping street, which makes you wonder how big the average Viennese top draw is.

Boutique Charme (Map pp83-5; ☎ 512 91 39; 01, Operngasse 2) Well placed between the Staatsoper and the Albertina is this shrine to the delicate creations of La Perla. Lacy bras, stockings, nighties, suspenders, accessories – it's all here.

Markets

Flohmarkt (flea market; Map pp80-2; 05, Kettenbrücken-gasse; ☽ dawn-5pm Sat) This atmospheric flea market, in the mould of an Eastern European market, shouldn't be missed, with goods piled up in apparent chaos on the walkway. You can find anything you want (and everything you don't want): books, clothes, records, ancient electrical goods, old postcards, ornaments, carpets … you name it. Bargain for prices here.

From around the middle of November, *Christkindlmärkte* (Christmas Markets) start to pop up all over Vienna. Ranging from kitsch to quaint in style and atmosphere, the markets all have a few things in common: plenty of people, loads of Christmas gifts to purchase, mugs of *Glühwein* (mulled wine) and hot-plates loaded down with *Kartoffelpuffer* (hot potato patties) and *Maroni* (roasted chestnuts). Most close a day or two before Christmas day. Some of the best include:

Freyung market (Map pp83-5) Austrian arts and crafts and an old-worldly feel.

Heiligenkreuzerhof market (Map pp83-5) Oft-forgotten market which is arguably the most authentic and quaint of all the *Chrsitkindlmärkte*.

Karlsplatz market (Map pp83-5) Mainly sells arty gifts and is situated close to the Karlskirche.

Rathausplatz market (Map pp83-5) Easily the biggest and most touristy Christmas market in Vienna, held on the square in front of the Rathaus, but most of the Christmas gifts on sale are kitschy beyond belief unfortunately.

Schönbrunn market (Map pp80-2) Circle of upmarket stalls, loads of events for the kids and daily classical concerts at 6pm (more on weekends).

Spittalberg market (Map pp83-5) Traditional market occupying the charming cobblestone streets of the Spittalberg quarter. Stalls sell quality arts and crafts, but not at the cheapest prices.

Music

Black Market (Map pp83-5; ☎ 533 76 17-0; 01, Gonzagagasse 9) This is Vienna's house, techno and electronic specialist. The vinyl selection is enormous and the staff are highly knowledgeable.

Rave Up (Map pp80-2; ☎ 596 96 50; 06, Hofmühlgasse 1) Friendly staff, loads of vinyl and a massive collection covering every genre of music in the world makes a trip to Rave Up a real pleasure.

Teuchtler (Map pp83-5; ☎ 586 21 33; 06, Windmühlgasse 10) This second-hand shop buys, sells and exchanges records and CDs, including rare and discontinued titles.

Photography

Lomoshop (Map pp83-5; ☎ 523 70 16; 07, Museumsplatz 1) What began in the '80s as a bit of fun for a handful of Lomo fanatics in Vienna has now turned into a worldwide cult, and the Lomoshop is considered the very heart of the global Lomo movement. Here you'll find Lomo cameras, gadgets and accessories for sale, including original Russian-made Lomos.

Orator (Map p86; ☎ 526 10 10-0; 07, Westbahnstrasse 23) Orator is one of a handful of specialist photography shops at the western end of Westbahnstrasse. Their range of digital, SLR, lense and second-hand stock is quite impressive.

Wine

Wien & Co (☎ 535 09 16; www.weinco.at; 01, Jasomirgottstrasse 3-5) Wein & Co is arguably the best place to buy wine in Vienna; prices are extremely competitive, the selection hard to

VIENNA

beat and the concentration of New World wines is impressive.

Unger und Klein (Map pp83-5; ☎ 532 13 23; 01, Gölsdorfgasse 2) Austrian wines make a great show at this wine bar/shop, with the best the country has to offer – whether expensive boutique varieties or bargain-bin bottles.

GETTING THERE & AWAY
Air

Vienna is the main centre for international flights. Up to four flights run daily from Graz (from €88 return) and Salzburg (from €88 return) and five from Klagenfurt (from €88 return), Linz (from €88 return) and Innsbruck (from €120 return). See p362 for more information.

Boat

Steamers head west (mostly from Krems) and fast hydrofoils head east – see p366 and p130.

Bus

Vienna currently has no central bus station and national Bundesbuses arrive and depart from several different locations, depending on the destination – many routes south (eg Eisenstadt) go from Südtiroler Platz. For information, call ☎ 711 01 (☼ 7am to 8pm).

Car & Motorcycle

All the major car rental companies are represented in Vienna.

Avis (Map pp83-5; ☎ 7007 32700; www.avis.at; 01, Opernring 3-5; ☼ 7am-6pm Mon-Fri, 8am-2pm Sat, 8am-1pm Sun)

Denzeldrive (Map pp80-2; ☎ 897 55 28; www .denzeldrive.at; 15, Europlatz (Westbahnhof); ☼ 8am-8pm Mon-Fri, 8am-2pm Sat)

Europcar (Map pp83-5; ☎ 714 67 17; www.europcar .at; 01, Schubertring 9; ☼ 7.30am-6pm Mon-Fri, 8am-1pm Sat, 8am-noon Sun)

Hertz (Map pp83-5; ☎ 512 86 77; www.hertz.at; 01, Kärntner Ring 17; ☼ 7.30am-6pm Mon-Fri, 9am-3pm Sat & Sun)

Train

Vienna has excellent rail connections with Europe and the rest of Austria. Not all destinations are served by one station, and schedules are subject to change. The following stations (except Meidling) have lockers, currency exchange, *Bankomats* and places to eat and buy provisions for your journey.

WESTBAHNHOF

Trains to the west and north depart from Westbahnhof. Half-hourly services head to Salzburg (€36.50, three hours); four continue onto Munich (€63.10, 4½ hours). Three daily direct trains run to Zürich (€77.90, nine hours), four travel to Frankfurt (€92, seven hours) and six to Budapest (from €19, 2¾ hours). Westbahnhof is on U-Bahn lines U3 and U6, and many trams stop outside.

SÜDBAHNHOF

From Südbahnhof trains travel to Italy, the Czech Republic, Slovakia, Hungary and Poland. One direct train daily leaves for Rome (€109, 13½ hours; via Klagenfurt, Venice and Florence); more services require a change at Venice. Hourly trains go to Bratislava (€16, one hour), five a day to Prague (€42, 4½ hours) and one daily heads for Berlin (€90, 9¾ hours).

Trams D (to the Ring and Franz Josefs Bahnhof) and O (to Wien Mitte and Praterstern) stop outside. Transfer to Westbahnhof in about 20 minutes by taking tram No 18, or the S-Bahn to Meidling and then the U6.

FRANZ JOSEFS BAHNHOF

This handles regional and local trains, including to Tulln (p138), Krems an der Donau (p137), and the Wachau region. From outside, tram D goes to the Ring, and tram No 5 goes to Westbahnhof (via Kaiserstrasse) in one direction and Praterstern (Wien Nord) in the other.

OTHER STATIONS

Smaller stations include Wien Mitte (Map pp83-5), Wien Nord (Map pp80-2) and Meidling (Map pp80-2). All have U-Bahn stops and the former two have connections to the airport.

GETTING AROUND
To/From the Airport

Getting to/from the airport is possible using the following transport options:

Bus Link (☎ 05 17 17; www.oebb.at; one-way/return €5.80/10.90, child under 6 free, child 6-15 €2.90/5.40; from Westbahnhof ☼ 5.30am-11pm, from Wien-Mitte ☼ 4.30am-12.30am, every 20-30 min) The Westbahnhof service calls in at Wien Südbahnhof station; the Wien-Mitte service is direct.

C&K Airport Service (☎ 444 44; one-way €22) C&K car service is a better and cheaper option than a taxi as its rates are fixed. On arrival at the airport, head to its stand to the left of the exit hall; when leaving Vienna, call ahead to make a reservation.

City Airport Train (☎ 252 50; www.cityairporttrain.com; return adult/child up to 15 €15/free; ◷ 5.37am-11.07pm, every 30 min) Departs from Wien-Mitte; luggage check-in facilities and boarding card issuing service.

Schnellbahn 7 (☎ 05 17 17; www.oebb.at; one-way €3, with city transport passes €1.50; ◷ 4.35am-9.39pm Mon-Sat, every 30 min) Cheapest way to get to the airport; departs from Wien Nord and passes through Wien-Mitte.

Buses run between MR Stefánika airport in Slovakia and Schwechat seven times daily; a return fare costs €14.30.

Bicycle

Over 700km of cycle tracks crisscross Vienna, making it a great city to get around by bicycle. Bikes can be rented from **Pedal Power** (Map pp80-2; 1hr/half-/full-day rental €5/17/27; ◷ 8am-7pm Apr-Oct) or from **Vienna City Bike** (☎ 0810-50 05 00; www.citybikewien.at; 1st hr free, 2nd hr €1, 3rd hr €2, 4th hr €4), which has blue and yellow bike racks across the city. Unfortunately only an Austrian bank card or city bike card can be used to rent bikes; the latter is available from **Royal Tours** (01, Herrengasse 1-3; ◷ 9-11.30am & 1-6pm) for €2 per day. But make sure you don't lose the bike, or €600 will be deducted from your card.

Bicycles can be carried on carriages marked with a bike symbol on the S-Bahn and U-Bahn (9am to 3pm and after 6.30pm Monday to Friday, after 9am Saturday, and all day Sunday) for half the adult fare. It's not possible to take bikes on trams and buses.

Car & Motorcycle

You're better off using the excellent public transport system in Vienna. The city administrators have a penchant for one-way streets, the Viennese are particularly impatient drivers and parking is difficult and/or expensive in the centre. Most Viennese themselves completely avoid driving in the Innere Stadt because of its notorious one-way system.

If you do plan to drive in the city, take special care of the trams; they always have priority and vehicles must wait behind trams when they stop to pick up or set down passengers.

Districts one to nine and 20 are pay zones and display *Kurzparkzone* (short-stay parking zones) where a *Parkschein* (parking voucher) is required. These come in 30-/60-/90-minute lots (€0.40/0.80/1.20) and can be purchased from most *Tabaks* (tobacconist shops), banks, train stations and Wiener Linien ticket offices. A free 10-minute voucher is also available. To validate a voucher, just cross out the appropriate time, date and year and display it on your dashboard.

Public Transport

Vienna has a comprehensive and unified public transport network that is one of the most efficient in Europe. Flat-fare tickets are valid for trains, trams, buses, the underground (U-Bahn) and the S-Bahn regional trains. Services are frequent, and you will rarely have to wait more than five or 10 minutes.

Public transport kicks off around 5am or 6am. Buses and trams finish between 11pm and midnight, and S-Bahn and U-Bahn services between 12.30am and 1am. Twenty-one Nightline bus routes crisscross the city from 12.30am to 5am. Schwedenplatz, Schottentor and the Oper are starting points for many services; look for buses and bus stops marked with an 'N'. All tickets are valid for Nightline services.

Transport maps are posted in all U-Bahn stations and at many bus and tram stops. Free maps and information pamphlets are available from **Wiener Linien** (☎ 7909 105; www .wienerlinien.at; information line ◷ 6am-10pm Mon-Fri, 8.30am-4.30pm Sat & Sun), located in 25 U-Bahn stations. The Karlsplatz, Stephansplatz and Westbahnhof information offices are open from 6.30am to 6.30pm Monday to Friday and 8.30am to 4pm Saturday and Sunday. Those at Floridsdorf, Spittelau, Praterstern, Philadelphiabrücke, Landstrasse and Volkstheater are closed on weekends.

TICKETS & PASSES

Tickets and passes can be purchased at U-Bahn stations – from automatic machines (with English instructions and change) and occasionally-staffed ticket offices – and in *Tabaks*. Once bought, tickets need to be validated before starting your journey (except for weekly and monthly tickets); look for small blue boxes at the entrance to U-Bahn stations and on buses and trams. Just pop the end of the ticket in the slot and wait for the 'ding'. It's an honour system and ticket inspection is infrequent, but if you're caught without a ticket you'll be fined €62, no exceptions.

Tickets and passes are as follows:

8-Tage-Karte (Eight-day Ticket) €24, valid for eight days, but not necessarily eight consecutive days; punch the card as and when you need it

"24-Stunden Wien" -Karte (24-Hour Ticket) €5; 24 hours unlimited travel from time of validation.

Die Wien-Karte (The Vienna Card) see p90.

Fahrschein (Single Ticket) €1.50, good for one journey, with line changes; costs €2 if purchased on trams and buses (correct change required).

Monatskarte (Monthly Ticket) €45, valid from the 1st of the month to the last day of the month.

Streifenkarte (Strip Ticket) €6; four single tickets on one strip.

Wiener Einkaufskarte (Vienna Shopping Card) €4, for use between 8am and 8pm Monday to Saturday; only good for one day after validation.

Wochenkarte (Weekly Ticket) €12.50, valid Monday to Sunday.

Children aged six to 15 travel for half-price, or for free on Sunday, public holidays and during Vienna school holidays (photo ID necessary); younger children always travel free. Senior citizens (women over 60, men over 65) can buy a €2 ticket that is valid for two trips; inquire at transport information offices.

Taxi

Taxis are reliable and relatively cheap by West European standards. City journeys are metered; flagfall costs €2.50 from 6am to 11pm Monday to Saturday and €2.60 any other time, plus a small per kilometre fee. A small tip is expected; add on about 10% to the fare. Taxis are easily found at train stations and stands all over the city, or just flag them down in the street. To order one call ☎ 31 300, ☎ 60 160, ☎ 40 100 or ☎ 81 400. Don't count on taxis taking credit cards.

AROUND VIENNA

KLOSTERNEUBURG

Realistically, much of Lower Austria can be visited as a day trip from Vienna. Klosterneuburg, a small town only 12km north of the Innere Stadt, is one exception; it's an easy half-day trip.

Without doubt the biggest attraction is Klosterneuburg's **Augustinian Abbey** (☎ 02243-411 212; www.stift-klosterneuburg.at; Stiftplatz 1, Klosterneuberg; adult/concession & child €5.50/3.20; ☺ 10am-5pm Tue-Sun May–mid-Nov). Founded in 1114, the abbey's baroque facelift didn't begin until 1730, and wasn't completed until 1842. The plans actually called for something much more grand, but fortunately these were not realised, leaving large sections intact in their original medieval style. The abbey's museum is an eclectic mix of religious art from the Middle Ages to the present, but you're better off including a guided tour on your itinerary, which takes in the cloister and the church (tours in English require advanced notice). The tour's highlight is the **Verdun Altar** in St Leopold's Chapel, an annexe of the church. Made in 1181 by Nicholas of Verdun, it is an unsurpassed example of medieval enamel work and is gloriously adorned with 51 enamelled panels showing biblical scenes.

Not far from the abbey, but light years away in its displays, is **Sammlung Essl** (☎ 0800-232 800; www.sammlung-essl.at; Kunst Der Gegenwart, An der Donau-Au 1, Klosterneuburg; adult/concession/child €6.50/5/4, free Wed 7-9pm only; ☺ 10am-7pm Tue-Sun, 10am-9pm Wed). This gallery houses the extensive contemporary art collection of the Essl family, and includes the likes of Gerhad Richter, Hermann Nitsch, Georg Baselitz and Elke Krystufek.

Getting There & Away

Klosterneuburg is on the S-Bahn route from Vienna (Franz-Josef-Bahnhof) to Tulln. Klosterneuburg-Kierling is the station closest to the abbey (€4.10; 15 minutes; every 30 minutes).

Lower Austria

Bordering Vienna on all sides is Lower Austria (Niederösterreich), Austria's largest province and Vienna's gargantuan outdoor playground. Historically overshadowed by the country's capital, it seems the tourist board is happy to stick with the status quo; tourist literature proudly proclaims Lower Austria as 'The Land Round Vienna'.

But this is a province with enough going for it to warrant a change in marketing strategy. It's a region of changing landscapes; to the north you'll find a veritable Garden of Eden, where cultivated pastures, forested glens and vineyards intermingle on the slopes of gentle rolling hills. To the south you'll see what many tourists come to Austria for: mountains. They're not as impressive as those to the west, but the highest climb over the 2000m mark.

Carving Lower Austria in two is the mighty Danube (Donau). Long ago its winding path created the Danube Valley, the region's premiere attraction. This is a place of supreme natural beauty and human endeavour; the Wachau, which stretches from Melk to Krems an der Donau, is arguably the prettiest section along the entire length of the Danube and is justly praised for its wines, castles, abbeys and medieval villages.

St Pölten, Lower Austria's largest town, is at first glance nothing special, but it's come a long way since it became the provincial capital in 1986. Once a sleepy backwater town, it can now lay claim to an excellent *Landesmuseum* (provincial museum) and some progressive architecture.

South of Vienna are more historic settlements and vineyards. The spa town of Baden bei Wien can trace its roots back to the Romans, who craved its curative waters. Semmering and Schneeberg (2076m), the first a health resort and the second Lower Austria's highest peak, are both within striking distance of Vienna and offer hiking, skiing and plenty of fresh air.

HIGHLIGHTS

- Exploring the historical **Danube Valley** (p130) by train, boat or bicycle

- Meandering through **Stift Melk** (p131), a magnificent baroque monastery on the banks of the Danube

- Appeasing the palate at one of the multitude of *Heurigen* (wine taverns) in **Krems an der Donau** (p136) or **Dürnstein** (p134)

- Riding the **Semmering railway** (p151), a remarkable engineering feat and Unesco World Heritage site

- Travelling by 'Salamander' train or cogwheel steam-engine to the top of **Schneeberg** (p152), Lower Austria's highest peak

- POPULATION: 1,544,000 ■ AREA: 19,178 SQ KM ■ HIGHEST ELEVATION: SCHNEEBERG 2076M

History

The inhabitation of Lower Austria can be traced back to prehistoric times; some of the earliest archaeological finds in Europe, such as the 25,000-year-old *Venus of Willendorf* (p43), come from the region. The Romans thought quite a bit of Lower Austria, particularly the area south of the Danube, and built fortifications at Ybbs, Melk, Mautern and Carnuntum (p143).

Lower Austria's borders were not truly defined until well into the 13th century under Babenberg rule, but it wasn't long (1278) before the region fell to the Habsburgs. Lower Austria's flat plains to the north were a favourite of marauding foreigners; it was often overrun with Bohemian Hussites in the early 15th century, the Turks in the 16th century and the Swedes during the Thirty Years War. Things quietened down after the threat of the Turks dissipated and Lower Austria prospered through its fertile soil.

After WWII, the region lay in the hands of the Russians, and once again suffered. With the creation of an independent Austria in 1955, however, the situation improved, but it wasn't until 1986 that Lower Austria gained its own provincial capital, St Pölten (Vienna had played the role until then).

Climate

Lower Austria has a mix of climates; to the north and east you'll find a Pannonian climate and to the south more alpine weather,

LOWER AUSTRIA

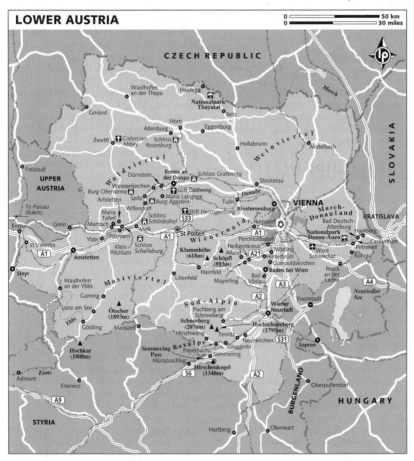

with rapid changes in temperature common. The Danube Valley is marked by a continental climate.

Getting There & Away

Much of Lower Austria has great connections to the rest of Austria. The A1 autobahn, running from Upper Austria to Vienna, splits the province into two unequal halves to the south of the Danube (which also connects Upper Austria and Vienna by boat). The A2 runs south from Vienna to Graz through its lower region; off this branches the A3 towards Eisenstadt and Hungary and the S6 to northern Styria. Passing through Lower Austria's eastern fringe is the A4, which links Vienna with northern Burgenland and eventually Budapest.

Shadowing most of the major roads is an extensive rail system.

Getting Around

Without your own wheels, the best way to get around Lower Austria is by train. Due to the region's relatively flat landscape, it has the best connections of any province in Austria. Well-maintained autobahn and *Bundesstrasse* (alternative routes) make it simple and safe to explore the entire region by car.

THE DANUBE VALLEY

The Danube, which enters Lower Austria from the west near Ybbs and exits in the east at Bratislava, Slovakia's capital, carves a winding path through the province's hills and fields. The stretch of river between Ybbs and Tulln, a historic town 30km west of Vienna, is known as the Danube Valley, which scenically peaks in the Wachau, a section between Krems and Melk. Here the landscape is characterised by vineyards, forested slopes, wine-producing villages and imposing fortresses at nearly every bend. In 2000 the Wachau became a World Heritage site due to its harmonious mix of natural and man-made beauty.

Tourismusverband Wachau-Nibelungengau (☎ 02713-300 6015; www.wachau.at; Schlossgasse 3, Spitt an der Donau; ☻ 8am-4.30pm Mon-Thu, 8am-2.30pm Fri) can help with information on the Wachau and its surrounds.

This section covers the main Danube Valley attractions from west to east.

Getting Around

A popular way of exploring the region is by boat, particularly between Melk and Krems, but it's also possible to travel from Passau to Vienna; see p174 for more details. The most popular time to take a boat trip on the Danube is between May and September, when a number of companies compete for tourist euros.

DDSG Blue Danube (☎ 01-588 80; www.ddsg-blue danube.at; 01, Friedrichstrasse 7, Vienna; Vienna-Dürnstein one-way/return €19/25, Melk-Krems one-way/return €15.80/20.50, Melk-Spitz & Spitz-Krems one-way/return €9.20/12.20) operates steamers between Melk and Krems, Spitz and Melk or Spitz and Krems from early April to October, up to three times daily, and between Vienna and Dürnstein every Sunday from May till September.

Brandner (☎ 07433-25 90-25; www.brandner.at; Ufer 50, Wallsee) offers the same services as DDSG for around the same price, but only puts on two boats daily mid-April to late October.

More popular is exploring the region by bicycle. A wonderfully flat cycle path runs along both sides of the Danube from Vienna to Melk, passing through Krems, Dürnstein, Weissenkirchen and Spitz (these are all on the northern bank). Many hotels and pensions (B&Bs) are geared towards cyclists, and most towns have at least one bike-rental shop. For more information pick up a copy of *The Donauradweg – Von Passau bis Bratislava*, which provides details of distances, hotels and information offices along the route.

Roads hug the contours of the Danube between Melk and Krems. Note that there are no bridges crossing the river between the two and the handful of ferries, for instance between Rossatz and Dürnstein, normally only take passengers and bicycles. A rail track runs along the Danube's northern bank and while it's a scenic trip, it's quite slow.

MELK

☎ 02752 / pop 6500

Nothing prepares you for the sheer size and majesty of the imposing abbey-fortress of Melk, which rises above the Danube and the small town. It's an essential stop along the Danube Valley route, but it may not be as rewarding as other abbeys across the country, simply due to the bus-loads of tourists you'll have to fight through to explore the place. Don't neglect the town itself, with its pretty *Platz* (town square) and cobblestone streets.

Orientation & Information

The train station is 300m south of Rathausplatz, the town centre. From the station, take Bahnhofstrasse directly north until it turns into Bahngasse, which leads directly to the *Platz*. The post office is halfway up Bahnhofstrasse.

The **tourist office** (☎ 523 07-410; www.tiscover .com/melk - in German; Babenbergerstrasse 1; ☻ 9am-7pm Mon-Sat, 10am-2pm Sun Apr-Oct, 9am-noon & 2-6pm Mon-Fri, 10am-2pm Sat Nov-Mar) is east of Rathausplatz, as are a couple of *Bankomats* (ATMs).

Stift Melk

Of the plethora of abbeys across the length and breadth of Austria, **Stift Melk** (Benedictine Abbey of Melk; ☎ 555-232; www.stiftmelk.at; Abt Berthold Dietmayr Strasse 1; adult/student/family €6.90/4.10/13.50, with guided tour €8.50/5.70/16.70; ☻ 9am-6pm Mar-Sep, 9am-5pm Apr & Oct) is the best known, possibly because of its location near the A1 autobahn between Vienna and Salzburg.

This however takes nothing away from the complex, which is a classic example of baroque architecture. Historically, Melk was of great importance to both the Romans and the Babenbergs, who built a castle here. In 1089 the Babenberg margrave Leopold II donated the castle to Benedictine monks, who converted it into a fortified abbey. Fire destroyed the original edifice, which was completely rebuilt between 1702 and 1738 according to plans by Jakob Prandtauer and his follower, Josef Munggenast.

The huge **monastery church** is enclosed by the buildings, but still dominates the complex with its twin spires and high octagonal dome. The inside is baroque gone mad, with endless prancing angels and gold twirls, but is still extremely impressive. The theatrical high altar scene, depicting St Peter and St Paul (the two patron saints of the church), is by Peter Widerin. Johann Michael Rottmayr did most of the ceiling paintings, including those in the dome.

Other highlights include the **library** and the **mirror room**; both have painted tiers on the ceiling (by Paul Troger) to give the illusion of greater height. The ceilings are slightly curved to aid the effect. **Imperial rooms**, where various dignitaries stayed (including Napoleon), contain museum exhibits.

During winter, the monastery can only be visited by guided tour. Even in summer, phone ahead to ensure you get an English-language tour.

Old Town Centre

While the old town suffers under the huge weight of tourists during summer, it's still a pleasant place to spend an hour or two wandering its cobblestone streets. Most buildings date from the 16th and 17th centuries; don't miss the excellent façade of the **Altes Posthaus** (Old Posthouse; Linzer Strasse 3-5), with its animals and farming tools. The popularity of the Danube cycle trail is nowhere more apparent than in Melk; there are easily more bike racks than car parks around the old town centre.

Sleeping & Eating

The tourist office accommodation leaflet lists inexpensive private rooms, most of which are away from the centre of town.

Gasthof Goldener Stern (☎ 522 14; Sterngasse 17; s/d from €25/42; ℗) Even though Stern is very central, it still has a quiet and secluded atmosphere, due to its high position above the main square and homely décor. Rooms are individually decorated and a good size. There is also a fine restaurant on site.

Gasthof zum Goldenen Hirschen (☎ 552 57; Rathausplatz 13; s/d €32/50; ℗) This 16th-century house has pleasant but compact rooms right on the main square (ask for a room at the back if you're sensitive to noise). Its restaurant, **Rathauskeller** (mains €6-12), has Austrian food and outdoor tables.

Stadt Melk (☎ 525 47; hotel.stadtmelk@netway.at; Hauptplatz 1; s/d from €50/72; ℗) This three-star place has stylish, modern-style rooms complete with balcony, but the service can sometimes be a little stiff. The **restaurant** (mains €12-20) is gourmet quality, and the proprietor maintains an extensive wine cellar – the wine menu is as thick as a book!

Tom's Restaurant (☎ 524 75; Hauptplatz 1; mains €10-20; ☻ lunch & dinner) Tom's is a relaxed yet refined dining experience in the heart of town.

The town also sports a **camping ground** (☎ 532 91; Kolomaniau 3; camp sites per person/tent €3.75/2.75; ℗) right on the Danube, a **Jugendherberge** (☎ 526 81; melk@noejhw.at; Abt Karl Strasse 42; dm €16.20; ℗) HI hostel which is 10 minutes' walk east of the station, and a **Spar** (Rathausplatz 9) supermarket.

LOWER AUSTRIA

Getting There & Away

Boats leave from the canal by Pionierstrasse, 400m north of the abbey; see p130 for more information. Seven trains daily travel direct to Melk from Vienna's Westbahnhof (€13.90, 1¼ hours); others require a change at St Pölten.

WEST OF MELK

The stretch of the river from Melk to Ybbs is known as the Nibelungengau, after the medieval epic poem, the *Nibelungenlied*, which was mostly set in these parts (see p43). On the northern bank, some 20km from Melk, is the pilgrimage church of **Maria Taferl** (☎ 07413-278; Maria Taferl 1; admission free; ☯ 7am-7pm) high above the Danube Valley. Created by Jakob Prandtauer (of Melk fame), this baroque church is notable for its two onion domes and dark dome-frescoes. Its altar is a complicated array of figures in gold. Because of its fixed position on the tourist trail from Vienna to Salzburg, the town around the church has a number of pensions and restaurants, most of which sport fine views of the valley below.

About 5km northeast of Maria Taferl, taking minor roads, is **Artstetten** (☎ 07413-83 02; Artstetten 1; adult/senior/student/child €6.20/5.50/4.70/3.60; ☯ 9am-5.30pm Apr-Oct), unusual for its many onion domes. The castle has endured a plethora of modifications over the past 700 years but gained fame through a former owner, the one and only Archduke Franz Ferdinand. Inside is a museum devoted to the luckless heir, which displays photos and stories of his and his wife's time at the castle and their fateful trip to Sarajevo. Their tomb is in the church.

Without your own transport, getting to either Artstetten or Maria Taferl is a bit of a headache unless you're happy to walk the few kilometres uphill from the train station at Klein Pöchlarn or Marbach respectively. Only one direct bus calls at both villages from Melk (9.50am Monday to Friday).

SCHLOSS SCHALLABURG

A splendid Renaissance castle-cum-palace, **Schloss Schallaburg** (☎ 02754-6317; www.schallaburg .at; Schallaburg 1; adult/senior/student/family €7/5/3/14; ☯ 9am-5pm Mon-Fri, 9am-6pm Sat & Sun May-Oct), 5km south of Melk, is one of the highlights of a region packed with gems. Just beyond the entranceway is the castle's architectural centrepiece, a two-storey arcaded Renaissance courtyard with magnificent terracotta arches and rich red-brown carvings that cry out to be photographed. There are some 400 terracotta images, completed between 1572 and 1573; the largest figures support the upper-storey arches, of which the court jester sniggering in the corner is the most intriguing. Below these are pictorial scenes and a series of mythological figures and masks. Annually the castle hosts a prestigious exhibition – in past years artwork from Tibet, Egypt and the Habsburgs has been shown. Combined tickets with nearby attractions which change yearly are usually on offer.

There's an excellent mid-range restaurant in the castle and irregular buses journey from Melk to Schallaburg (€1.90, 10 minutes).

MELK TO DÜRNSTEIN

The stretch of river between Melk and Dürnstein is hard to beat scenery-wise; the steep hills enclosing the Danube are often topped with castles (both in use or lying in ruin) while their lower reaches are covered with vineyards, fruit orchards and pretty villages.

Most of the attractions here are located on the north bank of the Danube, but a couple are to be found on the south. **Schloss Schönbühel** (admission free; ☯ dawn-dusk), a 12th-century castle standing high on a rock some 5km northeast of Melk, officially marks the beginning of the Wachau region.

A further 10km on and the ruins of **Burg Aggstein** (admission €2; ☯ dawn-dusk) soon swing into view. Another 12th-century castle, Burg Aggstein was built by the Kuenringer family and now offers a grand vista of the Danube far below. Both castles, or 'robber barons' as they were once known, are said to have imprisoned their enemies on a ledge of rock (the Rosengärtlein), where the hapless captives faced starvation (unless they opted for a quicker demise by throwing themselves into the abyss below). From Burg Aggstein it's a further 25km to Krems, either along the river or via winding back roads; the back roads allow you to take in the baroque church at **Maria Langegg**, known for its impressive ceiling frescoes.

Heading northeast along the northern bank from Melk, the small village of **Willendorf** soon appears, where a 25,000-year-old sandstone statuette of Venus was discovered (see the boxed text 'The Venus of Willendorf' p43). A further 5km brings **Spitz** into view, a peaceful village surrounded by vineyards and lined with quiet, cobblestoned streets. Its Gothic **parish church** (☎ 02713-2231; Kirchenplatz; ☼ 8am-6pm) is unusual for its chancel, which is out of line with the main body of the church. Other noteworthy features are the 15th-century statues of the 12 apostles lining the organ loft; most wear an enigmatic expression, as if being tempted by an unseen spirit to overindulge in the communion wine. Nearby, the Tausendeimerberg hill is so-named for its reputed ability to yield a thousand buckets of wine per season. The town's **tourist office** (☎ 02713-23 63; info@spitz-wachau.at; Mittergasse 3a; ☼ 10am-1pm & 2-8pm Mon-Sat, 2-6pm Sun Easter-Oct, 2-4pm Mon-Fri Nov-Easter) can provide information about accommodation, but consider treating yourself to a night in **Burg Oberranna** (☎ 02713-82 21; burg-oberranna@aon.at; s/d €66/102; tours Sat & Sun €2; P), 6km west of Spitz in Mühldorf. Surrounded by woods, this solid castle overlooking the valley is furnished with period pieces and has a refreshing old-worldly feel.

Six kilometres further along the north bank is **Weissenkirchen**. Its centrepiece is a hilltop fortified **parish church** (☎ 02715-2203; Weissenkirchen 3; ☼ 8am-7pm Easter-Oct, 8am-5pm Sat & Sun Nov-Easter), whose front doors are approached by a labyrinth of covered pathways. This Gothic church was built in the 15th century and has a baroque altar and a peaceful garden terrace which provides good views of the Danube. Below the church is the charming **Teisenhoferhof** arcaded courtyard, with a covered gallery and lashings of flowers and dried corn. The **Wachau Museum** (☎ 02715-2268; Weissenkirchen 32; adult/child €2.20/1.10; ☼ 10am-5pm Tue-Sun Apr-Oct) is here, containing work by artists of the Danube school. Close to the river is the **Raffelsberger Hof** (☎ 02715-22 01; raffelsberger@nextra.at; s/d from €62/98; P), a four-star hotel in a small but beautifully renovated Renaissance castle (severe flooding in 2002 destroyed many of the fittings).

From Weissenkrichen, it's only 6km to Dürnstein.

Getting There & Away

All scheduled boats (see p130) stop at Spitz, but only the westward Brandner boats call at Weissenkirchen. By train, Spitz (€4.10, 30 minutes) and Weissenkrichen (€4.10, 20 minutes) are best approached from Krems; services from Melk usually require at least one change.

Buses to Schönbühel and Aggstein from Melk are almost non existent; you're better off hiring a bike. Bikes can be hired from **Hotel zur Post** (☎ 2752-523 45; Linzer Straße 1; per half/full day €7/10).

DÜRNSTEIN

☎ 02711 / pop 1000

The pretty town of Dürnstein, on a curve in the Danube, is not only noted for its beautiful buildings but also the castle above the town which at one time imprisoned Richard I (the Lionheart) of England.

Orientation & Information

The train station and **tourist office** (☎ 200; Dürnstein Bahnhof; ☼ 1-7pm Mon, Thu & Fri, 11am-7pm Sat & Sun mid-Apr–Oct) are about five minutes' walk east of Hauptstrasse, the town's main street. The **Rathaus** (town hall; ☎ 219; Hauptstrasse 25; ☼ 8am-noon & 1.30-4pm Mon-Fri), near the heart of the town, also offers information.

The boat-landing stage is below the dominating feature of the village centre, the blue-and-white parish church.

Sights

Kuenringerburg, the castle high on the hill above the town, is easily the most photographed castle in the Wachau – not because of its incredible beauty or dominating position (which isn't bad in both respects), but because it was here, between 1192 and 1193, that Richard the Lionheart was incarcerated. His crime was to have insulted Leopold V; his misfortune was to be recognised despite his disguise when journeying through Austria on his way home from the Holy Lands; his liberty was achieved only upon the payment of an enormous ransom of 35,000kg of silver (which partly funded the building of Wiener Neustadt). It was here that the singing minstrel Blondel attempted to rescue his sovereign. There's not a lot to see but a bunch of rubble, but the view is worth the 15- to 20-minute climb.

Of the picturesque 16th-century houses and other prominent buildings lining Dürnstein's streets, the meticulously restored **Chorherrenstift** (☎ 375; Stiftshof; admission €2.20; ☼ 9am-6pm Apr-Oct) is the most impressive. It's all that remains of the former Augustinian monastery that was founded in 1410; it received its baroque facelift in the 18th century (overseen by Josef Munggenast, among others). The exterior has plenty of saints and angels adopting pious poses on and around the pristine blue-and-white steeple; the interior combines white stucco and dark wood balconies. Kremser Schmidt did many of the ceiling and altar paintings. Entry includes access to the porch overlooking the Danube and an exhibition on the Augustinian monks who once ruled the roost here (up until the monastery was dissolved by Joseph II in 1788).

Sleeping & Eating

The tourist office can supply a list of private rooms, pensions and *Gasthöfe* (inns with accommodation) in Dürnstein and neighbouring Oberloiben and Unterloiben.

Pension Böhmer (☎ 239; pension.boehmer@i-one .at; Hauptstrasse 22; s/d €30/40) Right in the heart of the town is this pension/wine shop, with comfy, newly renovated rooms.

Hotel Sänger Blondel (☎ 253; www.saengerblondel .at; Klosterplatz; s/d €61/85; P) Even more central and luxurious is Blondel, a traditionally furnished hotel with good-sized rooms and a fine tree-shaded garden where **meals** (mains €7-15) are served.

Pension Altes Rathaus (☎ 252; pension.fuertler@ duernstein.at; Hauptstrasse 26; r €42-60) This quiet pension with large rooms occupies a lovely 16th-century building; it's reached through an attractive courtyard.

Goldener Strauss (☎ 267; Hauptstrasse 18; mains €6-10; ☽ 10am-9pm Wed-Mon) This old *Gasthaus* (inn) turns out inexpensive regional food, and its small garden is perfect for a cool drink after the descent from the castle.

Alter Klosterkeller (☎ 378; Anzuggasse; mains €5-15; ☽ 3-11pm Wed-Mon Apr-Nov) This attractive *Heurigen* (wine tavern) is just outside the village walls (on the eastern side) and overlooks the vineyards close to the town. It's the perfect place to sample the local cuisine and wines.

Restaurant Loibnerhof (☎ 828 90; Unterloiben 7; mains €7-15; ☽ 11.30am-9.30pm Wed-Sun) This lakeside restaurant is 1.5km east of Dürnstein in Unterloiben; it's highly regarded, reasonably priced and has a large garden.

Getting There & Away

Krems and Weissenkirchen are both about 20 minutes away by Brandner boat (€6,

twice daily May to September); it's cheaper and quicker by train though (€2.60, 11 minutes to Krems, 7 minutes to Weissenkirchen, hourly). Dürnstein's train station is called Dürnstein-Oberloiben.

KREMS AN DER DONAU
☎ 02732 / pop 23,400

Krems an der Donau is one of the larger towns in the Wachau region and has a historical core dating back over 1000 years. It reclines on the northern bank of the Danube, surrounded by terraced vineyards, and has been a centre of the wine trade for most of its history.

Orientation & Information

Krems comprises three parts: Krems to the east, the smaller settlement of Stein (formerly a separate town) to the west, and the connecting suburb of Und. Hence the local witticism: *Krems und Stein sind drei Städte* (Krems and Stein are three towns).

The centre of Krems stretches along a pedestrian-only street, Obere and Untere Landstrasse. The **tourist office** (☎ 826 76; www .tiscover.com/krems; Undstrasse 6; ☽ 8.30am-6.30pm Mon-Fri, 10am-noon & 1-6pm Sat, 10am-noon & 1-4pm Sun May-Oct, 8.30am-5pm Mon-Fri Nov-Apr), part of the Austropa travel agency, is about halfway between Krems and Stein; staff will make room reservations on your behalf free of charge.

The **main post office** (Brandströmstrasse 4-6) is near the *Hauptbahnhof* (main train station), approximately three blocks south of Obere Landstrasse. The boat station is near Donaustrasse, about 2km west of the train station.

Sights

One of the best things to pass your time in Krems is to enjoy the peaceful ambience and wander around the cobbled streets, quiet courtyards and ancient city walls; the tourist office can supply you with a map pinpointing all the architectural and cultural attractions around town. Of particular note is the distinctive **Steinertor** (Obere Landstrasse), which dates from the 15th century; this triple-towered gate is the town's emblem.

Krems has several churches worth poking around in. The **Pfarrkirche St Veit** (☎ 832 85; Pfarrplatz 5; ☽ about 7am-7.30pm) on the hill at Pfarrplatz is baroque in style, though it had earlier Gothic and Romanesque incarnations. Its frescoes are by Martin Johann

LOWER AUSTRIA

KREMS AN DER DONAU

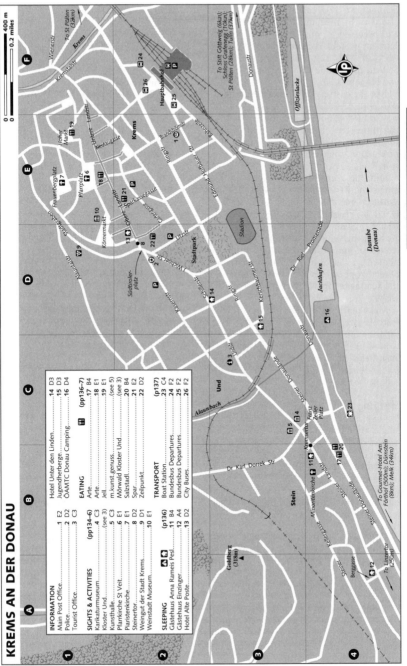

INFORMATION	
Main Post Office	1 E2
Police	2 D2
Tourist Office	3 C3

	Hotel Unter den Linden	14 D3
	Jugendherberge	15 D3
	ÖAMTC Donau Camping	16 D4

SIGHTS & ACTIVITIES	(pp134–6)
Karikaturmuseum	4 C3
Kloster Und	(see 3)
Kunsthalle	5 C3
Pfarrkirche St Veit	6 E1
Piaristenkirche	7 E1
Steinertor	8 D2
Weingut der Stadt Krems	9 D1
Weinstadt Museum	10 E1

EATING	(pp136–7)
Arte	17 B4
Arte	18 E1
Jell	19 E1
m.kunst.genuss	(see 5)
Mörwald Kloster Und	(see 3)
Salzstadl	20 B4
Spar	21 E2
Zeilpunkt	22 D2

SLEEPING	(p136)
Gästehaus Anna Rameis Pesl	11 B4
Gästehaus Einzinger	12 A4
Hotel Alte Poste	13 D2

TRANSPORT	(p137)
Boat Station	23 C4
Bundesbus Departures	24 F2
Bundesbus Departures	25 F2
City Buses	26 F2

LOWER AUSTRIA

Schmidt, an 18th-century local artist who also went by the name of Kremser Schmidt and occupied a house from 1756 near the Linzetor in Stein. **Piaristenkirche** (☎ 820 92; Frauenbergplatz; ☼ about 7am-6pm), behind Pfarrkirche St Veit, has Gothic vaulting, huge windows and baroque altars.

Not far east is the **Weinstadt Museum** (Dominikanerplatz; adult/child €4/3; ☼ 9am-6pm Tue & 1-6pm Wed-Sun Mar-Nov), housed in a former Dominican monastery; inside you'll find displays on the town's pride and joy (wine) and its production, and paintings by its favourite son, Kremser Schmidt.

Offering something completely different is the **Karikaturmuseum** (☎ 908 020; www .karikaturmuseum.at; Steiner Landstrasse 3a; adult/child €7.50/3.50; ☼ 10am-6pm), near the eastern entrance to Stein. The only one of its kind in Austria, this museum features a large collection of humorous caricatures of prominent Austrian and international figures. Directly opposite is the town's arts centre, the **Kunsthalle** (☎ 908 010-19; Steiner Landstrasse 3; admission €5; ☼ 9am-5pm Mon-Fri).

Much of Krems' economic strength comes from its wine culture, and it's a perfect venue for wine tasting; both **Kloster Und** (☎ 704 493; Undstrasse 6; ☼ 1-7pm Wed-Sun) and **Weingut der Stadt Krems** (☎ 801 441; Stadtgraben 11; ☼ 9am-noon & 1-5pm Mon-Sat) have a plethora of wines to sample (for free) and buy.

Sleeping

Many places charge a small surcharge for a single-night stay. As ever, private rooms are a good deal, and details of these are in the tourist office's accommodation brochure.

Hotel Alte Poste (☎ 822 76; www.altepost-krems .at; Obere Landstrasse 32; s/d €42/70; **P**) This quaint guesthouse is located in a historic 500-year-old house and provides comfortable rooms, an enchanting courtyard and a traditional restaurant.

Gästehaus Anna Maria Rameis Pesl (☎ 851 69; gaestehaus-rameis@utanet.at; Steiner Landstrasse 16; s/d from €30/56) This lovely *Gasthaus* on Stein's cobblestoned main street has a traditional feel, a warm welcome and very cosy rooms.

Gästehaus Einzinger (☎ 823 16; gaestehaus.einzing er@aon.at; Steiner Landstrasse 82; s/d €27/52) This is another excellent pension in Stein, offering elegant, old-style rooms arranged around a quiet, attractive courtyard.

Gourmet-Hotel Am Förthof (☎ 833 45; hotel.foert hof@netway.at; Förthofer Donaulände 8; s/d from €60/100; **P** 🔧) About 500m west of Stein, this small hotel combines cosy rooms, romantic ambience, garden and a superb gourmet **restaurant** (mains €7-23) to create one of the better hotels in Krems.

Hotel Unter den Linden (☎ 821 15; www.udl.at; Schillerstrasse 5; s/d from €43/62; **P**) This big, yellow, family-run hotel not far west of the town centre has comfy rooms, a friendly welcome and a shady garden for guests.

Jugendherberge (☎ 834 52; oejhv.noe.krems@aon.at; Ringstrasse 77; dm €15; ☼ Apr-Oct; **P**) This HI hostel close to the tourist office is well geared for cyclists; it features a garage, an onsite repair service and offers packed lunches. It costs an extra €2.20 for stays of less than three nights.

ÖAMTC Donau Camping (☎ 844 55; donaucamping krems@aon.at; Wiedengasse 7; camp site per person/tent €5/2.50; ☼ Easter–mid-Oct; **P**) This flat lakeside campsite is sandwiched between the boat station and the town's yacht harbour.

Eating

Salzstadl (☎ 703 12; Steiner Donaulände 32; mains €6-12; ☼ lunch & dinner Mon-Sat, lunch Sun) This traditional *Beisl-Gasthof* (tavern-hotel) has a relaxed air, patio seating and highly recommended regional cuisine.

Jell (☎ 823 45; Hoher Markt 8-9; mains €12-18; ☼ lunch & dinner Tue-Sun) Occupying a gorgeous stone house, Jell is hard to beat for its rustic and warm atmosphere, fine wine from its own vineyard and excellent Austrian food.

Mörwald Kloster Und (☎ 704 930; Undstrasse 6; mains €17-20; ☼ 10am-10pm Wed-Sun) With an impressive wine selection, creative European cuisine and stylish interior, Mörwald rates among the best restaurants in the Wachau.

m.kunst.genuss (☎ 908 010-21; Steiner Landstrasse 3; mains €10-20; ☼ 10am-10pm) Choose between the glass box or modern interior of this upmarket restaurant-café-bar beside the Kunsthalle.

Arte (☎ 806 230; Steiner Donaulände 34; snacks €3-8; ☼ 11-1am Mon-Sat) This modern wine bar/art gallery is a fine spot to sample the local wines; a second Arte can be found at Obere Landstrasse 4.

Supermarkets include **Spar** (Obere Landstrasse) and Zeilpunkt in the shopping centre by the Steinertor.

Don't omit a *Heurigen* visit; most are out of the centre and provide an authentic experience in eating and drinking. They're

A floral display with a musical theme at Schloss Esterházy (p156), Burgenland

Entrance to a *Buschenschank* (wine tavern) at Rust (p160), Burgenland

Local vintner at work, Burgenland (p160)

WITOLD SKR

Stadtpfarrkirche (town parish church; p177) and town centre on Enns River, Steyr, Upper Austria

MARK HONAN

Memorial at KZ Mauthausen (p175), Upper Austria

The spires of Augustiner Chorherrenstift (p174), St Florian, Upper Austria

MARK

only open for two- or three-week bursts during the year; get the timetable from the tourist office.

Getting There & Away

Frequent daily trains depart from Krems for Vienna's Franz Josefs Bahnhof (€12.20, one hour). The quickest buses to Melk require a change at St Pölten (€6, 1½ hours).

Getting Around

From the train station, bus No 4 heads for the heart of Krems and bus No 1 for Stein. Bikes can be hired at ÖAMTC Donau Camping (opposite) and some hotels. Cyclists are very welcome in Krems; many hotels have bike garages and repair facilities.

AROUND KREMS
Stift Göttweig

Due to its impressive hilltop position 6km south of Krems, it's very hard to miss **Stift Göttweig** (Göttweig Abbey; ☎ 02732-85581 231; Furth bei Göttweig; adult/senior/student €6.50/6/3, full/part-guided tour €2.50/1.50; ☆ 10am-6pm mid-Mar–mid-Nov, tours 11am & 3pm). Founded in 1083 and given to the Benedictine order 11 years later, the abbey you see today is mostly baroque due to work that took place after a devastating fire that all but gutted it in the early 18th century. Aside from the grand view back across the Danube Valley from its garden terrace and restaurant, the abbey's highlights include the elaborate **Imperial Staircase** with a heavenly ceiling fresco painted by Paul Troger in 1739, and the over-the-top baroque interior of the **Stiftskirche** (which has a Kremser Schmidt work in the crypt). Fully guided tours take in the abbey's Imperial wing, church and summer vestry; shorter tours explore either the Imperial wing or the church and vestry.

Only three direct buses on weekdays travel between Krems train station and Göttweig (€2.60, 30 minutes). The train is another possibility, but it's a steep walk up hill from the Klein Wien station (€2.60, 10 minutes).

Schloss Grafenegg

About 10km east of Krems near the road to Tulln is **Schloss Grafenegg** (☎ 02735-220 522; www.grafenegg.com; Haitzendorf; adult/concession/family €5/3/7.50; ☆ 10am-5pm Wed-Sun mid-Apr–Oct), which has the look and feel of an ornate Tudor mansion in English woods more so than a solid Austrian castle. Built in neogothic style

by Leopold Ernst in the mid-19th century and surrounded by a dry moat, its façade is graced with steeped gables and devilish gargoyles. It is now a venue for exhibitions and concerts, but it's also possible to explore the interior, which includes a neogothic *Schloss* (castle) chapel and decadent state rooms, weighed down with plenty of wood, period furniture, carpets and fireplaces.

The castle's manicured gardens are perfect for a picnic, but for fine dining don't pass up **Restaurant & Hotel Schloss Grafenegg** (☎ 02735-261 6-0; schloss_grafenegg@moerwald.at; r €118; ☆ 10am-10pm Wed-Sun; Ⓟ) directly opposite the castle. Owned and run by wine makers Mörwald, the restaurant and hotel are of the highest standard.

To get to Schloss Grafenegg, catch one of the four daily trains to nearby Wagram-Grafenegg (€4.10, 18 minutes) and walk 2km northeast to the *Schloss*.

TULLN

☎ 02272 / pop 12,900

It's hard to imagine that the quiet, modern town of Tulln, 30km northwest of Vienna, has a past dating back to Roman times, when it began life as camp known as Comagena. Nowadays, it plays host not to legions of soldiers but to an army of cyclists exploring the Danube Valley. Tulln's fame also comes from seminal painter Egon Schiele, who was born here.

Orientation & Information

Tulln is centred on pedestrian-only *Hauptplatz* (main square), a 15-minute walk northwest of the main train station; turn right into Bahnweg, right at Brückenstrasse, and left onto Wiener Strasse. The **tourist office** (☎ 658 36; www.tulln.at - in German; Minoritenplatz 2; ☆ 9am-7pm Apr-Oct, 8am-3pm Mon-Fri Nov-Mar) is one block north of the southern end of the Hauptplatz. Tulln Stadt, an S-Bahn station (for suburban trains from Vienna), is just five minutes' walk south of *Hauptplatz* along Bahnhofstrasse.

Sights

The town's pretty main square doubles as a parking place and is dominated by the *Rathaus* (town hall). For lovers of art, a trip to the **Egon Schiele Museum** (☎ 645 70; Donaulände 28; adult/child €3.50/2; ☆ 10am-6pm Tue-Sun Feb-Nov), near the river bank of the Danube, is in order. Housed in a former jail, the museum vividly presents the story of the life of the Tulln-born artist – ask for the extensive English notes – and includes around 100 of his paintings and sketches and a mock-up of the cell he was briefly imprisoned in (he was however jailed in Neulengbach). He fell foul of the law in 1912 following the seizure of 125 erotic drawings; some were of pubescent girls, and Schiele was also in trouble for allowing children to see his explicit works. Schiele aficionados should also not miss the Leopold Museum in Vienna (p95).

Tulln's other two museums unfortunately can't compete with the house devoted to Schiele; the **Römermuseum** (☎ 659 22; Marc-Aurel-Park 1b; adult/child €3/2; ☒ 10am-6pm Tue-Sun Mar-Nov), to the east of the Egon Schiele Museum, contains a small collection of Roman finds, while the **Tullner Museen** (☎ 619 15; Minoritenplatz 1; adult/child €3/2; ☒ 10am-6pm Tue-Sun May-Sep), next to the tourist office, delves into the history of the town. The highlight of the Tullner Museen is a bunch of well restored historic fire engines. Of the few Roman ruins remaining, the oldest is the **Römerturm** (Donaulände), a watch tower built in 360 under the direction of Emperor Diocletian.

Take a peek in the **Pfarrkirche St Stephan** (☎ 623 38-0; Wiener Strasse 20; admission free; ☒ 7.30am-7.30pm summer, 7.30am-5pm winter), a Romanesque church east of *Hauptplatz* with alterations in Gothic and baroque style. Its crypt has ghoulish stacks of exhumed bones and behind is a 13th-century polygonal funerary chapel, where frescoes depict some not so evil-looking devils.

The town and its tourist office are well set up for cyclists as the Danube cycle-way cuts between the river the town's northern border; bicycles are available for rent at the Donaupark Camping. On hot summer days follow the rest of the town to the **Aubad** (☎ 686 67; Donaulände; ☒ 8am-8pm Jul & Aug, 10am-8pm Mon-Fri & 8am-8pm Sat & Sun May & Jun), a man-made lake to the east of the town near Donaupark Camping.

Sleeping & Eating

The tourist office can help with a list of accommodation options (including private rooms), and a map of the town.

Hotel-Restaurant Zur Rossmühle (☎ 624 11-0; www.rossmuehle.at; Hauptplatz 12; s/d from €52/66; P) If you're into plants, Rossmühle has possibly the best foyer of any hotel in Austria; it's a

veritable Amazon jungle. Rooms have an imperial air about them, complete with period furniture, and the **restaurant** (mains €8-12) is first class.

For more basic accommodation try **Alpenvereins Herberge** (☎ 626 92; Donaulände 1; mattress on floor €11, dm €15; ☒ May-Oct), a haven for cyclists 300m west of the town centre by the river, **Familien und Jugendgasstehaus Tulln** (☎ 651 65; tulln@noejhw.at; Marc-Aurel-Park 1; dm €15.70-24.70; P), occupying the same building as the Römermuseum, or **Donaupark Camping** (☎ 652 00; camp tulln@oeamtc.at; Hafenstrasse 4; camp sites per person/tent €6/4.50; ☒ Apr-Oct; P), east of the centre.

S'Pfandl Dreh' dich Satt (☎ 616 70; Hauptplatz 12; mains €8-12; ☒ lunch & dinner) Occupying the same building as Hotel-Restaurant Zur Rossmühle is this family-run restaurant, with buffet-style Austrian cuisine and a grand midday menu.

Getting There & Away

Tulln is reached hourly by train (€7, 25 minutes) or S-Bahn (line 40; €7, 45 minutes) from Vienna's Franz Josefs Bahnhof. The train is quicker, but only stops at the main Tulln station, while the S-Bahn stops at Tulln Stadt. Heading west, trains go to Krems (€8.40, 30 to 45 minutes, hourly) or St Pölten (€8.40, 40 to 50 minutes, hourly).

ST PÖLTEN

☎ 02742 / pop 49,000

St Pölten, a destination few stop at as they scream down the A1 on their way from Vienna to Salzburg, may be Lower Austria's capital but it still has the feel of a sleepy town. The city does have a few things going for it, however, such as an attractive *Altstadt* (old town), with pedestrian-only cobblestone streets, and its new Landhaus Viertel (Landhaus Quarter), which is filled with contemporary architectural delights and first-rate entertainment centres.

History

Nearly 2000 years ago St Pölten was known as Aelium Cetium, but the town all but disappeared with the departure of the Romans. The arrival of the Augustinians in the 8th century saw it regain importance, and the country's newest provincial capital has the oldest municipal charter, granted in 1159. The *Altstadt* is noted for its baroque buildings: baroque master Jakob Prandtauer lived and died in the city.

Orientation & Information

The centre of town is a compact, mostly pedestrian-only area to the west of the Traisen River. Its main square, Rathausplatz, is home to the *Rathaus* and **tourist office** (☎ 353 354; tourismus@st-poelten.gv.at; Rathausplatz 1; 🕓 8am-5pm Mon-Fri, 9am-5pm Sat, 10am-5pm Sun Apr-Oct, 8am-5pm Mon-Fri Nov-Mar). Ask for the *St Pölten Gäste-service* booklet (in German, but with useful listings) and the city map; outside is an accommodation map and a telephone you can use to make free calls to hotels and guesthouses. About 500m north of Rathausplatz is the *Hauptbahnhof*, which has money-exchange counters and a *Bankomat*; next door is the main post office. Internet access is available in Cinema Paradiso (see p141). The Landhaus Viertel is 700m east of Rathausplatz.

Sights

The quaint city centre is easily tackled by foot; the tourist office produces a *Your City Guide* (in English) which outlines two walking tours of the city and can be complemented by an audio guide (€1.55).

Rathausplatz is lined with eye-catching pastel-coloured buildings and dominated by the **Rathaus** and **Franziskanerkirche** (☎ 352 6211; Rathausplatz 12; 🕓 dawn-dusk), which was completed in 1770 and has a grandiose altar offset by side altar paintings by Kremser Schmidt. Playing truce-maker between the two is the tall **Dreifaltigkeitssäule** (Trinity Column). Note the house at **Rathausgasse 2**, with its baroque façade and Schubert relief (the composer was a frequent visitor).

Not far south and west of Rathausplatz are several places of interest, including the **Institut der Englischen Fräulein** (☎ 352 188-0; Linzer Strasse 11; admission free; 🕓 dawn-dusk), a convent founded in 1706, which has a classic baroque façade, black-and-gold organ and several frescoes by Paul Troger in the chapel. The tiny **Museum im Hof** (☎ 353 477; Hess Strasse 4; admission free; 🕓 9am-noon Wed, Fri & Sat) dwells on recent history, particularly from a worker's viewpoint. Just around the corner is the **Stadtmuseum** (☎ 333-26 43; Prandtauerstrasse 2; adult/student €2/1; 🕓 10am-5pm Tue-Sat), which has a rather bland history of the city from Roman times to the mid-19th century.

To the east of Rathausplatz is Domplatz, which hosts a morning market every Thursday and Saturday and is home to the **Domkirche** (☎ 353 402-0; Domplatz 1; 🕓 dawn-dusk). Originally built in the 13th-century, it received a major baroque make-over in the early 18th century; its interior, with lashings of fake marble and gold, was designed by Jakob Prandtauer and is easily the most impressive in St Pölten. Note the painted figure that seems about to fall on you if you stand before the altar, and the hole in the organ that captures the stained glass image behind. Not all the architecture in town is exclusively baroque – **Kremser Gasse 41** is graced with an Art Nouveau façade by Josef Olbrich, the creator of the Secession building in Vienna.

From Domplatz it's an easy walk down Lederergasse past the town's **synagogue** (Lederergasse 11; admission free; 🕓 9am-3pm Mon-Fri) to the Landhaus Viertel. The Viertel's pride and joy is the **Landesmuseum** (☎ 90 80 90-153; Franz Schubert-Platz 5; adult/concession/child €8/7/3.50; 🕓 10am-6pm Tue-Sun), devoted to the history, art and environment of Lower Austria. A wave made from glass, frozen in movement above the entrance, sets the mood for the museum; water is a common theme throughout. Of particular note in the extensive art collection, which spans the medieval ages to the present day, is the 13th-century Lion of Schöngrabern from a Romanesque parish church.

For a birds-eye view of the entire quarter take the lift to the top of the **Klangturm** (☎ 90 80 50; Landhausplatz; adult/child €7.50/3.50; 🕓 10am-6pm Tue-Sun).

Sleeping

The tourist office has a complete list of accommodation options, including private rooms.

Stadthotel Hauser Eck (☎ 733 36; www.hausereck.at; Schulgasse 2; s/d from €42/84; **P**) This lovely Art Nouveau hotel is the best place in town, with a fine restaurant (p140) downstairs serving Austrian cuisine, a friendly welcome and neat, comfy rooms.

Mariazellerhof (☎ 76995; www.pension-mariazellerhof.at; Mariazeller Strasse 6; s/d from €29/58; **P**) The pink façade of family-owned Mariazellerhof faces a busy intersection, but inside most of the noise is blocked out by double-glazed windows. Many of the good-sized rooms come with kitchen facilities.

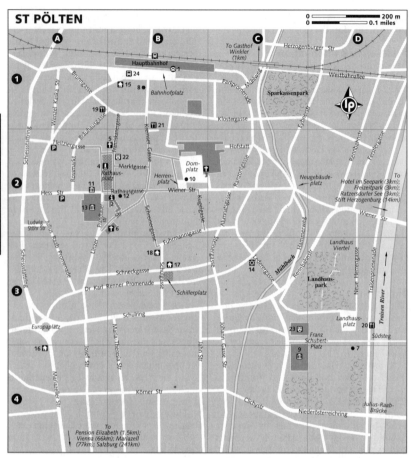

ST PÖLTEN

0 ————— 200 m
0 ————— 0.1 miles

Pension Elisabeth (☎ 727 14; Mariazeller Strasse 164; s/d €26/52; Ⓟ) Run by the owners of Mariazellerhof; rooms are cheaper here but have no cooking amenities.

Metropol (☎ 707 00-0; metropol@austria-trend.at; Schillerplatz 1; s/d €85/121; Ⓟ ⊠ ▢) The town's only central four-star hotel; expect modern, standardised rooms and excellent service.

Gasthof Graf (☎ 352 757; office@hotel-graf.at; Bahnhofplatz 7; s/d €34/68; Ⓟ) Convenient to the *Hauptbahnhof* is this quiet *Gasthof*, with well-renovated rooms and a homely atmosphere, which unfortunately is dampened by the owner's slightly suspicious attitude towards her guests.

Hotel im Seepark (☎ 251 510; www.hotel-seepark .at; Am Ratzersdorfer See; camp sites per person/tent €4/3; Ⓨ year-round; Ⓟ) This lakeside hotel, 3km to the northeast of the centre in the Freizeitpark, has the closest camping ground to the city. It's a fine place to spend the day sunning and swimming.

Eating

Mundwerk (☎ 720 20; Schulgasse 2; mains €7-12; Ⓨ 7am-11pm Mon-Sat, 7-11am Sun) Taking up the ground floor of Stadthotel Hauser Eck is this quality restaurant, serving great Austrian cuisine and big breakfasts in modern, orange-and-black surroundings.

Landhaus Stüberl (☎ 245 24; Landhausboulevard 27; midday menu €4-6; mains €7-12; Ⓨ lunch & dinner Mon-Sat) Landhaus is certainly catering for the Viertel office workers, but it has good, cheap midday menus and a terrace overlooking the Traisen.

Zum Roten Krebs (☎ 352 606; Kremser Gasse 18; snacks €3-8; ☻ lunch & dinner Mon-Sat) Taking up a side-alley of Kremser Gasse is this modern café-bar with a refined air and great coffee.

Gasthof Winkler (☎ 364 944; Mühlweg 64; mains €7-18; ☻ lunch & dinner Mon-Sat, lunch Sun) This upmarket restaurant is about 1km north of the *Hauptbahnhof* and offers good regional and seasonal dishes.

Self-caterers should head for **Billa** (cnr Brunngasse & Bräuhausgasse).

Entertainment

The **FestSpielHaus** (☎ 90 80 80-222; www.festspielhaus .at; Franz Schubert-Platz 2) is a newly built theatre which features an impressive array of music, theatre and dance performances from both Austria and abroad. **Cinema Paradiso** (☎ 214 00; www.cinema-paradiso.at; Rathausplatz 14; ☻ 9-1am) combines arthouse cinema and fine café.

Getting There & Away

Trains run about every half hour from Vienna to St Pölten (€9.70, 45 to 75 minutes), continuing on to Linz (€17.70, one hour) and Salzburg (€29.50, 2½ hours). From St Pölten, trains run to Krems (€7, 45 minutes, hourly) and Mariazell (€12.90, 2½ hours, three direct daily).

St Pölten has equally good road connections: the east-west A1/E60 passes a few kilometres south of the city and the S33 branches north from there, bypassing St Pölten to the east, and continuing to Krems.

AROUND ST PÖLTEN

The land around Lower Austria's capital is not particularly enthralling, but it does contain one of Austria's five Augustinian abbeys, **Stift Herzogenburg** (☎ 02782-831 13; Herzogenburg; adult/senior/student/child €5/3.60/3/1.50; ☻ 9-11am & 1-5pm Apr-Oct). Like many castles and abbeys in Austria, Herzogenburg's current baroque look from the early 18th century belies a long history; the abbey can trace its beginnings back to 1112. Its interior can only be visited by guided tour (English tours can be arranged in advance; tour cost is included in admission costs), which winds its way through many of the abbey's holy rooms; the *Bildersaal* (picture room), with 144 paintings adorning the walls, is suitably breathtaking, but is overshadowed by the *Bibliothek* (library), home to almost 80,000 books, some of which are beautifully illustrated and date from the 13th century.

For a bite to eat and a glass of local wine under a shady tree, look no further than the abbey's small but inviting *Heurigen*.

Herzogenburg lies on the main train line between Krems (€4.10, 30 minutes) and St Pölten (€4.10, 15 minutes); at least a dozen trains pass through the town's train station (which is 10 minutes' walk from the abbey) on a daily basis.

MOSTVIERTEL

The Mostviertel, in Lower Austria's southwestern corner, gains its name from cider which is produced and consumed in the area. By Lower Austrian standards, the landscape is spectacular; the eastern Alps are ever-present in its southern reaches. It's largely ignored by international tourists and is certainly an area off the beaten track.

For a snapshot of the Mostviertel it's best to hire a car and head south on Bundestrasse 121 from **Amstetten**, a city of little tourist interest. First port of call is the stunning riverside town **Waidhofen an der Ybbs**, with historic gabled houses, arcaded courtyards and dramatic onion domes. Staff at its **tourist office** (☎ 07442-511 255; tourismus@waidhofen.at; Freisingerberg 2; ☻ 9am-noon & 1-6pm Mon-Fri, 9am-noon & 1-5pm Sat) can fill you in on the town and its surrounds. At Gstadt, Bundestrasse 31 branches off to the right and heads south; this road will lead you into mountainous country and through

LOWER AUSTRIA

a string of pretty little villages such as **Gös-tling**, **Lunz am See** and **Gaming**.

In the eastern fringes of the Mostviertel, and only 23km south of St Pölten, is the **Cistercian monastery** (☎ 02762-524 24; Klosterrotte 1; tours adult/student/child €7/6/4, admission without tour €3/2.50/1; ☺ 8am-noon & 1-5pm, tours 10am & 2pm Mon-Sat, 2pm Sun) of Lilienfeld. Founded in 1202, the foundations of the monastery are Romanesque, but like so many churches and abbeys in Austria, it first received a Gothic, andthen a baroque make-over. Fortunately though, all three styles are still visible in the complex. Without forking out any cash, you'll only be able to peek through locked glass doors at the abbey's church, which is Romanesque-Gothic in structure, but decorated in black-and-gold baroque fixtures. Its highlight though is its main entrance; this *Trichterportal* (funnel portal) is early Gothic in style and consists of 16 slender marble columns. The tour takes you through the church, Kreuzgang (stunning Romanesque-Gothic cloisters), medieval dormitory and baroque library; without joining a tour you'll only visit the Kreuzgang.

Getting There & Away

If you don't have your own transport, there are six daily trains to Waidhofen an der Ybbs (€13.90, one hour, change at Amstetten) from St Pölten; services to Göstling, Lunz and Gaming and rare and time-consuming. Frequent buses and trains travel between St Pölten and Lilienfeld Monday to Saturday (€5.50, 35 to 50 minutes) but this drops to one on Sunday.

WALDVIERTEL & WEINVIERTEL

Between them, the Waldviertel (Wood Quarter) and Weinviertel (Wine Quarter) take up most of the land north of the Danube in Lower Austria. The Waldviertel to the northwest is a region of rolling hills and rural villages, and while there isn't actually much forest to speak of, there are a number of fine attractions. The Weinviertel, north and northeast of Vienna, is invariably flat and agricultural, and has little of interest for the average tourist (unless you're crazy about Austrian wine). Both regions

are certainly places to escape the madding crowds.

Waldviertel's central **tourist office** (☎ 02822-541 09-0; info@waldviertel.ro.at; Hauptplatz 4) is located in Zwettl, a small town near a baroque **Cistercian Abbey** (☎ 02822-550; Stift Zwettl 1; tours adult/child €6/3; tours 10am, 11am, 2pm & 3pm Mon-Sat, 11am, 2pm & 3pm Sun May-Oct). Staff can provide you with enough information on the area.

Some 40km east of Zwettl is a grouping of enticing sites. First up is the Benedictine **Stift Altenburg** (☎ 02982-3451; www.stift-altenburg .at; Stift 1; adult/senior/student/family €7/6/3/14, guided tours extra €1.50; ☺ 10am-5pm Apr-Oct, to 6pm mid-Jun–Aug, tours 11am, 2pm & 3pm Sat & Sun), which can trace its foundations back to 1144. In the ensuing centuries it was all but destroyed by plundering hordes, until extensive baroque rebuilding began in 1650. The abbey library (with ceiling frescoes by Paul Troger) and the crypt (featuring frescoes by Troger's pupils) are among the most impressive examples of their kind in Austria. The abbey's church, which is free to enter, contains some of Troger's best frescoes (in the central dome, and above the high and side altars). Note the bizarre statues scattered around the complex, including what looks like Mary knocking an evil-doer off the roof in the first inner courtyard, and a drunkard barely able to stand up, let alone hang onto his hat and tankard, in the second.

A few kilometres southeast of Altenburg is **Schloss Rosenburg** (☎ 02982-2911; www.rosenburg .at - in German; Rosenburg am Kamp; tours adult/senior/child/family €8/7/4/18, extra €2 for falconry & pageantry; ☺ 9am-5pm Mon-Fri, 9am-6pm Sat & Sun May-Sep, 9.30am-4.30pm Apr & Oct), a Renaissance castle with medieval ancestry. This multiturreted edifice is notable for its large grassy inner courtyard, where splendid falconry shows take place at 11am and 3pm when the Schloss is open.

A further 18km east of Rosenburg, the quaint town of **Eggenburg** comes into view. It's still surrounded by much of its original defensive walls, but more intriguing is its **Österreiche Motorradmuseum** (Motorbike Museum; ☎ 02984-2151; www.motorradmuseum.at - in German; Museumgasse 6; adult/concession/child €5/4/2; ☺ 8am-4pm Mon-Fri, 10am-5pm Sat & Sun mid-Jan–mid-Dec). This masterpiece of motorbike dedication has over 300 immaculately restored bikes on show. You'll find extensive collections of BMWs, including 'suicide-shift' models from the late-'20s, and Austrian-made Puchs, but almost any motorbike manufacturer you care to name is represented here; around 200 in fact. More unusual models include the NSU Max Sportversion, with its sharp angles, and the Böhmerland 600, the longest bike in the world.

Getting There & Away

Zwettl is best reached by bus from Krems (€11.30, 1½ hours); there is one bus daily on weekends and more Monday to Friday. Five direct trains travel from Krems to Horn daily (€8.40, one hour), stopping at Rosenburg along the way. From Horn, very irregular buses run to Altenburg (€1.90, 10 minutes). Eggenburg has plenty of daily connections to Tulln (€8.40, 40 minutes).

NATIONALPARK THAYATAL

Straddling the border of Austria and the Czech Republic in the northwestern reaches of the Weinviertel is Austria's smallest national park, Thayatal. This unique stretch of land is actually two parks; its other half, Podyjí National Park, is located across the border. What makes Thayatal so special is its climatic conditions, caught between the hot, dry Pannonian winds from the east and the wet Atlantic storms from the west. This has created a perfect environment for flora diversity; of the 3000 plant species found in Austria, about 1300 occur here. Thayatal's landscape consists of a deep canyon cut by the Thaya river, a plethora of rock formations and steep slopes. Walking is the most popular activity in the park.

The **Nationalparkhaus** (☎ 02949-70 05-0; www.np-thayatal.at - in German; exhibition adult/concession €3.80/2.20; 🕑 10am-6pm Tue-Sun Apr-Sep, 10am-4pm Thu-Sun Oct-Dec & Mar), near Hardegg, has loads of information and an exhibition on the park's ecology. Hardegg, the natural jump-off point for the park, is not easy to get to without your own transport; it's best approached by train from Vienna to Retz (€12.90, 1¼ hours), from where the occasional bus runs to the town (€3.30, 20 minutes).

MARCH-DONAULAND

The March-Donauland stretches from the eastern border of Vienna to the Slovakian border, an area dominated by the Danube and it natural flood plains. It's an area rich in history and natural wonder – Carnuntum, an important Roman camp, and Nationalpark Donau-Auen are found here.

CARNUNTUM

Vienna may stand head and shoulders above any village, town or city in Austria, but in Roman times it was overshadowed by Carnuntum, a military camp of the Roman province of Upper Pannonia. With a population of over 50,000 at its peak, it was a powerful base from AD 40 until it was abandoned some 400 years later. Its ruins are spread out over 4km, between the villages of Petronell and Bad Deutsch-Altenburg.

Orientation & Information

Carnuntum basically consists of three parts: an archaeological park in Petronell (the main attraction), an amphitheatre halfway between Bad Deutsch-Altenburg and Petronell, and a museum in Bad Deutsch-Altenburg. Petronell's *Bahnhof* (train station) is 1km south of the main street, Hauptstrasse, which is home to the archaeological park, its **information office** (☎ 02163-337 70; www.carnuntum.co.at; Hauptstrasse 3; 🕑 9am-5pm mid-Mar–mid-Nov) and the **Regionalbüro March-Donauland** (☎ 02163-355 5-10; www.marchdonauland.at; Hauptstrasse 3; 🕑 10am-4pm Mon-Fri).

Bad Deutsch-Altenburg also has its own **tourist office** (☎ 02165-624 59; baddeutschaltenburg@netway.at; Erhardgasse 2; 🕑 7am-4pm Mon-Fri).

Sights

One ticket (adult/concession €7/5, tours extra €3/2) covers all three attractions of Carnuntum, which, on the face of it, aren't particularly stunning, but with an audio guide or organised tour, they soon come to life.

The **archaeological park** (☎ 02163-337 70; www.carnuntum.co.at; Hauptstrasse 3; 🕑 9am-5pm mid-Mar–mid-Nov, tours 11am & 2pm Sat & Sun, also 10am, noon & 2pm Mon-Fri Jul & Aug) lies on the site of the old civilian town. It includes ruins of the public baths, a reconstructed temple of Diana and a viewing platform which helps to put it all into perspective. The **Heidentor** (Heathen Gate; admission free) was once the southwest entrance to the city and now stands as an isolated anachronism amid fields of corn.

About 1km on from the park towards Bad Deutsch-Altenburg is the grass-covered **amphitheatre** (Wienerstrasse 52; 🕑 9am-5pm mid-Mar–mid-Nov, tours 3.30pm Sat) that formerly seated 15,000. It now hosts a theatre festival over summer.

Bad Deutsch-Altenburg's **Museum Carnuntinum** (Badgasse 40-46; ☺ noon-5pm Mon & 10am-5pm Tue-Sun mid-Mar–mid-Nov, 11am-5pm Sat & Sun mid-Nov–mid-Dec) is the largest of its kind in Austria, having amassed over 3300 Roman treasures in its 100-year existence. Its highlight is the *Tanzende Mänade* (Dancing Maenad), a marble figure with a perfect bum. The town is also a health spa, with 28°C iodine sulphur springs.

Hainburg, 3km further east, is a possible additional excursion. It has more ancient relics, in the form of sturdy city gates and hilltop ruins. **Bratislava**, the Slovakian capital, is also an easy day trip from Carnuntum.

Sleeping & Eating

Bad Deutsch-Altenburg, with its pretty *Kurpark* (Spa Gardens), spa facilities and location near the Danube, is far more appealing than Petronell for overnighting. Much of the accommodation is found on Badgasse. If you do want to stay in Petronell though, try **Hotel Marc Aurel** (☎ 02163-22 85; www.marcaurel .at; Hauptstrasse 10; s/d €45/64, mains €7-12), a few steps from the archaeological park.

Pension Madle (☎ 02165-627 63; Badgasse 22; s/d €20/40; P) Madle is a simple pension with no frills, but the rooms are absolutely fine and the family owners welcoming and friendly.

Pension Riedmüller (☎ 02165-624 73; pension-ried mueller@aon.at; Badgasse 28; s/d from €21/42; P) This is another basic pension with decent rooms, which offers free use of bicycles for guests and organises tours to Bratislava.

Hotel König Stephan (☎ 02165-647 11; Badgasse 34; s/d €22/44; P) Stephan is closer to the river and has a fine **restaurant** (mains €7-15) which serves Austrian cuisine in its large conservatory. Rooms are the same standard as both pensions mentioned above.

The Donaustüberl, right next to the Danube, is a very relaxed eatery with a peaceful, tree-shaded garden and local wines.

Getting There & Away

From Vienna, the S7 train (direction Wolfsthal) departs Wien Floridsdorf hourly, via Wien Nord and Wien Mitte on its way to Petronell (€8.40, 56 minutes), Bad Deutsch-Altenburg (€8.40, one hour) and Hainburg (€9.70, 67 minutes).

The cycle path from Vienna goes along the north bank of the Danube, crosses to the south at Bad Deutsch-Altenburg, and continues into Slovakia.

NATIONALPARK DONAU-AUEN

Nationalpark Donau-Auen is a thin strip of natural floodplain on either side of the Danube, running from Vienna to the Slovakian border. Established as a national park in 1997, it was the culmination of 13 years of protest and environmentalist action against the building of a hydroelectric power station in Hainburg. You'll find plentiful flora and fauna, including 700 species of fern and flowering plants, and a high density of kingfishers (feeding off the 50 species of fish). Guided tours by foot or boat are available; for more information contact **Nationalpark Donau-Auen** (☎ 02212-34 50; www.donauauen .at; Schlossplatz 1, Orth an der Donau).

Nationalpark Donau-Auen is best explored by bicycle from Vienna; see p125 for details of bicycle hire in Vienna.

WIENERWALD

The Wienerwald (Vienna Woods) encompass gentle wooded hills to the west and southwest of Vienna, and the wine growing region directly south of the capital. For the Viennese, it's a place for walking and mountain biking, but it is often overlooked by tourists. Numerous walking and cycling trails in the area are covered in the *Wienerwald Wander und Radkarte*, available free from local tourist offices and the region's main office, **Tourismusregion Wienerwald** (☎ 02231-621 76; www .wienerwald.info; Hauptplatz 11, 3002 Purkersdorf).

Attractive settlements, such as the grape-growing towns of **Perchtoldsdorf** and **Gumpoldskirchen**, speckle the Wienerwald. Picturesque **Mödling**, only 15km south of Vienna, was once favoured by the artistic elite escaping from Vienna: Beethoven's itchy feet took him to Hauptstrasse 79 from 1818 to 1820, and Schönberg stayed at Bernhardgasse 6 from 1918 to 1925. More information is available from the **Tourismus-Information Mödling** (☎ 02236-267 27; tourismus@moedling.at; Elisabeth-strasse 2).

The road from Mödling to Mayerling, the Bundestrasse 23, shadows a small river, cutting through the forested hills and round rocky outcrops. Only a few kilometres out of Modling is **Seegrotte Hinterbrühl** (☎ 02236-263 64; www.seegrotte.at; Grutschgasse 2a; boat tours adult/ child €6/4; ❍ 9am-noon & 1-5pm Apr-Oct, 9am-noon & 1-3.30pm Nov-Mar), Europe's largest underground lake. This former mine flooded with 20 million litres of water in 1912 and consequently shut down. Reopened to tourists as a display mine in 1932, it was then used by the German army to build aircraft during WWII. The 40-minute boat tours may be in English if you phone ahead.

Another 12km from Hinterbrühl is **Heiligenkreuz** and its 12th-century Cistercian abbey, **Stift Heiligenkreuz** (☎ 02258-87 03; www .stift-heiligenkreuz.at; Heiligenkreuz 1; tours adult/senior/ child €6/5/2.90; tours 10am, 11am, 2pm, 3pm & 4pm Mon-

Sat, 11am, 2pm, 3pm & 4pm Sun). It's an excellent example of Romanesque-Gothic architecture. The chapter house is the final resting place of most of the Babenberg dynasty, which ruled Austria until 1246. The grave of Maria Vetsera (ill-fated mistress of Archduke Rudolf) is also here, and can be seen without joining the tour. The abbey museum contains 150 clay models by Giovanni Giuliani (1663–1744), a Venetian sculptor who also created the Trinity column in the courtyard. Within the abbey's grounds is a restaurant, complete with chandeliers, a cellar and a terrace. Note that tours in English are by request only.

Mayerling, which lies 6km southwest of Heiligenkreuz, has little to show now, but

---

MYSTERY AT MAYERLING

It's the stuff of lurid pulp fiction: the heir to the throne found dead in a hunting lodge with his teenage mistress. It became fact in Mayerling on 30 January 1889, yet for years the details of the case were shrouded in secrecy and denial. Even now a definitive picture has yet to be established – the 100th anniversary of the tragedy saw a flurry of books published on the subject, and Empress Zita claimed publicly that the heir had actually been murdered.

The heir was Archduke Rudolf, 30-year-old son of Emperor Franz Josef, husband of Stephanie of Coburg, and something of a libertine who was fond of drinking and womanising. Rudolf's marriage was little more than a public façade by the time he met the 17-year-old Baroness Maria Vetsera in the autumn of 1888. The attraction was immediate, but it wasn't until 13 January the following year that the affair was consummated, an event commemorated by an inscribed cigarette case, a gift from Maria to Rudolf.

On 28 January, Rudolf secretly took Maria with him on a shooting trip to his hunting lodge in Mayerling. His other guests arrived a day later; Maria's presence, however, remained unknown to them. On the night of the 29th, the valet, Loschek, heard the couple talking until the early hours, and at about 5.30am a fully dressed Rudolf appeared and instructed him to get a horse and carriage ready. As he was doing his master's bidding, he reportedly heard two gun shots; racing back, he discovered Rudolf lifeless on his bed, with a revolver by his side. Maria was on her bed, also fully clothed, also dead. Just two days earlier Rudolf had discussed a suicide pact with long-term mistress Mizzi Caspar. Apparently he hadn't been joking.

The official line was proffered by Empress Elisabeth, who claimed Rudolf died of heart failure. The newspapers swallowed the heart failure story, though a few speculated about a hunting accident. Then the rumours began: some believed Maria had poisoned her lover, that Rudolf had contracted an incurable venereal disease, or that he had been assassinated by Austrian secret police because of his liberal politics. Even as late as 1982, Empress Zita claimed the heir to the throne had been killed by French secret agents. Numerous books have been written on the subject, but no-one can say what exactly occurred on that ill-fated morning.

Through all the intrigue, the real victim remains Maria. How much of a willing party she was to the suicide will never be known. What has become clear is that Maria, after her death, represented not a tragically curtailed young life but an embarrassing scandal that had to be discreetly disposed of. Her body was left untouched for 38 hours, after which it was loaded into a carriage in such a manner as to imply that it was a living person being aided rather than a corpse beyond help. Her subsequent burial was a rude, secretive affair, during which she was consigned to the ground in an unmarked grave (her body was later moved to Heiligenkreuz). Today the hunting lodge is no more – a Carmelite nunnery stands in its place.

the bloody event that occurred there (see the boxed text 'Mystery at Mayerling' p145) still draws people to the site. The **Carmelite convent** (☎ 02258-8703-2275; Mayerling 1; admission €1.50; ⏰ 9am-noon & 2-6pm) can be visited, but it's not really worth the effort; all you see is a chapel and a couple of rooms of mementos.

Getting There & Away

To explore this region, it's best if you have your own transport. Trains skirt either side of the woods and the bus service is patchy. The Baden–Alland bus passes through Heiligenkreuz (€1.50, 35 minutes) and Mayerling (€3, 45 minutes) on an hourly basis Monday to Friday, but this drops to a trickle on weekends. From Mödling (reached on the Vienna Südbahnhof–Baden train route), there are frequent buses going to Hinterbrühl (€1.50, 11 minutes) which sometimes continue on to Alland via Heiligenkreuz (€3, 30 minutes).

The main road through the area is the A21 that loops down from Vienna, passes by Heiligenkreuz, then curves north to join the A1 just east of Altlengbach.

BADEN BEI WIEN
☎ 02252 / pop 24,000

The spa town of Baden bei Wien, on the eastern fringes of the Wienerwald, has a long history. The Romans were prone to wallow in its medicinal springs and it was initially named *Padun* in 869. Beethoven

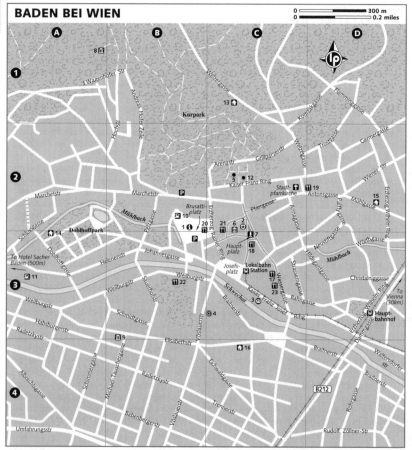

BADEN BEI WIEN

frequented the town in hope of a cure for his deafness, and in the early 19th century it flourished as the favourite summer retreat of the Habsburgs. Much of the town centre is in the 19th century Biedermeier style, resulting from rebuilding after Turkish invasions and severe fires. Note that Baden mostly closes down in winter.

Orientation & Information

The town is centred on pedestrian-only Hauptplatz; the *Lokalbahn* (tram) station is just south of the Hauptplatz, while the *Hauptbahnhof* is 500m southeast. A couple of minutes' walk west of *Hauptplatz* is **Baden Tourismus** (☎ 226 00-600; www.baden.at; Brusattiplatz 3; ⊙ 9am-6pm Mon-Sat, 10am-1pm Sun May-Sep, 9am-5pm Mon-Fri Oct-Apr); ask about the VIP Card (free if you stay three nights or more in any type of accommodation), which gives very useful benefits, such as discounts on entry prices and free walking tours. South of the *Hauptplatz* the video-rental store **Videowelt** (☎ 476 88; Vöslauerstrasse 9; per hr €4.30; ⊙ 9am-9pm Mon-Sat, 2-9pm Sun) has Internet access. The post office is squeezed between the Schwechat river and Kaiser Franz Josef Ring, 150m south of Hauptplatz.

Sights

Baden exudes health and 19th-century affluence, an impression endorsed by the many Biedermeier-style houses. Its reputation is however based firmly on the existence of its 14 **hot springs**, with a daily flow of 6.5 million litres. The waters emerge at a temperature of 36°C and are enriched with sulphur, chlorine and sulphates. The town has various indoor and outdoor pool complexes, for medicinal or frivolous purposes. In the latter category is the **Thermalstrandbad** (☎ 486 70; www.baden-bei-wien.at; Helenenstrasse 19-21; all-day entry Mon-Fri €5.70, Sat & Sun €6.60; ⊙ May–mid-Sep) with sulphur and normal pools, plus imported sand. Other bathing options include the **Römertherme** (Roman baths; ☎ 450 30; www.roemer

therme.at; Brusattiplatz 4; 2hr/all-day entry €8.50/19.30; ⊙ 10am-10pm) by Baden Tourismus.

The town attracts plenty of promenading Viennese at the weekends. All and sundry make for the **Kurpark**, a magnificent setting for a stroll. Rows of white benches are neatly positioned under manicured trees in front of the **bandstand**, where free *Kurkonzerte* (spa concerts) are performed from May to September. Elaborate flower beds complement monuments to famous artists (Mozart, Beethoven, Strauss, Grillparzer etc). Near the southern entrance to the park, the **Undine Brunnen** (fountain) is a fine amalgam of human and fish images.

To the northwest of the *Kurpark* is the **Emperor Franz Josef Museum** (☎ 02252-411 00; Hochstrasse 51; adult/child €2.50/1; ⊙ 2-6pm Tue-Sun Apr-Oct) which displays a rather eclectic collection of folk art, armour and uniforms dating from the 17th to 20th centuries and Habsburg memorabilia.

Back in the town centre, one of the houses Beethoven stayed in has inevitably been turned into the **Beethovenhaus** (Rathausgasse 10; adult/child €2.50/1; ⊙ 4-6pm Tue-Fri, 9-11am & 4-6pm Sat & Sun), but unfortunately there isn't a lot to see. Nearby, the **Dreifaltig-keitssäule**, dating from 1714, dominates the Hauptplatz.

The **Rollett Museum** (☎ 02252-482 55; Weikersdorfer Platz 1; adult/child €2.50/1; ⊙ 3-6pm Wed-Mon), southwest of the town centre, covers important aspects of the town's history, such as bomb damage in WWII. The most unusual exhibit is the collection of skulls, busts and death masks amassed by the founder of phrenology, Josef Gall (1752–1828). This apparently cranky science, which held that criminal characteristics could be inferred from the shape of a person's skull, disturbingly brings to mind modern claims of the discovery of a 'criminal gene'.

Festivals & Events

June is a big month for Baden; it sees the start of **Operetta Metropolis**, an operetta festival than runs till the beginning of September, and is the time of **Baden Rosentage** (Rose Days), a rose festival held in the Rosarium gardens in the Doblhoffpark.

Sleeping

The tourist office produces a handy accommodation booklet, listing a whole gamut of hotels and pensions.

Hotel Kurpark (☎ 891 04; www.hotel-kurpark.at; Welzergasse 29; s/d from €38/68; P ⚤) This small hotel backing onto the *Kurpark* is more a pension than anything else, with a large garden, indoor and outdoor pools and bright, spacious, rooms.

Pension Maria (☎ 430 33; Elisabethstrasse 11; s/d €38.50/60; P ⚤) Sporting three stars, this place is only a short walk south of the town centre on a quiet suburban, tree-lined street.

Pension Garni Margit (☎ 897 18; www.pension -margit.at; Mühlgasse 15-17; r from €55; P) Margit, 500m east of Hauptplatz, has a homey ambience, a garden and old-style rooms with high ceilings. A couple of *Heurigen* are also located on the street.

Hotel Sacher Baden (☎ 48400-0; www.sacher-baden .at; Helenstrasse 55; s/d from €74/106; P) This modern, four-star hotel, associated with Hotel Sacher in Vienna (p109), is suitably plush and accommodating, and has a lovely café-restaurant and garden.

Hotel Schloss Weikersdorf (☎ 483 01; www.hotel schlossweikersdorf.at; Schlossgasse 9-11; s/d from €65/98; P ⚤) Stay here to experience a genuine Renaissance-castle ambience and appearance, which is usually reflected in room furnishings. The hotel adjoins Doublhoff-park and has a sauna and indoor swimming pool.

Eating

Café Central (☎ 48 454; Hauptplatz 19; coffee €2.40-3; 7am-9pm Tue-Sat, 8am-9pm Sun) Central is indeed central, taking pride of place on the Hauptplatz. It's a '60s-style café that's a bit on the dark side but full of character.

Gasthaus Zum Reichsapfel (Spiegelgasse 2; mains €6-11; dinner Mon, Wed & Fri, lunch & dinner Sat & Sun) This rustic restaurant is a mix of beer hall and wine tavern, with beer on tap, plenty of local wine and daily Austrian specials.

Venezia (☎ 443 20; Wassergasse 16; pizza €5-8, mains €9-12; 11.30am-11pm) Occupying a quiet courtyard with ivy-covered walls, this pleas-

ant Italian restaurant has a Mediterranean feel and bigger-than-average pizzas.

Pauli's (☎ 430 24; Beethovengasse 10; mains €9-23; 6pm-2am Mon-Sat) This modern restaurant offers a variety of international cuisine, specialises in steaks, and has a grassy outdoor seating area. It's also a nice spot for a drink in the evening.

Rauhenstein (☎ 412 51-6, Weilburgstrasse 11-13; mains €8-20; dinner) Rauhenstein offers international cuisine and the best dining in town. Also within the same hotel complex is **Café Sauerhof** (7am-6pm) which has extensive Sunday brunches; on the first Sunday in the month there's also live jazz.

There's a **Billa** (Wassergasse 14) supermarket in town, but the best places for compiling hot or cold snacks are the **market stalls** (Brusattiplatz).

Baden is not known for its nightlife, but to combine wine and dining, ask at Baden Tourismus for the opening schedule of the various *Heurigen* in and around town.

Getting There & Away

Regional and S-Bahn trains run to and from Baden up to four times an hour from Vienna's Südbahnhof (€5.50, 20 to 30 minutes). The *Lokalbahn* tram (€5.50, 62 minutes, every 15 minutes) and buses (€4.50, 40 minutes, hourly) from Karlsplatz in Vienna do the same job, but take a bit longer. Two to four trains per hour run to Wiener Neustadt (€5.50, 20 minutes).

The north–south road routes, Hwy 17 and the A2, pass a few kilometres to the east of the town.

SÜD-ALPIN

Landscape-wise, the southern corner of Lower Austria, known as the Süd-Alpin (Southern Alps), is the province's most appealing region. Here the hills rise to meet the Alps, peaking at Schneeberg (2076m), a mountain popular with the Viennese for its skiing and hiking possibilities. Nearby Semmering has long been a favourite of the capital's burghers, due mainly to its alpine air. One of the greatest highlights of the area though is the journey there; the winding railway over the Semmering Pass has been designated a Unesco World Heritage site.

WIENER NEUSTADT

☎ 02622 / pop 37,400

First known simply as Neustadt (New City) or Nova Civitas, Wiener Neustadt was built by the Babenbergs in 1194 with the help of King Richard the Lionheart's ransom payment (see p133). It became a Habsburg residence in the 15th century, during the reign of Friedrich III, whose famous AEIOU (*Alles Erdreich Ist Österreich Untertan*; Austria rules the world) engraving can be found in a number of places throughout the city. Severely damaged in WWII (only 18 homes were left unscathed), Wiener Neustadt has bounced back over the ensuing centuries and is once again home to a pretty Altstadt.

Orientation & Information

The town is centred on the large Hauptplatz, where you'll find the **tourist office** (☎ 373-311; www.wiener-neustadt.at; Hauptplatz 3; ☒ 8am-5pm Mon-Fri, 8am-noon Sat) which provides the free booklet, *Cultural Promenade*, describing the central sights and giving their locations on a map. Much of the town centre, including the Hauptplatz, is pedestrian-only.

The *Hauptbahnhof* is less than 1km to the southwest of the Hauptplatz; regional buses also stop here. It has bike rental, a travel agency and a *Bankomat* and, as with many small cities, the main post office is next door.

Sights

While the **Hauptplatz** is too big to be truly charming, it is lined with elegant buildings, not least of which are the three parts of the **Rathaus** (first mentioned in 1401), featuring an arcade and colourful crests. East of *Hauptplatz* is **Neukloster** (☎ 231-02; Ungargasse; admission free; ☒ dawn-dusk), a 14th-century Gothic church with striking baroque fittings and a dark-wood pulpit. The finely carved tomb of Empress Eleonore, wife to Friedrich III, is found behind the high altar.

To the north of the *Hauptplatz* is the Romanesque **Dom** (☎ 373-440; Domplatz; admission free; ☒ dawn-dusk), erected in 1279 but subsequently much rebuilt. It has a rather bare and grey exterior, and two severe-looking square towers, and the interior has an unbalanced look, caused by the chancel being

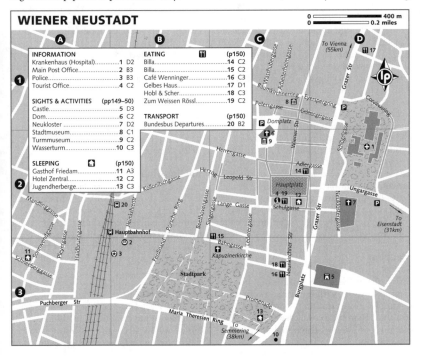

WIENER NEUSTADT

| | | 0 — 400 m |
| | | 0 — 0.2 miles |

| INFORMATION | |
| Krankenhaus (Hospital)...........1 D2 |
| Main Post Office........................2 B3 |
| Police..3 B3 |
| Tourist Office............................4 C2 |

| SIGHTS & ACTIVITIES (pp149–50) |
| Castle.......................................5 D3 |
| Dom..6 C2 |
| Neukloster................................7 D2 |
| Stadtmuseum............................8 C1 |
| Turmmuseum.............................9 C2 |
| Wasserturm..............................10 C3 |

| SLEEPING 🏠 (p150) |
| Gasthof Friedam........................11 A3 |
| Hotel Zentral.............................12 C2 |
| Jugendherberge........................13 C3 |

| EATING 🍴 (p150) |
| Billa..14 C2 |
| Billa..15 C2 |
| Café Wenninger........................16 C3 |
| Gelbes Haus.............................17 D1 |
| Hobl & Scher.............................18 C3 |
| Zum Weissen Rössl....................19 C3 |

| TRANSPORT (p150) |
| Bundesbus Departures...............20 B2 |

LOWER AUSTRIA

out of line with the nave, and the asymmetric arch that connects the two. Fifteenth-century wooden apostles peer down from pillars, and there's a baroque high altar and pulpit. At the Dom's southwest corner is the **Turmmuseum** (☎ 373-441; admission €2; ⏱ 10am-5pm Tue & Wed, 10am-8pm Thu, 10am-noon Fri, 10am-4pm Sat May-Oct), a free-standing tower that provides grand views over the city's rooftops. The key for the Turmmuseum is available from the **Stadtmuseum** (☎ 373-950; Petergasse 2a; adult/child €3/1.50; ⏱ 10am-5pm Tue & Wed, 10am-8pm Thu, 10am-noon Fri, 10am-4pm Sat May-Oct), housed in the former St Peter's monastery. Its showcase displays include artefacts from the Dom and photos of the devastation Allied bombing wrought on the town.

Heading south from the Hauptplatz, the imposing **castle** (☎ 381-0; Burgplatz 1; admission free) soon comes into view. Its four towers and walls date from the 13th century, though it had to be completely rebuilt after WWII. From the mid-18th century it has housed a military academy (founded by Empress Maria Theresia) which at one time was commanded by the young Rommel, pre-'desert fox' days. Visits are by appointment only. Within the complex is **St Georgs Kapelle** (admission free; ⏱ 10am-5pm), with a fine late-Gothic interior. Maximilian I, who was born in the castle, is buried under the altar. On the outside wall is the **Wappenwand** (Heraldic Wall) comprising 15th-century carvings of 107 coats of arms. This wall was all that survived the bombing during WWII (the stained glass had already been removed to the Altaussee salt mines in the Salzkammergut). The statue below the window is Friedrich III, whose AEIOU motto also appears on the wall.

Further south, rising between the convergence of two busy roads, is the town's **Wasserturm** (water tower), built between 1909 and 1910. Its shape intentionally apes the gilded goblet donated to the townsfolk by King Matthias Corvinus of Hungary after he took the town in 1487.

Sleeping

Gasthof Friedam (☎ 230 81; Schneeberggasse 16; s/d €32/44; **P**) Friedam is one of the best budget choices in town, with renovated rooms and a simple pub-restaurant downstairs. It's less than 10 minutes' walk west of the train station. For stays of three nights or more, prices drop.

Hotel Zentral (☎ 237 93; www.hotel-zentral.tos.at; Hauptplatz 27; s/d from €40/60) Zentral is about as central as you can get, and its stylish rooms have a distinct modern feel. Room prices depend on their size and view (those overlooking the *Hauptplatz* cost more).

Jugendherberge (☎ 296 95; oejhv-noe@oejhv.or.at; Promenade 1; dm €12.50, s/d €16/32; **P**) This HI hostel is the pale house in the Stadtpark, near the *Wasserturm*. Phone ahead as reception is not always open and the place is often full.

Eating

Hobl & Scher (☎ 269 69; Neunkirchner Strasse 34; mains €8-15; ⏱ dinner Mon-Sat) The dark red interior of this stylish restaurant is a perfect complement to the excellent wine selection and Italian, Asian and Austrian menu.

Gelbes Haus (☎ 264 00; Kaiserbrunngasse 11; menus from €40; ⏱ lunch & dinner Tue-Sat) This noble restaurant is the best in town, with four- to seven-course menus of divine Austrian cuisine. Thursday evening is a good time to visit; every second person dines free.

Zum Weissen Rössl (☎ 233 04; Hauptplatz 3; mains €6-10; ⏱ 7am-8pm Mon-Fri, 7am-5pm Sat) This *Gasthaus* may look a little dusty from the outside, but it's cosy and welcoming and serves solid Austrian food. There are outside tables on the Hauptplatz.

Café Wenninger (☎ 223 37; Neunkirchner Strasse 36; coffee €2-5; ⏱ 7am-11pm Mon-Thu, 7am-midnight Fri, 8.30am-midnight Sat, 8.30am-10pm Sun) The warm atmosphere of this traditional café is helped along by soft lighting, games, booths and good coffee.

Billa supermarkets can be found on Bahngasse and Hauptplatz, which also has several *Würstel* (sausage) stands.

Getting There & Away

Half-hourly trains connect Wiener Neustadt with Vienna (€8.40, 45 minutes) and the Hungarian town of Sopron (€6, 25 to 45 minutes) daily. Bundesbuses depart from the northern end of Wiener Neustadt train station for Forchtenstein (€4, 30 minutes, three times daily on weekdays) and other destinations.

SEMMERING

☎ 02664 / pop 1100

Semmering has long been an alpine resort, famed for its clean air. It's also a popular destination with those Viennese eager for a bit of skiing on weekends but unwilling to travel long distances; artificial snow guarantees white slopes all winter.

Orientation & Information

Semmering sits on a south-facing slope above the Semmering Pass. There's no real centre to the resort: it's mostly ranged along Hochstrasse, which forms an arc above the train station.

Outside the unstaffed train station, which is a 20-minute walk from the **Kurverwaltung tourist office** (☎ 200 25; www.semmering.at; Passhöhe 248; 8am-4.30pm Mon-Fri), is a map of the resort. At the same location as the tourist office is a bank and the regional tourist office, **Tourismusregion Süd-Alpin** (☎ 2539; www.noesued .at; 8am-4pm Mon-Fri).

Sights

There's not a lot to do at the resort except relax, breathe in the air and do a bit of walking or skiing. The tourist office has Wanderkarte maps (text in German) and brochures outlining scenic walks. Overlooking Semmering to the south is the **Hirschenkogel** (1340m), where a modern cable car whisks walkers (one-way €8, return €11.50) or skiers (day pass €26) up to the top. Regional skiing day passes are also available (€28.50).

The resort has a couple of ski schools, a golf course (with some of the steepest holes you'll ever play), mini golf and tennis courts. The swimming pool, sauna complex and fitness room in the four-star **Hotel Panhaus** (☎ 818 10; Hochstrasse 32) can be used by non-guests (€9 weekdays, €14 weekends).

Sleeping & Eating

Of the plethora of sleeping options, most are situated on Hochstrasse. Many have their own restaurants, which makes things easy and convenient.

Hotel Wagner (☎ 25 12-0; www.panoramahotel -wagner.at; Hochstrasse 267; r from €52;) This hotel is the epitome of health – rooms come with wood furniture, natural cotton bedding and grand views of the valley below. Yoga, meditation and Qi Gong courses are offered and there are sauna, spa and massage facilities. Needless to say, its highly rated **restaurant** (mains €8-16) only uses organic products.

Pension-Restaurant Löffler (☎ 23 04; www.pen sion-loeffler.com; Hochstrasse 174; s/d €36/66;) Löf-

fler is a fresh, colourful and modern pension with pristine rooms. Its **restaurant** (mains €8-16) serves above-average Austrian cuisine, displays local artwork and has a large outdoor patio.

Gasthof Edelweiss (☎ 2284; edel-weiss@aon.at; Hochstrasse 57; s/d €33/66;) This quaint wooden chalet is set back from the road in a grove of trees, and has decent rooms, a basic restaurant, a children's playground and lovely secluded garden.

Hotel-Restaurant Belvedere (☎ 22 70; hotel.bel veder@telecom.at; Hochstrasse 60; s/d from €32/64, mains €6-18;) This family-run hotel has a friendly atmosphere and alpine décor, and excellent facilities; swimming pool, sauna, large garden and patio area. Rooms are modern and come with balcony. The restaurant has regional dishes, including fish and seasonal specialities.

There is a Billa supermarket between Hotel Belvedere and the main highway.

Getting There & Away

There are two direct trains daily on weekends from Graz to Semmering (€16.20, 1½ to two hours) and many more Monday to Friday. For trains from Vienna, see the boxed text (below).

SEMMERING PASS BY TRAIN

For its time, it was an incredible feat of engineering, something which took more than 20,000 workers years to complete. Even today, it never fails to impress with its switchbacks, 15 tunnels and 16 viaducts. This is the **Semmering railway** (www.semmering bahn.at), a 42km stretch of track that begins at Gloggnitz and rises 455m to its highest point of 896m at Semmering Bahnhof.

Completed in 1854 by Karl Ritter von Ghega, the Semmering line was Europe's first alpine railway, and due to its engineering genius, gained Unesco World Heritage status in 1998. It passes through some impressive scenery of precipitous cliffs and forested hills en route (make sure you sit on the right); the most scenic section is the 30-minute stretch between Semmering and Payerbach (€5.50). If you're leaving from Vienna, there are four direct services daily to Semmering (€17.20, 1¾ hours) and frequent trains with a change at Wiener Neustadt.

LOWER AUSTRIA

If you're under your own steam, consider taking the small backroad northwest of Semmering to the Höllental via Breitenstein; the road winds its way down the mountain, passing under the railway line a number of times and taking in the spectacular scenery you see on the train trip.

SCHNEEBERG, RAXALPE & HÖLLENTAL

Lying to the north of Semmering are two of Lower Austria's highest points, Schneeberg (2076m) and the Raxalpe. The area is a hugely popular destination for hiking due to its relative proximity to Vienna.

The ascent of Schneeberg by cogwheel steam train or diesel 'Salamander' train is a full-day excursion from the capital, providing excellent views and good walks. The **Schneebergbahn** (☎ 02636-36 61-20; www.schneeberg bahn.at; Salamander one-way/return €19/27, steam train €25/33; ✆ late Apr-Oct) leaves from Puchberg am Schneeberg and takes about an hour with the Salamander and around 1¼ hours with the stream train; check the website for the train timetable.

Near the top station, Hochschneeberg (1795m), is a hotel and restaurant, and a viewing terrace by a chapel dedicated to the Empress Elisabeth (wife of Franz Josef). From the station, a path leads to **Klosterwappen** (2075m) and the mountain hut **Fischerhütte**; these are each about a 70-minute walk from the station, and 20 minutes from each

other. Above Fischerhütte is the **Kaiserstein viewpoint** (2061m), with a beehive-shaped monument to Emperor Franz I. The most impressive part of the view from here is the Breite Ries, a bowl-shaped area of erosion with stark grey and red cliffs.

On the southern side of Schneeberg is the scenic **Höllental** (Hell's Valley), a deep, narrow gorge created by the Schwarza River. Rising to the south of Höllental is the **Raxalpe**, another point of interest for walkers; from Hirschwang, a small village in Höllental, the **Raxseilbahn** (☎ 02666-524 97; www.raxseilbahn .at; adult/concession €9.40/8.30; ✆ year-round) cable car ascends to 1547m and hiking trails. The Raxseilbahn is the site of Austria's first cable car, built in 1926.

Puchberg am Schneeberg has places to stay and eat – ask the **tourist office** (☎ 02636-2256; www.puchberg.at). In Höllental, the **Hotel Marienhof** (☎ 02666-529 95; www.marienhof.at; Reichenau; s/d from €62/94; Ⓟ ✆), a grand old dame with a silver-service restaurant, is not far from the Raxseilbahn.

Getting There & Away

There are nine daily direct trains from Wiener Neustadt to Puchberg am Schneeberg (€5.50, 46 minutes). Hirschwang (€5.40, 50 minutes) is only a little harder to get to; a train must first be taken to Payerbach, from where regular buses run up the Höllental valley.

Burgenland

CONTENTS

BURGENLAND

Most tourists to Austria give Burgenland, Austria's easternmost province, a wide berth. At first glance, it's easy to see why; this long strip of land bordering Hungary and Slovenia doesn't have the bombastic architecture of Austria's major cities or the soaring mountains of the Austrian Alps in its armoury. But what it does have is more sun and wine than any other place you'll find within the borders of Austria. This is certainly reason enough alone to make a detour east, at least for one day.

The province receives a reputed 300 days of sunshine a year; couple this with a rich soil base and a wine history dating back to pre-Roman days, and you have Austria's best wine-producing region. What better way to spend an afternoon, sampling local *Weine* (wines) in a *Heurigen* (wine tavern) under a warm sun? But the sun's influence extends not only to wine. Shallow Neusiedler See, the largest steppe lake in Central Europe, is a water-sports lover's dream come true, and when the sun burns the clouds away hoards of Viennese descend on the lake, hungry for a taste of a holiday by the sea. The lake is also home to a plethora of bird species and is part of one of the six national parks of Austria, the Neusiedler See-Seewinkel National Park.

Culture and castles are two more words that could easily make the cut for Burgenland's dictionary definition. Eisenstadt, the provincial capital, is a pocket-sized town, complete with its own majestic *Schloss* (castle) and famous former-resident, Joseph Haydn. And while the province didn't receive its name from the plethora of *Burgen* (castles) dotting its landscape, it would be an easy mistake to make. This, a former frontier land in the best traditions of a John Wayne western, is filled to overflowing with these stolid protectors, either lovingly restored to their former glory or left in peaceful ruin.

HIGHLIGHTS

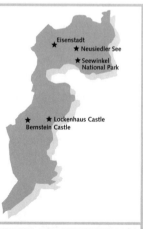

- Sampling the excellent wine in one of the thousand **Heurigen** (p160) dotted across Burgenland

- Swimming, splashing or sailing in the **Neusiedler See** (p159), Central Europe's only steppe lake

- Taking a cycle-trip through the **Neusiedler See-Seewinkel National Park** (p162), a haven for birdlife

- Spending the night as a noble in **Lockenhaus** (p163) or **Bernstein Castle** (p163)

- Exploring **Eisenstadt** (p156), the provincial capital and home of Haydn

- POPULATION: 277,000　- AREA: 3966 SQ KM　- HIGHEST ELEVATION: GESCHRIEBENSTEIN 884M

History

Burgenland is the youngest of Austria's provinces, only gaining such an elevated title after the collapse of the Austrian empire at the end of WWI. It's so named, not for the numerous castles, but for the 'burg' suffix of the four western Hungarian district names at that time – Pressburg (Bratislava), Wieselburg (Moson), Ödenburg (Soporn) and Eisenburg (Vasvär).

The region was first settled some 7000 to 12,000 years ago, and over the ensuing millennia many peoples tried their hand at settling permanently, including the Illyrians, Celts and Romans. The arrival of the Hungarians in the 10th century however changed the face of Burgenland forever. The region soon became a buffering zone between the Hungarians and the Austrian Germans, each vying for the upper hand over their adversary and trading uneasy peace with outright war throughout the centuries.

The arrival of marauding Turks in the 16th century neutralised both the Hungarians and the Austrians, but also devastated the local population. Landlords, without anyone to tend their farms, invited substantial numbers of Croats to settle the land. Their presence is still felt today – around 10% of the population is Croatian, Croatian is an official language and a few small towns in middle Burgenland sport Croat signs.

With the defeat of the Turks at the gates of Vienna in 1683, relative peace settled over the area. With the demise of the Habsburg empire after WWI Austria lost control of Hungary, but managed to retain the German-speaking western region of Hungary under the Treaty of St Germain. The new province of Burgenland was born, but all was not well. Hungary was loath to lose Ödenburg (Sopron) to Austria, and a plebiscite held in December 1921 (under controversial circumstances) resulted in the people of Ödenburg opting to stay in Hungary. Burgenland lost its natural capital, and Eisenstadt became the new *Hauptstadt* (capital).

Climate

Burgenland enjoys hot summers and rather mild winters compared to the alpine reaches of western Austria. This Pannonian microclimate is perfect for wine production. The Neusiedler See, to the north of the province, consistently records some of the highest sum-

mer temperatures in Austria, but the large expanse of water ensures high humidity.

Language

With its close proximity to Hungary, it's no surprise that some Burgenlanders speak German with a slight Hungarian accent. Burgenland is the only province to include Croatian and Hungarian alongside German as official languages.

Getting There & Away

Eisenstadt and the northern extension of Neusiedler See are easily reached by train from Vienna and Lower Austria. Lower and middle Burgenland are less accessible by train; here the bus is often your best option. The A2 autobahn, heading south from Vienna towards Graz and Carinthia, runs parallel to the western border of Burgenland. Its many off-ramps provide quick, easy access to much of the province.

Getting Around

Like the rest of Austria, destinations not connected to the country's extensive train network are covered by bus. From late April to October, ferries ply the Neusiedler See, linking Podersdorf with Rust and Breitenbrunn, and Illmitz with Mörbisch (p159).

Burgenland is a cyclist's dream – much of the landscape is flat or, at most, gentle rolling hills, and is crisscrossed with well-marked cycle paths. Local tourist offices can supply cycle maps, or simply log on to www .bikeburgenland.at – in German.

EISENSTADT

☎ 02682 / pop 12,000

After a quick glance at the town's tourist paraphernalia, you have to wonder whether Eisenstadt has anything to offer apart from its connection with its most famous former resident, seminal 18th-century musician and composer Josef Haydn. And while most tourists do visit Burgenland's capital and largest town to bathe in the glow of one of classical music's greatest sons, the town's *Altstadt* (old town) alone, with its cobblestone streets and proud houses, is worth a day trip from Vienna, or even an overnight stay.

History

The first documentary evidence of Eisenstadt dates from 1264 (although archaeological digs have confirmed settlement since the Stone Age). At the time, the town was under control of the Hungarians, but it wasn't until 1371 that it gained its charter from the ruling nobility. In the ensuing centuries the Hungarians and the Habsburgs fought for control of Eisenstadt, but it was the Turks who decided the town's fate by neutralising the Hungarian threat at the 1526 Battle of Mohács. In 1622 Eisenstadt became the residence of the Esterházys, a powerful Hungarian family, and in 1648 the town was granted the status of *Freistadt* (free city) by Ferdinand III. In 1925 it became the capital of Austria's newest province, Burgenland, after Sopron's citizens voted to join with Hungary (see p155).

Orientation

Eisenstadt's pretty *Altstadt*, centred on the pedestrian-only Hauptstrasse and Schloss Esterházy, is surrounded by a modern, uninteresting urban sprawl. It's about a 10-minute walk north along Bahnstrasse from the train station to the *Altstadt*. The main bus station is on Domplatz, one street south the Hauptstrasse.

MAPS

Eisenstadt Tourismus hands out free maps which are highly adequate for most tourist needs.

Information

INTERNET ACCESS

Ricky's Cafe (☎ 661 77; Pfarrgasse 18; ⓦ 9.30am-2pm)

MEDICAL SERVICES

Hospital & Pharmacy (☎ 601; Esterházystrasse 26)

MONEY

There are a number of banks with ATMs on the Hauptstrasse and along its side streets.

POST

Main Post Office (☎ 62 27 10; Ignaz P Semmelweis-Gasse 7)

TOURIST INFORMATION

Burgenland Tourismus (☎ 02682-633 84-0; www .burgenland.info; Schloss Esterházy, Eisenstadt; ⓦ 9am-5pm Apr-Oct, 9am-2pm Mon-Fri Nov-Mar)

Eisenstadt Tourismus (☎ 673 90; www.eisenstadt .at - in German; Schloss Esterházy; ⓦ 9am-5pm Apr-Oct, 9am-2pm Mon-Fri Nov-Mar) Provides a useful brochure listing hotels, private rooms, restaurants, festivals and details of museum opening times and prices.

Sights & Activities

The most outstanding building in Eisenstadt is Schloss Esterházy (☎ 719 3000; www.schloss -esterhazy.at; Schloss Esterházy; adult/child €5/4, grand tours €7.50/6.50; ⓦ 9am-5pm Apr–mid-Nov, 9am-5pm Mon-Fri mid-Nov–Mar), a giant, Schönbrunn-yellow castle/palace that dominates Esterházyplatz. Dating from the 14th century, the *Schloss* received an initial makeover in baroque, and later in Neoclassical style. Much of it is now occupied by the provincial government and only a few rooms are open to the public for viewing by guided tour.

Egotists will enjoy the multiple reflections in the mirrored corridor but the highlight

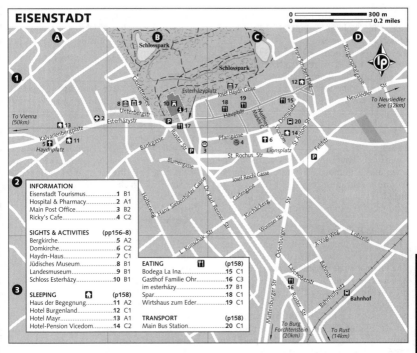

of any tour is the highly-frescoed **Haydn Hall**. The hall's former marble floor was replaced by an aesthetically inferior but acoustically superior wooden floor (it's rated the second-best concert hall in Austria, after Vienna's Musikverein). During Haydn's employment by the Esterházys from 1761 to 1790, he conducted an orchestra on a near-nightly basis in this wonderful hall. Tours then continue on to a rather standard exhibition on the Esterházy family. Note that grand tours only take place at 10am and 2pm in July and August; tours in English are rare so call ahead to enquire when the next one is planned.

Josef Haydn revealed that Eisenstadt was 'where I wish to live and to die'. He achieved the former, being a resident for 31 years, but it was in Vienna that he finally tinkled his last tune. He also rather carelessly neglected to give any directive about his preferred residence after death. His skull was stolen from a temporary grave shortly after he died in 1809, after which it ended up on display in a Viennese museum. The headless cadaver was subsequently returned to Eisenstadt (in 1932), but it wasn't until 1954

that the skull joined it. The white marble tomb that now contains his reunited parts can be viewed in the **Bergkirche** (☎ 628 38; Haydnplatz 1; adult/senior/student €2.50/2/1; ☒ 9am-noon & 1-5pm Apr-Oct). The church itself is remarkable for the Kalvarienberg, a unique calvary display; access is via a separate entrance to the rear of the church. Life-sized figures depict the Stations of the Cross in a series of suitably austere, dungeon-like rooms.

For more on Haydn, visit the **Haydn-Haus** (☎ 719 3900; www.haydnhaus.at; Josef Haydn Gasse 21; adult/concession/family €3.50/2.50/8; ☒ 9am-5pm Apr-Oct), the great composer's former residence to the east of the *Schloss*. It now contains a small museum of unexciting Haydn memorabilia that only true Haydn fanatics will probably enjoy.

More intriguing are two museums just west of the *Schloss*, the **Landesmuseum** (☎ 600 1209; Museumgasse 1-5; adult/concession/family €3/1.50/5.80; ☒ 9am-5pm Tue-Sat, 10am-5pm Sun mid-Feb–Dec) and the **Jüdisches Museum** (☎ 651 45; www.ojm.at; Unterbergstrasse 6; adult/concession €3.70/2; ☒ 10am-5pm Tue-Sun May-Oct). The former delves into the local history of the region, and includes a collection of Roman mosaics, ancient arte-facts, wine-making equipment and some im-pressive propaganda posters from the 1920s. There's also a room devoted to Franz Liszt, complete with a warty death mask of the Hungarian composer. The latter primarily hosts temporary and permanent exhibitions on Jewish culture, and includes one of the few synagogues to survive the *Reichskristallnacht* (p27) of 1938.

Tours

Eisenstadt Tourismus offers tours of the town and a number of wine cellars, but all require a minimum of eight persons to go ahead. It may, however, be possible to join a group; call the tourist office to check.

Festivals & Events

The high point on Eisenstadt's cultural cal-endar is, of course, associated with Haydn. The **Internationale Haydntage**, staged through much of September, attracts both local and international acts and features anything from chamber pieces to full-scale orchestra performances. Most events take place in the Haydn Hall or the Bergkirche; for more in-formation contact the **Haydnfestspiele Büro** (☎ 618 66-0; www.haydnfestival.at - in German).

Behind the palace is the **Schlosspark,** a large, relaxing park and the setting for the **Fest der 1000 Weine** (Festival of 1000 Wines) in late August.

Sleeping

Staff at the tourist office are happy to sup-ply tourists with a complete list of accom-modation options.

Hotel-Pension Vicedom (☎ 642 22; www.krato .at; Vicedom 5; s/d from €36/62) This comfortable hotel-pension occupies a quiet corner in the heart of town. Rooms are tasteful in their simplicity.

Hotel Mayr (☎ 627 51; www.tiscover.com/hotel .mayr; Kalvarienbergplatz 1; s/d €31/57) Aside from private rooms, this simple hotel is one of the cheapest options in town. The rooms are a decent size.

Haus der Begegnung (☎ 632 90; www.hdb-eisen stadt.at; Kalvarienbergplatz 11; s/d from €44/74; **P**) Close to the Bergkirche is this large three-star hotel, which sports modern, well-kept rooms.

Hotel Burgenland (☎ 6960; www.hotelburgenland .at; Franz Schubert-Platz 1; s/d from €85/120; **P** **♨**) Bur-genland is top-dog in town, and Eisenstadt's

only four-star hotel. Its services are tailored to business people and while it doesn't look like much from the outside, the rooms are quite modern.

Eating

Bodega La Ina (☎ 623 05; Hauptstrasse 48; tapas €3-8; ☺ 8am-midnight Tue-Thu, 8am-1am Fri & Sat) Occupy-ing a quiet courtyard off the main street, this modern tapas bar is overwhelming friendly and stocks some excellent Spanish wines.

im esterhäzy (☎ 628 19; Esterhäzy Platz 5; mains €8-20; ☺ 8am-midnight Mon-Thu, 8am-2am Fri & Sat, 9am-midnight Sun) This fine eatery directly opposite the *Schloss*, with above-average international cuisine and cellar-like surroundings, has a distinct touch of class about it.

Gasthof Familie Ohr (☎ 624 60; Ruster Strasse 51; mains €8-16; ☺ 8am-11pm Tue-Sun) Close to the train station, this *Gasthof* offers consistently good food, and a spattering of Pannonian (west Hungarian) cooking.

Wirtshaus zum Eder (☎ 626 45; Hauptstrasse 25; mains €7-15; ☺ 9.30am-midnight) Seasonal dishes and a large conservatory are the big attrac-tions here, but if you'd like a break from Austrian cuisine, there is also a colourful sushi bar out front.

A **Spar** (Hauptstrasse 13) supermarket on the main street is handy for self-caterers.

Getting There & Away

Bus is the best option for travel between Eisenstadt and Vienna; eight direct buses leave from Vienna's Südtiroler Platz daily (€6, one hour), with plenty more on week-days. Ten trains make the same trip daily (from Südbahnhof), but a change is required at either Neusiedl am See or Wulkaprod-ersdorf (€11.50, 1¼ hours). Again, there are more connections Monday to Friday.

AROUND EISENSTADT
Burg Forchtenstein

Resting atop a dolomite spur some 20km southwest of Eisenstadt, **Burg Forchtenstein** (☎ 02626-812 12; www.burg-forchtenstein.at - in German; Melinda Esterhazy-Platz 1; guided tour of 1 exhibition adult/senior/student €4.75/4/3.10, treasury & weapon exhibitions €11.85/11.10/6.50; ☺ 9am-6pm, last entry 5pm Apr-Oct) is one of the most imposing castles in Burgen-land. This large, solid stronghold was built in the 14th century and enlarged by the Ester-häzys in 1635, in whose hands it still remains. Apart from the grand view from its ramparts, the castle's highlights include an impressive collection of armour and weapons, portraits of regal Esterházys and spoils from the Turkish wars (the castle curators will proudly tell you Forchtenstein was the only castle in the area not to fall to the Turks). Its *Schatzkammer* (treasury) contains a rich collection of jewellery and porcelain.

GETTING THERE & AWAY

Four buses run directly from Eisenstadt (€4.60, 40 minutes) and three from Wiener Neustadt (€4, 30 minutes) to Forchtenstein on weekdays.

Wiesen

About 5km north of Forchtenstein is the small town of Wiesen which, during summer, transforms itself into Austria's version of Glastonbury. The series of summer festivals hosted here are the biggest in the country and range from jazz to reggae. For more information, log on to www.wiesen.at – in German.

Wiesen can be reached by bus or train from Vienna's Südbahnhof (€11, 1½ hours) on a regular basis Monday to Saturday.

NEUSIEDLER SEE

Neusiedler See, the only steppe lake in Central Europe, is the lowest point in Austria. But what it lacks in height, it certainly makes up for in other areas. Ringed by a wetland area of reed beds, it's an ideal breeding ground for nearly 300 bird species and its Seewinkel area is a particular favourite of birdwatchers. The lake's average depth is 1.5m, which means the water warms quickly in summer. Add to this a prevalent warm wind from the northwest and you have a water enthusiast's dream come true, which explains the thousands of tourists who flock to the lake for windsurfing and sailing during the summer months. The best swimming beaches are on the eastern side of the lake as the western shore is thick with reed beds. The lake's shallowness also attracts many families – the only drawback is that the water has a slightly saline quality, as there is no natural outlet.

The area is also made for cycling; a flat cycle track winds all the way round the reed beds, the ferries crisscrossing the lake carry bikes and most hotels and pensions cater well to cyclists and their bikes. It's possible to make a full circuit of the lake but as the southern section stretches into Hungary, remember to take your passport (path open April to November).

To top it all off there are acres upon acres of vineyards, producing some of the best of Austria's wines. Rust, on the western shore of the lake, is a perfect place to sample one fine glass after another.

Neusiedler See is best visited in summer; the tourist trade is much reduced in the winter, when many hotels and restaurants close down. If you're overnighting, inquire at tourist offices or hotels about the useful *Neusiedler See Gästekarte* which provides free admission to swimming areas and museums (including many in Sopron), plus free use of public transport (travel on ferries is half-price).

Getting Around

There is at least one *Radverlieh* (bike hire shop) in every town on the lake; rental costs around €10 to €15 per day. Pick up a copy of the handy *Radtouren* map, available from tourist offices, which lists all *Radverlieh* and marks out cycle routes around the lake.

Ferry services across the Neusiedler See are provided by a number of companies from around 9am to 6pm May to the beginning of October; it costs between €5 and €7 for ferries between Podersdorf and Breitenbrunn, Podersdorf and Rust and Möbisch and Illmitz.

Bus connections are frequent; see the separate towns below for specific details.

RUST

☎ 02685 / pop 1700

Rust, 14km east of Eisenstadt, is arguably the prettiest town on Neusiedler See. Its prosperity has been based on wine for centuries; in 1524 the emperor granted local vintners the right to display the letter 'R' on their wine barrels and today the corks still bear this insignia. It's best to sample this history in one of the town's many *Heurigen*. It's also famous for storks, which roost on dozens of chimneys throughout the town.

Orientation & Information

Bundesbuses stop at the post office, 100m from Conradplatz, a small square that leads

BURGENLAND

to the town hall and Rathausplatz, the focal point of the village.

The **tourist office** (☎ 505; www.rust.or.at - in German; Conradplatz 1, Rathaus; ☒ 9am-6pm Mon-Fri, 9am-4pm Sat, 9am-noon Sun Jul-Aug, 9am-5pm Mon-Fri, 9am-noon Sat & Sun Apr-Jun & Sep, 9am-4pm Mon-Thu, 9am-noon Fri Oct-Mar) has a list of wine growers offering tastings, plus hotels and private rooms in the town.

Sights & Activities

Rust's affluent past has left a legacy of attractive burghers' houses on and around the main squares. **Storks**, which descend on the town from the end of March to rear their young, take full advantage of these houses and their kindly owners; metal platforms are built atop many chimneys to entice the storks to build a nest. The clacking of expectant parents can be heard till late August. A good vantage point is attained from the tower of the **Katholische Kirche** (Haydengasse; admission €1; ☒ daylight hr summer) at the southern end of Rathausplatz. The **Fischerkirche** (☎ 502; Rathausplatz 16; admission €1; ☒ daylight hr summer), at the opposite end of Rathausplatz, is the oldest church in Rust, built between the 12th and 16th centuries.

Access to the **lake** and **bathing facilities** (☎ 591; Seebad; per day €4; ☒ 9am-7pm May–mid-Sep) is 1km down the reed-fringed Seepromenade. If you want to play in the lake, however, you're better off going elsewhere.

Sleeping

Storkencamp (☎ 595; office@gmeiner.co.at; Ruster Bucht; per adult/tent/car €5.50/3.50/3.50; ☒ Apr-Oct) With a large children's playground, bike rental, close proximity to the lake and free access to the bathing area, this campsite is a great place for families.

Ruster Jugendgästehaus (☎ 591; www.seebadrust .at - in German; Ruster Bucht 2; dm from €14.50; ☒ year-round) This HI hostel is only a few years old, which accounts for the pristine modern rooms. It's part of the bathing complex by the lake.

Alexander (☎ 301; www.pension-alexander.at - in German; Dorfmeistergasse 21; s/d from €29.50/59; P ☒) Though the Alexander has four stars, prices are very reasonable, plus guests can take advantage of its sauna, garden and outdoor swimming pool.

Hotel Sifkovits (☎ 276; Am Seekanal 8; s/d €67/102; P) Close to the centre of town, the Sifkovits is a fine family-run hotel with large rooms and a quiet ambience. It also has one of the finest **restaurants** (mains €8-17) in town.

Eating

When in Rust, do as the locals do and head for one of the many *Heurigen* around town. They're easy to spot – just look for the *Buschen* (small bush) hanging in front of doorways – highly enjoyable and more often than not have outside tables. Food is very Austrian and the excellent wine is from the surrounding hills.

Peter Schandl (☎ 265; Hauptstrasse 20; mains €5-10; ☒ 4pm-midnight Mon-Fri, 11am-midnight Sat & Sun Apr-Oct) Just off the Rathausplatz is this frequented *Buschenschank* (wine tavern), with top-notch food and a sunny garden.

Rathauskeller (☎ 261; Rathausplatz 1; mains €6-15; ☒ 11.30am-11pm Thu-Tue) If you'd prefer 300-year-old cellar-like surroundings, rustic décor and local specialities, head for the Rathauskeller instead.

THE WINES OF BURGENLAND

A trip to Burgenland without trying at least one glass of wine is a sin. From its most northern point to its most southern extreme, this small province is covered in vineyards, and the wine produced here is arguably the best in Austria. This is easy to understand when you realise that viticulture has been around since the Roman times, and possibly even before the arrival of Bacchus. Add 300 days of sunshine per year, rich soil and excellent drainage and you have the perfect recipe for great wine.

Burgenland produces mainly whites – Grüner Veltliner, Riesling, Chardonnay, Müller-Thurgau Weissburgunder – but reds, such as Blaufränkisch, Zweigelt, St Laurent, Pinor Noir and Cabernet Sauvignon, are fast making inroads. The area around Neusiedler See is known for its superb sweet wines, and more recently for its dry, full-bodied whites and reds. Middle Burgenland, in particular around the villages of Horitschon and Deutschkreutz, is the place to head for Blaufränkisch, a dry wine rich in tannin and full of character. Blaufränkisch is also the leading variety in southern Burgenland, but this area is better known for Uhudler, a wine with a distinctly fruity taste.

BURGENLAND

Inamera (☎ 64 73; Oggauer Strasse 29; mains €9-21; ☹ lunch & dinner Wed-Fri, 11.30am-10pm Sat & Sun) Inamera rates among the best restaurants to be found in the Neusiedler See region. Prices are above the norm, but the food, and its fantastic tree-shaded garden, make up for the price difference.

Getting There & Away

From Monday to Saturday there are hourly buses between Eisenstadt and Rust (€3, 25 minutes); on Sunday, only three make the same journey. For Neusiedl am See, a change is required in Eisenstadt. Ferries cross the lake to Podersdorf from mid-May to September (€6.90).

MÖRBISCH AM SEE

☎ 02685 / pop 2400

Mörbisch am See, a quiet town 6km south of Rust, and only a couple of kilometres short of the Hungarian border, is worth a stopover to soak up the relaxed atmosphere and take in the quaint whitewashed houses with hanging corn and flower-strewn balconies.

The town's ambience changes dramatically during the evening from mid-July to August due to the **Seefestspiele** (www.seefestspiele-moerbisch .at), a summer operetta festival which attracts some 200,000 each year and takes pride of place on the town's social calendar. Its biggest competitor is the **Opern Festspiele** (www .ofs.at; ☹ mid-Jul–Aug), an opera festival held in an old Roman quarry near St Margareten, 7km northwest of Mörbisch.

The local **tourist office** (☎ 8430; tourismus@ moerbisch.com; Hauptstrasse 23; ☹ 9am-5pm Mon-Fri, 9am-noon Sat & Sun Apr-Jun & Sep-Oct, 9am-6pm Jul-Aug) can fill you in on the festival, accommodation, *Heurigen* and lakeside facilities.

All buses pass through Rust on their way to Möbisch from Eisenstadt (€4.50, 40 minutes, hourly Monday to Friday). A foot- and cycle-only **border crossing** (☹ 6am-10pm Jun-Sep, 8am-8pm Apr, May & Oct) into Hungary, under 2km south of Mörbisch, is handy for those wishing to circumnavigate the lake. For those who've forgotten their passport, or don't have the energy for such an excursion, a ferry zips across to Illmitz (€5) from May to October.

PURBACH AM SEE

☎ 02683

Purbach am See, 17km north of Rust, is one of the prettiest towns on the lake. Its small, compact centre is filled with strong, squat houses and is still guarded by bastions and three gates, left over from the Turkish wars. While there isn't anything specific to see and do in the town – there is no direct access to Neusiedler See – it's worth spending time here soaking up the slow pace of life and wandering from one **wine cellar** (☹ from 4pm 1st Sat in month Apr-Oct) to the next along historic Kellergasse and Kellerplatz outside the town's walls.

The **tourist office** (☎ 5920-4; www.tiscover.at/pur bach; Hauptgasse 38; ☹ 9am-noon & 3-6pm Mon-Sat May-Sep, 9am-noon Mon-Fri Oct-Apr) has information on accommodation and wine. If you need a place to stay, look no further than **Camping Purbach & Jugendberge** (☎ 51 70; office@gmeiner .co.at; Türkenhain; per adult/tent/car €3/2.20/2, dm €11.70) on the edge of the reed beds, or **Purbachhof** (☎ 55 64; www.tiscover.com/purbachhof; Schulgasse 14; s/d from €30/60), a converted wine-maker's house which could easily double as a folk museum. For food, **Türken Keller** (☎ 5112; Schulgasse 9; mains €8-16; ☹ 5pm-midnight Thu & Fri, 11am-midnight Sat & Sun Jul & Aug, 11am-midnight Sat & Sun Sep-Dec & Mar-Jun, closed Jan & Feb), in the heart of Purbach, has one of the loveliest courtyards around and a lively, convivial atmosphere. Its name supposedly originates from a Turkish soldier who hid in the chimney to avoid being hauled off back to his homeland.

Seven daily trains heading for Neusiedler See from Eisenstadt pass through Purbach (€3, 20 minutes).

NEUSIEDL AM SEE

☎ 02167 / pop 5300

Neusiedl am See is the region's largest town and the most accessible from Vienna. Its good transport connections and central location at the northern point of the lake make it a perfect springboard for the rest of the region. Otherwise, there's no real reason to linger here.

Neusiedl's **tourist office** (☎ 86 00-0; www.neu siedlersee.com; Obere Hauptstrasse 24; ☹ 8am-5pm Mon-Fri, 9am-5pm Sat, 9am-noon Sun Jul-Aug, 8am-4pm Mon-Sat, 9am-noon Sun Apr-Jun & Sep-Oct) has more than enough information on the town. If you need a place to stay or eat look no further than **Rathausstüberl** (☎ 2883; www.rathaussttueberl .at; Kirchengasse 2; s/d from €28/56), a real gem just around the corner from the tourist office. Rooms are bright and airy and the **restaurant** (mains €8-15) serves local specialities

BURGENLAND

in its conservatory or tree-shaded inner courtyard.

Neusiedl has good train connections from Vienna's Südbahnhof (€9.70, 40 minutes, seven daily); there are also buses from Vienna, but a change is required in Simmering. Hourly buses travel down the eastern side of the lake, passing through Podersdorf (€4, 15 minutes) and Illmitz (€4.50, 30 minutes) before terminating in Apelton. Regular trains to Eisenstadt (€7.10, 40 minutes) pass through Purbach (€5.70, 15 minutes); you'll have to travel all the way to Eisenstadt to take a connecting bus to Rust though.

PODERSDORF AM SEE

☎ 02177 / pop 2100

Podersdorf am See, on the eastern shore, is the only town which can truly claim to be *Am See* (on the lake). It's easily the most popular holiday destination in the Neusiedler See region (and Burgenland), due to its position by the lake, lack of reed beds, fair share of wind and good infrastructure.

The town's **tourist office** (☎ 2227; www.podersdorfamsee.at; Hauptstrasse 2; ☽ 8am-noon & 1-4pm Mon-Thu, 8am-noon Sat Apr-Sep) can help find accommodation, of which there is plenty to choose from.

Sights & Activities

Podersdorf offers the most convenient bathing opportunities on Neusiedler See, with a long grassy **beach** (adult/child €4/2; ☽ 7.30am-6pm Apr-Sep) for swimming, boating and windsurfing. Windsurfing is an extra €3.50, even with your own board, and paddle/electric boat hire is €6/10 per day. The Südstrand (South Beach) is the place to head for wind and water enthusiasts; **Fun & Sail** (☎ 0676-407 23 44; www.fun-and-sail.at; boards per hr/day €9/45, courses per hr/day €34/44) has boards for hire and offers courses, while **Segelschule** (☎ 0676-378 57 53; funsail@ycn.at; boats per hr/day from €15/64) rents out sailing boats and takes weekly sailing courses (from €185).

Bicycles – the perfect way to see the Seewinkel wetlands which start some 5km south of town – are available from five rental shops around town for between €7 and €10 per day, depending on the category of bike.

Sleeping & Eating

It's worth booking ahead for July and August when the place is heavily invaded. Seestrasse, the street leading from the tourist office to the lake, has many small places to stay.

Steiner (☎ 2790; www.steinergg.at; Seestrasse 33; s/€24/48; **P**) This *Gästehaus* has loads going for it – friendly staff, a quiet, homey atmosphere and super clean rooms with modern bathrooms and balcony.

Ettl (☎ 2226; Seestrasse 77; s/d €24/48; **P**) Ettl is another *Gästehaus* in the mould of Steiner but has the added bonus of producing its own wine.

Seewirt (☎ 2415; www.seewirtkarner.at - in German; Strandplatz 1; s/d from 39/78; **P**) Four-star Seewirt has been taking care of holiday-makers since 1924, so the staff really know what they're doing. It occupies a prime spot right next to the ferry terminal and beach.

Strandcamping (☎ 2279; Strandplatz 19; per adult/tent/car €6.80/4.80/4.90; ☽ end-Mar–Oct) Right by the beach, this popular camping ground is one of the largest around; there's plenty of flat ground and shade.

Zur Dankbarkeit (☎ 22 23, Hauptstrasse 39, Podersdorf; mains €6.50-19; ☽ lunch & dinner Mon, Tue, Fri, 11.30am-9pm Sat & Sun) Zur Dankbarkeit occupies a lovely old guesthouse and serves up some of the best regional cooking around. The inner garden, with its mature trees and country ambience, is perfectly complimented by a glass of wine.

Gasthof Kummer (☎ 2263, An der Promenade 5; meals €6-15; ☽ 11am-9pm Apr-Oct) This is just one of several places to eat near the beach, with lots of outside tables and fine food. The fish specialities are particularly good.

Getting There & Away

Hourly buses make the journey between Neusiedl and Podersdorf on weekdays but are infrequent on the weekend (€4, 15 minutes). Ferries connect Podersdorf with Rust (€6) and Breitenbrunn (€5.10) on the western shore.

SEEWINKEL

☎ 02175

Seewinkel is the heart of the Neusiedler See-Seewinkel national park, a grassland and wetland of immense importance to the thousands of birds who call it home. The vineyards, reed beds, shimmering waters and constant bird calls make this an enchanting region for an excursion. Even if you're not an ornithologist, this is an excellent area to explore on foot or by bicycle.

The protected areas cannot be directly accessed by visitors, so to really get into the castle you need a pair of binoculars. There are viewing stands along the way.

The park has its own information centre, the **Nationalparkhaus** (☎ 344 20; www.nationalpark -neusiedlersee.org - in German; ☺ 8am-5pm Mon-Fri, 9am-5pm Sat, 9am-noon Sun Jul-Aug, 8am-4pm Mon-Sat, 9am-noon Sun Apr-Jun & Sep-Oct). It has a small display on the ecology and staff can inform you on the best places to spot local wildlife.

The town of **Illmitz**, 4km from the lake, is surrounded by the national park area and makes for a good base. Staff at its **tourist office** (☎ 2383; www.tiscover.at/illmitz; Obere Hauptplatz 2-4; ☺ 8am-noon & 1-5pm Mon-Fri, 9am-noon & 2-5pm Sat, 9am-noon Sun Jul & Aug, 8am-noon & 1-4pm Mon-Fri Sep-Jun) can provide information on the town, Seewinkel and the multitude of pensions and private rooms in the area. Illmitz is connected to Mörbisch by ferry (€5) and Neusiedler See by bus (€4.50, 30 minutes, hourly on weekdays).

MIDDLE & SOUTHERN BURGENLAND

Heading south, the flat expanse of the Neusiedler See is soon forgotten as the land begins to undulate; rolling hills and forested glens now create the landscape and hilltop castles dot the horizon. It's a region often forgotten by local and international tourists alike; a place where life is still very much connected to the land and the influence of long-resident Hungarian and Croatian settlers can still be felt.

LOCKENHAUS & AROUND

Lockenhaus, in the centre of Burgenland, is famous for its **castle** (☎ 02616-23 94; www.tiscover .com/burg.hotel.lockenhaus; adult/senior/child €5/4/2.50; ☺ 8am-5pm Apr-Nov, 8am-4pm Dec-Mar), or more accurately, for its former resident Elizabeth Báthory. Better known as the 'Blood Countess', she will forever go down in history for her reign of terror early in the 17th century, when she reputedly tortured and murdered over 600 women, mainly peasants, for her own sadistic pleasure. The castle has long been cleansed of such gruesome horrors but still contains an impressive torture chamber, complete with an Iron Maiden.

If you require a place to stay, seven of the castle's rooms have been converted into a **hotel** (s/d €60/90); there's also a standard **hotel** (s/d €50/70) just outside the castle walls. A cellar-like tavern off the castle's first inner courtyard will satisfy the strongest hunger.

Some 13km east of Lockenhaus is the tiny village of **Klostermarienberg**, home to a now-defunct monastery housing the only dog museum in Europe, the **Europäisches Hundemuseum** (☎ 2611-22 92; www.kulturimkloster .at - in German; Klostermarienberg; adult/child/family €4/2/8; ☺ 2-5pm Thu, Sat & Sun May-Oct). The odd collection of dog paraphernalia includes paintings, statues and intriguing photos of dogs dressed for war during WWI and WWII, complete with gas masks. Take a few minutes to visit the monastery's crypt, a chamber containing archaeological finds dating from the 13th and 14th centuries.

Bernstein, 15km west of Lockenhaus, is yet another town dominated by an impressive **castle** (☎ 03354-63 82; www.burgbernstein.at; r from €130; ☺ end Apr–mid-Oct; 🅿). Ten of the castle's rooms, all of which are tastefully decorated with period furniture, are now used to accommodate paying guests. The castle, whose foundations date from 1199, is a delightful retreat from the stress of modern-day living and a time warp back to nobler days. In the town centre is a small **Felsenmuseum** (☎ 03354-66 20-14; Hauptplatz 5; adult/child €4.50/2.50; ☺ 9am-6pm Jul & Aug, 9am-noon & 1.30-6pm Mar-Jun & Sep-Dec), which concentrates its displays on serpentine and its mining (the gemstone was first mined in the town in the mid-19th century).

If your body needs a bit of TLC after all this travelling, stop in at the spa-town of **Bad Tatzmannsdorf**, 15km south of Bernstein. Aside from taking the waters at the **Burgenland Therme** (☎ 03353-89 90; www.burgen landtherme.at - in German; Am Thermenplatz 1; daycard €19; ☺ 9am-10pm), you can visit the **Freilichtmuseum** (☎ 03353-83 14; Bahnhofstrasse; admission €1; ☺ 10am-6pm May-Oct), a small but rewarding open-air museum filled with thatched buildings from 19th-century Burgenland. The local **tourist office** (☎ 03353-70 15; www.bad.tatzmannsdorf.at; Joseph Haydn Platz 1; ☺ 8am-5.30pm Mon-Fri, 9.30-11.30am Sat & Sun Jun-Aug, 8am-4.30pm Mon-Fri, 9.30-11.30am Sat Sep-May) can help with accommodation.

Getting There & Away

You're better off with your own transport in this area as getting from one place to another usually requires at least one bus change and the railway is practically non-existent. Lockenhaus–Eisenstadt is an exception; four direct buses travel to Lockenhaus from Eisenstadt (€11.30, 1½ hours) on weekdays; on Saturday this drops to two.

Only five buses on weekdays travel between Klostermarienberg and Lockenhaus (€3, one to two hours). For Bernstein (€4, 30 minutes) and Bad Tatzmannsdorf (€1.90, 10 minutes), it's best to train it to Oberwart (from Vienna: €19.50, two hours) and then catch one of the four buses on weekdays heading north through both towns.

GÜSSING & AROUND

If you're not castled-out by this stage head 40km south of Bad Tatzmannsdorf to Güssing, a peaceful town on the banks of the Strembach river. Here the arresting sight of **Burg Güssing** (☎ 03322-434 00; www.burgguessing .info - in German; adult/senior/child €5.50/4/3.50; ☉ 10am-5pm Tue-Sun May-Oct) rises dramatically over both the river and town. The castle, which is an aesthetically pleasing mix of ruins and renovations, contains plenty of weapons from the Turks and Hungarians, striking portraits from the 16th century and a tower with 360° views. Also on display is an iron safe, the heaviest object in the exhibition, which has a tiny statue of a dog at the bottom – a sign that the owner had *auf den Hund gekommen* (gone to the dogs). A **funicular railway** (tickets €1; ☉ 10am-10pm May-Oct) helps those with weary legs reach the castle.

The **Auswanderer Museum** (☎ 03322-425 98; Stremtalstrasse 2; adult/child €2/1; ☉ 2-6pm Sat & Sun), to the north of the castle, is also worth seeing; it relays the story of the mass exodus of *Burgenlander* to America before and after WWI (including Fred Astaire's father). Most emigrated due to lack of work or poor living conditions.

If you missed the open-air museum in Bad Tatzmannsdorf, head 5km west of Güssing to the **Freilichtmuseum** (☎ 03328-322 55; Gerersdorf bei Güssing 66; adult/child €4/1.50; ☉ 9am-5pm Mon-Fri, 10am-6pm Sat & Sun Apr-Oct) at **Gerersdorf**. You could easily spend an hour or two exploring the 30-odd buildings and their traditional furniture and fittings, which capture the rural culture of Burgenland in the 18th and 19th centuries.

The **tourist office** (☎ 03322-440 03; www.tiscover .at/guessing; Hauptplatz 7; ☉ 9am-noon Mon-Fri) in Güssing can help with private rooms, otherwise try **Landgasthof Kedl** (☎ 03322-42 40 30; gasthofkedl@burgenland.org; Urbersdorf 33; s/d €27/44; **P**) 3km north of Güssing in Urbersdorf. The castle's restaurant, **Die Burg Güssing** (☎ 03322-444 74; mains €6-16; ☉ 10am-10pm Tue-Sun May-Oct), is an excellent spot for a meal or snack; its terrace has far-reaching views over the countryside.

Getting There & Away

Four direct buses on weekdays connect Güssing (€6, 45 minutes) with Oberwart. Only one bus daily during summer travels between Güssing and Geresdorf (€1.90, 10 minutes).

Upper Austria

Upper Austria (Oberösterreich) is the country's northwestern corner, with Germany to the west and the Czech Republic to the north. Aside from the Salzkammergut in the southwest, which warrants its own chapter, much of the province is overlooked by tourists.

Geographically, Upper Austria has a lot in common with its close neighbour Lower Austria. This is also a fertile land, characterised by undulating hills, cultivated fields and the Danube (Donau), which enters the province in its northwestern corner at Passau and exits into the Donautal (Danube Valley) in the east. The scenery along the river's banks cannot match the Danube Valley, but what it does have is a refreshing lack of tourists.

Occupying centre stage is Linz, Upper Austria's capital. It's thought of as an industrial backwater by most Austrians, and while it certainly has its fair share of industry, it's by no means provincial. With an attractive *Altstadt* (old town), thriving nightlife and excellent museums, Linz certainly has the ability to entertain.

The region has its fair share of abbeys, two of which are within easy reach of the capital. To the west of Linz is Wilhering and its elaborate rococo church, but it's overshadowed by St Florian, the high point in Austria's baroque monasteries. To the east is a reminder that humanity also has an ugly face – the former Nazi concentration camp at Mauthausen.

A little further from Linz, and deserving of an overnight stay, are towns of surprising beauty. To the south is Steyr, a highly appealing city at the confluence of two alpine rivers, the Enns and the Steyr, and to the north is Freistadt, with the country's best-preserved fortifications and great beer. Directly on the border with Germany far to the west is Schärding, a town of striking pastel colours and baroque houses.

HIGHLIGHTS

- Wandering the rooms of Linz's two world-class museums, the **Ars Electronica Center** (p171) and the **Lentos Kunstmuseum** (p171)
- Discovering baroque at its best at St Florian's **Augustiner Chorherrenstift** (p174)
- Roaming the historic centre of **Steyr** (p176), tucked between the Enns and Steyr Rivers
- Enjoying the perfectly preserved medieval walls and locally brewed beer of **Freistadt** (p180)
- Experiencing a stark reminder of the horrors of Nazi atrocities at **Mauthausen** (p175)

★ Freistadt

★ Linz
★ Mauthausen
St Florian ★

★ Steyr

| ▪ POPULATION: 1,198,000 | ▪ AREA: 9480 SQ KM | ▪ HIGHEST ELEVATION: GROSSE PRIEL 2515M |

Climate

The climate of the Mühlviertel is characterised by long summers and harsh winters. Heading south, milder temperatures are more prevalent until the Alps rise from the east.

Getting There & Away

Upper Austria has good connections in all directions; the A1 autobahn runs east–west to Vienna and Salzburg, the A8 north to Passau and the rest of Germany and the A9 south into Styria. Express trains between Vienna and Salzburg pass through Linz and much of southern Upper Austria, and there are also express trains heading south from Linz to St Michael in Styria, from where connections to Klagenfurt and Graz are possible.

Getting Around

Upper Austria's excellent bus and train services are covered by **Oberösterreichischer Verkehrsverbund tickets** (☎ 0810-240 810; www.ooevv .at - in German). Prices depend on the number of zones you travel (one zone is €1.50, 10 zones is €40), and alongside single tickets, daily, weekly, monthly or yearly passes are available for however many zones you require.

LINZ

☎ 070 / pop 203,000

In the eyes of many Austrians, Linz is a city to avoid, a provincial backwater with heavy

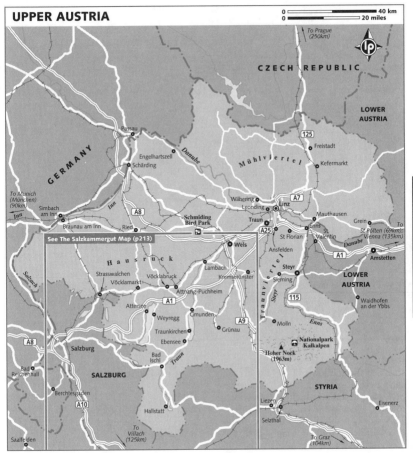

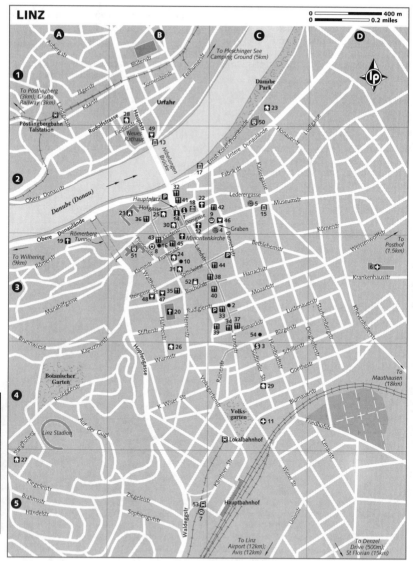

LINZ

0 ——————— 400 m
0 ——————— 0.2 miles

industry. The skyline of belching smoke-stacks to the southeast of the city certainly can't be ignored, but it seems that many prefer to overlook the highlights the city has to offer, which come as a pleasant surprise. This is a city with a highly attractive *Altstadt*, two world-class museums and a lively buzz; a city striding into the future rather than living in its past, which cannot be said for every place in Austria.

History

Linz was a fortified Celtic village by the time the Romans arrived, who then took over and named it Lentia. By the 8th century, when the town came under the control of Bavaria, its name had changed to Linze, and by the 13th century it was an important trading town for raw material out of Styria. In 1489 Linz became the imperial capital under Friedrich III, but this was to last only until his death in 1493.

Like much of Upper Austria, Linz was at the forefront of the Protestant movement in the 16th and 17th centuries, attracting prominent figures such as the astronomer Johannes Kepler. However, the Counter-Reformation made a spectacular and assertive comeback, knocking the stuffing out of the place for the following century. Its resurgence in the 19th century was largely due to the development of the railway, when Linz became an important junction.

Adolf Hitler may have been born in Braunau am Inn (p182), but Linz was his favourite (he spent his schooling days here, moving to Vienna at the age of 18), and his (largely unrealised) plans for the city were grand. His Nazi movement did build massive iron and steel works here, which still employ many locals. After WWII, Linz was at the border between the Soviet- and the US-administered zones, with land north of the Danube in Soviet control. Since 1955, Linz has become an important industrial city and port and provincial capital.

Orientation

Linz lies on both sides of the Danube, with the *Innenstadt* (inner town) and most attractions on the south bank. Almost all the sights on the north bank are within the district of Urfahr. Hauptplatz, an elongated, spacious square, is the hub; it is mostly car-free and abuts Landstrasse, a shopping street with a long pedestrian-only section. The *Hauptbahnhof* (main train station) is about 1km south of Hauptplatz.

MAPS

A free map, with information in both German and English and an enlargement of the *Innenstadt*, is available from Tourist Information Linz.

Information

BOOKSHOPS

Amadeus (☎ 76 15-0; Landstrasse 41; ☺ 9am-5pm Mon-Fri, 9am-noon Sat) A small selection of English-language books.

INTERNET ACCESS

Ars Electronica Center (☎ 7272-0; www.aec.at; Hauptstrasse 2; adult/concessions €6/3; ☺ 9am-5pm Wed, Thu, 9am-9pm Fri, 10am-6pm weekends) Free Internet access with entry ticket.

Bignet Internet.café (☎ 796 820 10; Graben 17; ☺ 10am to midnight) Internet access per hour €4.50.

Hauptbücherei (☎ 7070-1831; Museumstrasse 15; ☺ 11am-7pm Mon, 9am-2pm Tue, 9am-5pm Wed & Thu, 9am-7pm Fri) Internet access per hour €1; bookings are normally required.

INTERNET RESOURCES

Linz.info.at (in German) Links to some of the city's more prominent cultural venues, firms and transport providers.
www.linz-termine.at (in German) Listings of cultural events and exhibitions throughout the year.

MEDICAL SERVICES

Krankenhaus der Stadt Linz (☎ 78 06-0; Krankenhausstrasse 9) The main hospital, 1km east of the centre.

UPPER AUSTRIA

Unfallkrankenhaus (☎ 69 20-0; Blumauerplatz 1) Emergency hospital.

MONEY
American Express (☎ 66 90 13; Bürgerstrasse 14; ⊙ 9am-5.30pm Mon-Fri) Financial and travel services under one roof.

There are a number of banks with ATMs in the *Innenstadt*; the airport also has a bank. The *Hauptbahnhof* has an ATM and a **money exchange office** (⊙ 7.30am-4pm Mon-Thu, 7.30am-1.30pm Fri).

POST
Main Post Office (☎ 69 60-0; Bahnhofplatz 11; ⊙ 7am-9pm Mon-Fri, 9am-1pm Sat) Near the Hauptbahnhof; has an ATM.
Post Office (☎ 7711-800; Domgasse 1; ⊙ 8am-6pm Mon-Fri) This post office is handier to the centre.

TOURIST INFORMATION
Tourist Information Linz (☎ 7070-1777; www.linz.at - in German; Hauptplatz 1; ⊙ 8am-7pm Mon-Fri, 10am-7pm Sat & Sun May-Oct, 8am-6pm Mon-Fri, 10am-6pm Sat & Sun Nov-Apr) Brochures, accommodation listings, room reservation service and a separate Upper Austria information desk can be found here.

TRAVEL AGENCIES
STA Travel (☎ 77 58 93; Herrenstrasse 7; ⊙ 9am-5.30pm Mon-Fri)

Sights & Activities
Before setting off on an excursion around the city, consider purchasing the Linzer Museumskarte (€12), which allows entry to 12 museums in the city, or the Linzer City Ticket (€20), which provides entry to all museums covered by the Museumskarte, a €10 restaurant voucher, a city tour and a return trip on the Pöstlingerbergbahn. The Junior Linz Ticket (€8, ages six to 14) is also available, but has limited benefits. All three tickets are valid the entire year.

INNENSTADT
The walking tour of the *Innenstadt*, outlined in the free map from the tourist office covers all the major sights south of the river.

The focal point of Linz is its large, open **Hauptplatz**, which is lined with pastel-coloured baroque buildings. The **Altes Rathaus** is by far the most interesting building on the square, which still retains some of its earlier Re-

naissance elements. It now houses **Linz-Genesis** (☎ 7070-1920; Rathausgasse 8; admission free; ⊙ 9am-1pm & 2-6pm Mon-Fri), an impressively modern museum (displays activate themselves as you approach) focused on the town's history. It covers various periods in the town's architectural history and highlights some of Linz's famous sons, such as Johannes Kepler, Adalberrt Stifler and Anton Bruckner. Pride of place on the square goes to the **Dreifaltigkeitssäule** (trinity column), a baroque pillar of Salzburg marble carved in 1723 to commemorate the town's deliverance from war, fire and plague. Behind the Altes Rathaus you'll find the baroque **Stadtpfarrkirche** (town parish church; ☎ 77 61 20; Pfarrplatz 4; ⊙ 8am-6pm); inside is a tomb with a few leftovers from Friedrich III, namely his heart and intestines.

Just west of the *Hauptplatz* (main square) is the **Landhaus** (Klosterstrasse), the seat of the provincial government constructed between 1564 and 1571. Wander into the arcaded courtyard to see the **Planet Fountain** (1582), which predated the arrival of the great German astronomer Johann Kepler, who taught for 14 years in a college once sited here.

Also not far west of the *Hauptplatz* is **Schloss Linz**. Its foundations lie in the 8th century, but it was rebuilt by Friedrich III in the 1470s, and even later by Rudolph II. It now houses the **Schlossmuseum** (☎ 77 44 19; Tummelplatz 10; adult/child €3/1.70; ⊙ 9am-5pm Tue-Fri, 10am-4pm Sat & Sun), displaying a fine collection of weapons, artefacts and the obligatory religious art, the highlight of which is the detailed Eggelsberger Altar, painted in 1480 and depicting biblical tales. Behind the Schlossmuseum is the **Martinskirche** (☎ 77 74 54; Römerstrasse; ⊙ services 8.30am Wed, 8.15am Sun), Austria's oldest church. First documented in 799, it was built using debris from Roman buildings and displays Romanesque and Gothic touches. Unfortunately the church can only be visited during Mass, or on an organised city tour.

A few blocks south of the *Schloss*, the neo-Gothic cathedral, **Neuer Dom** (☎ 77 78 85, Herrenstrasse 26; ⊙ 7.30am-7pm Mon-Sat, 8am-7pm Sun), rises impressively from among shops and residential houses. Built in 1855, its façade is vaguely reminiscent of St Vitus Cathedral in Prague, but without the supreme grace. The interior features exceptional stained glass, including a window depicting the history of the town. At 131m high, its spire is the second highest in Austria after Stephansdom in Vienna (p89), yet the cathedral itself can hold more churchgoers.

Back towards *Hauptplatz* along Landstrasse is the **Alter Dom** (☎ 770 866-0; Domgasse 3; 🕑 7am-7pm), where Anton Bruckner served as church organist. Originally built by the Jesuits in the 1670s, its style is 17th-century baroque, with some exceptional stucco and marble décor. A few streets east is the **Landesmuseum** (☎ 77 44 82-0; Museumsstrasse 14; adult/concessions €4/2.20; 🕑 9am-6pm Tue-Fri, 10am-5pm weekends), housed in a lovely 19th-century building. It hosts temporary exhibitions, usually from the contemporary genre.

Along the southern bank of the Danube is the greenery of the **Donaupark** (Danube Park) and the first of Linz's world-class museums, the unmissable **Lentos Kunstmuseum** (☎ 7070-3600; www.lentos.at - in German; Ernst-Koref-Promenade 1; adult/concessions €6.50/4.50; 🕑 10am-6pm Wed-Mon, 10am-10pm Thu). The clean lines of this glass and steel construction were designed by Zurich architects Weber & Hofer, who decided to leave a large gap in the base of its rectangle shape. Inside, its open, stark-white rooms are perfectly suited for exhibits of the museum's involving collection of contemporary art, which focuses its attention on German and Austrian artists. The likes of Schiele, Klimt, Kokoschka, Corinth and Pechstein are on display, along with works by Andy Warhol and Maria Lassing. The ground floor hosts temporary exhibitions.

URFAHR
On the northern bank of the Danube is the suburb of Urfahr, home to Linz's second world-class museum, the **Ars Electronica Center** (☎ 7272-0; www.aec.at; Hauptstrasse 2; adult/concessions €6/3; 🕑 9am-5pm Wed & Thu, 9am-9pm Fri, 10am-6pm weekends). This is a museum devoted to interactive computer wizardry, where everything is somehow connected to the world of technology (the lift features projected graphics and the entrance-hall flower garden is tended to by a remote-controlled robotic arm). There are loads of computer simulations on its four floors, with numerous staff on hand to explain what's going on. By far the most impressive exhibit is the Cave of Virtual Reality, which allows you to take a 3D trip though space and time (explore the universe, visit a Renaissance city). There's also a virtual reality flying machine that will whisk you around the museum and over a virtual Linz.

Clearly visible from the old town is the **Pöstlingberg** (537m) on the north bank. The views from the summit, which is topped by an 18th-century twin-spired baroque church, are quite impressive. The walk is quite gentle, but you can take the narrow-gauge **Pöstlingbergbahn** (adult/child €5.60/2.80, combined ticket with Tram No 3 €3.50/1.70; 🕑 every 20-30min 5.20am-8pm Mon-Sat, 7.15am-8pm Sun). Tram No 3 goes from the *Hauptbahnhof*, via the town centre to the Pöstlingbergbahn Talstation (lower station). At the top is a **grotto railway** (☎ 3400-7506; Am Pöstlingberg 16; adult/child €4/2.20; 🕑 10am-6pm Jun-Aug, 10am-5pm Sep-Nov & Mar-May) that trundles past scenes from fairy stories, followed by a walk along a miniature fairy-tale street. It will certainly keep small children entertained.

Tours
Tourist Information Linz organises **walking tours** (€7; 🕑 10.30am May-Sep) of the city, which go ahead no matter the weather or the number of people. Tours leave from outside the information office.

Festivals & Events
Linz's most celebrated festival is the **Brucknerfest** (☎ 7612-2170; www.brucknerhaus.at; tickets €11-92) in September. Concerts are held at the Brucknerhaus or in the *Stiftskirche* (monastery church) in St Florian. It's preceded by the **Ars Electronica Festival** (a technology exhibition), which takes place in early September. Both festivals coincide with free **Klangwolke** (cloud of sound) concerts in Donaupark.

The **Linz Fest**, starting in late May or early June and running for three or four weeks, brings free rock, jazz and folk to the city.

Sleeping
Tourist Information Linz offers a free accommodation booking service for visitors, but only face-to-face and not over the phone.

BUDGET
Goldenes Dachl (☎ 77 58 97; goldenesdachl@web.de; Hafnerstrasse 27; s/d €22/44) For price and proximity to the city centre, the Goldenes Dachl is the best Linz has to offer. Rooms are not flash but they're highly adequate, and there's a traditional *Gästehaus* (guesthouse) and beer garden on the ground floor.

Wilde Mann (☎ 65 60 78; wilder-mann@aon.at; Goethestrasse 14; s/d from €27/48; P) This simple pension has rooms with no frills, but they're accommodating, clean and some of the cheapest around.

Jugendgästehaus (☎ 66 44 34; jgh.linz@oejhv.or.at; Stanglhofweg 3; dm €15; s/d €26.50/38; **P**) About 1½km from the city centre near the Linz Stadion is this HI hostel. It's housed in a modern block and rooms are fairly plain, and there is food available (for which advanced booking is needed on weekends).

Pleschinger See (☎ 24 78 70; Seeweg 11; camp sites per adult/child/tent €4/2.50/3, showers €1; **P**) This site is in a protected area (no motor vehicles) about 5km northeast of the Nibelungen Brücke. It's on the north bank by the lake and the Danube cycle track.

MID-RANGE & TOP END

Drei Mohren (☎ 77 26 26-0; www.drei-mohren.at; Promenade 17; s/d €98/130; **P** ✗) This well-established hotel has a touch of class about it and excellent personal service. Its 25 rooms are large and individually furnished.

Goldener Anker (☎ 77 10 88; goldeneranker@nusurf .at; Hofgasse 5; s €28-50, d €54-80) This family-run place just off *Hauptplatz* is a superb deal if you can land rooms with shared facilities, but they're usually booked well ahead. Otherwise you'll have to settle for the cosy en-suite rooms.

Wolfinger (☎ 77 32 91; www.hotelwolfinger.at; Hauptplatz 19; s/d from €42/64; **P**) The Wolfinger is a family-run hotel with the best location of any hotel in Linz. Its historical ambience is accentuated by archways, stuccowork and period furniture. Ask for a room at the back with balcony. Parking is in a garage nearby.

Zum Schwarzen Bären (☎ 77 24 77; baer@linz-hotel .at; Herrenstrasse 9-11; s/d from €68/90; **P**) Located on a quiet pedestrian street, this three-star hotel has good-sized rooms and a convenient location. Higher-priced rooms have designer open-plan bathrooms.

Arcotel Hotel Nike (☎ 76 26-0; www.arcotel.at/nike; Untere Donaulände 9; rooms €160; **P** ✗ ✈) The Nike is set up for business clients and doesn't have a lot of character, but it does have great views of the Danube, an indoor swimming pool, a steam room and a fitness centre.

Spitz Hotel (☎ 73 64 410; www.spitz.at/hotel; Fiedlerstrasse 6; s/d €106/122; **P** ✗) This Best Western hotel in Urfahr has a modern ambience and suitably plush rooms.

Eating

Linz's restaurant selection comes as a pleasant surprise; the city offers up a healthy variety of cuisine types and its fair share of top restaurants. The *Linz is(s)t gut* booklet, available from the tourist office, lists the majority of eateries in town.

RESTAURANTS

p'aa (☎ 77 64 61; Altstadt 28; mains €7-11; ☉ 11am-midnight Mon-Sat) p'aa is a rarity not only for Linz but for Austria – it serves vegan dishes and the cuisine is a grand mix of Tibetan, Indian and Mexican. Choose between outdoor seating on *Altstadt* cobblestones or an indoor table under low, arched ceilings.

Mia Cara (☎ 78 57 28; Pfarrplatz 13; mains €8-16; ☉ 8am-midnight Mon-Sat) Nestled behind the *Stadtpfarrkirche* is this refined *osteria* (Italian tavern), serving Italian cuisine with plenty of flair on its outdoor patio.

Alte Welt (☎ 77 00 53; www.altewelt.at - in German; Hauptplatz 4; lunch menu from €6.20; mains €9; ☉ lunch & dinner) Alte Welt is a bit of a Jekyll & Hyde – during the day it attracts a mixed crowd of diners with its traditional Austrian cooking and rural *Gästehaus* atmosphere, while at night it becomes a meeting place for students, artists and musicians (often hosting live music).

Klosterhof (☎ 77 33 73; Landstrasse 30; mains 6-16; ☉ 9am-midnight) Klosterhof's glorious tree-shaded beer garden is arguably the best of its kind in the heart of an Austrian city. If this isn't enough to tempt you, the 17th-century building out front and the quality Austrian cuisine should.

Mangolds (☎ 78 56 88; Hauptplatz 3; meals €7-10; ☉ 11am-8pm Mon-Fri, 11am-5pm Sat) Healthy salads, freshly squeezed juices, soups and hot meals are the order of the day at this self-service vegetarian restaurant.

Herberstein (☎ 78 61 61; Altstadt 10; mains €12-20; ☉ dinner) Herberstein is one of the classiest restaurants around, serving refined international cuisine. Aside from the restaurant, it's possible to lose yourself in the bar, cigar lounge, Asia lounge, Oriental lounge and inner courtyard.

Josef Stadtbräu (☎ 77 31 65; Landstrasse 49; brunch €6.90, mains €5-12; ☉ 10am-4am) This is an excellent choice for decent beer (this establishment makes its own) and hearty food in a buzzing environment. There's a big beer garden and live music on Sunday (April to October),

UPPER AUSTRIA

and the all-you-can-eat brunch (11am-3pm Monday to Friday) packs 'em in.

Other recommendations include:

La Gondola (☎ 78 23 10; Magazingasse 11; mains €6-10; ⏰ 11am-11pm) Simple Italian/Greek with large pizzas and sun-warmed terrace.

Los Caballeros (☎ 77 89 70; Landstrasse 32; mains €7-22; ⏰ 11am-2am) Mexican place with excellent T-bone steaks, spare ribs and secluded green courtyard.

CAFÉS

While in Linz, don't pass up an opportunity to try the *Linzer torte*, an almond pastry and raspberry cake. The recipe has been around since the 18th century, and it's the greatest rival to the *Sacher torte* in Vienna.

Cafe Jindrak (☎ 77 92 58; Herrenstrasse 22; lunch menus €5-7; ⏰ 8am-6pm Mon-Fri, 7.30am-12.30pm Sat) Join the old dames for a slice of the famous *Linzer torte* at this, Linz's most celebrated café. It's been serving up the people of Linz since 1929.

Traxlmayr (☎ 77 33 53; Promenade 16; coffee & cake €2-5; ⏰ 8am-10pm Mon-Sat) What Traxlmayr lacks in tradition it makes up for with an enormous patio, '60s décor and a buzzing atmosphere.

Both the Lentos Kunstmuseum and Ars Electronica Center have suitably modern cafés; Ars Electronica has fine views over the city.

SELF-CATERING

Self-caterers will have no problem finding a supermarket; there are two Billas and a Spar on Landstrasse. Otherwise head to the *Bauernmärkte* (farmers markets) on *Hauptplatz* (9am to 2pm Tuesday and Friday) and outside the Neuen Rathaus (8am to noon Saturday). There are plenty of cheap *würstel* (sausage) stands lining the Volksgarten on Landstrasse.

Drinking

Linz's nightlife scene is harder than anywhere else in Austria, possibly due to the city's industrial base. There is however something for everyone; the *Linzer Nacht Meile*, available from the tourist office, maps many bars on or near *Hauptplatz* and Landstrasse. A large concentration of bars can be found one block west of the Hauptplatz, nicknamed the 'Bermuda Triangle', and while the area is highly atmospheric, its bars can often be a little tired and tardy.

Strom (☎ 73 12 09; Kirchengasse 4; ⏰ about 8pm-3am) This bar attracts a wide range of alternative music aficionados and students; upstairs is rather rough and ready, while downstairs is more appealing and chilled, with people spilling out onto quiet Kirchengasse. Next door is **Stadtwerk**, which hosts clubbing events.

Cafe Ex-Blatt (☎ 77 93 19; Waltherstrasse 15; ⏰ 10am-2am Mon-Fri, 6pm-2am Sat & Sun) More of a bar than a café, this relaxed place attracts a crowd mainly in their 20s to 40s, including many students. It has candles on the tables and walls crammed with pictures.

Places also worth trying:

Cheeese (☎ 79 28 27; Waltherstrasse 11; ⏰ 6pm-4am Tue-Sun) Popular bar with a younger crowd; live music Wednesdays and Saturdays.

Bluu Club (☎ 78 5528; Graben 18; ⏰ 4pm-4am Fri & Sat, 4pm-midnight Tue-Thu) Offers good cocktails and a sophisticated atmosphere.

Entertainment

Brucknerhaus (☎ 7612-0; www.brucknerhaus.linz.at; Untere Donaulände 7) The Brucknerhaus is the city's premier music venue, hosting regular classical concerts.

Posthof (☎ 77 05 48-0; www.posthof.at - in German; Posthofstrasse 43) Near the docks is this centre for contemporary music, dance and theatre, particularly avant-garde events. Raves are occasionally held at the venue.

Landestheater (☎ 76 11-0; www.landestheater-linz .at - in German; Promenade 39) Programmes at Linz's main theatre are generally more traditional in nature.

Shopping

A good street to pick up quality goods, such as paintings, jewellery and antiques, is Bischofstrasse, running west off Landstrasse. You'll also find **Klosterladen** (☎ 78 13 21; Bischofstrasse 4; ⏰ 9am-1pm, 2-6pm Mon-Fri, 9am-noon Sat) here, a shop stocking products, including schnapps, beer, wine and pasta, from monasteries around Upper Austria.

At the other end of the scale is the city's *Flohmärkte* (flea markets), which spring forth in front of the **Neues Rathaus** (⏰ 6am-2pm Sat Nov-Feb) and on the **Hauptplatz** (⏰ 6am-2pm Sat Mar-Oct).

Getting There & Away

AIR

Austrian Airlines and Lufthansa are the main airlines servicing the **Blue Danube Airport**

UPPER AUSTRIA

(☎ 07221-600-0; www.flughafen-linz.at). There are flights to Vienna, Salzburg and Graz, as well as Berlin, Frankfurt, Düsseldorf, Stuttgart and Zürich. Ryanair has daily flights to London Stansted; see p363.

BOAT
The **Schiffsstation** (Untere Donaulände 1) is on the south bank next the Lentos Kunstmuseum. **Wurm + Köck** (☎ 78 36 07; www.donauschiffahrt.de - in German) sends boats westwards to Passau (one-way/return €21/24, six to seven hours, 8am and 2.20pm Tuesday to Sunday May to late October) and east to Vienna (€52/59, 11½ hours, 9am Saturday May to September).

BUS
Bundesbuses depart from stands near the *Hauptbahnhof*, beyond the small park to the west. Information can be obtained from the **bus information counter** (☎ 61 71 81; 7.50am-5.30pm Mon-Fri).

TRAIN
Linz is on the main rail route between Vienna (€23.50, two hours) and Salzburg (€17.70, 1⅓ hours), and express trains run hourly in both directions. Slower trains also service this route and others. At least three trains depart daily for Prague (€58, five hours). Aside from the obligatory **information desk** (8am-6.50pm), there are also some snack bars and an ATM at the *Hauptbahnhof*.

Getting Around
TO/FROM THE AIRPORT
Linz airport is 12km southwest of the town. A direct airport bus connects the *Hauptbahnhof* (€2.20, 20 minutes) with the airport hourly.

BICYCLE
Bikes can be hired at the **Lokalbahnhof** (local train station; ☎ 65 43 76; Coulinstrasse 30; half-day/full-day/week €5/7/45; 7am-noon & 1-6pm Mon-Fri, 7am-12.30pm Sat).

CAR
Linz has offices for all the major car hire firms:
Avis (☎ 66 28 81; Flughafenstrasse 1)
Denzel Drive (☎ 60 00 91; Wiener Strasse 91)
Hertz (☎ 78 48 41; Bürgerstrasse 19)

PUBLIC TRANSPORT
Linz is extensively covered by trams and buses (☎ 3400-7000, www.linzag.at), but by early evening some services stop or become infrequent. Single tickets (€1.50), day passes (€3) and weekly passes (€10) are available from pavement dispensers; *Tabak* (tobacconist) shops also sell daily and weekly passes. Drivers don't sell tickets – buy and validate your tickets before you board.

AROUND LINZ

The following places are close to Linz and can be visited as a day trip.

WILHERING
☎ 07226 / pop 5190
The small village of Wilhering, 9km west of Linz along the southern bank of the Danube, is the home to a **Cistercian Abbey** (☎ 07226-23 11-0; Linzerstrasse 4; admission free; daylight hours), which at first glance isn't particularly striking. However, if you enjoy rococo interiors, then its *Stiftskirche* is well worth making a detour for. It is breathtaking for its extremely elaborate but delicate ornamentation, and almost nothing of the interior is left untouched by twirls of gold.

There are frequent buses (€1.80, 10 minutes) between Linz and Wilhering.

ST FLORIAN
☎ 07224 / pop 5600
Unassuming St Florian, a market town 15km southeast of Linz, hides one of the best abbeys in Upper Austria, if not the whole country. St Florian was a Roman who converted to Christianity and was drowned in the Enns River (in 304) for his pains. In many Austrian churches he is represented wearing Roman military uniform and dousing flames with a bucket of water.

The centre of town is Marktplatz, which is just below the abbey. Here you'll find a small **tourist office** (56 90; st.florian@oberoesterreich.at; Marktplatz 2; 9am-1pm Mon-Fri), a few *Gästehäuse* and the local post office.

Sights & Activities
AUGUSTINER CHORHERRENSTIFT
The baroque spires of the **Augustiner Chorherrenstift** (Augustinian Abbey; ☎ 89 02; www.stift-st-florian .at, Stiftstrasse 1; tours adult/concession €5.30/4.50; tours

10am, 11am, 2pm, 3pm & 4pm Apr–Oct) are visible from anywhere in town. The abbey dates from at least 819 and has been occupied by the Augustinians since 1071, but its baroque appearance, created by Carlo Carlone and Jakob Prandtauer, only appeared between 1688 and 1751. The main entrance, framed by statues, is especially impressive, particularly when bathed in afternoon sunlight. The abbey's interior can only be visited by guided tour.

The abbey features lavish apartments, resplendent with rich stucco and emotive frescoes. They include 16 emperors' rooms (once occupied by visiting popes and royalty) and a library housing 125,000 volumes. The Marble Hall is dedicated to Prince Eugene of Savoy, a Frenchman who led the Habsburg army to victory over the Turks in many battles. Prince Eugene's Room contains an amusing bed featuring carved Turks.

The high point of the interior is the **Altdorfer Gallery**, displaying 14 paintings by Albrecht Altdorfer (1480–1538) of the Danube school. There are eight scenes of Christ and four of St Sebastian – all vivid and dramatic with an innovative use of light and dark. Altdorfer cleverly tapped into contemporary issues to depict his biblical scenes (for example, one of Christ's tormentors is clearly a Turk).

The **Stiftskirche** (admission free; approx 7am–10pm) is almost overpowering in its extensive use of stucco and frescoes. The altar is made from 700 tonnes of Salzburg marble, and the huge organ (1774), which is literally dripping with gold, was the largest in Europe at the time it was built. Anton Bruckner was a choir boy in St Florian and was church organist from 1850 to 1855; he is buried in the crypt below his beloved organ. Also in the crypt are the remains of 6000 people, their bones and skulls stacked in neat rows. The crypt is normally locked and can only be visited as part of the abbey tour. To hear the wonderful organ in full song, attend one of the regular **concerts** (adult/concession with tour €6.80/6.20, without tour €2.50/2; 2.30pm Mon, Wed-Fri & Sun mid-May–mid-Oct).

Opposite the *Stiftskirche* is the **Historisches Feuerwehrzeughaus** (Fire Brigade Museum; 42 19; Stiftstrasse 2; adult/concession €2.20/2; 9am-noon & 2-4pm Tue-Sun May-Oct), which houses historic fire engines, hoses, buckets and other fire-fighting paraphernalia.

SCHLOSS HOHENBRUNN

Less than 2km west of town is Schloss Hohenbrunn, built between 1722 and 1732 in the baroque style by architect Jakob Prandtauer. This stately home houses the fairly interesting (though unusual) **Jagd Museum** (hunting museum; 200 83; Hohenbrunn 1; adult/concession €2.20/1.90; 10am-noon & 1-5pm Tue-Sun Apr-Oct). Blood sports are celebrated everywhere here: in art, ornaments, implements, weapons and even the castle stuccowork.

Sleeping & Eating

If you wish to overnight, there are a few places on and around Marktplatz.

Zum Goldenen Pflug (42 26; Speiserberg 3; s/d €23/40; P) This is your basic no-frills accommodation near the abbey gates. Phone ahead to guarantee a room.

Gasthof Erzherzog Franz Ferdinand (42 45-0; office@hotel-st-florian.at; Marktplatz 13; s/d from €40/62, mains €7-13; P) Opposite the tourist office is this, the largest (98 beds) and fanciest (three stars) accommodation option in St Florian. Rooms are suitably comfortable and the restaurant serves Austrian and local specialities in wood-panelled surroundings.

Gasthof Zur Traube (42 23; Speiserberg 1; mains €8-13, midday menus €8; lunch & dinner Fri-Wed) This traditional, comfortable *Gasthof* (inn) with rural décor and ambience is a great place to enjoy Austrian food.

Getting There & Away

St Florian (officially Markt St Florian) is not accessible by train. There are a zillion buses departing from opposite Linz Hauptbahnhof on workdays (€2.20, 22 minutes), but only five on Sunday.

MAUTHAUSEN

07238 / pop 4845

Nowadays Mauthausen is a pleasant small town on the north bank of the Danube east of Linz, but its status as a quarrying centre prompted the Nazis to site **KZ Mauthausen** (07238-2269; Erinnerungsstrasse 1; adult/concession €2/1; tours 2pm Mon-Fri, in English with one week's prior arrangement; 9am-5.30pm), a concentration camp here. Prisoners were forced into slave labour in the granite quarry and many died on the so-called *Todesstiege* (stairway of death) leading from the quarry to the camp. In all, some 100,000 prisoners died or were executed in the camp between 1938 and 1945.

The camp, about 3km northwest of the town centre, has now been turned into a museum of sorts, retelling its history, and the history of other camps (such as those at Ebensee and Melk). Texts are in German, but an audio guide, in various languages, is included in the entry price.

Visitors are able to walk through the remaining living quarters (each designed for 200, but housing up to 500) and the see the cramped and disturbing gas chambers. The former Sick Quarters now houses most of the camp's harrowing material – charts, artefacts and many photos of both prisoners and their SS guards. Also on display are numerous poignant memorials to the deceased – the camp was not only a life sentence for Jews, but also for many Soviets, Poles and a handful of non-Jewish Austrians and Germans. It is a stark reminder of human cruelty, and most, if not all visitors, will be moved.

At the car park is the camp's information centre, which shows a film (free with camp admission, every hour, on the hour, last film 4pm) on the history of the camp and has video and audio recordings of camp survivors.

Getting There & Away
From Linz the most direct way to Mauthausen is by bus (€4.40, 50 minutes); the camp is still another 2km walk uphill from the bus stop. Buses run every half-hour Monday to Friday. By train (€7, 30 minutes), a change is required at St Valentin. You can rent a bike from the station, which eases the 5km journey to the camp (follow the KZ Mauthausen signs).

THE TRAUNVIERTEL

The Traunviertel is a large swathe of land to the south of Linz, and some of the most fertile in Upper Austria. The landscape consists of gentle hills which rise slowly as they roll south towards the Salzkammergut and Nationalpark Kalkalpen. Among the hills and valleys are pretty towns and villages; over the centuries, two of the region's main towns, Steyr and Wels, have grown into cities.

STEYR
☎ 07252 / pop 40,100
At the convergence of the Rivers Enns and Steyr 30km south of Linz stands Steyr, the prettiest of Upper Austria's cities. Like Linz, it's a city with heavy industry on its outskirts, but Steyr easily compensates for the ugly smoke stacks with a heart-warming main square, streets that front the rivers and cobblestone back alleys. The iron industry has been the backbone of its prosperity since the Middle Ages and it made armaments in WWI and WWII and, in 1944, was bombed for its trouble. It was also the first town in Europe to have electric street lighting (1884).

Orientation & Information
The picturesque town centre is caught between the fast flowing Enns and Steyr Rivers, while the *Hauptbahnhof* is situated on the eastern bank of the Enns, about eight minutes' walk from the pivotal Stadtplatz. The **tourist office** (☎ 532 29-0; www.tourism-steyr.at; Stadtplatz 27; ☺ 8.30am-6pm Mon-Fri, 9am-noon Sat) is on the main square in the Rathaus.

Not far from the *Hauptbahnhof* is the **main post office** (Dukartstrasse 13; ☺ 7.30am-7pm Mon-Fri, 8am-11pm Sat), but the post office at Grünmarkt 1 is more handy to the Stadtplatz. Internet access is available at **Telefon** (Jägergasse 4; ☺ 10am-6pm Mon-Fri) northeast of the *Hauptbahnhof*.

Sights & Activities
Many of Steyr's main points of interest are clustered on or around the long Stadtplatz, which is centred on a 17th-century fountain. Of particular note is the 18th-century **Rathaus**, with its church-like belfry and a rococo façade. Opposite, and in stark contrast to the Rathaus, is the **Bummerlhaus** (Stadtplatz 32); this 15th-century symbol of the town has a Gothic appearance and steep gable. Further round the square is the house where Franz Schubert lived (Stadtplatz 16), a notable baroque façade at No 9 and, depending on your tastes, the most striking of all, the façade of **Stadtplatz No 12**, whose blue and yellow hues are perfectly complemented by angels and crests.

To the north of Stadtplatz is the **Schloss Lamberg** (Berggasse), rising high above the Steyr River. It was restored in baroque style in 1727 after a fire damaged the town centre, and is now mainly inhabited by bureaucrats. Next door is the small but attractive **Schlosspark**.

UPPER AUSTRIA

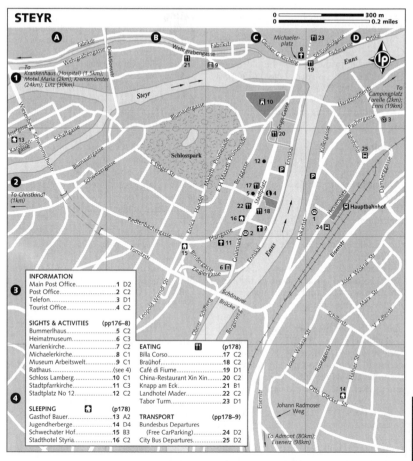

STEYR

0   300 m
0   0.2 miles

To Krankenhaus (Hospital) (1.5km); Motel Maria (2km); Kremsmünster (24km); Linz (30km)

To Christkindl (1km)

To Campingplatz Forelle (2km); Enns (19km)

To Admont (80km); Eisenerz (98km)

Hauptbahnhof

Schlosspark

Johann Radmoser Weg

UPPER AUSTRIA

Further north, across the Steyr River, it's hard to miss the **Michaelerkirche** (Michaelerplatz; daylight hours), whose tall steeple casts its shadow almost as far as the river bank. The bright church has a particularly high and open nave, and a large gable fresco. To the west of Michaelerkirche – through cobblestoned streets with one house piled on top of the next – is the **Museum Arbeitswelt** (773 51; Wehrgrabengasse 7; adult/concession €4.75/3.30; 9am-5pm Tue-Sun mid-Mar–mid-Dec). This excellent museum delves into the topic of Steyr's industrial past and its effect on society, through displays on working-class history, forced labour during WWII and the rise of the Socialist party.

Back on Stadtplatz, its southern end is dominated by the **Marienkirche** (531 29;

Grünmarkt 1; daylight hours), a mix of Gothic and baroque styles, with an extremely ornate high altar and pulpit. The alcoves for the side altars are rich in stucco; to the left of the entrance is a statue of St Florian.

Up the hill to the west is the **Stadtpfarrkirche** (Brucknerplatz 4; daylight hours), a Gothic creation from the 15th century. It shares some features with Stephansdom in Vienna, just as it shared the same architect, Hans Puchsbaum, but it's a cruder work. Down the steps to the south is the **Heimatmuseum** (575 548; Grünmarkt 26; admission free; 10am-4pm Tue-Sun, 10am-4pm Wed-Sun Nov-Mar, 10am-5pm Dec). Housed in the 17th-century granary Innerberger Stadel, it has displays on the history, culture and folklore of the town, including some impressive mechanical puppets.

If you happen to arrive in town over Christmas be sure to head for the suburb of **Christkindl**, to the west of the old centre. During this time, a special **post office** (Schulweg; ☉ 9am-5pm 28 Nov-6 Jan) is set up in the Christkindlkirche to handle the almost two million letters posted around the world.

Sleeping

The tourist office can help with arranging private rooms.

Jugendherberge (☎ 455 80; jugend@steyr.gv.at; Hafner Strasse 14; dm €7.70; ☉ year-round) This HI hostel is behind and to the south of the *Hauptbahnhof*: bus No 3 runs close. It's housed in a rather unexciting building in the middle of suburbia, but the rooms are totally fine.

Gasthof Bauer (☎ 544 41; Josefgasse 7; s/d €31/56; P ☒) Situated on an island in the Steyr River, this small, family-run *Gasthof* has a homey ambience, comfortable rooms and an inexpensive restaurant. It's about 10 minutes' walk from the town centre.

Stadthotel Styria (☎ 515 51; info@styriahotel.at; Stadtplatz 40; s/d €77.60/113.20; P ☒) Accommodation in Steyr doesn't get any more plush than this; rooms are full of personal touches and the Renaissance breakfast room is quite impressive.

Motel Maria (☎ 710 62; www.motel-maria.at - in German; Reindlgutstrasse 25; s/d €30/60; P ☒) This peaceful place is 2km west of the town centre, a short walk beyond the *Krankenhaus* (hospital), where bus No 2B stops. Rooms are large, well kept and come with balcony, and the motel backs onto a big garden.

Schwechater Hof (☎ 530 67; schwechaterhof .steyr@aon.at; Leopold Werndl Strasse 1; s/d €48/72; P) This hotel offers standard three-star accommodation that is a little overpriced, but its location, up behind the *Stadtpfarrkirche*, is good. Its restaurant has all the trappings of a traditional *Gästehaus*.

Campingplatz Forelle (☎ 780 08; www.forelle steyr.com - in German; Kermatmüllerstrasse 1a; campsites per adult/tent or car €4.70/5.80) On the eastern bank of the Enns, 2km north of town in the suburb of Münichholz, is this tree-shaded camping ground. There's a children's playground and facilities for cyclists (take bus No 1 from the centre).

Eating

Stadtplatz has lots to offer self-caterers; it hosts an open-air market on Thursday and Saturday mornings, has snack stands, as well as a **Billa Corso** (Stadtplatz 30).

Knapp am Eck (☎ 762 69; Wehrgrabengasse 15; mains €5-12; ☉ lunch & dinner Tue-Sat, lunch Sun) Next to the fast-flowing side arm of the Steyr is this lovely *Wirtshaus* (inn/tavern) with simple Austrian fare and a fine wine selection. Best of all is its quiet back garden, with its tree shade and ivy-covered walls.

Café di Fiume (☎ 871 21; Michaelerplatz 11; lunch menu €5; ☉ 8am-7pm Tue-Sat) Mismatching chairs, relaxed staff, great coffee, European cuisine and views of the Enns all combine to create a wonderful Bohemian atmosphere in this little gem of a café.

China-Restaurant Xin Xin (☎ 470 34; Enge Gasse 20; lunch menu €5-6, mains €6-15; ☉ lunch & dinner) This decent restaurant has the usual range of Chinese dishes, but has the added bonus of a secluded, tree-shaded garden.

Braühof (☎ 420 00; Stadtplatz 35; mains €8-12; ☉ 10am-1am) This Austrian eatery has daily specials, a nice little vegetarian selection and covers all the bases, combining a restaurant, café, cocktail bar, wine cellar and outdoor seating.

Landhotel Mader (☎ 533 58; Stadtplatz 36; mains €7-18; ☉ 10.30am-midnight Mon-Fri, 3.30-10pm Sat) Mader is another reliable restaurant on Stadtplatz offering solid Austrian fare. Choose from the wine cellar, bar or winter garden to feast on your meal.

Tabor Turm (☎ 729 49; Taborweg 7; mains €11-19; ☉ 10.30am-midnight Wed-Sun, 10.30am-5pm Mon) The best feature of Tabor Turm is the view of Steyr and the mountains of Nationalpark Kalkalpen far to the south. It occupies a former church on a hill behind Michaelerkirche.

Getting There & Away

Trains from Linz (€6.70, 50 minutes) are direct every two hours, or require a change at St Valentin; there are far fewer on Sundays. Trains then continue south into Styria. The *Hauptbahnhof* has a restaurant, a travel information office and left-luggage lockers. For Wels (€11, 1½ hours, hourly), most trains and buses require a change in St Valentin or Linz; only four buses daily (€8, one on Sunday) are direct, and all pass through Kremsmünster (€5.20, 50 minutes).

Bundesbuses leave from above the *Hauptbahnhof* (where there's also free car parking) while city buses leave from outside the *Hauptbahnhof* to the north. Buses run to Linz (€6, 70 minutes) approximately hourly Monday to Friday, less on weekends. Steyr is on Hwy 115, the road branching from the A1/E60 and running south to Leoben.

NATIONALPARK KALKALPEN

Near the border to Styria directly south of Steyr is Nationalpark Kalkalpen, Austria's second-largest national park after Hohe Tauern. The park features large expanses of untouched forest, broken up by peaceful alpine meadows, and its valleys and gorges cut their way through classic alpine landscapes, which rise to **Hoher Nock** (1963m), the park's highest peak. It's particularly popular with hikers and cyclists, but there is also a smattering of rock-climbing, and during winter the pristine snow is crisscrossed by the tracks of cross-country skiers.

Information on the park is available from **Nationalpark Zentrum Molln** (☎ 07584-36 51; www .kalkalpen.at - in German; Nationalpark Allee 1; ⏰ 7.30am-5pm mid-Apr–Oct), a purpose-built centre near the northern entrance to the park; staff can help with accommodation, including the 15 mountain huts within the park. A good map covering walking, cycling and cross-country skiing trails of the park is Kompass map No 70 (1:50,000). Regular direct buses from Steyr to Molln (€4.70, one hour) normally only run on weekdays.

KREMSMÜNSTER

☎ 07583 / pop 6440
Overlooking the Krems Valley about halfway between Steyr and Wels is the **Benedictine abbey** (☎ 07583-52 75-150; www.kremsmuenster.at /stift - in German; Stift 1; adult/child/family €4.80/2.20/11.70; ⏰ tours 10am, 11am, 2pm & 3.30pm Mon-Fri, 10am, 11.30am, 1pm, 2pm & 4pm Sat & Sun Easter-Oct, 11am, 2pm & 3.30pm Mon-Sat Nov-Easter) of Kremsmünster, another bombastic conception worthy of a visit. Although it was established in 777, it too owes much to baroque remodelling in the early 18th century. Stuccowork and frescoes are much in evidence in the long, low **Bibliothek** (library) and **Kaisersaal** (Emperor's Hall), while the most acclaimed piece in the **Schatzkammer** (treasury) is the Tassilo Chalice, made of gilded copper and donated to the monks by the Duke of Bavaria in about 780.

All three can be visited only on a one-hour guided tour.

The 50-m-high **Sternwarte** (observatory tower; adult/child/family €5.10/2.20/12.40; ⏰ tour 10am & 2pm May-Oct), built in 1758, houses a museum devoted to a number of schools of natural history. It's certainly an interesting collection, but you have to endure a 1½-hour tour in German to see it.

What can be seen without greasing the palms of the abbey with silver are the **Stiftskirche** (⏰ daylight hours) and **Fischbehälter** (Fish Basin; ⏰ 10am-4pm). The baroque church interior is quite unusual; its arched ceiling is crisscrossed with highly ornate white stucco, its columns draped with Flemish tapestries and on its walls hang dark, brooding paintings. The Fischbehälter comes as quite a surprise; built between 1690 and 1692, it consists of five fish ponds enclosed in an inner courtyard, with each pond centred on a fountain-statue. The sound of the water is loud but calming, and you can feed the carp (for €0.20).

Getting There & Away

Kremsmünster is on the rail line between Linz and Graz (from Linz €7, 40 minutes); the longest you'll have to wait for a train is 1½ hours. Buses from Wels (€3, 30 minutes, workdays only) and Steyr (€4.40, 50 minutes) run on a regular basis.

WELS

☎ 07242 / pop 55,500
Steyr may well be the most attractive city in the Traunviertel, but Wels is the largest, and second only to Linz in Upper Austria. It's an agricultural hub with an appealing centre and a history dating back to Roman times, when it was known as Ovilava.

Information, maps and audio guides (free) of the city are available from **Tourismusverband Wels** (☎ 434 95; office@tourism-wels.at; Kaiser Josef Platz 22; ⏰ 9am-6pm Mon-Fri), two blocks north of the main square, Stadtplatz.

Sights & Activities

The focal point of the town is the long **Stadtplatz**, lined with historic buildings, eye-catching façades and several attractive courtyards (for example, at Stadtplatz 34). Easily the most striking though is the **Haus der Salome Alt** (House of Salome Art; Stadtplatz 24), gaining its name from one-time occupant

Salome Alt, mistress of Salzburg's Prince-Archbishop Wolf Dietrich. Its Renaissance façade is a colourful combination of red-and-cream brickwork. Opposite is the refreshingly simplistic **Stadtpfarrkirche** (☿ daylight hours), with a fine Romanesque porch and Gothic stained glass. The western end of Stadtplatz is guarded by the **Ledererturm**, constructed in 1376.

No city would be complete without a castle, and so it is with Wels. **Burg Wels**, to the south of the Haus der Salome Alt, isn't much of a castle by Austrian standards, but it was here that Maximilian I breathed his last breath in 1519. It now houses a **museum** (☎ 235 7350; Burggasse 13; adult/concession €3.70/1.45; ☿ 10am-5pm Tue-Fri, 2-5pm Sat, 10am-4pm Sun) which mainly sticks to agricultural and bakery themes.

Sleeping & Eating

Staff at the tourist office can help you find somewhere to stay. There are plenty of eating options on Stadtplatz and its tributaries.

Jugendherberge (☎ 235 7570; jugendherberge@wels.at; Dragonerstrasse 22; dm with/without shower €10.10/9.10; P) This HI hostel is just five minutes' walk northwest of Stadtplatz, and has spacious rooms.

Kremsmünstererhof (☎ 466 23; Stadtplatz 62/63; s/d €37/54; P) Directly on the main square is this three-star hotel, with spacious rooms and a large inner courtyard.

For coffee and cake, stop in at **Café Urban** (Schmidtgasse 20; ☿ 8.30am-6.30pm Mon-Fri, 8am-1pm Sat), a café in the same mould of its traditional Viennese counterparts. Something more substantial can be had at **Altstadt Weinstube** (cnr Altstadt & Hafergasse; mains €7-12; ☿ lunch & dinner Mon-Sat), a wine bar with rustic character, or at the more upmarket **Da Leone** (☎ 797 85-10; Hafergasse 1; mains €10-18; ☿ lunch & dinner Mon-Sat), which serves Italian specialities in an intimate setting. A Spar supermarket is located just beyond the Ledererturm.

Getting There & Away

Trains and buses arrive at the *Hauptbahnhof*, 1¼km north of Stadtplatz. The town is on the InterCity (IC) and EuroCity (EC) express rail route between Linz and Salzburg, just 15 minutes southwest of Linz (€4.40, several per hour). There's also a line running to Passau (€12.90, one hour and 20 minutes, hourly) on the German border.

LAMBACH

☎ 02745

And yet another small town dominated by an abbey. The **Benediktinerstift** (Benedictine abbey; ☎ 02745-217 10; Klosterplatz 1; tours adult/child €4.40/1.80; ☿ 2pm Easter-Oct) at Lambach, 10km southwest of Wels, was founded in 1056 though much of the present edifice dates from the 17th century when the church was rebuilt in baroque style. The abbey's highlights (by tour only) include a baroque theatre (the only one of its kind in Austria) and library, but more striking are the Romanesque frescoes from the 11th century. They are extremely well preserved and betray the influence of the styles of southeastern Europe, unusual in Austria.

From Wels there are frequent buses (€3, 20 minutes) and trains (€3, 10 minutes) to Lambach.

THE MÜHLVIERTEL

Separating Linz from the Czech Republic is the Mühlviertel, a region of woodlands and pastures often forgotten by local and international tourists alike. It's a stronghold of folk traditions and an area influenced by Bohemia to the north. Apart from getting off the beaten track, the Mühlviertel's main attractions are the walled town of Freistadt and the Gothic altar of Kefermarkt's church.

FREISTADT

☎ 07942 / pop 7200

Of all the medieval towns in Austria, Freistadt has the best-preserved fortifications of them all. But this is not the town's only drawcard; the old centre is a pretty arrangement of cobblestoned streets lined with neat houses, and its fine burghers have been brewing their own beer for centuries. The town is a mere 17km from the Czech border, and 35km to Linz.

Orientation & Information

The compact town centre, within the old city walls, is centred on Hauptplatz. Here you'll find the **Mühlviertler Kernland tourist office** (☎ 757 00; kernland@oberoesterreich.at; Hauptplatz 14; ☿ 9am-5pm Mon-Fri), which has information on the town and its surrounds. The main north–south route, connecting Linz with the Czech border, skirts the western

---

BUYING INTO YOUR FAVOURITE BEER

It's not particularly unusual that Freistadt has a brewery; some 65 towns in Austria can make the same claim. But what gives this town special status in the plethora of proud brewing towns is the relationship between its citizens and its brewery.

Freistadt is known as a *Braucommune*, a town where the citizens actually own their brewery. It's quite a grand scheme if you like your beer – buy a house and you automatically buy a share of your favourite tipple. Not every landowner in the town has shares, though; ownership is limited to the 149 households located within the town walls. People who sell lose their stake to the purchaser, so don't expect to find too many of these homes on the market. Realistically, the brewery cannot be taken over by any competitor, as the business would have to buy the whole town in order to take control.

The arrangement started way back in 1777 when the brewery first opened. In the ensuing centuries the lucky owners would receive their share of the profits in liquid form, which would be distributed in *Eimer Bier* containers holding 56L. Each owner might get up to 130 containers! Nowadays, for better or worse, owners instead get a cash payment of equivalent value (which, on Friday and Saturday nights, often goes straight back to the brewery).

Every bar and guesthouse in town serves the local brew, so it's not hard to sample the beer, or to see why the brewery remains a profitable business. If you'd like to learn more about Freistadt beer, there are **tours** (☎ 757 77; Promenade 7; www.freistaedter-bier.at; brewery tours €6.50; ☼ tours 2pm Wed; tourist office tours €6; ☼ 6pm & 8pm 1st Thu of month) of the brewery; two beers are thrown in with the price of the tour. Call ahead if you'd like to take a tour.

---

section of the city walls; the local **post office** (Promenade 11) is located here.

Sights & Activities

The tourist office produces a handy *City Walk* brochure, which highlights the best the city has to offer. Of its specific sights, the city walls, complete with several gates and turrets and bordered by a grassy moat, top the list. As Freistadt developed as an important staging point on the salt route to Bohemia, so did the need for strong defences; the current walls were built in the 14th century.

The expansive **Hauptplatz** has some interesting old buildings with ornate façades, including the 14th-century **Stadtpfarrkirche** (☼ daylight hours) on the southern side of the square. The main construction is Gothic, but its tower is baroque. Waaggasse, just west of the Hauptplatz, is lined with striking architecture, including some with sgraffito designs.

Just beyond the northeastern corner of *Hauptplatz* is the city's 14th-century **Schloss**, with a square tower topped by a tapering red-tiled roof. Inside is the **Schlossmuseum** (☎ 722 74; Schlosshof 2; adult/senior €2.50/2; ☼ tours 9am, 10.30am, 2pm & 3.30pm Mon-Fri, 10.30am & 2pm Sat, 2pm Sun May-Oct, 10.30am & 2pm Mon-Fri, 2pm Sat & Sun Nov-Apr) which contains a ho-hum collection of historical and cultural displays as well as 600 works of engraved painted glass (*verre églomisé*).

Sleeping & Eating

Freistadt is one of the most pleasant towns in Upper Austria to overnight in, and enjoys a very high standard of both accommodation and eating options. All the following recommendations (apart from Camping Freistadt) are in the old centre.

Pension Pirklbauer (☎ 724 40; pension.pirklbauer .at; Höllgasse 2-4; s/d from/€18/36) In the southwest corner of the old centre is this traditional and welcoming pension which has been in operation since 1867. Rooms are large and supremely comfortable.

Café Pension Hubertus (☎ 723 54; www.café -pension-hubertus.at - in German; Höllplatz 3; s/d €18/36; P) This is another great choice, offering friendly service, a big welcome and big, cosy rooms. The only advantage over nearby Pirklbauer is that it has parking facilities.

Hotel Zum Goldenen Adler (☎ 721 12; goldener .adler@hotels-freistadt.at; Salzgasse 1; mains €6-16; s/d €45/74; P ⚹) Goldenen Adler is a step up from the pensions above, with modern rooms, steam room, sauna whirlpool and fitness room. The elegant restaurant specialises in dishes with beer as an ingredient, and has a quiet courtyard.

Vis à Vis (☎ 742 93; Salzgasse 13; pizzas €6-7; ◯ 9am-2am Mon-Fri, 5pm-2am Sat) This unpretentious pizzeria-bar is certainly a local hangout, and has a sunny conservatory and rustic cellar.

Stadtwirtshaus (☎ 776 20; Salzgasse 5; mains €9-12; ◯ lunch & dinner Mon-Sat) Stadtwirtshaus is a few steps away from Vis à Vis, and a few steps up in formality and quality. It's a highly traditional place, offering great Mühlviertel cuisine.

Hotel-Gasthof Deim (☎ 722 58; Böhmergasse 8-10; mains €8-15; ◯ 11.30am-midnight) This rambling, medieval place is the top restaurant in town. Its large conservatory overlooks a section of the disused moat.

Camping Freistadt (☎ 725 70; www.freistadt.at/ffc - in German; Eglsee 12; campsite per adult/car/tent €2/1.50/2.50; **P**) About five minutes' walk northeast of the town centre is this quiet camping ground on the banks of the Feldaist River.

Getting There & Away

Freistadt is on a direct rail route from Linz (€6.70, one hour, two-hourly). This line then wriggles its way north to Prague; Czech rail fares are lower than those in Austria, so you can save money if you're travelling north by waiting and buying (in Czech currency) your onward tickets once you've crossed the border.

Freistadt train station is 3km southwest of the centre so a better option from Linz is to take the bus, as these stop in the centre (€6.70, one hour, hourly Monday to Friday, infrequent at weekends). Bicycles can be rented from most of the pensions and hotels for around €4 per day.

Hwy 125, the main route to and from Linz, runs adjacent to the walled centre and then continues its way northwards towards Prague.

KEFERMARKT
☎ 07947

There's one particular reason to visit Kefermarkt: the **Pfarrkirche St Wolfgang** (☎ 62 03; Oberer Markt 1; ◯ approx 7am-8pm), also known as the Wallfahrtkirche. Although this is not as famous as the pilgrimage church in the village of St Wolfgang in Salzkammergut, its Gothic *Flügelaltar* (winged altar) is of comparable beauty and similar design. The altarpiece of limewood is 13.5m high, with latticework fronds rising towards the ceiling. At the centre are three expressive figures, carved

with great skill (left to right as you face them): St Peter, St Wolfgang and St Christopher. The wings of the altar bear religious scenes in low relief. The rest of the decorations in the church are baroque.

If you want to stay, there are a couple of places down the hill from the church. Freistadt, however, is a prettier town to overnight in.

Gasthof Horner (☎ 62 20; Oberer Markt 13; mains €6-10; s/d €28/48; ◯ Wed-Mon; **P**) Horner is a good bet for an overnight stay; rooms are clean and fresh and the restaurant warm and cosy. Note that no arrivals are accepted on Tuesday when the restaurant is closed.

Four daily trains (more on weekdays) travel between Kefermarkt and Freistadt (€2.60, 10 minutes). The church is about 1km north of the train station.

THE INNVIERTEL

The Innviertel is Upper Austria's western corner, stretching from Salzburgerland to the banks of the Danube. It gains its name from the Inn River, a tributary of the Danube that forms a natural border between Germany and Austria. While there isn't a whole lot to see and do, the Innviertel's fertile farmland and small, colourful towns – Braunau am Inn and Schärding stand head and shoulders above the rest – are suited for escaping the madding crowds of Austria's more popular destinations.

BRAUNAU AM INN
☎ 07722 / pop 16,700

Across the Inn River from Simbach am Inn in Germany, towards the southern end of the Innviertel, is Branau am Inn. This border town has achieved unwanted attention as the birthplace of Hitler, though it would prefer to be described as *die gotische Stadt* (the Gothic city).

The long main square, **Stadtplatz**, is lined with elegant homes in pastel shades. At the northern end is the town's **tourist office** (☎ 626 44; tourismusverband.braunau@netway.at; Stadtplatz 9; ◯ 8.30am-6pm Mon-Fri, 9am-noon Sat), while its southern end narrows to the **Torturm**, a medieval gate tower dating from 1260. To the west of Stadtplatz the spire of the parish church, **Stadtpfarrkirche St Stephan** (Kirchenplatz; ◯ daylight hours), can clearly be seen.

UPPER AUSTRIA

At almost 100m, it's one of the tallest in Austria.

Not far south of the Torturm is **Hitler's Geburtshaus** (birth house); born in 1889 with the unprepossessing moniker of Adolf Schicklgruber, he only spent two years of his life in the town before moving with his family to Linz. The inscription outside his birthhouse simply reads *Für Frieden Freiheit und Demokratie, nie wieder Faschismus, millionen Tote Mahnen* (For peace, freedom and democracy, Never again fascism, millions of dead admonish).

Sleeping & Eating

Jugendherberge (☎ 81638; int.osternberg.braunau@aon .at; Osternbergerstrasse 57; dm €14; ☻ Feb-Nov; **P**) About 1km south of the Stadtplatz is this hostel, which is well set up for cyclists.

Hotel Gann (☎ 632 06; Stadtplatz 23; s/d €29/46) This small-scale hotel has certainly seen better days, but it still exudes a homey atmosphere and rooms are large and comfy.

Bogner (☎ 683 43; Stadtplatz 47; mains €7-10; ☻ 9am-1am) Supposedly Austria's smallest brewery, Bogner is a rustic pub-restaurant with solid Austrian fare and several home-brewed beers to guzzle.

Getting There & Away

By train, at least one change is normally required from either Linz (€17.60, 2¼ hours) or Salzburg (€10, 1½ hours) by train. From Wels, there are two daily direct trains (€15.30, 1½ hours).

Braunau receives plenty of touring cyclists because it lies on two bike routes: the Innsbruck–Passau Inntal Radweg and the Salzach River track to Salzburg.

SCHÄRDING
☎ 07712 / pop 5200

If you follow the Inn River a further 40km downstream you hit Schärding, a town of striking pastel colours and baroque houses. While there aren't any specific attractions to draw you here, it's a pleasant town to overnight in, and it's certainly easier on the eye than Braunau.

The **tourist office** (☎ 43 00-0; www.barockstadt -schaerding.at; Innbruckstrasse 29; ☻ 9am-6pm Mon-Fri & 10am-3pm Sat & Sun late Apr-Oct, 8am-noon & 1-5pm Mon-Fri Nov-late Apr), near the bridge spanning the river into Germany, has plenty of information on the town and the surrounding area.

STANDING BY YOUR NAME

In the far western corner of the Innviertel stands a tiny village with a big name, Fucking (pronounced 'fooking'). Naturally the name has caused a few giggles, and a few problems along the way (signs go missing all the time), but the village is *stolz* (proud) of its unique name. Recently residents were asked to vote on a name change but decided to stick with it; village spokesman Siegfried Hoeppl stated that 'Everyone here knows what it means in English, but for us Fucking is Fucking – and it's going to stay Fucking'. The name derives from a certain Herr Fuck who settled in the area some 100 years ago.

Look no further than the **Silberziele** (silver row), a line of richly coloured houses with identically shaped gables, for accommodation and food. **Pension Lachinger** (☎ 22 68; café .lachinger@aon.at; Silberzeile 13; s/d €21/42; **P**) and **Haus Mayr** (☎ 30 80; Silberzeile 8; s/d €24/48) are two uncomplicated pensions with comfy rooms and friendly staff.

If you have a chance, nip over to **Stift Engelhartszell** (☎ 0771-80 10-0; 30/60min tours in German only €1.50/2.30; ☻ tours 8-11.30am, 1-5pm Mon-Sat, 9-10.30am Sun), 28km east of Schärding. It started life as a Cistercian abbey in 1295, but since 1975 it has operated as a Trappist monastery, the only one of its kind in Austria. Tours of this working abbey stick to its **church** (admission free; ☻ daylight hours), unusual for its combination of abstract frescoes and rococo ornamentation. Stop in at the abbey's shop, which sells surprisingly good schnapps and liquor produced by the monks.

If you have your own transport, the approach to Schärding from Linz, via Engelhartszell along the eastern bank of the Danube, is quite beautiful, and certainly off the beaten track. Another good option is to combine a trip to Passau by boat (see p174), then onto **Schärding** (☎ 73 50; www.innschifffahrt .at - in German; Carossastrasse 2; adult/child one way €6/3, adult/child return €9/4; ☻ 9am & 6.30pm Tue-Sun year-round, also 11am, 2pm & 4pm Apr-Oct). Trains connect Linz with Schärding (€15.30, one hour) four times daily. Only two direct buses travel between Schärding and Engelhartszell (€5.20, one hour) Monday to Friday.

UPPER AUSTRIA

Styria

CONTENTS

Styria (Steiermark) is the country's best-kept secret. When you ask an Austrian for advice on the best places to visit in their beloved country, and they answer with the mountains of Tyrol, the lakes of Salzkammergut and the cultural joys of Vienna, they're lying through their teeth, just to keep you out of Styria.

This, the second-largest province in Austria, is a perfect combination of everything the country has to offer: culture, architecture, gentle rolling hills, vine-covered slopes, and of course mountains. Its capital Graz, Austria's second-largest city and one of the county's most attractive, has one of the highest standards of living in Europe.

Head south from Graz and you're in wine country. Dubbed the Styrian Tuscany for its uncanny resemblance to that land of glorious wine and golden sun, this green, fertile area is crisscrossed with *Weinstrassen*, well-marked wine trails. This is also *Kürbiskernöl* country; a strong, dark pumpkin-seed oil ubiquitous in Styrian cooking.

The eastern stretch of Styria is dotted with rejuvenating thermal spas and century-old castles. If you're a fan of the former, Bad Blumau is a mandatory stop, not only to take the waters but also to appreciate its unusual architecture, created from the rich imagination of Hundertwasser. If you prefer the later, Schloss Riegersburg stands head and shoulders above most castles, not only in Styria, but in the entire country.

The landscape of Styria's northern and western reaches take on a more traditional Austrian role. This is the province's untamed region, where cold, fast-flowing alpine rivers have carved valleys through towering mountains. Complementing the area's natural wonders is a handful of manmade gems; Admont Abbey, deep in the Enns valley, is possibly the best of its kind in Austria, and the Erzberg open-cast mine is a sight to behold.

Note that the northwestern reaches of Styria stretch into Salzkammergut (p210).

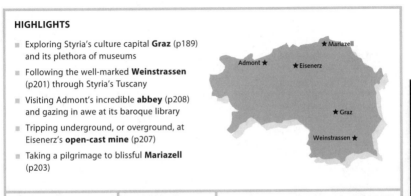

HIGHLIGHTS

- Exploring Styria's culture capital **Graz** (p189) and its plethora of museums
- Following the well-marked **Weinstrassen** (p201) through Styria's Tuscany
- Visiting Admont's incredible **abbey** (p208) and gazing in awe at its baroque library
- Tripping underground, or overground, at Eisenerz's **open-cast mine** (p207)
- Taking a pilgrimage to blissful **Mariazell** (p203)

- POPULATION: 1,183,000   - AREA: 16,392 SQ KM   - HIGHEST ELEVATION: HOCHGOLLING 2862M

History

Habitation of Styria dates back to the Stone Age, and findings from the Bronze and Iron Age are on display in Grossklein (p201). The Celts, then the Romans, followed by the Avars and Slavs, settled in the area, but it wasn't until the 11th century that Styria as a region gained its current name. At the time Ottakar I, whose base was in the Upper Austrian town of Steyr, acquired the area through succession and stamped his seal *Marchia Styriae* (Styrian Mark) on the province. The name stuck.

When Duke Ottokar IV died without an heir in 1192, Styria passed to the Babenberg duke Leopold V as an inheritance. Control subsequently fell to King Ottokar II of Bohemia and then finally, in 1276, into the hands of the Habsburgs. In the next century the population grew, but there followed two centuries of local conflicts and invasions by the Turks and Hungarians. The year 1480 was particularly dire; it was known as the year of the 'Plagues of God' – the Turks, the Black Death and locusts all paid unwelcome visits. Exactly 200 years later one-quarter of the population of Graz was wiped out in a further epidemic of the Black Death.

The 16th and 17th centuries were also less than peaceful for Styria; Reformation and Counter-Reformation gripped the province, with the Habsburg army running riot and burning anything Protestant it could find. Once the religious upheavals were settled, and the Turkish threat removed after 1683, the economy and infrastructure of the region developed. Then, in 1779, and again in 1805 and 1809, it was the turn of the French to invade. After the Nazi occupation of WWII, the first Allied troops to liberate the area were from the Soviet Union, followed by the British, who occupied Graz until 1955.

Climate

Styria's climate is a tale in two parts; southern Styria enjoys a relatively kind climate, influenced by the Pannonian (west Hungarian) plain to the east, while much of northern Styria is subject to alpine climatic conditions.

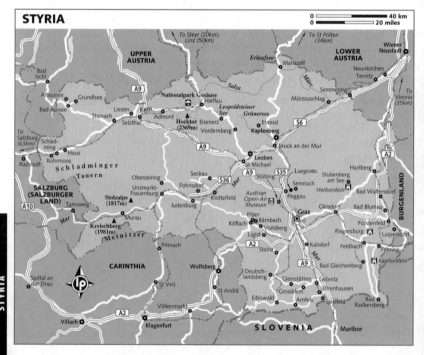

Getting There & Away

The A2, running from Vienna to Villach in Klagenfurt, cuts a path through southern Styria, passing just below Graz, while the A9 runs an almost north–south course through the middle of Styria, making it straightforward to travel from Linz and Salzburg to Graz. The A9 also connects Graz with Slovenia, 40km to the south.

Unlike much of eastern Austria, Styria's train lines are relatively sparse; the main line between Carinthia and Vienna passes well north of Graz through the region's main railhead, Bruck an der Mur. For Linz and Salzburg, a change is usually required at St Michael, 25km southwest of Bruck.

Getting Around

Regional transport (☎ 0316-82 06 06; www.verbund linie.at - in German), including city transport, is integrated under a zonal ticketing system. Zonal tickets are valid for trains and buses, including those run by the private transport company GKB. Single tickets are valid for periods varying from one hour (one zone) to five hours (22 zones). Weekly, monthly and yearly, as well as 24-hour, passes are also available.

GRAZ

☎ 0316 / pop 240,000

Of all Austrian cities, it could be argued that Graz has the best of everything. For starters, it's an attractive city; the green of the parks, the red of the rooftops and the blue of the river are a picturesque combination. Then there's the architecture; Renaissance courtyards, baroque palaces and groundbreaking modern constructions amazingly complement each other. Culturally, Graz is leagues ahead of many of its European contemporaries, with a full festival calendar, a plethora of galleries and opera and theatre. Its size is also a bonus: big enough to offer plenty of variety, but not too big to overwhelm. The surrounding countryside, a mixture of vineyards, mountains, forested hills, and thermal springs, is within easy striking distance. Last but by no means least, a strong student population (some 50,000 in four universities) helps drive a kicking nightlife and vibrant art scene.

This all combines to create a lively, yet laid-back city; a city worth lingering in for a few days.

History

Graz is a derivation of the Slav word *gradec*, meaning small fortress, but the original town developed from a Bavarian settlement, first documented in 1128. By 1189 Graz had grown enough to be considered a city, and in 1379 it became the seat of the Leopold line of the Habsburgs. Friedrich III, king of Germany, emperor of Austria and holy roman emperor, resided here and left his famous motto, AEIOU (*Austria Est Imperare Orbi Universo*; Austria rules the world) inscribed all over town. In 1564, Graz became the administrative capital of Inner Austria, an area covering present-day Styria and Carinthia, plus the former possessions of Carniola, Gorizia and Istria. Over the next few centuries the importance of the town faded, and in 1784, with the threat of the Turks gone, Graz dismantled its city walls.

Early in the 19th century Archduke Johann, brother to Franz I, founded the first museum in Austria, the Joanneum, in Graz. Johann's benign influence was strong in the city, which may help account for some of the relaxed air the city has today. The historic centre of Graz was awarded Unesco World Heritage status in 1999 and the city was the European City of Culture in 2003, the first city to hold such a title alone (normally two cities are awarded the title each year).

Orientation

Graz is dominated by the Schlossberg, which rises over the medieval town centre. The river Mur cuts a north–south path west of the hill, dividing the old centre from the *Hauptbahnhof* (main train station).

Tram Nos 3 and 6 run from the *Hauptbahnhof* to *Hauptplatz* (main square) in the town centre. Radiating from *Hauptplatz* is Sporgasse, an important shopping street, and Herrengasse, the main pedestrian thoroughfare. At the southern end of Herrengasse is Jakominiplatz, a major transport hub for local buses and trams.

MAPS

Graztourismus hands out a free map of the central city, which is highly adequate for most tourist needs. For anything more, Freytag & Berndt's *Graz* (€3.50; scale 1:15,000) map is the best option; it has a comprehensive street index.

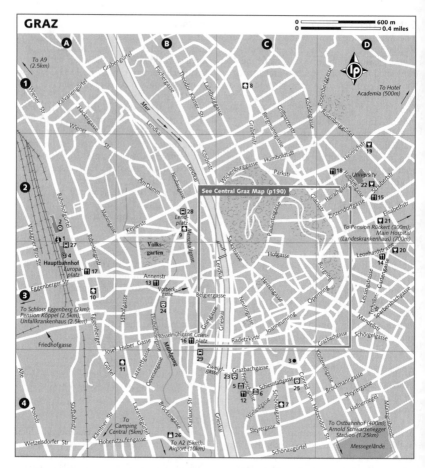

GRAZ

0 _____ 600 m
0 _____ 0.4 miles

See Central Graz Map (p190)

Information

BOOKSHOPS

English Bookshop (Map pp190-1; ☎ 82 62 66; Tummelplatz 7; ⏰ 9am-6pm Mon-Fri, 9am-noon Sat) The largest collection of English books in Graz at the steepest prices.

Freytag & Berndt (Map pp190-1; ☎ 81 82 30; Sporgasse 29; ⏰ 9am-6pm Mon-Fri, 9am-noon Sat) The best source of maps and guide books in town.

Moser (Map pp190-1; ☎ 83 01 10; Herrengasse 23; ⏰ 9am-6pm Mon-Fri, 9am-noon Sat) Sells travel guides and has a concise collection of foreign-language books.

INTERNET ACCESS

Medien.kunstbar (Map pp190-1; Kunsthaus, Lendkai 1; ⏰ 10am-6pm Tue-Sun, 10am-8pm Thu) Free access.

SIT Cafe (Map pp190-1; ☎ 81 45 65; Hans Sachs Gasse 10; per hr €4.50; ⏰ 8am-midnight Mon-Sat, 9am-9pm Sun)

Speednet Cafe (Map pp188-9; www.speednet-cafe.com - in German; Europaplatz 4; per hr €5.80; ⏰ 8am-10pm Mon-Sat, 9am-9pm Sun) Located in the train station.

INTERNET RESOURCES

www.graz.at Provides a snapshot of the political, social, cultural and financial standing of the city (German only).

www.graztourismus.at The city's official tourist information portal, with loads of information in English.

www.info-graz.at List upon list of practical information covering every aspect of life in Graz (German only).

LAUNDRY

Putzerei-Rupp (Map pp188-9; ☎ 82 11 83; Jakoministrasse 34; ⏰ 8am-5pm Mon-Fri) One of the very few places in Graz with self-service washers and dryers.

INFORMATION			EATING	🍴	(pp195–6)	ENTERTAINMENT	🎭	(p197)
Hauptbahnhof Informationsbüro	**1**	A2	Anschlössl	**12**	C4	Augartenkino	**23**	C4
Post Office	**2**	A2	Billa	**13**	B3	Bang	**24**	B3
Putzerei-Rupp Laundry	**3**	C4	Girardikeller	**14**	D3	Royal English		
Speednet Cafe	**4**	A3	Mensa	**15**	D2	Cinema	**25**	C4
			Zu den 3 Goldenen Kugeln	**16**	B3			
SIGHTS & ACTIVITIES		(pp189–92)	Zu den 3 Goldenen Kugeln	**17**	A3	SHOPPING	🛍	(pp197–8)
FriDa & FreD	**5**	C4	Zu den 3 Goldenen Kugeln	**18**	D2	Citypark	**26**	B4
Museum der Wahrnehmung	**6**	C4	Zu den 3 Goldenen Kugeln	(see 26)				
						TRANSPORT		(p198)
SLEEPING	🛏	(pp194–5)	DRINKING	🍸	(pp196–7)	Airport Bus	(see 27)	
Augarten Hotel	**7**	C4	Bierbaron	**19**	D2	Bundesbuses	**27**	A3
Das Wirtshaus Greiner	**8**	C1	Goldene Kugel	**20**	D3	Denzel	(see 1)	
Gasthof-Pension zur Steirer-Stub'n	**9**	B2	Kulturhauskeller	(see 21)		GKB & Watzke		
Hotel Strasser	**10**	A3	Orange	**21**	D2	Bus Stops	**28**	B2
Jugendgästehaus	**11**	B4	Three Monkeys	**22**	D2	GKB Bus Stop	**29**	B4

LEFT LUGGAGE
Lockers (€2.60 for 24 hours) can be found at the train station.

LIBRARIES
Steiermärkische Landesbiblothek (Map pp190–1; ☎ 801 64-600; Kalchberggasse 2; ☺ 8.30am-5pm Mon-Fri) The main library of Graz.

MEDICAL SERVICES
Landeskrankenhaus (Map pp188-9; ☎ 385-0; Auenbruggerplatz 1) The city's largest hospital, provides emergency treatment. It's about 3km from the town centre.
Unfallkrankenhaus (Map pp188-9; ☎ 505; Göstingersrasse 24) Emergency hospital at tram No 1 terminus.

MONEY
Graz is littered with banks and ATMs. The *Hauptbahnhof* has a money exchange, Western Union office and two ATMS.
Bankhaus Krentschkar Hamerlinggasse (Map pp190–1; ☎ 80 30-0; Hamerlinggasse 8; ☺ 8.30am-4.15pm Mon-Wed, 8.30am-5.30pm Thu, 8.30am-3pm Fri) Am Eisernen Tor (Map pp190–1; ☎ 80 30-0; Am Eisernen Tor 3; ☺ 8.30am-4.15pm Mon-Wed, 8.30am-5.30pm Thu, 8.30am-3pm Fri) American Express representative in Graz; will exchange American Express travellers cheques without charging commission.

POST
Hauptbahnhof post office (Map pp188-9; Bahnhofgürtel 48; ☺ 8am-midnight Mon-Fri, 7am-2pm Sat, 3-10pm Sun) This post office is just to the north of the main entrance to the train station.
Main post office (Map pp190-1; Neutorgasse 46; ☺ 6.30am-8pm Mon-Fri, 8am-noon Sat)

TOURIST INFORMATION
Graztourismus (Map pp190-1; ☎ 80 75-0; www.graztourismus.at; Herrengasse 16; ☺ 9am-7pm Mon-Fri, 9am-6pm Sat, 10am-6pm Sun Jun-Sep, 9am-6pm Mon-Sat, 10am-6pm Sun Oct-May) Graz's main tourist office, with loads of information on the city and its surrounds. Most of it's free, although there is a charge of €1 for the *World Heritage Site Graz* booklet, which describes central sites.
Hauptbahnhof Informationsbüro (Map pp188-9; ☎ 80 75-21; Grazer Hauptbahnhof; ☺ 8.30am-1pm & 2-5.30pm Mon-Wed & Fri, 8.30am-1pm & 2-6.30pm Thu) Located in the main train station.

TRAVEL AGENCIES
STA (Map pp190-1; ☎ 82 62 62-0; graz@statravel.at; Raubergasse 20; ☺ 9am-5.30pm Mon-Fri) Nation-wide travel agency specialising in student travel; often has cheap deals.

UNIVERSITIES
Universität Graz (Map pp188-9; ☎ 380-0; www.kfuni graz.ac.at; Universitätsplatz 3) Of the four universities in Graz, this is the largest.

Sights
Graz is a bonanza of museums, galleries, noble buildings, modern architecture, grand parks, churches and unusual, on-off pieces. If you plan to visit a few museums while in town, don't pass over purchasing a Joanneum pass (one-/seven-days €10/€15), which covers some 20 museums throughout Styria, including the Landeszeughaus, Schloss Eggenberg, Alte Galerie, Neue Galerie and Volkskundemuseum. The pass is available for purchase at each museum.

HAUPTPLATZ & AROUND
The **Landesmuseum Joanneum** (Map pp190-1; ☎ 8017 9716; www.museum-joanneum.at; Raubergasse 10; adult/child €4.50/3; ☺ 9am-4pm Tue-Sun), founded in 1811, is Austria's oldest museum. Its massive collection is devoted to natural history, which is displayed in four separate departments – Geology and Palaeontology, Mineralogy, Botany and Zoology. It's a rather static and old-fashioned museum, but the volume of the collection is highly impressive.

Depending on your taste, the **Landeszeughaus** (provincial armoury; Map pp190-1; ☎ 80 17-9810;

STYRIA

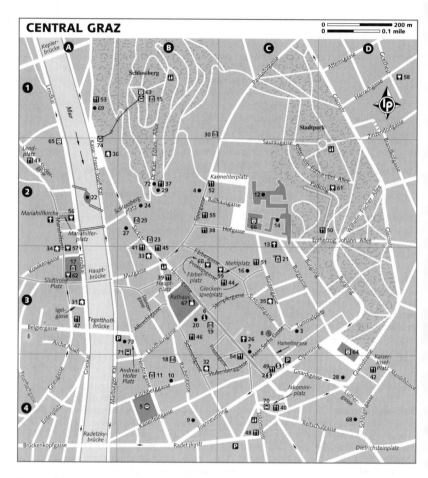

CENTRAL GRAZ

Herrengasse 16; adult/concession €4.50/3, with tour €6/4.50; 10am-6pm Tue-Sun, 10am-8pm Thu Apr-Oct, 10am-3pm Tue-Sun Nov-Mar) could possibly rate as the best museum in Austria. It houses an incredible array of gleaming armour and weapons, more than 30,000 pieces in fact. Most of it dates from the 17th century when the original armoury was built. Some of the armour is beautifully engraved; other exhibits, which are crude and intimidating, look as though they are freshly returned from battle. The sheer weight of the metalware (such as the two-handed swords) is quite staggering.

Don't miss the **Landhaushof** (Map pp190-1; Herrengasse 16) behind the Landeszeughaus, a stunning Italian Renaissance courtyard. Its three-tiered gallery, connected by walk-ways, is one of the best examples of Renaissance architecture in Austria.

Stop in for a peek at the stained glass window of the **Stadtpfarrkirche** (town parish church; Map pp190-1; Herrengasse 23; admission free; dawn-dusk), southeast of the Landeszeughaus. The fourth panel from the bottom on the right (left of the high altar) clearly shows Hitler and Mussolini looking on as Christ is scourged.

WEST OF THE MUR

Sitting splendidly on the bank of the Mur river is Graz's newest pride and joy, the **Kunsthaus** (Map pp190-1; ☎ 8017 9200; www.kunsthausgraz.at; Lendkai 1; adult/child €6/2.50, with tour €8.50/4; 10am-6pm Tue-Sun, 10am-8pm Thu, tours 11am & 4pm). Designed by British architects Peter Cook and

STYRIA

Colin Fournier, this world-class contemporary art space is a bold creation which looks something like a space-age sea slug. Exhibitions change every three to four months, and tours cover not only the exhibitions but also the building.

Not to be outdone by the Kunsthaus is the **Murinsel** (Map pp190-1), a man-made island of metal and plastic in the middle of the Mur. With plenty of curves and hardly any sharp points, this modern floating landmark is extremely eye-catching and a relaxing place to while away an hour. The island contains a café (p196), a kids' playground and a small stage.

SCHLOSSBERG

Dominating Graz is the Schlossberg, a hill that climbs to a height of 473m. Its wooded slopes can be reached by a number of paths, or with the funicular **Schlossbergbahn** (Castle Hill Railway; Map pp190-1; free with public transport ticket) from Franz Josef Kai or with the **Glass Lift** (Map pp190-1; free with public transport ticket) from Schlossberg-platz. Scattered across the hill is an **open-air theatre** (Map pp190-1; ☎ 82 73 48; Schlossberg 5a; adult/child €1.45/0.73; ☺ 10am-5pm Tue-Sun), remains of the now-demolished castle (Napolean was to blame for that) and some restaurants. Perched on the southern edge of Schlossberg is the emblem of Graz, the **Uhrturm** (Clock Tower; Map

pp190-1). The large hand on the clock face shows the hours; the minute hand was added much later. The townsfolk paid the French a ransom of 2987 florins and 11 farthings not to destroy the clock tower during the 1809 invasion.

THE BURG & AROUND

To the southeast is the city's 15th-century **Burg** (Map pp190-1; Hofgasse), now containing government offices. At the far end of the courtyard, on the left under the arch, is an ingenious **double staircase** (1499; Map pp190-1) – the steps diverge and converge as they spiral. To the east of the Burg is **Stadtpark** (Map pp190-1), the city's largest green space.

Opposite the Burg is the **Domkirche** (Map pp190-1; ☎ 82 16 83-0; Burggasse 3; admission free; ☺ dawn-dusk), a late-Gothic building dating from the 15th century, though it only became a cathedral in 1786. The interior combines Gothic and baroque elements, with reticulated vaulting on the ceiling and many side altars. The highlight is the faded *Gottesplagenbild* fresco on the cathedral's exterior, which dates from 1485. It depicts life in the early 1480s when Graz was besieged by the Turks, the plague and locusts.

Next door is a more impressive sight, the mannerist-baroque **mauseoleum of Ferdinand II** (Map pp190-1; ☎ 82 16 83; Burggasse 2; adult/senior/child €4/3/2; ☺ 10.30am-12.30pm & 1.30-4pm May-Oct,

11am–noon Nov–Apr). Construction was started in 1614 by an Italian architect, Pietro de Pomis, who spent nearly 20 years on the project. After Pomis died, Pietro Valnegro completed the structure. Inside, the exuberant stucco and frescoes were the work of Johann Bernhard Fischer von Erlach. Ferdinand, his wife and his son are interred in the crypt below, their tomb modestly set into the wall. Pride of place in the crypt goes to the red marble sarcophagus of Ferdinand's parents, Charles II and Maria. However, only Maria lies within; Karl II rests in Seckau Abbey (p209)

About midway between the Domkirche and Herregasse is **Glockenspiel** (Map pp190–1; Glockenspielplatz); at 11am, 3pm and 6pm daily figures emerge from the clock's upper window and twirl to music.

SCHLOSS EGGENBERG

On the western fringes of the city (tram No 1 for the centre) is **Schloss Eggenberg** (☎ 58 32 64-0; Eggenbergen Allee 90; state rooms tour €6; individual museums €4.50; ⏰ 10am–5pm Tue–Sun Apr–Oct), built by the Eggenberg dynasty in 1625. This splendid baroque palace was constructed by de Pomis at the request of Johann Ulrich (1568–1634), who required an appropriate dwelling after his appointment as governor of Inner Austria in 1625.

The dominating theme of the 24 **Prunkräume** (staterooms) is astronomy and mythology. The Planet Hall, which is a riot of white stucco surrounding baroque frescoes, is particularly impressive; the frescoes portray the seven planets (all that were then discovered), the four elements and the 12 signs of the zodiac. Most rooms are devoted to one theme, including a Chinese room and a games room. Guided tours are conducted in German every hour on the hour, though an English translation is possible (inquire in advance).

Of the three museums housed within the palace, the most interesting is the **Pre- and Early-History Collection**. The prize exhibition here is the exceptional bronze *Strettweg Chariot*, which dates back to the Hallstatt period (7th century BC). The **Coin Collection** covers coins and money from Styria, while **Collection of Roman Provincial Antiquities** displays Roman finds in the province.

The palace is set in **parkland** (admission €1; ⏰ 8am–7pm summer, 8am–5pm winter) where pea-

cock and deer roam, and Roman stone reliefs can be seen.

OTHER SIGHTS

Graz has more museums and galleries than you can shake a stick at; below is a list of other intriguing establishments:
Alte Galerie (Map pp190–1; ☎ 80 17-9770; Neutorgasse 45; admission €4.50; ⏰ 10am–6pm Tue–Sun, 10am–8pm Thu) Old masters from Romanesque to late Baroque.
Museum der Wahrnehmung (Museum of Perception; Map pp188–9; ☎ 81 15 99; Friedrichgasse 41; adult/concession/child/family €3.50/2.50/1.50/8, samadhi bath €45; ⏰ 2–6.30pm Wed–Mon) Small but unusual collection that explores sensory illusions; the samadhi (meditative) bath is a therapeutic bath that relieves the body of all sensory input.
Neue Galerie (Map pp190–1; ☎ 82 91 55; Sackstrasse 16; adult/concession/child/family €6/4.50/2.50/12; ⏰ 10am–6pm Tue–Sun, 10am–8pm Thu) Temporary modern art exhibitions, housed in baroque Palais Herberstein.
Stadtmuseum (Map pp190–1; ☎ 82 73 48; Sackstrasse 18; adult/child €3.65/2.20; ⏰ 10am–9pm Tue, 10am–6pm Wed–Sat, 10am–1pm Sun) History of the city and temporary exhibitions.
Volkskundemuseum (Map pp190–1; ☎ 80 17 98 99; Paulustorgasse 11-13a; adult/senior & child €4.50/1.50, tours extra €1.50; ⏰ 10am–6pm Tue–Sun, 10am–8pm Thu) Museum devoted to folk art and lifestyle; highlights include 2000 years of traditional clothing.

Graz for Children

With its green spaces, playgrounds and relaxed atmosphere, Graz is a good place for children. The creation of **FriDa & FreD** (Map pp188–9; ☎ 87 27 700; www.fridaundfred.at - in German; Friedrichgasse 34; adult & child over 6/child under 6/family €4/1.50/11; ⏰ 9am–5pm Mon, Wed & Thu, 9am–7pm Fri, 10am–5pm Sat & Sun), Graz's first museum devoted to children, made it even better. This small but fun-packed museum is aimed at children up to the age of 12, and hosts workshops, exhibitions and theatre. Like any good children's museum, the aim is learning through doing, which equates to loads of hands-on tasks and interactive displays.

The **Schlossberg Cave Railway** (Map pp190–1; Schlossbergplatz; admission €3; ⏰ 10am–5pm), the longest grotto railway in Europe, is another highlight for the little 'uns. The trip, taking about 20 minutes, winds its way around fairy-tale scenes through tunnels once used as a safe haven from the allied bombings during WWII.

STYRIA

THE TERMINATOR FROM GRAZ

Arnold Schwarzenegger may be the king of America and a household name worldwide, but his meteoric rise to fame and fortune started humbly in the small village of Thal, 6km west of Graz.

Born on 30 July 1947, to police chief Gustav Schwarzenegger and his wife Aurelia, Arnie spent his formative years attending school in Graz before starting a very short career in the timber business. It was around this time, in the summer of 1961, that he visited a gym for the first time and discovered his passion for bodybuilding. Naturally talented at the sport, he was winning titles by the age of 15, and in 1967 he conquered the bodybuilding world, capturing the Mr Universe title for the first time (he has five such titles, and an extra seven Mr Olympia titles under his belt).

It seems bodybuilding was just a launching pad for Arnie's attempt to conquer the world. In 1970, soon after moving to America, he made his silver screen debut in *Hercules in New York,* under the pseudonym Arnold Strong. He had to wait another 12 years however for his first big breakthrough, in the comic-book adaptation *Conan the Barbarian*. His greatest screen role, that of a killer robot from the future in the *Terminator*, came two years later. His physique and thick Austrian accent were made for the role, and his character, and the movie, became cult classics overnight.

His next giant step towards immortalisation came in 1986 when he married into America's royal family, tying the knot with Maria Shriver (niece of John F Kennedy). The next years involved a string of movies, including *Commando* (1985), *Predator* (1987; also starring future Minnesota Governor Jesse Ventura), *Twins* (1988), *Terminator 2* (1991) and *Terminator 3* (2003; with *Mannerschnitten* product placement).

But Arnie's greatest coup was yet to come. Since the late 80s, he has often affiliated himself with political figures, including former President George Bush, and made noises about a possible future political career. The latter became reality in October 2003 when Arnie convinced the people of California that he was the best choice for governor. Speculation is rife that his next goal is the White House itself and when it comes to Arnold Schwarzenegger, anything is possible.

Those wishing to get a bit more 'up-close and personal' with the Terminator can visit the **gym** (☎ 48 24 82; Stadionplatz 1; admission free; ⏰ 5.45am-10pm Mon-Fri, 10am-9pm Sat, Sun & holidays) where he lifted his first weights. Unfortunately there's not a lot to see, apart from a few photos and some old equipment; it's at the southern end of the No 4 tram in the **Arnold Schwarzenegger Stadion**.

Tours

Graztourismus (☎ 80 75-0; www.graztourismus.at; Herrengasse 16; ⏰ 9am-7pm Mon-Fri, 9am-6pm Sat, 10am-6pm Sun Jun-Sep, 9am-6pm Mon-Sat, 10am-6pm Sun Oct-May) offers a guided walking tour (adult/child €7.50/3.75) of the old town at 2.30pm on Tuesday, Wednesday, Friday, Saturday and Sunday. It also runs bus tours (€11.50/5.75) of the city and its many architectural delights at 2.30pm and 6pm on Monday, Wednesday and Thursday from April to October, plus excursions to the Lipizzaner Stud Farm in Piber (adult/child €24/9) at 2pm on Saturday from April to October, and through the wine country of southern Styria (€24/9) at 2pm on Sunday from April to October.

Cabrio Bus (☎ 88 74 99), an open-top bus, undercuts the Graztourismus bus tours of the city with its tours (adult/child €10/5) at 11am weekdays, as well as 2.30pm Tuesday, Wednesday and Friday, but they wouldn't be much fun in rainy weather. Tours leave from Jakominiplatz.

Note that tours are not always carried over to the next year, so some of the tours mentioned here may not be available.

Festivals & Events

Graz's biggest bash is **Styriarte**, a festival featuring one classical concert after another in June and July. Information is available at the **Styriarte Kartenbüro** (Map pp190-1; ☎ 82 50 00; www .styriarte.com; Sackstrasse 17).

Something more entertaining for the whole family is **Graz Erzählt** (www.graz.tales.org), a storytelling festival of epic proportions (it's the largest of its kind in the world). Running from late May to early June, it attracts acts from across the globe.

Steirischer Herbst, an avant-garde festival of new art held during October, includes performances in music, theatre, films, exhibitions and art installations. Contact **Steirischer Herbst Informationsbüro** (Map pp190-1; ☎ 81 60 70; www.steirischerbst.at; Sackstrasse 17) for more information.

STYRIA

Jazz Sommer Graz (www.jazzsommergraz.at - in German), a collection of free jazz concerts (often with an impressive international line up), takes place on Mariahilferplatz from early July to late August.

The **Graz marathon** (www.grazmarathon.at) takes place sometime in October.

Sleeping
BUDGET

Budget accommodation in central Graz is very thin on the ground, so it's best to plan ahead. The tourist office has a list of private rooms and will book accommodation for free.

Jugendgästehaus (Map pp188-9; ☎ 70 83 50; jgh .graz@jgh.at, Idlhofgasse 74; 2-/4-bed dm €20/17, new 4-bed dm €20, d €47; P 🖳) This big, colourful and friendly HI hostel is easily the cheapest deal in Graz. There's a small playground for kids and a football field. Breakfast is included in the price and stays under three nights require an extra €3 supplement.

Hotel Strasser (Map pp188-9; ☎ 71 39 77; hotel@ clicking.at; Eggenberger Gürtel 11; s/d from €29/45; P) Don't judge this book by its cover; Strasser may not look like much from the outside, but the rooms are very good for the price and there is private parking. Ask for a room facing the courtyard as it's on a busy road close to the train station.

Camping Central (Map pp188-9; ☎ 0676-378 51 20; freizeit@netway.at; Martinhofstrasse 3; 1/2 person sites €12/ 18; ☼ Apr-Oct; P 🐾) The name is a little misleading, being 6km southwest of the city centre (bus No 32 from Jakominiplatz), but the campsite's facilities, with a cinema, kids' playground and swimming pool, make up for it.

MID-RANGE
Gasthof-Pension zur Steirer-Stub'n (Map pp188-9; ☎ 71 68 55; www.pension-graz.at; Lendplatz 8; s/d €37/66; mains €8-9) Its price, homely ambience, rural décor and good-sized rooms make this *Gasthöfe* (inn) one of the best accommodation options in town. Its restaurant, serving Austrian fare, is the icing on the cake.

Pension Rückert (Map pp188-9; ☎ 32 30 31; Rückertgasse 4; s/d €37/63; P) In the villa district of Graz east of the town centre, this blue pension features lovingly renovated rooms, a bright breakfast room and a lift. Take tram No 1 to Tegetthoffplatz, walk 100m in the direction of the tram route then turn right.

Das Wirtshaus Greiner (Map pp188-9; ☎ 68 50 90; das .wirtshaus.greiner@eunet.at; Grabenstrasse 64; s/d €46/72; P 🗙) North of Schlossberg, this small-scale place is a little oasis at the confluence of two busy streets. Rooms are cosy and clean, and there's a small garden for guests (though the noisy street may disturb some). Reception is not always open so phone ahead to check.

Pension Köppel (Map pp188-9; ☎ 58 55 47; Göstinger Strasse 25; s/d €35/56; P) Köppel may be a long way from town, at the terminus of tram No 1, but it has the advantage of a peaceful setting, forested hills nearby and a welcoming and comfortable atmosphere.

Hotel Academia (Map pp188-9; ☎ 32 35 58; graz@ academia-hotels.co.at; Untere Schönbrunngasse 7-11; s/d €37/58; ☼ Jul-Sep; P) This large student residence near Graz university has good-sized and clean rooms over the summer break. It's located in a quiet residential area.

Hotel Mariahilf (Map pp190-1; ☎ 71 31 63; www .hotelmariahilf.at; Mariahilferstrasse 9; s/d from €51/88) Mariahilf's big plus is its close proximity to the Kunsthaus and the old town of Graz. Rooms are large but some could do with a bit of an upgrade.

Grazerhof (Map pp190-1; ☎ 82 43 58; www.grazerhof .at; Stubenberggasse 10; s/d from €47/60) The Grazerhof is one of only three hotels in the very heart of Graz, which means it can demand higher prices. Rooms are decent though some are on the small side.

TOP END
Augarten Hotel (Map pp190-1; ☎ 20 800-0; www .augartenhotel.at; Schönaugasse 53; s/d €120/1600; P 🗙 🐾) This thoroughly modern hotel looks out of place in suburban Graz, but that takes nothing away from its restful ambience. Individually decorated rooms, contemporary art installations, an indoor pool and top-class service combine to make the Augarten one of the better choices in town.

Schlossberg Hotel (Map pp190-1; ☎ 80 70-0; www .schlossberg-hotel.at; Kaiser Franz Josef Kai 30; s/d from €139/191, suite €375; P 🗙 🐾 🐾) Four-star Schlossberg's location is perfect – walking distance to all the action but secluded enough to guarantee privacy and peace. It's also small enough for guests to receive personal service and the rooftop terrace is made for an evening glass of wine.

Hotel zum Dom (Map pp190-1; ☎ 82 48 00; www.dom hotel.at - in German; Bürgergasse 14; s/d €90/165, ste from €200; P 🗙) Hotel Zum Dom is a charming, graceful hotel, with tastefully and individually furnished rooms of the highest standard. Rooms either come with steam/power showers or whirlpools (the grandaddy suite comes complete with a whirlpool on the terrace). Note the ceramic art throughout the hotel, produced by a local artist.

Hotel Erzherzog Johann (Map pp190-1; ☎ 81 16 16; www.erzherzog-johann.com; Sackstrasse 3-5; s/d from €112/175; (P) (X)) It's hard to find a more central hotel than the Johann. Its large, well furnished, baroque-style rooms are built around a pleasant, plant-strewn atrium, which houses a superb winter-garden restaurant, one of the better eateries in town. Prices drop during the winter months.

Grand Hotel Wiesler (Map pp190-1; ☎ 70 66-0; www.weitzer.com; Grieskai 4; s/d from €170/223; (P) (X) (X)) This Art Nouveau gem is the only five-star hotel in town. Elegant rooms exhibit subtle touches, though they vary greatly in size. Guests have free use of the sauna.

Eating

Whether you're after a bite on the run, coffee and cake, a cheap, filling meal, hearty Styrian fare or gourmet cuisine in equally splendid surroundings, Graz will certainly satisfy your tastebuds.

RESTAURANTS

Aiola (Map pp190-1; ☎ 81 87 97; Schlossberg 2; mains €8-16; (Y) 9-2am Mon-Sat, 9am-midnight Sun summer, 9am-midnight winter) Ask any local where to find the best outdoor dining experience in Graz, and more often than not they'll answer with Aiola. This wonderful restaurant is basically a huge patio on top of the Schlossberg, with great views, top-rate international cuisine, a superb wine list, spot-on cocktails and very chilled music.

Landhaus Keller (Map pp190-1; ☎ 83 02 76; Schmiedgasse 9; mains €8.50-19.50; (Y) 11.30am-midnight Mon-Sat) What started as a spit-and-sawdust pub in the 16th century eventually evolved into an atmospheric and high-quality restaurant serving Styrian specialities. Flowers, coats of arms and medieval-style murals contribute to the historical ambience. In the summer, outside tables overlook the stunning Landhaus courtyard.

Stern (Map pp190-1; ☎ 81 84 00; Sporgasse 3; lunch menu €6, mains €6-12; (Y) 9-3am Mon-Sat) This little 'star' of Sporgasse is a true chameleon; during the day and early evening, it's a fine

restaurant serving international cuisine at outdoor tables on Kameliterplatz, and when the sun sets, its cellar-like interior transforms itself into a bar, featuring DJs every Friday and Saturday, and live acts on Sunday.

Krebsen Keller (Map pp190-1; ☎ 82 93 77; Sackstrasse 12; daily menus €6-8; mains €6-12; (Y) 10am-midnight) The Krebsen Keller sticks to what it knows best, Styrian cuisine (which generally means a lot of pumpkin seed oil). It appeals to locals and tourists alike, not only for its home-style cooking, but also for its peaceful inner courtyard and traditional atmosphere.

Taj Mahal (Map pp190-1; ☎ 82 77 99; Kaiser-Franz-Josef-Kai 58; lunch menus €6, mains €10-14; (Y) dinner Tue, lunch & dinner Wed-Sun) Expect spicy Indian curries, a large vegetarian selection, smart Indian trappings and prompt service at this, one of the better Indian restaurants in town.

Gamlitzer Weinstube (Map pp190-1; ☎ 82 87 60; Mehlplatz 4; (Y) 9am-11pm Mon-Fri) Gamlitzer is one of a plethora of restaurants on Mehlplatz, but it stands out for its home-made Styrian dishes, which it has been serving for quite a long time. As with every other place nearby, there are outside tables on the square.

Nagoya (Map pp190-1; ☎ 81 14 45; Jakominstrasse; lunch menu €4.80-7.20; sushi & maki sets €7-12; (Y) lunch & dinner Mon-Sat, dinner Sun) This unpretentious sushi bar is small, quiet and authentic with bargain lunch menus or sushi and *maki*.

Zur Goldenen Pastete (Map pp190-1; ☎ 82 13 12; Landhausgasse 1; lunch menu €6.50, mains €9-18; (Y) 11am-midnight) This place was established in 1723, making it the oldest inn in Graz. Styrian home cooking is the order of the day here and its shaded outdoor seating is a welcome respite from the bustling city centre.

Girardikeller (Map pp188-9; ☎ 38 29 15; Leonhardstrasse 28; mains €5-8; (Y) 5pm-2am Tue-Fri, 6pm-2am Sat & Sun) This humble and welcoming restaurant-bar is known for its pizzas, which are big, cheap and tasty.

Other recommended restaurants include:
Altsteirische Schmankerlstubn (Map pp190-1; ☎ 83 32 11; Sackstrasse 10; mains €8-16; (Y) 10am-midnight) Rustic restaurant serving traditional Styrian cuisine at the foot of the Schlossberg.
Stainzerbauer (Map pp190-1; ☎ 82 11 06; Bürgergasse 4; mains €8-18; (Y) 11am-midnight Mon-Sat) Styrian and Austrian specialities in a lovely courtyard garden.

CAFÉS
Edegger-Tax (Map pp190-1; ☎ 83 02 30; Hofgasse 8; coffee & cakes €2-5; (Y) 7am-8pm Mon-Fri, 7am-3pm Sat)

This modern café is perfectly complemented by its historical **bakery** (🕐 7am-6pm Mon-Fri, 7am-noon Sat) next door, which has been in operation since 1569. Apart from the yummy goodies baked on the premises, its stunning wood-carved façade is reason enough to drop by; note the small doors in the frontage, concealing ingenious hiding places.

Aiola Island (Map pp190-1; 🕿 81 86 69; Murinsel; mains €5-12; 🕐 10am-10pm Tue, Wed & Sun, 10-2am Thu-Sat) Kick back with a drink and a snack as the Mur river rushes by below your feet, at this appealing café.

Promenade (Map pp190-1; 🕿 81 38 40; Erzherzog Johann Allee 1; coffee & cakes €2-5; 🕐 9am-midnight) Popular with all walks of life, the Promenade has good coffee and very pleasant surroundings; it's situated on a tree-lined avenue in the Stadtpark.

Auschlössl (Map pp188-9; 🕿 81 33 68; Friedrichgasse 36; coffee about €3; 🕐 10am-midnight Mon-Sat) Auschlössl is another small café on the edge of a park, but this time on the other side of town. It's perfect for an evening drink or a coffee break after an exhausting visit to FriDa & FreD. It often hosts art exhibitions.

Les Vipéres (Map pp190-1; 🕿 80 17 92 92; Lendkai 1; coffee €3; 🕐 9-2am Tue-Sun) This, the ultra modern café of the Kunsthaus, is minimalist in style and often hosts music events, particularly on its 'savage' Tuesday.

Operncafé (Map pp190-1; 🕿 82 04 36; Opernring 22; coffee & cakes €2-5; 🕐 7.30am-9pm Mon-Sat, 9am-9pm Sun) Operncafé is a traditional coffee house in every sense; it comes complete with good coffee, homemade pastries, suited waiters and elderly ladies.

QUICK EATS

Aside from the listings below, there are plenty of cheap eateries near **Universität Graz** (Map pp188-9), particularly on Halbärthgasse, Zinzendorfgasse and Harrachgasse.

Zu den 3 Goldenen Kugeln (most mains under €5; 🕐 lunch & dinner) Heinrichstrasse (Map pp188-9; 🕿 36 16 36; Heinrichstrasse 18); Griesplatz (Map pp188-9; Griesplatz 34); Bahnhofgürtel (Map pp188-9; Bahnhofgürtel 89); Citypark (Map pp188-9; Lazarettgürtel 55) An institution in Graz, the Goldenen Kugeln serves up possibly the cheapest schnitzel around, but still manages to make it tasty. There are four branches, but the Heinrichstrasse branch, with its rustic feel, is the nicest.

Temmel Eissalon (Map pp190-1; Herrengasse 28; ice cream from €1.50; 🕐 9am-10pm Mon-Fri, 11am-10pm Sat) For the best ice cream in town, head to Temmel on the main street.

Mangolds (Map pp190-1; 🕿 71 80 02; Griesgasse 11; meals €5-10; 🕐 11am-8pm Mon-Fri, 11am-4pm Sat) Look no further than Mangolds' buffet for over 40 different vegetarian salads and delightful freshly squeezed juices.

Other fine quick-eats include:

Feinspitz (Map pp190-1; 🕿 870-0; 2nd fl Kastner & Öhler department store, Sackstrasse 7-11; meals €5-8; 🕐 9am-6.30pm Mon-Fri, 9am-5pm Sat) Buffet-style restaurant with healthy salads and ready meals; also offers a kids' menu from €4.

Mensa (Map pp188-9; 🕿 33 362; Sonnenfelsplatz 1; meals from €3.70; 🕐 8.30am-2.30pm Mon-Fri, closed early–mid-Aug) Reasonable food at cheap prices.

SELF-CATERING

The freshest fruit and vegetables are available at the **farmers markets** (🕐 7am-noon Mon-Sat) on Kaiser Josef Platz (Map pp190-1) and Lendplatz (Map pp188-9). For fast-food stands, head for *Hauptplatz* (Map pp190-1) and Jakominiplatz (Map pp190-1). Supermarkets are plentiful throughout the city; there's a **Billa** (Map pp188-9; Annenstrasse 23), a **Eurospar** (Map pp190-1; Sackstrasse 7-11) and a **Spar** (Map pp188-9; 🕐 daily) is located in the *Hauptbahnhof*.

Drinking

The nightlife in Graz is propelled along by a healthy student population, and an ex-student set that has a bit more cash to burn and more refined tastes. Most bars are concentrated in three areas; around the university, on Mehlplatz and Prokopigasse (dubbed the 'Bermuda Triangle') and near the Kunsthaus.

Like Vienna, the line between restaurant, café and bar is quite often blurred, so don't dismiss a place for a good night out just because it serves food. Classic examples of this include Aiola, Stern and Insel Café.

Orange (Map pp188-9; 🕿 0676-790 46 30; Elisabethstrasse 30; 🕐 8-3am) This modern cocktail bar is popular with a young, trendy student crowd and has a perfect patio for warm summer evenings. DJs regularly feature.

Kulturhauskeller (Map pp188-9; Elisabethstrasse 30; admission Tue-Sat €2; 🕐 9pm-5am Mon-Sat) Next door to Orange, the Kulturhauskeller is a cellar bar that heaves with young students on weekends.

Café Harrach (Map pp190-1; 🕿 32 26 71; Harrachgasse 26; 🕐 9am-midnight Mon-Fri, 7pm-midnight Sat &

Sun) Harrach is a well-established café-bar, and a good place to mix with students.

Bierbaron (Map pp188-9; ☎ 32 15 10, Heinrichstrasse 56; 🕑 11am-2am Mon-Sat) This large, busy bar, just north of the university, is a well-known student haunt. There are rows of gleaming silver beer pumps, and a relaxing garden.

Goldene Kugel (Map pp188-9; ☎ 32 31 08; Leonhardstrasse 32; 9-1am) Also close to the university, this is the Bierbaron's second bar, and it offers much the same as the original.

Three Monkeys (Map pp188-9; ☎ 31 98 10; www.three -monkeys.at; Elisabethstrasse 31; 🕑 9pm-6am Mon-Sat, 7pm-6am Sun) Three Monkeys is possibly the most popular student bar near the university; it's generally known as a pick-up joint but it's also loud and lots of fun.

Parkhouse (Map pp190-1; Parkring; 🕑 11am-late Tue-Sun) If you wonder where all the people have disappeared to on balmy summer evenings, the answer is they're all at Parkhouse. It occupies a peaceful spot in the middle of Stadtpark and attracts a mixed crowd, all of whom flock here for the chilled tunes (live music Tuesday and Sunday) and relaxed air.

M1 (Map pp190-1; ☎ 81 12 33; 3rd fl, Färberplatz; 🕑 10-2am Mon-Thu, 10-4am Fri & Sat, 11-2am Sun) In the heart of the Bermuda Triangle is M1, a modern three-storey café-bar complete with rooftop terrace and a mixed crowd. Its spiral staircase can cause a few problems after sampling a couple of the bar's 200 or so cocktails.

Lukullus (Map pp190-1; ☎ 81 59 98; Mehlplatz 1; 🕑 8-2am Mon-Sat, 9am-midnight Sun) Centrally located in the Bermuda Triangle, Lukullus attracts a trendy set with its stylish interior and the people-watching patio.

Cafe Centraal (Map pp190-1; ☎ 0699-172 13 415; Mariahilferstrasse 10; breakfast €3-6, snack €5-7; 🕑 8am-midnight Sun-Mon) This traditional bar and *beisl* (small tavern or restaurant), with a dark-wood interior and outside seating, is a relaxed spot for a drink, and the perfect place for a hangover breakfast-cure the next morning.

03 Bar (Map pp190-1; ☎ 72 19 44; Mariahilferplatz 2; 🕑 9-2am Mon-Sat, 9-1am Sun) This modern cocktail bar near the Kunsthaus is a favourite of the upwardly mobile, and has an enormous patio with the Schlossberg as its backdrop.

Vipers im Thienfeld (Map pp190-1; www.vipers.at - in German; Mariahilferstrasse 2; 🕑 10-1am Tue-Sun) Thienfeld is *the* place to be seen, so the crowd can often be snooty and the atmosphere a little stifled at times. All the same, it's a stylish bar

with regular DJs and large breakfasts every Sunday till 5pm.

Entertainment

To find out what's on where in the city, pick up a copy of the free monthly *das eventmagazin*, available from tourist offices, or buy *Megaphon* (€2), a monthly magazine that combines entertainment listings with political and social commentary. It's sold on most street corners.

CINEMAS

Augartenkino (Map pp188-9; ☎ 82 11 86; Friedrichgasse 24) Regularly shows films (mostly art-house) in their original language.

Royal English Cinema (Map pp188-9; ☎ 82 61 33; Conrad von Hötzendorf Strasse 10) This cinema screens English-language films.

NIGHTCLUBS

Bang (Map pp188-9; ☎ 71 95 49; Dreihackengasse 4; 🕑 9pm-2am Wed, Thu & Sun, 9pm-4am Fri & Sat) Bang is a small club that attracts a mixture of gay and straight party-goers. It also hosts the occasional cabaret show.

Dom im Berg (Map pp190-1; ☎ 8008 333; www.domim berg.at - in German; Schlossbergplatz) The Dom im Berg is a large art-clubbing venue that makes good use of the old tunnels under Schlossberg. The sound system and light show are the best in Graz, so it's no surprise the place is often full when it hosts clubbings.

p.p.c (Map pp190-1; ☎ 83 08 62; www.popculture.at - in German; Neubaugasse 6; 🕑 9pm-late Wed & Thu, 10pm-late Fri & Sat) This, one of the better clubs in Graz, attracts top DJs from both Austria and abroad.

THEATRE & OPERA

Graz is an important cultural centre, hosting musical events throughout the year. The main venues in town are the **Schauspielhaus** (theatre; Map pp190-1; ☎ 80 00; Hofgasse 11) and the **Opernhaus** (opera; Map pp190-1; ☎ 8008-0; Kaiser-Josef-Platz 10). Performance details and tickets (no commission) for both venues are available at **Theatrekasse** (Map pp190-1; ☎ 80 00; www.theater-graz.com; Kaiser-Josef-Platz 10; 🕑 8am-6.30pm Mon-Fri, 8am-1pm Sat). Both venues close in August and there are discounts for students.

Shopping

Aside from its divine pumpkin-seed oil, Styria is known for painted pottery and

STYRIA

printed linen. A good place to pick up quality handicrafts is **Steirisches Heimatwerk** (Map pp190-1; ☎ 82 90 45; Herrengasse 10; ☺ 9am-6pm Mon-Fri, 9am-1pm Sat) or **Kastner & Öhler** (Map pp190-1; ☎ 870-0; Sackstrasse 7-11), a department store north of Hauptplatz. If you're just looking for high street names, head for **Citypark** (Map pp188-9; ☎ 71 15 80-0; Lazarettgürtel 55), a large shopping centre to the south of the centre.

Getting There & Away

AIR

The **airport** (☎ 29 02-0; www.flughafen-graz.at - in German) is 10km south of the town centre, just beyond the A2; see p362. **Austrian Airlines** flies to/from Vienna and Innsbruck on a daily basis, while **Welcome Air** (☎ 0800-210 211) flies to Linz on weekdays. Lufthansa connects Graz with Frankfurt and Munich, and Ryanair has two flights daily to London Stansted. Facilities at the airport include an **information desk** (☎ 2902-172; ☺ 5am-11.30pm), travel agents and a bank with an ATM and exchange machine.

BUS

Bundesbuses (Map pp188-9; ☎ 82 06 06; www.verbundlinie.at - in German) depart from outside the *Hauptbahnhof* (Map pp188-9) and from Andreas Hofer Platz (Map pp190-1) to all parts of Styria; fares are charged per zone, ranging from one zone (€1.70), covering Graz, to 22 zones (€25.40), which reaches the province's furthest corners. **GKB buses** (Map pp188-9; ☎ 59 87-0; www.gkb.at - in German) run to Piber (€5.60; one hour), Bärnbach and Deutschlandsberg (€7; two hours) from the *Hauptbahnhof* and Griesplatz (Map pp188-9).

TRAIN

Trains (☎ 05-17 17; www.oebb.at - in German) to Vienna's Südbahnhof depart hourly (€26.90, 2¾ hours) and two-hourly to Salzburg (€36.50, four hours). All trains running north or west go via Bruck an der Mur (€9.70, 40 minutes, every 20 minutes), where it's sometimes necessary to change for onward travel. Amazingly, there is only one direct train daily to Klagenfurt (€27.70, three hours); all other trains pass through Bruck. Trains to eastern Styria via Graz's Ostbahnhof originate at the Hauptbahnhof.

International trains from Graz include Zagreb (€35, 3½ hours), Ljubljana (€34, four hours), Szentgotthárd (€11, 1½ hours) and Budapest (€55; 6¼ hours).

CAR RENTAL

Car rental companies include **Avis** (Map pp190-1; ☎ 81 29 20; Schlögelgasse 10), **Hertz** (Map pp190-1; ☎ 82 50 07; Andreas Hofer Platz 1; also at the airport) and **Denzel** (Map pp188-9; ☎ www.denzeldrive.at - in German; Europlatz). See p369 for rates.

Note that much of Graz is a *Kurzparkzone* (short-term parking zone); tickets are available from parking machines on streets (€0.60 per 30 minutes).

Getting Around

Buses run regularly from Jakominiplatz between 5am and 11.14pm (€1.70, 20 minutes); four of these start from the *Hauptbahnhof* (Map pp188–9). Trains from here leave every one or two hours (€1.70, 10 minutes).

All of Graz is covered by one zone, zone 101. Single tickets (€1.70), which cover buses and trams, are valid for one hour, but you're better off buying a 24-hour pass (€3.40) if you plan to use the public transport more than once. Ten one-zone tickets cost €11.65, and weekly/monthly passes cost €8.20/28.30. Hourly and 24-hour tickets can be purchased from the driver; other passes can be purchased from *Tabak* (tobacconist) shops, pavement ticket machines or the tourist office.

Bicycle rental is available from **Bicycle** (Map pp190-1; ☎ 82 13 57-15; Kaiser Franz Josef Kai 56; per 24hr €9; ☺ 7am-1pm & 2-6pm Mon-Fri). To call a taxi, dial ☎ 2801, ☎ 878 or ☎ 889.

AROUND GRAZ

All the following sights are within easy distance of Graz.

ÖSTERREICHISCHEN FREILICHTMUSEUM

Consisting of almost 100 farmstead buildings from across the country, the **Österreichischen Freilichtmuseum** (Austrian Open-Air Museum; ☎ 03124-53 700; www.freilichtmuseum.at; adult/student/child €7/4.50/3.50; ☺ 9am-5pm Tue-Sun Apr-Oct) in Stübing is one of the best of its kind in Austria. The complex is about 2km in length and at least two hours is needed to fully appreciate the entire museum; it's a good idea to pick up an English-language guidebook (€2.50) at the entrance before setting out. The museum is arranged in order as if the visitor is walking through Austria from east to west. The solid buildings from all regions are sure to impress, but some of the unmissable farmhouses include the Salzburg *Rauchhaus*, or smoke house, so-called due to the absence of a chimney – smoke was supposed to seep through chinks in the ceiling and dry grain in the loft; and a west Styrian grocery, with old-fashioned goods on display and a few modern items for sale. A notice board by the ticket office announces when country-craft demonstrations take place. As these don't occur on a regular basis, it's worth inquiring (by telephone or Internet) before planning your visit. At the end of September, **Erlebnistag**, a special fair with crafts, music and dancing, is held at the complex.

The museum is about a 20-minute walk from the Stübing train station; turn left out of the train station and pass over the tracks, then under them before hitting the entrance. Hourly trains make the journey from Graz (€3.30; 15 minutes).

LURGROTTE

These, the largest caves in Austria, are 20km north of Graz. They are particularly noted for their impressive range of stalactites.

Entrance to the caves is possible from the villages of Peggau or Semriach. **Tours from Peggau** (☎ 03127-25 80; www.lurgrotten.com; Lurgrottenstrasse 1/2; 1hr-tours adult/child €5/3, 2hr-tours €8/4.50) depart on the hour from 9am to 4pm from April to October, and are offered by appointment only from November to March. **Tours from Semriach** (☎ 03127-83 19; www.lurgrotte-semriach .at - in German; 1hr-tours adult/child €5/3) leave from 10am to 4pm from mid-April to October, and at 11am and 2pm on weekends (by arrangement on weekdays) from November to mid-April. If you want to combine a day trip to the caves with a visit to the open-air museum you're better off entering from the west at Peggau. Both offer adventure tours (€11) by arrangement only, which take you deeper into the caves. The temperature in the caves remains a cool 9°C, so remember to bring something warm.

Peggau is a little further down the railway line from Stübing and there are regular trains (€4.40, 20 minutes, hourly); the caves are 15 minutes' walk from the station. Buses to Semriach depart from Lendplatz and *Hauptbahnhof* in Graz three times a day from Monday to Saturday, and twice on Sunday (€4.40, 40 minutes).

BUNDESGESTÜT PIBER

Horse fans will want to make the trip to the small village of Piber, home to the world-famous Lipizzaner stallion stud farm **Bundesgestüt Piber** (Piber Stud Farm; ☎ 03144-33 23; www .piber.com - in German; Piber 1; guided tour adult/senior/ student €11/9/6; tours 9am-noon & 1-5pm Apr-Oct, 9-10.30am & 1.30-3.30pm Nov-Mar).

The farm has been at its current location since 1920; originally it was based in Lipizza, but had to be moved when Slovenia was annexed after WWI. About 40 foals are born at the farm every year, but of these only about five stallions are of the right height and aptitude to be sent to the Spanische Hofreitschule (Spanish Riding School) in Vienna for training. Foals are born dark and take between five and 12 years to achieve their distinctive white colouring. Even before training, each stallion is worth a cool €15,000.

Tours of the farm depart as soon as enough interested participants are assembled (which doesn't take long). Visitors see a film (with English commentary on the English tour – phone ahead for details) and museum exhibits, then tour the stables to meet some of the equine residents.

For information on the surrounding area, head to the **Tourismusverband Lipizzanerheimat** (☎ 03144-2519 750; www.lipizzanerheimat.com - in German; Bahnhofstrasse 6) in Köflach, 3km south of Piber. The perfect place to overnight is **Gasthof Bardel** (☎ 03144-34 22; guenter.bardel@onemail.at; Fesselweg 1; s/d €30/50; **P**), right next to the stud farm. Each of the modern rooms comes with a balcony overlooking one of the parading areas. There's also a restaurant on the premises, but if you would prefer a snack and coffee, there's a café on the stud farm's grounds. The best eating option however is **Restaurant Caballero** (☎ 03144-33 23-70; mains €14-20; 9am-7pm Tue, Wed & Sun, 9am-midnight Thu-Sat), on the ground floor of Schloss Piber within the confines of the farm.

Getting There & Away

To get to Piber, you'll need to catch a **GKB** (www.gkb.at - in German) private train (€5.60; one hour; hourly on weekdays, on weekends every two hours) from Graz to Köflach. From Köflach station, walk up Bahnhofstrasse, turn right along *Hauptplatz* (300m) and then left for a 3km walk along Piberstrasse (signposted). Walking is a better option than cooling your heels at a bus stop, cursing the non-appearance of infrequent buses.

It's also possible to take a GKB bus, leaving from Graz's *Hauptbahnhof* and Griesplatz; the fare, duration and frequency of buses match those of GKB trains.

BÄRNBACH

☎ 03142 / pop 5160

Bärnbach's claim to fame is its St Barbara Kirche, which is highly unusual for a small, rural town; it was designed by the one-and-only Hundertwasser, and is certainly hard to miss. The town is also known for its glass-making centre and the delicate products it creates.

Tourist information is available from the glass-making centre and **Bärnbach Information** (☎ 615 50; tourismus@gv.baernbach.at; ☼ 9.30am-noon & 2-5pm Mon-Sat) in the town hall. The church and glass centre are an equal distance west and east respectively from the Hauptplatz.

Sights

Although built after WWII, **St Barbara Kirche** (☎ 625 81; Piberstrasse; admission free, tours adult/child €2/1; ☼ dawn-dusk) needed renovating in the late 1980s. About 80% of the town population voted to commission the maverick Viennese artist Friedensreich Hundertwasser (p40) to undertake the redesign; work began in 1987 and was completed in 1988. It was a bold move: Hundertwasser was known for his unusual design concepts, particularly in discarding the straight line in building projects. The gamble paid off; the church is a visual treat inside and out, yet is still clearly a place of worship rather than a pseudo–art gallery. Leave a donation and pick up the explanation card in English, which reveals the symbolic meaning behind the architectural design features. Tours run by appointment only.

The church is surrounded by 12 gates, each representing a different faith, and all connected by an uneven pathway. By the west façade is a powerful mosaic war memorial by Franz Weiss. The distinctive church steeple is topped by a gold onion dome. Features you wouldn't see in any other church include the bowed roof with green splodges along its flanks, the irregular windows, and the grass growing on the side porch roofs. The interior unfortunately doesn't match the exterior, although Hundertwasser's 'spiral of life' window (which reflects the after-

noon sun onto the font), on the left as you enter, is striking. Also note the glass altar and podium filled with 12 layers of different types of earth representing the 12 tribes of Israel, created by Erwin Talker.

Bärnbach, a glass-making centre for the last three centuries, is home to the **Stölzle Glas Center** (☎ 629 50; www.stoelzle.com; Hochtregisterstrasse 1; adult/child/family €5.50/3/13; ☼ 9am-5pm Mon-Fri, 9am-1pm Sat & Sun Apr–mid-Dec, closed Sun Apr & Nov-mid–Dec), a working glass-blowing factory and museum. Try to get there in the morning as the entrance fee includes a guided tour (leaving 9am, 10am, 11am and noon Monday to Thursday, 9am, 10am and 11am Friday) of the glass-making facilities and the small museum filled with delicate pieces. In the afternoon the factory is off-limits.

Sleeping & Eating

Bärnbach is an easy day trip from Graz, and not a particularly exciting place at night, so you're better off returning to Graz or continuing on to Piber. If you need a bite to eat, there are a couple of cheap eateries near the church, including **Pizzera Casa Verona** (☎ 03142-61 5 65; Hauptplatz 1; pizzas €5-10; ☼ 10am-midnight). A **Billa supermarket** (Hauptplatz 2) is close by.

Getting There & Away

Bärnbach (€5.60, 50 minutes, hourly Monday to Friday, every two hours Saturday and Sunday) is on the Graz-Köflach train line, one stop (five minutes) before Köflach. The train station is 2km south of the town centre; Dr Nieder Strasse leads directly to the *Hauptplatz* from the station. GKB Graz-Köflach buses (€5.60; one hour) stop in Bärnbach town centre.

Bundesgestüt Piber (Piber Stud Farm) is close to Bärnbach; from the church, head west on Piberstrasse for 2km and after about 30 minutes you'll reach it.

SOUTHERN STYRIA

Southern Styria is known as *Styrische Toscana* (Styrian Tuscany), and for good reason. Not only is this wine country, but the landscape is reminiscent of Chianti and Crete; gentle rolling hills, cultivated with vineyards or farmland and topped by a huddle of trees. It's also famous for *Kürbiskernöl*, a rich pumpkin-seed oil generously used in Styrian cooking.

STYRIAN WEINSTRASSEN

Crisscrossing much of Southern Styria, and pushing their way into East Styria, are Styrian **Weinstrassen** (wine routes; www.steirischerwein .at), trails whose direction is dictated by wine. The *Steirische Weinführer* booklet, free from the Graz tourist office (p189), is a comprehensive guide to all eight trails, providing a map and a list of *Buschenschänken* (wine taverns) and vineyards along the way. You really need your own wheels to explore the routes, as trains and buses will take you to only one or two points on a certain route.

The most travelled wine route is the *Schilcher-Wienstrasse*, which runs north–south from Ligist to Eibiswald, passing through the Stainz and Deutschlandsberg. The wine of choice here is *Schilcher*, a light, dry rosé. Other popular wine-roads include the *Klöcher Wienstrasse*, stretching from Fehring to Bad Radkersburg (try the *Gewürztraminer*, a dry white wine typical of the region), the *Südsteirische Wienstrasse*, looping its way from Ehrnhausen to Spielfeld near the Slovenian border, and the *Sausaler Weinstrasse*, which runs west from Leibnitz to Gleinstätten.

Aside from Graztourismus, information can be obtained from the **Tourismusregionalverband Südsteirisches Weinland** (☎ 03452-767 11; www .steiermark.com/suedsteirisches-weinland; Hauptplatz 24, Leibnitz) or the **Tourismusregionalverband West-steiermark** (☎ 03463-49 50; www.steiermark.com/west steiermark; Ettendorfer Strasse 3, Stainz).

DEUTSCHLANDSBERG

☎ 03462 / pop 8000

In the heart of the Schilcher wine region is Deutschlandsberg, a bustling little town dominated by a well-restored castle, some 25 minutes' walk uphill from the town centre. Inside the castle is a **museum** (☎ 56 02; www.burg museum.at - in German; Burgplatz 2; adult/concession/child €9/8/4; ☽ 9.30am-5pm Mar–mid-Nov) split into four parts; ancient history, the Celts, historical weapons and antique jewellery. The extensive collection, whose highlights include a delicate gold necklace from the 5th century BC, takes about 1½ hours to see. Like any good castle, there's a torture chamber in the underground vaults.

The **tourist office** (☎ 75 20; tourismus.deutschlands berg@utanet.at; Hauptplatz 37; ☽ 9am-noon & 3-6pm Mon-Fri, 10am-1pm Sat Apr-Oct, 9am-3pm Mon-Fri, 9am-

noon Sat Nov-Mar) is a good source of information on the surrounding area.

For sleeping arrangements, look no further than the **Burg Hotel** (☎ 56 56-0; www .burghotel-dl.at - in German; Burgplatz 1; s/d from €53/86, mains €8-20; ℗), which is located in the castle. Rooms are large, quiet and have views of the woods. Its restaurant serves Styrian cuisine in medieval surroundings.

If Burg is too pricey then the newly built **HI Hostel** (☎ 0662-84 29 84; jgh.deutschlandsberg@ jgh.at; dm from €14.50, d from €20.50) should do the trick. Facilities here include a sauna and kids' play area.

Four daily trains travel between Graz and Deutschlandsberg (€7.40; 50 minutes).

GROSSKLEIN

Southern Styria was at one time favoured by the Celts, who left much of their culture for archaeologists to discover. Some of their findings are housed in the small but worthwhile **Hallstattzeitliches Museum** (Hallstatt Period Museum; ☎ 03456-50 38; www.archaeo-grossklein.com - in German; adult/concession €4/2; ☽ 10am-noon & 1.30-4.30pm Tue-Sun May-Oct) in the small town of Grossklein, 26km southeast of Deutschlandsberg. On display is a collection of exceptional artefacts, including coins, pottery and tools, and a copy of a bronze mask dating from 600 BC (the original is housed in Schloss Eggenberg in Graz; see p192). If the museum fails to sate your appetite for Celtic culture, a 9km walking route heading northwest from the town towards Kleinklein, passing by approximately 700 Celtic grave mounds, should.

Up to nine buses on weekdays travel from Leibnitz to Arnfels, stopping at Grossklein on the way (€4.40; 25 minutes).

EHRENHAUSEN

☎ 03453 / pop 1200

The picturesque town of Ehrenhausen, near the A9 which connects Graz with the Slovenian border, is in the heart of the wine region and makes a fine base for exploring the southern reaches of Styria.

The town is basically one street, which is lined with pastel-coloured houses and dominated by the **Pfarrkirche** (Hauptplatz; admission free; ☽ dawn-dusk). The church interior is vividly baroque; a combination of painted statues and shiny gold. Before embarking on excursions into the wine country, be sure to follow the path (less than 10 minutes' walk) to the right of the Rathaus, which leads up to the **mausoleum** (admission free) of Ruprecht von Eggenberg (1546–1611), hero of the Battle of Sisak against the Turks. Resting high above Hauptplatz, this white and yellow building is guarded by two strong statues gazing imperiously down on the town. The stucco inside is starkly white, with many embellishments clinging to the central dome and vines swirling around supporting pillars. The mausoleum is normally locked; get the key from the **manse** (Pfarrhof; ☎ 2633) next to the Pfarrkirche. Schloss Ehrenhausen, a little further up the hill from the mausoleum, is closed to the public.

Sleeping & Eating

There are several private rooms available in Ehrenhausen, but you'll probably need to book them through the tourist office in Leibnitz (p201). Otherwise there's two places almost next to each other on the *Hauptplatz* which are reasonably priced and have tidy, accommodating rooms; **Zur Goldenen Krone** (☎ 26 40; Hauptplatz 24; s/d €26/48; closed Thu; **P**) and **Die Burg zum Goldenen Löwen** (☎ 20 4 15; Hauptplatz 28; s/d €38/76; mains €6-15; **P**). The latter has a quiet restaurant with courtyard seating.

The *Hauptplatz* has most of the facilities travellers require, including a Nah & Frisch

supermarket and a bank. To purchase wine, head to **Erzherzog Johann Vinothek** (☎ 0699-100 64 654; Hauptplatz 35; ⏲ 7.30am-noon & 1.30-5pm Mon-Fri, 11am-6pm Sat, 11am-3pm Sun).

Getting There & Away

The best way to get from Graz to Ehrenhausen is by train (€8.40; 45 minutes; every two hours). The train station is about four minutes' walk east of Hauptplatz.

RIEGERSBURG
☎ 03153 / pop 2560

Arguably one of the most striking castles in Austria is located at Riegersburg, 50km southeast of Graz. **Schloss Riegersburg** (☎ 821 31; adult/senior/child/family €9.50/8.50/7/25; ⏲ 10am-5pm Apr-Oct), rising high above the surrounding landscape on a rocky outcrop, is a hugely impressive 13th-century castle that offers fine views of the Grazbach Valley. Formerly a crucial bastion against invading Hungarians and Turks, it now has a couple of museums among its numerous rooms; the **Hexenmuseum** features witchcraft and the **Burgmuseum** expounds the history of the owners, the Liechtenstein family. A **war memorial** is a reminder of fierce fighting in 1945, when Germans occupying the castle were attacked by Russian troops.

THERMAL SPAS OF STYRIA

East Styria is well known throughout Austria for its thermal activity, and in particular the spa centres that have sprung up around its thermal springs. Offering a combination of wellness treatments, sporting activities and relaxation therapies, many Austrians take full advantage of such places for a weekend, or possibly a whole week. A nights' accommodation is generally not cheap, but many spas offer specials and packages throughout the year.

Fans of the architectural style of Friedensreich Hundertwasser won't want to miss the unusual spa **Rogner-Bad Blumau** (☎ 03383-51 00-0; www.blumau.com; d from €168), near the town of Bad Blumau 50km east of Graz. The spa has all the characteristics of his art, including uneven floors, grass on the roof, colourful ceramics and golden spires. Overnight accommodation includes entry to the spa. Those looking for something more traditional should travel to **Parktherme Bad Radkersberg** (☎ 03476-26 77-0; www.parktherme.at - in German; daycard €16.25) in the southern regions of Styria. While the spa itself is a modern complex, the town of Bad Radkersberg is a quaint market town with parts of its 16th-century fortifications still intact.

Other well-established spas in Styria's thermal lands include:

- **Bad Waltersdorf** (☎ 03333-50 01; www.heiltherme.at - in German; daycard from €15.50, d from €154) Seven thermal baths and sports facilities; 55km east of Graz.

- **Loipersdorf** (☎ 03382-82 04; www.therme.at - in German; daycard €19) One of the largest in Europe, complete with water- and sports-park; 60km east of Graz.

- **Bad Gleichenberg** (☎ 03159-22 03; www.bad-gleichenberg.at - in German; daycard €18) Small spa in a rural setting, with 20 hectares of parklands; 60km southeast of Graz.

For more information on the Schloss or activities, contact the **tourist office** (☎ 86 70; touris mus@riegersburg.com). Riegersburg is also known for its culinary delights, namely chocolate, schnapps and vinegar. **Gölles Schnapsbrennerei & Essigmanufaktur** (☎ 75 55; Stang 52; ✆ 10am-noon & 1-5pm Mon-Sat), 3km south of town on the road to Bad Radkersburg, makes good use of the natural abundance of apples in the area by producing apple vinegar and schnapps, while nearby **Zotter Schokoladen** (☎ 55 54; Bergl 56a; ✆ 8am-6pm Mon-Fri, 9am-1pm Sat) produces heavenly chocolate creations.

If you have your own transport, consider stopping in at **Schloss Kapfenstein** (☎ 03157-300 30-0; www.schloss-kapfenstein.at - in German; Kapfenstein 1; s/d from €65/130; mains €10-16; **P** 🗶), a hotel-restaurant 17km south of Riegersburg. Its plush rooms are furnished with antiques and its restaurant serves delightful Styrian cuisine on its outer courtyard overlooking the valley below.

Getting There & Away
The nearest train station is Feldbach (€9.70 from Graz; 50 minutes); from there, five weekday buses head for Riegersburg (€1.70; 20 minutes).

NORTHERN STYRIA

Heading north from Graz the landscape of Styria begins to change; gentle hills and flat pastures are replaced by jagged mountains, virgin forests, deep valleys and cold, clear mountain streams. This is also the region's industrial heartland, home to the *Steirische Eisenstrasse* (Styrian Iron Rd), where for centuries iron mining was the backbone of the economy and in places, such as Eisenerz, left the landscape scarred.

Huddled beneath the soaring peaks are the towns of northern Styria, home to impressive houses of worship; the pilgrimage church of Mariazell and the abbey of Admont stand out among the crowd.

MARIAZELL
☎ 03882 / pop 2000
Settling itself gently into the slopes of the lower reaches of the eastern Alps is Mariazell, one of the prettiest towns in Styria. The abundance of nature on its borders is however not the town's main attraction for

many; this is the most important pilgrimage site in Austria. Its Basilika, founded in 1157, holds a sacred statue of the Virgin, and busloads of Austrians flock to the site on weekends and on 15 August (Assumption) and 8 September (Mary's 'name day').

Orientation
Mariazell is in the extreme north of Styria, a stone's throw from Lower Austria. The town is centred on *Hauptplatz*, which is opposite the Basilika. The train station is in St Sebastian, 1km north of *Hauptplatz*, the centre of Mariazell.

Information
Staff at Mariazell's **tourist office** (☎ 23 66; tour ismus@mariazellerland.at; Hauptplatz 13; ✆ 9am-5.30pm Mon-Fri, 9am-4pm Sat, 9am-12.30pm Sun May-Sep, 9am-5.30pm Mon-Fri, 9am-4pm Sat Oct, 9am-noon & 2-5pm Mon-Fri, 9am-noon Sat Nov-Apr) has loads of information about the town and the surrounding area and will find rooms without charging; ask about reductions given with the Mariazellercard.

The **post office** (Ludwig Leber Strasse) is located just west of *Hauptplatz* next to the bus station. **Café Faro** (☎ 37 13; Hauptplatz 8; per hr €5; ✆ 9am-11pm Mon, Tue & Thu-Sat, 3-11pm Wed & Sun), has Internet access. Mariazell has a couple of Bankomat machines.

Sights
Proudly dominating the small town is Mariazell's *raison d'être*, the **Basilika** (☎ 25 95; Kardinal Eugen Tisserant Platz 1; admission free; ✆ 8am-8pm). Originally Romanesque, the church underwent a Gothic conversion in the 14th century and then a massive baroque facelift in the 17th century. The result from the outside is a strange clash of styles, with the original Gothic steeple bursting like a wayward skeletal limb from between two baroque onion domes. The interior works better, with Gothic ribs on the ceiling combining well with baroque frescoes and lavish stuccowork. Both Johann Bernhard Fischer von Erlach and his son Josef Emmanuel had a hand in the baroque face-lift; the crucifixion group (1715) on the high altar is by Lorenzo Mattielli.

Unusually, the church is centred on a small but exquisite chapel, known as the **Gnadenkapelle** (Chapel of Miracles). This gold and silver edifice houses the Romanesque statue of the Madonna, whose healing

STYRIA

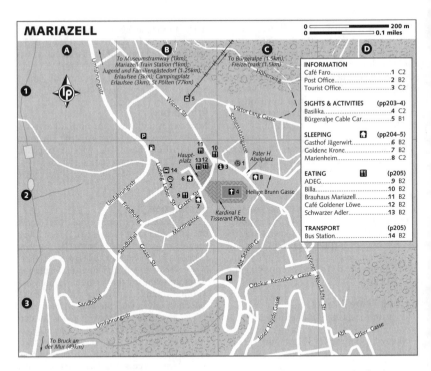

powers reputedly helped King Louis of Hungary defeat the Turks in 1377. Taking up the upper galleries of the church is the **Schatzkammer** (treasury; ☎ 25 95; Kardinal Eugen Tisserant Platz 1; adult/student/child €3/1.50/1; ☷10am-3pm Tue-Sat, 11am-4pm Sun & holidays May-Oct), which contains votive offerings spanning six centuries, mainly naive paintings.

Activities
Bürgeralpe (1270m), Mariazell's outdoor playground, offers hiking in the summer and skiing in the winter. Fortunately its **cable car** (☎ 2508; www.mariazell-buergeralpe.at - in German; adult/child return €9.90/6.20) runs all year round so your legs can at least have a rest going up to the top. At the summit are a few restaurants, trails leading off in all directions and a **Freizeitpark** (Erlebniswelt Holzknechtland; entry & cable car adult/child €12.50/7.30; ☷ 9am-5pm May-Oct), a small museum devoted to wood and all its wonderful uses. During winter, daily/weekly ski passes are available (€23/109).

Mariazell's second outdoor playground is **Erlaufsee**, a small lake on the border of Styria and Lower Austria, a few kilometres to the northwest of the town. Aside from swimming, there are good opportunities for water sports such as windsurfing and scuba diving; contact addresses of bodies running such sports are listed in the booklet *Mariazellerland von A-Z*, available at the tourist office. A novel way of getting to the lake is by the steam Museumstramway (one-way/return €8/€5), which runs at weekends and on holidays between July and September. It leaves from the Museumstramway Bahnhof.

Sleeping
The only time you should have problems finding a room in Mariazell is around the pilgrim days. Aside from hotels and pension, there is a smattering of private rooms.

Goldene Krone (☎ 2583; www.mariazell.at/krone - in German; Grazer Strasse 1; s/d from €30/60, mains €6-12) Directly opposite the Basilika is this hotel, which is more of a homely *Gasthöfe*. Rooms are big and bright and come with their own bathroom and breakfast area. The ground floor is taken up by an excellent kid-friendly restaurant with traditional Austrian cuisine and streetside seating.

Marienheim (☎ 25 45; Pater H Abelplatz 3; s/d from €23/42; closed Mar & Nov) Run by nuns, this peaceful place has spotless rooms (some with bathrooms, some without) and a friendly welcome.

Jugend und Familiengästedorf (☎ 26 69; jgh .mariazellerland@jgh.at; Erlaufseestrasse 49; dm from €17.50; P 🖳) Located halfway between Mariazell and Erlaufsee, this HI hostel is quite new and has loads of facilities, including a café, sauna, solarium, fitness room and sports areas.

Gasthof Jägerwirt (☎ 23 62; jaegerwirt@mariazell .at; Hauptplatz 2; s/d €28/56) With a central position, clean rooms and a restaurant with solid Austrian fare, Jägerwirt is a fine choice for overnighting.

Campingplatz Erlaufsee (☎ 49 37; sankt.sebastion@ aon.at; camp site per adult/tent €3.60/3; 🕑 May–mid-Sep; P) At the southeastern end of Erlaufsee is this small camping ground, with a ring of pine trees providing a semblance of privacy.

Eating

Aside from restaurants at the accommodation options, there are plenty of places to eat on and around *Hauptplatz*.

Brauhaus Mariazell (☎ 25 23-0; Wiener Strasse 5; r from €47, mains €7-17; 🕑 10am-11pm Mon-Thu, 10am-midnight Fri & Sat, lunch Sun) This highly pleasant restaurant has Styrian food, a garden out back and its own beer, Girrer (named after the family that owns the place). There are also a few rooms available upstairs.

Café Goldener Löwe (☎ 24 44; Hauptplatz 1a; mains €6-12; 🕑 9am-7pm Tue-Sun) Meals at this café-restaurant are served outside on its large terrace overlooking the church.

Schwarzer Adler (☎ 28 63-0; Hauptplatz 1; mains €7-15; 🕑 9am-11pm) Sidling up to the Goldener Löwe is this decent restaurant on the ground floor of a four-star hotel. Its outside terrace also overlooks the Basilika.

Supermarkets in the town include an **ADEG** (Grazer Strasse) and a Billa just north of the tourist office.

Getting There & Away

A narrow-gauge train departs from St Pölten, 77km to the north, every two to three hours. It's a slow trip (€12.90, 2½ hours), but the scenery is good for the last hour. Bus is the only option for further travel into Styria; three direct buses daily head for Bruck an der Mur (€8.30, 1½ hours), from where three head for Graz (€15.20, 2½ hours).

There are also direct buses from Vienna (€19.40, three hours) daily.

BRUCK AN DER MUR
☎ 03862 / pop 13,700

Bruck, at the confluence of the Mur and Mürz rivers, is the Mur valley's first real town and an important railway junction for Styria. It's certainly not the valley's best attraction, but if you have a few hours to kill between trains, it's worth heading into town for a look around.

Orientation & Information

The train station and a post office are at the eastern end of Bahnhofstrasse; money can be exchanged at the station only; there's also a Bankomat here. At the western end of Bahnhofstrasse is the beginning of the town centre. Koloman Wallisch Platz, Bruck's main square, is home to the Rathaus, which in turn houses the town's **tourist office** (☎ 890-121; www .bruckmur-tourismus.at; Koloman-Wallisch-Platz 1; 🕑 9am-4pm Mon-Fri). Updated computerised information is accessible daily. There's also another post office on the Platz.

Sights

Several paths wind up to **Schloss Landskron**, a castle-ruins of which only a clock tower and a few cannons remain, but the view back across the town's rooftops is worth the 10-minute climb. One path leads to Bauernmarkt, where there's a **food and flower market** (Wed & Sat) beside the 15th-century Gothic **Pfarrkirche** (Kirchplatz; admission free; 🕑 dawn-dusk), which is notable for its lack of ceiling decoration and 14th-century frescoes on its northern wall.

The remaining sights in Bruck are found on Koloman-Wallisch-Platz. The quaint **Rathaus**, with its arcaded courtyard, is suitably attractive, but it's the **Kornmesserhaus** that steals all the limelight. Its delicate arches and arcaded frontage with fussy ornamentation is a mixture of Gothic and Renaissance influences that combine well. This late-15th-century building was erected at the behest of a rich merchant, Pankraz Kornmess, for whom it is named. Other historic pieces on the square include the **Art Nouveau façade** above the ice cream shop at No 10 and the fine Renaissance-style **wrought-iron well** created by Hans Prasser in 1626.

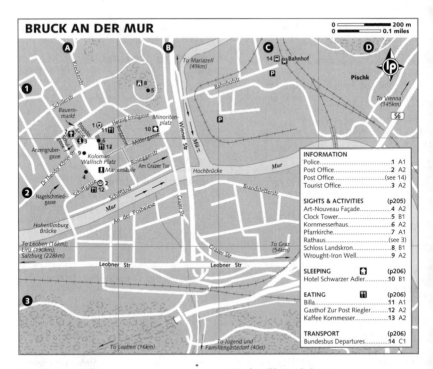

BRUCK AN DER MUR

INFORMATION	
Police	1 A1
Post Office	2 A2
Post Office	(see 14)
Tourist Office	3 A2

SIGHTS & ACTIVITIES	(p205)
Art-Nouveau Façade	4 A2
Clock Tower	5 B1
Kornmesserhaus	6 A2
Pfarrkirche	7 A1
Rathaus	(see 3)
Schloss Landskron	8 B1
Wrought-Iron Well	9 A2

SLEEPING	(p206)
Hotel Schwarzer Adler	10 B1

EATING	(p206)
Billa	11 A1
Gasthof Zur Post Riegler	12 A2
Kaffee Kornmesser	13 A2

TRANSPORT	(p206)
Bundesbus Departures	14 C1

Sleeping & Eating

Jugend und Familiengästedorf (☎ 584 58; jgh.bruck@ oejhv.or.at; Stadtwaldstrasse 1; dm from €14.30; P ☐) This family-friendly HI hostel, 10 minutes' walk south of the centre, was recently overhauled and now includes a café and a restaurant. It's in the heart of Weitental, Bruck's woodland playground.

Hotel Schwarzer Adler (☎ 567 68; minoriten@aon .at; Minoritenplatz 8; s/d €33/66) In the heart of the town above a tiny shopping mall is this small hotel, with large rooms and friendly staff.

Gasthof Zur Post Riegler (☎ 549 04; Koloman-Wallisch-Platz 11; mains €7-16; 🕑 9am-midnight Mon-Sat) This informal *Gasthöfe* has outdoor seating on the main square and a menu loaded with Styrian cuisine and local seasonal specialities.

Kaffee Kornmesser (☎ 584 44; Koloman-Wallisch-Platz 22; coffee €2-5) Occupying half of the Kornmesserhaus' ground floor is this very lovely café, complete with pleasant outdoor seating.

If you want to stock up on provisions, try **Billa** (Herzog Ernstgasse 6).

Getting There & Away

Bruck is the region's main rail hub; all fast trains to Graz (€8.30, 40 minutes, hourly) go via Bruck. Other major destinations include Klagenfurt (€22.30, two hours, hourly), Vienna's Südbahnhof (€20.80, two hours, hourly) and Linz (€25.10, three hours, every two hours, change at Leoben or Selzthal).

By road, the main autobahn intersect to the southeast of the town. If you're planning to cycle in the region, the tourist office can supply some useful maps.

Bundesbus buses arrive and depart form next to the train station.

LEOBEN

☎ 03842 / pop 27,100

Leoben is yet another town that successfully hides a pretty Altstadt away from the casual passer-by with ugly factories on its outskirts. It's a centre for metallurgical industries and home to Gösser beer, and achieved fame with the peace treaty signed here in 1797 by Napoleon and Emperor Franz II.

Information on the town can be gathered at the local **tourist office** (☎ 48 148; www.leoben.at;

Peter-Tunner-Platz 2). The long, wide *Hauptplatz* is lined with elegant 17th-century façades, including the baroque **Hacklhaus** (Hauptplatz 9), while Leoben's connection with the iron industry is seen in the curious town motif displayed on the **Altes Rathaus** (Hauptplatz 1) façade, which shows an ostrich eating horseshoes. Nearby, the dreary exterior of **Pfarrkirche St Xaver** (☎ 432 36; Kirchplatz 1; ☾ 8am-7pm) belies a harmonious interior of white walls and black-and-gold baroque altars.

Of more interest is the late-Gothic **Stiftskirche** (☎ 22 148; Gösser Platz; admission free; ☾ dawndusk, tours 8am-noon) in Göss, a suburb to the south of Leoben's heart. The unusual twisted columns, green-and-gold ornamentation, dainty pulpit and heavily gold-laden altar all work well together. Unfortunately the 1000-year-old crypt and paintings in the Bishops chapel can only be visited by guided tour. Directly behind the Stift is the **Brauerei Göss** (☎ 20 90-5802; s.schneeweis@brauunion.com; Brauhausgasse 1; adult/child €4/2, with tour €7/5; ☾ 9am-6pm Sat & Sun Apr-Oct), which brews the ubiquitous Gösser beer.

If you require a place to sleep, try the simple **Gösserhof** (☎ 26 001; Turmgasse 1; s/d €31.50/56; Ⓟ), opposite the Stift. The **Arkedenhof** (☎ 42 074; Hauptplatz; mains €6-11), a pub-restaurant with Styrian food, a large atrium and a medieval look, is one of the better places to eat.

Getting There & Away
Leoben is 16km west of Bruck (€3.30; 15 minutes) and is on the main rail route from there to Klagenfurt or Linz. The town centre is 10 minutes' walk from Leoben Hauptbahnhof: cross the Mur and bear right. The Stift and brewery is another 30 minutes' walk south of the centre, or a short bus ride (€1.70).

EISENERZ
☎ 03848 / pop 6000
Eisenerz is one of the main destinations along the **Steirische Eisenstrasse**, and lies at the foot of the extraordinary **Erzberg** (Iron Mountain), a mine literally eating its way into the mountains. While the town has certainly seen better days, it's still a fine place to stop by; the narrow, cobblestone streets, solid houses and noise of alpine streams all combine to create a relaxed atmosphere.

The **tourist office** (☎ 37 00; www.eisenerz-heute .at; Freiheitsplatz 7; ☾ 9am-1pm & 3-5pm Mon-Fri May-

Oct, 10am-noon & 2-5pm Mon-Fri Nov-Apr) is in the centre of the town.

Sights
The main reason to come to Eisenerz is the **Erzberg** (☎ 32 00; info@abenteuer-erzberg.at; Erzberg 1; tour adult/child €13/6.50, combined ticket €22/11, tour & Stadtmuseum €15/7.50; ☾ tours 10am-3pm May-Oct), a peak that has been completely denuded by opencast stope mining to such an extent that it resembles a step pyramid. The outcome is surprisingly beautiful, with its orange and purple shades contrasting with the lush greenery and grey crags of surrounding mountains. The ironworks can be seen up-close and personal in two ways; with a 90-minute 'Schaubergwerk' tour which burrows into the mountain to the underground mines, abandoned in 1986 (guaranteed tours at 10am, 12.30pm and 3pm), or with a 60-minute 'Hauly Abenteuerfahrt' tour, which explores the surface works aboard an enormous truck, with fine views along the way (reserve ahead). Both tours are usually in German, with English-language notes available. The departure point is a 10-minute walk from the centre, following the course of the river.

The town itself is not to be dismissed though. Its old centre is full of charm, and some of its buildings, particularly around Bergmannsplatz, sport *sgraffito* (mural or decoration in which the top layer is scratched off to reveal the original underneath) designs. Near Bergmannsplatz is the **Wehrkirche St Oswald** (☎ 22 67; Kirchenstiege 4; admission free; ☾ 9am-7pm summer, 9am-5pm winter), more a fortress than a Gothic church, which gained its heavy walls in 1532 as protection against the Turks. Near the tourist office is the **Stadtmuseum** (☎ 36 15; Schulstrasse 1; adult/senior/student €3.60/1.45/3.10; ☾ 10am-noon & 2-5pm Tue-Fri May-Oct), once the hunting lodge of Franz Joseph I. Its wood-panelled walls now contain displays of religious paraphernalia, including a delicate 16th-century Renaissance goblet. Upstairs is devoted to the strange combination of local artists' exhibitions and mining, including a reconstructed mining tunnel, explanations on backbreaking mining methods in the late 19th and early 20th centuries, and current mining techniques.

The town is surrounded by **hiking trails**, and only 3km north on the road to Admont is idyllic **Leopoldsteiner See**, a small lake with a wall of granite rising to 1649m as a backdrop.

Sleeping & Eating

Aside from the places listed below, there are a number of fine pensions and restaurants in the old centre, all within a few minutes walk of each other.

Jugend & Familiengästehaus (☎ 605 60; jgh.eisen erz@jhg.at; Ramsau 1; dm €14; **P** **☐**) About 5km south of Eisenerz in a quiet valley is this new HI hostel. Each room has its own bathroom and there is a restaurant on site.

Gästehaus Tegelhofer (☎ 20 86; www.gaestehaus -tegelhofer.at - in German; Lindmoserstrasse 8; s/d €29/48; **P**) This modern *Gästehaus* (guesthouse) is quite a find, with its spacious, spotless rooms, free sauna and fitness room, and welcoming staff.

Bräustüberl (☎ 23 35; Flutergasse 5; mains €5-12; s/d €21/36; **P**) Bräustüberl is a more traditional place, with a few new-looking rooms. Its decent restaurant is complimented with an excellent, open beer garden.

Getting There & Away

Two-hourly direct buses run from Leoben to Eisenerz (€5.60; one hour). They're about the same frequency from Eisenerz to Hieflau (€3.30; 25 minutes), where there are train connections to Selzthal via Admont.

Trains no longer operate to Eisenerz, except for the special Vordernberg–Eisenerz **Nostalgie** (nostalgic train; ☎ 03849-832; www.erzberg bahn.at - in German; adult/child €9/4.50) which runs at 10.25am and 2.30pm on Sunday from late June to early October.

NATIONALPARK GESÄUSE

Only established in 2003, Gesäuse is Austria's newest national park, a pristine region of jagged mountain ridges, rock towers, deep valleys, alpine pastures and dense spruce forests. Unusually for a protected landscape, traditional farming is still allowed on selected meadows.

Dividing the park in two uneven halves is the Enns, a fast-flowing alpine river that eventually spills into the Danube near Mauthausen in Upper Austria. It's a favourite of rafting connoisseurs, and a number of companies offer rafting trips during the summer months. Hiking and mountain climbing, and to a lesser extent mountain biking, also feature highly in the park's outdoor activi-

ties; of the six peaks over 2000m within the park, **Hocktor** (2369m) rises above the rest and is the goal of many hikers. The occasional spelunking excursion is also available; around 150 caves burrow under the high limestone mountains, the deepest of which descends 600m below the surface.

More information on activities in the park can be found at the **Nationalpark Gesäuse Information Centre** (☎ 03613-21 000; www.nationalpark .at; Weng im Gesäuse 2). The best gateways to the park can be reached by train from Selzthal. They are Gstatterboden (€5.60, 30 minutes, up to four daily) and Johnsbach (€5.60, 30 minutes, one daily).

ADMONT
☎ 03613 / pop 2900

Depending on your taste, Admont's **Benedictine Abbey** (☎ 23 12-601; www.stiftadmont.at; Admont 1; adult/senior/student & child €9/8/5, library only €4.50/4/3.50; ☯ 10am-5pm Apr-Oct, 10am-1pm Fri-Sun Dec-Mar) pips St Florian's Augustinian Abbey at the post for the best in Austria.

Recently renovated, expanded and upgraded, Admont's abbey is an impressive combination of museums, religious art and baroque architecture which is actually worth the €9 entrance fee. Pride of place goes to the **Stiftsbibliothek** (abbey library), the largest abbey library in the world. Survivor of a fire in 1865 that severely damaged the rest of the abbey, it displays 150,000 volumes, heavenly ceiling frescoes by Bartolomeo Altomonte and statues (in wood, but painted to look like bronze) by Josef Stammel (1695–1765). Pick up a leaflet in English at the ticket desk to understand the symbolism inherent in these works.

On the same floor is the abbey's **art history museum**. The impressive collection features some unusual pieces, including a tiny portable altar from 1375, made from amethyst quartz and edged with gilt-silver plates, Gerhard Mercator globes from 1541 and 1551 and a Festival Monstrance from 1747, set with a king's ransom of 2175 gems. In between the museum and library is a highly innovative **multimedia show**, retelling the story of St Benedict and the abbey through video, slides and a spacey mirror room whose effect is similar to Dr Who's Tardis.

The 2nd floor begins with contemporary art exhibitions, but more importantly moves on to the **natural history museum**.

Started in 1674, the collection is small but enthralling, and includes rooms devoted to flying bugs (one of the largest collections in the world), butterflies, stuffed animals, wax fruits (bizarrely) and reptiles.

The **tourist office** (☎ 21 64; info@xeis.at; Hauptplatz 36; ☉ 8am-noon & 2-6pm Mon-Fri, 9am-noon Sat) is housed in the Rathaus near the abbey church. There are also a couple of pensions and places to eat nearby, including homely **Gasthof Zeiser** (☎ 21 47-4; gasthof.zeiser@aon.at; Hauptstrasse 147; s/d €32/53).

Admont is 15km to the east of Selzthal, on the train route to Hieflau; four direct trains (€3.30, 15 minutes) run from Monday to Friday.

WEST STYRIA

Like northern Styria, west Styria is a mountainous region divided by jagged ranges and alpine streams which gather speed and volume as they head east. It's an area for enjoying Austria's natural splendour and escaping the madding crowds.

Murau, high up in the Mur valley, is a picturesque town well placed for hikes and cycle-trips into the surrounding forests. If you're heading this way from Graz, consider a detour to **Seckau** or **Oberzeiring**. The former is famous for its **Benedictine Abbey** (☎ 03514-23 4-0; Seckau 1; basilica admission free; tours adult/child €4/2.50; ☉ 10am-5pm May-Oct), stunning Romanesque Basilica and mausoleum of Karl II, while the latter is known for its old **silver mine** (☎ 03571-23 87; www.silbergruben.at; adult/child/family €5/3.50/12; ☉ tours 9.45am, 1.45pm & 3pm May-Oct, 4pm Wed Nov-Apr), now resurrected as a small health resort for sufferers of respiratory diseases.

MURAU
☎ 03532 / pop 2500

Murau, in the western reaches of the Mur valley on the banks of the fast-flowing Mur, is an attractive town filled with pastel-coloured houses and surrounded by forested hills and alpine meadows. Its close proximity to Stolzalpe to the north and Metnitzer mountains to the south make it an excellent base for hiking and cycling during the summer months.

The **tourist office** (☎ 27 20-0; tourismus@murau .at; Bundesstrasse 13a; ☉ 9am-6pm Mon-Fri, 10am-noon Sat), on the main road into town, has loads of brochures on the town and its surrounds, including hiking trails and bicycle-ways.

The Liechtenstein family once dominated the Murau region and built **Schloss Obermurau** (☎ 230 258; Schlossberg 1; tours adult/child €2.50/1.50; ☉ 3pm Wed & Fri mid-Jun–mid-Sep) in 1250. Given a Renaissance makeover by the Schwarzenberg family in the 17th century, it is now in great shape for a castle.

Just below the castle is **Stadtpfarrkirche St Matthäus** (St Matthew's Church; ☎ 24 89, Schlossberg 8; ☉ dawn-dusk), yet another Gothic church remodelled in baroque style. Both elements work well together, as in the combination of the Gothic crucifixion group (1500) and the baroque high altar (1655). The beautiful frescoes date from the 14th to 16th centuries.

Murau is also famous for its Murau Brewery, which has a **brewery museum** (☎ 32 66; Raffaltplatz 19-23; admission €3; ☉ 3-5pm Wed & Fri Jul-Sep). Entry includes a glass of the local brew. Don't despair if it's closed, the **Murau Brauerei** next door has Murau on tap.

Bike rental is available from **Intersport Pintar** (☎ 23 97; Bundesstrasse; half-day/full-day/weekend/ week rental €7/10/25/39), near the tourist office.

Sleeping & Eating

Jugend & Familiengästehaus (☎ 23 95; jgh.murau@ jgh.at; St Leonhard Platz 4; 2-6 bed dm €14-17.30) This 190-bed HI hostel is situated in three historic buildings near the train station and has a sauna and peaceful inner courtyard.

In the heart of the town are two fine options; **Gasthof Bärenwirt** (☎ 20 79; Schwarzenbergstrasse 4; s/d €26/50, mains €6-10), an uncomplicated place with basic rooms and solid Austrian cuisine, and **Hotel Lercher** (☎ 24 31; www.lercher .com; Schwarzenbergstrasse 10; s/d €40/80, mains €8/14; ℗), a plush, four-star hotel with a highly rated restaurant.

Getting There & Away

If you're coming from Salzburgerland, the most pleasant mode of transport is the **Murtalbahn** (☎ 22 31; www.stlb.at - in German; one-way/return €15.80/31.60), a steam train that chugs its way between Tamsweg and Murau once every Tuesday and Wednesday in July and August, on a private narrow-gauge line.

Normal ÖBB trains to Murau require a change at Unzmarkt (€4.80; 40 minutes), from where five make the trip daily (three on weekends).

STYRIA

The Salzkammergut

CONTENTS

As its name suggests, the Salzkammergut rose to fame and fortune through the mining of salt – the 'white gold' that has been mined all over this mineral-rich lake region since Celtic times, laying the foundations of Salzburg's wealth. Disputes over salt had far-reaching effects: Salzburg's 'salt war' with Maximilian, Duke of Bavaria, over the profits from the salt trade led to the downfall of Wolf Dietrich, Prince-Archbishop of Salzburg.

The white gold is still being extracted in the Salzkammergut today – there are working mines at Hallstatt, Bad Ischl and Altaussee. Brine from these mines goes to Ebensee, where the salt is extracted.

The Salzkammergut's modern-era reputation centres around its privileged position as the favourite holiday spot of the Habsburg emperors and their hangers-on. Emperor Franz Josef declared the region to be 'an earthly paradise' and spent a large part of every summer at Bad Ischl, whose healing waters were credited with his conception. The salt mines which made the region famous are also open to the public – attractions typically include sliding down wooden miners' slides (overalls provided) and floating in boats on illuminated underground lakes.

Today, it's the Salzkammergut's myriad lakes that bring visitors in droves from Salzburg and further afield – the peaceful, glassy waters provide limitless opportunities for boating, swimming, fishing or just sitting on the shore and chucking stones into the water. Favourite lakeside beauty spots include the picturesque villages of Hallstatt and St Wolfgang and the Riviera-style port of Gmunden.

HIGHLIGHTS

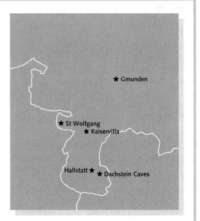

- Wandering around **Hallstatt** (p216), not just a beauty spot, but a jewel of a small village that was once a centre of Celtic culture

- Exploring **St Wolfgang** (p226), another lakeside village with another dimension; this one has a pilgrimage church filled with priceless works of art

- Visiting the **Kaiservilla** (p213), Franz Josef's summer residence, now a handsome museum set in wild parkland

- Meeting a 300-year-old miner at Hallstatt's **Salzbergwerk** (p217), a working salt mine

- Plunging into the depths of the **Dachstein Caves** (p218), where glittering towers of ice are masterfully illuminated in the depths of a mountain

- Visiting the **Museum für Historische Sanit-ärobjeckte** (p222), Gmunden – a museum dedicated to loos? They must be potty …

| ▦ POPULATION: 179,000 | ▦ AREA: 2888 SQ KM | ▦ HIGHEST ELEVATION: DACHSTEIN 2988M |

Orientation & Information

The Salzkammergut is split between three provinces: Upper Austria, which takes the lion's share; Styria, comprising the small area around Bad Aussee; and Salzburg province. For general information, check out www.salz kammergut.at.

History

Mining has been the principal activity in the Salzkammergut since Celtic times, when primitive tunnels were hacked into the rock and water sloshed down them to release the brine. After the demise of the Celts, the prince-archbishops of Salzburg took over the mining trade and used the profits from the dark, dank mines to build their elaborate palaces and pleasure gardens.

Ironically, considering its later popularity as a tourist area, the whole of the Salzkammergut region was banned to visitors until the early 19th century because the Salzburg government, which held a monopoly on salt mining here, wanted to prevent salt from being smuggled out. Later, Emperor Franz Josef's patronage brought central European aristocracy to the region in their droves. They came to promenade around the parks of the elegant spa towns like Bad Ischl, or to tramp through the snowy mountain forests in search of unwary deer.

Climate

Summers down by the Salzkammergut region's lakes tend to be quite warm, with an average temperature of 15°C–25°C. In spring and autumn especially, beware of the so-called 'string rain' – a soft, yet drenching rain that seems to soak you through before you've noticed it's begun. During winter (mid-November to February) the average lies around −4°C.

Getting There & Away

To reach the Salzkammergut from Salzburg by car or motorcycle, take the A1 to reach the north of the region, or Hwy 158 to Bad Ischl. Travelling north–south, the main road is Hwy 145 (the Salzkammergut Bundesstrasse) which follows the rail line for most of its length. By train, the main rail routes into the province are from Salzburg or Linz, with a change at Attnang-Puchheim onto the regional north–south railway line.

Getting Around

The Salzkammergut is crossed by regional trains on a north–south route Attnang-Puchheim on the Salzburg–Linz line and Stainach-Irdning on the Bischofshofen–Graz line. The rail line linking these two access points is 108km long, and hourly trains take 2½ hours to complete the journey (and they're often late). Smaller stations on this route are *unbesetzter Bahnhof* (unstaffed stations; look for the crossed-through rectangle icon on timetables); at these you'll have to use a platform ticket machine or pay on the train. Attersee is also accessible by rail.

Regular bus services connect all towns and villages in the area, though less frequently at weekends. Timetables can be seen at stops and tickets can be bought from the driver. For bus times and prices from Salzburg to the various towns in the region, see p248.

Passenger boats ply the waters of the Attersee, Traunsee, Mondsee, Hallstätter See and Wolfgangsee.

The Salzkammergut Erlebnis Card, available from tourist offices and hotels, costs €4.90. It is valid between 1 May and 31 October for the duration of your holiday in the region. Cardholders are entitled to a 25% discount on about 110 attractions – sights, ferries, cable cars and some of the Bundesbus routes. It's not transferable.

BAD ISCHL

☎ 06132 / pop 14,100

This spa town's reputation snowballed after the Habsburg Princess Sophie took a treatment here to cure her infertility in 1828. Within two years she had given birth to Emperor Franz Josef I; two other sons followed and were nicknamed the Salzprinzen (Salt Princes).

Rather in the manner of a salmon returning to its place of birth, Franz Josef made an annual pilgrimage to Bad Ischl, making it his summer home for the next 60 years and hauling much of the European aristocracy in his wake. The fateful letter he signed declaring war on Serbia and sparking off WWI bore a Bad Ischl postmark.

Today's Bad Ischl is a handsome, dignified town with many buildings still painted imperial yellow. It makes a handy base for visiting the region's five main lakes.

THE SALZKAMMERGUT

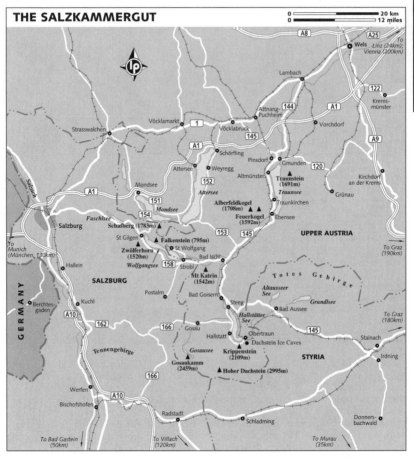

Orientation & Information

Bad Ischl's town centre is compactly contained within a bend of the Traun River. There are moneychanging facilities at the post office and train station.

Post office (Bahnhofstrasse; 8am-6pm Mon-Fri, 9am-12pm Sat) In the centre of town.

Salzkammergut Info-Center (☎ 240 00-0; www.salz kammergut.co.at; Gützstrasse 12; ☼ 9am-8pm) A helpful private agency, which can provide region-wide information & hotel bookings (no commission). It also has bike rental (€7.30 for 24hrs) and Internet access (per 10 min €1.10).

Tourist office (☎ 277 57-0; www.badischl.at; Bahnhofstrasse 6; ☼ 8am-6pm Mon-Fri, 9am-3pm Sat, 10am-1pm Sun) The government tourist office is west of the train station. The phone line is manned from 8am to 8pm every day to help find rooms and provide local info.

Sights & Activities
KAISERVILLA

Franz Josef's summer residence was the **Kaiservilla** (☎ 232 41; Jainzen 38; www.kaiservilla.com - in German; adult/child €9.50/5.50, grounds only €3.50/2.50; ☼ 9.30am-4.45pm summer, winter by appointment only), an Italianate building that was actually bought by his mother, the Princess Sophie, as an engagement present for her son and Princess Elisabeth of Bavaria. Elisabeth, who loathed the villa and her husband in equal measure, spent little time there, but the emperor came to love it and it became his permanent summer residence for over 60 years. His mistress, Katharina Schratt, lived nearby in a house chosen for her by the empress.

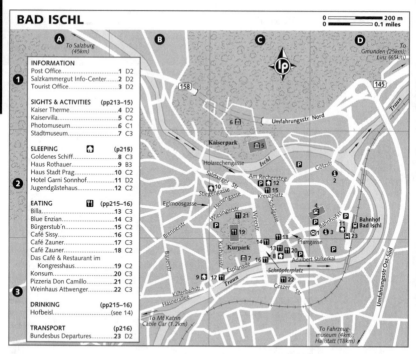

BAD ISCHL

0 — 200 m
0 — 0.1 miles

Ⓐ To Salzburg (45km)   Ⓑ   Ⓒ   Ⓓ To Gmunden (25km); Linz (65km)

The interior of the villa can only be seen by guided tour (which leave every half-hour in summer) and sheets of English information are available. You'll learn of the emperor's habit of rising at 3.30am each morning to take a bath before beginning his day's work punctually at 4am. The only recreation he allowed himself was hunting – the walls of the villa are liberally studded with the fruits of his labours, including the stuffed corpse of the 2000th chamois he shot. There are various other objects of interest, including a bust of the Empress Elisabeth, made when she was in her mid-40s (a grandmother and still an internationally-famous beauty), and a death mask made after she was killed by a knife-wielding madman at the age of 60. The natural-style parkland surrounding the villa contains a small **Photomuseum** (☎ 244 22; adult/child €1.50/0.70; ⏱ 9.30am-5pm early Apr-end Oct).

STADTMUSEUM

If you walk along the Esplanade, you'll reach the **Stadtmuseum** (city museum; ☎ 254 76; Esplanade 10; adult/child €4.20/2; ⏱ 10am-5pm Tue & Thu-Sun, 2-7pm Wed, 10am-5pm Mon Jul & Aug only).

This is the building where Franz Josef and Elisabeth got engaged (the day after they met at a ball). Today it holds various exhibits on the history of the town, plus national costumes; on the second floor there's a display of Far Eastern treasures brought home from the 'Orient' by a globetrotting 19th-century resident.

FAHRZEUGMUSEUM

With displays of motorised transport, such as airplanes, helicopters, motorcycles, cars and army vehicles, the **Fahrzeugmuseum** (Transport Museum; ☎ 266 58; Sulzbach 178; admission adult/child €7/3; ⏱ 9am-6pm 1 Apr-31 Oct) is approximately 4km south of the town centre; Bad Goisern/Hallstatt Bundesbuses stop 200m away.

MT KATRIN

Bad Ischl's local peak is **Mt Katrin** (1542m), which provides views and walking trails. It's reached by a summer **cable car** (☎ 237 88; return ticket adult/child €12/8, ⏱ closed Easter–mid-May, Nov 1-Dec 7). In winter, there are 3km of pistes for downhill skiing on the mountain. The area also has some cross-country skiing trails.

KAISER THERME

If you'd like to follow in Princess Sophie's footprints, take a spa treatment at the **Kaiser Therme** (☎ 061-33; www.kaisertherme.co.at - in German; Bahnhofstrasse 1; adult/child €10.40/6.20; ☺ 9am-10pm) The entry price gets you into the indoor and outdoor salt-water swimming pools, but there's also a gym, sauna and brine Jacuzzi, plus mud treatments and massage. If you're interested, you can down a mug of the mineral-rich waters here (€1.50).

Festivals & Events

Free *Kurkonzerte* (spa concerts) are performed once or twice a day from 16 June to 30 September; they take place in an open-air pavilion in the Kurpark or inside the nearby Congresshaus. Bad Ischl was the home of operetta composer Franz Lehár, and the **Lehár Festival** (www.leharfestival.at - in German) takes place every year in July and August, with stagings of his productions and those of other composers being put on in the Congresshaus and various churches in town.

Sleeping

Staff at both the tourist offices will help find rooms, or you can use the 24-hour accommodation board in the government tourist office foyer.

Hotel Garni Sonnhof (☎ 230 78; www.sonnhof.at; Bahnhofstrasse 4; s/d with breakfast €45/90; P) Nestled in a leafy glade of maple trees next to the station, this is an excellent option – it has cosy, traditional décor, a lovely garden (complete with a pond), a sunny conservatory and large bedrooms with interesting old furniture, rag rugs and wooden floors. There's a billiard room, sauna and a steam bath on site.

Goldenes Schiff (☎ 242 41; www.goldenes-schiff.at; Stifterkai 3; s/d with breakfast €54-122/60-134; P X ▣) Overlooking the river, this four-star hotel has modern and soulless rooms, but great views of the river and town. The best are the corner rooms, with balconies. There's also a wellness centre with solarium and sauna, and a good restaurant.

Haus Stadt Prag (☎ /fax 236 16; stadt-prag@aon.at; Egelmoosgasse 9; s/d €32/60; ☺ closed Nov; P) This private pension outside the town centre has a peaceful, old-world atmosphere and the spacious, modern rooms are good value. Add 10% to the price if you're only staying one night.

Haus Rothauer (☎ 236 28; Kaltenbachstrasse 12; s/d with breakfast €25/55) Convenient for the town centre, this private house has well-furnished, good-value rooms. Do phone ahead to check availability and make sure someone is there when you intend to arrive.

Jugendgästehaus (☎ 265 77; www.oejhv.or.at; Am Rechensteg 5; dm/s/d €13/26.50/38; ☺ reception 8am to 1pm & 5pm to 7pm, hostel closed 6-21 Jan & 7-27 Dec) This nondescript HI hostel is in the town centre behind Kreuzplatz.

Eating & Drinking

Weinhaus Attwenger (☎ 233 27; Lehárkai 12; mains €6.90-17.80; ☺ lunch & dinner, closed Mon & Tue in low season) This quaint chalet with a relaxing garden next to the river serves prime-quality Austrian cuisine from a seasonal menu, with wines to match. There are a couple of set menus (three/four courses €23/€26.50).

Café Zauner (☎ 237 22; Esplanade & Pfarrgasse 7; cakes €3-10; ☺ lunch) Founded in 1832, this was Franz Josef's bakery of choice – his mistress ordered their pastries for their breakfast every morning when the emperor was in residence. There are now two branches in town, both with suitably glittering chandeliers, marble floors and fantastical displays of confectionary.

Das Café & Restaurant im Kongresshaus (☎ 233 220; Kurpark; mains €4-14.60; ☺ lunch & dinner) In the delicate, pink Kongresshaus, surrounded by the greenery of the Kurpark formal gardens, this place is one of the most atmospheric places to eat in Bad Ischl. Enjoy a big bowl of strawberries and cream or a fresh river trout while listening to classical music from the park pavilion or the adjoining theatre.

Café Sissy (☎ 241 73; Pfarrgasse 2; mains €5-9; ☺ breakfast, lunch & dinner) Sissy was the nickname of the Kaiserin Elisabeth, unhappy wife of Emperor Franz Josef, and her pictures hang on the walls of this popular riverside bar/café. Come here for an 'imperial breakfast' (€36), which includes a bottle of champagne. Cheaper and plainer fare is also available.

Blue Enzian (☎ 289 92; Wirerstrasse 2; mains €6-12; ☺ lunch & dinner) This informal bar/restaurant, set back from the main street in a courtyard, offers pasta, regional and national food and salads. Almost next door is the popular **Hofbeisl** (☺ 9am to 4am), an atmospheric bar with baroque décor.

Pizzeria Don Camillo (☎ 277 35; Wiesingerstrasse 5; mains €6-7.40; ☺ lunch & dinner) This Italian restaurant has a nice garden overlooking the Kurpark and serves real stone-baked pizzas, plus house specialities like veal in red wine sauce (€9.80).

Bürgerstub'n (☎ 235 68; Kreuzplatz 7; 2-course menu €9; ☻ lunch Mon-Sat) Back from the street in a courtyard, this cheap and cheerful place has lots of plants, an outside terrace and filling Austrian food.

Supermarkets in Bad Ischl include Billa on Pfarrgasse and Konsum on Auböckplatz.

Getting There & Away
Bundesbuses depart from outside the train station. There are hourly buses to Salzburg (€8.90, 85 minutes) between 5am and 7.20pm (6.20pm on weekends), via St Gilgen. To St Wolfgang (€4.50), you often have to change at Strobl (the bus will be waiting and the same ticket is valid). Buses travel to Hallstatt every couple of hours (€5.10, 50 minutes), with some continuing to Obertraun.

Trains depart hourly to Hallstatt (€4.10), but unlike the bus, you must add the cost of the boat from Hallstatt station (€1.90). There are also hourly trains to Gmunden (€7, 45 minutes), as well as to Salzburg via Attnang-Puchheim (€16, two hours, hourly).

Most major roads in the Salzkammergut go to or near Bad Ischl; Hwy 158 from Salzburg and the north–south Hwy 145 intersect just north of the town centre.

SOUTHERN SALZKAMMERGUT

The Dachstein mountain range provides a stunning 3000m backdrop to the lakes in the south. Transport routes go round rather than over these jagged peaks.

HALLSTÄTTER SEE
The big draw in the south is this lake, tucked in between the mountains at an altitude of 508m. Hallstatt is the most spectacularly situated of the villages that surround the lake, and it can get very busy with day trippers in summer. Just 5km round the lake lies Obertraun, the closest resort to the Dachstein ice caves. Such is its environmental importance that the whole Hallstatt–Dachstein region became a Unesco World Cultural Heritage site in 1997.

Circular, 75-minute excursions round the lake are offered by **Hemetsberger** (☎ 6134-8228; Am Hof 126; €7; operates Jul–mid-Sep weather depending), the same company that runs the train-town ferry. There are boats three times a day from Hallstatt, and it's possible to get on and off en route.

HALLSTATT
☎ 06134
With pastel-coloured houses casting shimmering reflections onto the glassy, green waters of the lake, swans floating by and towering mountains on all sides, Hallstatt's beauty alone would be enough to guarantee it fame. Boats chug tranquilly across from the train station to the village itself, which clings precariously to a tiny bit of land between mountain and shore. So small is the patch of land occupied by the village that its annual Corpus Christi procession takes place largely in small boats on the lake.

Today, Hallstatt's prettiness attracts coach parties of tourists, but the salt in the hills above the town once attracted primitive miners in equal numbers. The Hallstatt Period (800 to 400 BC) refers to the early Iron Age in Europe, named after the village and the Celtic settlers who worked the salt mine here. No one is sure what happened to the early miners – theories speculate that fatal rockslides led the area to be abandoned.

Orientation & Information
The train station is across the lake from Hallstatt – to get into town you have to take a short ferry ride (€1.90). Seestrasse is the main street in Hallstatt; some other streets are mere pedestrian paths.

Internet access (Seestrasse 145; ☻ 9am-10pm; per 15 min €1) A few terminals at a small 'umbrella bar' just down the road from the Bräu Gasthof. Summer only.

Post office (☻ 8am-12pm & 1.30-5.30pm) Around the corner from the tourist office.

Tourist office (☎ 8255-0; www.hallstatt.at - in German; Seestrasse 169; ☻ 9am-12pm & 2-5pm Mon-Fri, 9am-5pm Mon-Fri, 10am-5pm Sat & 10am-2pm Sun Jul & Aug). Turn left from the ferry to reach the office, which sells an English-language walking guide (€5.85).

Sights & Activities
BEINHAUS
You should not miss the macabre beauty of the **Beinhaus** (Bone House; ☎ 8279; Kirchenweg 40; admission €1; ☻ 10am-6pm 1 May-27 Oct) behind

the church. This small charnel house contains rows of neatly stacked skulls, painted with flowery designs and the names of their former owners. These human remains have been exhumed from the too-small graveyard since 1600 in a practice that recalls the old Celtic pagan custom of mass burial. The last skull in the collection was added in 1995. The Beinhaus stands in the grounds of the 15th-century Catholic **Pfarrkirche** (parish church; ☎ 8279; Kirchenweg 40) and has Gothic frescoes and three winged altars; arguably the best one, on the right, dates from 1510 and shows saints Barbara and Katharina, with Mary in the middle.

STADTMUSEUM

The revamped, high-tech **Stadtmuseum** (city museum; ☎ 8206; www.museum-hallstatt.at - in German; Seestrasse 56; adult/child €7/3.50; ☿ 10am-4pm daily Apr & Oct, 10am-6pm May-Sep, 11am-3pm Nov-Mar, closed Mon Jan-Mar) covers the region's history of Celtic occupation and salt mining. All explanations are in German, but you can still admire the drama of the fatal rockslides that may have led to the area being abandoned. There's one of the Iron Age skeletons on display, along with the weapons and pots buried alongside for the journey into the afterlife.

Celtic and Roman excavations can be seen downstairs in **Dachsteinsport Janu** (☎ 8298; Seestrasse 50; admission free; ☿ 8am-6pm), a shop opposite the tourist office.

SALZBERGWERK

Above Hallstatt on the Salzberg (Salt Mountain) is the **Salzbergwerk** (Salt Mine; ☎ 06132-200 24 90; adult/child €19.90/11.95; ☿ 9am-6pm 26 Apr-21 Sep, 9.30am-4.30pm 22 Sep-26 Oct, closed 27 Oct-25 Apr). In 1734 the fully preserved body of a prehistoric miner was found in the Hallstatt Salt Mine, known today as the 'Man in Salt'. The tour revolves around his fate, with visitors travelling down an underground railway and wooden miner's slides to an illuminated subterranean salt lake, peeking into caves of glittering salt crystals. The last tour is at 4.30pm from late April to mid-September; at other times it's at 3pm.

To get there, a funicular railway (one-way/return €5/7.90) will take you to **Rudolfsturm** (Rudolf's Tower), 15 minutes' walk from the mine. Alternatively, either of two scenic walking trails will get you from Hallstatt to the tower in 45 minutes. There's an

excellent view from the public terrace of Rudolfsturm.

Gasthof Hallberg is the base for Hallstatt's **scuba diving school** (www.zauner-online.at - in German). If you're longing to get out onto the lake, boat hire is available from **Rieder Bootverleih** (☎ 8320; electric boat per hr €9) next to the ferry terminal.

Sleeping

Some private rooms in the village are only available in summer; others require at least a three-night stay. Your best bet is to elicit the help of the tourist office, which will willingly ring round for you without charge. Rooms get booked out in high season, so reserve ahead if possible. There's an accommodation board with free phone in Lahn (the southern part of the village). Lahn has the cheapest private rooms.

Gasthof Hallberg (☎ 8286; www.pension-hallberg.at .tf; Seestrasse 113; s with breakfast €45-55, d with breakfast €60-110; **P**) Hallberg is the base of Hallstatt's dining room, so interesting artefacts rescued from the lake line the staircase leading up to the rooms. The best of these are fabulous – light and airy, furnished with pale wood and boasting superb views over the lake on both sides. The more ordinary rooms are still excellent quality, many with quaintly sloping ceilings and views of the mountains.

Gasthof Zauner (☎ 8246; www.zauner.hallstatt.net; Marktplatz 51; s/d with breakfast €38-49/76-98; ☿ closed mid-Nov–mid-Dec; **P** ✗) Gasthof Zauner is a quaint, ivy-covered place in the nearest square to the ferry terminal. Has traditional pine-embellished rooms – some with a balcony and a view of the lake. The **restaurant** (mains €13-18) is renowned for its good food (especially fish) and wines.

Bräu Gasthof (☎ 8221; Seestrasse 120; s/d with breakfast €35/75) This simple bar/restaurant has a few rooms upstairs; many have antique furniture and a balcony.

TVN Naturfreunde Herberge (☎ /fax 8318; toeroe .f@magnet.at; Kirchenweg 36; dm €11; ☿ check-in 11am-1.30pm & 4-9pm Wed-Mon, closed Tue) This youth hostel is run by the Zur Mühle Gasthaus, which shares the building. It's handily situated on the way up to the church, and the dorms are reasonable.

Jugendherberge (☎ 8212; biene1005@aon.at; Salzberg-strasse 50; dm €8; ☿ open 1 May-30 Sep, check-in approx 5-6pm) Some dorms in this hostel have lots of beds and can be cramped. Phone ahead as reception hours are irregular; it's usually full with groups in July and August. Opening does depend on the weather.

Campingplatz Höll (☎ 8329; camping.klausner@ magnet.at; Lahnstrasse 7; per adult €6; 🕑 15 Apr-15 Oct) This campsite is conveniently located south of the centre.

Eating

Bräu Gasthof Restaurant (☎ 200 12; Seestrasse 120; mains €6.50-15.50; 🕑 lunch & dinner May-Oct) The menu here promises 'hearty local fare' and turns out dishes such as sirloin steak with onions (€13) or game goulash (€12), served in vaulted rooms or on tables outside by the lake. There are also a few salads if all the stodge gets too much.

Pferdestall (☎ 200 00; Seestrasse 156; mains €6.80-19; 🕑 lunch & dinner Thu-Tue) Once a stable (tables are built into the old horse stalls, complete with wooden partitions and iron bars), this small bar/trattoria turns out cheap pizza and pasta, and pricier meat dishes.

Zur Mühle (☎ 8318; Kirchenweg 36; mains €6.40-10.80; 🕑 dinner Wed-Mon) This restaurant has good prices for Austrian and Italian food, but when we visited the staff weren't helpful.

Kongress Stuberl (☎ 83 11 59; Seestrasse 169; daily menu €9; 🕑 lunch & dinner, closed Tue Oct-Apr) This restaurant next door to the tourist office has filling, cheap daily menus.

Getting There & Away

There are around six buses a day to/from Obertraun and Bad Ischl, but not after about 5pm. Get off the Bundesbus at the Parkterrasse stop for the centre and the tourist office, or at Lahn (at the southern end of the road tunnel) for the Jugendherberge hostel.

Hallstatt train station is across the lake. The boat service from there to the village coincides with train arrivals – the whole trip takes about 45 minutes. The last ferry connection leaves Hallstatt train station at 6.44pm. Car access into the village is restricted from early May to late October: electronic gates are activated during the day. Staying overnight in town gives free parking and a pass to open the gates.

OBERTRAUN
☎ 06131

This spread-out village appears to be totally enclosed within a crater of mountains, a pleasing trick of perspective. Within the mountains lie the Dachstein ice caves, which are the main reason for a visit here.

Orientation & Information

The resort's *Gästekarte* (guest card) entitles you to a variety of useful discounts. The ice caves are a 20-minute walk uphill through the woods from the village – turn right along the main road and then follow the signposts for path No 7.

Tourist office (☎ 351; tourismus@obertraun.or.at; Gemeindeamt; 🕑 8am-12pm & 2-5pm Mon-Fri, 9-11.30am Sat Jul & Aug) On the way to the Dachstein ice caves from the train station.

Sights & Activities

The Dachstein caves are millions of years old and extend for nearly 80km in places. The ice itself is no more than 500 years old but is increasing in thickness every year – the 'ice mountain' is 8m high, twice as high now as it was when the caves were first explored in 1910.

Both sets of **caves** (☎ 8400-1830; www.dachstein .at; each cave/combined ticket €8.20/12.70; 🕑 early May-late Oct, tours 9.20am-4pm, 9.20am-4.30pm 10 Jun-5 Sep) are 15 minutes' steep walking from the first stage of the Dachstein cable car (station Schönbergalm) at 1350m; near the station is the ticket office for the caves. The cable car operates every 20 minutes; a return ticket costs €13.40. Each tour takes nearly an hour; be at the ticket office at the latest by 3pm in summer and 2pm in spring and autumn to have time to do both tours.

The best of the caves are the **Rieseneishöhle** (Giant Ice Caves). The enormous ice formations here are illuminated with coloured light and the shapes they take are eerie and surreal. The caves can only be seen on a guided tour (every 30 minutes), which takes about 55 minutes. Ask at the ticket office about tours in English – if none are available you can take a sheet of printed information around the caves with you.

The **Mammuthöhle** (Mammoth Caves) are basically more of the same, except without the ice formations. They are worth seeing, if only for the atmospheric slide show projected within a far cavern, accompanied by swelling music mingling with the sound of ceaselessly dripping water.

The **Koppenbrüllerhöhle** (☎ 8400-1830; guided tour €7; 🕑 1 Jun-30 Sep) are water-filled caves, and are all part of the same Dachstein cave system. They're down the valley towards Bad Aussee.

The Dachstein cable car has three stages, the highest being **Krippenstein** (2109m), which gives access to various viewpoints and walking trails. In winter this is also a ski and snowboard free-riding area (it's €28 for a day pass). Apparently you can also indulge in nude cross-country skiing up here – inquire at the tourist office if you're feeling brave.

Obertraun has a grassy **beach area** (admission free) with changing huts, a small waterslide, a children's play area and boat rental.

Sleeping & Eating

Obertraun has many private rooms (from €19) and holiday apartments, plus a couple of small hotels.

Gasthof Höllwirt (☎ 394; gasthof.hollwirt@aon.at; Hauptstrasse 29; d without/with bathroom €44/60; mains €5.70-12.30) This traditional restaurant also has some double rooms upstairs – those with private bathroom also have TV and room rates include breakfast. The restaurant specialises in fresh lake fish and game meat.

Gasthof/Pension Dachsteinhof (☎ 393; fax 393-4; Winkl 22; s/d with breakfast €33/66; mains €2.80-12; ⓟ) This simple, traditional pension has an idyllic setting by the river on the way up to the ice caves. The good-sized rooms are clean and functional, with the sound of the rushing water to lull you to sleep at night. The restaurant serves up the usual schnitzels, steaks and trout dishes.

Restaurant Pizzeria Kegelbahnen (☎ 335; Obertraun 178; mains €5.40-10.80; dinner Tue-Fri, lunch & dinner Sat & Sun) This place is near the beach and boat-landing point. The pizzas are good and there's a skittles alley to keep you occupied.

Jugendherberge (☎ 360; obertraun@jutel.at; Winkl 26; dm with breakfast €18; ⓨ check-in 5-8pm) This HI hostel is a 15 minutes' walk from the train station: cross the river and take the first street on the left. Doors are locked during the day.

Campingplatz Hinterer (☎ 265; camping.am.see@ chello.at; Winkl 77; per adult €6.50; ⓨ May-Oct) This informal, grassy campsite is by the lake south of the river.

Getting There & Away

Bus connections between Obertraun and Hallstatt (€1.70, 10 minutes) are patchy, with only six or fewer per day; the walk takes 50 minutes. Three or four boats per day travel between Obertraun and Hallstatt in summer (€4, 25 minutes).

Obertraun-Dachsteinhöhlen is the train station for the village. Obertraun-Koppenbrüllerhöhle is the station for the water caves (€1.70, four minutes); trains only stop here in summer when the caves are open. There are trains to Bad Ischl (€4.50, 30 minutes, hourly) via Hallstatt (€1.70, three minutes).

For taxis to the ice caves, call ☎ 542.

GOSAUSEE

☎ 06136 / elevation 923m

This small lake is flanked by the impressively precipitous peaks of the **Gosaukamm range** (2459m). The view is good from the shores (it takes a little over an hour to walk around the lake). The Gosaukammbahn cable car goes up to 1475m (€9.50 return), where there are further views and walking trails. Before reaching the lake you pass through the village of **Gosau**, which has its own **tourist office** (☎ 8295; www.oberoesterreich .at/gosau - in German; ⓨ 8am-12pm & 2-6pm Mon-Fri year-round, 9am-12pm Sat May-Oct), with an accommodation board situated outside.

Getting There & Away

Gosau is at the junction of the only road to the lake and can be reached by Hwy 166 from Hallstätter See. Bundesbus services run to the lake from Bad Ischl (€6.20, 65 minutes, every one to two hours) via Steeg.

BAD AUSSEE

☎ 03622 / pop 5200

Quiet, staid Bad Aussee is the chief Styrian town in the Salzkammergut and provides access to two lakes. Wearing national dress is a big tradition here, so you'll see plenty of people in *Dirndls* (women's traditional dress) and lederhosen walking around the town. If this inspires you to buy your own, dozens of shops on the main street can oblige.

Orientation & Information

The train station is 1.5km south of the town centre. Buses run into town hourly, and there are taxis outside – the taxi trip to town is €7.

Internet Eck (☎ 53250; Bahnhofstrasse 115; per 10 min €1; ⓨ 4-11pm Mon-Fri)

Post office (Ischlerstrasse 94; ⓨ 8am-12pm & 2-5.30pm Mon-Fri, 8-11am Sat 1 Jul-6 Sep) Provides bus information and timetables.

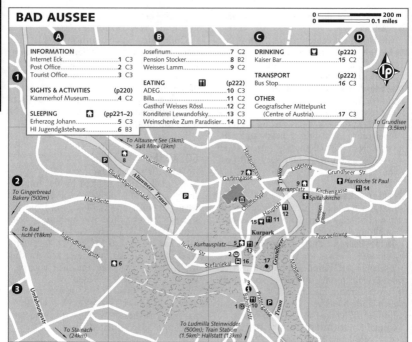

BAD AUSSEE

| | | 0 | 200 m |
| | | 0 | 0.1 miles |

INFORMATION
Internet Eck.................................1 C3
Post Office..................................2 C3
Tourist Office.............................3 C3

SIGHTS & ACTIVITIES (p220)
Kammerhof Museum..................4 C2

SLEEPING (pp221-2)
Erherzog Johann.........................5 C3
HI Jugendgästehaus....................6 B3

Josefinum..................................7 C2
Pension Stocker.........................8 B2
Weisses Lamm............................9 C2

EATING (p222)
ADEG.......................................10 C3
Billa...11 C2
Gasthof Weisses Rössl..............12 C2
Konditerei Lewandofsky...........13 C3
Weinschenke Zum Paradiser...14 D2

DRINKING (p222)
Kaiser Bar................................15 C2

TRANSPORT (p222)
Bus Stop...................................16 C3

OTHER
Geografischer Mittelpunkt
(Centre of Austria)...............17 C3

To Grundlsee (3.5km)

To Altausee See (3km); Salt Mine (3km)
Altausseer Str
Elisabethpromenade
Altausseer Traun
Marktleite
To Gingerbread Bakery (500m)
To Bad Ischl (18km)
Jugendherbergsstr
Umfahrungsstr
To Stainach (24km)
Gartengasse
Habsburgerstr
Traun
Ledererg
Grundlseer Str
Pfarrkirche St Paul
Meranplatz
Kirchengasse
Spitalskirche
Gamser Gasse
Haupstr
Kurpark
Tauscherweg
Mühleitle
Ischler Str
Kurhausplatz
Stefaniekai
Grundlseer
Praterg
Bahnhofstr
Traun
To Ludmilla Steinwidder (500m); Train Station (1.5km); Hallstatt (13km)

Tourist office (☎ 523 23; www.ausseerland.at - in German; Bahnhofstrasse 132; ⏰ 9am-7pm Mon-Fri, 9am-4pm Sat summer, 9am-12pm & 1-6pm Mon-Fri, 9am-12pm Sat winter) The entrance is on Pratergasse, close to the Kurpark, which marks the exact geographical centre of Austria.

Sights & Activities

The largest rock-salt deposit in Austria, **Altaussee Salzbergwerk** (☎ 6132 200 2490; tours adult/concession €11.50/6.90; ⏰ hourly tours 10am-4pm daily), is still a working salt mine and was the secret hiding place of art treasures stolen by the Nazis during WWII. Tours include the treasure chambers, an underground lake and a chapel made of blocks of salt and dedicated to St Barbara, the patron saint of miners. Guided tours in English are available.

Kammerhof Museum (☎ 525 11-20; Chlumeckyplatz 1; adult/child €3/1.50; ⏰ 10am-noon & 3-6pm) in a beautiful 17th-century building, covers local history and salt production. There are also some portraits of Anna Plöchl, the local postmaster's daughter who scandalously married a Habsburg prince. All explanations are in German but there's an English guide available.

There are great views across the town and the mountains beyond it from **Ausseer Lebkuchen** (Gingerbread Bakery; ☎ 52 943; www.lebkuchen.at - in German; admission free; ⏰ 8am-12pm & 1-6pm Tue-Sat, 1-6pm Sun, Mon closed), a working gingerbread bakery that offers tours. Buy some gingerbread to take home, or eat it on the spot in the pleasant **café** (⏰ 9am-10pm Wed-Mon).

Five kilometres northeast of Bad Aussee, **Grundlsee** is a longer, thinner lake, with a good viewpoint at its western end as well as walking trails and water sports (including a sailing school). Extending from the eastern tip of the lake are two smaller lakes, **Toplitzsee** (opposite) and **Kammersee**. Between May and October, **boat tours** (☎ 03622 8613; www.3-seen-tour.at - in German; full tour €14) are available.

A scenic road, the **Panoramastrasse**, climbs most of the way up **Loser** (1838m), the main peak overlooking the Altausser See. The toll for the return trip is €6.70 per adult for cars and €2.20 per child. You'll need snow chains if you wish to travel the road during the winter.

TOPLITZSEE TREASURE

In 1945, with defeat staring them in the face, the Nazis were faced with a problem – where to hide $4.5 billion in counterfeit currency, forged in an attempt to destabilise the economies of Britain and her allies. They settled on Toplitzsee, a tiny lake hidden deep in the Salzkammergut countryside. Boxes of forged notes were brought to the edge of the lake in a horse-drawn wagon, loaded into boats in the dead of night, then tipped overboard.

No one is sure exactly what else was deposited in Toplitzsee during those last desperate days of the Third Reich. For more than half a century rumours have whispered that the loot in the lake included gold, precious stamp collections, diamonds and other valuables looted by the Nazis from Jews in occupied Europe.

Over the years several diving expeditions have braved the oxygen-free depths of the lake in an attempt to recover the lost booty. After one treasure-hunter died in the attempt, the lake was put off-limits to private divers by the government. However, various expeditions have searched the lake using specially adapted submarines, recovering dozens of chests of fake notes and documents detailing the counterfeiting operation (skilled Jewish printers at the concentration camps were forced to produce the fake notes), together with weapons and heavy artillery pieces.

But the allure for mystery-lovers and treasure hunters hasn't dimmed. Speculation that the region's lakes held yet more treasure deepened in 2003, when an amateur diver discovered a solid-gold cauldron at the bottom of Chiemsee in neighbouring Bavaria. The cauldron was worth almost a million dollars and is thought to have been commissioned by a top Nazi official.

Today, interest is centred around the chance of finding the so-called 'Amber Room' – a mysterious crate decorated with Russian markings, which was photographed by a submarine at the bottom of the lake but never retrieved. The plot thickens …

Festivals & Events

Ascension Day, usually in late May/early June, sees the start of the **Narzissenfest**, a four-day festival celebrating the Narcissus flower, with processions, music and animals made of flowers. Entry costs €10.

Sleeping

Staff at the tourist office will help to find accommodation free of charge; there's a 24-hour information touch screen nearby. Many homes around Altausseer See and Grundlsee offer cheap private rooms, which are listed along with pensions and campsites in the Bad Aussee brochure available from the tourist office.

Erherzog Johann (☎ 52507; www.erzherzogjohann .at; Kurhausplatz 62; s with breakfast €75-103, d with breakfast €126-182; P 🖳 🗟) Bad Aussee's four-star hotel has a great position right opposite the Kurpark. Inside, rooms are modern and corporate-looking, but well equipped. There's a well-regarded **restaurant** (mains €8-22) serving up hearty Styrian food with an international slant, a wellness centre with sauna and a salt-water swimming pool.

Weisses Lamm (☎ 524 04; fax 524 04-4; Meranplatz 36; s with breakfast €30-32, d with breakfast €58; P) Run by the English-speaking Strenberger

sisters, this is a friendly place with modern, clean and well-maintained rooms, although some of the singles are a bit small.

Josefinum (☎ /fax 521 24; ba.josefinum@graz.kreuz schwestern.at; Gartengasse 13; s/d with breakfast €21.50/ 41.90, s with breakfast without bathroom €19.50; 🗶) This peaceful retreat has lovely clean, bright rooms with good views of the mountains. It's run by nuns so be on your best behaviour. Telephone ahead for evening arrival.

Pension Stocker (☎ 524 84; www.badaussee.net /pension.stocker - in German; Altausseer Strasse 245; s/d with breakfast €23/46, with breakfast & shared bathroom €15.50/31; P) Located 500m northwest of Kurhausplatz, this is a very pretty pension with wooden balconies and flower-filled window boxes. It has pristine rooms and a large garden that overlooks tennis courts.

Ludmilla Steinwidder (☎ 551 24; alexandra.stein widder@chello.at; Bahnhofstrasse 293; s/d with breakfast €16/32; P) This private house, opposite the Kegelbahn, is 500m towards the train station from town. The elderly hostess is friendly but doesn't speak English. If you book ahead she'll pick you up from the station.

HI Jugendgästehaus (☎ 522 38; www.jgh.at - in German; Jugendherbergsstrasse 148; dm €17.40; 🕑 reception all day Jul-Aug, closed 1pm to 5pm Sep-Jun, hostel closed 1 Nov-24 Dec; P 🗶) This modern building is on the town's hill. It's 15 minutes' walk by road, but there are shorter (unlit) footpaths.

Eating & Drinking

The best place in town for a gourmet meal is the restaurant of the hotel Erzherhog Johann (see p221).

Gasthof Weisses Rössl (☎ 521 77; Hauptstrasse 156; mains €4-11; lunch & dinner Fri-Wed) A family-friendly (but rather smoky) restaurant, this place serves national fare including fish meals and omelettes.

Konditerei Lewandofsky (☎ 532 05; Kurhausplatz 144; lunches €3-10; breakfast & lunch Mon-Sat, lunch Sun) This is the best place in town for coffee and cakes, plus light lunches during the week. There's an outside terrace looking over the Kurpark.

Weinschenke Zum Paradisier (☎ 2135 038; Kirchengasse 28; meals €2.40-6.50; 4pm-late Mon-Sat) This cosy and appealing *Heurigen* (wine tavern), with a red-brick floor and calico draped on the ceiling, specialises in smoked trout. It's an atmospheric place for an evening drink or snack.

Kaiser Bar (☎ 0664 305 3547; Hauptstrasse 152; 6pm-3am Tue-Sat) This slick, well-decorated but tiny bar does a few pizzas but it's mainly a drinking venue.

There's an ADEG supermarket on Bahnhofstrasse, by the tourist office, and a Billa on Hauptstrasse.

Getting There & Away

Bad Aussee is on the rail route from Bad Ischl (€6, 40 minutes) to Stainach-Irdning (€5.50; 35 minutes), with trains running hourly in both directions.

Buses run every one or two hours from the train station to both lakes (€1.70; around 15 minutes), calling at Bad Aussee en route; the fare is the same to either lake or to Bad Aussee.

NORTHERN SALZKAMMERGUT

The two most popular of the northern lakes are Traunsee – with the three resorts of Gmunden, Traunkirchen and Ebensee on its shores – and Wolfgangsee, home to the villages of St Wolfgang and St Gilgen (it also provides access to the **Schafberg**; 1783m).

TRAUNSEE

Traunsee is the deepest lake in Austria, reaching a maximum depth of 192m. The eastern flank is dominated by rocky crags, the tallest of which is the imposing **Traunstein** (1691m). The resorts are strung along the western shore and are connected by rail.

Infrequent Bundesbuses also run between the Traunsee's main towns, sometimes continuing to Bad Ischl. Boats operated by **Traunsee Schiffahrt** (☎ 07612-667 00; www.traunseeschiffahrt .at - in German, Traungasse 12a, Gmunden) tour the shoreline from Gmunden to Ebensee, between late April and late October; frequencies peak in July and August. The full one-way trip costs €5.50. The famous paddle steamer *Gisela*, once boarded by Franz Josef, takes to the waves on weekends and holidays in July and August (a €1.50 surcharge applies).

GMUNDEN

☎ 07612 / pop 13,200

Gmunden is a laid-back town known for its castles and ceramics, a former administration centre for both the Habsburgs and the salt trade. Today the town centre has a breezy, Riviera-like ambience thanks to a yacht marina and a flower-fringed esplanade that runs along the lake, where swans float past a lake Geneva-style jet of water spurting heavenwards.

Orientation & Information

The town centre is on the western bank of the Traun River and has the Rathausplatz at its heart. The main tourist office is at Toscanaparkplatz 1 in Toscana park, south of the town centre – contact details are the same as for the one listed below.

Espresso 10 (☎ 777 44; Kirchenplatz 4; Internet access per hr €3; 9am-7pm daily Mon-Fri, 9am-12pm Sat)
Post office (Bahnhofstrasse; 8am-12pm & 2-5.30pm Mon-Fri) Two hundred metres up the hill.
Tourist office (☎ 643 05; info@traunsee.at; Rathausplatz 1; 8am-9pm Mon-Fri, 10am-8pm Sat & Sun Jul & Aug) A small summer office in the Rathaus. Staff will find rooms free of charge.

Sights & Activities

Gmunden is a famous centre of ceramics, so what better place for the **Museum für Historische Sanitärobjeckte** (Klo & So Museum, Museum for Historical Sanitary Objects; ☎ 794 293; Traungasse 4; adult/child €4/1 10am-noon & 2-5pm Tue-Sat, 10am-2pm Sun & holidays May-Oct), a museum dedicated to all

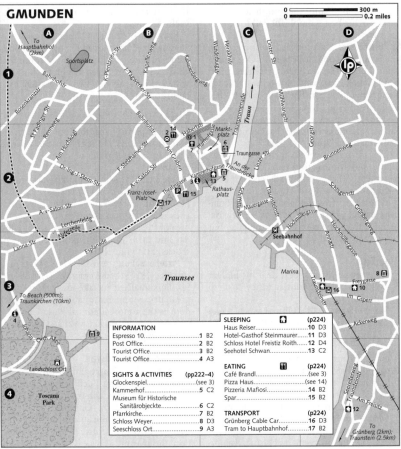

GMUNDEN

0 _____ 300 m
0 _____ 0.2 miles

INFORMATION	
Espresso 10.............................1	B2
Post Office.............................2	B2
Tourist Office.........................3	B2
Tourist Office.........................4	A3

SIGHTS & ACTIVITIES	(pp222–4)
Glockenspiel.......................(see 3)	
Kammerhof...........................5	C2
Museum für Historische	
Sanitärobjekte.....................6	B2
Pfarrkirche...........................7	B2
Schloss Weyer.......................8	D3
Seeschloss Ort.......................9	A3

SLEEPING	(p224)
Haus Reiser.........................10	D3
Hotel-Gasthof Steinmaurer.....11	D3
Schloss Hotel Freistiz Roith.....12	D4
Seehotel Schwan...................13	C2

EATING	(p224)
Café Brandl......................(see 3)	
Pizza Haus.....................(see 14)	
Pizzeria Mafiosi...................14	B2
Spar..................................15	B2

TRANSPORT	(p224)
Grünberg Cable Car................16	D3
Tram to Hauptbahnhof............17	B2

things toilet related? Rows of antique and primitive toilet bowls, commodes and chamber pots (including one belonging to Franz Josef) provide hours of scatological fun.

The 17th-century **Seeschloss Ort** (☎ 654 99; Ort 1; www.schlossorth.com; admission free; tours adult/child €2/1.50; ♥ 24hr), jutting into the lake, is visible from the Esplanade and forms a fine picture. The castle has achieved recent fame being portrayed as a hotel in a German-language TV series, *Schlosshotel Orth* – look for excitable German fans trying to check in. The attractive arcaded courtyard is often flooded – look for the water levels marked on the wall. There are guided tours in English on the hour, a café/restaurant and a small chapel.

Kammerhof (☎ 794-420; Kammerhofgasse 8; adult/child €4/1; ♥ 10am-noon & 2-5pm Mon-Sat, 10am-noon Sun & holidays May-Oct & Dec-Jan), the town museum, covers antique Gmunden ceramics and local history and has an art gallery on the top floor. Apart from some handsome, iron Celtic jewellery and ornaments, there's not much excitement here.

Porcelain, silver and jewellery can be seen in the elegant environment of this Renaissance castle **Schloss Weyer** (☎ 650 18; Freygasse 27; admission €5; ♥ 10am-noon & 2-6pm Tue-Fri, 10am-1pm Sat May-Sep), east of the Traun.

North of the Rathausplatz is the 12th-century **Pfarrkirche** (parish church; ☎ 642 17; Kirchplatz), a Gothic building later remodelled as baroque and noted for an altar (dating from 1678) by Thomas Schwanthaler, said to be one of the best examples of gothic carving in Austria.

Toscana Park is a protected nature area on the peninsula opposite Seeschloss Ort. It contains a castle (Landschloss Ort), now a forestry school. Head south down the esplanade for 1.5km to reach it. The main tourist office is situated in the car park at the entrance.

The Rathausplatz in the town centre contains a ceramic **glockenspiel** that chimes tunes at 10am, noon, 2pm, 4pm and 7pm.

The town has schools for sailing, waterskiing and windsurfing (ask for details at the tourist office) and a **beach** (adult/child €4.70/ 2.40 per day) just south of Toscana Park.

Gmunden provides access to the **Grünberg lookout** (984m). A **cable car** (€10.60 return) ascends from the east side of the lake, but it's easy to walk up.

Sleeping

Private rooms are the best deal for budget travellers – ask the tourist office to help you find one.

Seehotel Schwan (☎ 633 91; www.seehotel-schwan .at; Rathausplatz 8; s/d with breakfast €70/110; [P] [X] [🖵]) This upmarket hotel is slap in the middle of the town and has lake views from all rooms. The rooms are large, with modern furniture and a balcony, but the corridors are a bit gloomy. There's a smart **restaurant** (mains €7.80-16.60; ❤ lunch & dinner) downstairs, serving fresh lake fish on a daily changing menu.

Schloss Hotel Freistiz Roith (☎ 649 05; www.schloss hotel.at; s with breakfast €62-76, d with breakfast €124-162; [P] [X] [🖵]) One of several hotels spread along the eastern lakeshore, this place is about 1.5km from town. The rooms are comfortable but rather plain, with fantastic views. There's an elegant glassed-in **restaurant** (mains €11-25; ❤ lunch & dinner) serving an Austrian and international menu, and a small spa with a sauna.

Hotel-Gasthof Steinmaurer (☎ 704 88; steinmau rer@aon.at; Traunsteinstrasse 23; s with breakfast €52, d with breakfast €82-90; [P]) This place is by the Grünberg cable car and across the road from a public beach. The rooms are modern, clean and for the most part large – many doubles have a balcony or terrace. The busy **restaurant** (mains €5.80-11; ❤ breakfast, lunch & dinner) serves well-cooked, imaginative meals such as vegetable cakes with tomato ragout, and smoked trout and prawn salad.

It has great outside seating overlooking the yacht marina.

Haus Reiser (☎ /fax 724 25; pension.reiser@aon.at; Freygasse 20; s/d with breakfast €27/48) This good-value, private pension has a TV room and garden. There are seven bright, fresh rooms with radios – all but two have their own bathrooms.

Eating

The main places to eat in Gmunden are the hotel restaurants. For ice cream and snacks, there are several outdoor cafés lining the esplanade.

Café Brandl (☎ 641 85; Rathausplatz 1; lunches €2-5; ❤ breakfast, lunch & dinner) This smart café/bar has bright yellow walls, black leather sofas and cubist artworks dotted around. It serves breakfast, cakes and light meals during the day and turns into a drinking venue (with snacks) at night.

Pizzeria Mafiosi (☎ 666 02; J-Tagwerker-Strasse 1; pizza €3.30-6.60; ❤ lunch & dinner Mon-Fri, dinner Sat & Sun) This small eat-in/take-away place offers great prices and reasonable quality. Next door is the almost identical Pizza Haus.

A Spar supermarket awaits self-caterers at Kursaalgasse 5.

Getting There & Away

The Gmunden Hauptbahnhof on the Salzkammergut Attnang-Puchheim to Stainach-Irdning line, is the main train station for the town. The Bad Ischl–Gmunden train fare (€7, 45 minutes, hourly) also includes the tram ride to the centre. The Seebahnhof, near the marina, services the slow, private train line from Vorchdorf-Eggenburg.

Getting Around

The *Hauptbahnhof* is 2km northwest of the town centre: tram G (€1.50) departs from outside it to Franz Josef Platz after every train arrival. Bus rides in town cost €1.50. The Bummelzug (an electric train on wheels) will take you to Seeschloss Ort from the Rathausplatz for €2. It runs every half hour from 9am to 7pm.

TRAUNKIRCHEN

☎ 07617 / pop 1700

The attractive hamlet of Traunkirchen sits on a spit of land about halfway along the western shore of the Traunsee. It's chiefly famous for the wooden **Fischerkanzel** (Fisherman's Pulpit; ☎ 2234; Klosterplatz 1; ☺ 8am-5pm or 6pm daily) in the Pfarrkirche (parish church). It was carved in 1753 and depicts the miracle of the fishes, with the apostles standing in a tub-shaped boat and hauling in fish-laden nets. The composition, colours (mostly silver and gold) and detail (even down to wriggling, bug-eyed fish) create quite a vivid impression.

For information on accommodation, contact the **tourist office** (☎ 2234; www.traunsee.at; Ortsplatz 1; ☺ 8am-12pm & 1-5pm Mon-Fri Sep-Jun, 8am-6pm Mon-Fri, 9am-12pm, 2-6pm Sat Jul & Aug).

Traunkirchen Ort is on the north–south train line, about 12km from Gmunden (€2.60, 12 minutes, hourly). It's a four-minute walk to the centre from this unstaffed train station; take the path that passes under the tracks. The main Traunkirchen station is further from the resort.

EBENSEE
☎ 06133 / pop 8700

Ebensee lies on the southern shore of the Traunsee. There is little to see in the town itself, so head into the hills – take the cable car (adult/child €16/€9.30 hourly) that climbs up to **Feuerkogel** (1592m), where there are walking trails leading across a flattish plateau. Within an hour's walk is **Alberfeldkogel** (1708m), with an excellent view over the two Langbath lakes. Feuerkogel also provides access to winter **skiing** (€30 for a day pass) with easy to medium slopes.

In early January every year, the men of Ebensee don giant illuminated head-dresses made of tissue paper in a bizarre ritual known as Glöcklerlaufen.

For details of water sports and accommodation, contact the local **tourist office** (☎ 8016; www.ebensee.at - in German; Hauptstrasse 34; ☺ 8am-6pm Mon-Fri, 9am-12pm & 2-6pm Sat Jul & Aug, 8am-12pm & 1-5pm Mon-Fri Sep & Oct, 9am-12pm Mon-Fri Nov), by the Landungsplatz train station.

The train station for the centre and the boat landing stage is Ebensee-Landungsplatz, rather than the larger Ebensee station. The town is 17km north of Bad Ischl (€3.10 by train, 20 minutes, hourly) and the same distance south of Gmunden.

GRÜNAU
If you want to get off the beaten track, consider going to Grünau, east of Traunsee. Trains run there from Wels (€8.40, one hour,

two-hourly) and buses run from Gmunden (€3.70, 1 hour, hourly).

The small, friendly **Tree House Backpacker Hotel** (☎ 07616-84 99; www.treehousehotel.net; Schindlbachstrasse 525; dm/d without bathroom €14.50/37) offers bike hire (per day €6), horse riding, canyoning, rafting, skiing and snowboarding (plus clothes and equipment rental), among many other activities. Home meals are available, and there are two bars for partying.

ATTERSEE
The largest lake in the Salzkammergut is flanked mostly by hills, with mountains in the south. It's one of the less scenic and less visited of the Salzkammergut's lakes, but a few resorts cling to the shoreline, offering the usual water-leisure activities. The main resort is **Attersee**, which has a museum and a couple of churches. Its **tourist office** (☎ 07666-7719; www.attersee.at - in German; Nussdorferstrasse 15) will help you to find accommodation.

Attersee-Schifffahrt (☎ 07666-7806; www.atterseeschifffahrt.at) does boat circuits of the lake: one covers the north (€6.50, 1¼ hours) from mid-April to early October, and the other circles around the south (€11, 2½ hours) from early May to late September. Both tours stop at Attersee town four to six times daily in high season.

Getting There & Away
Two lakeside towns, Attersee and Schörfling, are connected to the rail network, each by a line branching from the main Linz–Salzburg route (though only regional trains stop): for Kammer-Schörfling change at Vöcklabruck, and for Attersee town change at Vöcklamarkt.

WOLFGANGSEE
Named after a local saint, this lake holds two main resorts, St Wolfgang and St Gilgen, of which St Wolfgang is the most appealing. The third town on the lake, **Strobl** (population 2750), is an unremarkable place at the start of a scenic toll road (€3 per car and per person) to Postalm (1400m).

A **ferry service** (☎ 01638 22 32-0; www.wolfgangseeschifffahrt.at; ☺ early May-late Oct) operates from Strobl to St Gilgen, stopping at various points en route. Services are more frequent between early June and early September. Boats run from St Wolfgang to St Gilgen (€5, 45 minutes, hourly from 9.14am

---

IN THE FOOTSTEPS OF THE PILGRIMS

A historic path, the pilgrim's way, connects St Gilgen and St Wolfgang via the western shore. In the past pilgrims followed this path in honour of St Wolfgang, the bishop who was said to have founded the church in St Wolfgang village by throwing his axe from the Falkenstein hill into the valley below and building on the spot where it fell.

The walk takes half a day and route maps are available from the tourist offices in St Wolfgang and St Gilgen. The path starts from Furberg, near St Gilgen, and climbs the Falkenstein (795m) before continuing through the village of Reid to St Wolfgang. Apart from the fairly steep climb to the top, the walk isn't too strenuous (remind yourself that many pilgrims did it with lentils in their shoes or naked with iron rings around their necks as a sign of penance!). There are various things to see along the way, including a stone that still apparently bears the marks of the saint's buttocks. It became as soft as wax in a miracle sent by God to help the saint rest his weary bones.

---

to 8.15pm, half-hourly from July to September). In the other direction, the first departure from St Gilgen is at 9.15am.

Schafberg

Wolfgangsee is dominated by the 1783m **Schafberg** mountain on its northern shore. At the summit you'll find a hotel, a restaurant and phenomenal views over mountains and lakes (especially Mondsee, Attersee and, of course, Wolfgangsee). If you don't fancy the three- to four-hour walk from St Wolfgang (early tourists were carried up in sedan chairs), ride the **Schafbergbahn** (cogwheel railway; ☎ 06138 2232-0; one-way/return €13/22, 40 min), which runs from early May to late October. Departures are approximately hourly between 8.25am and 5.40pm, but the trip is so popular that you probably won't be able to get on the next train to leave. Queue early, purchase a ticket for a specified train and then go for a wander along the lake or around St Wolfgang until your train departs.

ST WOLFGANG

☎ 06138 / pop 3000

St Wolfgang is a peaceful and charming little village built on the steep banks of the Wolfgangsee. On summer evenings there's nothing like a tranquil stroll along the wooded lakeshore past the gently creaking wooden boathouses.

The village's main fame came as a place of pilgrimage (see above) and today's visitors still come to see the 14th-century pilgrimage church, packed with art treasures.

Orientation & Information

The main streets of Pilgerstrasse and Michael Pacher Strasse join at the pilgrimage church. A road tunnel bypasses the village centre, and there are car parks at either end of it.

Tourist office (☎ 8003; www.wolfgangsee.at; Au 140; ☉ 9am-8pm Mon-Fri, 9am-12pm & 2-6pm Sat, 1-5pm Sun Jul & Aug only) At the eastern tunnel entrance.

Pilgerstrasse Branch (Michael Pacher Haus, Pilgerstrasse; ☉ 9am-12pm & 2-5pm Mon-Fri) At the other end of town, near the road tunnel.

Sights & Activities

St Wolfgang's incredible **Wallfahrtskirche** (☎ 2321; donation €0.80; ☉ 9am-6pm) was built in the 14th and 15th centuries and is virtually a gallery of religious art, with several altars (from Gothic to baroque), a showy pulpit, a fine organ and many statues and paintings. The most impressive piece is the winged high altar, built by celebrated religious artist Michael Pacher between 1471 and 1481 – it's a perfect example of the German gothic style, enhanced with the technical achievements of Renaissance Italy. The luminous colours of the paintings on the wings are as impressive as the gilded figures in the centre and the detail is incredible, right down to the notes of the music played by the hovering angels. So important was the altar that the wings were traditionally kept closed except for important festivals. Now they are always open, except for eight weeks before Easter.

Another altar, made 200 years later, stands over the spot where St Wolfgang's axe is supposed to have landed. There's also a small museum containing more religious works of art, including folk art pieces donated by pilgrims.

A tourist office booklet details the many **water sports** on offer. A few minutes' walk anticlockwise round the lake is the start of the Schafberg railway.

Sleeping

St Wolfgang has some good private rooms in village homes or in farmhouses in the surrounding hills. Lists are available from the tourist office, which will phone places on your behalf.

Im Weissen Rössl (☎ 2306-0; www.weissesroessl .at; Im Stöckl 74; s with breakfast €117-127, d with breakfast €92-102; **P** ▯ ▤) This is St Wolfgang's most famous hotel, the setting for Ralph Benatzky's operetta *The White Horse*. The lake-view rooms are done in a modern, bland style, but the more rustic 'romantic' rooms are more interesting, with wooden ceilings and dark-wood furniture. Some of the bathrooms are rather small.

Hotel Peter (☎ 2304; www.tiscover.at/hotel.peter; s with breakfast €65-70, d with breakfast €104-110; **P** ⊠ ▤) The generous-sized rooms at this four-star place have balconies looking onto the lake, large bathrooms and tasteful décor. The **restaurant** (mains €3.30-15) also has a terrace overlooking the lake, with an interesting menu – try the fish soup.

Gästehaus Raudaschl (☎ 2329; raudaschl-158@inter aktive.com; Pilgerstrasse 4; s/d with breakfast €27/52) This central place next to the Raudaschl supermarket offers convenient, homey and reasonably comfortable rooms.

Haus am See (☎ 2224; Michael Pacher Strasse 98; s/d without bathroom €25/50; **P**) The Haus am See offers basic rooms (with saggy mattresses!) but exudes a run-down charm, with views over the lake from the sloping garden. It's also conveniently right opposite the Au bus stop.

Camping Appesbach (☎ 2206; Au 99; per adult/tent €5/4; ☾ Easter-1 Oct). This campsite is on the lakeside, 1km from St Wolfgang in the direction of Strobl.

Eating & Drinking

There are dozens of hotels and cafés in St Wolfgang's compact village centre; stroll around and make your choice.

Im Weissen Rössl (☎ 2306-0; Im Stöckl 74; mains €7.50-17; ☾ lunch & dinner) There are two restaurants in this well-regarded hotel – the Kaiserterrasse (upstairs) is uninterestingly decorated, without much atmosphere, but the downstairs brasserie is a bit brighter and very popular with day-trip parties.

Kraftstoff-Bar (☎ 2491; Markt 128; mains €5-11; ☾ lunch & dinner) This informal bar/restaurant next door to Haus am See has a tiny but rather charming lake balcony and excellent, plain food – try the sumptuous smoked fish platter (€9).

There's a Konsum supermarket 200m from the Schafbergbahn.

Getting There & Away

The only road to St Wolfgang approaches from the east from Strobl. The Bundesbus service from St Wolfgang to St Gilgen (€4, 50 minutes, 11 daily) and Salzburg (€8.20, 100 minutes, 11 daily) goes via Strobl, where you usually have to change buses. Wolfgangsee ferries stop at the village centre (stop: Markt) and at the Schafberg railway.

ST GILGEN

☎ 06227 / pop 3700

The ease of access to St Gilgen, 29km from Salzburg, has boosted its popularity. Apart from the very scenic setting and the usual lake watersports, the main attraction of the town is the charming musical-instrument museum.

Information

Café Donner (☎ 2208; Pichlerplatz 4; per min €0.20; ☾ 11am-11pm summer only) Internet access, near the Rathaus.

Tourist office (☎ 2348; www.wolfgangsee.at; Mondsee Bundesstrasse 1a; ☾ 9am-noon & 2-5pm Mon-Fri 16 Oct-30 Apr, 9am-noon & 2-6pm Mon-Fri May, 9am-7pm 1 Jun-17 Sep, 9am- noon & 2-5pm Mon-Fri 18 Sep-15 Oct) Helps find rooms.

Sights & Activities

The cosy little **Muzikinstumente Museum der Völker** (Folk Music Instrument Museum; ☎ 8235; Sonnenburggasse 1; admission €4; ☾ 9-11am & 3-7pm Tue-Sun) contains 1800 musical instruments from all over the world, which were all collected by one family of music teachers. The son of the family, Askold zum Eck, knows how to play them all and will happily demonstrate for hours. Visitors are welcome to have a go anything from an African drum to an Indian sitar. There are some truly beautiful objects here and the family's enthusiasm is infectious.

Like all Austrian lakeside resorts, St Gilgen offers **water sports** such as windsurfing, water-skiing and sailing. There's a town swimming pool and a small, free beach with a grassy area beyond the yacht marina.

The mountain rising over the resort is **Zwölferhorn** (1520m); a cable car (€17 return) will whisk you to the top where there are good views and walks. Skiers ascend in winter.

Sleeping & Eating

Gasthof Zur Post (☎ 2157; www.gasthofzurpost.at; Mozartplatz 8; s with breakfast €61-63, d with breakfast €92-96; P ☒ ▣) The 'post-gesichte' rooms at this old inn are beautifully designed, with open-plan bathrooms and a rustic but contemporary style, managing to be minimalist and cosy at the same time. There are heavy wooden beds, interesting colour schemes and pale-wood floors. The rest of the rooms are also very comfortable, just not so interestingly decorated. The **restaurant** (mains €7.20-21; ☒ lunch & dinner) here serves national and regional specialities in a low-ceilinged, whitewashed dining room or outside on the elegant terrace.

Pension Falkensteiner (☎ 6227; www.pension-falkensteiner@aon.at; Salzburgerstrasse 13; s/d with breakfast €28/56; P) This convenient pension has spotless, large and comfortable rooms for reasonable prices.

Gasthof Rosam (☎ 2591; rosam@aon.at; Frontfestgasse 2; s with breakfast €25, d with breakfast €42-66; ☒ Easter-late Oct) This family-run place down by the lake has fresh, new-looking rooms and a small **restaurant** (mains €5-12; ☒ lunch & dinner, closed Wed Apr-May) serving hearty portions of Austrian food.

Jugendgästehaus Schafbergblick (☎ 2365-75; www.oejhv.or.at; Mondseestrasse 7; dm €13-18.80, d €15.20-21; ☒ reception 8am-1pm & 5-7pm Mon-Fri, 9am & 5-7pm Sat & Sun; P) This upmarket youth hostel has a good position near the town swimming beach. Night keys are available.

Fischer-Wirt Restaurant (☎ 2304; Ischlerstrasse 21; mains €8.80-35; ☒ lunch & dinner Tue-Sun, daily Jul & Aug, closed 1 Jan-Ash Wednesday) This is the place to come for a fish feast – the menu features delights such as fresh trout (€13.70) and seafood spaghetti (€10.50), plus a fish platter for two. There are some meat dishes, as well.

San Giorgio (☎ 203 90; Ischler Strasse 18; pizza €5.80-7.90; ☒ lunch & dinner) This Italian restaurant by the lake has eat-in (inside or in the garden) or take-away food. It also has a bar/disco downstairs, the **Zwolfer Alm Bar** (☒ from 9pm summer only) which claims to be the oldest nightclub in Austria (it was founded in 1930!).

Getting There & Away

St Gilgen is 50 minutes from Salzburg by Bundesbus (€4.40), with hourly departures until early evening; some buses continue on to Stobl and Bad Ischl. The bus station is near the base station of the cable car. Highway 154 provides a scenic route north to Mondsee. For details on the ferry service to/from St Wolfgang, see p227.

MONDSEE
☎ 06232 / pop 3100

The village of Mondsee is on the northern tip of the crescent-shaped lake, noted for its warm water; coupled with its closeness to Salzburg (30km away), this makes it a popular lake for weekending Salzburgers to come for swimming and watersports.

The village **tourist office** (☎ 2270; www.mondsee.at; Dr Franz Müller Strasse 3; ☒ 8am-12pm & 1-5pm Mon-Fri Oct-May, 8am-12pm & 1-6pm Mon-Fri, 8am-12pm & 3-6pm Sat Jun-Sep) is between the church and the lake.

Sights & Activities

The lemon-yellow baroque façade of the 15th-century **Parish church** (☒ 8am-7pm) was added in 1740. This large church achieved brief fame when featured in the wedding scenes of *The Sound of Music*, but it's worth visiting in any case for its black and gold altars and many statues.

The rather small **Museum Mondseeland und Pfahlbaumuseum** (Wrede Platz; adult/student €3/1.50; ☒ 10am-6pm Tue-Sun 1 May-end Oct) next door to the church has displays on the Stone Age finds and the monastic culture of the region (Mondsee is the site of the oldest monastery in Austria). There's also a replica of a traditional farmhouse.

The **Segelschule Mondsee** (☎ 3548-200; www.segelschule-mondsee.at - in German; Robert Baum Promenade 3) is the largest sailing school in Austria. It offers sailing (one week €205) and windsurfing (two days €99) courses.

Sleeping

For lists of hotels and restaurants, ask at the tourist office.

Leitner Bräu (☎ 6500; www.leitnerbraeu.at; Steinerbachstrasse 6; s with breakfast €69-82, d with breakfast €112-150; P X Q) This four-star hotel faces the Marktplatz. Some of the light and airy rooms have a view of the square and the church – ask when booking. There's a sauna, steam bath and small gym on site. The restaurant, **Jedermann's** (Marktplatz 9; mains €7.60-16.80; ⏰ lunch & dinner Tue-Sat, lunch Sun, dinner Mon), has tables outside on the square.

Gasthof Grüner Baum (☎ 2314; gruenerbaum.mond see@aon.net; Herzog Odilo Strasse 39; s/d with breakfast €55/66) This pension has large, modern and clean rooms, but it's a bit overpriced and the landlady isn't friendly.

Jugendgästehaus (☎ 2418; www.oejhv.or.at; Kran-kenhausstrasse 9; dm/s/d €16.80/26.50/38; ⏰ 1 Feb–mid-Dec, reception 8am-1pm & 5-7pm Mon-Fri, 5-7pm Sat & Sun & holidays; P X) This HI hostel has 70 beds and is conveniently close to the town centre.

Eating
Gasthof Blaue Traube (☎ 2237; Marktplatz 1; mains €6-14.60; ⏰ lunch & dinner) This restaurant, opposite the church, serves Austrian food and great ice creams.

Shrimps Krimps & Co (☎ 6009; Herzog Odilo Strasse 25; mains €7.90-12.50; ⏰ lunch & dinner Thu-Mon, dinner Wed, closed Tue) Strange choice of name for a restaurant that specialises in steaks – although there is a lighter weekday menu available.

For self-caterers, there's a Spar supermarket on Rainerstrasse 5.

Getting There & Away
Plenty of Bundesbus routes run to/from Mondsee, including an hourly service from Salzburg (€4.60, 45 minutes). However, there are only three buses a day to St Gilgen (€4.50, 20 minutes).

Salzburg & Salzburger Land

SALZBURG &
SALZBURGER LAND

The city of Salzburg, famous as Mozart's birthplace and home to a world-famous classical-music tradition, is second only to Vienna in popularity with visitors. Devotees of a rather different musical genre are also drawn to the region in surprising numbers: in 1964 Salzburg and its surrounding hills were alive with the making of the blockbuster Hollywood film, *The Sound of Music*.

Salzburg itself, with its baroque architecture and cultural events, merits a stay of at least a week, but it's well worth allowing some time to explore the wider area of Salzburg province too. Surrounding the city is a scenic landscape filled with dramatic mountain ranges, salt mines, monumental ice caves and fairytale hilltop castles. Excellent transport links in the region mean that it's easy to combine a bit of urban bustle and sophistication with wide-open spaces, physical adventure and pastoral tranquillity in the course of a single visit.

Historically, Salzburg Province was part of the domain of a succession of all-powerful prince-archbishops, who lorded it over parts of Bavaria and Italy at the same time. The province's munificent wealth was built on humble origins – the mining of salt, the so-called 'white gold' that had been more valuable than the real thing since Celtic times. There are still several salt mines to visit in the area around Salzburg and the region's place names (salt being *Salz* in German) reflect the importance of salt in the province's long history.

Salzburg Province also has the largest part of the magnificent Hohe Tauern National Park. In the southwest of the province, the Salzach river marks the border with Germany, making it easy to combine a trip to Salzburg with southern Germany, a region which retains strong cultural links with Austria.

HIGHLIGHTS

- Taking in a Mozart operetta or a string quartet in the Marble Hall of **Schloss Mirabell** (p238), with chandeliers twinkling overhead
- Strolling around the trick water fountains of **Schloss Hellbrunn** (p250), the most magnificent of Salzburg's lordly residences
- Quaffing beer from giant earthenware mugs in the down-to-earth surroundings of the **Augustiner Bräustübl** (p247)
- Watching falcons wheel and sweep over the medieval ramparts of Werfen's **Burg Hohenwerfen** (p252)
- Gazing at sparkling towers of ice, brilliantly lit up in the chilly confines of the **Eisriesenwelt ice caves** (p252)

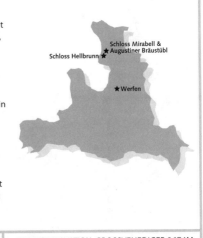

- POPULATION: 523,500
- AREA: 7154 SQ KM
- HIGHEST ELEVATION: GROSSVENEDIGER 3674M

History

Salzburg was the chief town in the region as far back as Roman times, when a town named Iuvavum stood on the site of the present-day city. This bastion of the Roman empire came under constant attack from warlike Celtic tribes and was ultimately destroyed by them or abandoned due to disease.

The first Christian kingdom in this part of Austria was established in about 696 by St Rupert. As the centuries passed, the successive archbishops of Salzburg gradually increased their temporal power, eventually being given the grandiose titles of princes of the Holy Roman Empire.

Wolf Dietrich von Raitenau (1587–1612), one of Salzburg's most influential archbishops, instigated the baroque reconstruction of the city, commissioning many of its most beautiful buildings. He fell from power after losing a dispute over salt with the powerful rulers of Bavaria and died a prisoner.

Another of the city's archbishops, Paris Lodron (1619–53), managed to keep the principality out of the Europe-wide destruction that was the Thirty Years' War. Salzburg also remained neutral during the War of the Austrian Succession that came a century later, but the province's power was gradually weakening; during the Napoleonic Wars Salzburg was controlled by France and Bavaria. It became part of Austria in 1816.

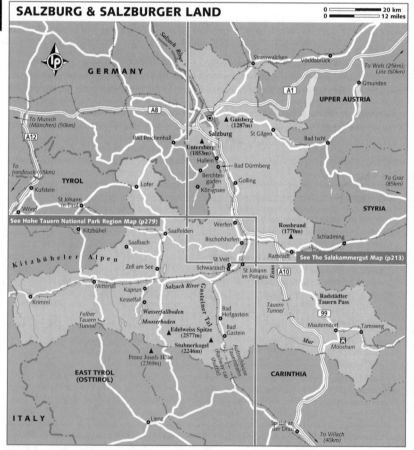

SALZBURG & SALZBURGER LAND

MARK HONAN

The winged high altar of Wallfahrtskirche (p226), St Wolfgang,
Salzkammergut

Overleaf:
The façades of *Hauptplatz*
(main square), Mariazell
(p203), Styria

MARK HONAN

MARK HC

The rooftops of Graz (p187), Styria

The town of Hallstatt (p216) overlooking Hallstätter See, Salzkammergut

MARK HO

Climate

Average temperatures in Salzburg range from 23°C in July and August to -1°C in January. In the mountains winter brings heavy snowfalls and much lower temperatures, with cooler but sunny days in summer. Spring is the wettest time, with an average of 13 rainy days per month.

National Parks

A large part of the famous Hohe Tauern National Park lies within Salzburg province. This area is dealt with separately (p277).

Getting There & Away

Salzburg is well connected by public transport to the rest of Austria, with good rail and road connections to the neighbouring area of Salzkammergut and down into Hohe Tauern National Park. Germany, Italy and the Czech republic have good train connections from Salzburg's *Hauptbahnhof* (main train station; p249).

By road, the main routes into the region are the A8 from Munich and the A1 from Linz. To enter Salzburg Province from Carinthia and the south, you can use the A10 from Spittal an der Drau or the Autoschleuse Tauernbahn (Railway Car Shuttle) south of Bad Gastein.

Both normal and no-frills flights from Europe and the USA come into Salzburg airport (p362), a half-hour bus ride from the city.

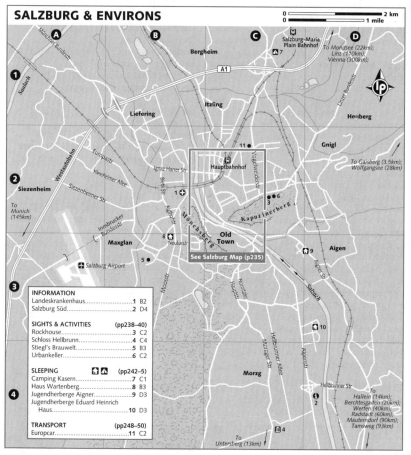

SALZBURG & ENVIRONS

```
INFORMATION
Landeskrankenhaus.............................1  B2
Salzburg Süd........................................2  D4

SIGHTS & ACTIVITIES         (pp238–40)
Rockhouse..........................................3  C2
Schloss Hellbrunn...............................4  C4
Stiegl's Brauwelt................................5  B3
Urbankeller........................................6  C2

SLEEPING                      (pp242–5)
Camping Kasern...................................7  C1
Haus Wartenberg................................8  B3
Jugendherberge Aigner.........................9  D3
Jugendherberge Eduard Heinrich
    Haus...........................................10  D3

TRANSPORT                     (pp248–50)
Europcar..........................................11  C2
```

Getting Around

Salzburg's efficient network of bus and train routes should make it relatively easy to reach even the province's smaller villages. Salzburg itself is small enough to walk around but also has a network of city buses and trains (p249). Tourist offices in the province sell the **Salzburgerland Card** (www.salzburgerlandcard.com), which gives discounts on attractions in the province (six-day card adult/child €34/17).

SALZBURG

☎ 0662 / pop 145, 800

The delicate, slender spires of Salzburg's old town nestle up against the craggy cliff face of the Mönchsberg mountain, with the forbidding fortress of Festung Hohensalzburg glowering down on them. In the narrow streets of the old town, elegant shop façades are festooned with elaborate iron-and-gilt signs, and horse-drawn carriages clop past elaborate churches that pay tribute to the city's history as a spiritual centre. Inside the marble-and-gold coffee shops, smartly dressed locals take refuge from the ubiquitous tour groups, while nibbling the town's signature chocolate, *Mozartkugeln* (Mozart balls), and sipping frothy coffee.

Salzburg's popularity with tourists is not a new phenomenon. Its decline into poverty in the 18th century was a blessing in disguise, ensuring that the historic buildings were repaired rather than replaced. The city began attracting well-heeled visitors from the early 19th century onwards.

Another fortuitous event for Salzburg's tourist industry was the birth in 1756 of a certain Wolfgang Amadeus Mozart, who spent his childhood in a modest apartment in the city centre. Ironically, the city that gave the composer scant encouragement during his lifetime is now defined by him – Mozart's works stream out from every shop and café, and his music dominates both the festival performances of world-class orchestras and the hopeful scrapings of street buskers.

Orientation

The city centre is split by the Salzach River. The compact, pedestrianised old town (officially called the Salzburg Historic Centre and known to locals as the Altstadt) is on the *linkes Salzachufer* (left/west bank). Most of the obvious tourist attractions are on this side of the river. The new town is on the *rechtes Salzachufer* (right/east bank), along with most of the cheaper hotels.

Mirabellplatz, on the right bank, is a hub for both local buses and city tours. A little further north is the *Hauptbahnhof*, with the Bundesbus station outside it. Bus 2 runs from the airport to the *Hauptbahnhof*.

MAPS

The tourist offices sell a city map for €0.70, but you could just as easily get by with the free central-city map on offer at most hotels. City maps are also on sale at most bookshops and souvenir kiosks.

Information
BOOKSHOPS

Motzko (Map p235; ☎ 88 33 11; Elisabethstrasse 1) Stocks English-language books.
Motzko Reise (Map p235; Rainerstrasse) Across the road from Motzko; sells maps and guidebooks.
News and Books (Map p235; Hauptbahnhof platform 2a) International newspapers and magazines.

EMERGENCY

Ambulance (☎ 144)
Hospital (Landeskrankenhaus; Map p233; ☎ 44 82-0; Müllner Hauptstrasse 48) Just north of the Mönchsberg.
Police headquarters (Map p235; ☎ 63 83-0; Alpenstrasse 90)

INTERNET ACCESS

Internet cafés are scattered all over Salzburg. Those in the area around the train station are much cheaper than those in the old town.
Piterfun (Map p235; ☎ 878 414; office@piterfun.at; Ferdinand Porsche Strasse 7; per hr €5; ⏰ 11am-11pm)
International Telephone Discount (Map p235; ☎ 88 31 94; Kaiserschützenstrasse 8; per hr €4.20; ⏰ 9am-11pm) Also has cheap international telephone calls.
Bignet (Map pp236-7; ☎ 841 470; www.bignet.at; Judengasse 5-7; per hr €9; ⏰ 9am-10pm) Discounted phone calls, drinks and snacks.

LAUNDRY

Norge Exquisit (Map pp236–7; ☎ 87 63 81; Paris Lodron Strasse 16; self-service wash €10; ⏰ 7am-6pm Mon-Fri, 8am-12pm Sat)

LEFT LUGGAGE

In addition to the usual luggage lockers in the station, the tourist office can hold luggage for €1 per day (deposit of €5).

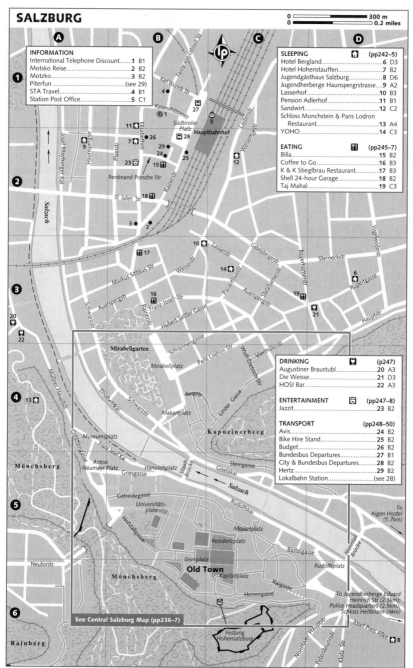

SALZBURG

| 0 | 300 m |
| 0 | 0.2 miles |

INFORMATION
International Telephone Discount......**1** B1
Motsko Reise...........................**2** B2
Motzko................................**3** B2
Piterfun..........................(see 29)
STA Travel...........................**4** B1
Station Post Office...................**5** C1

SLEEPING (pp242–5)
Hotel Bergland...........................**6** D3
Hotel Hohenstauffen.......................**7** B2
Jugendgästhaus Salzburg...................**8** D6
Jugendherberge Haunspergstrasse....**9** A2
Lasserhof.............................**10** B3
Pension Adlerhof......................**11** B1
Sandwirt.............................**12** C2
Schloss Monchstein & Paris Lodron
  Restaurant........................**13** A4
YOHO..................................**14** C3

EATING (pp245–7)
Billa.................................**15** B2
Coffee to Go..........................**16** B3
K & K Stieglbrau Restaurant...........**17** B3
Shell 24-hour Garage..................**18** B2
Taj Mahal.............................**19** C3

DRINKING (p247)
Augustiner Braustubl..................**20** A3
Die Weisse............................**21** D3
HOSI Bar..............................**22** A3

ENTERTAINMENT (pp247–8)
Jazzit................................**23** B2

TRANSPORT (pp248–50)
Avis..................................**24** B2
Bike Hire Stand.......................**25** B2
Budget................................**26** B2
Bundesbus Departures..................**27** B1
City & Bundesbus Departures...........**28** B2
Hertz.................................**29** B2
Lokalbahn Station..................(see 28)

SALZBURG &
SALZBURGER LAND

See Central Salzburg Map (pp236–7)

MONEY

Normal banking hours are from 8.30am to 12.30pm and 2pm to 4.30pm Monday to Friday, although some branches and exchange offices are open for longer hours, particularly in the summer. Western Union changes money at its branch in the **Hauptbahnhof** (Map p235; ☎ 9300 03-162; 🕑 8.30am-7pm Mon-Fri, 8.30am-4.30pm Sat). At the airport, exchange booths are open all day every day. There are also plenty of exchange offices downtown, but beware of high commission rates. *Bankomats* (ATMs) are all over the place.

American Express (Map pp236-7; ☎ 80 80; Mozartplatz 5; 🕑 9am-5.30pm Mon-Fri, 9am-12pm Sat & Sun) is next to the tourist office. Amex travellers cheques are cashed here free of charge. **Hotel Weisse Taube** (Kaigasse 9) also exchanges Amex cheques at the same rate (with no commission).

TOURIST INFORMATION

The **main tourist office** (Map pp236-7; ☎ 889 87-330; www.salzburg.info; Mozartplatz 5; 🕑 9am-6pm Mon-Sat 1 Jan-30 Apr & 15 Oct-30 Nov, 9am-7pm 1 May-14 Oct & 1-31 Dec). There's a ticket booking agency in the same building. This office mostly has information about the city and immediate surroundings – for information about the rest of the province, contact **Salzburgerland Tourismus** (☎ 66-880; www.salzburgerland.com).

Other information offices are at arrival points to the city:

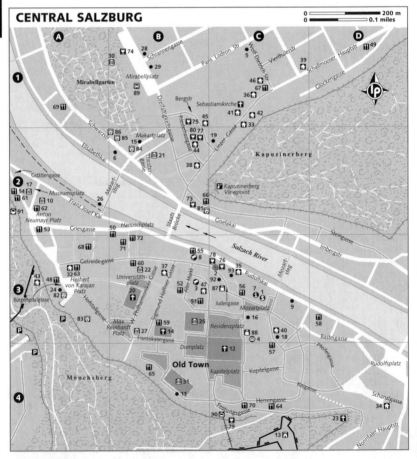

Hauptbahnhof (Map p235; ☎ 889 87-340; Platform 2a; ⌚ 8.30am- 8pm May & Sep, 8.30am-8.30pm Jun & Jul, 8.30am-9pm Aug, 8.30am-7pm Sep-Apr)

Salzburg Süd (Map p233; ☎ 889 87-360; Park & Ride Parkplatz, Alpensiedlung Süd, Alpenstrasse; ⌚ 10am- 6pm Mon-Sat Apr-15 Oct)

Staff at all of the branch tourist offices will book rooms in hotels and pensions; a normal commission is €2.20.

Salzburg Information (☎ 889 87-0; fax 889 87-32; www.salzburginfo.at) is the head tourism office for the region. Advance hotel reservations placed through this office (☎ 889 87-314; fax 889 87-32) are free. It also deals with marketing and congress inquiries and sends out tourist brochures (☎ 889 87-430; fax 889 87-435), but for in-person inquiries go to the Mozartplatz office.

Salzburg's tourist offices provide a comprehensive booklet in English and German entitled *Salzburg – Barrierfrei Erleben*, which contains information on Salzburg's facilities for disabled people. It goes into great detail, including dimensions of hotel rooms and availability of roll-under tables in restaurants, plus information on lifts, wheelchair access and disabled toilets.

Tourist offices and hotels sell the **Salzburg Card** (low/high season for a 24hr card €19/21, for 48hrs €26/28, for 72hrs €32/34). This provides free entry to every sight in town and reduced entry to a further 24 attractions plus free public transport for the duration.

Salzburg Plus is a prepaid card that has the Salzburg Card benefits but also covers meals, accommodation and shows. The price starts at €111 but depends on what you include; inquire at tourist offices. The free *Salzburg Card* booklet details opening hours and entry fees for important sights.

POST

Station post office (Map pp236-7; Bahnhofspostamt 5020, Südtiroler Platz 17; ⌚ 7am-8.30pm Mon-Fri, 8am-2pm Sat, 1-6pm Sun)

Main post office (Map p235; Hauptpostamt 5010, Residenzplatz 9; ⌚ 7am-7pm Mon-Fri, 8am-10am Sat)

TRAVEL AGENCIES

STA Travel (Map p235; ☎ 45 87 33; www.statravel.at; Fanny-von-Lehnert Strasse 1) Student and budget travel agency.

Salzburger Landesreisebüro (Map pp236-7; ☎ 87 34 03; www.verkehrsbuero.at - in German; Schwarzstrasse 11) Also issues train tickets.

SALZBURG & SALZBURGER LAND

Sights

Many of Salzburg's sights, as well as a lot of restaurants, remain open every day or extend their opening hours during the Salzburger Festspiele (p241) in August. The hours given here are for non-festival times.

FESTUNG HOHENSALZBURG

A steep 15-minute walk from the city centre, **Festung Hohensalzburg** (Hohensalzburg Fortress; Map p235; ☎ 84 24 30 11; Mönchsberg; admission to courtyards adult/child €3.60/2, to interior extra adult/child €3.60/2; ⏰ 9.30am-5.30pm Feb-May, 9.30am-6pm Jun-Sep, 9.30am-5pm Oct-Jan) was built over the centuries by successive prince-archbishops, with the greatest influence on its present form coming from Leonard von Keutschach, Archbishop of Salzburg from 1495 to 1519. His rather prosaic symbol was the turnip and this peculiar motif appears 58 times around the castle, usually as a wall relief. The deposed Archbishop Wolf Dietrich died in 1612 a prisoner within the walls of the fortress he helped to create.

The outlook to the north over the city is simply stupendous, with the view to the south presenting a vista of Alpine peaks, including the **Untersberg** (1853m). Inside, the English audio guide included in the entry price will take you through a series of opulent rooms, providing an excellent idea of the late-Gothic ducal style of living. There are also two small museums (allow about 20 minutes for each) covering arms, puppets, WWII photos and tools of the torturer's trade.

If you don't want to walk up to the fortress, you can take the expensive **Festungsbahn funicular** (Map pp236-7; ☎ 84 26 82; Festungsgasse 4; one-way/return €5.60/8.50; ⏰ 9am-5pm Feb-Apr, 9am-10pm May-Aug, 9am-9.30pm Sep, 9am-5pm Oct-Dec, closed 7-30 Jan), which whisks you to the top in just 60 seconds.

SCHLOSS MIRABELL

The palace in Mirabellgarten, **Schloss Mirabell** (Map pp236-7), was built by the less-than-chaste Prince-Archbishop Wolf Dietrich for his mistress, the fabulously named Salome Alt, in 1606. Salome bore the archbishop at least 10 children (sources disagree on the exact number – poor Wolf was presumably too distracted by spiritual matters to keep count himself). Johann Lukas von Hildebrandt gave the building a more baroque appearance in 1727. Its ornate **Mirabellgar-**ten (formal gardens) were featured in *The Sound of Music* and today are one of the city's most attractive green spaces, popular with locals and tourists as a place to stroll or relax. The interior is now home to the mayor's offices, but is worth a peep for the **marble staircase** (⏰ 8am-4pm Mon-Fri), adorned with baroque sculptures. The best way to experience the Mirabell magic is to attend one of the lunchtime or evening concerts (p247) in the magnificent marble hall, with its chandeliers and wall reliefs.

MOZART'S HOUSES

There are two Mozart museums in Salzburg; they're popular, pricey and cover similar ground. Both contain musical instruments, sheet music and other memorabilia of the great man. You can save money by buying a combined ticket for both (adult/concession €9/3).

Mozarts Geburtshaus (Mozart's Birthplace; Map pp236-7; ☎ 84 43 13; www.mozarteum.at - in German; Getreidegasse 9; adult/concession €6/1.50; ⏰ 9am-7pm Jul & Aug, 9am-6pm Sep-Jun) is where he lived for the first 17 years of his life. Modest displays include the mini-violin that little Wolfgang played as a toddler.

The **Mozart-Wohnhaus** (Mozart's Residence; Map pp236-7; ☎ 87 42 27-40; www.mozarteum.at; Makartplatz 8; adult/concession €6/1.50; ⏰ 9am-7pm Jul & Aug, 9am-6pm Sep-Jun) is more interesting, with a more high-tech, imaginative approach. Commentary and musical excerpts are delivered via hand-held devices activated by infrared signals and there's a slide show that concentrates on Mozart's early years and extensive travels. In the same building is the **Mozart Ton-und Filmmuseum** (Map pp236-7; ☎ 88 34 54; Makartplatz 8; admission free; ⏰ 9am-1pm Mon, Tue & Fri, 1-5pm Wed & Thu), an archive of film and musical material mostly of interest to the ultra-enthusiast or research student.

HAUS DER NATUR

Salzburg's Natural History Museum, the **Haus der Natur** (Map pp236-7; ☎ 84 26 53; www.hausdernatur.at; Museumplatz 5; adult/child €4.50/2.50; ⏰ 9am-5pm) is a particularly fine example of the genre that will account for hours of a rainy afternoon, particularly if you have kids in tow. The best feature is an extensive and imaginatively designed aquarium on the ground floor, complete with piranhas, 'Nemo'-style clownfish and some beautiful living coral. The live-reptile house on the second floor has an interesting, pale-coloured Burmese python plus iguanas and freshwater crocodiles. In between, there are interactive displays on everything from astronomy to glaciers. Some of the explanations are in English.

RESIDENZ STATE ROOMS AND GALLERY

Overlooking Residenzplatz, the **Residenz** (Map pp236-7; ☎ 80 42-26 90; www.salzburg-burgen.at; Residenzplatz 1; adult/concession €7.30/2.50; ☼ 10am-5pm) is a less-than-modest home that allows you to see the baroque luxury Salzburg's archbishops went home to after a hard day preaching about humility and poverty. An audio guide takes you round the opulent staterooms, festooned with valuable tapestries and works of art, including frescoes by Johann Michael Rottmayr (p40). The admission price includes the **Residenz Galerie** (☎ 84 04 51; www.residenzgalerie.at; Residenzplatz 1; ☼ 10am-5pm, closed Mon), though this can also be visited separately (adult/concession €5/2). It's an art gallery that displays European art from the 16th to 19th centuries and includes a good selection of Dutch and Flemish works.

STIEGL'S BRAUWELT

Austria's largest private **brewery** (Map p233; ☎ 83 87-14 92; Bräuhausstrasse 9; adult/concession €9/8.30; ☼ 10am-5pm Wed-Sun Jun-Sep). The extensive museum takes you through the brewing process (it tries very hard to make this interesting, but mostly fails) and persuasively makes the case that beer is a very good thing indeed. It's pretty good value, considering the entry price includes a small gift and a trip to the bar for two free beers and a fresh pretzel. Take bus No 1 or 2 to Bräuhausstrasse.

RUPERTINUM

Also of interest in the old town is the **Rupertinum** (Map pp236-7; ☎ 80 42-36; www.museumdermoderne.at; Wiener Philharmoniker Gasse 9; adult/concession €9/5.50; ☼ 10am-6pm Thu-Tue, 10am-9pm Wed), a modern art museum in which most space is devoted to rolling temporary exhibitions. Check the website for news of a new, bigger modern art museum due to open in October 2004 at the top of the Mönchsberg lift.

CAROLINO AUGUSTEUM MUSEUM

Opposite the Haus der Natur, the **Carolino Augusteum Museum** (Map pp236-7; ☎ 84 11 34-0; Museumsplatz 1; adult/senior/child €3.50/2.70/1.10; ☼ 9am-

5pm Fri-Wed, 9am-8pm Thu) covers local history and includes Roman mosaics and some fine bronze Celtic statuettes. All explanations are in German.

Activities

The old town is squeezed between Kapuzinerberg and Mönchsberg hills, both of which have a good network of footpaths for **walking**. There is a **viewpoint** (Map pp236-7) at the western end of the Kapuzinerberg, with ramparts built during the Thirty Years' War; the climb up from the stairs near the southern end of Linzer Gasse takes 10 minutes. On Mönchsberg, a good walk is from Festung Hohensalzburg down to the Augustiner Bräustübl (p247). There are also plenty of **cycling routes**; bikes are for hire in various places in Salzburg (p249).

Relatively new and extremely popular are **River Cruises** (☎ 82 58 58; www.salzburgschifffahrt.at; adult/child €11/7, to Schloss Hellbrunn €14/10). They depart almost hourly throughout the summer and several times a day in April, May, September and October. The boats start from the Makart bridge (Map pp236-7) and take about an hour, with some going further on to Schloss Hellbrunn (p250; entry to the palace is not included in the ticket price).

Walking Tour

Start this two- to three-hour walk by absorbing the bustle of **Domplatz (1)** and the adjoining **Kapitelplatz (2)** and **Residenzplatz (3)**. The hubbub from the market stall in these wide-open squares competes with the clip-clop of horses' hooves and the music of buskers. Residenzplatz also has a rooftop **Glockenspiel (4)** that chimes at 7am, 11am and 6pm.

The vast 15th-century **Dom (5**; cathedral; Domplatz) has three bronze doors symbolising – from left to right as you face them – faith, hope and charity. The cupola was rebuilt after being destroyed by a bomb in 1944. Inside, admire the dark-edged stucco, the dome and the Romanesque font where Mozart was baptised. Ecclesiastical treasures are exhibited in the attached **Dommuseum** (☎ 84 41 89; adult/child €5/1.50; ☼ 10am-5pm Mon-Sat, 11am-6pm Sun).

From here, turn left at the first courtyard off Franziskanergasse for the fabulously ornate **Stiftskirche St Peter (6**; St Peter Bezirk). Beneath a pretty green stuccoed ceiling lit by chandeliers, the walls are studded with

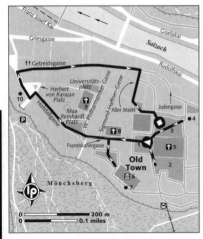

works of religious art and baroque swirls. Look out for a dramatic statue of the Archangel Michael shoving a crucifix through the throat of a goaty demon. The graveyard contains some so-called **catacombs** (**7**; Katakomben; ☎ 84 45 78-0; adult/child €1/0.60; ☿ 10.30am-5pm May-Sep, 10.30am-3.30pm Wed & Thu, 10.30am-4pm Fri-Sun Oct-Apr), which are caves used as chapels and crypts.

Returning to Franziskanergasse, you will come to the tall and elegant **Franziskanerkirche** (**8**; Franciscan Church; ☎ 84 36 29-0; Franziskanergasse 5; admission free; ☿ daylight hours), with a baroque, high altar surrounded by five pillars.

The western end of Franziskanergasse opens into Max Reinhardt Platz, where you'll see the back of Fischer von Erlach's **Kollegienkirche** (**9**; Collegiate Church; Universitätsplatz; admission free; ☿ daylight hrs), also known as the Universitätskirche. This church is considered an outstanding example of the baroque for its overall structure, but the interior is bare and almost austere compared with the ornamentation of Stiftskirche St Peter.

Walk left on leaving the church to reach Herbert von Karajan Platz and the **Pferdeschwemme** (**10**; horse trough), a rather elaborate drinking spot for the archbishops' mounts. Created in 1700, this is a horselover's delight, with rearing equine pin-ups surrounding Michael Bernhard Mandl's statue of a horse tamer.

Turn right around the corner and you'll join the bustling crowds beneath the wrought-iron shop signs along **Getreide-**gasse**. Turning right down Alter Markt will bring you back to Residenzplatz.

Courses

German-language courses are offered at **Inlingua** (Map pp236-7; ☎ 87 11 01; www.inlingua-salzburg .at; Linzer Gasse 17-19; 2/4 weeks €298/563). Salzburg Card holders get a €25 discount.

Quirky Salzburg

Don't pass **Easter in Salzburg** (Map pp236-7; ☎ 841 794; Judengasse 13) without popping in for a gawk. Spread over two glittering floors are an incredible 140,000 real eggs, each individually hand blown and hand painted by art students and housewives. Eggs are a traditional Austrian gift for New Years Eve as well as Easter, but there are eggs here of every conceivable colour and design, all hung by ribbons from artfully arranged dead branches or stacked floor to ceiling in cartons. Prices range from €2 for a modestly painted hen's egg to €146 for an ostrich egg painted with a portrait of Mozart. The shop will ship them home for you if you're too afraid to put them in your luggage. Across the road is **Christmas in Salzburg**, no less spectacular but with delicate glass baubles replacing the eggs. Just, for goodness sake, don't trip …

Tours

One-hour **walking tours** (☎ 84 04 06; www.salz burg-guide.at; €8) of the old city leave at 12.15pm daily (except Sunday during winter) from the main tourist office. You can buy tickets just before you set off from the counter in the tourist office.

Several companies run tours of the city and environs, usually with a free hotel pickup. Some also leave from Mirabellplatz.

Competition is hot, but the following three companies offer broadly the same products, the most popular of which is the *Sound of Music* Tour.

Salzburg Panorama Tours (Map pp236-7; ☎ 87 40 29; www.panoramatours.com; Schrannengasse 2) Boasts the 'original *Sound of Music*' Tour' with letters from Maria Von Trapp to prove it. Tours booked through the YOHO youth hostel are 10% cheaper.

Salzburg Sightseeing Tours (Map pp236-7; ☎ 88 16 16; www.salzburg-sightseeingtours.at; Mirabellplatz 2) This company claims one of its buses was used in the film.

Bob's Special Tours (Map pp236-7; ☎ 84 95 11; www .bobstours.com; Rudolfskai 38) Also offers a *Sound of Music* Tour in a light aircraft.

EVERYTHING YOU NEVER KNEW ABOUT *THE SOUND OF MUSIC* …

- **DO** – Director Robert Wise considered Yul Brynner, Sean Connery and Richard Burton for the role of Captain Von Trapp. Doris Day was offered the part of Maria, but declined.

- **RE** – Julie Andrews was knocked off her feet every time by the helicopter downdraft while filming the opening sequence.

- **MI** – Romantic lead Christopher Plummer hated the final movie and for ever after referred to it as 'The Sound of Mucus'.

- **FA** -The film flopped in Austria just three days after it was released. The Austrians resented their portrayal as pawns of the Nazis.

- **SO** – Charmian Carr (Liesl) slipped on the first take while leaping across a bench in the gazebo and fell through a pane of glass. The scene was later reshot with her leg strapped and makeup covering the bandages.

- **LA** – The real Maria Von Trapp (on whose life the film was based) has a cameo appearance in the movie as an Austrian peasant woman in the background of one scene.

- **TI** – One of Captain von Trapp's nephews said in a 1990 interview that his uncle was 'the most boring man who ever lived'.

- **D'OH** – A South Korean cinema owner once decided that the movie was too long, so he shortened it by cutting out all the musical scenes.

These tours last from three to four hours and all cost around €33. They take in major city sights featured in the movie and include a visit out into the Salzkammergut countryside for more movie locations. You'll see the **Nonnberg Abbey**, the church in **Mondsee** (p228) used for the wedding scenes, and Liesl's gazebo, now relocated to the gardens of **Schloss Hellbrunn** (p250). Needless to say, the soundtrack to the film is played in the buses as they bowl merrily along.

The success or otherwise of a *Sound of Music* tour really depends on the people in the bus – if you have a good crowd who are prepared to get into the whole thing with the right sense of kitsch irony, singing along and acting out scenes from the film at the various locations, it can be a real scream.

If you'd rather pedal around town in a carefree manner warbling songs from the film, opt for **Fräulein Maria's Cycling Tours** (Map pp236-7; ☎ 34 26 97; incl bike hire €16; ⌚ 9.30am 15 May-31 Aug). These tours start at 9.30 daily during the summer and last a leisurely three hours, taking in the main film locations along the route. No advance booking is necessary, so you can just turn up at the meeting point at the entrance to the Mirabell Gardens.

Festivals & Events

The **Salzburger Festspiele** (Salzburg Festival) takes place from late July to the end of August and includes music ranging from Mozart (of course!) to contemporary. This is the high point in Salzburg's cultural calendar, a time when the city takes on a new vitality and a few thousand extra tourists, too. Several events take place each day in different locations, with as many as 180 orchestral, operatic and theatrical events staged. The 2006 festival will celebrate Mozart's 250th anniversary by staging performances of all 22 of his operas – the Festspielhaus (festival hall) is being extended for the purpose.

Prices vary from €4 to €360; the cheapest prices are for standing-room tickets, which can usually be prebooked. Most tickets sell out months in advance. You can see the programme as early as the previous November on the festival's website, www.salzburg festival.at.

People under 26 years old are eligible for reduced-price deals for two or more events. Try checking closer to the event for cancellations – inquire at the **ticket office** (Map pp236-7; ☎ 84 45-500; info@salzburgfestival.at; Herbert von Karajan Platz 11; ⌚ 9am-start of last performance of the day).

Small-scale music festivals are held every Pfingstkon-zerte (Whit Sunday weekend,

ROCK ME AMADEUS

- Aged 2, Mozart identified a pig's squeal as G sharp. He presented his first public recital aged 5.
- Aged 23 Mozart fell in love with the soprano Aloysia Weber. When she rebuffed him, he promptly married her sister.
- When not composing, Mozart enjoyed billiards, heavy drinking sessions and teaching his pet starling to sing operettas.
- A boy once asked Mozart how to write a symphony. He replied that a symphony was too difficult at such a young age. 'You wrote symphonies at my age!' exclaimed the boy. 'But I didn't have to ask how' replied Mozart.
- Modern psychologists believe that Mozart suffered from Tourette's Syndrome, a disorder leading to uncontrolled outbursts of swearing and obscene behaviour.

the seventh Sunday after Easter) and Easter (www.osterfestspiele-salzburg.at). **Mozartwoche Salzburg** (Mozart Week; www.mozarteum.at - in German) is held in late January. Fittingly for the city where Silent Night was composed, Salzburg is also known for its splendid Christmas Market, which fills the Domplatz and surrounding squares every December.

Sleeping

Staying in the old town is generally more expensive and not always good value – the old, low-ceilinged rooms can get stiflingly hot on summer days and the crowds surging past the door when you step outside are hardly relaxing either. Since Salzburg is compact and easily walkable, staying on the right bank may be a more cost-effective option.

Prices in Salzburg go up sharply in high season, which comprises Easter, summer, Christmas and New Year. Accommodation is at a premium during Salzburger Festspiele so book well ahead. The price ranges shown here indicate different room sizes as well as high and low season prices.

BUDGET
HOSTELS

YOHO Salzburg (Map p235; ☎ 87 96 49; www.yoho.at; Paracelsusstrasse 9; per person in 8-/6-bed dm €15/16, q/tr/d/s per person €17/18/20/27, 1st night €1.50 extra; ☯ reception 24hr; P ☒ ☐) If you're travelling to party, this is the place to meet like-minded backpackers – there's a cheap bar and no school groups. The Sound of Music is shown at 10.30am daily and guests here get a 10% discount on Panorama's tours. Adventure activities can also be booked here. Phone reservations in busy times are accepted no

earlier than one day before. Cheap breakfasts and evening meals are also available. Prices include one shower token.

Institut St Sebastian (Map pp236-7; ☎ 87 13 86; Linzer Gasse 41; www.st-sebastian-salzburg.at; dm/s/d with breakfast €16/30/48) More expensive rooms with private bathrooms are also available at this clean and well-kept church hostel. It doubles as a student residence and has a roof terrace and kitchens. Prices are marginally lower in winter and you can check in during the day (ring the bell if reception is unstaffed).

Naturfreundehaus Stadtalm (Map pp236-7; ☎ 84 17 29; Mönchsberg 19; q/tw per person €12.35/13.30; ☯ 1 May-15 Sep, check-in 9am-9pm, curfew 1am). This basic place with marvellous views is clearly visible high on the hill west of the fortress. Take the stairway up from near Max Reinhardt Platz, or the Mönchsberg lift from Anton Neumayr Platz. It's sometimes too cold to open the dorms (no heating), so phone ahead and check availability. The restaurant provides hot meals and breakfasts.

In addition to the places above, Salzburg also has four traditional HI hostels, all clean, institutionalised and sometimes full with school groups. Prices quoted are for HI members. Non-members pay on average €3 extra.

Jugendgästehaus Salzburg (Map p235; ☎ 84 26 70-0; www.jgh.at; Josef Preis Allee 18; dm with breakfast high/low season €14/16, d per person €24/25; P ☐) Offers bike rental and discounts on Salzburg Sightseeing Tours. Half- and full-board also available.

Jugendherberge Aigen (Map p233; ☎ 62 32 48; www.lbsh-aigen.at; Aigner Strasse 34; per person in dm/q/d with breakfast €15/18/21). Open year-round, all day check-in. South of the Kapuzinerberg in Aigen, 20 minutes walk from the old town or take bus 49.

Jugendherberge Eduard Heinrich Haus (Map p235; ☎ 62 59 76; www.hostel-ehh.at; Eduard Heinrich Strasse 2; dm/s/d with breakfast €15/18/36; ☺ check-in 7am-midnight Mon-Fri, 7-10am & 5pm-midnight Sat, Sun & public holidays) South of town; bus No 51 or 95 will get you within 400m (stop: Polizeidirektion). Rooms with private bathrooms also available.

Jugendherberge Haunspergstrasse (Map p235; ☎ 87 50 30; www.lbsh-haunspergstrasse.at; Haunspergstrasse 27; dm/q/d/s per person with breakfast €15/18/20/23; ☺ 7am-midday & 5pm-midnight). West of the *Hauptbahnhof*.

PRIVATE ROOMS
Salzburg's private rooms aren't quite the bargain they are elsewhere in Austria: they cost a minimum of €20 per person anywhere near the city centre. Check the websites www.privatvermieter.com or www.salzburg.info or ask at the tourist office for a list. Prices generally go down the longer you stay.

HOTELS & PENSIONS
Sandwirt (Map p235; ☎ /fax 87 43 51; Lastenstrasse 6a; s/d/tr €23/38/54; ℗) This good-value pension is in an ugly part of town, but it's convenient for the train station (cross the tracks via the footpath bridge) and it's set back from the street. The good-sized rooms are reasonably quiet and the friendly landlady will let you use her washing machine and even the kitchen. Book well ahead.

Junger Fuchs (Map pp236-7; ☎ 87 54 96; Linzer Gasse 54; s/d/tr without bathroom €28/44/55) Despite being above a kebab shop (handy for the late-night munchies), the rooms in this conveniently located little pension are clean and spacious, with wooden floors.

Schwarzes Rössl (Map pp236-7; ☎ 87 44 26; www.academia-hotels.co.at; Priesterhausgasse 6; s/d/tr without bathroom €33/54/72) This student residence welcomes tourists from July to September. The rooms are ramshackle but big, with cute painted furniture. Other plus points: a great location and generous breakfast buffet. The shared bathrooms are rudimentary and only one shower per floor means long waits and cold water at busy times.

Hinterbrühl (Map pp236-7; ☎ 84 67 98; Schanzl-gasse 12; s/d without bathroom €42/54; ☺ reception 8am-midnight) You're paying dearly here for an old-town location, as the rooms (some with TV) are generally basic. Try to get room 14 – it's the biggest and has a balcony, private bathroom and lounge area; reception is in

the downstairs restaurant. Triple and quad rooms are also possible.

Camping Kasern (Map p233; ☎ /fax 45 05 76; www.camping-kasern-salzburg.com; Carl Zuckmayer Strasse 26; per adult/child €4.50/2.50, tent hire €10; ℗) Just north of the A1 Nord exit, within walking distance of Salzburg-Maria Plain train station.

MID-RANGE
Haus Wartenberg (Map p233; ☎ 84 42 84; www.hauswartenberg.com; Riedenburger Strasse 2; s €55-92, d €75-115; ℗ ✗ ▯) This is a fabulously eccentric and cosy hotel, brimming with character and fun and housed in a 400-year-old building. The rooms aren't terribly plush, but cosy, comfortable and imaginatively furnished with antiques and family heirlooms. It's within walking distance of the old town, and many bus routes run along nearby Neutorstrasse. The **restaurant** (mains €6.40-15.50; ☺ closed Sun) serves hearty Austrian dishes.

Hotel Bergland (Map p235; ☎ 87 23 18; www.berglandhotel.at; Rupertgasse 15; s/d €56/86; ℗ ✗ ▯) A very good option in the mid-range price category. The light, airy rooms in this friendly, stylish hotel/pension are decorated with traditional Austrian furnishings given a modern twist. The owner painted most of the pictures that hang on the walls. Bikes are available for hire at €6 per day. It is about 10 minutes' walk east of the city centre.

Lasserhof (Map p235; ☎ 87 33 88; www.lasserhof.com; Lasserstrasse 47; s €55-95, d €85-165) Sizable rooms with eye-catching features such as handmade Venetian chandeliers and traditional ceramic stoves. Some also have balconies. The staff here are friendly and efficient and prices are negotiable depending on how busy the place is.

Hotel Amadeus (Map pp236-7; ☎ 87 14 01; www.hotelamadeus.at; Linzer Gasse 43-45; s €72-82, d €112-150, q €180-220; ✗ ▯) A good three-star option on the right bank, halfway up the attractive Linzer Gasse with its smart shops. The cosy, well-maintained rooms are modern and comfortable without being soulless – they're well decorated and some even have iron four-poster beds.

Pension Adlerhof (Map p235; ☎ 87 52 36; www.pension-adlerhof.com; Elisabethstrasse 25; s/d €52/80, reductions in low season) This is another good choice, friendly and handy for the train station but not in a very pretty part of town. The more old-fashioned rooms have painted furniture and some have four-poster beds.

Cheaper rooms with shared bathrooms are available. No credit cards are accepted.

Trumer Stube (Map pp236-7; ☎ 84 47 76; www.trumer -stube.at; Bergstrasse 6; €56-89, d €89-103; ☒ ▣) This family-run pension is on the right bank, but is close to the old town, and provides clean, modern rooms with flouncy floral furnishings. Single occupancy is not usually possible in August, when double rooms go up to €118-132.

Goldene Krone (Map pp236-7; ☎ 87 23 00; office@ hotel-goldenekrone.com; Linzer Gasse 48; s with IV €55-71, d with TV €75-95; ℗) Some of the rooms here are on the small side, with cramped bathrooms, but some have church-like vaulted ceilings that add a bit of character. The walled roof terrace is a good place for a coffee on a sunny day. Receptionists don't always speak English or know much about the city.

Hotel Hohenstauffen (Map p235; ☎ 87 21 93; www .hotel-hohenstauffen.at; Elisabethstrasse 19; s €58-94, d €94-144; ℗ ☒ ▣) This hotel is convenient for the train station but could really benefit from a bit of redecoration – certain rooms are looking very tired and outdated. Even canopy beds in some rooms can't make up for ugly wallpaper, '70s bathroom tiles and nylon carpets That said, it's still comfortable, with friendly and helpful owners.

Hotel Restaurant Hofwirt (Map pp236-7; ☎ 87 21 72-0; www.hofwirt.net; Schallmooser Hauptstrasse 1; s €54-86/ d €75-120; ℗) The lobby and restaurant of this three-star hotel are dreadful: dark, gloomy and straight out of the '70s. Thankfully the rooms are perfectly clean, modern and pleasant, though hardly brimming with warmth and character.

The following places are in the old town, where parking can be limited, though many places have an arrangement for reduced prices at parking garages.

Zur Goldenen Enten (Map pp236-7; ☎ 84 56 22; www .ente.at - in German; Goldgasse 10; s €70-80, d €100-120; ☒) Charming staff preside over this 700-year-old former townhouse. Each of the fairly plain rooms is slightly different, but all are very comfortable, with welcome extra touches such as bathrobes and slippers. The downstairs **restaurant** (mains €8.50-18.50; ⌚ lunch & dinner) serves well-cooked Austrian cuisine, with great puddings.

Hotel Wolf (Map pp236-7; ☎ 84 34 53-0; www.hotel wolf.com; Kaigasse 9; s €58-98, d €80-158; ☒) A smart, classy three-star hotel with good-sized rooms in a converted old townhouse. Décor varies

from modern to rustic, but all the rooms have a bit of character, making this one of the best old-town choices.

Blaue Gans (Map pp236-7; ☎ 84 13 17; www.blauegans .at; Getreidegasse 43; s €99-119, d €135/185; ☒ ▣) The lobby of this smart designer hotel is cool and contemporary, but the bedrooms, although comfortable, are disappointingly bland and corporate. The well-regarded **restaurant** (mains €16.50-19.80; ⌚ closed Tue except Aug) is smart and simple, with vaulted ceilings and an imaginative menu.

TOP END
All prices in this section include breakfast.

Schloss Mönchstein (Map p235; ☎ 84 85 55-0; www .monchstein.at; Mönchsberg Park 26; d €335-395, ste €625-980; ℗ ☒ ▣) This gabled, yellow medieval castle nestles in woods about 10 minutes' walk from the Mönchsberg lift, with great views over the surrounding hills. The differently sized rooms are furnished with Persian rugs, antiques and oil paintings. There's a restaurant with outside terrace, a cosy bar and a set of tennis courts on site. The tiny chapel is a favourite place for Japanese and American couples to get married.

Goldener Hirsch (Map pp236-7; ☎ 80 84-0; www.gold enerhirsch.com; Getreidegasse 37; s €204-376, d €274-538; ☒ ☒ ▣) The prices here don't buy much space – the low-ceilinged rooms, spread out across four old townhouses in the heart of the Altstadt, are quaint and rustic rather than palatial, with pink-marble bathrooms. Service is predictably excellent – discreet and attentive. Downstairs are two award-winning restaurants (see p246).

Hotel Altstadt Radisson SAS (Map pp236-7; ☎ 84 85 71-0; www.austria-trend.at; Rudolfskai 28/Jugendgasse 15; s €149-265, d €220-390; ℗ ☒ ▣) Built over three converted townhouses overlooking the river, this hotel has more character than most chain places. The smart rooms have parquet floors and modern furniture, while the suites at the top are more interesting, with low half-timbered ceilings. There are plenty of sitting areas and cosy corners to curl up in, plus a large dining room with views of the river.

Wolf Dietrich (Map pp236-7; ☎ 87 12 75; www.salz burg-hotel.at; Wolf Dietrich Strasse 7; s €54-109, d €79-149; ▣) This hotel has excellent facilities including an indoor pool, sauna, solarium, bar and a great organic restaurant (see p245). The decor is elegant downstairs and heavy on the floral fabrics and chandeliers in the bedrooms. There are also a couple of fabulously over-the top suites full of romantic frills and loosely based on Mozart's opera the *Magic Flute*.

Hotel Gablerbräu (Map pp236-7; ☎ 889 65; www
.gablerbrau.com; Linzer Gasse 9; s €70-98, d €108/158;
✖ 🖵) This comfortable and classy place, just across the bridge from the old town, has large, modern rooms and a good-value **restaurant** (mains €12-20). It's been a hotel for nearly 600 years.

Hotel Elefant (Map pp236-7; ☎ 84 33 97; www.elefant
.at; Sigmund Haffner Gasse 4; s €100, d €140-185; 🅿
✖ 🕸 🖵) The rooms at this Best Western Hotel don't contain any surprises, being modern, corporate and plain, but fairly large by the standards of the old town area.

Eating
BUDGET
Salzburg need not be expensive for food. You can fill up on the giant pretzels hanging in every bar, buy cheese and sausages from the market stalls on Universitätsplatz and Kapitelplatz, or get your fast-food fix in the many kebab shops dotted around town.

Republic (Map pp236-7; ☎ 84 16 13; Anton Neumayr
Platz 2; mains €6.70-7.90; 🕑 lunch & dinner) This stylish, trendy bar/restaurant has a good-value and interesting menu, with dishes such as red snapper on wild garlic linguine. There's breakfast all day and lots of dips, snacks, beer food and healthier options.

SKS Spicy Spices (Bio Bistro; Map pp236-7; ☎ 87 07
12; Wolf Dietrich Strasse 1; mains €5.50; 🕑 lunch & dinner)
This small and basic, but friendly, Indian vegetarian restaurant has outside tables, a daily curry special and a range of organic products for sale.

Vegy Vollwertstube (Map pp236-7; ☎ 87 57 46;
Schwarzstrasse 21; lunch €2.50-5.70; 🕑 lunch Mon-Fri)
This friendly little place has been providing home-cooked vegetarian food to Salzburg for over 23 years. There are some wholesome products on sale too.

Il Sole (Map pp236-7; ☎ 84 32 84; Gstattengasse 15;
mains €5.50-8.50; 🕑 lunch & dinner) This simple Italian trattoria is recommended by readers for reasonably priced and good-quality pizzas and pasta dishes. There are a few tables outside on the pavement.

Stadtalm (Map pp236-7; ☎ 84 17 29; Mönchsberg
19; mains €4.50-8.50; 🕑 lunch & dinner mid-May–mid-
Sep) The restaurant of the Naturfreundehaus hostel up on Mönchsberg is worth visiting

for the view, though the hearty food's good value too.

Wilder Mann (Map pp236-7; ☎ 84 17 87; Getreidegasse 20; mains €5.50-8.50; 🕑 lunch & dinner Mon-Sat)
With surprisingly low prices considering its location in the old town, this small and smoky place dishes up dumplings, fried sausages and other light and airy fare.

The best budget lunch deals are in the university Mensas on the left bank. The courtyard **Mensa Toscana** (Map pp236-7; ☎ 8044-
6909; Sigmund Haffner Gasse 11; lunch menu €3.70; 🕑 lunch
Mon-Fri) is the most convenient place. The **Mensa GesWi** (Map pp236-7; ☎ 8044-6905; Rudolfskai
42; set lunch €3.90; 🕑 lunch Mon-Fri, closed Jul & Aug) has similar deals on offer.

For self-caterers there are several supermarkets, including **Billa** (Map pp236-7; Griesgasse
19) and a couple on Schallmooser Hauptstrasse. A fruit-and-vegetable market occupies Mirabellplatz on Thursday morning. The **Shell** (Map p235; St Julien Strasse 33) garage has a shop open 24 hours, with snacks, provisions and alcohol.

MID-RANGE
St Paul's Stub'n (Map pp236-7; ☎ 84 32 20; Her-
rengasse 16; mains €7-14; 🕑 dinner Mon-Sat) This small wood-panelled restaurant on the 1st floor has good-value meals with an excellent variety of fish dishes, including fresh tuna steaks. There are also a couple of meat and veggie options, and a lovely garden for warm evenings.

St Peter's Stiftskeller (Map pp236-7; ☎ 84 12
68-0; St Peter's Bezirk 1/4; mains €9.80-21.90; 🕑 lunch
& dinner) This historic, attractive restaurant is in a courtyard by Stiftskirche St Peter. Though firmly tourist territory, the food and regular Mozart lunch and dinner concerts (lunch €29.50, dinner €45) have good reports from visitors.

Sternbräu (Map pp236-7; ☎ 84 21 40; Griesgasse 23;
mains €6.50-14.10, set menus €11.50-18.50; 🕑 lunch &
dinner) Tucked away in a courtyard between Getreidegasse and Griesgasse, Sternbräu has several dining rooms and a garden seating area. It serves good Austrian food, including fish specials. The restaurant also incorporates an Italian Trattoria and a self-service snack bar. *The Sound of Music* dinner show takes place here (see p248).

K+K StieglBräu Restaurant (Map p235; ☎ 87 76
94; Rainerstrasse 14; mains €8.90-20.10; 🕑 lunch & dinner)
This large, traditional restaurant has several

smart dining rooms and a garden, serving classical Austrian cuisine. Most dishes are unadventurous but well prepared.

Weisses Kreuz (Map pp236-7; ☎ 84 56 41; Bierjodlgasse 6; mains €8.70-17.50; ❤ lunch & dinner) This place offers a menu of meaty Balkan specialities alongside the usual Austrian fare. *Djuvec* (rice, succulent pork, capsicum and paprika) is excellent, or try the Balkan Plate for an introduction to this kind of food.

Lemon & Olives (Map pp236-7; ☎ 84 16 26; Kaigasse 8; mains €3.90-12.90; ❤ lunch & dinner Mon-Sat, daily Jul & Aug) This stylish, friendly bistro is recommended by readers for pizza and Sicilian-style Italian food.

Humboldt Stub'n (Map pp236-7; ☎ 84 31 71; Gstattengasse 4-6; mains €6.90-12; ❤ lunch & dinner) The newest bar/restaurant in town promises a 'traditional kitchen and Austria's finest wine'. It's a good place for a fun dinner with a group, with funky music and an upbeat, pre-clubbing vibe.

Shrimps Bar (Map pp236-7; Steingasse 5; 87 44 84; mains €7-10; ❤ dinner) This tiny but trendy yellow-painted bar has a good selection of pasta and salads and some tables outside.

Taj Mahal (Map pp236-7; ☎ 88 20 10; Bayerhamerstr 13; mains €7-12; ❤ lunch & dinner Tue-Sun) A reasonably priced Indian with lots of veggie options and a cheap lunch menu (€6.50).

TOP-END

Paris Lodron (Map p235; ☎ 84 85 55-0; Mönchsberg Park 26; mains €25-30; ❤ lunch & dinner) At the top of the range is the hotel Schloss Mönchstein's dark, gothic-looking formal restaurant, which also has a garden terrace. The elaborate food is dished up in suitably opulent surroundings amid shining silverware and soft classical music. Service is impeccable. Reserve in advance.

Restaurant Goldener Hirsch (Map pp236-7; ☎ 80 84-0; Getreidegasse 37; mains €21-27; ❤ lunch & dinner, closed Sun in winter) This is the formal, gourmet restaurant in the Golderner Hirsch hotel, offering award-winning food in hushed surroundings. The house speciality is venison saddle with cabbage and dumplings.

S'Herzl (Map pp236-7; ☎ 80 84-0; Getreidegasse 37; mains €10.90-19; ❤ lunch & dinner, closed Sun in winter) In the same building is this cheaper, cosier and more informal dining room. The food is excellent and mostly traditional Austrian, with plenty of sausages, sauerkraut and scrumptious puddings.

K+K Restaurants am Waagplatz (Map pp236-7; ☎ 84 21 56; Waagplatz 2; mains €9.20-19.20; ❤ lunch & dinner) A well-regarded complex of restaurants just off Mozartplatz, with a series of small and traditionally furnished dining rooms spread over four floors. The menus vary from upmarket Austrian to cheaper, lighter dishes depending on which section you eat in. Medieval-style banquets are held in the 900-year-old cellar vault.

Alt Salzburg (Map pp236-7; ☎ 84 14 76; Bürgerspitalgasse 2; mains €10.20-22.90; ❤ lunch & dinner Tue-Sat, dinner Mon, closed Sun) A very cosy and quaint restaurant tucked into a cobblestone courtyard at the base of the Mönchsberg. The menu is traditional Austrian and the service old-fashioned and courteous.

Restaurant Ärlich (Map pp236-7; ☎ 871 275-60; Wolf Dietrich Strasse 7; mains €12.80-16.80; ❤ dinner Tue-Sat, closed Feb & Mar) This excellent organic restaurant has friendly staff, fresh ingredients and an imaginative menu of mostly traditional Austrian food.

Pan e Vin (Map pp236-7; ☎ 844 666; Gstattengasse 1; mains €15-30; ❤ lunch & dinner Mon-Sat, trattoria closed Mon) This upmarket place combines a trattoria downstairs with a mediterranean restaurant upstairs. It's beautifully decorated in a modern style and the mostly Italian-influenced dishes use fresh ingredients.

Zum Eulenspiegel (Map pp236-7; ☎ 84 31 80; Hagen-auerplatz 2; mains €12.40-20.40; ❤ lunch & dinner Mon-Sat) By Mozarts Geburtshaus, this rickety old place occupying several floors has cosy surroundings and good food including several fish specialities. There's a tiny, cosy bar downstairs that serves lighter, cheaper meals, eaten at tables in the courtyard.

CAFÉS

To experience the best of Salzburg's coffeehouse culture, go to Alter Markt.

Café Tomaselli (Map pp236-7; ☎ 84 44 88; Alter Markt 9; pastries €4; ❤ breakfast & lunch) This is the city's most famously elegant café.

Café Konditorei Fürst (Map pp236-7; ☎ 84 37 59; Brodgasse 13; cakes €3; ❤ breakfast & lunch) Just opposite, this café has a unique claim to fame – it was here in 1890 that the ubiquitous *Mozart Kugeln* chocolate balls were invented. They're still made here to the original recipe.

For organic sandwiches, sushi, muffins and salads, try **Indigo** (Map pp236-7; ☎ 843 480; Rudolfskai 8; salad €5; ❤ lunch & dinner). Just off Mirabellplatz, **Coffee to Go** (Map p235; ☎ 878 256; Franz

Josef Strasse 3; bagels €3; ☺ breakfast, lunch & dinner, Wed & Sun breakfast & lunch; ☒) has fresh bagels, salad and smoothies.

Drinking

It shouldn't be too hard to find a place for a beer or a glass of fine Austrian wine in Salzburg. Most bars tend towards the traditional, with wooden floors and tables, but there are a couple of more contemporary options too.

Augustiner Bräustübl (Map p235; ☎ 43 12 46; Augustinergasse 4-6; ☺ 3-11pm Mon-Fri, 2.30-11pm Sat & Sun) This place proves that monks know how to enjoy themselves – the quaffing clerics have been running this huge beer hall for years. Beer is dispensed from pumps in the foyer into huge stone mugs, and when the munchies hit you, the on-site stalls sell meat, bread, cheese and salad. It's atmospheric, cheap and a great place for people watching – Austrians of all ages drink here alongside parties of tourists. There's a massive beer garden under shady chestnut trees for those long, lazy summer afternoons.

Die Weisse (Map p235; ☎ 87 22 46; Rupertgasse 10; ☺ 10.30am-midnight Mon-Sat) This is the Gasthof of the Salzburger Weissbierbrauerei, a small brewery which creates its own very palatable dark and cloudy brew. The beer is the main attraction and can be imbibed in the wooden-floored pub or outside in the shady garden.

Zum Fidelen Affen (Map pp236-7; ☎ 87 73 61; Priesterhausgasse 8; mains €8.90-11.80; ☺ 5pm-midnight Mon-Sat) This popular old-style drinking venue with monkey-themed décor (!) has decent Austrian food plus tables on the pavement.

StieglKeller (Map pp236-7; ☎ 84 26 81; Festungsgasse 10; ☺ 10am-11pm May-Sep) This beer hall next to the Festungsbahn funicular has a garden overlooking the town. Beer is cheapest from the self-service taps outside.

Schnaitl Pub (Map pp236-7; ☎ 87 56 68; Bergstrasse 5; ☺ 7pm-2am Mon-Sat) In the same building as the Schwarzes Rössl, this grungy, laid-back place is popular with students who come to play on the games machines and table football.

Vis-à-Vis (Map pp236-7; ☎ 84 12 90; Rudolfskai 24; ☺ from 8pm) This neon-lit cellar bar is also a bit more sophisticated – and less crowded – than many of the sweaty, packed places nearby. **Bellini's** (Map pp236-7; ☎ 87 13 85; Mirabellplatz 4; ☺ 9am-1am Mon-Fri, 11am-1am Sat & Sun) is a cool Italian café/bar with a good range of cocktails. It also serves snacks such as tramezzinis and crostinis. Shrimps Bar (Map pp236-7) is also a stylish place for a drink.

If you're tired of wooden floors and gingham fabrics as a backdrop for your drinking, Republic (p245) and Humboldt's (opposite) are two relatively new, hip and very popular bars, near the bottom of the Mönchsberg lift, which double as restaurants and have a selection of fliers detailing club nights around town.

The tourist office distributes a guide to Salzburg's fairly limited gay scene. More listings can be found on the web at www.gaynet .at – in German.

The Homosexuelle Initiative, HOSI, runs a **gay bar** (Map p235; ☎ 43 59 27; www.hosi.or.at - in German; Müllner Hauptstrasse 11; ☺ evenings Wed, Fri & Sat). Other gay bars in town are **Diva** (Map pp236-7; ☎ 0664-431 53 17; Priesterhausgasse 22; www.divabar .at - in German; ☺ from 3pm/6pm summer/winter), which runs weekly parties and special events, and **2 Stein** (Map pp236-7; ☎ 877 179; Giselekai 9; ☺ from 6pm), which has a dance floor and occasional live music.

Entertainment
MUSIC

Schlosskonzerte (☎ 84 85 86; www.salzburger-schloss konzerte.at; tickets €8-31) It would be a shame to come to Mozart's birthplace and not take the opportunity to hear classical music played in a suitably baroque venue. The top choice for this kind of thing are the recitals given by international soloists and chamber musicians in the beautiful, ornate marble hall of Schloss Mirabell (p238). Most are in the evenings but there are also recitals at 11am most Sundays. Tickets and information can be obtained from Mozarts-Wohnhaus (p238).

The works of Mozart and other classical composers are performed at the **Mozarteum** (Map pp236-7; ☎ 87 31 54; Schwarzstrasse 26-28; tickets €15-60). Lower-brow but still of a good standard are the Mozart lunch-and-dinner concerts at **St Peter's Stiftskeller** (Map pp236-7; ☎ 84 12 68-0; St Peter's Bezirk 1/4; lunch/dinner €29.50/45). Concerts, some with dinner, are also held at the **Festung Hohensalzburg** (www.mozartfestival.at).

If you're lucky enough to be in Salzburg during the Festspiele in August, you can try to get tickets for concerts, operas and plays at the **Festspielhaus** (Map pp236-7; ☎ 84

SALZBURG & SALZBURGER LAND

45-579, Hofstallgasse 1), built into the sheer sides of the Mönchsberg.

Inevitably, there's also a **Sound of Music Show** (☎ 82 66 17; without/with dinner €29/43; ⏰ nightly May-Oct), with Austrian folk music and classical pieces being performed alongside hits from the show. It takes place in an old-fashioned dining room at Sternbräu restaurant (p245) – the higher price includes a four-course meal (featuring foods mentioned in the song 'My Favourite Things') and coffee.

More contemporary tastes are catered for at **Rockhouse** (Map p233; ☎ 88 49 14; Schallmooser Hauptstrasse 46; admission €10-20; ⏰ 6pm-2am Mon-Sat), Salzburg's main venue for rock and pop bands – check the website (www.rockhouse.at – in German) or the local press for details of what's on. There's also a tunnel-shaped bar that has DJs (usually free) and live bands.

There are also two jazz venues in town.

Jazzit (Map p235; ☎ 87 68 91; Elisabethstrasse 11/5; www.jazzit.at - in German) This jazz bar has regular live acts and a happy hour from 5pm to 8pm daily. Check the website for details of upcoming gigs.

Urbankeller (Map p233; ☎ 87 08 94; Schallmooser Hauptstrasse 50; admission €9-15; ⏰ 5pm-midnight Mon-Sat) This place incorporates a Jazzclub, which hosts live jazz every second Friday from about September to April.

THEATRE & CINEMA

Das Kino (Map pp236-7; ☎ 87 31 00; www.daskino.at - in German; Giselakai 11; tickets €7.50) Hollywood and independent films are shown here in their original language two or three times a day. It's also a good place to pick up fliers for clubs and happenings around town.

Landestheater (Map pp236-7; ☎ 87 15 12-0; www.theater.co.at - in German; Schwarzstrasse 22; tickets €5-42) Musicals, ballets, plays and operas, mostly in German, are performed here.

Marionettentheater (Marionette Theatre; Map pp236-7; ☎ 87 24 06-0; www.marionetten.at; Schwarzstrasse 24; tickets €18-35; ⏰ May-Sep, Christmas, Easter & Mozart Week in Jan) Not just for children – the performing puppets here are voiced by classically trained singers and musicians performing a repertoire of well-known operas. The baroque auditorium seats 350.

Szene (Map pp236-7; ☎ 84 34 48; www.sommerszene.net - in German; Anton Neumayr Platz 2; tickets €10-45) This art and music venue stages avant-garde productions encompassing dance, theatre, live music and DJs.

Shopping

Getreidegasse is the main street for shopping and souvenirs.

Elsewhere, try **Kopfberger** (Map pp236-7; ☎ 84 56 36; Judengasse 14) for woodcarvings and *Dirndl* (traditional women's dress), which many Austrians still wear.

Salzburger Heimatwerk (Map pp236-7; ☎ 84 41 19; Residenzplatz 9) also sells both, plus glassware, CDs, books, china and fabrics relating to the province.

Not many people leave Salzburg without sampling *Mozartkugeln* (Mozart balls) – delicious chocolate-coated combinations of nougat and marzipan. They're on sale in almost every shop, but they are cheaper in supermarkets. Only in Salzburg will you find whole window displays devoted to Mozart merchandise, with the chocolate joining forces in extravagant displays with liqueurs, mugs and other items. Or, for a truly extravagant shopping spree, check out the fabulously odd Easter in Salzburg (see p240).

Getting There & Away

AIR

Salzburg airport (Map p233; ☎ 85 80-251; www.salzburg-airport.com), half an hour by bus from the city centre, has regular scheduled flights to destinations all over Europe and main Austrian cities. Low-cost flights from the UK are provided by **Ryanair** (☎ 0900 210 240; www.ryanair.com). Other airlines flying into Salzburg are **British Airways** (☎ 0179 567 567) and **KLM** (☎ 85 809 69).

BUS

Bundesbuses depart from just outside the *Hauptbahnhof* (Map p235) on Südtiroler Platz, where timetables are displayed. Bus information and tickets are available from the information points on the main station concourse.

Hourly buses leave for the Salzkammergut between 6.30am and 8pm – destinations include Bad Ischl (€7.60, 1¾ hours), Mondsee (€4.60, 50 minutes), St Wolfgang (€6.90, 1¾ hours) and St Gilgen (€4.60, 50 minutes). All prices are one way. Return tickets include travel on the city-bus network. For information on bus travel further afield and an online timetable see www.postbus.at – in German.

TRAIN

Salzburg is well served by InterCity (IC) and EuroCity (EC) services. For train information call ☎ 05-1717 (8am to 8pm daily), or visit the office in the *Hauptbahnhof*. Tickets (no commission) and train information are also available from **Salzburger Landesreisebüro** (Map pp236-7; ☎ 87 34 03; www.verkehrsbuero.at - in German; Schwarzstrasse 11).

Fast trains leave hourly for Vienna's West-bahnhof (€36.50, 3¼ hours), travelling via Linz (€17.70, 1¼ hours). The two-hourly express service to Klagenfurt (€27.70, three hours) runs via Villach.

The quickest way to Innsbruck is by the 'corridor' train through Germany; trains depart at least every two hours (€29.50, two hours) and stop at Kufstein. Trains to Munich take about two hours and run every 30 to 60 minutes (€25.80, but ask about special deals at counters Nos 1 or 2); some of these continue to Karlsruhe via Stuttgart.

If you hop on the train in Salzburg you can also hop off in Berlin (€86.40, 11 hours), Budapest (€67.70, seven hours), Prague (€45.80, seven hours), Rome (€119.80, 10½ hours) or Venice (€48.60, 6½ hours). There may be cheaper ticket deals for all these destinations at off-peak times – enquire at the ticket counter.

CAR & MOTORCYCLE

Three autobahns converge on Salzburg and form a loop around the city: the A1 from Linz, Vienna and the east, the A8/E52 from Munich and the west, and the A10/E55 from Villach and the south. The quickest way to Tyrol is to take the road to Bad Reichenhall in Germany and continue to Lofer (Hwy 312) and St Johann in Tyrol. Parking is difficult and expensive in the city centre, so it may be better to avoid taking your car in – there are three park-and-ride points to the west, north and south of the city from where you can get the bus into the centre.

Getting Around

TO/FROM THE AIRPORT

Salzburg airport is less than 4km west of the city centre at Innsbrucker Bundesstrasse 95.

Bus No 2 (€1.70, 30 minutes) leaves from outside and terminates at the *Hauptbahnhof*. This bus runs from about 5.30am to 1am and doesn't go via the old town, so you'll have to take another bus once you arrive, or walk (15-20 minutes). A taxi to the airport from the centre costs about €12.

BUS

Bus drivers sell single tickets for €1.70 and daily (24-hour) tickets (adult/child €4/2). Weekly cards cost €10 and must be bought from *Tabak* (tobacconist) shops or tourist offices. Single tickets bought in advance from these places are cheaper (€1.40 each) and are sold in units of five. Children under six years travel free.

Bus routes are shown at bus stops and on some city maps; bus Nos 1 and 4 start from the *Hauptbahnhof* and skirt the pedestrian-only old town.

BUS TAXI

'Bus taxis' operate nightly from 11.30pm to 1.30am (3am on weekends) on fixed routes, dropping off and picking up along the way, for a cost of €3. Hanuschplatz is the departure point for suburban routes on the left bank, and Theatergasse for routes to the right bank.

CAR & MOTORCYCLE

Driving in the city centre is hardly worth the effort. Parking places are limited and much of the old town is only accessible by foot. The largest car park near the centre is the Altstadt Garage under the Mönchsberg. Attended car parks cost around €13 per day. Rates are lower on streets with automatic ticket machines (blue zones); a three-hour maximum applies (€3 or €0.50 for 30 minutes) 9am to 7pm on weekdays and perhaps also on Saturday (it'll say on the machine).

Car rental offices include:

Avis (Map p235; ☎ 87 72 78; Ferdinand Porsche Strasse 7)
Budget (Map p235; ☎ 87 34 52; Elisabethstrasse 8a)
Europcar (Map p233; ☎ 87 16 16; Vogelweiderstrasse 69)
Hertz (Map p235; ☎ 87 66 74; Ferdinand Porsche Strasse 7)

FIACRE

Rates for a fiacre (horse-drawn carriage) for up to four people are €33 for 25 minutes. The drivers line up on Residenzplatz. Not all speak English, so don't expect a guided tour.

TAXI

Taxis cost €3.60 plus around €0.90 per kilometre. To book a radio taxi (€0.75 surcharge), call ☎ 81 11 or ☎ 17 15. There's a huge taxi rank outside the main train station.

AROUND SALZBURG

Hellbrunn, Gaisberg and Untersberg are excursions of less than a day from Salzburg. Hallein merits a whole day trip, while Werfen can also be visited as a day/overnight trip or explored en route to sights further south.

HELLBRUNN

Four kilometres south of the centre of Salzburg's old town is the magnificent **Schloss Hellbrunn** (Map p233; ☎ 0662-82 03 72-0; www.hellbrunn.at; Fürstenweg 37; combined ticket adult/child €7.50/3.50; ☺ 9am-4.30pm Apr & Oct, 9am-5.30pm May & Jun, 9am-6pm Jul & Aug), an imposing yellow-painted baroque palace built in the 17th century by bishop Marcus Sitticus, Wolf Dietrich's nephew. You can tour the interior with an English audio guide, but the biggest draw is the **Wasserspiele** (water games) section in the grounds. This contains many ingenious trick fountains and water-powered figures. They were installed by the bishop following an Italian fashion of the time and are activated by the tour guides, who all seem to share the same infantile sense of humour. Expect to get wet! **Tours** (€7; ☺ hourly 7-10pm Jul & Aug) run every 30 minutes. Evening tours are also possible.

There is no charge to stroll round the attractive Schloss gardens; these are open year-round till dusk. On the hill overlooking the grounds is the small **Volkskundemuseum** (Folklore Museum; ☎ 0662-620808-500; adult/child €2/0.80; ☺ 10am-7.30pm mid-Apr–mid-Oct), affiliated to the **Carolinum Augustum Museum** (p239) in Salzburg and containing examples of the extravagant traditional costumes worn at festivals in the province.

Also in the grounds is **Tiergarten Hellbrunn** (☎ 0662-82 01 76; adult/child €7/3.50; ☺ 8.30am-6.30pm Sun-Thu, 8.30am-11pm Jun-Sep). This zoo is naturalistic and open-plan in summer; the more docile animals are barely confined.

Getting There & Away

Bus No 25 stops directly outside the Schloss every half-hour (€1.70, city passes valid). Pick it up from Salzburg's *Hauptbahnhof* or Rudolfskai in the old town.

UNTERSBERG

This is the peak to the south of the town (Map p232), reaching a height of 1853m. The panorama of the Tyrolean and Salzburg Alpine ranges is spectacular, and the area is rich in local legends. One such myth relates that a mysterious king with a long white beard sleeps beneath the mountain. The summit is accessible by cable car (up/down/return €10.50/9/17), which runs every half hour year-round except for two weeks in April and six weeks from 1 November. Get to the valley station by taking city buses 25 or 16 to St Leonhard.

GAISBERG

The peak of **Gaisberg** (Map p232; 1287m) is east of Salzburg old town, at the edge of the city limits. A lookout point provides an excellent panorama of the town and the Salzkammergut.

Unless you have your own transport, the only way up is to take the 151 bus (☎ 0662-42 40 00), which leaves four or five times a day in summer from the northern end of Mirabellplatz (pp236-7; €2.60 return, 30 minutes). From November to March the bus only goes as far as Zistelalpe, about 1.5km short of the summit.

HALLEIN

☎ 06245 / pop 18,500 / elev 461m

The main reason to visit Hallein (Map p232) is the Salzwelten Salzburg salt mine museum at Bad Dürrnberg (Map p232), on the hill above the town. The town was once settled by Celts, who provided its name.

Orientation & Information

The train station is east of the Salzach River: walk ahead, bear left and then turn right to cross the river for the town centre (five minutes). The post office is opposite the train station. The **tourist office** (☎ 853 94; www.hallein-tourism.at - in German; Mauttorpromenade; ☺ 8.30am-5pm Mon-Fri, 9am-3pm Sat) is on the narrow Pernerinsel island adjoining the Stadtbrücke.

Sights

The sale of salt from the **Salzwelten Salzburg** (☎ 200 2490; Ramsaustrasse 3; adult/child €15.90/9.55; ☼ 9am-5pm) show-mine filled Salzburg's coffers during its princely heyday. Early settlers were mining salt 4500 years ago, but production has now been replaced by guided tours taking in an underground railway, a wooden slide and a brief raft trip on the salt lake. Just by the mine entrance is a reconstructed Celtic village. Only children over four are admitted to the mine.

Bus 41 (€1.70, 12 minutes) departs from outside the train station every hour on weekdays, less often on weekends. Alternatively, it's a steep 40-minute climb to the mine; from the centre, walk up to the church with the bare concrete tower, turn left along Ferchl Strasse and follow the 'Knappensteig' sign pointing to the right after the yellow Volksschule building.

Hallein has some elegant 17th- and 18th-century houses in Salzach style, as well as the **Keltenmuseum** (Celtic Museum; ☎ 807 83; Pflegerplatz 5; adult/child €4/1.50; ☼ 9am-5pm Apr-Oct). The museum displays beautiful green-bronze Celtic artefacts and details the history of salt extraction in the region (English notes are available).

Festivals & Events

The **Halleiner Stadtfestwoche** is the biggest folk-music festival in Austria and comprises 10 days of diverse events in mid-September every year, including live folk music from all over Europe. Some events are free. Contact the tourist office for details.

Sleeping & Eating

Most people visit Hallein as a day trip from Salzburg, but if you do decide to stay overnight there are a few decent options, as well as a couple of restaurants.

Hotel Hafnerwirt (☎ 803 19; hafnerwirt@aon.at; Salzachtal Bundesstrasse Süd 3; s €40-46, d €60-72; **P**) Conveniently located three-star place between the train station and the centre.

Pension Mikl (☎ 802 29; Ederstrasse 2; s/d without bathroom €30/45) Reception (in café) open 6am-9pm Mon-Sat. Eight-bed place in the town centre.

Jugendherberge Schloss Wispach (☎ 803 97; www.jgh.at; Wiespachstrasse 7; dm €12.90) HI hostel in a former stately home 1.4km north of both the station and the town centre.

Halleiner Stadtkrug (☎ 830 85; Thunstrasse; ☼ lunch & dinner Mon-Fri, dinner Sun; mains €7.50-11.80) Offers plain Austrian cooking and good-value lunch buffets.

Getting There & Away

Hallein is 30 minutes or less south of Salzburg by bus or train with departures every 30 to 60 minutes. The main train station in Salzburg sells the Salz Erlebnis Ticket (€18) covering the train to Hallein, a bus transfer and entry to the salt mine.

BERCHTESGADEN

This German town about 25km from Salzburg achieved infamy for the **Eagle's Nest** (☎ 0049-86 52 29 69; parking per car €1.50; ☼ mid-May–Oct), a retreat given to Adolf Hitler on his 50th birthday. The imposing building, with its National Socialist architecture, is reached via a brass-lined lift that travels more than 120m up through sheer rock into the building itself, which now houses a restaurant.

For more information, contact the Berchtesgaden **tourist office** (☎ 0049 86 52/9 44 53 00; www.berchtesgadener-land.com) or refer to Lonely Planet's *Germany* guidebook.

Getting There & Away

Berchtesgaden is about 30km south of Salzburg, on Hwy 160. Direct buses and trains run hourly from the city (€6.90, one hour). From Berchtesgaden, a bus (€13.50) runs to the Eagles Nest every 30 minutes between 8.30am and 4.50pm during summer. Salzburg's tour operators offer a five-hour tour to the Eagle's Nest (€45).

WERFEN

☎ 06468 / pop 3200 / elev 525m

The small and pretty village of Werfen is chiefly used as a base for visiting two of the province's top attractions – the Eiseriesenwelt ice caves and the spectacular castle of Hohenwerfen. It's well worth a day trip or an overnight stay.

Orientation & Information

The town stands on the northern side of the Salzach River, five minutes' walk from the train station – cross the river and head towards the castle. The **tourist office** (☎ 5388; www.werfen.at; Markt 24; ☼ 9am-5pm Mon-Fri, 9am-7pm Mon-Fri, 5-7pm Sat Jul & Aug) will book accommodation for no commission.

SALZBURG & SALZBURGER LAND

Sights

BURG HOHENWERFEN

When it comes to location, few castles can beat **Burg Hohenwerfen** (☎ 7603; adult/student/family €9.50/5/20; ⊗ 9am-6pm Jul & Aug; 9am-5pm May, Jun, Sep; 9am-4.30pm Apr, Oct & Nov, closed Mon in Apr) for sheer drama. Perched on the very top of its own hill in the centre of the valley, it's surrounded on all sides by towering grey peaks. Pennants flutter from turrets that look fit for a medieval prince, but the present fortress was actually built in the 16th century for an archbishop of Salzburg.

The entry fee includes a falconry museum (look for interesting photos of modern-day falconers flying their hunting birds against an industrial backdrop of factory chimneys) and a guided tour of the interior (audio handsets in English are €4.50); this covers the chapel, dungeons, arsenal and belfry. A highlight is a dramatic 20-minute falconry show in the grounds (11am and 3.15pm). Falconers in medieval costume release eagles, owls, falcons and vultures to wheel in front of the ramparts and the surrounding Tennengebirge mountain range. It's exhilarating to watch, although no substitute for observing these supreme predators in the wild. There's a commentary in English and German.

Both the fortress and the ice caves can be fitted into a day trip from Salzburg if you start early; visit the caves first, and be at the fortress for the last falconry show. The stiff walk up from the village takes 20 minutes. For taxis, call ☎ 5293.

EISRIESENWELT HÖHLE

The largest accessible ice caves in the world, **Eisriesenwelt Höhle** (Eisriesenwelt Caves; ☎ 5248; ⊗ 9am-4.30pm Jul & Aug, 9am-3.30pm May, Jun, Sep-26 Oct) contain 30,000 sq m of ice and about 42km of known passages. During a one-hour tour (€8), visitors are led up wooden stairs and along dim, chilly underground passageways, with guides periodically lighting magnesium flares to illuminate beautiful and elaborate ice formations. The name Eisriesenwelt means 'world of the ice giants' and some of these fantastical shapes do look almost supernatural – many are named after the gods of Nordic myths. In a cave known as the 'cathedral' lies a plaque marking the resting place of Alexander von Mörk, the explorer who pioneered the cave's early exploration.

This is not a trip for the unfit or infirm – the tour takes in 1400 steep steps, plus the walk uphill from the bus stop or car park and from the cable car to the caves (as you puff up both you'll be rewarded by fantastic views). Take warm clothes – the temperature sinks past freezing inside the caves. If there are enough English-speaking visitors, guides will also do the tour in English.

A minibus service (€5.60 return) operates every two hours from the train station along the very steep 6km road to the caves' car park, which is as far as vehicles can go. If your arrival doesn't coincide with the bus from the station, turn right and walk along the river to the town car park, from where the minibuses depart every half hour. A 15-minute uphill walk brings you to the cable car (€9 return); from the top station it's another steep 15-minute walk to the caves. Allow at least four hours for the return trip from the train station (including tour), or three hours from the car park (peak-season queues may add an hour). The whole route can be walked, but it's a hard four-hour ascent, rising 1100m above the village.

Sleeping & Eating

All Werfen's sleeping and eating options are lined up along the village's main street, the Markt.

Restaurant-Hotel Obauer (☎ 5212-0; www.obauer.com; Markt 46; s €70-130, d €120-210; P ✗) This is Werfen's smartest option – the **restaurant** (set three-course lunch or dinner €48) is acclaimed as one of the finest in Austria. The creative dishes are mostly Austrian in origin, but with French and Italian influences and made using refined regional produce. Rest days vary, so book in advance. The stylish rooms upstairs are a bit '80s in their décor, but very comfortable – the radios in the bathrooms are a nice touch.

Pension Obauer (☎ 5224-0; www.obauer.at - in German; Markt 36; s/d €32/64; P ✗) Not to be confused with the smarter place above, this is the best of Werfen's pensions. The rooms are fairly small, but well decorated, and the breakfast room is cosy. The pension also runs the excellent delicatessen next door.

Weisses Rössl (☎ 5268; www.salzburgerland.com /weisses roessl werfen; s/d/tr/q €28/48/58/68) This popular place also has good-quality rooms and a couple of family apartments.

Zur Stiege (☎ 5256; www.restaurant-zur-stiege.at - in German; Markt 10; mains €13-23) Another restaurant with an excellent culinary reputation, at the far end of the village towards the castle.

There are several cheaper restaurants on Markt, the main street, as well as an **ADEG** (Markt 28) supermarket.

Getting There & Away

Werfen can be reached from Salzburg by Hwy 10. Trains from Salzburg (€8.60, 50 minutes) run approximately hourly.

SOUTHERN SALZBURG PROVINCE

The main attractions in the south are covered in the Hohe Tauern National Park Region chapter (p277), but the following are worth a look if you're passing through the southeast of the province. Tamsweg and Mauterndorf are both in the Lungau region; staff at the **Lungau tourist office** (☎ 06477-8988; www.lungau.co.at; Postfach 19, A-5582, Lungau) can tell you about ski passes and accommodation.

TAMSWEG

☎ 06474 / pop 5000 / elev 1024m

Tamsweg is the main town in the Lungau. You may want to stop off to look at **St Leonhardkirche** (☎ 06474-6870), a 15th-century Gothic church on a hill outside the town. It has some impressive stained-glass windows, particularly the Goldfenster (gold window) to the right of the chancel.

Tamsweg is known for its Samsonumzug (Samson Procession), which takes place on two days in late July and on a couple of other variable dates in summer. The biblical character and other famous figures are depicted in giant size and paraded through the streets.

Getting There & Away

Tamsweg is a 10km detour from Hwy 99, which connects Radstadt and Spittal an der Drau. It's at the terminus of a private rail line that branches off from the Vienna-Klagenfurt main line at Unzmarkt. See p209 for details.

MAUTERNDORF

☎ 06472 / pop 1600 / elev 1122m

Both a summer and winter resort, Mauterndorf has the added attraction of **Burg Mauterndorf** (Mauterndorf Caste; ☎ 7426; adult/child/family €8/5/20; ☉ 10am-6pm May 1-Oct 30). This 13th-century castle was built by the archbishops of Salzburg on the site of a Roman fort. The castle houses a regional museum and is the venue for various cultural events. It is believed that in the Middle Ages the main road passed directly through the castle courtyard and tolls were extracted from road users.

Getting There & Away

Mauterndorf is on Hwy 99. Bus number 780 runs from Radstadt to the Mauterndorf post office (50 mins, three times daily).

RADSTADT

☎ 06452 / pop 4800 / elev 856m

Radstadt has an attractively walled town centre, with round turrets and a **Stadtpfarrkirche** (town parish church) that combines Gothic and Romanesque elements. Most visitors, however, come to Radstadt and the surrounding resorts to ski or snowboard.

Together, the resorts form the huge Salzburger Sportwelt skiing area; 100 lifts give access to 300km of pistes, mostly suitable for intermediate and beginner skiers, plus several snowboard parks and high-altitude cross-country trails. For information, contact the **Salzburger Sportwelt Tourist Office** (☎ 06457-29 29; www.sportwelt-amade.com).

The same mountains attract sporty types in summer, too, with over 1000km of walking trails and opportunities for canyoning, climbing, white-water rafting and mountain biking.

Getting There & Away

Radstadt is on the route of two-hourly IC trains running between Innsbruck and Graz – both are about three hours away. Zell am See (€11.20, 70 minutes) and Bruck an der Mur (€21.60, 2½ hours) are also on this route.

From Radstadt, Hwy 99 runs into Carinthia, then climbs to the Radstädter Tauern Pass (1739m); caravans not recommended. Just to the west is a busier north–south route, the A10/E55, which avoids the high parts by going through a 6km tunnel.

Carinthia

CONTENTS

With its warm and sunny climate, Carinthia (Kärnten) is Austria's summer province, the holiday playground of many of the country's wealthy and fashionable set. Its position on Austria's southern border with Italy contributes to a relaxed, almost Mediterranean atmosphere in many places. The beautiful people of Vienna and Salzburg come here to sunbathe and party on the shores of the region's 1270 clean, clear lakes, some of which, like the famous Wörthersee, have waters warmed to a comfortable swimming temperature by thermal springs.

Boating, fishing and high-adrenaline sports like waterskiing and jet boating are also popular, while on summer nights some of the sleepy lakeside resorts are home to a surprisingly stylish, Riviera-style outdoor bar and restaurant scene. In the extreme south of the province is Villach, famous for its rejuvenating thermal waters and for years a centre of spa tourism.

Away from the lakes, Carinthia's medieval heritage is celebrated in picturesque walled villages such as Friesach and Gmund and impressive castles like the hilltop fortress of Hochosterwitz. Many of the towns and villages nestled amid Carinthia's rolling hills hold an annual summer festival, with folk-music groups and bands of roving performers coming from neighbouring Italy and Slovenia to take part alongside locals. The province's proximity to Slovenia (the border between Austria and Slovenia has been redrawn several times over the centuries) means that many of the place names are of Slavic origin and Slavic surnames are common among the local inhabitants.

Culturally, prosperous and semi-rural Carinthia is one of the more conservative and politically right-wing of Austria's provinces – the region is the political home of controversial politician Jörg Haider, often seen in streetside posters around the smaller towns.

CARINTHIA

HIGHLIGHTS

- Visiting the innovative Die Spur des Einhorns exhibition in **Friesach** (p268), Carinthia's prettiest medieval village
- Sunbathing, waterskiing and partying with Austria's fashionable crowd on the shores of the **Wörthersee** (p263) or **Millstättersee** (p275)
- Watching an open-air concert on the lake stage at Klagenfurt's **Europapark** (p259)
- Transporting yourself to the tranquil ambience of Tibet at the Heinrich Harrer museum in **Hüttenberg** (p270)

Friesach ★ ★ Hüttenberg
Millstättersee ★   Burg
                    ★ Hochosterwitz
           Wörthersee
Warmbad Villach ★   ★ ★ Klagenfurt

- Sinking into a hot Jacuzzi full of healing waters in the famous spa of **Warmbad Villach** (p267)
- Admiring the views from the top of **Burg Hochosterwitz** (p271), a spectacular medieval castle

■ POPULATION: 556,300   ■ AREA: 9,533 SQ KM   ■ HIGHEST ELEVATION: GROSSGLOCKNER 3797M

History

Carinthia (then called Carantania) belonged to Slovenian tribes until the 800s, when the Avars, an eastern tribe, invaded. The locals called upon the might of the Bavarian empire to help them, leading to the gradual replacement of Slavic culture with a Germanic one. Carinthia became part of Austria in 1335.

The Slovenes attempted to reclaim the southern part of Carinthia after WWI, with a Yugoslav army crossing the border and occupying Klagenfurt, the provincial capital. On October 10, 1920, the province was restored to Austria after a popular vote.

Climate

Carinthia gets the most sunshine of anywhere in Austria – in summer it can get blazingly hot, with lake water temperatures of 25° to 28°C. The mild climate means winters are less harsh than elsewhere, too, leading to a shorter ski season (late December to March). The best months for hiking are September and October.

National Parks

Carinthia shares an area of outstanding natural beauty, the Hohe Tauern National Park (p277), with neighbouring Salzburg province and Tyrol.

Getting There & Around

Klagenfurt airport receives cheap flights from the UK (www.ryanair.com) and Ger-many (www.hlx.com), and Austrian domestic flights (www.aua.com). Klagenfurt and Villach are the main hubs for trains from elsewhere in Europe.

As in other provinces, Carinthia is divided into regional zones for public transport, with the option of buying single tickets or passes valid for 24 hours, seven days, 30 days or one year. Ticket clerks will advise you, or you can call Kärntner Linien in Klagenfurt (☎ 0463-500 830). Many of the lakes are served by efficient boat services in summer.

The **Kärnten Card** (www.kaerntencard.co.at; 2/5-week card €32/45) gives free or reduced access to the province's major sights and 50% discounts on buses and trains. It's sold at hotels and tourist offices from May to October.

KLAGENFURT

☎ 0463 / pop 89,700

It's not an urban centre comparable with Salzburg or Vienna, but Klagenfurt, Carinthia's provincial capital, is an enjoyable, sunny city, handy as a base for exploring the Wörthersee's lakeside villages and the attractive medieval towns to the north.

Ring roads today mark the site of the old city walls, pulled down in 1809 on the orders of Napoleon, while the city centre provides Renaissance courtyards, alleyways and arcades to explore, many filled with smart boutiques and cafés.

At the town's western limit is the wide green space of Europapark, home to a cou-

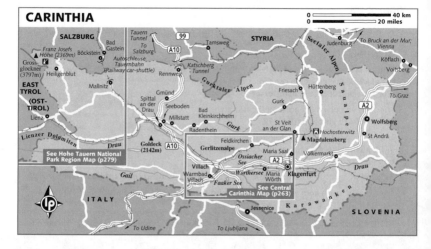

ple of indifferent children's attractions including the bizarre world-in-miniature of Minimundus.

Orientation

Klagenfurt lies 30km from Slovenia and 60km from Italy. The **airport** (☎ 415 00-0; Flughafenstrasse 60-66) is 3km north of the city

centre – take bus No 45, then 40 (€1.60, 30 minutes) to get into town.

The *Hauptbahnhof* (main train station; Map p257) is just over 1km south of Neuer Platz, which marks the heart of the city centre. One block west of Neuer Platz is Heiligengeistplatz, the hub for local buses.

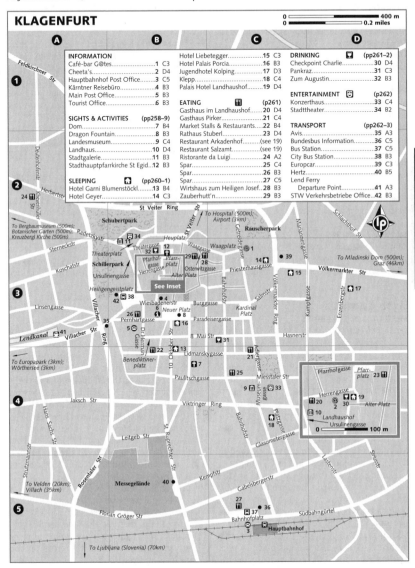

KLAGENFURT

INFORMATION	
Café-bar G@tes	1 C3
Cheeta's	2 D4
Hauptbahnhof Post Office	3 C5
Kärntner Reisebüro	4 B3
Main Post Office	5 B3
Tourist Office	6 B3

SIGHTS & ACTIVITIES	(pp258–9)
Dom	7 B4
Dragon Fountain	8 B3
Landesmuseum	9 C4
Landhaus	10 D4
Stadtgalerie	11 B3
Stadthauptpfarrkirche St Egid	12 B3

SLEEPING	(pp260–1)
Hotel Garni Blumenstöckl	13 B4
Hotel Geyer	14 C3

Hotel Liebetegger	15 C3
Hotel Palais Porcia	16 B3
Jugendhotel Kolping	17 D3
Klepp	18 C4
Palais Hotel Landhaushof	19 D4

EATING	(p261)
Gasthaus im Landhaushof	20 D4
Gasthaus Pirker	21 C4
Market Stalls & Restaurants	22 B4
Rathaus Stuberl	23 D4
Restaurant Arkadenhof	(see 19)
Restaurant Salzamt	(see 19)
Ristorante da Luigi	24 A2
Spar	25 C4
Spar	26 B3
Spar	27 C5
Wirtshaus zum Heiligen Josef	28 B3
Zauberhutt'n	29 B3

DRINKING	(pp261–2)
Checkpoint Charlie	30 D4
Pankraz	31 C3
Zum Augustin	32 B3

ENTERTAINMENT	(p262)
Konzerthaus	33 C4
Stadttheater	34 B2

TRANSPORT	(pp262–3)
Avis	35 A3
Bundesbus Information	36 C5
Bus Station	37 C5
City Bus Station	38 B3
Europcar	39 C3
Hertz	40 B5
Lend Ferry	
Departure Point	41 A3
STW Verkehrsbetriebe Office	42 B3

CARINTHIA

Wörthersee is about 4km west of the city centre, with Europapark on its eastern shore.

Information

EMERGENCY & MEDICAL SERVICES

Hospital (Map p257; ☎ 538-0; St Veiter Strasse 47)

INTERNET ACCESS

Café-bar G@tes (Map p257; ☎ 50 97 77; gates@gates .at; Waagplatz 7; per 10 min €0.75; ☺ 9am-1am Mon-Fri, 7pm-1am Sat & Sun)
Cheeta's (Map p257; Herrengasse 7; per hr €3; ☺ 4pm-2am) Also has games & TV.

POST

Main Post Office (Map p257; Pernhartgasse 4; ☺ 7.30am-6pm Mon-Fri, 8am-11am Sat) One block west of Neuer Platz with another branch by the station.

TOURIST INFORMATION

Tourist office (Map p257; ☎ 53 722 23; www.info.klagen furt.at; Rathaus, Neuer Platz 1; ☺ 8am-8pm Mon-Fri, 10am-5pm Sat & Sun May–mid-Oct, 8am-6.30pm Mon-Fri, 10am-1pm Sat & Sun mid-Oct–Apr) Sells Kärnten cards and books accommodation free of charge.

TRAVEL AGENCIES

Kärntner Reisebüro (Map p257; ☎ 56 4 00-0; www.krb .at; Neuer Platz 2; ☺ 9am-6pm Mon-Fri, 9am-noon Sat) Helpful and central. Student fares available and ISIC cards (€10) issued.

Sights & Activities

MUSEUMS & GALLERIES

Landesmuseum (Map p257; ☎ 305 52; Museumgasse 2; adult/family €5/11.50; ☺ 10am-6pm Tue-Wed & Fri-Sun, 10am-8pm Thu, closed Mon) features the *Lindwurmschädel*, a fossilised rhinoceros head, which was the model for the head of the Dragon Fountain. The most interesting stuff is generally on the top floors including lots of Celtic armour and jewellery, roman busts and bronzes and religious art (look out for a bizarre painting of Mary Magdalene ascending to heaven covered in hair!). All explanations are in German.

Rolling art exhibitions are held in the various rooms of the **Stadtgalerie** (Map p257; ☎ 537 5532; www.stadtgalerie.net; Theatergasse 4; adult/concession €5/2.90; ☺ 10am-7pm Tue-Fri, 10am-5pm Sat & Sun), with several shows at once taking place in the one bright, attractive building. This is also a good place to pick up leaflets about art and culture events

taking place around town and further afield.

Bergbaumuseum (Mining Museum; Map p257; ☎ 51 12 52; Prof-Dr Kahler Platz 1; adult/concession €5/2.50; ☺ 9am-6pm 1 Apr-31 Oct) is a good option for a rainy day. Exhibits including tools and drilling equipment are housed in tunnels that lead from the grounds of the botanical gardens deep into the hill. The locals took shelter here from Allied bombing during WWII.

Neuer Platz, Klagenfurt's central square, is dominated by the **Dragon Fountain** (Map p257), the emblem of the city. The blankeyed, wriggling statue is modelled on the *Lindwurm* (dragon) of legend, said to have resided in a swamp here long ago, devouring cattle and virgins. The *Lindwurm* is depicted with the local hero who eventually clubbed it to death, wearing a scanty lion skin and sporting a truly terrifying moustache.

The provincial government headquarters, **Landhaus** (Map p257; ☎ 577 57-0; Landhaushof 1; ☺ 9am-5pm 1 Apr-31 Oct), stands just to the west of Alter Platz. Go through the archway into the cobbled two-storey courtyard to admire the building's two steeples. The ceiling of the **Wappensaal** (interior chamber; adult/concession €3/2) has a trompe l'oeil gallery painted by Carinthian artist Josef Ferdinand Fromiller (1693–1760), and depicting Carinthian landowners paying homage to Charles VI. Stand in the centre of the room for the best effect.

Alter Platz is the oldest square in the city and contains a number of historic buildings. It's a good place to watch the world go by from behind an ice cream or a glass of beer. Nearby is the **Stadthauptpfarrkirche St Egid**, with an ornate gold-leaf interior and fine ceiling frescos. Its **Stadtpfarrturm** (tower; €1; ☺ 10am-5.30pm Mon-Fri, 10am-12.30pm Sat Apr 9-Oct 9) can be climbed for a good view of the city and surrounding countryside. The **Dom** (cathedral; Domplatz 1), with its ornate marble pulpit and pink-and-white stuccoed ceiling, is also worth a look.

At the far end of Radetzkystrasse is a set of limp **Botanischer Garten** (Botanical Gardens; Map p257; admission free; ☺ 9am-6pm May-Sep). Adjoining the gardens is the **Kreuzbergl Kirche**, perched on a hillock with a set of very pretty mosaic stations of the cross on the path leading up to it.

EUROPAPARK VICINITY

The large, green expanse of Europapark and the *Strandbad* (beach) on the shores of Wörthersee are centres for summer activities, particularly for kids. Boating and swimming are generally available from May to September, although balmy weather can extend the season. Bus Nos 10, 11, 12, 20, 21 and 22 from Heiligengeistplatz run to Minimundus, though usually only Nos 10, 11 and 12 continue the short distance to Strandbad.

The slogan at **Minimundus** (Map p259; ☎ 211 94-0; Villacher Strasse 241; adult/child 6-16/under 6 €11/6/free; ⏱ 9am-6pm Apr & Oct, 9am-7pm May, Jun & Sep, 9am-10pm Jul & Aug) is: 'In one day, you can see the whole world!' It's a typical example of Austrian efficiency: why trek around the world admiring architecture when you can come to this theme park to see the planet's most impressive buildings handily rendered in miniature? Lying on the floor with a camera can give the impression that you've been to the real Taj Mahal, Eiffel Tower or Arc de Triomphe. English guides to the less recognisable models are on sale for €4. There's a café and restaurant (normal size) on site.

Strandbad (Map p259; ☎ 26 25 00; Metnitzstrand 2; day card adult/child €3.20/1.10, 3-8pm €1.45/0.75; ⏱ 8am-8pm approx early May-late Sep) is Klagenfurt's private beach, with cabins, wooden piers, shady grassy areas, a nude sunbathing terrace (for men on Tuesday, Thursday and Saturday; for women on other days) and a restaurant.

Next to the Strandbad (on the north side) are places where you can hire rowing boats (€1.85), pedal boats (€3.05) and motorboats (€5.25); rates are for 30 minutes.

At **Happ's Reptilienzoo** (Reptile Zoo; Map p259; ☎ 235 25; Villacher Strasse 237; adult/concession/child €8.50/4.30/3; ⏱ 8am-5pm winter, 8am-6pm summer), crocodiles of schoolchildren come to stare wide-eyed at the real thing, plus all manner of creepers, crawlers and slitherers. Some signs are in English.

Opposite the zoo is **Freizeitzentrum** (Map p259; ☎ 236 59; Villacher Strasse 235; ⏱ 9am-7pm Easter-31 Oct), which has a crazy-golf course, table tennis and pool tables and bikes for rent (per day/five hours €16/10).

WALKS

To take a walking tour, pick up the relevant brochure in English from the tourist office. It has a map and detailed descriptions of monuments, historic buildings and hidden courtyards. Free guided tours depart from the tourist office at 10am during July and August.

Festivals & Events

Klagenfurter Stadtfest is a two-day music and theatre festival that takes place every year in early July. The **Wörthersee Festival** (Wörtherseefestspiele; ☎ 507355-0; www.woertherseefestspiele.com) happens every summer between late June and mid-August, with operas, ballets and concerts taking place on a huge lakeside stage in the Wörthersee.

Sports events include the **Kärnten Ironman Triathlon** (www.ironmanaustria.com) in early July

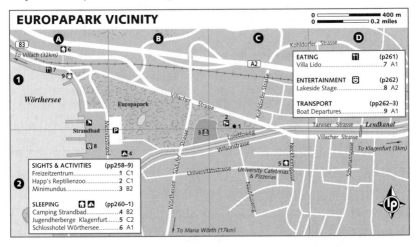

EUROPAPARK VICINITY

0 — 400 m
0 — 0.2 miles

EATING 🍴	(p261)
Villa Lido	7 A1
ENTERTAINMENT	(p262)
Lakeside Stage	8 A2
TRANSPORT	(pp262-3)
Boat Departures	9 A1

SIGHTS & ACTIVITIES	(pp258-9)
Freizeitzentrum	1 C1
Happ's Reptilienzoo	2 C1
Minimundus	3 B2

SLEEPING	(pp260-1)
Camping Strandbad	4 B2
Jugendherberge Klagenfurt	5 C2
Schlosshotel Wörthersee	6 A1

Wörthersee
Strandbad
Europapark
To Villach (32km)
To Klagenfurt (3km)
To Maria Wörth (17km)
Lendkanal

and **beach volleyball** (www.beachvolleyball.at) at the beginning of August. The tourist office will happily supply details of all these and more.

Sleeping

When you check into accommodation in Klagenfurt, ask for a copy of your *Gästekarte* (guest card), which entitles you to a range of discounts on local attractions and public transport.

BUDGET

Hotel Liebetegger (Map p257; ☎ 569 35; www.liebe tegger.com - in German; Völkermarkter Strasse 8; s with breakfast €35.50-52, d with breakfast €75; **P** 🖵) This good three-star hotel can serve as a budget choice if you skip breakfast (deduct €7.50 from the prices). The décor here is modern, but not bland, with interesting touches like cast-iron door handles and Gustav Klimt prints on the walls. There's a smart **café/bar** (mains €7-10; 🕑 24hr) attached. A wellness centre is planned for 2005.

Jugendherberge Klagenfurt (Map p257; ☎ 23 00 20; www.oejhv.or.at; Neckheimgasse 6; dm/s/d €17.50/21/42; **P** 🖵) This modern HI hostel is near Europapark. The four-bed dorms are clean and modern, with bathrooms. To get there from the centre, take bus Nos 10, 12 or 22 and get off at Jugendgästehaus or (depending on the bus route) Neckheimgasse. Reception is closed from noon to 5pm, though you can leave your bags during the day. Front-door keys are available and the friendly staff will make bookings for other hostels in the area. Book ahead as it's usually busy with school groups.

The other two youth hostels in Klagenfurt only open in summer: **Jugendhotel Kolping** (Map p257; ☎ 569 65; kolpinghaus_klagenfurt@yahoo .de; Enzenbergstrasse 26; s €22-32, d €32-52; **P**), from 1 July to 30 September, and **Mladinski Dom** (Map p257; ☎ 356 51; mlandinski.dom@chello.at; Mikschalle 4; s/d €22/36; **P**), 1km east of Völkermarkter Ring, from 1 July to 31 August.

About a dozen homes in Klagenfurt offer private rooms for €15-25 per person, but these are mostly in the suburbs. An exception is **Klepp** (Map p257; ☎ 322 78; Platzgasse 4; s/d/tr with shared bathroom €22/37/45), which has clean, reasonably sized and quiet rooms. Laundry facilities are available.

Campers at the big, well-equipped **Camping Strandbad** (Map p259; ☎ 211 69; www.caravan interland.nl; Metnitzstrand 5; site with electricity & shower per person €5.50; 🕑 1 May-30 Sep **P** 🏊) have free use of the Strandbad swimming complex. Caravans can also be rented here.

MID-RANGE & TOP END

Palais Hotel Landhaushof (Map p257; ☎ 59 09 59; www.landhaushof.at; Landhaushof 3; s/d with breakfast €130/190; ✗ 🖵 🖵) Klagenfurt's grandest hotel is a very stylish affair. Housed in a converted Renaissance palace, its décor features lots of snazzy granite, chrome and leather. The rooms range from elegant and traditional to kitsch and funky, with original baroque furniture given a new lease of life via innovative use of fabrics and colours. The restaurant, café and bar are no less attractive, with an airy, glass-roomed atrium in the main restaurant and café tables outside in the cobblestone courtyard.

Hotel Geyer (Map p257; ☎ 578 86; www.hotelgeyer .com; Priesterhausgasse 5; s with breakfast €55-75, d with breakfast €80-106, tr with breakfast €95-114; **P**) This three-star hotel has recently had a complete revamp and is now an excellent, central mid-range option. The smart interior has modern art on the walls and lots of funky and colourful touches. The bedrooms are plainer, but still well furnished. There's an outside patio for summer breakfasts.

Hotel Palais Porcia (Map p257; ☎ 51 15 90; www .hotel-palais-porcia.org; Neuer Platz 13; s with breakfast €84-182, d with breakfast €113-197; **P** ✗ 🏊) A marvellously ornate and old-fashioned hotel on the second floor of an old building, right in the town centre. Expect lots of gilt, mirrors and red-velvet couches, with pink marble and gold taps in the bathrooms. Some of the rather dark rooms have four-poster beds. There's no restaurant, but a huge lounge complete with leather armchairs, oil paintings and chandeliers.

Schlosshotel Wörthersee (Map p259; ☎ 211 58-0; www.schloss-hotel.at; Villacher Strasse 338; s/d with breakfast €48/76; **P**) The prices at this lakeside hotel go down in winter. The handsome yellow-painted exterior is better than the rather faded rooms, although they are slowly being refurbished. Not all rooms have a lake view, so check this when booking. There's a stretch of private beach and a restaurant.

Hotel Garni Blumenstöckl (Map p257; ☎ 577 93; www.blumenstoeckl.at; 10 Oktober Strasse 11; s with breakfast €42.10-50.85, d with breakfast €76.70) This two-star, family-run place is in a 400-year-old building, with rooms ranged around a plant-filled courtyard. The traditionally furnished rooms aren't terribly grand, but a central position and very friendly owners make up for this.

Eating

Restaurant Arkadenhof (Map p257; ☎ 590 959; Landhaushof 3; mains €11-21; ⟨ lunch & dinner) This is the more formal of the two restaurants in the up-market Palais Hotel Landhaushof. Here you can dine on Austrian dishes and Asian fusion food in chic surroundings – reserve ahead at busy times. Next door is a smart bar and **Restaurant Salzamt** (mains €4-17; ⟨ breakfast, lunch & dinner), a more informal 'kitchen' serving grills, wok noodles and pasta dishes.

Gasthaus im Landhaushof (Map p257; ☎ 502 363; Landhaushof 1; mains €10-19; ⟨ lunch & dinner) Tucked into a corner of the Landhaus square, this is another upmarket and stylish eating option, with tables and booths in a cosy vaulted cellar. The menu specialises in locally bred beef, with dishes like pepper steak flambéed in cognac and salted ox tongue. Don't be afraid to use your spoon for the sauces – the Austrian emperors apparently did!

Villa Lido (Map p259; ☎ 21 07 02; Friedelstrand 1; mains €8-16; ⟨ lunch & dinner) A short walk along the lakeshore from Europapark is this classy and attractive lakeside restaurant, with tables on a wooden deck overlooking the water. There's a daily risotto choice, a sumptuous ice-cream menu and some fish options alongside the usual meat dishes.

Ristorante da Luigi (Map p257; ☎ 51 66 51; Khevenhüller Strasse 2; mains €12-20; ⟨ dinner Mon, lunch & dinner Tue-Sat) This top-notch Italian restaurant has won numerous accolades for its excellent food and warm atmosphere. Don't expect pizza – giant prawns, calamari and escalope of veal are more the speciality.

Wirtshaus zum Heiligen Josef (Map p257; ☎ 500 807; Osterwitzgasse 7; mains €5-12; ⟨ lunch & dinner Mon-Fri) This great-value restaurant with outside tables serves excellent Austrian food, plus a few Italian vegetarian options such as risotto and gnocchi. There are daily soups and lunchtime specials and a very friendly, English-speaking owner.

Zauberhutt'n (Map p257; ☎ 547 95; Osterwitzgasse 6; mains €5-17; ⟨ dinner Sat, lunch & dinner Mon-Fri) This cheap, family-run Italian restaurant has a rustic interior and outside tables. It's

---

CARINTHIAN CULINARY SPECIALITIES

- **Käsnudel**: pockets of ravioli filled with curd cheese, mint and meat or vegetables

- **Saure Suppe**: 'sour soup' made from meat, herbs and sour cream, flavoured with saffron, fennel and aniseed

- **Kletzennudel**: pasta pockets filled with dried pears and served with melted butter, cinnamon and sugar, a favourite at Christmas

- **Reindling**: a cake made of yeast dough filled with cinnamon, sugar and raisins, traditionally served at Easter

- **Frigga**: a woodcutter's dish made from cured ham, cheese and polenta, cooked slowly in a heavy cast-iron pan

---

also the headquarters of the Magic Club of Klagenfurt, so expect the unexpected…

Gasthaus Pirker (Map p257; ☎ 571 35; Adlergasse 16; mains €6.40-11; ⟨ breakfast, lunch & dinner Mon-Fri) This family-orientated restaurant is a good place for kids, with high chairs and a children's menu. There are a couple of vegetarian options too.

Rathaus Stuberl (Map p257; ☎ 573 47; Pfarrplatz 8; mains €6.50-12; ⟨ lunch & dinner Mon-Sat) A cosy, very traditional bar/restaurant serving Carinthian specialities like *Nudeln* and steaks. The kitchen closes about 8.30pm when it's quiet.

A fruit and vegetable market (Map p257) occupies Benediktinerplatz from Monday to Saturday, bolstered by a flower market on Thursday and Saturday mornings. There are several tiny restaurants in the market square and a set of food stalls inside, making it a very cheap and atmospheric place to pick up a lunch of sausages, stew or cheese.

Out near Europapark, several student cafeterias and pizzerias line Universität-strasse, all a good option for cheap eats if you're staying in the youth hostel.

Self-caterers can stock up at the Spar supermarkets on Dr Hermann Gasse (Map p257), Bahnhofstrasse (Map p257) or in the station itself.

Drinking

Klagenfurt's nightlife is livelier in winter than during the summer, when most people decamp to the bars and nightclubs in the Wörthersee resorts of Pörtschach (opposite) or Velden (opposite). Even in summer, however, there are always at least a few people out in the bars lining the eastern end of Herrengasse.

Readers have recommended **Checkpoint Charlie** (Map p257; ☎ 0664 3572819; Herrengasse 3; ⌚ 5pm-2am, closed Sun), which occasionally hosts live rock and blues gigs.

Another good option for music lovers is **Pankraz** (Map p257; ☎ 516 675; 8 Mai Strasse 16; ⌚ 9am-4am Mon-Sat, 1pm-1am Sun), a funkily decorated place that sometimes features DJs and live jazz. There's a shop selling house and electronica CDs here, too.

More traditional in character, **Zum Augustin** (Map p257; ☎ 51 39 92; Pfarrhofgasse 2; mains €1-12; ⌚ 11am-12am Mon-Sat) has an attractive, copper-plated bar and a wooden floor. It brews its own beer and has eight different ales on tap. There's a cobbled courtyard at the back for alfresco eating.

Entertainment

Klagenfurt isn't exactly brimming with entertainment in the evenings. You can see plays, musicals and operas at the **Stadttheater** (Map p257; ☎ 540 64; www.stadttheater-klagenfurt.at - in German; Theaterplatz 4; tickets €20-70; box office ⌚ 8am-4pm Mon-Fri mid-Sep–mid-Jun). The **Konzerthaus** (Map p257; ☎ 542 72; Miesstaler Strasse 8) puts on other musical events. There's a booklet with a timetable of events available from the tourist office. In summer, the best place to see stage performances is at the **lakeside stage** by the Europapark (p259).

Getting There & Away

AIR
Flights leave Klagenfurt airport for destinations in the UK, Austria and Germany (p362).

BOAT
The departure point for boat cruises on the lake is only a few hundred metres north of Strandbad. See opposite for information on timetables and lakeside resorts.

BUS
Bundesbuses depart from outside the *Hauptbahnhof* (Map p257), where there's an **information office** (Map p257; ☎ 543 40; ⌚ 7.30am-1pm Mon-Fri) with a timetable board outside. See p264 for information on buses going to lake resorts.

CAR & MOTORCYCLE
Since the opening of a bypass, the A2/E66 between Villach and Graz skirts the north of Klagenfurt.

Car rental offices include:
Avis (Map p257; ☎ 559 38; Villacher Strasse 1c)
Europcar (Map p257; ☎ 351 4538; Völkermarkter Ring 9)
Hertz (Map p257; ☎ 561 47; St Ruprechter Strasse 12)

TRAIN
Direct IC (InterCity) trains run from Klagenfurt station to Vienna (€37.30, four hours, every two hours) and Salzburg (€27.70, 2¼ hours, every two hours). Trains to Graz depart every one to two hours (€27.70, two to three hours); these go via Bruck an der Mur (€22.30, 2¼ hours, 170km). Trains to western Austria, Italy, Slovenia and Germany go via Villach (€7, 30 to 40 minutes, two to four per hour).

Getting Around

TO/FROM THE AIRPORT
To get to the airport, take bus No 40 from the main train station or Heiligengeistplatz to Annabichl (€1.60, 25 minutes), then change to bus No 45 (10 minutes).

BOAT
A **motor ferry** (☎ 0664 34 25 788; €4) chugs along the Lendkanal between the centre of Klagenfurt, through Europapark and up to the shore of the Wörthersee (55 minutes, three times daily Monday to Saturday).

BUS
Single bus tickets (which you buy from the driver) cost €0.90 for two or three stops or €1.60 for one hour. Drivers also sell 24-hour passes for €4, but these cost only €3.35 when purchased in advance from ticket machines or the **STW Verkehrsbetriebe office** (Map p257; ☎ 521 542; Heiligengeistplatz 4; ⌚ 7.30am-1.30pm Mon-Fri), which also hands out free timetables. A strip of 10 tickets costs €13 when bought in advance. The advance purchase tickets and passes must be validated in the machine after boarding the bus.

CYCLING
As well as renting bikes, the tourist office provides a Radwandern cycle map, listing

CARINTHIA

sights and distances. Tours (the longest being 34km) are arranged by themes.

TAXI
For taxi services in Klagenfurt, call ☎ 311 11 or ☎ 27 11.

CENTRAL CARINTHIA

WÖRTHERSEE
The Wörthersee is one of the warmer lakes in the region owing to thermal springs: the average water temperature between June and September is 21°C. Summers in this part of Carinthia are very hot in any case, so it's an ideal location for frolicking amid the lapping waves, or for the serious pursuit of water sports. The lake stretches from west to east between Velden and Klagenfurt and the long, thin shoreline provides unfolding vistas on a boat trip.

The northern shore has the best transport access and is the busiest section, with a packed programme of summer events, from go-kart rallies to avant-garde festivals of tattoo and body painting.

Pörtschach
The most exclusive of the resorts is Pörtschach, with a distinctive tree-lined peninsula with a curving bay on either side. Here you'll find some upmarket bars and restaurants, a golf course and the usual water sports. It's a favourite spot for wealthy

citizens of Salzburg and Vienna, many of whom own private villas here.

Contact **Pörtschach Information** (☎ 04272-23 54; www.tiscover.at/poertschach; Hauptstrasse 153; ☼ 7.30am-4pm Mon-Thu, 7.30am-1pm Fri) for details of (mostly upmarket) accommodation and sports activities.

The biggest nightclub on the lake is **Fabrik** (☎ 0664 44 000 45; www.fabrik.at; ☼ from 11pm Fri-Sun), in the tiny village of Saag between Pörtschach and Velden. Shuttle buses run to here from both places.

Velden
Velden enjoys a reputation as the Wörthersee's top nightlife resort and is also the venue of various high-adrenaline sports events on summer weekends. It's a brash, lively place packed with a strange combination of young and beautiful people nursing cocktails and parties of old-age pensioners nibbling ice cream.

Veldener Tourismus (tourist office; ☎ 2103-0; www .velden.at; Villacher Strasse 19; ☼ 8am-8pm Jul & Aug, 8am-6pm May-Jun & Sep-Oct, 8am-5pm Mon-Sat Nov-May) can advise on accommodation and provide lists of events and bike hire locations.

Five kilometres south of Velden is Rosegg, with **Wildpark** (animal park; ☎ 04274-523 57; www .rosegg.at; adult/child €6.50/3.60; ☼ 9am-6pm Jul & Aug, 9am-5pm Apr-Jun & Sep-Oct) and a **Schloss** (palace; ☎ 04274-30 09; www.rosegg.at; adult/child €5.50/3.30; ☼ 10am-6pm Tue-Sun, daily Jul & Aug). Both of these are closed in winter.

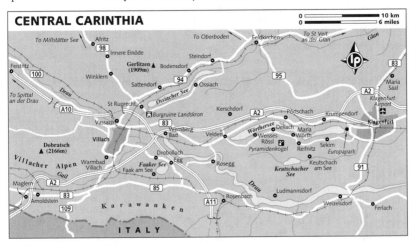

CENTRAL CARINTHIA

Maria Wörth

On the southern shore lies Maria Wörth, a small resort dominated by two medieval churches. The larger Pfarrkirche combines Gothic, baroque and Romanesque elements; the smaller 12th-century Winterkirche features frescoes of the apostles.

On the hill southwest of Maria Wörth is the **Pyramidenkogel** (☎ 04273-2443; adult/child €4.75/1.85; 10am-6pm Apr & Oct, 9am-7pm May & Sep, 9am-8pm Jun, 9am-9pm Jul & Aug), a hill topped by a rather avant-garde tower that provides fine views of Wörthersee and the surrounding mountain ranges. Further details are available from the Maria Wörth **tourist office** (☎ 04273-22400; www.tiscover.at/maria-woerth; Süduferstrasse 110; 8am-4.30pm Mon-Thu, 8am-12.30pm Fri winter, 8am-7pm Mon-Fri, 10am-7pm Sat & Sun spring-autumn).

Getting Around

BICYCLE

A circuit of the lake is about 50km, well within the limits of most casual cyclists, especially with an overnight stop somewhere. There is a *Fahrrad Verleih* (Rent a Bike) scheme in the summer; rent a standard bicycle at one of several outlets round the lake and return it at any other outlet (five hours/24 hours/one week €5/9/35). Mountain bikes (€10/16/75) can also be hired.

BOAT

STW (☎ 0463-211 55; schiffahrt@stw.at; St Veiter Strasse 31, Klagenfurt) runs motorboats and steamers on the lake from early May to early October. Boats call at both sides, stopping at Klagenfurt, Krumpendorf, Sekirn, Reifnitz, Maria Wörth, Pörtschach, Dellach, Weisses Rössl, Auen and Velden. They return by the same route, departing from Klagenfurt at least every two hours.

You can get on and off the boat en route if you buy a *Rundfahrtkarte* (return) ticket, which allows unlimited trips in one day (adult/child €12.80/6.40). The longest trip (Klagenfurt–Velden) takes 1¾ hours on a steamer (motorboats are quicker) and costs €8.80 one-way.

BUS & TRAIN

Bundesbuses travel along both shores of the lake, stopping at all the main resorts; for information call ☎ 0463-500 830. Buses run between Villach and Klagenfurt (€5.20, 1¼ hours, eight times a day) travelling along the northern shore. Buses also run along the southern lakeshore between Klagenfurt and Velden via Maria Wörth (€5.20, 35 minutes, four times daily Monday to Saturday).

Trains between Klagenfurt and Villach run along the northern shore of the lake every 30 to 60 minutes. Regional trains from Klagenfurt stop at Krumpendorf (€1.60, seven minutes), Pörtschach (€3.10, 15 minutes) and Velden (€4.50, 20 minutes); express trains stop at only one or two of those stations.

CAR & MOTORCYCLE

The A2/E66 and Hwy 83, which runs closer to the shore, are on the northern side of the lake. On the southern side, the route is classified as a main road, but it's much smaller.

VILLACH

☎ 04242 / pop 57,900

Lively Villach is an important transport hub for routes into Italy and Slovenia, with visitors from both countries much in evidence during the summer holidays. It's not a very picturesque town, but serves as a handy base for exploring the nearby lakes, beaches and beauty spots. Warmbad Villach is a suburb famous for its rejuvenating spa waters (p267).

Orientation & Information

The old town centre is south of the Drau River. The train and bus stations are north of the river.

Amadeus Bookshop (Hauptplatz 4) Provides maps of the area.

Café Nicolai (☎ 22 511; Nikolaigasse 16; per 10 mins €1; 7am-9pm Mon-Fri, 7am-2pm Sat) Fast but expensive Internet access.

Tourist office (☎ 205-2900; www.villach.at; Rathausplatz 1; 8am-noon & 1-5pm Mon-Fri, 8am-6pm July & Aug, 9am-noon Sat May-Oct) Can find accommodation in town.

Sights

Stadtpfarrkirche St Jakob (parish church of St Jakob; ☎ 205 3540; Obere Kirchenplatz 8), an enormous, monolithic church, dominates the small old town, which otherwise has a modest spread of smart shops and outdoor cafés. Inside, the far end of the nave has an impressive stuccoed ceiling and a vast rococo altar in gold leaf, arrayed with fresh cream flowers. The walls are studded with the ornate memorial plaques of the region's noble families. Every summer a pair of falcons nests

View of Grossglockner peak from Franz Josefs Höhe (p286), Hohe Tauern National Park

MARK HONAN

GARETH MCCORMACK

The Grossglockner peak towering over Heiligenblut (p286), Hohe Tauern National Park

Burg Hochosterwitz (p271), Carinthia

MARK HONAN

MARK HONAN

Friesach (p268), Carinthia

Ski resort, Lech (p345), Western Arlberg, Vorarlberg

Schloss Ambras (p303), Innsbruck, Tyrol

Silvretta Alps (p334), Vorarlberg

Skier, St Anton am Arlberg (p329), Tyrol

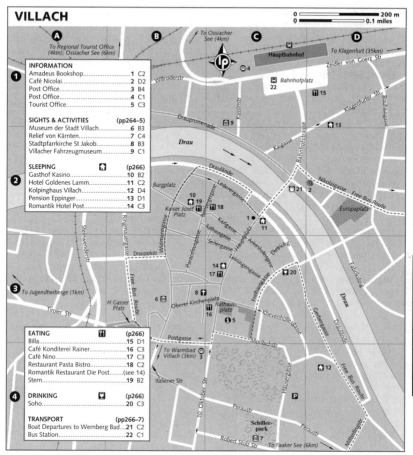

VILLACH

0 — 200 m
0 — 0.1 miles

To Regional Tourist Office
(4km); Ossiacher See (6km)

To Ossiacher
See (4km)

Hauptbahnhof

To Klagenfurt (35km)

Zeidler von Goerz Str

INFORMATION
Amadeus Bookshop........................1 C2
Café Nicolai................................2 D2
Post Office...................................3 B4
Post Office...................................4 C1
Tourist Office................................5 C3

SIGHTS & ACTIVITIES (pp264–5)
Museum der Stadt Villach..............6 B3
Relief von Kärnten........................7 C4
Stadtpfarrkirche St Jakob..............8 B3
Villacher Fahrzeugmuseum............9 C1

SLEEPING (p266)
Gasthof Kasino............................10 B2
Hotel Goldenes Lamm..................11 C2
Kolpinghaus Villach......................12 D4
Pension Eppinger..........................13 D1
Romantik Hotel Post......................14 C3

EATING (p266)
Billa...15 D1
Café Konditerei Rainer..................16 C3
Café Nino..................................17 C3
Restaurant Pasta Bistro.................18 C2
Romantik Restaurant Die Post.....(see 14)
Stern.......................................19 B2

DRINKING (p266)
Soho..20 C3

TRANSPORT (pp266–7)
Boat Departures to Wernberg Bad...21 C2
Bus Station................................22 C1

Bahnplatz

Drau

Draupromenade

Europaplatz

To Jugendherberge (1km)

Tiroler Str

Burgplatz

Kaiser Josef
Platz

Rathausplatz

Oberer-Kirchenplatz

Postgasse

To Warmbad
Villach (3km)

Italiener Str

Schiller-
park

To Faaker See (6km)

CARINTHIA

---

in the **Stadtpfarrturm** (steeple; adult/student €1.80/1; 10am-4pm Mon-Sat May & Oct, 10am-6pm Mon-Fri, 12-5pm Sat Jun-Sep), the highest in Carinthia. You can watch their domestic life on a closed-circuit TV screen in the square opposite.

Relief Von Kärnten (relief map; ☎ 20 53 550; Peraustrasse; adult/student €1.80/1; 10am-4.30pm Mon-Sat 2 May–31 Oct) is a huge relief model of Carinthia housed in Schillerpark, south of the old town. It covers 182 sq metres and depicts the province at a scale of 1:10,000 (1:5000 vertically, to exaggerate the mountains). It could help you plan your trip (or track your progress) through the region.

Villacher Fahrzeugmuseum (☎ 25 530; Draupromenade 12; admission €5.50; 9am-5pm mid-Jun–mid-Sep, 10am-noon & 2-4pm mid-Sep–May) displays ever-

increasing numbers of vintage motorcycles and cars, all rather crammed together.

Museum der Stadt Villach (☎ 20 53 500; Widmanngasse 38; adult/student €2.50/1.80; 10am-4.30pm Mon-Sat 2 May–31 Oct) is a fairly unexciting museum covering local history, archaeology and medieval art.

Festivals & Events
On the first Saturday in August, the pedestrian centre is taken over by the **Kirchtag** (☎ 205 3211; www.villacherkirchtag.at - in German; tickets €7), a folk-music festival featuring groups from Italy, Latvia and Slovenia as well as local musicians. There are plenty of costumes, food stalls and fireworks. Some events begin during the preceding week.

CARINTHIA

Sleeping

As well as the options listed below, it's also possible to stay in Warmbad Villach (opposite) – there are actually more hotels and pensions there than in Villach itself.

Romantik Hotel Post (☎ 261 01-0; www.romantik -hotel.com; Hauptplatz 26; s/d with breakfast €63/115; P ⊠ 🖳) The corridors of this smart hotel are atmospheric, with chandeliers and oriental rugs, but the rooms could do with a refit: they currently have rather nasty pastel-painted furniture and garish bathroom tiles. Those overlooking the square can be noisy thanks to the old, ill-fitting windows. There's a good restaurant downstairs (above).

Gasthöf Kasino (☎ 244 49; www.hotel-kasino.at; Kaiser Josef Platz 4; s/d €43.60/83.60; P ⊠ 🖳) The rooms at this three-star hotel are ultra-modern and functional but entirely devoid of character, with smallish bathrooms. It has an inexpensive **restaurant** (mains €4-10; ⊗ closed Sun). There's no lift.

Hotel Goldenes Lamm (☎ 241 65; www.goldenes lamm.at; Hauptplatz 1; s/d/tr with breakfast €60/94/120, without breakfast €53/80/99; P ⊠) This is a central, plain and modern three-star hotel with a range of room prices and standards – if possible ask to see a few before you book.

Pension Eppinger (☎ 243 89; Klagenfurter Strasse 6; s/d with bathroom €24/32, without bathroom €18/21; P) This small pension is set back from the street through a green gate. It has a few simple, good-value rooms and a friendly hostess who doesn't speak English (and may go out occasionally, so phone ahead).

Jugendherberge (☎ 563 68; www.oejhv.or.at; Dinzlweg 34; dm/s/d €16.80/23.80/40.60; ⊗ reception 7-10am & 5-10pm, doors open all day) This HI hostel is about 1km west of the pedestrian centre. From H Gasser Platz, head west along Tyroler Strasse over the railway tracks and then bear right on St Martiner Strasse. Dinzlweg is the first on the left, but car drivers need to stay on Tyroler Strasse, which eventually loops round.

Another budget option in summer is **Kolpinghaus Villach** (☎ 270 71-0; Hausergasse 5; s/d €23.65/36; ⊗ reception 8-10am & 4-9pm), a student residence offering functional rooms to tourists from the end of July to the beginning of August.

Eating & Drinking

Stern (☎ 24 755; Kaiser Josef Platz 5; mains €10-13.90; ⊗ lunch & dinner Mon-Fri) This is the pick of Villach's restaurants – a stylish and contemporary space with leather sofas in the bar and modern art and poetry on the walls. The menu features a modern take on traditional Austrian food and Carinthian specialities, plus monthly themes such as middle-eastern or oriental cooking. It also holds occasional art exhibitions and events.

Romantik Restaurant Die Post (☎ 261 01-0; Hauptplatz 26; mains €5.90-16.50; ⊗ lunch & dinner Tue-Sat) The restaurant of the Romantik Hotel Post is more old-fashioned and traditional than Stern, but it serves acclaimed regional specialities and has a cosy and intimate atmosphere. Midday meat or veg *Menüs* (set menus) are good value and there's also a good selection of salads.

Restaurant Pasta Bistro (☎ 0676 33 86313; Kaiser Josef Platz 7; mains €5-12.80; ⊗ lunch & dinner Sun-Fri, dinner Sat) This new restaurant in a cosy, vaulted room offers an unusual and extensive menu of fish specialities alongside fresh, filled baguettes (as a main course) and a selection of salads and pastas. There are a couple of meat and vegetarian dishes, also.

Café Nino (☎ 24 802; Hauptplatz 28; mains €3-9.80; ⊗ breakfast, lunch & dinner Mon-Sat) A friendly, buzzy café on the old town square, with plenty of tables outside and fresh calamari on the menu every Friday. It also serves great ice cream and extravagant coffees.

Café Konditerei Rainer (☎ 243 77; Oberer Kirchenplatz 5; lunches €4.40-5.70; ⊗ lunch) Villach's oldest café has a sumptuous array of more than 50 different cakes, daily lunch specials, diabetic options and a kid's play area, plus in summer a screen with live pictures from the 'falcon cam' at the top of the church steeple opposite (p265).

Soho (☎ 0664 14 54 222; Freihausgasse 13; ⊗ 7pm-2am) Under the same management as Stern, this is Villach's trendiest bar/club, with live jazz on Monday, cocktail specials on Thursday and DJs on Friday and Saturday, plus plenty of sponsored special events.

For self-caterers, there's a Billa supermarket opposite the train station, with various snack places close by.

Getting There & Around

A small **city bus** (☎ 205 6400; free; ⊗ every 20 min during shopping hours Mon-Fri) runs around the city centre – look for the blue bus stops.

Villach is on three Austrian ICE rail routes, serving Salzburg (€23.50, 2½ hours, every two hours), Lienz (€16.20, 1½ hours, hourly) and Klagenfurt (€7, 30 to 40 minutes, two to four per hour). Direct services go to many destinations, eg Venice, Italy (€18.40, 3½ hours, three per day), Ljubljana, Slovenia (€24.50, 1¾ hours, four daily), and Zagreb, Croatia (€44.10, 4½ hours, three daily).

Various bus routes radiate from Villach; call ☎ 500 830 for Bundesbus information. For information about bus services to the Wörthersee resorts, see p264.

AROUND VILLACH
WARMBAD VILLACH
Three kilometres south of the town centre is **Warmbad Villach**, a complex of thermal pools and rejuvenating radioactive mineral waters, reputed to give relief to health problems from rheumatism to constipation. Nearly 40 million litres of water gush daily from six springs, and despite the old-fashioned image of 'taking the cure', the resort remains very popular.

Kinetotherapy, mud baths, aquatherapy, massage, saunas and more are on offer in plush hotels and at the state-sponsored **Kurzentrum Heilbad Thermalbad Warmbad** (☎ 370 00; Kadischenallee 24-26; day pass for pool €9.50; ☺ 8am-7pm). In the latter you can also swim in the thermal pool or lounge in the hot baths (€7.90). **Erlebnistherme Warmbad** (☎ 378 89; Kadischenallee 25-27; sauna & pool pass €12; ☺ 9am-8pm) is a more conventional, non-thermal swimming pool with a water slide, indoor and outdoor swimming areas and a sauna complex. City bus No 1 goes to Warmbad (€1.60) from central Villach.

FAAKER SEE & OSSIACHER SEE
Six kilometres east of Villach, the **Faaker See**, close to the Karawanken range, and the **Ossiacher See**, 4km to the northeast, offer lower-key holidays than the flash resorts of the Wörthersee, with plenty of camping, boating and swimming opportunities. On the Ossiacher See, **boats** (☎ 04242 58071; www.schiffahrt.at/drau - in German) complete a crisscross tour between St Andrä and Steindorf (€10.50, 2½ hours, approximately hourly from May to October).

Boats run by the same company also navigate the Drau River between Villach Kongresshaus and Wernberg Bad (€10 return) up to four times a day between late April and early October.

SIGHTS & ACTIVITIES
Adler Flugschau (Falconry show; ☎ 04242-428 88; www.adlerflugschau.com; Burgruine Landskron, Schlossweg; adult/child €6/3; ☺ 11am & 3pm May, Jun, Sep, 11am, 3pm & 6pm Jul & Aug) a 40-minute birds-of-prey show that takes place in the ruins of Landskron Castle between Villach and the Ossiacher See. During the show captive-bred falcons, eagles and vultures are released to soar and swoop in the upcurrents above the crumbling stone walls. Also in the grounds of the castle is **Affenberg** (Monkey Mountain; ☎ 04242-31 97 02; adult/child €6/3; ☺ 9.30am-5.30pm 1 Apr-31 Oct), a monkey reserve where cute simians roam free. There's a café here and a souvenir shop selling 'miscellaneous monkey things'.

If you have young kids, you might want to check out one of several puppet museums in the region: **Elli Riehl's Puppenwelt** (☎ 04248-23 95; Buchholzer Str 4, Einöde; adult/child €4.20/2.10; ☺ 9am-6pm Jun-Sep, 9am-noon & 2-4pm Apr, May, 1-15 Oct) and **Puppenmuseum** (☎ 04242-228 55; Vassacher Strasse 65, Vassach; ☺ Apr-Dec).

Walkers and mountain bikers should head for the **Dobsbratsch** (2166m) area, in the Villacher Alpen about 12km west of Villach. Just south of here, hiking trails go from the small town of Arnoldstein to the Dreiländereck – the point where Austria, Italy and Slovenia meet. At 1500m there's an **Alpine garden** (☎ 0664 91 42 953; adult/child €2/1; ☺ 9am-6pm 1 Jun-31 Aug) containing flora from the southern Alps. To reach the garden, follow the Villacher Alpenstrasse from the town. This is a toll road (per car €13), though from about November to mid-March it's free. It's closed to caravans. Dobratsch is popular for cross-country skiers, but the main downhill area is **Gerlitzen** (1909m), whose peaks form the northern backdrop to the Ossiacher See. Day pass €29.50.

Sleeping
You could quite happily base yourself in Villach to explore the whole region, though there are also numerous accommodation options around Ossiacher See and Faaker See, including campsites, hotels, pensions, private rooms and holiday apartments. Staff at the **Warmbad Villach tourist office** (☎ 04242-372 44; therme.warmbad@villach.at; ☺ 8am-1pm & 2-6pm Mon-Fri 9am-1pm Sat) find rooms commission free.

Refer to the region-wide accommodation brochure obtainable from the Villach tourist office, or contact the **regional tourist office**

(☎ 04242-420 00; www.da-lacht-das-herz.at; Töbringer Strasse 1, Villach). The local tourist offices at the specific lake resorts can also help out.

Getting There & Around

From Villach train station hourly trains and buses run to Warmbad Villach (€1.60) and along the northern shore of Ossiacher See; trains to Faaker See are less frequent. Bundesbuses run to both lakes from Villach bus station. You can also explore the region by bicycle. You can hire bikes at Villach and Bodensdorf train stations and from various hotels and campsites around the region.

EASTERN CARINTHIA

Eastern Carinthia's prettiest medieval towns and most impressive castles lie north of Klagenfurt, on or close to Hwy 83 and the rail route between Klagenfurt and Bruck an der Mur. There are mountain ranges on either side: the Seetaler Alpen and Saualpe to the east and the Gurktaler Alpen to the west.

FRIESACH

☎ 04268 / pop 5400

Friesach is Carinthia's oldest town, once a key staging post on the Vienna–Venice trade route. Its claim to fame in the middle ages was as the home of the silver 'Friesach penny', the first widespread currency in the southwest Alps, which was minted from silver mined near the town.

The hills on either side of Friesach bristle with ruined fortifications and the town centre is surrounded by a moat (it's the only town in Austria that still has one) and a set of imposing, grey-stone walls. These have been tested to the fullest over the centuries, with successive invasions by the Bohemians, Hungarians, Turks and French before the town came under the wing of the Habsburgs in 1803.

These days, Friesach is a peaceful, laid-back little place with pastel buildings lining the tiny town square, green hills on all sides and an annual medieval summer festival. The town's medieval heritage is very much alive and well all-year round – it's not unusual to see kids in medieval costume scampering around or grownups cycling by in pointed hats and smocks. It's well worth heading up here for the day or overnight.

Orientation & Information

Friesach lies in the Metnitz Valley. At the centre of town, the picturesque *Hauptplatz* (main square) is a few minutes' walk from the train station along Bahnhofstrasse: turn left on leaving the station and follow the road as it branches right, then turn a corner and step back in time as the moat and ramparts come into view.

There's a free touch-screen Internet point opposite the Goldener Anker guesthouse and a bank with an ATM on the town square.

Tourist office (☎ 43 00; www.friesach.at; Fürstenhofplatz 1; ☺ 8am-5pm Mon-Fri, 10am-4pm Sat & Sun 1 May-Sep 30, 8am-noon Mon-Fri 1 Oct-21 Apr) Walk towards the main square and then follow the signs leading off to the right. The Spur des Einhorns exhibit is in the same complex.

Sights & Activities

Die Spur des Einhorns (☎ 43 00; www.friesach.at; Fürstenhofplatz 1; adult/student/child €5.50/3.50/2.50; ☺ 9am-6pm May-Oct) is Friesach's main attraction, a contemporary and dreamlike art installation, housed in a 15th-century bishop's palace and loosely based on the myths and stories of the medieval age in Europe. Visitors move from room to room, assailed with ambient music, disembodied voices and a variety of sound and light effects. The voiceovers are all in German, but there's an English information sheet explaining the different rooms you'll walk through: from an 'enchanted forest' made of mirrors to the final resting place of the mighty sword, Excalibur. It's fascinating, beautiful and perfect for children and adults alike.

In the moat behind the exhibition is the Wheel of Life, another installation by the same artist. It's a giant water wheel adorned with rusted-metal human figures, apparently charting mankind's progress from birth to death.

The rest of Friesach's attractions are more conventionally historic. Ranged along the hills rising above *Hauptplatz* to the west stand four ancient fortifications, all providing excellent views of the town and valley. The northernmost is Burg Geyersberg; the furthest south is the Virgilienberg Ruins. The middle two are the most easily visited from the town. The best view is from **Peterskirche**, accessible by paths ascending from in front of the *Stadtpfarrkirche*. To see the Gothic interior of Peterskirche, ask for the key at the house next door (☎ 23 19).

Behind Peterskirche, **Petersberg** houses the small town **museum** (☎ 26 00; adult/child/concession €3/0.75/1.50; ⏰ 1-5pm Tue-Sun 1 May-30 Jun & 1 Sep-10 Oct, 10am-5pm Tue-Sun Jul & Aug), with exhibits covering the town's medieval history and religious art. The Petersberg castle is also the site for open-air theatre performing anything from Shakespeare to Brecht in summer. Obtain details and tickets (prices ranging from €10.20 to €18.50) from the tourist office.

North of the moat is a **Dominican monastery** (Stadtgrabengasse 5; admission free). Its 13th-century Gothic church is open to the public from dawn till dusk daily and is noted for its wooden crucifix and a sandstone statue of the Virgin.

Just to the north is the **Stadtpfarrkirche**, on Wienerstrasse, which has a fine 12th-century font and a distinctive tiled roof. To see the interior of the slender 14th-century **Heiligblutkirche** (Church of the Holy Blood; Seminarpark; ⏰ by arrangement), visible on the hill to the southwest of Hauptplatz, you need to join one of the tourist office's guided tours (€3.50 per person, minimum 15 people).

Festivals & Events

The **Spectaculum** is one evening in early August where the Middle Ages lives again: electric lights are extinguished and the town is lit by torches and flares as jesters, princesses and knights in shining armour stroll around juggling, fire-eating and staging jousting tournaments and duels. The town reverts to the currency that made it famous, with medieval meals from street stalls being paid for with Friesach Pennies. Contact the tourist office for dates and event information.

Friesach also holds an annual **jazz festival** (www.friejazz.com), with performances taking place in various historical venues around town.

Sleeping

Zum Goldenen Anker (☎ 23 13; www.goldeneranker .at; Bahnhofstrasse 3; s/d with breakfast €30/50) This small *Gasthöf* just off the main town square is the best deal in town. Some of the spick-and-span rooms have antique furniture and traditional ceramic stoves. The food in the wood-panelled restaurant next door is also good value. Reception is in the restaurant.

Weisser Wolf (☎ 22 63; www.weisser-wolf.at; Hauptplatz 8; s/d €35/62) This *Gasthöf* has plain, clean rooms, some overlooking the square,

and a vaulted **restaurant** (mains €6.55-12; ⏰ lunch & dinner, closed Mon in winter) with outside terrace.

Metnitztalerhof (☎ 25 10-0; www.metnitztalerhof .at - in German; Hauptplatz 11; s/d with breakfast €48-96; P ☒ ▣) This pastel-pink edifice at the far end of the town square is the only four-star hotel in Friesach; the rather ordinary wooden-floored rooms have a big balcony with good views. There's a sauna, Jacuzzi and steam room on site. The **restaurant** (mains €6.20-18; ⏰ lunch & dinner, closed Fri in winter) serves Austrian and Carinthian dishes. There's a fine view of the square from the raised terrace tables.

Getting There & Away

Friesach is on the railway line between Vienna's Südbahnhof (€33, 3¾ hours) and Villach (€13.90, 1½ hours). Bruck an der Mur (€17.70, 1¾ hours) and Klagenfurt (€9.70, 40 to 60 minutes) are also on this route. Bundesbuses run to Friesach from Klagenfurt via St Veit several times a day.

GURK

☎ 04266 / pop 1340

This small town, some 18km west of the Friesach–Klagenfurt road, is notable for its **Dom** (cathedral; ☎ 82 36-12; Domplatz 11; ⏰ closed during services). It was built between 1140 and 1200 and is one of the finest examples of Romanesque architecture in Austria. The pale-pink exterior of the cathedral is dominated by two huge onion domes that cap square-sided twin towers. The interior has Gothic reticulated vaulting on the ceiling and most of the church fittings are baroque or rococo. The early-baroque high altar is particularly impressive, laden with 72 statues and 82 angel heads.

The frescoes in the **Bischofskapelle** (Episcopal Chapel; adult/concession €3.60/2.95; ⏰ guided tour 1.20pm, 2.20pm & 3.50pm), dating from around 1200, are made all the more affecting by their primitive colours. This chapel can be viewed by guided tour only. Guided tours are also possible of the cathedral and the 100-pillared crypt.

Getting There & Away

Gurk cannot be reached by rail and Bundesbuses only go there from Klagenfurt (via St Veit an der Glan, 1¾ hours) three times a day (twice on Sunday). Private transport makes a visit much easier: the town is on Hwy 93.

HÜTTENBERG

☎ 04263

Step off the bus in the tiny mining village of Hüttenberg and you might be forgiven for thinking you'd landed in Tibet – fluttering prayer flags climb up the cliff at the entrance to the town, and a giant painting of the Buddha gazes benevolently down on the populace. The reason for all this is that Hüttenberg is the birthplace of Austria's most famous explorer, Heinrich Harrer (below), who famously spent Seven Years in Tibet and was immortalised by Brad Pitt for his efforts.

Outside the **Heinrich Harrer Museum** (☎ 8108; Bahnhofstrasse 12; adult/concession €7.50/4; ☉ 10am-5pm 1 Apr-31 Oct) you can sip on a bowl of butter tea and listen to the rush of water through wooden prayer wheels, before going inside the beautiful stone and wood building to see the huge collection of objects and photographs Harrer brought back from his world travels. There's a cinema inside showing a film about Harrer's life (in German), plus a replica of a Tibetan ceremonial chamber complete with the sound of prayer horns and chanting. All explanations are unfortunately in German, but there's enough interesting stuff here to pass a good few hours.

Opposite the museum is the Lingkor, a metal walkway built up the cliff face as an aid to prayer and meditation. The colourful prayer wheels made from oil drums are a fitting testament to Hüttenberg's strange mixture of heavy industry (this is an iron-ore mining area).

Getting There & Away

Huttenberg can be reached by bus from St Veit an der Glan (€6, one hour, five times daily Monday to Friday) but buses are very infrequent at weekends. Services are more frequent from Klagenfurt (€8, 1¼ hours, 10 buses daily Monday-Friday).

ST VEIT AN DER GLAN

☎ 04212 / pop 12,700

St Veit was historically important as the seat of the dukes of Carinthia from 1170 until 1518, when the dukes skipped down the road to Klagenfurt and the town diminished in status. These days it's a handsome, mid-sized town that makes an agreeable base for explorations of the medieval towns and other attractions further north.

Orientation & Information

St Veit is near the junction of primary road routes to Villach (Hwy 94) and Klagenfurt (Hwy 83). To get to the pedestrian-only town centre from the *Hauptbahnhof*, walk left down Bahnhofstrasse for 600m and then go one block right.

The **tourist office** (☎ 5555-668; www.stveit.carinthia.at; Rathaus, Hauptplatz 1; ☉ 8am-8pm) sells maps of the town for €1.

Sight & Activities

The most impressive façade on St Veit's long *Hauptplatz* belongs to the **Rathaus**. Its baroque stuccowork was applied in 1754 and features a double-headed eagle on the pediment. St Veit (the saint, not the town) stands between the eagle's wings. Walk through the Gothic vaulted passage to admire the arcaded courtyard, bedecked with sgraffito (a mural or decoration in which the top layer is scratched off to reveal the original underneath).

The *Hauptplatz* itself has a fountain at either end and a central column erected in

---

HEINRICH HARRER – HERO OR NAZI?

When WWII broke out in 1939, a young Austrian mountaineer named Heinrich Harrer, in India on a climbing expedition, found himself rounded up and imprisoned by the British. In 1944 Harrer and a fellow internee, Peter Aufschnaiter, escaped, trekking on foot across the Tibetan plateau to the forbidden city of Lhasa. He stayed for five years, beginning a lifelong friendship with the teenage Dalai Lama and teaching him the ways of the then-unknown outside world (he built the kingdom's first cinema at the boy's request). He left soon after the Communist invasion of China and wrote a bestselling book, *Seven Years in Tibet*, before going on to further explorations on six continents.

In 1997 the release of the film of his book, starring Brad Pitt, was dogged by controversy following allegations by a German magazine that Harrer was a member of the Nazi party. Whatever the real facts of the story, Harrer is today an outspoken advocate of human rights and remains a steadfast champion of Tibetan freedom.

1715 as a memorial to plague victims. The northeastern fountain, the **Schüsselbrunnen,** is surmounted by a bronze statue, created in 1566. This figure is the town mascot: its hand is raised as if in greeting, yet at the same time a jet of water spits forth from its mouth. The southwestern fountain bears a statue of a local medieval poet, Walther von der Vogelweide.

For an antidote to the ubiquitous classical architecture, have a look at the crazily tiled **Rogner Hotel Ernst Fuchs Palast** (below), a surrealist structure designed by mystical artist Ernst Fuchs.

Close to the *Rathaus* is the **Verkehrs-museum** (Transport Museum; ☎ 5555-64; Hauptplatz 29; adult/ student €3/1.50; ☒ 9am-6pm Jul & Aug, 9am-noon & 2-6pm 1 Jun-30 Oct). It tries hard to make the development of transport in the region seem interesting, but unless you're a die-hard trainspotter you can probably give it a miss.

Sleeping

Rogner Hotel Ernst Fuchs Palast (☎ 4660-0; www .fuchspalast.com; Friesacher Strasse 1; s/d with breakfast €82/130; ☒ ☒ ☒) The incredible exterior of this four-star hotel has to be seen to be believed – it's studded with blue and red glass tiles in fantastical and astrological designs. Inside, the surrealist theme continues into the public areas, with fluted columns and jewel-like mosaics, but the corporate-style rooms are disappointingly normal, despite being named after signs of the zodiac. The hotel attempts to marry art and wellbeing, with a health centre on site offering holistic therapies such as hot stones, aromatherapy massage and reflexology. There's one room adapted for disabled use.

Hotel Garni Mosser (☎ 3223; fax 322310; Spital-gasse 6; s/d with breakfast €23/46) This budget hotel is excellent value – the rooms are extremely comfortable, it's bang in the centre of town and there's a generous breakfast buffet. The downstairs **restaurant** (mains €6.40-14; ☒ lunch & dinner Mon-Sat) is an equally good bet for a hearty meal of Austrian specialities.

Weisses Lamm (☎ 23 62; www.weisseslamm.at - in German; Unterer Platz 4-5; s/d with breakfast €40/70; ☒ ☒) This central, four-star place has rather poky rooms arranged around an atmospheric arcaded courtyard. There's also a sauna and a therapeutic massage service. The **restaurant** (mains €6.10-14, menus €9.90-13.50; ☒ lunch & dinner) is a good place

for cheap local eats, with several set-menu options.

Gasthöf Sonnhof (☎ 2447; Völkermarkter Strasse 37; s/d with breakfast €30/53; ☒) South of the rail tracks (15 minutes from the centre), the Sonn-hof has light and modern, though slightly impersonal, rooms, some with a balcony. The good-value **restaurant** (mains €7-13.50; ☒ breakfast, lunch & dinner Tue-Sun) has more character, with an outside terrace and a good range of kids' menus. From the station, leave by the south-eastern exit, take the path to the right (which soon joins a road); at the main road junction, turn left.

Eating

St Veit is blessed with two quality restaurants, plus plenty of outdoor cafés on the *Hauptplatz* and around.

La Torre (☎ 39250; Grabenstrasse 39; mains €10.50-20; ☒ lunch & dinner Tue-Sat) This magnificent Italian restaurant is set in one of the towers of the 14th-century town wall. As well as the smart, romantic interior there's a beautiful, walled garden and terrace and an Italian owner who exudes bonhomie. The food is quite superb, from swordfish carpaccio to homemade pasta with calamari.

Pukelsheim (☎ 24 73; Erlgasse 11; mains €9.10-19.50; ☒ lunch & dinner Tue-Sat). This place serves Austrian and regional specialities prepared with flair and using fresh herbs and vegetables from its own garden plot next door.

Getting There & Away

St Veit is 33km south of Friesach and 20km north of Klagenfurt. Hourly express trains run to Villach (€8.40, 45 minutes), stopping at Friesach (€7, 23 minutes) and Klagenfurt (€4.10, 20 minutes).

Bundesbuses run to Klagenfurt, Maria Saal and Friesach about every hour.

BURG HOCHOSTERWITZ

This fairytale fortress (it claims to be the inspiration for the castle in *Sleeping Beauty*) drapes itself around the slopes of a hill, with 14 gate towers on the path up to the final bastion. These were built between 1570 and 1586 by Georg Khevenhüller, the then owner, to protect against Turkish invasion. It certainly looks impregnable and the information booklet (in English; €2.50) outlines the different challenges presented to attackers by each gate – some have spikes embedded in them,

CARINTHIA

which could be dropped straight through unwary invaders passing underneath. The fortress is particularly imposing when viewed from the northeast – sit on the left of the train heading south from Friesach.

A small **museum** (☎ 20 20; adult/child €7/4; ⊙ 9am-6pm Palm Sunday-31 Oct) features the suit of armour of one Burghauptmann Schenk, who measured 2m 25cm at the age of just 16. There's a small café serving sausages, soup, rolls and coffee at the top.

Getting There & Away

Regional trains on the St Veit–Friesach route stop at Launsdorf Hochosterwitz station, a 3km walk from the car park and the first gate, where a lift (€3) will take you directly to the castle. Infrequent buses from either Klagenfurt or St Veit (€1.60, 29 minutes, two daily) will get you 1km closer (to the Brückl crossroads).

MARIA SAAL
☎ 04223 / pop 3400

Maria Saal is a small town perched on a fortified hill 10km north of Klagenfurt. It's famous for it's pilgrimage church, whose twin spires can be seen for miles around.

The road from the train station splits in two and encloses the church hill. Behind the church is Hauptplatz, the main square with a bank and several restaurants. The **tourist office** (☎ 22 14-25; www.maria.saal.at; Am Platzl 1; ⊙ 8am-noon) is in the centre of Hauptplatz.

Sights & Activities

The **church** (☎ 22 14-12; Domplatz 1; ⊙ 8am-4.30pm), sometimes known as the Wallfahrtskirche, was built in the early 15th century from volcanic stone, some of it filched from a nearby Roman ruin. Originally Gothic, it later received Romanesque and baroque modifications. The exterior south wall is embedded with relief panels and ancient gravestones – look for the Roman mail wagon carved into one of the stones and the weird frescoes of people growing out of bulbous flowers on the church ceiling (they represent the genealogy of Christ). There's an explanatory pamphlet in English available in the church.

Getting There & Away

There are no official left-luggage facilities in the small train station, but if you're just passing through on the way somewhere else, the ticket clerk might watch your bags if you ask nicely. Regional trains stop hourly en route to St Veit (€3.10, nine minutes) and Klagenfurt (€2.60, eight minutes). Buses run to both places from below the church.

WESTERN CARINTHIA

Besides Hohe Tauern National Park (p277), the main attractions of Western Carinthia are Millstatt with its serene lake, abbey and famous music festival (p275), and Spittal an der Drau, with its stately Renaissance palace and pretty, floral park (opposite).

Both Millstatt and Spittal an der Drau are close to the primary road route north from Villach, the A10/E55 which ultimately leads to Salzburg. It has a toll section between Rennweg and a point north of the Tauern Tunnel (€14/9 summer/winter, €8 for motorcycles); to avoid the toll, take Hwy 99.

GMÜND
☎ 04732 / pop 2700

Gmünd's is an attractive 11th-century village with a walled centre and a 13th-century castle, the **Alte Burg**, on a hill above it. There's a restaurant inside the partially-ruined building, which is the setting for various plays and musical events.

Of an entirely different era is the privately owned **Porsche Museum** (☎ 24 71; Riesertratte 4a; admission €6; ⊙ 9am-6pm 15 May-15 Oct, 10am-4pm 16 Oct-14 May). A Porsche factory was sited in Gmünd from 1944 to 1950 and the first car to bear that famous name (a 356) was hand-

---

THE AUTOSCHLEUSE TAUERNBAHN

If you're driving to Bad Gastein from Spittal an der Drau, you'll need to use the *Autoschleuse Tauernbahn* (railway car–shuttle service) through the tunnel from Mallnitz to Böckstein. The fare for cars is €15 one-way or €24 return (valid for two months). The price is €8 one-way or €13 return for motorcycles and €5 return for bicycles. For information on services through this tunnel, telephone ☎ 05 717. Departures are every 30 minutes in summer or 60 minutes in winter, with the last train departing at 10.55pm. The journey takes 13 minutes.

made here. One of these models is on display (only 52 were built), together with about 15 other models and a couple of the wooden frames used in their construction. There's a film (in German) on Dr Porsche's life and work. Unless you're a car buff, it might be a bit pricey for such a small museum.

Gmünd has a range of inexpensive accommodation, including hotels specifically geared towards families with young children. Staff at the **tourist office** (☎ 22 22; www.familiental.com - in German), in the *Rathaus* on Hauptplatz, can outline accommodation options. There are a couple of places on *Hauptplatz* with affordable restaurants.

Getting There & Away

Gmünd is not on a rail route, though buses do go there from Spittal an der Drau (€3.15, 30 minutes); departures are usually every two hours, though there are only two buses on Sunday.

SPITTAL AN DER DRAU

☎ 04762 / pop 16,000

Spittal is an important economic and administrative centre in upper Carinthia. Its name comes from a 12th-century hospital and refuge that once succoured travellers on this site. Today it's an unremarkable town with an impressive Italianate palace at its centre and a small, but attractive, park with splashing fountains and bright flowerbeds. To get into town from the station, walk straight up the road, then cut through the Stadtpark on your right.

Information

Café Erni (☎ 4750; Bahnofstrasse 15; per 10 mins €1; 🕒 7am-noon Sun-Thu, 7am-1am Fri & Sat) Internet access.
Post office (SüdTyrolerplatz 3; 🕒 8am-noon & 2-6pm Mon-Fri, 9-11am Sat) Near the train station.
Tourist office (Kulturamt Spittal; ☎ 56 20 220; tourismusbuero@spittal-drau.at; Burgplatz 1; 🕒 9am-6pm Mon-Fri, 9am-noon Sat) Round the side of Schloss Porcia. From the train station, cut across Stadtpark, a 10-minute walk.

Sights & Activities
SCHLOSS PORCIA

An eye-catching Renaissance edifice, **Schloss Porcia** (🕒 8am-8pm) was built between 1533 and 1597 by the fabulously named Duke of Salamanca. Inside, Italianate arcades run around a central courtyard used for summer **theatre performances** (☎ 42020-20; ksporcia@aon.at).

The top floors contain the enormous **Museum für Volkskultur** (Local Heritage Museum; ☎ 28 90; museum@spittal-drau.at; adult/child €4.50/2.25; 🕒 9am-6pm 15 May-31 Oct, 1-4pm Mon-Thu 1 Nov-14 May). This high-tech regional museum has information panels in English, but the text is dense and academic. Exhibits to look out for are the reproduced mountain huts, a pair of antique skis and some rather bawdy paintings by local artist Karl Truppe.

GOLDECK

Spittal's nearest mountain, offering inspiring views, is the **Goldeck** (2142m) to the southwest. In summer, the peak can be reached by cable car (€8/14.50 one-way/return, 15 minutes) or by the Goldeckstrasse toll road (cars/motorbikes €12/6; reductions with *Gästekarte*). The road stops 260m short of the summit. In winter, the peak is the domain of skiers (lift pass adult/child €25/12). The cable car doesn't run from mid-April to mid-June or from mid-September to mid-December.

Festivals & Events

On one weekend in late June every odd-numbered year (2005 etc), the historical legend of Katharina von Salamanca (said to haunt Schloss Porcia in retribution for the violent death of her son) is re-enacted in the **Salamanca Festival**, held in the palace. Admission is free.

Sleeping

Staff at the tourist office will track down accommodation free of charge.

Hotel Ertl (☎ 204 80; info@hotel-ertl.at; Bahnhofstrasse 26; s/d with breakfast €53/94; P ⋒) This three-star hotel is aimed at the coach-party trade, meaning that the restaurant staff are frequently swamped. Rooms are variable – some bathrooms are on the small side. Ask for a room overlooking the hotel's peaceful garden and swimming pool.

Gasthöf Brückenwirt (☎ /fax 27 72; An der Wirtschaftsbrücke 2; s/d with breakfast €21/42) This chalet is a few minutes' walk east of the town centre, by the Lieser River. Most of the old-fashioned but comfortable rooms have a balcony and some have a view of the river. There's also a garden, cheap restaurant and friendly staff.

Gasthaus Klingan (☎ 31 65; fax 3165-65; Rizzistrasse 5a; s/d €20/40; P) This little guesthouse is a real bargain – spacious, clean rooms

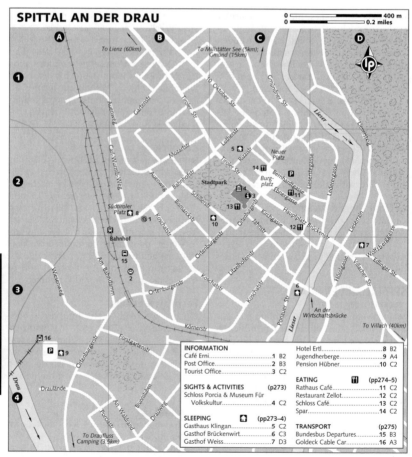

SPITTAL AN DER DRAU

INFORMATION		Hotel Ertl.................................8 B2
Café Erni....................................1 B2		Jugendherberge.......................9 A4
Post Office.................................2 B3		Pension Hübner......................10 C2
Tourist Office............................3 C2		
		EATING 🍴 (pp274–5)
SIGHTS & ACTIVITIES (p273)		Rathaus Café.........................11 C2
Schloss Porcia & Museum Für		Restaurant Zellot...................12 C2
Volkskultur........................4 C2		Schloss Café.........................13 C2
		Spar.....................................14 C2
SLEEPING 🏠 (pp273–4)		
Gasthaus Klingan.....................5 C2		**TRANSPORT** (p275)
Gasthof Brückenwirt................6 C3		Bundesbus Departures............15 B3
Gasthof Weiss.........................7 D3		Goldeck Cable Car..................16 A3

with good facilities for very low prices. Breakfast isn't available.

Gasthöf Weiss (☎ 23 41; Edlingerstrasse 1a; s/d with breakfast €26/52) This quaint little place, just over the river Lieser and handy for the Brückenstrasse bars, has a few budget rooms.

Pension Hübner (☎ 21 12; huebner.spittal@aon .at; Schillerstrasse 20; s €27-35, d €47-59) This central, peaceful pension, near Schloss Porcia, is run by the owners of the shop of the same name. Prices depend on the season and length of stay. There are also apartments with kitchens (minimum stay five days).

Jugendherberge (☎ 32 52; stadionbuffet@aon.at; Zur Seilbahn 2; dm €9.50) This HI hostel is near the base of the Goldeck cable car. From the train station, turn right and cross under the rail

tracks. There are basic cooking facilities and a good-value restaurant. Check-in is 5pm to 9pm, but call ahead as this hostel may close in off-season. There's another HI **Jugendherberge** (☎ 27 01; goldeck@gmx.at) at the Goldeck mid-station (1650m), accessible only by cable car.

Draufluss Camping (☎ 24 66; Schwaig 10; per site €15; ☿ Apr-Oct) This camping ground is about 3.5km from the town centre on the southern bank of the Drau River.

Eating

Restaurant Zellot (☎ 21 13; Hauptplatz 12; mains €6.60-20; ☿ lunch & dinner Tue-Sat) This is a funky and rather eccentric restaurant serving Austrian staples alongside daily specials and monthly themes. The walls display rolling exhibitions of contemporary art by up-and-coming local artists.

Schloss Café (☎ 47 07; Burgplatz 1; mains €3.50-8; ⏰ 7.30am-9pm Mon-Fri, 8.30am-9pm Sat, 2-8pm Sun) This bakery/café occupies one end of Schloss Porcia, with a terrace overlooking the fountains and greenery of the Stadtpark. It's the best place in town to be on a summer's evening.

Rathaus Café (☎ 49 18; Ebnergasse 5; mains €5.85-14.50; ⏰ 7am-midnight Mon-Sat) This place has a 1st-floor terrace, a pub ambience and some cosy leather booths to sit in while you tuck into the usual Austrian fare.

Gasthöf Brückenwirt (☎ 27 72; An der Wirtschaftsbrücke 2; mains €4.95-10; ⏰ lunch & dinner). This is an unpretentious, friendly local hangout with low prices serving Austrian food (schnitzels are a bargain at €7) and pizzas.

On Neuer Platz is a Spar supermarket.

Getting There & Away

Spittal-Millstättersee train station is at an important rail junction: two-hourly ICE services run north to Bad Gastein (€8.70, 40 minutes, every two hours) and west to Lienz (€10, one hour, hourly). There are also frequent trains to Villach (€6, 30 minutes, hourly), 37km to the southeast. The route north via Mallnitz-Obervellach yields some excellent views as the railway track clings high to the side of the valley (sit on the left).

Bundesbuses leave from outside the train station to Gmünd (€3.15, 30 minutes, hourly; fewer on Sundays). Call ☎ 39 16 for schedule information.

For taxis, call ☎ 5580.

MILLSTATT

☎ 04766 / pop 3200

The genteel lakeside village of Millstatt lies 10km east of Spittal an der Drau on the northern shore of tranquil Millstättersee. It got its name from Emperor Domition, an early Christian convert, who threw *mille statuae* (1000 heathen statues) into the lake. A gaunt and crazed-looking sculpture of the emperor himself stands in the lake, portrayed in the act of consigning a buxom-looking Venus to a watery grave.

Orientation & Information

Millstatt is roughly in the middle of the 12km-long northern shore of Millstättersee. **Millstätter See tourist office** (☎ 37 00; www .millstatt-see.co.at - in German; Marktplatz 14; ⏰ 8am-noon, 1-5pm Mon-Fri) Touch-screen computer information outside.

Town tourist office (☎ 20 22-0; www.millsee.info - in German; Marktplatz 8; ⏰ 8am-noon, 1-5pm Mon-Fri)

Sights & Activities

The Millstatt skyline is dominated by a Romanesque **Benedictine abbey**, founded in 1070. The exterior of the abbey, with two onion towers, is plain and looks surprisingly new for an 11th-century building. Look out for the grotesque faces peering from the columns around the inner doorway. In the arcaded courtyard stands an old linden tree; there's an even more ancient tree (about 1000 years old) outside, along with a harrowing modern crucifix.

Stiftsmuseum (Abbey Museum; ☎ 0676-46 06 413; Stiftgasse 1; adult/child € 2.50/1.20; ⏰ 9am-noon & 2-6pm 1 Jun-30 Sep) This deals with the history of the town, with a section on the culture of knot-making (explanations in English).

The lake itself is up to 141m deep and teems with possibilities for **water sports** such as sailing, scuba diving, swimming, water-skiing, windsurfing and fishing. Several types of boat are available for hire from **Wassersport Strobl** (☎ 22 63; Seemühlgasse 56a; motorboat/sailing boat/kayak per day €11/10/5).

East of Millstatt is **Bad Kleinkirchheim**, a spa resort and winter skiing centre. Its **tourist office** (☎ 04240-82 12; info@badkleinkirchheim) can provide details.

Festivals & Events

MUSICWOCHEN

If two Carinthians meet, they start a choir, according to a local saying. If two Millstätters get together, they start a music festival, and one that's put this minute place firmly on the classical music map is the **Musikwochen Millstatt** (Millstatt music weeks; ☎ 2022-35; www .musikwochen.com - in German; tickets €10-34). It happens every year from May to September, with most performances taking place in the Abbey.

Sleeping & Eating

The summer season is from Easter to mid-October, with the highest prices from June to September. Millstatt has some winter tourism, but most hotels, pensions and private rooms close at this time. The winter hibernators don't open until sometime in May, including some of the places mentioned following –

check availability with the tourist office in the non-winter months.

Villa Verdin (☎ 374 74; www.villaverdin.at - in German; Seestrasse 69; s with breakfast €35-65, d with breakfast €70-130; P ☐) This converted 19th-century villa hotel mixes contemporary design style with antiques and interesting junk to create a comfortable, informal yet stylish atmosphere. The rooms are all different, some with funky, red furniture and zebra-print accessories, some with buddhas and Japanese screens. Several have enclosed verandas or balconies with views of the lake. The clientele is stylish fashion and media types, who come to relax by the lake in summer or sip red wine in front of blazing fires in winter. There's also a retro beach café for daytime snacks and a low-key restaurant for evening meals.

Hotel See-Villa (☎ 21 02; see-villa@hotel.at; Seestrasse 68; s €48-73, d €105-175; P ☐) Next door to Villa Verdin, this staid, old-fashioned hotel is a complete contrast: it's a handsome old building right on the lake, with a huge terrace restaurant, a private sauna and a swimming jetty. The rooms are wooden floored, creaky and quaint, with a variety of different styles and colour schemes, all very traditional. The **restaurant** (mains €8.90-19.80; ☒ lunch & dinner) serves a high-class menu featuring dishes such as calves liver flambéed with dried plums, accompanied by a

selection of fine wines. The clientele here is mostly elderly gents, some accompanied by glamorous (second or...) wives.

In addition to these and several other upmarket hotels along the lake promenade, many quiet, mid-priced B&Bs line Alexanderhofstrasse and Tangernerweg, to the west of the resort centre. Try **Pension Pleikner** (☎ 20 36; pension-pleikner@newsclub.at; Seemühlgasse 57; d with breakfast €43-57.50; P), between Kaiser Franz Josef Strasse and the boat station. It's above and part of **Pizzeria Peppino** (mains €5.20-€12; ☒ dinner), which serves pizza, schnitzel and spaghetti. Rooms are available in summer only, but the restaurant is open 4pm to midnight daily, year-round.

Several other mid-priced restaurants overlook the lake; alternatively, compile a picnic at the **ADEG** (Kaiser Franz Josef Strasse 24) supermarket, near Schwarzstrasse.

For pub entertainment, try **Full House** (☎ 20 73; Kaiser Franz Josef Strasse; ☒ 2pm-2am summer, 7pm-2am winter), near Seemühlgasse.

Getting There & Away

Bundesbuses to Millstatt depart from outside Spittal train station (€3.10, 20 minutes, two hourly), with some continuing to Bad Kleinkirchheim (from Spittal €6, one hour). The road from Spittal gives good views of the lake – sit on the right.

Hohe Tauern National Park Region

CONTENTS

Austria's highest peak and its tallest waterfall, the longest glacier in the eastern Alps, snow-capped crags, larch forests, soaring vultures, meadows full of edelweiss, burrowing marmots – the *Nationalpark Hohe Tauern* (Hohe Tauern National Park) is the jewel of Austria's natural landscapes and the site of some of the most spectacular views in Europe.

At 1787 sq km, Hohe Tauern is in fact Europe's largest national park and includes the most famous route in Austria, the Grossglockner road, which starts in Salzburg province and ends in Carinthia. The park's highest point is the mighty Grossglockner (3797m), which straddles the border between Osttirol (East Tyrol) and Carinthia. On the western side of the park stands the second-highest peak in the region, Grossvenediger (3674m), the high point of the border between East Tyrol and Salzburg. The park is open all year round and free to enter. Wildlife abounds, with alpine mammal species such as marmots and ibex easily spotted on walks and birds of prey such as bearded vultures and golden eagles lording it over the skies.

Despite being a National Park, Hohe Tauern isn't an empty wilderness area. First signs of human habitation go back to the Stone Age and today over 60,000 people live here in 30 or so farming communities. The popular holiday towns of Zell am See, Bad Gastein and Lienz each border the park and are also covered in this chapter.

The park is an outdoor enthusiast's dream, with endless opportunities for hiking, plus a bit of serious mountaineering. In the towns, adventure sports take priority over history or culture, with companies offering everything from canyoning to kayaking and paragliding. Mountain-biking routes crisscross the park and maps are available from tourist offices.

HIGHLIGHTS

- Climbing the snowy **Grossglockner** (p282), the highest peak in Austria
- Or taking the easier option and driving the winding **Grossglockner road** (p285), with staggering views on all sides
- Winter skiing through the pine forests of the Schmittenhöhe above Zell am See, or summer snowboarding on the **Kitzsteinhorn glacier** (p280)
- Soaking in the exhilarating spray of **Krimml Falls** (p284), the longest waterfall in Austria
- Strolling through the charming streets and admiring the pilgrimage church of **Heiligenblut** (p286), a village with a grisly legend at its core
- White-water rafting, canyoning and kayaking in the mountains around **Lienz** (p293)

★ Schmittenhöhe
★ Krimml Falls
★ Grossglockner Road
★ Kitzsteinhorn Glacier
Grossglockner ★
★ Heiligenblut
Lienz ★

| AREA: 1787 SQ KM | HIGHEST ELEVATION: GROSSGLOCKNER 3797M |

History

The Austrian Alps once formed the boundary between the more established, southern Roman territories and their newer, less stable conquests to the north. The main trade route for pack animals ran along the pass at the end of the Tauern valley, but few permanent settlements were established due to the Roman's distrust of the treacherous climate (tales of malevolent, snowy spirits abounded) and difficult topography of the mountains.

In 1971 the provinces of Carinthia, Salzburg and Tyrol agreed to the creation of a national park; regions were added in stages between 1981 and 1991 until it became Europe's largest national park. Today it's widely regarded as one of Europe's biggest conservation success stories, an example of 'eco-realism', and an approach where the needs of the local population are addressed right from the start.

Information

All tourist offices in places bordering the park have information on and maps of Hohe Tauern. The Experience in Nature map (in English) shows information offices, overnight accommodation spots and tour suggestions. You could also investigate the national park's website at www.hohetauern .org, which lists the various provincial tourist offices responsible for the National Park.

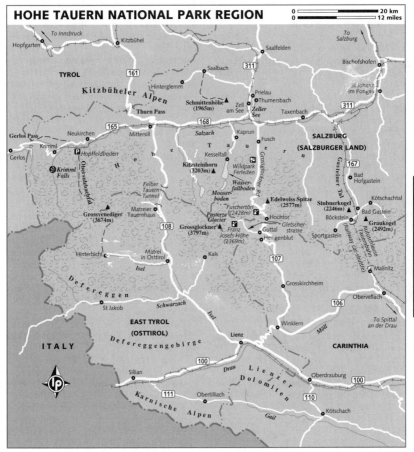

Climate

The national park has an alpine climate with high rainfall, short summers and long winters with heavy snowfall. Avalanches are common in spring. Be aware that the sun is intense at high altitudes.

Dangers & Annoyances

Extremes of climate and terrain make parts of the park potentially dangerous for walkers and climbers. Always come prepared for abrupt changes in weather conditions and visibility, with warm clothing and adequate maps, and consider taking a guide on more difficult routes.

The number for emergency mountain rescue services is ☎ 140. Call ☎ 0512-291600 for weather information.

Getting There & Around

The main hubs for train services are Zell am See (for services to Salzburg and points north via St Johann im Pongau) and Lienz (for trains east and west into Tyrol and Carinthia).

The authorities are determined to limit the flow of traffic through the park, so most of the roads through it have toll sections and some are closed in winter. The main north–south road routes are Felber Tauern Rd, open year-round, and the Grossglockner road (p285). The 5.5km-long Felber Tauern Tunnel is at the East Tyrol–Salzburg border: the toll is €10 for cars and €8 for motorcycles. Bundesbuses and those on the Lienz–Kitzbühel route operate along this road.

Getting around by Bundesbus is made more attractive by special passes; such deals change periodically, so make inquiries upon arrival. Buying zonal day or week passes for provincial transport should work out significantly cheaper than buying single tickets.

ZELL AM SEE

☎ 06542 / pop 9700

Zell am See's handiness as a base for excursions to Krimml Falls and the Grossglockner road – plus a picturesque location between its namesake lake, the Zeller See, and the ridged slopes of **Schmittenhöhe** (1965m) – have made it one of the region's most popular holiday spots.

The streets of the town are thronged with visitors (mostly English) in summer and winter alike – together with Kaprun, the town

forms the Europa Sports Region, with endless ski and snowboard opportunities. Kaprun itself can be lively and it has good access to ski slopes, but isn't so convenient for water sports. Sports brochures, available from the tourist office in either place, usually cover the whole region.

Orientation & Information

Almost adjacent to the compact main resort of Zell am See is the residential area of Schüttdorf, which is generally cheaper for accommodation. Both are on the western shore of the Zeller See. You should ask to be given the *Gästekarte* (guest card) wherever you stay and show it for discounts on activities, sights and transport.

Café Estl (☎ 726 10; Bahnhofstrasse 1; per 10 mins €1; ⏱ 7.30am-10pm Mon-Sat) Internet access.

Kaprun branch (☎ 06547-86 43; www.kaprun.net - in German; Salzburger Platz, Kaprun) For advice on accommodation in Kaprun.

Tourist office (☎ 770-0; www.europasportregion.info - in German; Brucker Bundesstrasse 1; ⏱ 9am-6pm Mon-Fri, 9am-12pm, 2-6pm Sat, 10am-12pm Sun in winter & summer high seasons). Can find rooms and has an accommodation board in the foyer with a free telephone (24 hr).

Sights & Activities

SKIING

This region has a long history of skiing. In 1927 the first cable car in Salzburg province (the fifth in Austria) was opened on Schmittenhöhe and the first glacial ski run was opened on Kitzsteinhorn in 1965. The Europa Sports Region operates 58 cable cars and lifts, giving access to over 130km of runs for people of all abilities. Combined ski passes for the Schmittenhöhe and Kitzsteinhorn region cost per adult/child €66/33 for a two-day minimum period (passes are cheaper in the low season); ski buses are free for ski-pass holders. Ski/boot rental prices are about €25/33 for one day.

Cable cars from Zell am See ascend to the ridge on either side of the **Schmittenhöhe cable car** (return adult/child €19.30/6.95, with guest card €17.30), which reaches 1965m. These operate from mid-December to mid-April. There are several black (difficult) runs that twist between the tree-lined flanks of the mountain.

Kaprun is the closest resort to **Kitzsteinhorn** (3203m), offering year-round glacier skiing and snowboarding – as many as 13 runs can be open all summer in a good year.

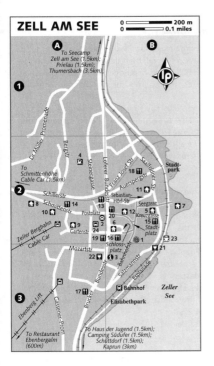

ZELL AM SEE

Start early in the day during the high season to avoid long queues.

The Gletscherbahn underground railway, which caught fire in 2000 (p29), is no longer used to carry people; a memorial to the victims is planned. First-timers can try a cheap taste of winter skiing on the Maiskogel lift for €15. The short Lechnerberg lift costs just €2.50 for one ride (medium difficulty).

HIKING

The summer walk, **Pinzgauer Spaziergang**, from the Schmittenhohe peak, takes 8 to 10 hours and exploits to the full the magnificent views; the path is marked, and a map is available from the tourist office. There is very little change in altitude along the way. You descend via the Schattbergbahn cable car to Saalbach (part of the excellent Saalbach-Hinterglemm skiing area) and take the Bundesbus back from there to Zell am See (last departure at 7pm). From June to mid-October there are guided walks (free with a lift ticket) from Schmittenhöhe to other places.

Freizeitzentrum (☎ 785-0; Steinergasse 3-5; ⏰ 10am-10pm daily; pool €7.40), a sports centre in the centre of town, has a **swimming pool**, saunas, steam room and massage, as well as tenpin bowling and an ice rink.

Adventure Service (☎ 735 25; www.adventureservice.at; Steinergasse 9; rafting/canyoning/paragliding €41/46/100), near Freizeitzentrum, is one of several places providing high-adrenaline activities in the surrounding mountains.

Boat trips (☎ 789-0; adult/child €7.40/3.70; ⏰ early May-early Oct) on the lake depart from Zell am See Esplanade and complete a 40-minute 'panorama round trip'. Boats also shuttle passengers across the lake, occasionally stopping at **Seecamp Zell am See** (one-way/return €2.60/4.30). Rowing boats, pedal boats and motorboats can be hired from various places by the shore between April and October. Anglers need a fishing permit.

Of the **water sports** available at other resorts around the lake, Thumersbach has a water-skiing school and Prielau has a windsurfing and sailing school.

The tourist office can provide details and maps on all walking paths and **cycling** in the area; the staff can also provide information on where to play **golf** and **tennis**.

Festivals & Events

Zell am See celebrates two lake festivals. The first, in mid-July, features sporting events

---

HIKING AND CLIMBING IN HOHE TAUERN NATIONAL PARK

Walking through the unspoiled environment of mountains, ravines, lakes, forests and glaciers is the main activity in Hohe Tauern. There are trails of every level, from gentle strolls through the pine forests to extreme expeditions to scale inaccessible peaks and ridges. As this is a conservation area, there are several things *not* to do, such as straying from the marked trails, littering, lighting fires or disturbing the flora and fauna.

Freytag & Berndt produces nine 1:50,000 walking maps covering the national park and surrounding areas. If you plan to undertake major walking expeditions, you should schedule your overnight stops in advance – some small-scale guesthouses provide food and accommodation, but they are widely scattered. Contact the regional or local tourist offices for accommodation lists.

Popular walking trails include the ascent of the **Grossvenediger**, a peak permanently coated with ice and snow and flanked by glaciers. The closest you can get by road is the Matreier Tauernhaus Hotel (1512m) at the southern entrance to the Felber Tauern Tunnel. You can park here and within an hour's walk gain fine views of the mountain.

Anyone with mountain-climbing experience and a reasonable level of fitness can climb the mighty **Grossglockner** via the 'ordinary' route without a guide, although guides are recommended. The authorities also strongly recommend that hikers allow two days to conquer the Grossglockner. The main route for hikers begins from the Adlersruhe (Eagles Rest) **overnight hut** (☎ 04876-500), a four- to five-hour hike from Heiligenblut. From here, the route to the summit crosses ice and rocks, following a steel cable over a narrow snow ridge. The final ascent to the cross at the summit is relatively easy. The easiest descent is via the same route. It's essential to have the proper equipment (including maps, ropes and crampons) and to check the weather conditions before setting out. For guides, contact the tourist offices in Heiligenblut or Kals, or ring the mountain guides association on ☎ 04824 2700.

For information on walking the Grossglockner Rd, see p285.

---

and the second, in early August, has music and costume parades. The **Zell Summer Night** festival runs from June to August and features bands, clowns and theatre performances every Wednesday night in the town centre. Details from the tourist office.

Sleeping

As in other ski resorts, many hotels close between seasons, so be sure to phone ahead at these times. Prices are higher in winter than in summer.

BUDGET

Private rooms are the best cheap option in Zell am See. The tourist office can provide a list.

Haus Haffner (☎ 723 96; haffner.at; Schmittenstrasse 29; s/d with breakfast €23/42, summer/winter €26.50/42; P ⊔) This place, just west of the Zeller Bergbahn cable car, has 12 charming and clean rooms with rag rugs, carved wooden furniture and balconies, as well as a few larger family apartments. Cheaper rooms with shared bathrooms are also available.

Jugendherberge (☎ 470 36; www.lbsh-zell.at - in German; Schmittenstrasse 27; dm with breakfast €20, one night supplement €2; P ⊔ ⊠) This is the most central of Zell's HI youth hostels, with clean four-bed dorms, as well as a gym and a restaurant. Reception is open 8am-12pm and 4-10pm. Bike hire (per day €10) is also available here.

Haus der Jugend (☎ 571 85; www.hostel-zell.at - in German; Seespitzstrasse 13, Schüttdorf; 6/4/2-bed dm with breakfast €16/18/20; ☸ reception 7.30am-9.30pm & 4pm-10pm, hostel closed Nov; P) This HI hostel is a 15-minute walk around the lake. Exit the train station on the lakeside (Zum See), take the footpath along the shore and turn left at the end.

Jugendgästhaus Kaprun (☎ 06547-85 07; www .jgh.at; Nikolaus Gassner Strasse 448; dm with breakfast summer/winter €15.70/18.70; P ⊔ ⊠) This 114-bed hostel is 1km east of the centre.

Seecamp Zell am See (☎ 721 15; www.seecamp .at; Thumersbacher Strasse 34, Prielau; per adult €7.40; P) This huge complex with a shop and restaurant is on the northern shoreline (head clockwise from the town).

Camping Südufer (☎ 562 28; www.camping -suedufer.at; Seeuferstrasse 196; per adult €5.80) Though cheaper, this camping ground to the southeast of town is not by the lake.

MID-RANGE & TOP END

The difference in price between the low and high seasons is more marked in this category of accommodation. High-season prices are quoted here; there are high seasons in both summer and winter.

Romantik Hotel zum Metzgerwirt (☎ 7 2520; www.romantik-hotel.at/en; Sebastian-Hörl-Strasse 11; s with breakfast summer €96-164, s with breakfast winter €57-130, d with breakfast winter €114-260; P ⬛) This very charming and well-decorated hotel has a rose garden and ivy-draped whitewashed walls. As well as elegant, comfortable and tasteful rooms, there's a superb lounge area that looks like a huge farmhouse sitting room, with an open fire under a huge chimney in winter and a carved wooden bar. There's also a wellness centre with sauna, steam room and several Jacuzzis. Half board costs just €10 extra per night.

Grand Hotel (☎ 788; www.grandhotel.cc; Esplanade 4-6; s with breakfast summer €83-107, d with breakfast summer €104-194, s with breakfast winter €94-107, d with breakfast winter €140-184; P ⬛ ⛲) Zell's most upmarket hotel, on a promontory on the lake, has unbeatable views from almost all sides, but not much flair in decorating. Lots of the plain, rather corporate rooms have internal staircases. Suites and apartments are also available. The hotel closes for two weeks from April to November.

Hubertus (☎ 724 27; www.hubertus-pension.at; Gartenstrasse 4; s with breakfast €30, d with breakfast €52-60; P ⬛ ⬛) This quiet, friendly and convenient hotel is the best of the mid-range options. It's been in the same family for three generations, but has recently been completely redecorated with taste and attention to detail. The whitewashed rooms haven't lost their cosy and traditional character – they have rag rugs, painted wooden beds and in some cases views of the lake. There's a sauna and a spacious garden with swings and slides for kids.

Sporthotel Lebzelter (☎ 776-0; www.hotel-lebzelter .at; Dreifaltigkeitsgasse 7; s with breakfast summer €40-53, d with breakfast summer €72-98, s with breakfast winter €63-76, d with breakfast winter €118-144; P ⬛ ⬛) The downstairs restaurants and bar at this central hotel are very traditional, with staff in *Dirndls* (women's traditional dress) and lederhosen, vaulted ceilings and wood-panelled walls. The well-equipped rooms, however, are plain, light and modern. There's a sauna and steam bath on site.

Gasthof Steinerwirt (☎ 725 02; www.steinerwirt .com; Schlossplatz 1, s with breakfast €22 35, d with breakfast €44-70; P ⬛) The rooms in this central and popular hotel are variable – some of them could do with a lick of paint, but the best are large and comfortable, with cream décor and sepia photos on the walls. There's a well-regarded outdoor restaurant here, with tables under shady chestnut trees.

Buchner (☎ /fax 726 36; Seegasse 12; s/d with breakfast €29/58; P) This English-speaking pension has light and airy rooms with wood furnishings and comfortable beds. Some have a balcony. Cheaper rooms with shared bathrooms are also available.

Eating

Salzburger Stuben (☎ 765-0; Auerspergstrasse 11; mains €18.20-23; ⊗ lunch & dinner, closed Nov) The award-winning restaurant in this five-star hotel serves some of the area's best local cuisine, incorporating smoked meats, lake fish and fresh regional vegetables.

Einkehr (☎ 723 63; Schmittenstrasse 12; mains €9.50-18.90; ⊗ winter lunch & dinner, summer dinner Mon-Sat) A classy restaurant with an imaginative menu (try seafood lasagne or glazed spare ribs) and a stylish interior featuring lots of wood and cast iron. There's also a small courtyard for summer dinners outside.

Zum Hirschen (☎ 774; Dreifaltigkeitsgasse 1; mains €11-25; ⊗ lunch & dinner) This hotel-restaurant serves high-quality, high-priced Austrian and international fare in a spacious, light, wood-panelled dining room or outside on a street terrace.

Octopussy (☎ 470 42; Schlossplatz 2; mains €8-15; ⊗ dinner) This large restaurant has an ambitious menu featuring lots of fish – try lemongrass soup with giant prawn skewers or stuffed cuttlefish. There's also a good salad buffet and fast service.

Restaurant Ebenbergalm (☎ 0664 351 2307; Schmitten 38, Ebenburg; mains €10; ⊗ lunch & dinner) Bearded Günter and his sister Gudrun serve very well-cooked mountain fare in this little hut near the top of the Ebenberglift. You can also walk up (about one hour) or call for a lift (free pickup from the town hotels). Book in advance.

Gasthof Steinerwirt (☎ 725 02; Schlossplatz 1; mains €6-20; ⊗ lunch & dinner) This hotel restaurant serves inexpensive and hearty Austrian fare using meat from the Hohe Tauern pastures and fresh fish from the lake. There are a couple of vegetarian options (try the tomato risotto) and live music weekly in the garden.

Restaurant Kupferkessel (☎ 727 68; Brucker Bundesstrasse 18; mains €3.25-10; lunch & dinner Mon-Sat, dinner Sun) This crowded and smoky, but family friendly, restaurant serves up cheap 'n' cheerful pizzas, salads and steaks in huge portions. There's a kid's play corner outside.

China-Restaurant Fünf Planeten (☎ 701 34; Loferer Bundesstrasse 3; lunch menu €4.90-5.90; mains €7-8; lunch & dinner) Weekday lunches at this decent Chinese are the best deal: they include a starter of soup or a huge, crispy spring roll.

Moby Dick Fischrestaurant (☎ 733 20, Kreuzgasse 16; mains €6.55-13.50; lunch & dinner Mon-Fri) There's a dazzling variety of fish dishes available at this restaurant/café, from smoked salmon to live trout plucked from a tank. Old-fashioned fish and chips are also available. The interior smells of cooking oil, but there are some tables outside.

For self-caterers, there are several central supermarkets, including a **Spar** (Brucker Bundesstrasse 4).

Entertainment

Zell's nightlife is considerably livelier in winter than in summer thanks to the ski-and-snowboard crowd.

B17 (☎ 474 24; Salzmannstrasse; 2; 5pm-2am Mon-Sat) This retro bar has a 1950s Americana theme, with pictures of B17 bombers adorning the walls. Half the bar has a glass front, while the other is a shabby-chic corrugated iron hut. The clientele are mostly young and stylish, and there's a small upstairs roof terrace for summer nights.

Crazy Daisy (☎ 7630; Brucker Bundesstrasse 10-12; from 8pm summer, 4pm winter) The resort's best-known after-ski venue is a raucous drinking hole beloved of snowboard dudes and ski bunnies. There are live bands, beer promotions and, in winter, an upstairs restaurant. It might be changing venue to a site near the Grand Hotel in 2005; check with the tourist office or your hotel.

Getting There & Away

Train destinations from Zell am See include Salzburg (€16.20, 1¾ hours, hourly), Kitzbühel (€8.70, 45 minutes, every two hours) and Innsbruck (€20.80, two hours, every two hours). The town is also at the head of the narrow-gauge railway line to Krimml

Falls (opposite). You can hire bikes at any of the sports shops in town.

Bundesbuses leave from outside the train station and the bus station behind the post office. They run to various destinations, including hourly to Kaprun (€2.90, 20 minutes) and to Krimml Falls (€7.30, 1½ hours). For details of buses to Lienz via Franz Josefs Höhe, see p286.

Zell am See is on Hwy 311 running north to Lofer, where it joins Hwy 312 connecting St Johann in Tyrol with Salzburg (passing through Germany). It's also just a few kilometres north of the east-west highway linking St Johann im Pongau with Tyrol (via the Gerlos Pass).

KRIMML FALLS

About 55km west of Zell am See, the **Krimmler Wasserfälle** (Krimml Falls), with their rainbow-filled clouds of spray hanging in the air and pine forests all around, are an inspiring sight and attract hordes of visitors in summer. The combined height of the falls is 380m (the highest in Europe), spread over three levels connected by a fast-flowing, twisting river and rapids. While this lessens the immediate impact, it means that you can ascend for 1½ hours with a different spectacular view at every turn.

In winter, the slopes above the village of Krimml become a ski area and the falls just a big lump of ice.

Orientation & Information

The Krimml Falls are on the northwestern edge of the national park, within the protected area.

Krimml Ort (that is, Krimml village), at an elevation of 1076m, is about 500m north of the path to the falls, on a side turning from Hwy 165, which goes towards the falls. There are parking spaces (€3.65 per day) near the path to the falls, which branches to the right just before the toll booths for the Gerlos Pass road (see opposite).

The **tourist office** (☎ 06564-72 39; www.krimml .at - in German; 8am-12pm, 2.30-5.30pm Mon-Fri, 8.30-10.30am Sat) is in the village centre next to the white church. The post office is next door.

Sights & Activities

The **Wasserfallweg** (Krimml Falls path) is 4km long. The highest free fall of water is 65m, in the lower falls. The middle section is mostly dissipated into a series of mini-falls, the highest being 30m, and the upper section has a free fall of 60m. The trail is steep in certain sections, but many elderly people manage the incline. Every few hundred metres, small paths deviate from the main trail and offer alternative viewpoints of the falls; each gives a worthwhile perspective. The excellent view back towards Krimml can often be seen through the treetops.

The **ticket & information offices** (☎ 06564 20 113; www.wawuwe.at - in German; admission adult/child €1.50/0.50, free Dec-Apr; ⏰ 8am-6pm May-Nov) are a few minutes' walk along the path. At the entrance to the falls is the new **Wasserwunderwelt** (Water Wonderland; admission inc waterfalls adult/child €7/3.50; ⏰ 10am-5pm 1 May-31 Oct), a watery theme park, with exhibits about the waterfall, water games and some art installations based on the same theme.

After about an hour's walk you'll reach the Gasthof Schönangerl, where you can get food and buy souvenirs. This point is just above the middle level of the falls. After another five to 10 minutes the terrain opens out and you can see the final, upper section of the falls. A steep, further 20-minutes' walk will bring you to the top of that level (known as the **Bergerblick viewpoint**) for a truly memorable view over the lip of the falls and back down to the valley.

If you stop off at all or most of the viewpoints on the way up, it'll take two to three hours to reach Bergerblick – more if you stop for food. A fast, straight descent can take as little as 40 minutes. If you don't want to walk up to the falls, a national park taxi can take you as far as Schönangerl; ask the village's tourist office to make a reservation in advance. Private cars are not allowed on this route.

Sleeping & Eating

Unless you want to continue walking past the third level of the falls and along the Krimmler Ache (Krimml river), Krimml is easily visited as a day trip from Zell am See. There are places to stay either in the village or on the way up to the falls; staff at the Krimml Ort tourist office can advise on accommodation options, or use its 24-hour accommodation board.

Near the church in Krimml is an ADEG supermarket, useful for creating a picnic. There are snack stands and restaurants

(with reasonable prices) on the walk to the falls. **Gasthof Schönangerl** (☎ 06564 7228; mains €4-9; ⏰ lunch & dinner) above the middle section of the falls, is open year-round except for a few weeks in November and December.

Getting There & Away

Krimml can be reached from either the west or the east. The only rail route is the scenic narrow-gauge Pinzgauer Lokalbahn from Zell am See (€7.60, 1½ hours, every two hours). It calls at many places (including Schüttdorf, near the Zell am See Haus der Jugend) on its slow trip past wooden huts and flower-studded meadows. The last train back to Zell am See leaves at 5.33pm.

In summer, Bundesbuses run from Krimml train station to the falls every two hours, but they only go as far as Krimml Ort (only about 500m short of the path to the falls) at other times; the bus fare is covered by your train ticket.

Bundesbuses run all year from Zell am See to Krimml (€7.90, 1½ hours, last return bus is at 5pm). The Krimml Falls path begins near the starting point of the *Tauernradweg* (cycle path) to Salzburg (175km) and Passau (325km).

GERLOS PASS

This pass is northwest of Krimml and is a scenic route to the Zillertal (Ziller Valley). Just southwest of Krimml there are fine views of the whole of the Krimml Falls; further on, peaks and Alpine lakes abound. There is a toll on this route: €7/4 for cars/motorcycles.

Bundesbuses make the trip from Krimml to/from Zell am Ziller (in Tyrol) (€10 each way including the toll, 1½ hours from 1 July to 30 September). By car, you can avoid using the toll road if you take the old route, signposted 'Alte Gerlosstrasse'. This 11km stretch of road branches off from Hwy 165 at Wald im Pingau, 9km east of Krimml (on the road to Zell am See) and joins the new Gerlos road just west of the toll section.

GROSSGLOCKNER ROAD

The Grossglockner Hochalpenstrasse, the region's most spectacularly scenic road, was originally conceived as a way of beating the depression of the 1930s. It was built by 3,000 men over the course of five years; those who died in the process are remembered in a tiny church at Fuschertörl. The road partly follows an important Roman trade and slave route between Italy and Germany. The present road takes visitors on a magical 50km journey between 800m and 2500m above sea level, traversing a range of valleys, glaciers and mountain peaks and passing through several climactic and environmental zones. You'll find a dozen restaurants along the route, some of which offer accommodation.

Just before reaching the park, you'll come to **Wildpark Ferleiten** (☎ 06456-220; admission adult/child €5/3; ☻ 8am-dusk May-Nov), home to more than 200 Alpine animals including chamois, marmots, wolves and bears.

Once through the tollgate near the Wildpark, the road rises steeply. At 2260m there's an **Alpine Nature Museum** (admission free; ☻ 9am-5pm daily), with a small cinema showing films about flora, fauna and ecology. A little further on is **Fuschertörl**, with the workers' monument and a restaurant with superb views on both sides of the ridge. From here a 2km side road (no coaches allowed) goes up to **Edelweiss Spitze** (2577m), where there's an even better panorama.

Hochtor (2503m) is the highest point on the road, after which there is a steady descent to Guttal (1950m). Here the road splits: to the east is Heiligenblut and the route to Lienz, to the west is the Gletscherstrasse (Glacier Rd). This 9km road ascends to **Franz Josefs Höhe** (2369m), the viewing area for Grossglockner.

Taking the Gletscherstrasse, the initial views south to the Heiligenblut valley are fantastic, yet you soon concentrate on the approaching massif of Grossglockner itself (sit on the left for the best views). At Franz Josefs Höhe, there's a panoramic restaurant, a car park and a visitor's centre with exhibitions on mountain themes covering four floors.

The Grossglockner looms from across a vast tongue of ice, the 10km-long **Pasterze Glacier**, with cracks and ridges creating a marvellous pattern of light and dark. Despite its timeless, majestic appearance, the glacier is actually receding at a disastrous rate, probably due to global warming. It is now officially classified as an at-risk environmental area.

Steps lead down to the edge of the glacier, or there's the **Gletscherbahn funicular** (one-way/return €4.40/7.20; ☻ every 10 min). There are several walks that start from Franz Josefs Höhe. The most popular is the Gamsgrubenweg,

winding above the glacier and leading to a waterfall; allow up to 1½ hours return.

Getting There & Away

The Grossglockner Rd (Hwy 107) is open from May to the beginning of November, daily between 5am and 10pm. There's a toll section between Wildpark Ferleiten and a point just north of Heiligenblut (€26 for cars, €17 for motorcycles). You can walk or cycle the road free of charge; the hills are steep (up to 12° gradient), but hardy mountain cyclists manage the trip. For recorded information on road conditions, call ☎ 06546 650.

Franz Josefs Höhe is accessible from north and south by Bundesbus No 5002, which runs from Lienz to Zell am See three times a day from 27 June 26 September – via Heiligenblut. The buses connect neatly so that you can spend some time in Heiligenblut and at Franz Josefs Höhe and still do the trip in one day. The toll charges are included in the ticket price (Lienz-Franz-Josefs Höhe €10.40, 1½ hours). The journey from Zell am See to Franz Josefs Höhe takes two hours and 10 minutes.

In the high season, you can get from Zell am See to Lienz (or vice versa) and still have plenty of time at Franz Josefs Höhe. Outside the high season this same-day trip is only possible travelling north (Lienz to Zell am See).

HEILIGENBLUT

☎ 04824 / pop 1200 / elevation 1301m

The slender, pale steeple of Heiligenblut's pilgrimage church stands out against the towering peaks all around it, making this pretty little village one of the most photographed spots in Austria. It's both a summer and winter resort, close to the boundaries of the national park and forming the usual lunch stop for coach parties heading up the Grossglockner Rd between Lienz and Zell am See. This means the village's streets are lined with souvenir shops selling felt hats, embroidered tea towels and crystal animals in high season. Even the staff in the tourist office are obliged to wear national costume to work every day!

Information

National park information office (☎ 27 00; www .hohetauern.at; ☻ 10am-5pm daily late May-early Oct, 3-6pm winter) In the Gästehaus Schober; has some museum

THE LEGEND OF HEILIGENBLUT

More than a thousand years ago, a certain Briccius and his three brothers left their native Denmark for Constantinople and the service of the Emperor Leo. Pious Briccius was distressed by the emperor's lack of faith and asked God for a sign to persuade his master of the True Way. He was soon rewarded – a passing trader decided to test the power of the Christian god himself by stabbing a picture of Christ with a knife, whereupon real blood flowed out. Seeing the miracle, the emperor was converted.

When Briccius decided to leave Constantinople and return to Denmark, he asked the emperor for a final boon: a phial of the holy blood from the painting. The emperor, loath to part with such a precious object, set Briccius a task: he must select a phial containing the real blood from two others containing the blood of mortals.

The emperor's daughter, who had fallen in love with Briccius, came to him in disguise and advised him to select the phial on which no flies landed. When Briccius obeyed and chose the true phial, the emperor dared not object any further.

Briccius and all three brothers then set out from Constantinople. To thwart the bandits sent out after him by the emperor to steal the phial, Briccius cut a wound in his own thigh to hide it. The wound healed over instantly, hiding the blood within his flesh.

When the brothers reached Carinthia, Briccius wanted to cross the Tauern pass and continue north. His brothers, however, elected to remain, moving down the Drautal and establishing themselves as local holy men. Trying to find his way alone over the Moelltal and through the high mountains, Briccius missed his way one stormy night and was buried by an avalanche.

When local peasants later came to the place, they found three beautiful green ears of corn growing out of the snow. They dug down and discovered the body of Briccius, with the ears of corn growing out of his heart. Convinced that this was a miracle, they decided to let God show the correct place for the body to be buried. They loaded it onto a cart, yoked up two young, untrained oxen and released them. The oxen galloped off and then stopped on top of a hill – the site of today's pilgrimage church – where the corpse was buried.

A few days later the peasants noticed a leg poking from the grave. On closer examination the phial of holy blood was discovered, hidden in the decomposed flesh of the saint. The phial was sent to the Archbishop of Salzburg, together with a ring and parchments found with the body. He went to the emperor in Constantinople for an explanation and thus the whole story was discovered and the pilgrimage church of Heiligenblut ('holy blood') was built. The phial of holy blood is still there.

exhibits. From 4pm to 5pm Monday to Friday someone from the Bergführerinformationsbüro (mountain guides office) gives advice on climbing and walking.

Tourist office (☎ 20 01-21; www.heiligenblut.at; ✆ 9am-12pm & 2-6pm Mon-Fri, 9am-12pm & 4-6pm Sat, 9am-6pm Mon-Fri Jul & Aug) On the main street, close to the 'Hotel Post' bus stop. Books mountain guides.

Sights & Activities

Heiligenblut's **church** was built between 1430 and 1483; its steeple is clearly visible from far away on the Gletscherstrasse. The church contains many statues of saints and its ceiling and altar are both Late Gothic in style. The tabernacle is purported to contain a tiny phial of Christ's blood, hence the name of the village (*Heiligenblut* means holy blood; see above). In the graveyard is a metal book containing the names of all those who have

died in the mountains since 1858. It's a sobering reminder of nature's power.

Most of the **skiing** above the resort is done from the Schareck (2604m) and Gjaidtroghöhe (2969m) peaks. A one-day local lift pass costs €29.50 and will also get you into other resorts in Carinthia and East Tyrol. In the summer, **mountaineering** is another popular local pursuit (see p282). The tourist office can provide details of mountain-biking trails in the park.

Sleeping & Eating

Staff at the tourist office can provide information about a wide variety of accommodation including hotels, pensions, private rooms, apartments and farmhouses.

Hotel Senger (☎ 22 15; www.romantic.at; Hof 23; s with breakfast €34-39, d with breakfast €70-108;

P ✗ ⬚) This lovely old farmhouse, with geraniums lining its wooden balconies, has been converted into a small, charming four-star hotel. Once inside, there's a real feeling of being up in the mountains, with stone floors, open fireplaces and plenty of nooks and corners to relax in (the walls show pictures of a party of Tibetan monks that came up here for a break during a visit to Austria!). The furnishings throughout manage to be very traditional, but stylish and classic at the same time. The whole place has the friendly, sociable atmosphere of a ski chalet and, indeed, skiing is possible from here in winter.

Jugendherberge (☎ /fax 22 59; www.oejhv.or.at; Hof 36; dm/r with breakfast €16.50/23.50; ☯ reception 7am-10am & 5pm-10pm) This HI hostel is located near the church, below the ADEG supermarket.

Grossglocknercamping (☎ /fax 20 48; Hadergasse 11; per site €17) This camping ground on the outskirts of the village is open year-round.

The village's main street is lined with restaurants and cafés serving Austrian and local food.

Café Dorfstüberl (☎ 20 19; Hof 5; mains €5-10, meals €6-14; ☯ breakfast, lunch & dinner). This handy café, near the tourist office, has a cosy interior and an outdoor terrace.

Getting There & Away
In addition to the Bundesbuses to the Franz Josefs Höhe viewing area, buses run year-round to/from Lienz (one-way/return €6/10.10, 70 minutes). They depart every one or two hours from Monday to Friday, though there's only one on Sunday.

BAD GASTEIN
☎ 06434 / pop 6100 / elevation 1000m

The genteel, Victorian-looking spa resort of Bad Gastein is the chief resort town in the scenic north–south Gasteiner Tal (Gastein Valley). The town's fame rests on its radon-rich hot springs, which have attracted cure seekers since the Middle Ages. In summer the town's visitors are a strange mixture of the aged and infirm, who come to take the waters, and hearty outdoor types who arrive to go canyoning, rafting or hiking in the surrounding mountains. In winter the town becomes a ski-and-snowboard centre and gains a much livelier atmosphere in the evenings.

Orientation & Information
Bad Gastein clings to the valley slopes – this means there are lots of hills and plenty of scenic vantage points. Tumbling through the centre in a series of waterfalls is the valley river, the Gasteiner Ache. The roar of its waters can be heard throughout the valley.

The train station is on the western side of town. The town centre, Kongressplatz, is down the hill to the east; make your way down near the Hotel Salzburger Hof. You can save some legwork by going to the Apcoa car park at the top of Haus Austria and taking the lift down.

Hotel Krone (per 20 mins €1) Internet access.

Post office (☯ 8am-12pm & 2-6pm Mon-Fri, 8-10am Sat) Next to the train station.

Tourist office (☎ 04632 3393 560; www.gastein.com; Kaiser Franz Josef Strasse 27; ☯ 8am-6pm Mon-Fri, 10am-4pm Sat & 10am-2pm Sun high season) To get here, go left from the train station exit and walk down the hill. Staff will find you accommodation free of charge. There's computer information on the national park in the foyer.

Sights & Activities
The tourist office can provide information in English on the beneficial effects of Bad Gastein's radon treatments. The radon-enriched water is the product of 3000 years of geological forces and is believed to have the ability to revitalise and repair human cells, alleviate rheumatism, improve male potency, reduce female menopausal problems and much more. The radon is absorbed through the skin and retained in the body for nearly three hours.

The usual way of taking the cure is by bathing in the radon-rich waters of the spa, but for more intensive treatment a 'vapour tunnel' is used – patients spend time in underground tunnels deep in the rock, which emit radon gases. The effects of this treatment were discovered by accident when miners working in the tunnels reported relief from symptoms of rheumatism and muscle fatigue.

Water-related health treatments are available at the more upmarket of Bad Gastein's hotels and pensions, or you can go to the recently rebuilt public **Felsentherme Gastein** (☎ 22 23-0; Bahnhofplatz 5; admission adult 3hr/1 day €15.50/19.50, child €8/12; ☯ 9am-10pm), opposite the train station, which has an indoor swimming pool (dug into sheer rock) and several steaming outdoor pools. Admission includes use

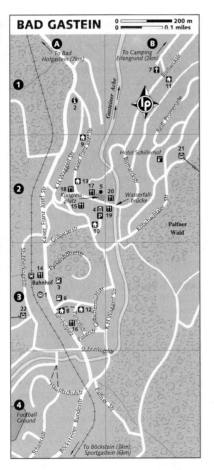

BAD GASTEIN

The small **Gasteiner Museum** (☎ 34 88; 2nd fl of Haus Austria, Kongressplatz; adult/child €3/free; ☻ 10.30am-12pm & 3.30-6pm, closed Nov & May) displays minerals, paintings, crafts and photos of historic events and famous visitors, including a shot of the infamous Nazi, Goebbels, taken in 1938. There are also some great vintage tourist posters from the Art Deco era and models and costumes from the Perchten Festival, when participants wear tall, incredibly elaborate hats. This festival occurs every four years on or around 6 January (the next is in 2006). All explanations are in German.

From the eastern bank by the *Wasserfallbrücke* (waterfall bridge), a path runs south up the hill. At the upper bridge, take Kötschachtaler Strasse and follow it eastwards up to the Hotel Schillerhof for one of the best views of the town and the valley. Work your way down via paths and roads to the Nikolauskirche.

Bad Gastein is a major area for winter **skiing** and **snowboarding**, and forms part of a wider area known as the Sportwelt Amadé, which has over 260 lifts and 800km of ski runs. If you'd like more information, check out the resort's website at www.skigastein.com. Bad Gastein's main peaks are Stubnerkogel (2246m) and Graukogel (2492m). Cross-country skiing is also possible in Bad Gastein.

of saunas, a kid's area and lockers. Curative massages, radon baths and electrotherapy are available next door in the **Kurzentrum** (Bahnhofplatz 7; ☻ 8am-4.30pm). The Gastein water can also be drunk here.

Many of the façades of Bad Gastein's hotels and apartment blocks reflect the grandeur of its 19th-century heyday – take a stroll around town to soak up the Belle Epoque ambience.

The small, solid **Nikolauskirche** was built in the 14th and 15th centuries around a central pillar. It's Gothic in style and charmingly simple inside, with an uneven flagstone floor and faded, child-like murals. Look out for the modern statue of 16th-century physician Paracelsus outside.

In summer, both peaks are excellent for **walking**. The two-section Stubnerkogelbahn cable car near the town's train station costs €14 return. The Graukogelbahn near Hotel Schillerhof is the same price.

Alpin Raft (☎ 2330-0; Hotel Krone, Bahnhofplatz 8) organises rafting, canyoning, paragliding and bungy jumping in the spectacular mountain terrain around the resort.

Sleeping

Phone ahead in the low season as many places close during that time. In addition to the places listed here, there are many private rooms – lists are available from the tourist office (see p288).

Villa Solitude (☎ 51 01; www.villasolitude.com; Kaiser Franz Josef Strasse 16; r with breakfast €100-260; P 🖳 ✖) This upmarket boutique hotel, housed in the former home of an Austrian countess, has just six suites. Each can sleep 3 or 4 people and all are elegantly decorated with antiques, dark wood panelling and oil paintings of the original inhabitants and their illustrious relatives. There's a more contemporary and stylish restaurant next door (see right).

Hotel Salzburger Hof (☎ 20 37-0; www.salzburger hof.com; Grillparzerstrasse 1; s with breakfast €102-174, d with breakfast €174-264; P 🖳 ✖ 🐾) This is a more standard, modern four-star hotel, very popular with people taking the cure. Some of the rather bland rooms are a bit small for the price. The lounges and restaurant have a rather staid, hushed atmosphere, with marble floors and leather armchairs. The hotel has a health centre with a (nonthermal) pool and sauna, plus thermal baths (which cost extra). There's also a **restaurant** (set menu €22) and a bar with live music almost every night.

Hotel Mozart (☎ 26 86-0; www.hotelmozart.at; Kaiser Franz Josef Strasse 25; s/d with breakfast 51/98; P 🖳) This reliable three-star hotel offers smart, sunny and spacious rooms, some with balconies. There are good views from the rooms at the front and a radon bath on site.

Pension Laura (☎ 27 04; www.pension-laura.com - in German; Bismarckstrasse 20; s/d €25/43) This small, good-value and rather rustic place near Nikolauskirche has cheerful rooms, a cosy restaurant, a sauna and radon baths in summer. It's open year-round, but usually pre-booked in winter.

Villa Charlotte (☎ 24 26 or 0664 906 2041; Paracelsusstrasse 6; s/d without bathroom €20/40) This friendly, homely pension, popular with hikers, has small but clean rooms and is convenient for the station. To get here on foot, take the path down the side of the Hotel Krone. Prices go up slightly in winter.

Euro Youth Hotel Krone (☎ 233 00; www.euro-youth -hotel.at; Bahnhofsplatz 8; dm/s/d with breakfast without bathroom €15.50/29/48; P 🖳) This new hostel has a backpacker vibe and is the place to come if you want to meet other travellers, many of whom are inter-railers on their way between northern Italy and Munich. It's very comfortable and well equipped, with cosy dorms, clean bathrooms and a big barbeque area outside. Adventure activities can be booked and bikes rented here, too. There's a lively bar and a **restaurant** (mains €5-11).

Camping Erlengrund (☎ /fax 27 90; www.kurcamp ing-gastein.at - in German; per adult €5.20; ☺ year-round) This place 2km north of Bad Gastein in Kötschachdorf. It's accessible by Bundesbuses, which depart from outside the train station.

Eating & Drinking

Restaurant Thom (☎ 510-11; Kaiser Franz Josef Strasse 16; mains €8.70-19; ☺ lunch & dinner Fri- Sun, dinner Tue-Thu) The restaurant of Villa Solitude (see left) has a colourful, modern and stylish interior and serves imaginative and well-prepared cuisine, making the most of local produce. Try mountain ox carpaccio (€8.70) or roast guinea fowl (€15.30). The menu changes every couple of months according to what's in season.

Jägerhäusl (☎ 20 33 2; Kaiser Franz Josef Strasse 9; mains €6.50-10.00; ☺ lunch & dinner) This well-decorated, two-storey restaurant produces fine Austrian cuisine and top-quality pizzas. There's a big outdoor seating area for summer.

Bahnhof Restaurant (☎ 21 66; Bahnhofplatz 10; mains €9-16.80; ☺ breakfast, lunch & dinner) Don't be put off by the fact that this restaurant is in the train station – it's actually a high-quality, comfortable and popular place, with an interesting menu. Try Norwegian smoked salmon (€11) or pepper steak with orange sauce (€16.80). There's also a tempting array of cakes.

Gastein Café/Don Carlos Pizzeria (☎ 50 97; Kaiser Franz Josef Strasse 4; mains €4.50-13.40; ☺ lunch & dinner) This place has a huge outdoor seating area, albeit within the brutal concrete surrounds of Kongressplatz. The pizzas it serves up are pretty average, but the ice creams are marvellous.

Wasserfall Pub (☎ 54 70; Kaiser Franz Josef Strasse 2; mains €5.90-13.80; ☺ lunch & dinner daily) This bar by the Wasserfallbrücke offers decent pizza, pasta and schnitzels alongside draught beer. There's a good view of the waterfall from the pavement tables.

Restaurant Sancho (☎ 217 62; Kaiser Franz Josef Strasse 1; ☺ lunch & dinner) You can also see the waterfall from the garden of Restaurant Sancho, which has Mexican food like steak in tequila sauce or fajitas. There are also a few Austrian dishes.

Bergfex (☎ 25 51-0; Kaiser Franz Josef Strasse 5; mains €6-18; ☺ breakfast, lunch & dinner) This bar/restaurant serves up decent Austrian specials and Italian dishes, as well as fondues. It's a lively place for an après-ski drink in winter.

Supermarkets in town include the Eurospar south of the train station.

Getting There & Away

InterCity (IC) express trains trundle through Bad Gastein every two hours, connecting the resort to points north and south including Spittal-Millstättersee (€8.15, 50 minutes), Salzburg (€10.90, 1¾ hours) and Innsbruck (€24.75, three hours). There are good views to the right of the train when travelling north from Bad Gastein to Bad Hofgastein. Travelling south, also sit on the right, as the view is good after the second tunnel.

To take your car south, you need to use the Autoschleuse Tauernbahn (railway car-shuttle service) through the tunnel that starts at Böckstein (€14.55 one-way). For more details, see p272).

AROUND BAD GASTEIN

Three kilometres south of Bad Gastein, at the head of the Gasteiner Tal, is **Böckstein**, a village with a museum and a baroque church. It also has a medieval gold mine, which has been converted into a lovely health treatment centre, the **Gasteiner Heilstollen** (Gastein Healing Gallery; ☎ 37 53-0; www.gasteiner -heilstollen.com; ☺ mid-Jan–late Oct). Patients are delivered by a small tunnel train 2.5km into the mountain, where they take in the healing radon vapours. The initial test admission is €25, then the full three-week cure costs €493 for 10 entries to the tunnel (book well in advance).

Leading west from Böckstein is a toll road (€4 per car, included in the ski pass) to **Sportgastein** (1588m), a centre for skiing

and other sports. Seven kilometres north of Bad Gastein is **Bad Hofgastein** (858m), another spa centre, with good winter-sports facilities. Bad Gastein, Bad Hofgastein and Böckstein are linked by bus and rail; Sportgastein has infrequent buses.

There are two access roads to the national park (with parking spaces at the terminus): the road to Sportgastein is one; the other turns east just south of Bad Gastein and follows the Kötschachtal.

LIENZ
☎ 04852 / pop 13,000

With the brooding, jagged grey peaks of the Dolomites crowding its southern skyline, Lienz is a relaxed small town, ideal as a base for winter sports or summer-adventure activities. Lienz, inhabited since Roman times, was granted a town charter in 1252. It's only 40km from here to the Italian border, a fact that brings plenty of Italian tourists to stroll around the streets in summer.

Orientation

The town centre is within a 'V' formed by the junction of the rivers Isel and Drau. The pivotal *Hauptplatz* (main square) is directly in front of the train station; three other squares lead from it. *Hauptplatz* has lots of parking – it's a *Kurzparkzone*, with a 90-minute limit during indicated hours.

Information

The Osttirol card, available from the tourist office, gives free access to local railways, cable cars and museums. It costs €30 for eight days.

Café Gietl (☎ 63 465; Beda Weber Gasse 38; ☺ 9am-10pm Wed-Mon). Free Internet if you're a paying customer.

Library (☎ 639 72; Muchargasse 4; per hr €1.80; ☺ 9am-12pm & 3-7pm Tue, 9am-12pm & 3-6pm Wed-Fri, 9am-12pm Sat) Internet access.

Osttirol Werbung (☎ 653 33; www.osttirol.com - in German; Albin Egger Strasse 17) For information about the wider East Tyrol area. They send out information, but aren't set up for visits.

Post office (Hauptplatz; ☺ 7.30am-6.30pm Mon-Fri, 8-11am Sat) Opposite the train station.

Tourist office (☎ 652 65; www.lienz-tourismus.at - in German; ☺ 8am-6pm Mon-Fri, 9am-12pm, 5-7pm Sat Jul-mid Sep, 10-12am Sun Jul & Aug) Just off Hauptplatz. Staff will find accommodation (even private rooms) free of charge. Wherever you stay, ask your host for the *Gästekarte* and get discounts on local sights and transport.

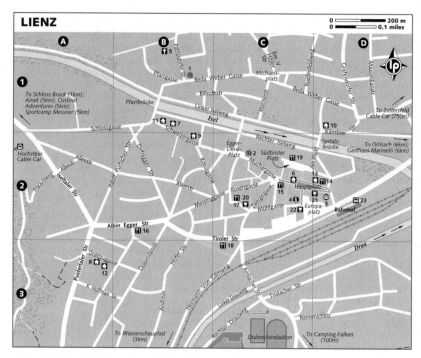

LIENZ

0 —————— 200 m
0 —————— 0.1 miles

Sights

SCHLOSS BRUCK

This well-preserved 13th-century castle overlooks Lienz from the west. It's the former seat of the counts of Görtz and houses the **Heimatmuseum** (☎ 625 80; Schlossberg 1; adult/child €6/2; ☼ 10am-6pm Palm Sunday-1 Nov), a well-thought-out and imaginative museum, which exhibits local crafts and items connected with folklore in atmospheric vaulted rooms. There are also several more abstract, contemporary displays, such as one on tattoo and body decoration, together with very spectacular exhibits from around the world including ritual costumes from West Africa and death's heads from Central America.

Don't miss the small private chapel, adorned with bright and beautiful 13th-century frescoes. A whole room is also devoted to the artist Albin Egger-Lienz (1868–1926), who dwelt on themes of toil, conflict and death. Expunge his morose vision with the exhilarating view from the castle tower.

STADTPFARRKIRCHE ST ANDRÄ

The handsome, Gothic **Stadtpfarrkirche St Andrä** (St Andrews church; ☎ 621 60; Pfarrgasse 4; ☼ daylight hours except during services) is north of the Isel River. The impressive terracotta-and-white church is noted for its murals (some dating from the 14th century), an organ loft (1616) with a winged organ and two 16th-century tombstones sculpted in red Salzburg marble. There's a magnificent altar lit by tall windows and a delicately vaulted ceiling. The walls of the graveyard are lined with arches containing family tombs, complete with oil paintings, flowers, candles and photos. There's a good view of the Dolomites from the church area – visit early evening when the sun turns the peaks a delicate pink.

Activities

South of the Drau River is the Dolomitenstadion, a sports complex comprising a stadium, swimming pool and tennis courts.

SKIING

Downhill skiing takes place on the Zettersfeld, where runs are mostly medium to easy. The Zettersfeld cable-car station is north of the Isel (signposted). The top section of the cable car is complemented by five ski lifts at elevations between 1660 and 2278m. **Hochstein** (2057m) is another skiing area, with its cable-car station west of the centre. A free bus runs from the train station to the two cable-car valley stations in summer and winter high seasons. One-day ski passes for the two mountains cost €29-32 and the ski lifts run from 1 December to Easter, depending on snow. Longer-term passes (eg two days for €56-60) include all of Osttirol's ski lifts (see www.topski.at - in German – for full ski pass details). There are also several cross-country trails in the valley. Ski rental (from various outlets in town and near the cable cars) starts at €18 per day, including boots, and cross-country equipment costs around €10.20.

WALKING

In the summer, good walking trails await in the mountains or along the valley to surrounding villages. The **Wasserschaupfad** (☎ 0664 1567 457; adult/child €2.90/1.90; ☼ 9am-6pm Jul & Aug, 10am-5pm Jun & Sep, 10am-5pm Sat & Sun May & Oct, closed winter) is a specially built walkway clinging to the sheer sides of the Dolomites above the gorge of the Drau River. To get there, head for Liesach, 3km from Lienz. If you're coming on the bus, ask to be dropped off at the point nearest the site.

The cable cars come back into service for the summer season. The two-section ride to Hochstein, which operates from late May to mid-September, costs €11 return. The Zet-

tersfeld cable car operates from mid-June to late September and costs €9, or €16 including the chairlift to 2214m. There are also family and child fares and the Osttirol Card is valid. Both lifts are run by **Lienzer Bergbahnen** (☎ 639 75; Zettersfeldstrasse 38).

CYCLING

Paths for city cycling and mountain bikes radiate from Lienz. Ask at the tourist office for the booklet *Radfahren in den Osttiroler Bergen*, which has routes and maps for mountain bikers. Bike rental from the various sports shops in town costs €18/7 per day for an adult's/child's bike.

ADVENTURE SPORTS

The foaming rivers, narrow gorges and pine forests of the Dolomites around Lienz are the perfect place for adrenaline-pumping sports such as white-water rafting, canyoning and kayaking. The following two companies, both based in the village of Ainet near Lienz, will set you up:

Osttirol Adventures (☎ 0664 356 0450; www.osttirol-adventures.at - in German)

Sportcamp Messner (☎ 0664 897 8259; www.raft company.at)

Festivals & Events

This town is the base for the **Dolomiten Mann** (www.dolomitenmann.com), a testosterone-fuelled, Red Bull–sponsored iron man competition that takes place every September and is billed as the world's hardest team challenge. Women are not permitted to enter the cross-country relay race, in which teams consisting of a mountain-runner, a paraglider, a kayaker and a mountain-biker compete. Lively open-air concerts, parties and celebrations are held every day during the weekend of the competition.

Not quite as strenuous, but still hardly relaxing, is the Dolomitenlauf, a famous cross-country skiing championship that takes place on the third Sunday in January.

At the end of July every year, Lienz hosts a free international street festival, with circus acts and theatre performances from around the world. Summer also sees a series of events representing Tyrolean culture, as well as free concerts on *Hauptplatz* and in other squares (at 8pm on Wednesdays and Sundays June to September).

Sleeping

BUDGET

Lienz offers plenty of inexpensive private rooms and a single night's stay is often possible. Several good choices are a few minutes west of the centre.

Goldener Stern (☎ /fax 621 92; www.tiscover.at /goldener.stern; Schweizergasse 40; s/d with breakfast €33/66; ☯ closed mid-Oct–early Dec & Easter-late May; ℗ ☒) This handsome 600-year-old *Gasthöfe* (inn) has light and sunny rooms that manage to be modern and well equipped while still maintaining their character. There's a charming courtyard for breakfast or afternoon snacks. Cheaper rooms with shared bathrooms are also available, making this the best of the budget choices.

Gästehaus Masnata (☎ 655 36; Drahtzuggasse 4; d with breakfast €36.50, apt with kitchen summer/winter €35/38.60) This place has very large and modern rooms with a balcony and a view. There are also several excellent apartments with a kitchen (minimum stay one week).

Haus Wille (☎ /fax 629 25; Drahtzuggasse 6; s with breakfast without bathroom €11-13, d with breakfast without bathroom €22-26, 2-night minimum) This is an excellent deal – the old-fashioned rooms in this private pension have a door onto the veranda and some have radios, too.

Gasthof Neuwirt (☎ 621 01; Schweizergasse 22; neuwirt-lienz@aon.at; s/d with breakfast €36.40/68; ℗ ☒) This large, lively and attractive hotel/restaurant is chiefly noted for its food (see right) but also has some big, plain rooms upstairs. Half board is also available.

Camping Falken (☎ 640 22; fax 640 22-6; camping .falken@tirol.com; Eichholz 7; per adult €5.60; ☯ mid-Dec–late Oct) South of the Drau, convenient to various sporting facilities.

MID-RANGE & TOP END

Hotel Traube (☎ 644 44; hotel.traube@tirol.com; Hauptplatz 14; s with breakfast €59-68, d with breakfast €118-136; ℗ ☒ ▢ ▣) Lienz's smartest hotel has a few token old artworks on the walls, but it's generally a modern and corporate place. The standard rooms are big, but fairly unimaginative when it comes to décor – the 'Romantik' rooms are more atmospheric and stylish (and more expensive), with painted furniture and a location on the sunny side of the building. There's a great rooftop indoor swimming pool.

Altstadthotel Eck (☎ 647 85; altstadthotel.eck@ utanet.at; Hauptplatz 20; s/d with breakfast €37/74; ℗)

This venerable old inn right in the town centre is a bargain considering the atmosphere and character it offers. Wood panels and oil paintings abound in the richly decorated corridors. The rooms are far from fashionable, but light and spacious, many with chairs and sofas, plus views over the square outside. There's an alfresco café-restaurant and an upstairs dining room.

Goldener Fisch (☎ 621 32; www.goldener-fisch.at; Kärntner Strasse 9; s/d with breakfast €45/88) The rooms in this sophisticated and modern hotel/restaurant are very good value considering you also get the use of a lovely mosaic sauna, a steam room and a small gym. There's also an excellent restaurant on site (see opposite). It's just over the river from the town centre, but still convenient.

Gästehaus Gretl (☎ 621 06; kawrza-ofen@aon.at; Schweizergasse 32; s/d with breakfast €31/54; ☯ closed approx March-May & Oct–pre-Christmas; ℗) Run by the same family as the ceramics shop out front, this place has big, well-furnished rooms. In future they may only be open in winter – check in advance.

Eating

Spice Tapas Bar (☎ 634 73; Südtiroler Platz 2; light dishes €4.10-6.50; ☯ dinner Wed-Mon) Despite its name, the dishes served until 1am in this very stylish bar aren't tiny like Spanish tapas – they're more like light suppers, delicately prepared and exquisitely presented. There's a daily changing menu of soups, fish and vegetarian options, plus a couple of meat dishes. Most of the tables are outside on the square, but its worth taking a look inside at the funky orange-and-red interior, which has local art on the walls. Highly recommended.

Gasthof Neuwirt (☎ 621 01; Schweizergasse 22; mains €8.50-12; ☯ lunch & dinner) This large and attractive hotel/restaurant has many different rooms with various décor themes; on the walls of the *Fischerstube* (Fisherman's Room) is a rogues' gallery of stuffed fish that didn't quite make it onto the dinner plate. Those that do, though, are very appetising: try the *forelle* (trout), fished out of a pond in the backyard (the menu features a handy diagram of how to eat it), or tuck into a good selection of cured local meats and cheeses.

Zum Weinhändler (☎ 644 44; Hauptplatz 14; mains €19-21; ☯ lunch & dinner Tue-Sun) The restaurant of the Hotel Traube (see above) is one of the best in town, offering creative versions of international and regional dishes. The same hotel also has a decent (and more affordable) pizza restaurant called **La Taverna** (pizza €12-20).

Goldener Fisch (☎ 621 32; Kärntner Strasse 9; mains €6-11.20; ⊙ lunch & dinner) The décor in this large *Gasthöfe* is a bit bland, but the various dining rooms are large and sunny and there's an attractive outside terrace. The menu features all the usual local and national specialities, plus a couple of kids' and vegetarian options. There are a couple of good-value set menus (two/three courses €7.50/11.50).

Pizzeria El Franco (☎ 699 09; Ägydius Pegger-Strasse; pizzas €6-20; ⊙ lunch & dinner) The Italian tourists who come to Lienz demand pizza worthy of their homeland and this is where they find it. The restaurant itself isn't terribly stylish, but the staff are friendly and the brick-oven pizzas are crisp and enormous.

Adlerstüberl Restaurant (☎ 625 50; Andrä Kranz Gasse 5; 2-person platter €11.50-27; ⊙ lunch & dinner) The speciality at this restaurant is plates for two people – try the platter of grilled meats and vegetables (€27) or the mixed-fish plate (€14.50), all served in attractive, vaulted rooms with ceiling paintings and wooden booths. There's also a good selection of ice creams and cakes. **S'Eck** (☎ 647 85; Hauptplatz 20; light meals €3.50-8.10; ⊙ breakfast, lunch & dinner) The bar-café of the Altstadthotel Eck has tables outside, a cosy old-style interior and lots of toasts, ice creams and cakes.

Gasthaus Marinelli (☎ 682 08; Dölsach 78, Dölsach; mains €5-10; ⊙ lunch & dinner Thu-Tue) Locals rave about the home-cooked local food at this tiny restaurant in the schnapps-making village of Dölsach, just outside Lienz. It's best to reserve in advance.

Imbissstube Ortner (☎ 623 91; Albin Egger Strasse 5; chickens €2.60; ⊙ lunch & dinner, closed Jan-Apr) This simple place specialises in tasty rotisserie *hendl* (half-chickens) sprinkled with delicious spices; in fact, excluding summertime, that's usually all it does.

For self-caterers, supermarkets in town include an ADEG at Hauptplatz 12 and a Spar at Tiroler Strasse 23.

Drinking

Pick Nick Ossi (☎ 710 91; Europaplatz 2; ⊙ 10am-11pm Mon-Sat) The downstairs room of this

cheap restaurant has some pool tables, table football, loud music and a mostly teenage clientele.

Petrocelli's (☎ 643 64-44; Hauptplatz 9; ⊙ 8am-12am) This snazzy ice-cream parlour turns into a bar in the evenings. There's a nightclub underneath, **Joy** (⊙ 10pm-4am Wed-Sun), which draws a slightly older crowd than Pic Nick Ossi.

Flair Musikpub (☎ 0676-602 57 85; Ägidius Pegger Strasse; ⊙ 5pm-1am) This smoky bar has live music once a week, mostly of the rock variety (some gigs have a cover charge of €5-10).

Getting There & Away

Regional transport in Tyrol comes under the wing of the Verkehrsverbund Tirol (VVT). For information on VVT transport tickets, valid for travel between Tyrol and East Tyrol, see p299.

BUS

The bus departure point is in front of the train station. The **Postbus information office** (⊙ 8am-12pm & 2-4pm Mon-Fri) is here. There are bus connections to the East Tyrol ski resorts of St Jakob, Sillian and Obertilliach, as well as northwards to the Hohe Tauern National Park (see p286 for more details). Buses to Kitzbühel (€13.60, 1½ hours) are quicker and more direct than the train, but they only go one to three times a day. Buses to Kufstein are also quicker than the train.

TRAIN

Most train services to the rest of Austria, including Salzburg (€29.60, 3½ hours), go east via Spittal-Millstättersee, where you usually have to change trains. This is also one route to Innsbruck, changing at Schwarzach-St Veit. However, a quicker and easier route to Innsbruck is to go west via Sillian and Italy. Some trains on this route are cheaper than others; holders of an Austrian rail pass may have to pay an international supplement.

CAR & MOTORCYCLE

To head south, you must first divert west or east along Hwy 100, as the Dolomites act as an impregnable barrier. For details of road routes to the north, see p280.

HOHE TAUERN NATIONAL PARK REGION

Tyrol

CONTENTS

If you're looking for picture-postcard Austria, then look no further than Tyrol (Tirol in German). This is a land of classic Austrian scenery, a place where deep, glacial valleys divide mountain ranges that crowd the skyline, and quaint wooden chalets huddle together on fertile foothills or hang precariously from steep slopes. And like the landscape, Tyroleans are a proud lot, as evidenced in the traditional saying: 'Bisch a Tiroler, bisch a Mensch' – 'If you're Tyrolean, you're a (real) person'.

The Inntal (Inn Valley), which runs almost the full length of the province, is Tyrol's major artery, from where smaller, steeper and more rugged valleys head off in all directions. Innsbruck, the vibrant capital, is a focal point of Tyrol and occupies a central position on the Inn River. Its *Altstadt* (old town) is a pure gem, filled with baroque façades and cobblestone alleyways. Close by, historical towns, such as Hall in Tirol and Schwaz, have managed to retain a medieval heart and oodles of charm, gained at the height of their power in the 15th century.

But Tyrol's monumental attraction is the Alps. Nowhere else in Austria are these majestic creations of nature more prominent, or more accessible. Numerous highly developed resorts line the valleys, offering myriad sporting opportunities; in winter, arguably Austria's best skiing is to be had in some of the country's top resorts, such as Kitzbühel and St Anton am Arlberg. In summer, walking takes over; the spectrum ranges from gentle valley strolls to tough, week-long tramps over windswept passes. Cable cars and chairlifts run year-round, providing a quick, painless ride to Alpine heights.

Tyrol's eastern region, Osttirol (East Tyrol), is cut off from the rest of the province by Salzburg and is dealt with in the Hohe Tauern National Park chapter (p277).

HIGHLIGHTS

- Skiing all day and partying all night in **St Anton am Arlberg** (p329), one of the Alp's top winter resorts

- Exploring the gardens and museum collections of **Schloss Ambras** (p303) in Innsbruck

- Soaking up the medieval atmosphere in historic **Hall in Tirol** (p311) and **Schwaz** (p312)

- Admiring Innsbruck's **Goldenes Dachl** (p305) against the spectacular backdrop of the Nordkette Mountains

- Escaping to the far reaches of Tyrol's numerous valleys, including **Zillertal** (p315) and **Ötztal (p325)**

Hall in Tirol ★ Schwaz
Innsbruck ★★
St Anton ★ am Arlberg
Zillertal Valley ★
Ötztal Valley ★

| ■ POPULATION: 636,400 | ■ AREA: 10,626 SQ KM | ■ HIGHEST ELEVATION: WILDSPITZE 3774M |

TYROL

TYROL

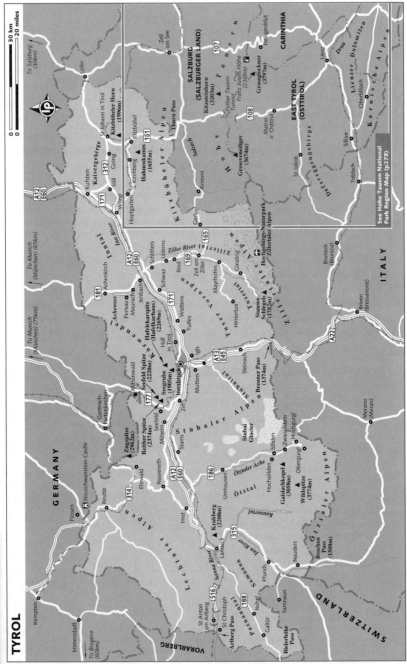

GERMANY

VORARLBERG

SWITZERLAND

ITALY

SALZBURG (SALZBURGER LAND)

CARINTHIA

EAST TYROL (OSTTIROL)

To Salzburg (30km)

To Munich (München) (65km)

To Munich (München) (75km)

To Munich (München)

To Bregenz (60km)

30 km
20 miles

Kempten

Immenstadt

Füssen

Neuschwanstein Castle

Reutte

Ehrwald

Nasserereith

Zugspitze (2962m)

Reither Spitze (2374m)

Garmisch-Partenkirchen

Mittenwald

Seefeld

Mösern

Lechtaler Alpen

Lermoos Alpen

Imst

Landeck

St Anton am Arlberg

St Christoph

Arlberg Pass

Paznauntal

Ischgl

Galtür

Bielerhöhe Pass

Samnaun

Pfunds

Nauders

Reschen Pass (1508m)

Kaunertal

Krahberg (2208m)

Inn River

Sanna River

Lofer

St Johann in Tirol

Kitzbüheler Horn (1996m)

Kitzbühel

Kirchberg

Hahnenkamm (1655m)

Going

Söll

Wörgl

Hopfgarten

Kufstein

Kaisergebirge

Inntal

Achenkirch

Pertisau

Maurach

Achensee

Jenbach

Schwaz

Schlitters

Uderns

Ried

Zillertal

Ziller River

Zell am Ziller

Mayrhofen

Ginzling

Hintertux

Tuxertal

Stans

Schlitters (1782m)

Zillertaler Alpen

Hochgebirgs-Naturpark Zillertaler Alpen

Karwendel

Hafelekarspitz (Hafelkarhaus) (2269m)

Hall (in Tirol)

Wattens

Tulfes

Igls

Innsbruck

Mutters

Zirl

Seegrube (1905m)

Seefeld Spitze (2220m)

Stubaier Alpen

Stubai Glacier

Starns

Umhausen

Ötztal

Ötztaler Ache

Hochsölden

Sölden

Obergurgl

Hochgurgl

Zwieselstein

Gaislachkogel (3058m)

Wildspitze (3774m)

Ötztaler Alpen

A13 E45

Sellraintal

Brenner Pass (1374m)

Steinach

A22

Brixen (Bressanone)

Merano (Meran)

Bruneck (Brunico)

Pustertal

Toblach

Sillian

St Jakob

Deferreggengebirge

Hohe Tauern

Kitzsteinhorn (3203m)

Felber Tauern Tunnel

Franz Josefs Höhe (2369m)

Grossglockner (3797m)

Grossvenediger (3674m)

Krimml

Gerlos

Zell am See

Thurn Pass

Saalfelden

Matrei in Osttirol

Lienz

Heiligenblut

Drau

Lienzer Dolomiten

Karnische Alpen

Obertilliach

107

108

312

171

181

177

186

315

188

516

314

171

165

169

151

A12 E60

A12 E60

See Hohe Tauern National Park Region Map (p279)

0

0

History

Despite the difficult Alpine terrain, Tyrol has experienced influxes of tribes and travellers since the Iron Age, verified by the discovery of a 5500-year-old body of a man preserved in ice in the Ötztaler Alpen (Ötztal Alps) in 1991 (see p326). The Brenner Pass (1374m), a high pass crossing into Italy, was a key to allowing the region to develop as a north–south trade route early in its history.

Tyrol fell to the Habsburgs in 1363 when Rudolf IV inherited it from his sister Magareta, widow of the last of the Görz-Tirol line. But the province had to wait for the rule of Emperor Maximilian I (1490–1519) to truly forge ahead. His fondness for Innsbruck increased the region's status and under his rule the town became an administrative capital and an artistic and cultural centre. He also drew up the Landibell legislation in 1511 that passed the defence of the province's borders over to the Tyroleans themselves, thus creating the celebrated *Schützen* (marksmen militia) which still exists today. The duchy of Tyrol was directly ruled from Vienna after the death of the last Tyrolean Habsburg, Archduke Sigmund Franz, in 1665.

In 1703 the Bavarians attempted to capture the whole of Tyrol in the War of the Spanish Succession, having contested control of parts of the north of the province for centuries. In alliance with the French, they reached as far as the Brenner Pass before being beaten back by the *Schützen*. But only a century later Tyrol passed into Bavarian hands under the command of Napoleon.

Bavarian rule of the province was short-lived and troublesome; in 1809 local innkeeper Andreas Hofer led a successful fight for independence, winning a famous victory at Bergisel (p304). His heroic stance was unfortunately not supported by the Habsburg monarchy and Tyrol was returned to Bavaria under a treaty later that year. Hofer continued the struggle, and was shot by firing squad on Napoleon's orders on 20 February 1810.

A further blow was dealt to the strong Tyrolean identity by the Treaty of St Germain (1919); prosperous South Tyrol was ceded to Italy and East Tyrol was isolated from the rest of the province.

Climate

With almost 90% of Tyrol's terrain given over to mountains, much of the province's climate is ruled by the Alps, with short summers, long cold winters and changeable weather. In the valleys the temperatures are surprisingly mild, helped no end by the *Föhn*, a warm south wind that sweeps down from the mountains.

Getting There & Away

Innsbruck receives international and national flights on a regular basis. The main road and rail route in and out of Tyrol follows the Inntal; the A12 autobahn runs east–west and cuts the province into almost equal halves, entering from Germany near Kufstein and exiting west of St Anton in Vorarlberg. The A13 connects Italy with Tyrol, crossing the Brenner Pass directly south of Innsbruck.

Getting Around

Regional transport comes under the wing of the **Verkehrsverbund Tirol** (VVT; ☎ 0512-56 16 16; www.vvt.at – in German; Bürgerstrasse 2, Innsbruck; ☀ 8am-noon Mon-Fri). Ticket prices depend on the number of zones you travel through; a single ticket for one zone costs €1.50 or €3 for a day pass. Monthly and yearly tickets are also available, and there are reductions for children, senior citizens and families. Tickets cover journeys on city buses, trams, Bundesbuses and also ÖBB (Austrian federal railway) trains.

Additionally, Tyrol is divided into 12 overlapping transport regions, which are individually covered by *Regio Ticket* (regional passes). A pass for individual regions costs €23.80/84 per week/month or €52.60/181.30 for all 12 regions. Innsbruck is an exception; see p311.

INNSBRUCK

☎ 0512 / pop 114,000

Of all Austria's provincial capitals, Innsbruck has arguably the best backdrop; mountains on its doorstep to the north and south, and a deep valley spreading to the east and west. The outdoor opportunities are obvious, with walking and skiing topping the lengthy list of things to do.

The city itself is a quietly confident place with a down-to-earth air, and its citizens enjoy a high standard of living. Architecturally there's plenty to see, and most of it is conveniently located in the city's compact, inviting *Altstadt*. With the setting sun, Innsbruck certainly doesn't sleep; the city

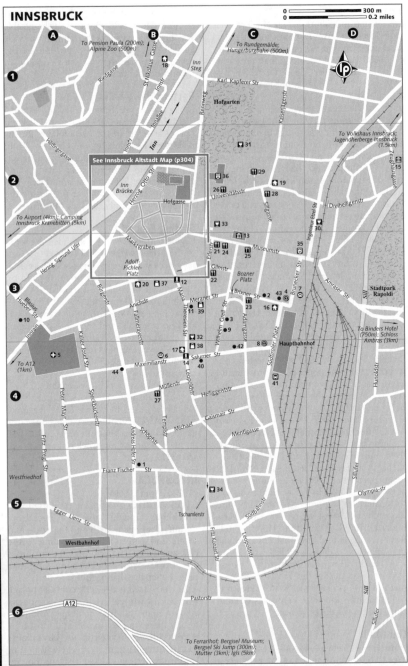

INNSBRUCK

0 _____ 300 m
0 _____ 0.2 miles

To Pension Paula (200m);
Alpine Zoo (500m)

To Rundgemälde;
Hungerburgbahn (500m)

Inn Steg

Karl Kapferer Str

Hofgarten

To Volkshaus Innsbruck;
Jugendherberge Innsbruck
(1.5km)

See Innsbruck Altstadt Map (p304)

Inn Brücke

Hofgasse

Universitätsstr

To Airport (4km); Camping
Innsbruck Kranebitten (5km)

Marktgraben

Adolf-
Pichler-
Platz

Museumstr

Bozner
Platz

Stadtpark
Rapoldi

Gilmstr

Meraner Str

Brixner Str

To Binders Hotel
(750m); Schloss
Ambras (3km)

To A12
(1km)

Maximilianstr

Salurner Str

Hauptbahnhof

Müllerstr

Heilggeiststr

Gaismair Str

Mentlgasse

Westfriedhof

Franz Fischer Str

Tschamlerstr

Westbahnhof

Pastorstr

A12

To Ferrarihof; Bergisel Museum;
Bergisel Ski Jump (300m);
Mutter (3km); Igls (5km)

entertains the third-largest student population in Austria, which helps to keep the place buzzing after dark.

With its position in the heart of the Inntal and enjoying excellent transport connections to the rest of Tyrol, Innsbruck makes a good base for exploring the province.

History

Innsbruck dates from 1180, when the small market settlement on the north bank of the Inn River expanded to the south bank. This was made possible by a bridge that had been built a few years previously and which gave the settlement its name, Ynsprugg.

In 1420 Innsbruck became the ducal seat of the Tyrolean line of the Habsburgs but it was under the reign of Emperor Maximilian I (1490–1519) that the city reached its zenith in power and prestige; many of the monuments, including the celebrated Goldenes Dachl (p305), can still be seen today. Maximilian was not the only Habsburg to influence the city's architectural skyline; Archduke Ferdinand II reconstructed the Schloss Ambras (p303) and Empress Maria Theresia the Hofburg (p302).

Aside from the two world wars, Innsbruck has enjoyed a relatively peaceful existence over the centuries. More recently, its importance as a winter sports centre reached the international stage – it held the Winter Olympics in 1964 and 1976.

Orientation

Innsbruck is in the valley of the Inn River, scenically squeezed between the northern chain of the Alps (the Karwendel) and the Tuxer Vorberge (Tuxer Mountains) to the south. Extensive mountain transport facilities radiate from the city and provide ample walking and skiing opportunities, particularly to the south and west. The town centre is compact, with the *Hauptbahnhof* (main train station) just a 10-minute walk from the pedestrian-only *Altstadt* (old town centre). The main street in the *Altstadt*, Herzog Friedrich Strasse, connects with Maria Theresien Strasse, which is a major thoroughfare but is closed to private transport.

MAPS

Tourist office maps are adequate for most tourist needs; they cost €1 but many hotels and pensions have the maps for free.

Information
BOOKSHOPS

The best source of international papers can be found at a handy newspaper stand on the corner of Riesengasse and Herzog Friedrich Strass (Map p304).

Freytag & Berndt (Map pp300-1; ☎ 57 24 30; Wilhelm Greil Strasse 15; ☽ 9am-1pm & 2-6pm Mon-Fri, 9am-noon Sat) Excellent source for maps and travel books.

Wagnersche Buchhandlung (Map p304; ☎ 595 05; Museumstrasse 4; ☽ 9am-6pm Mon-Fri, 9am-5pm Sat) University bookshop with Innsbruck's largest collection of English books.

INTERNET ACCESS

Innsbruck Information (Map p304; ☎ 53 56; www.innsbruck-information.at - in German; Burggraben 3; per 10min €1; ☽ 9am-6pm Apr-Oct, 8am-6pm Nov-Mar)

International Telephone Discount (Map pp300-1; ☎ 59 42 72 61; Bruneckerstrasse 12; per hr €4.20; ☽ 9am-11pm) Cheap phone calls as well.

IVB Kundenbüro (Map p304; ☎ 53 07-500; Stainerstrasse 2; ☽ 7.30am-6pm Mon-Fri) One free terminal with Internet connection.

SPÖ Internet Cafe (Map pp300-1; ☎ 53 66; Salurner Strasse 2; ⓨ 9am-4pm Mon-Thu, 9am-noon Fri) This place provides free Internet access, but donations are very welcome.

LAUNDRY

Bubble Point (☎ 565 0007 50; soap & wash €4; ⓨ 8am-10pm Mon-Fri, 8am-8pm Sat & Sun) Andreas Hofer (Map pp300-1; Andreas Hofer Strasse 37); Brixner (Map pp300-1; Brixner Strasse 1) Self-service laundries with Internet access for €6 per hour.

MEDICAL SERVICES

Landeskrankenhaus (Map pp300-1; ☎ 504-0; Anichstrasse 35) The University Clinic (Universitätklinik) at the city's main hospital has emergency services.

MONEY

The Hauptbahnhof and Innsbruck Information have exchange facilities and *Bankomats* are ubiquitous throughout the old centre.

POST

Main post office (Map pp300-1; Maximilianstrasse 2; ⓨ 7am-11pm Mon-Fri, 7am-9pm Sat, 8am-9pm Sun)
Post office (Map pp300-1; Brunecker Strasse 1-3; ⓨ 7am-7pm Mon-Fri, 8am-1pm Sat) This second post office is handy to the Hauptbahnhof.

TOURIST INFORMATION

City Tourist Board (Map p304; ☎ 598 50; www.innsbruck-tourism.com; Burggraben 3; ⓨ 8am-6pm Mon-Fri, 9am-noon Sat) Above Innsbruck Information; mostly fields telephone inquiries.
Hauptbahnhof (Map pp300-1; ☎ 583 766; ⓨ 9am-7pm) Smaller office in the main train station.

DISCOUNT CARDS

If you plan to experience Innsbruck in all its richness consider purchasing the Innsbruck Card, which allows one visit to most of the main attractions, a journey on the surrounding cable cars and free use of public transport, including The Sightseer (see p306). It's available from Innsbruck Information and costs €21/26/31 for 24/48/72 hours.

Free to those overnighting in Innsbruck, the Club Innsbruck card, available from your accommodation, gives various discounts on transportation and admission fees. It also entitles you to join free guided mountain walks, run from June to September; contact Innsbruck Information for details.

Innsbruck Information (Map p304; ☎ 53 56; www.innsbruck-information.at - in German; Burggraben 3; ⓨ 9am-6pm Apr-Oct, 8am-6pm Nov-Mar) Main tourist office with truckloads of info on the city and the surrounds, including skiing and walking. Sells ski passes, public-transport tickets, city maps (€1) and will book accommodation (€3 commission); has an attached ticketing service (ⓨ 9am-6pm Mon-Fri, 9am-noon Sat).

TRAVEL AGENCIES

STA Travel (Map pp300-1; ☎ 58 89 97; innsbruck@statravel.at; Wilhelm Greil Strasse 17; ⓨ 9am-5.30pm Mon-Fri) Friendly student-focused travel agency with occasional specials.

UNIVERSITIES

University of Innsbruck (Map pp300-1; ☎ 507-0; Christoph-Probst-Platz, Innrain 52) Main campus.

Sights

HOFBURG

Originally dating from 1397, the **Hofburg** (Imperial Palace; Map p304; ☎ 58 71 86; Rennweg 1; adult/senior/student €7/5/1.10; ⓨ 9am-4.30pm) has been rebuilt and extended several times since then. The Hofburg's greatest influence was Maria Theresia, who imposed her favourite baroque and rococo styles; it pales into insignificance, however, when compared with her other home, Schloss Schönbrunn in Vienna (p100). It's still suitably grand, with most rooms decorated with Habsburg family portraits. The impressive **Riesensaal** (Giant's Hall), a 31m-long state room with ceiling frescoes and marble, gold and porcelain embellishment, is the highlight; its walls are adorned with paintings of Maria Theresia and her large family. The faces of her 16 children (including Marie Antoinette, with head) look strangely identical – maybe the artist was intent on avoiding royal wrath arising from sibling rivalry in the beauty stakes.

Tours (included in the admission price) are available at 11am and 2pm, but they're usually conducted in German only; a booklet in English however is a worthwhile purchase at €2.20. Tours of the palace are also conducted by **Pedes** (☎ 53 56 30; without/with Innsbruck Card €5/8; ⓨ 12.15pm & 3.15pm May-Oct).

HOFKIRCHE & VOLKSKUNST MUSEUM

Both the following attractions are entered from Universitätstrasse 2, share the same opening times and can be visited with a combined ticket available from the **ticket** office (☎ 58 43 02; adult/concession/child €6.50/5.50/3; ☯ 9am-5pm Mon-Sat, 9am-noon Sun).

The **Hofkirche** (Imperial Church; Map p304; adult/student/child €3/2/1.50), opposite the Hofburg, is worthy of a visit solely for the massive, but empty, sarcophagus of Maximilian I (his wish was to be buried in Wiener Neustadt). The tomb is considered the finest surviving example of German Renaissance sculpture, though the overall display is only a partial realisation of the initial plans. It is beautifully decorated with scenes from his life; most of the reliefs were created by Flemish sculptor Alexander Colin (1527–1612), who also produced the kneeling bronze figure of the emperor (1584), while the Renaissance metal grille was designed in 1573 by Georg Schmiedhammer from Prague.

The twin rows of 28 sombre, giant bronze figures that flank the sarcophagus are memorable, if strangely unsettling. Habsburgs and other dignitaries are depicted, including König Artur (King Arthur), the legendary English king, which was designed by Albrecht Dürer. The bronze has been polished to a sheen in certain places by the hands that have touched it.

Tyrolean hero Andreas Hofer (1767–1810) is also entombed in the church. The steps by the entrance lead to the **Silberne Kapelle** (Silver Chapel), wherein stands an image of the Virgin with embossed silver. The tombs of Archduke Ferdinand II and his wife, a commoner, are also inside.

Next door to the church is the **Volkskunst Museum** (Folk Art Museum; Map p304; adult/student/child €5/3/1.50), which contains a fine collection of folk art from not only Tyrol, but also Südtirol in Italy. Alongside utensils, musical instruments, farming implements and traditional dress, there are complete rooms furnished in Gothic, Renaissance and baroque styles.

TIROLER LANDESMUSEUM FERDINANDEUM

This multilevel **museum** (Map pp300-1; ☎ 59 48 9-9; www.tiroler-landesmuseum.at - in German; Museumstrasse 15; adult/senior/student €8/6/4; ☯ 10am-6pm Fri-Wed, 10am-9pm Thu Jun-Sep, closed Mon Oct-May) houses a considerable collection covering a wide range of topics. Space on the ground floor is carved up into sections devoted to archaeological finds from the Stone, Bronze, Iron, Roman and early Middle Ages, while the 1st floor swiftly moves on to religious art, including Gothic statues and altarpieces and a collec-

tion of Dutch and Flemish masters. The top two floors contain paintings, sculpture, glass cutting and pewter creations from the baroque age through to the 20th century – depending on your taste, works from the likes of Klimt, Kokoschka (see p41) and Albin Egger-Lienz (see p95) are the highlights.

ZEUGHAUS

Not far northeast of the Hauptbahnhof is the **Zeughaus** (Map pp300-1; ☎ 59 48 9-311; Zeughausgasse; adult/senior/student/child €8/6/4/2; ☯ 10am-5pm May-Sep, 10am-5pm Tue-Sun Oct-Apr), the former imperial arsenal built by Maximilian around 1500. This low, solid structure now houses a museum, which chronologically runs through Tyrol's cultural history. It starts with the geological and mineral history of the province, including the rich silver deposits that made Hall and Schwaz medieval powerhouses. The museum however spends most of its time on one of Tyrol's greatest historical figures, Andreas Hofer, including a short film on the great man. If you're interested in Tyrolean music, this is also the place to come; a soundproof room houses over 100 CDs from the province's musical stars.

SCHLOSS AMBRAS

Southeast of the town centre, **Schloss Ambras** (☎ 01-525 24-745; Schlossstrasse 20; adult/concession/family €4.50/3/9 Nov-Mar, €8/6/16 Apr-Oct, guided tours €2; ☯ 10am-5pm Dec-Jul, Sep & Oct, 10am-7pm Aug, closed Nov) is a fine Renaissance castle and can easily occupy visitors for several hours. Archduke Ferdinand II acquired the castle in 1564, the year he became ruler of Tyrol, and greatly extended the original building, shifting the emphasis from fortress to palace. He was responsible for creating the impressive Renaissance **Spaniche Saal** (Spanish Hall), a long room with a wooden inlaid ceiling and frescoes of Tyrolean nobles gazing from the walls. Also note the *grisaille* (grey relief) around the courtyard of the upper castle.

Archduke Ferdinand was the instigator of the Ambras Collection, which has three main elements. The **Rüstkammer** (Armour Collection) mostly comprises 15th-century pieces, as well as Ferdinand's wedding armour, which inexplicably lacks a lapel for the carnation. The **Kunst und Wunderkammer** (Art and Wonders Collection) may be of more interest to most visitors; it is filled with some wondrous objects, including the *Tödlein*

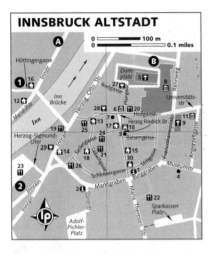

(Little Death), a small figure of death on the hunt, carved out of pear-tree wood.

The **Portraitgalerie** contains room upon room of portraits of the Habsburgs and other nobles. Portrait No 158 (Room 10) features a whiskered Charles VIII masquerading as a peasant while wearing a hat masquerading as an armchair. Maria Anna of Spain (No 126, Room 22) wins the prize for the most ludicrous hairstyle. When portraits of Habsburgs begin to pall, you can unwind by strolling in the extensive **castle gardens** (admission free; ☽ 6am-8pm), which are perfect for a picnic.

Guided tours are available; English tours however must be reserved. Entry is cheaper in winter as some parts of the castle may be closed. To get there take tram No 6 or bus K; tram No 3 will also take you reasonably close.

BERGISEL
On the southern outskirts of Innsbruck, Bergisel was the site of the famous battle in 1809 at which Andreas Hofer defeated the Bavarians. The **Bergisel Museum** (☎ 58 23 12; Bergisel 1; adult/student €3/1.50; ☽ 9am-5pm Apr-Oct) contains memorials to Tyrolean freedom fighters from this and other battles and a handful of paintings from WWI by Albin Egger-Lienz.

ALPENZOO & AROUND
North of the Inn River is the **Alpenzoo** (☎ 29 23 23; Weiherburggasse 37; adult/concession/children 6-15/children 4-5 €7/5/3.50/2; ☽ 9am-6pm), about 1.5km from the town centre. It features a comprehensive collection of Alpine animals, including amorous bears and combative ibexes. To get there, walk up the hill from the northern end of Rennweg or take the *Hungerburgbahn* (the funicular to Hungerburg), which is free if you buy your zoo ticket at the bottom.

Almost directly south across the cold Inn River is the **Rundgemälde** (☎ 58 44 34; Rennweg 39; adult/child €2.50/1.25; ☽ 9am-5pm Apr-Oct), a 1000-sq-metre panorama painting of the Battle of Bergisel. The circular building that houses the painting also contains an exhibition detailing epic overland trips by the Austrian travel writer Max Reisch (1912–85); though there's no English text, this is a surprising gem, and extremely evocative of the days before long-distance travel became so easy.

Activities
With the close proximity of so many mountainous peaks, Tyrol's provincial capital is a perfect base from which to enjoy a variety of Alpine activities. Aside from skiing and walking, rafting, mountain biking, paragliding and bobsledding are all available to the daring.

SKIING

There are seven ski fields nearby, and the quality of the pistes is not to be scoffed at; most have been used in Olympic competitions. The closest ski region to the city is the Nordpark-Seegrube area to the north while the rest are to the south or the west: Axamer Lizum, Patscherkofel, Kühtai, Rangger Köpfl, Glungezer, Schlick 2000 and Stubai Glacier. Skiing is varied, with most runs geared to intermediates, but with 270km of runs there is certainly something for everyone. At Bergisel there's a ski jump that, rather disconcertingly, overlooks a graveyard. Three-/ seven-day Gletscher Skipasses to all areas cost €90/172 and all are connected by ski buses, which are free to anyone with the Club Innsbruck card. In addition, the Innsbruck Super Skipass, which takes in all the above ski areas plus Kitzbühel and Arlberg areas – a massive 205 lifts and 750km of pistes – is available. Passes covering four out of six days cost €150, five out of six days cost €200.

Note that skiing is not only restricted to the winter months; the Stubai Glacier offers year-round skiing (p313).

WALKING

Hiking trails literally surround Innsbruck, all of which head into the mountains. The easiest way to reach any kind of altitude from the city though is to hitch a ride on the *Hungerburgbahn* (www.nordpark.com) in the northern part of the city. This train connects with the two-section Nordkette cable car; the first section rises to Seegrube (1905m) and the second to Hafelkarhaus (2269m), from where trails head off in all directions.

The cable car runs from about 8.30am to 4.30pm year-round and costs €2.90/4.30 one way/return to the top of the *Hungerburgbahn*, €12.20/20.30 to Seegrube and €13.10/ 21.80 to Hafelkarhaus.

Walking Tour

Innsbruck is easily explored on foot; this 1½-hour tour will help to point out some of the city's highlights.

A perfect place to start is by absorbing the baroque façades along Herzog Friedrich Strasse; most of these buildings were built in the 15th and 16th centuries and still retain their medieval charm. Of particular note is the **Helblinghaus (1)**, with its fussy

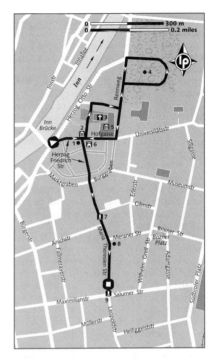

rococo ornamentation created in the 18th century.

Almost directly opposite the Helbling-haus is the **Goldenes Dachl (2**; Golden Roof), the absolute gem of Innsbruck's rich architectural collection. Its 2657 gilded copper tiles shimmer atop a Gothic oriel window (built in 1500); Emperor Maximilian used to observe street performers from the 2nd-floor balcony, which has a series of scenes depicted in relief (including, in the centre, the emperor himself with his two wives). Note the balustrade on the 1st floor, which bears eight coats of arms. Inside the building is a rather small but intriguing museum retelling the history of Maximilian, the **Maximilianeum** (☎ 58 11 11; Herzog Friedrich Strasse 15; adult/concession €3.60/1.80; ☺ 10am-6pm May-Sep, 10am-5pm Tue-Sun Oct-Apr).

From the Goldenes Dachl, turn left up Pfarrgasse and then head towards Dom-platz and **Dom St Jakob** (**3**; St James' Cathedral; Dom-platz; ☺ 7.30am-9.30pm Mon-Sat, 8am-7.30pm Sun). Its façade is nothing to write home about but its interior is another story; over-the-top baroque is everywhere to be admired. Much

TYROL

of the sumptuous art and stucco work were completed by the Asam brothers from Munich, though the Madonna above the high altar is by the German painter Lukas Cranach the Elder.

Not far northeast of St Jakob is the **Hofgarten (4)**, a peaceful park just perfect for a quiet stroll. From the park, head south on Rennweg to the **Hofburg (5)**, Innsbruck's imperial palace, before cutting down Hofgasse and back to Herzog Friedrich Strasse. Turn left and bear south once more, stopping at the 14th-century **Stadtturm (6**; city tower; ☎ 561 15 00; Herzog Friedrich Strasse 21; adult/concession/child €2.50/2/1; 10am-8pm Jun-Sep, 10am-5pm Oct-May); climb its 148 steps for 360-degree views of the city's rooftops and surrounding mountains.

Once again on Herzog Friedrich Strasse, continue south until the street turns into the equally imposing Maria Theresien Strasse. Directly in front of you lies the tall, slender **Annasäule (7**; St Anne's Column), which was erected in 1706 to mark the repulsing of a Bavarian attack in 1703. A statue of the Virgin Mary stands at the top, and St Anne is depicted at the base. After the next intersection, the fine baroque façade belonging to the **Altes Landhaus (8)** sails into view; built in 1728, it is now the seat of the provincial government. Walk another 200m south and you'll find the 1765 **Triumphpforte (9**; Triumphal Arch), which commemorates the marriage of the then emperor-to-be Leopold II.

Tours

Guided city walks, organised by Innsbruck Information (p302), take place mainly over the summer months and meander their way through the historical heart of the city for an hour or so. Tours leave at 11am and 2pm daily May to October and over the Christmas period, and cost €8 (€5 with an Innsbruck Card).

To capture more than the *Altstadt* in a tour, consider jumping on a bright-red **Sightseer** (www.sightseer.at) bus, which travels between the Alpenzoo and Schloss Ambras and back again. Buses depart from Maria Theresien Strasse every 30 minutes between 9am and 5.30pm May to October and 10am to 5pm November to April; a day pass costs €8/6 for adults/children. Innsbruck Information sells tickets.

Festivals & Events

For around three decades Innsbruck has been celebrating the **Festival of Early Music** (Festwochen der Alten Musik; ☎ 571 032; www.altemusik .at), which consists of a series of concerts conducted throughout much of July and August. It's normally dominated by baroque operas, and venues include Schloss Ambras (p303), the Landestheater (p310) and Dom St Jakob (p305).

Other big bashes in this city include the **Innsbruck Summer Dance Festival** (www.tanzsommer.at - in German), held in June and July; **Easter Celebrations**, which include concerts, markets and processions; and the ever-popular **Advent Christmas Markets**, which spring to life around the middle of November and run until 24 December. Brass-music lovers will be happy to know that from April to December **medieval brass-band music** is performed in various locations throughout the city; contact Innsbruck Information for details.

Sleeping
BUDGET

Aside from the budget options listed below, Innsbruck and the villages of Igls and Mutters, which are only a few kilometres away from the city centre, offer a bunch of private rooms to visitors. Such rooms will set you back anything between €15 and €30; Innsbruck Information (p302) can make the bookings for you and also provide information on the various student residences that open their doors to tourists over the university summer break.

Jugendherberge St Nikolaus (Map pp300-1; ☎ 28 65 15; www.hostelnikolaus.at; Innstrasse 95; dm/d/tr €15.80/ 40.40/52.80; P) This independent backpacker hostel lies within walking distance of the *Altstadt* and has simple, functional rooms. The restaurant occupying the ground floor serves cheap, decent Austrian food and has a large, overgrown garden and cellar bar attached.

Jugendherberge Innsbruck (Map pp300-1; ☎ 34 61 79; www.jugendherberge-innsbruck.at; Reichenauerstrasse 147; 6-/4-bed dm €14.50/17.20, s/d €31/46) From the outside this is possibly the ugliest HI hostel in Austria, but the rooms are absolutely fine, if a little plain. There's a kitchen, washing machines and bike rental on the premises. Bus O from Museumstrasse stops outside the hostel.

Volkshaus Innsbruck (Map pp300–1; ☎ 39 58 82; www.volkshaus.at; Radetzkystrasse 47; dm €15.80-18.80) Overlooking sports fields, this HI hostel doesn't have as many facilities as the other hostels in town, but the rooms are adequate and the staff friendly. To get there, take bus R from the Hauptbahnhof.

Ferrarihof (Map pp300–1; ☎ 57 88 98; Brennerstrasse 8; s/d €22/44; **P**) This simple pension is south of town, 500m from the last stop of tram No 1. Rooms have been recently renovated; breakfast is not included in the price.

Camping Innsbruck Kranebitten (Map pp300–1; ☎ 28 41 80; www.campinginnsbruck.com; Kranebitter Allee 214; per person/car/tent €6/3/3; ⊙ Apr-Oct; **P**) Camping Innsbruck is far enough away from the city centre to have a rural look and feel to it, but still close enough to make journeys into the city a simple task. There's a restaurant on site and good tree cover.

MID-RANGE

Pension Paula (Map pp300–1; ☎ 29 22 62; www.pension paula.at; Weiherburggasse 15; s/d from €27/47; **P**) This lovely, family-run pension occupies a traditional Alpine chalet and has homey rooms (many with balcony) and a quiet, relaxed air. It's up the hill towards the zoo and has views back across the city. It's popular so book ahead.

Weisses Rössl (Map p304; ☎ 58 30 57-5; www.roessl .at; Kiebachgasse 8; s/d from 69/110; **P**) This *Gasthöfe* (inn) is a pleasant mix of old and new; its restaurant and reception have retained all the charm developed over 600 years of service to visitors, but its bright, attractive rooms have been thoroughly modernised.

Hotel Weisses Kreuz (Map p304; ☎ 594 79; www .weisseskreuz.at; Herzog Friedrich Strasse 31; s/d from €35/ 91; **P** ⊠) The charming Weisses Kreuz has played host to guests of the city for 500 years, including a 13-year-old Mozart. This is probably the best three-star choice in the *Altstadt*, with modern, spacious and comfortable rooms. Prices quoted above are for rooms in high season (mid-June to September) with shared facilities.

Weinhaus Happ (Map p304; ☎ 58 29 80; www .weinhaus-happ.at; Herzog Friedrich Strasse 14; s/d from €51/88; **P**) Happ is about as central as you can get and, while the hotel itself has plenty of old-worldly atmosphere, its rooms are decked out in '80s style. For a bathroom with bathtub, you'll have to fork out a little extra than the prices quoted here.

Innbrücke (Map p304; ☎ 28 19 34; www.gasthof innbruecke.at; Innstrasse 1; s/d €30/50; **P**) Innbrücke has rather small, clinical rooms but you can't argue with the price and the fact that the *Altstadt* is only a stone's throw from the front door. Parking is an extra €5.

Gasthof Schwarzer Bär (Map p304; ☎ 29 49 00; www .gasthof-schwarzer-baer.at; Mariahilfstrasse 16; s/d €33/65; **P**) Convenience and price are the major advantages of this small *Gasthöfe*, which is only a few paces from the *Altstadt*. Rooms are fairly large, but they're also fairly plain. Like the Innbrücke, parking is an extra €5.

Hotel Innsbruck (Map p304; ☎ 598 68-0; www.hotel innsbruck.com; Innrain 3; s/d from €87.50/125; **P** ⊠ ⊠) The modern Innsbruck caters mainly to groups and business people, and has very comfy yet standard rooms. Its proximity to the *Altstadt* is a big bonus but parking is on the steep side (€14).

Goldene Krone (Map pp300–1; ☎ 58 61 60; www .goldene-krone.at - in German; Maria Theresien Strasse 46; s/d €68/105; **P**) This three-star hotel, near the Triumphpforte, is convenient for both the Altstadt and the Hauptbahnhof. It has smallish but well-equipped rooms with shower; prices drop over the winter period.

Binders Hotel (Map pp300–1; ☎ 334 36; www.binders .at; Dr Glatz Strasse 20; s/d €40/54; **P**) This amenable place, with colourful, comfy rooms, is behind the Hauptbahnhof, five minutes' walk along the route of tram No 3.

TOP END

Goldener Adler (Map p304; ☎ 57 11 11; www.goldener adler.com; Herzog Friedrich Strasse 6; s/d €87/128; **P**) It's hard to find a more beautiful, atmospheric hotel in Innsbruck – let alone Austria – than the Goldener Adler. Since opening in 1390, it's welcomed kings, queens and the famous (including Salzburg's two biggest exports, Mozart and Mrs Von Trapp) and is still doing the job exceptionally well. Rooms could do with a bit of character, but the stunning hallways, restaurant and bar make up for it.

Romantik Hotel Schwarzer Adler (Map pp300–1; ☎ 58 71 09; www.deradler.com; Kaiserjägerstrasse 2; s/d from €101/141; **P** ⊠) This beautiful hotel is arguably the top dog in town; the suites are a joy to behold, and even the standard rooms often have bathrooms that glitter with Swarovski crystals.

Europa Tyrol (Map pp300–1; ☎ 59 31; www.europa tyrol.com; Südtiroler Platz 2; s/d from €120/180; **P**) This hotel, opposite the Hauptbahnhof, is the only five-star place in town. The rooms and lobby are as grand as you would expect, and it has a top-class restaurant.

The Penz Hotel (Map pp300-1; ☎ 57 56 57-0; www .thepenz.com; Adolf-Pichler-Platz 3; s/d from €120/150; P) The Penz is possibly the most stylish and modern of all Innsbruck's hotels, with funky furniture and fittings and plenty of interior design. The atmosphere can be a little sterile and distant at times though.

Eating

Innsbruck's restaurant selection is certainly not enormous but there is enough to satisfy everybody's tastebuds.

RESTAURANTS

Sahib (Map pp300-1; ☎ 57 14 68; Sillgasse 3; mains €6-12, lunch menu €7.15; ☺ lunch & dinner) The wonderful aroma of Indian spices wafting from Sahib's open doorway should be enough to draw you inside this unpretentious Indian restaurant. Aside from that, there is a great vegetarian selection and midday buffet weekdays.

Mamma Mia (Map p304; Herzog Friedrich Strasse 4; pastas from €5, pizza slices from €2.40; ☺ lunch & dinner) This simple Italian eatery has a great buzz and plenty of life, alongside huge pizzas and healthy pasta servings, available for both take-away and sit-down meals.

Restaurant Philippine (Map pp300-1; ☎ 58 91 57; Müllerstrasse 9; buffet €4-7.50, mains & menus €8-11; ☺ lunch & dinner Mon-Fri, dinner Sat) The menu of this pleasant vegetarian restaurant is a healthy mix of international cuisine, including noodles, curries and rice dishes. Its buffet and set menus are particularly popular.

Cammerlander (Map p304; ☎ 58 63 98; Innrain 2; mains €7-14; ☺ lunch & dinner) One of the few eating establishments using the river as a backdrop is Cammerlander, a modern restaurant covering a whole gamut of international cuisine, from Schnitzel to chilli. Its large terrace attracts many happy diners during the summer.

Thai-Li (Map p304; ☎ 56 28 13; Marktgraben 3; mains €9-18; ☺ lunch & dinner) The highly rated Thai-Li cooks up a Thai-food storm on a daily basis and keeps Innsbruckers coming back again and again. Its small outdoor patio is perfect on warm evenings.

Goldener Adler (Map p304; ☎ 57 11 11; Herzog Friedrich Strasse 6; mains €10-20; ☺ lunch & dinner) It may be flooded with tourists and appear more

of an attraction than an eating establishment, but this 600-year-old restaurant still manages to churn out excellent Austrian and Tyrolean cuisine and create a friendly, warm ambience.

Romantik Hotel Schwarzer Adler Restaurant (Map pp300-1; ☎ 58 71 09; Kaiserjägerstrasse 2; mains about €20; ☺ lunch & dinner Mon-Sat) This upmarket eatery provides all the trimmings – flowers and candles on the table, attentive service and top-notch Austrian and international food.

Weisses Rössl (Map p304; ☎ 58 30 57-5; Kiebachgasse 8; mains €7-18; ☺ lunch & dinner Mon-Sat) Weisses Rössl serves some of the best Tyrolean cuisine in the Altstadt, but vegetarians will have a hard time find something suitable on the menu. It's advisable to book ahead in the high season.

Gasthaus Goldenes Dachl (Map p304; ☎ 58 93 70; Hofgasse 1; mains €7-18; ☺ lunch & dinner) Within sight of its namesake is the Goldenes Dachl, another *Altstadt* restaurant with a menu packed with Austrian and Tyrolean specialities. It's normally a little less hectic than the restaurants on busy Herzog Friedrich Strasse.

Hirschenstuben (Map p304; ☎ 58 29 79, Kiebachgasse 5; mains €9-20, midday menu €8; ☺ lunch & dinner Tue-Sat, dinner Mon) Hirschenstuben has a formal air, vaulted rooms and a selective menu encompassing both local and Italian dishes. Book ahead in the high season.

La Cucina (Map pp300-1; ☎ 58 42 29; Museumstrasse 26; mains €7-12; ☺ lunch & dinner) Friendly, colourful and relaxed, La Cucina is a great spot for pasta and pizza with Italian pizzazz.

Chilis (Map pp300-1; ☎ 56 73 30; Bozner Platz 6; mains €10-16; ☺ 11am-midnight) This colourful, upbeat restaurant is one of the very few places in town that serves Mexican food, and while the food is certainly good, don't expect too many hot spices and flavours.

Lotos (Map p304; ☎ 57 86 63; Seilergasse 5; lunch buffet Mon-Fri €7, mains about €9; ☺ lunch & dinner Sun-Fri, dinner Sat) One of the *Altstadt's* quiet back streets hides this fine Chinese restaurant, which dishes up a mammoth buffet lunch during the week. Unfortunately there's no outdoor seating and it can be a little stuffy on hot summer evenings.

CAFES

Café Central (Map pp300-1; ☎ 59 20; Gilmstrasse 5; coffee €2-4; ☺ 7.30am-11.30pm) This café is moulded in the best traditions of a Viennese-style coffee house; expect chandeliers, high ceilings, live piano music, newspapers, surly waiters and great coffee.

Hörtnagl Cafe (Map p304; ☎ 597 29-40; Hörtnagl Passage, Burggasse; cakes & ice cream from €1.50; ⏲ 6.30am-8pm Mon-Sat, 10am-8pm Sun) Tucked away in a small shopping mall is this simple café, with excellent cakes and ice cream and a secluded garden to enjoy them in.

QUICK EATS

Panino & Co (Map pp300-1; Universitätstrasse 3; paninis €3; ⏲ 9am-6pm Mon-Fri, 9am-1pm Sat) This quaint Italian deli has lovely coffee and cold paninis, and is the perfect place to stock up on picnic supplies – Italian bread, cheese and wine.

SOWI Lounge (Map pp300-1; ☎ 216 06 68; Universitätsstrasse 15; 2-course menu €4-5; ⏲ lunch Mon-Fri) This *Mensa* (university restaurant) for the business studies university has quick, cheap menus and outdoor seating on a grassy quarter.

SELF-CATERING

Pick up supplies at the large indoor food and flower **market** (Map p304; Herzog-Sigmund-Ufer; ⏲ 7am-6.30pm Mon-Fri, 7am-1pm Sat) by the river in Markthalle, or at Billa (Map pp300-1) and Hofer (Map pp300-1) supermarkets, close together on Museumstrasse.

Drinking

Innsbruck's nightlife can't quite match Vienna or Graz, but its healthy student population endeavours to keep the bar and clubbing scene lively and upbeat. Aside from the bars in and around the Altstadt, a concentration of drinking dens can be found nestled in the railway arches along Ingenieur Etzel Strasse, an area known as the Viaduktbögen. Most bars in this area are fairly lame, with the best of the bunch being Babalon at Bogen 22 on Ingenieur Etzel Strasse, perhaps because it receives divine help from the large Jesus statue in the middle of the establishment.

Treibhaus (Map pp300-1; ☎ 57 20 00; www.treibhaus.at - in German; Angerzellgasse 8; ⏲ 10am-1am Mon-Sat) This cultural complex attracts a more Bohemian crowd with its great Thai food, regular live music (jazz Tuesday, drum 'n bass Thursday, flamenco Friday), big open bar and accepting atmosphere. In August, Treibhaus also hosts an open-air cinema.

Hofgarten Café (Map pp300-1; ☎ 58 88 71; Rennweg 6A; ⏲ 11am-4am) Occupying a large pa-

vilion in the heart of the Hofgarten is this excellent café-restaurant. It's rated not only for its popular DJ sessions, big, open patio and top-notch cocktails, but also for its quality kitchen.

Dom Cafe-Bar (Map p304; ☎ 57 33 53; Pfarrgasse 3; ⏲ 11am-2am Jun-Sep, 5pm-2am Oct-May) Of the cluster of bars squeezed between the Goldenes Dachl and the cathedral, Dom is consistently the best option for a drink, with a relaxed vibe, outdoor seating and cosy interior rooms.

Utopia (Map pp300-1; ☎ 58 08 70; Tschamlerstrasse 3; ⏲ 6pm-1am Mon-Sat, 8pm-1am Sun) This café-bar has fixtures from its former incarnation as a factory still in place and has a cellar bar that regularly features live acts and clubbings, usually at weekends (these have a variable entry fee).

Marktbar (Map p304; ☎ 58 63 98; Innrain 2) Occupying the second half of Cammerlander restaurant is the Marktbar, an upmarket place attracting a mixed crowd eager to soak up the sun by the river, or kick back inside during the cold winter months.

Theresienbräu (Map pp300-1; ☎ 58 75 80; Maria Theresien Strasse 53; ⏲ 10.30am-1am Mon-Wed, 10.30am-2am Thu-Sat, 10.30am-midnight Sun) This massive establishment brews its own beer, has a secluded beer garden and attracts a boisterous, lively crowd eager for a good time and contact with the opposite sex.

Elferhaus (Map p304; ☎ 58 28 75; Herzog Friedrich Strasse 11; ⏲ 10am-2am) In the heart of town, with outdoor and live music on a regular basis, Elferhaus attracts a huge crowd of students and 20-somethings who throng around the narrow bar or spill out onto pedestrianised Herzog Friedrich Strasse.

Jimmy's (Map pp300-1; ☎ 57 04 73; Wilhelm Greil Strasse 19; ⏲ 11am-2am Mon-Sat) Hidden in an inner courtyard near the STA travel agency is this small, loud bar, popular with adrenaline junkies.

Entertainment

Innsbruck Information (p302) produces a helpful monthly guide (for free) to the city's main events, museums and exhibitions; it's mostly in German but is quite easy to navigate. The city has its own symphony orchestra which performs regularly in various venues. Classical music can also be heard at Schloss Ambras, which hosts a series of concerts in summer.

Landestheater (Map pp300-1; ☎ 520 74-4; www
.landestheater.at - in German; Rennweg 2; tickets €3-38; ticket
office ☺ 8.30am-8.30pm Mon-Sat, 5.30-8.30pm Sun)
Tyrol's seminal theatre stages year-round
performances ranging from opera and ballet
to drama and comedy.

Cinemas around town offer a special deal
on Monday, when all seats are sold at the
rate of the cheapest seats. For independent
films shown in their original language head
to **Cinematograph** (Map pp300-1; ☎ 57 85 00; www.cin
ematograph.at - in German; Museumstrasse 31; tickets €6-8).

Shopping

Tyrolean crafts include embroidered fabrics,
wrought iron and glassware. There are many
souvenir shops in the cobblestone streets of
the *Altstadt* offering loden hats, woodcarvings, grotesque masks and other Tyrolean
products.

Tiroler Heimatwerk (Map pp300-1; ☎ 58 23 20; Meraner Strasse 2; ☺ 9am-1pm & 2-6pm Mon-Fri, 9am-noon
Sat) This quality shop stocks locally produced
products, ranging from stained-glass knick-
knacks to wrought-iron candle-holders.

Tirol Haus (Map pp300-1; Maria Theresien Strasse 55;
☺ 8am-6pm Mon-Fri) Tirol Haus is another shop
selling products from the province; it mainly
stocks clothes and cloth.

Swarovski Crystal Gallery (Map p304; ☎ 57 31
00; Herzog Friedrich Strasse 39; ☺ 8am-6.30pm Mon-Sat,
8am-6pm Sun Apr-Oct, 8am-6pm Mon-Sat, 8am-5pm Sat &
Sun Nov-Jan, 8am-6pm Mon-Sat Jan-Mar) Nothing but
the finest Swarovski crystal products are on
display in this glittering shop, which is not a
place for uncoordinated people to shop.

Rathausgalerien (Map pp300-1; Maria Theresien
Strasse 18; ☺ 8am-6pm Mon-Fri, 8am-5pm Sat) This
modern shopping mall is packed with clothes
stores and cafés.

Franziskanerplatz, running south from
the Hofburg and Hofkirche, hosts a couple
of highly inviting markets; a flea market on
Saturday mornings and a farmers market
on Thursday mornings.

Getting There & Away
AIR

Innsbruck's **airport** (☎ 225 25-0; www.innsbruck-air
port.com; Fürstenweg 180) caters to a handful of national (Vienna and Graz) and international
flights (London, Amsterdam, Antwerp, Bern,
Frankfurt and Hannover), handled mostly
by Austrian Airlines and its subsidiaries and
Welcome Air (see p363).

BUS

The Bundesbus station (Map pp300–1) is at
the southern end of the Hauptbahnhof; its
ticket office can be found within the station.

CAR & MOTORCYCLE

The A12 and the parallel Hwy 171 are the
main roads heading west and east. Highway
177, to the west of Innsbruck, heads north
to Germany and Munich. The A13 is a toll
road (€8) running south through the Brenner Pass to Italy. En route you'll cross the
Europabrücke (Europe Bridge); it's 777m
long and passes over the Sill River at a
height of 190m, making it Europe's highest
bridge. Toll-free Hwy 182 follows the same
route, passing under the bridge.

TRAIN

The Hauptbahnhof is the most convenient
Innsbruck station, though some local trains
also stop at the Westbahnhof (which is actually to the south) and at Hötting (to the
west).

Fast trains daily depart every two hours
for Bregenz (€25.10, 2¾ hours) and Salzburg (€29.50, two hours). From Innsbruck
to the Arlberg, most of the best views are
on the right-hand side of the train. Two-
hourly express trains head north to Munich
(€32.40, two hours) and south to Verona
(€43.10, 3½ hours). Direct services to Kitzbühel also run every two hours (€12.20,
one hour) while six daily trains head for
Lienz (€18.40, three to five hours), of which
only two are direct; some pass through Italy
while others take the long way round via
Salzburgerland.

Getting Around
TO/FROM THE AIRPORT

The airport, which is 4km to the west of the
city centre, is served by bus F. Buses leave
every 15 or 20 minutes from Maria Theresien Strasse (€1.60); taxis charge about €8 to
€10 for the same trip.

CAR & BICYCLE

Most of central Innsbruck has restricted
parking, indicated by a blue line. You can
park within these areas for a maximum of
1½ or three hours during set times (approximately shop hours). The charge is
€0.50/1/1.50 for 30/60/90 minutes; tickets are
available from pavement dispensers. Parking

garages (such as the one under the *Altstadt*) will set you back about €15 per day.

The car rental agencies listed below each have an office at the airport:

Avis (Map pp300-1; ☎ 57 17 54; Salurner Strasse 15; ☺ 7.30am-6pm Mon-Fri, 8am-1pm Sat)

Denzeldrive (Map pp300-1; ☎ 58 20 60; Salurner Strasse 8; ☺ 8am-6pm Mon-Fri)

Hertz (Map pp300-1; ☎ 58 09 01; Südtiroler Platz 1; ☺ 7.30am-6pm Mon-Fri, 8am-1pm Sat)

Neuner (Map pp300-1; ☎ 561 501; Maximilianstrasse 23; ☺ 9am-6pm Mon-Fri, 9am-noon Sat) Rents mountain bikes for €16/20 per half-/full day.

PUBLIC TRANSPORT

Single tickets on buses and trams cost €1.60 (from the driver; valid upon issue), but if you plan to use the city's public transport more than once in a day you're better off buying a 24-hour ticket (€3.40). Weekly and monthly tickets are also available (€10.70 and €36.20 respectively). Tickets bought in advance, which are available from *Tabak* (tobacconist) shops, Information Innsbruck and the **IVB Kundenbüro** (Map p304; ☎ 53 07-500; Stainerstrasse 2; ☺ 7.30am-6pm Mon-Fri), must be stamped in the machines at the start of the journey.

TAXI

For a taxi call ☎ 0800 222 22 55 or 53 11.

AROUND INNSBRUCK

Innsbruck's surroundings have enough attractions to keep visitors entertained for a few days. If you're into historical towns, Hall and Schwaz are perfect destinations, but if you'd prefer communing with nature, then the Stubaital (Stubai Valley), running south from Innsbruck, is the place to head.

HALL IN TIROL
☎ 05223 / pop 11,600

It's hard to believe that this small, breathtakingly pretty town was one of the richest cities in Austria in the 15th century. It prospered from the salt mines to the north and its silver mint, and this wealth can still be seen in the compact medieval centre of the town. At little over 9km east of Innsbruck, Hall in Tirol is an easy, and highly rewarding, day trip from Tyrol's capital.

Staff at the **tourist office** (☎ 562 69; www.region hall.at; Wallpachgasse 5; ☺ 8.30am-12.30pm & 2-6pm Mon-Fri, 8.30am-12.30pm Sat) are friendly and knowledgeable and can point you in the direction of the town's attractions. They also organise **guided tours** (adult/child €6/3; ☺ 11am & 3pm Mon-Sat, 3pm Sun Apr-Oct) of Hall.

A good place to start exploring is Oberer Stadtplatz, the very heart of Hall. At the western edge of this square is the 15th-century **Rathaus** (☎ 58 45; Oberer Stadtplatz; admission free; ☺ 9am-5pm Mon-Thu, 9am-1pm Fri), with its distinctive courtyard, complete with crenated edges and mosaic crests. Ascend the stairs and turn left to take a peek at the building's impressive wood-panelled room, now used as council chambers.

Directly across the square, the spire of the 13th-century **Pfarrkirche** (parish church; admission free; ☺ daylight hours) rises skywards. Its off-centre chancel is predominantly Gothic in style but the highlight here is the Waldaufkapelle (p312). Less than 200m to the east is the **Damenstift**, a convent founded in 1557 and graced by a baroque tower; unfortunately the convent's church is often locked. Not far from the Damenstift is the small **Bergbaumuseum** (Fürstengasse; adult/child €3/1.50; ☺ tours 10am & 2pm Mon-Sat, 2pm Sun), which delves into the town's history of salt mining and can only be visited on a tour.

Directly to the south outside the medieval centre of Hall is **Burg Hasegg** (☎ 442 45; Burg Hasegg 6; admission €2; ☺ 2-6pm mid-Jul–mid-Sep), site of the tower that has become an emblem of the town; the castle can also be visited on a guided city tour outside the above hours. The castle had a 300-year career as a mint for silver *Thalers* (coins, the root of the modern word 'dollar'), and this long history can be explored in the **Münze Hall** (☎ 585 5165; Burg Hasegg 6; adult/child €6/4; ☺ 10am-5pm Tue-Sun Apr-Oct, 10am-5pm Tue-Sat Nov-Mar), which is contained within the castle complex. Audio guides are included in the price of the tour and you have the chance to mint your own coin.

Getting There & Away

Hwy 171 goes almost through the town centre, unlike the A12/E45, which is over the Inn River to the south. The train station is about 1km southwest of the centre; it is on the main Innsbruck–Wörgl train line, but only regional trains stop here. Buses take longer but it's the easiest option as they stop at the town centre. From Innsbruck (€2.30, 30 minutes), buses leave every 15 minutes.

WALDAUF'S COLLECTION

Many churches and cathedrals across Europe contain some rather strange objects within their four walls – skeletons of heroes and saints, body parts of kings and queens and even a nail or splinter from *the* crucifix. Hall's Pfarrkirche, in particular its small Waldaufkapelle, is certainly no exception.

Lining one wall of this small chapel is a glass case filled with a total of 45 skulls and 12 bones, picked from the remains of minor saints across the length and breadth of Europe. Each rests eternally on embroidered cushions, and the skulls are further capped with bizarre veils and elaborate headdresses, reminiscent of spiked haloes; the whole effect is both repulsive and enthralling. The collection dates from the 15th century and was collated by one Florian Waldauf von Waldenstein, a trusted advisor to the Emperor Maximilian I.

Born to a poor family in Anras, East Tyrol, Waldauf studied hard at a monastery school and used his intelligence to quickly rise through the ranks in court circles. In 1489, on a sea journey with Maximilian, he and the emperor nearly drowned; at this point, Waldauf swore an oath to God to collate as many religious artefacts as he could in his lifetime. He certainly did a good job of fulfilling his promise, reputedly gathering as many as 2000 such artefacts during his diplomatic travels across Europe.

WATTENS

The small town of Wattens has firmly cemented itself on the tourist trail through **Swarovski Kristallwelten** (Swarovski Crystal Worlds; ☎ 05224-510 80; Kristallweltenstrasse 1; adult/child €8/free; ☻ 9am-6pm late Nov-early Nov), a fantastical park/playground developed by crystal makers Swarovski. Inside you'll find a plethora of light and sound displays centred around the famous crystals, including an ice passage, Brian Eno Room and the largest kaleidoscope in the world. The world's biggest crystal, weighing in at 62kg, can also be seen, along with a sculptured giant's head spewing water into his pond. There are also a number of children's playgrounds scattered around the park.

Swarovski Kristallwelten is best visited by bus; from Wattens train station the park is a 20-minute walk. Buses (€3.30, 18 minutes), which leave every half hour (fewer on Sundays) from Innsbruck's *Busbahnhof* (bus station) heading for Schwaz, stop at Swarovski Kristallwelten.

SCHWAZ

☎ 05242 / pop 12,400

It's hard to believe that in the 15th century the small, pretty town of Schwaz was the second largest town in Austria after Vienna, but there it stands in the history books for all and sundry to read. Its wealth, like that of Hall, was based on mining, silver and copper to be specific (much of it finding its way to the Hall mint). Houses built during these prosperous years survive in and

around the central Stadtplatz and add substantial charm to the town.

Information

At only 18km east of Innsbruck, Schwaz is an easy day trip from the provincial capital. Information on the town and accommodation possibilities is available from the local **tourist office** (☎ 632 40; www.schwaz.at - in German; Franz-Josef-Strasse 2; ☻ 9am-6pm Mon-Fri, 9am-noon Sat May–mid-Oct, 9am-noon & 2-6pm Mon-Fri, 9am-noon Sat mid-Oct–Apr).

Sights & Activities

Aside from specific sights, Schwaz' biggest attraction is its labyrinth of small alleyways and cobblestone streets in and around the heart of the medieval centre. At one end of the main street, pedestrianised Franz-Josef-Strasse, is the 15th-century **Pfarrkirche** (admission free; ☻ daylight hours). Its large roof bears 15,000 copper tiles and, while the structure is Gothic, the interior has enjoyed a baroque makeover. One exception is the left side-altar which is an exquisitely carved piece dating from the early 1400s and depicting a Madonna and Child.

Not far south is the **Franziskanerkirche** (Gilmstrasse; admission free; ☻ daylight hours), which, like the Pfarrkirche, combines a Gothic exterior with a baroque inside. More interesting is the church cloisters next door; Gothic windows and unfinished frescoes line its inner courtyard.

Not far north of the centre is the **Haus der Völker** (☎ 660 90; St Martin; adult/child €6/4; ☻ 10am-

6pm), which houses the private collection of local photographer Gert Chesi. Inside you'll find artefacts from throughout Asia and Africa; the African masks and statues are particularly powerful, while the collection of voodoo ceremonial tools and photos is both fascinating and disturbing.

About 1.5km east of the town is **Schau Silberbergwerk** (☎ 723 72-0; Alte Landstrasse 3a; adult/senior/student/child/family €15/12/8/7/33; ⏰ 8.30am-5pm May-Oct, 9.30am-4pm Nov-Apr), a former silver mine that can only be visited by guided tour that includes a mini-train ride into the mountain; allow two hours.

Sleeping & Eating

Pension Clara (☎ 639 11; Winterstellergasse 20; s/d €19/38) For a place to stay look no further than Pension Clara, which has large but simple rooms, mountain views, a quiet garden and a peaceful ambience; it's just five minutes' walk east of the Pfarrkirche.

Goldene Löwe (☎ 623 73; www.goldenerloewe.at; Husslstrasse 4; s/d from €27/54; P ☻) With less charm but more frills, this place is just north of the Pfarrkirche.

Hellas (☎ 677 04; Burggasse 4; mains €7-18; ⏰ lunch & dinner Tue-Sun) If you need a break from schnitzel and *Tafelspitz* (boiled beef with apple and horseradish sauce), head to this small restaurant; it has a touch of class and serves Greek classics.

Gasthof Schaller (☎ 740 47; Innsbrucker Strasse 31; mains €7-14; ⏰ lunch & dinner) If you're happy with schnitzel, here you'll find a fine selection of regional specialities and a pleasant wood-panelled meal. The Rathaus' inner courtyard, with its ivy-clad galleries, is a perfect spot for an afternoon or early evening drink in summer.

Getting There & Away

The bus to Schwaz (€4.70, one hour) from Innsbruck also passes through Hall and Wattens; by rail, the journey is a lot quicker (16 to 25 minutes).

STUBAI GLACIER

It's possible to ski year-round on this glacier, which is a popular excursion 40km from Innsbruck. The pistes vary enough to cater for most skiers and summer skiing is limited to between 2900m and 3300m. Walkers are attracted to the network of footpaths lower down in the valley; a good hiking

map for the area is Kompass' *Stubaier Alpen Serleskamm* (scale 1:50,000). The Stubaital branches off from the Brenner Pass route (A13/E45) a little south of the Europabrücke and runs southwest.

Stubaitalbahn (STB) buses from Innsbruck's Bundesbus station journey to the foot of the glacier (one way/return €6.90/13.80, one hour) on an hourly basis; one-way tickets can be bought from the driver, return tickets need to be purchased in advance.

If you're based in Innsbruck and want to go skiing for the day on the glacier, consider purchasing a package tour offered by Innsbruck Information. For €49, you'll receive a return bus journey, ski or snowboard rental and a ski pass.

SEEFELD

☎ 05212 / pop 3000

This prosperous, attractively situated resort is a perfect place to appreciate the Alps in all their splendour, with barren peaks, Alpine meadows and forested hills everywhere you look. Seefeld is popular year-round, but especially in winter. Its ski slopes are world class; it hosted the Olympic Nordic-skiing competitions in 1964 and 1976.

The central **tourist office** (☎ 23 13; www.seefeld .at; Kloster Strasse 43; ⏰ 8.30am-6pm Mon-Sat, 10am-noon Sun mid-Jul–mid-Sep, 8.30am-6pm Mon-Sat rest of year) has loads of information on accommodation and outdoor activities.

Sights & Activities

Taking pride of place on the town's central square is the **Pfarrkirche St Oswald** (admission free; ⏰ daylight hours), a church dating from the 15th century. It's well worth taking a peek inside, but first stop to note the decorative tympanum depicting the 14th-century martyrdom of St Oswald and the miracle of the host above the Gothic doorway. The event (see p314) had such a strong impression on the local populace that the church soon became a pilgrimage site. Other features include the winged Gothic altar, the wooden font and the fine ceiling vaulting in the chancel. Ascend the inside stairway to view the **Blutskapelle** (Chapel of the Holy Blood), which houses some 18th-century stuccowork and paintings by Michael Huber.

Seefeld receives plenty of affluent, fur-clad tourists who take leisurely strolls round the streets and footpaths, opt for a horse-drawn carriage, or simply lounge around one of the five-star hotels. The walk south to the **Wildsee** is pleasant, or you could climb the small hill behind the church for good views of the resort, the lake and surrounding peaks. For longer, more adventurous walks, cable cars ascend part of the way to the top of nearby **Seefeld Spitze** (2220m) and **Reither Spitze** (2374m); consult the tourist office for more information or join one of its regular guided walks.

Downhill **skiing** here is mainly geared towards intermediates and beginners. Seefeld is linked with a number of ski fields, including Ehrwald (p327), Reith and Garmisch-Partenkirchen in Germany, all of which are covered by the Happy SkiPass (adult/child €83/50 for the minimum three days). The two main areas are Gschwandtkopf (1500m) and Rosshütte (1800m); the latter connects to higher lifts and slopes on the Karwendel range. The resort's speciality is cross-country skiing, with over 250km of *Loipe* (trails) across the valley. They go all the way to **Mösern**, 5km distant, where there are excellent views of the Inn River and the peaks beyond it.

THE MIRACLE OF THE HOST

These days miracles are thin on the ground, but back in the Middle Ages miracles such as that commemorated on the tympanum of Pfarrkirche St Oswald in Seefeld could make the reputation of a town or village.

During the Easter communion of 1384, local magnate Oswald Milser (no relation to the church's patron saint) decided he was far too important to settle for an ordinary communion wafer; instead, he demanded the wafer reserved only for clergy. The priest obeyed, whereupon the floor of the church softened beneath Oswald's feet and began to swallow him up. The priest quickly retrieved the wafer from the greedy citizen and the ground miraculously firmed up again, saving Oswald. He subsequently repented, and died penniless two years later. The wafer, once examined, was discovered to be marked with blood, not from foolish Oswald of course, but from Christ naturally; hence the apartment in the church which held the original wafer is called the Blutska-pelle (Chapel of the Holy Blood).

Sleeping

The resort is easily visited on a day trip from Innsbruck, though there are plenty of places to stay. The best value is a room in one of the many private houses; as is the case with hotels and pensions, prices are highest in winter.

Gruggerhof (☎ 32 54; http://members.aon.at/gruggerhof/; Leutascher Strasse 64; r €50-120; **P**) This pension is 500m west of Dorfplatz, and is perhaps the best budget option that is quite central. Its bright, large apartments come with balcony and guests enjoy free entry to the town's Olympia swimming pool.

Landhaus Seeblick (☎ 23 89; Innsbrucker Strasse 165; r from €60) Overlooking the Wildsee, Landhaus Seeblick has very comfy rooms, most of which come complete with balcony overlooking the lake.

Hotel Garni Dorothea (☎ 25 27; hotel.dorothea@aon.at; Kirchwald 391; s/d €36/70; **P** **☒**) This three-star hotel has well-appointed rooms, many of which have balconies and views of the village and surrounding mountains. Prices increase by a third in winter.

Eating

The hub of the resort, Dorfplatz, is a good place to start searching for something to eat.

Putzi's (☎ 49 55; Bahnhofstrasse 33; snacks €3-8; ☺ lunch & dinner) If you're looking for a quick bite to eat, Putzi's is a fine bet, with a mix of fast food, including schnitzels, pizzas and burgers.

Seefelder Stuben (☎ 22 58-90; Innsbrucker Strasse 23; mains €6-14; ☺ lunch & dinner) This traditional restaurant has a menu filled with Tyrolean, Austrian and Italian cooking. There's outside seating during the warmer months. Directly opposite is the Albrecht supermarket.

Luigi & Lois (☎ 22 58 67; Innsbrucker Strasse 12; mains €8-18; ☺ lunch & dinner) This is another place mixing Austrian and Italian cuisine on its menu; the place is generally bubbly and convivial with outdoor seating.

Wintergarten (☎ 25 71-0; Münchner Strasse 215; mains €10-20; ☺ lunch & dinner) This, the gourmet restaurant in Hotel Tümmlerhof, is popular with diners in search of creative international dishes.

Getting There & Away

Seefeld is 25km northwest of Innsbruck, just off the Germany-bound Hwy 177. The road follows the floor of the Inntal until it rises

TYROL

sharply (1:7 gradient) near Zirl. The train track starts climbing the north side of the valley much sooner after departing Innsbruck, providing spectacular views across the whole valley, especially if you sit on the left (€4, 40 minutes, 11 daily). Trains run to Mittenwald (€3.30, 20 minutes) every two hours and Garmisch-Partenkirchen (€5.40, 45 minutes), both in Germany.

NORTHEASTERN TYROL

Northeastern Tyrol is dominated by two east–west mountain chains, the Kitzbüheler Alpen and the Zillertaler Alpen. This is a region where the pursuit of the great outdoors takes centre stage and opportunities for walking and skiing are almost endless. One exception is Kufstein, a strategically important town with a proud castle over which Tyrol and Bavaria fought for centuries.

THE ZILLERTAL

The Zillertal (Ziller Valley), running south between the Tuxer Voralpen and the Kitzbüheler Alpen, is one of the most densely populated valleys in the region. It attracts plenty of tourists with its well-developed summer and winter sporting activities. Guarding the entrance to the valley is Jenbach, which stands on the north bank of the Inn River. The narrow Ziller River meanders along the length of the broad valley, passing by small resorts, farming pastures, chalets and church spires, but also unsightly lumber yards and electricity pylons. The valley's two biggest resorts are Zell im Zillertal (the commonly used name of Zell am Ziller) and Mayrhofen.

Almost every resort contains its own tourist office, but there is also a **tourist office** (☎ 05288-871 87; www.zillertal.at) that covers the whole valley in Schlitters, 6km from Jenbach. It stocks the usual guff on outdoor activities and accommodation you come to expect from Austria's well-organised information offices, along with the *Zillertaler Gästezeitung* (partially in English) magazine, which covers the valley in great detail. There's also the smaller-sized but no less informative *Zillertal Guide.*

Five camping grounds are found within the valley and there is a year-round **HI hostel** (☎ 05288-620 10; Finsingerhof, Finsing 73; dm €15.50; P)

at Uderns, 12km south of Jenbach. Accommodation prices at most places are usually slightly higher in the winter, which are the prices quoted here. Most beds are in chalet-style properties, such as pensions, private rooms, holiday apartments or farmhouses. Ask staff at the tourist offices for help in finding somewhere (they usually won't charge), as there are dozens of options in each resort. Wherever you stay, inquire about the resort's *Gästekarte* (guest card).

Note that many places close between seasons, usually early April to late June and early November to mid-December. This includes many of the hotels, restaurants and bars mentioned below.

Activities

The main **skiing** resort is Mayrhofen (including summer skiing), but there is downhill and cross-country skiing elsewhere. The Zillertaler Superskipass covers all 150-odd lifts in the valley; it starts at €118 for the minimum four days, or €131 for four out of six days. Ski buses connect the resorts.

Walking was highly developed well before skiing came on the scene and is strongly emphasised in summer. A famous network of trails is the Zillertaler Höhenstrasse in the Tuxer Voralpen, but trails lead off in all directions from the resorts of Ried, Kaltenbach, Aschau, Zell and Ramsau. Mountain huts at elevations of around 1800m provide overnight accommodation; the handy *Hütten-, Ausflugs- & Erlebnisführer* booklet (German only) lists all the huts in the valley, and includes a small location-finder map. A detailed walking map covering the entire region is the Kompass *Zillertaler Alpen & Tuxer Voralpen* (scale 1:50,000). If you plan to spend a week or more in the valley between June and October, the Zillertal Card (six/nine/12 days €39.80/54.80/68.80) is value for money; it covers public transport, one journey per day on any of the Zillertal cable cars and entry to swimming pools.

Other sporting possibilities include rafting, rock climbing, paragliding and cycling. The Ziller and its tributaries are also good for fishing, but permits are only valid for certain stretches.

Festivals & Events

From late September to early October the cow herds are brought down from the high pastures, an event known as the **Huamfahrerfest**. Cows are dressed in elaborate headdresses for the occasion, and the clanging of cow bells accompanies the efforts of amateur musicians. In Zell am Ziller the descent occurs on the first Sunday in October, an event called **Almabtrieb**. Mayrhofen celebrates the event on the first and second Saturdays in October, when the sprawling **Krämermarkt** takes over the village centre. Its wares include food, curios, crafts and cow bells.

Getting There & Away

The Zillertal is serviced by a private train line, the **Zillertalbahn** (☎ 05244-606-0; www.zillertalbahn.at), which travels the 32km from Jenbach to Mayrhofen.

Those with a thirst for nostalgia can take a *Dampfzug* (steam train) along the valley; it runs three times daily in summer (7.10am, 10.47am and 3.16pm) and once daily in winter (10.47am). It takes about 85 minutes to reach the last stop, Mayrhofen, and costs €10.40 one way to either Zell or Mayrhofen. If you just want to get from A to B, it's better to take the *Triebwagen* (train) or bus as it costs €5.40.

ZELL AM ZILLER

☎ 05282 / pop 1840

A former gold mining centre and now the main market town in the valley, Zell am Ziller retains its sense of fun, especially during the Gauderfest (see p315), and a semblance of rural charm. The town is usually marketed as Zell im Zillertal, as that includes the surrounding hamlets.

Orientation & Information

The **tourist office** (☎ 22 81; www.zell.at - in German; Dorfplatz 3a; ⏰ 8.30am-12.30pm & 2.30-6pm Mon-Fri, 9am-noon & 4-6pm Sat Jul-Sep, 8.30am-12.30pm & 2.30-6pm Mon-Fri, 9am-noon & 4-6pm Sat, 4-6pm Sun Mid-Dec-Easter, closed Sat & Sun Oct–mid-Dec & Easter-Jun) is near the train tracks: from the Zell am Ziller train station, turn right along Bahnhofstrasse and right again at the end, a five-minute walk. It stocks more than enough information on walking and skiing options (including maps) and also organises guided walks in the summer. Outside (on the train-track side) is a useful computer info screen and free accommodation telephone.

At the other end of Dorfplatz is the post office, with bus stops at the rear.

Sights & Activities

Just off Dorfplatz is the town's salmon and green **Pfarrkirche** (admission free; ⏰ daily). Built in 1782, it has an unusual circular design, with side altars all the way around and interior wall scenes in pastel colours by Franz-Anton Zeiller (1716–93). Outside, its cemetery is an arresting sight; a sea of black-grey distinctive metallic crosses with tracery surrounds greets you on entering the church grounds.

Abenteuer Goldbergbau (☎ 48 20; www.goldschaubergwerk.com - in German; Hainzernberg 73; adult/child €10/5; ⏰ 9am-5pm) is a two-hour tour of a gold mine 2km east of Zell on the road to Gerlos. The tour starts above ground with an exhibition on dairy products, including cheesemaking equipment from 150 years ago.

Aside from walking and skiing, the mountains around Zell are perfect for **paragliding**. Paragliding specialist **Pizza-Air** (☎ 22 89, 0664-200 42 29; www.zell.cc - in German; Zellbergeben 4) offers piloted trips descending 500m to 1500m (€55 to €99). It is based in Pizza-Café Reiter, on the western side of the Ziller River. Several rival firms offer similar deals; ask for details at the tourist office.

Bicycles can be rented from the train station (half-/full day €7.20/12).

Festivals & Events

Wafting around hot air currents (with or without the aid of a paraglider) is not recommended after a bellyful of Gauderbier, an incredibly strong beer (reputedly over 10% alcohol) brewed specially for the **Gauderfest** (www.gauderfest.at). The festival takes place on the first weekend in May, and participants show off long-established rural skills: playing music, dancing and drinking heavily. The lavish main procession (participants wear historical costumes) and wrestling take place on Sunday.

Sleeping & Eating

Zell is dotted with chalets offering accommodation; many can be found west of the river in Zellbergeben.

Hotel Bräu (☎ 23 13; hotel-braeu@telecom.at; Dorfplatz 1; s/d from €51/102; **P**) The 500-year-old Hotel Bräu is a step up from the many chalets in town, with large, well-appointed rooms, sauna and solarium. Its **restaurant** (mains €8-16) is full of rural trappings, wood-panelling, old stoves and serves Austrian and Tyrolean specialities and excellent fish dishes.

Gästehaus Brindlinger (☎ 26 71; brindlinger.zell@ aon.at; Gaudergasse 4; s/d from €24/48; P) A five-minute walk east of the town centre is this homely guesthouse, with a friendly welcome and big rooms.

Hotel-Restaurant Rosengarten (☎ 24 43; rosen garten@nextra.at; Rosengartenweg 14; s/d €35/70; P) This large chalet has well-equipped rooms with balconies and the advantage of a sauna, an inexpensive restaurant and great views to the south. It's a couple of minutes east of the train tracks, and open in the low season.

Camping Hofer (☎ 22 48; www.campinghofer.at; Gerlosstrasse 33; camp sites per adult/tent in summer €6/ 6.50, in winter €7.50/9.50, guesthouse s/d €19/29; P 🛁) This small camping area is east of the train tracks, has a restaurant, guesthouse and is surrounded by houses.

Pizza-Café Reiter (☎ 22 89-0; Zellbergeben 4; pizzas €7-9; 🕑 dinner) For big pizzas and fun après-ski (parties 5pm to 7pm Monday, Tuesday and Thursday) during the ski season, look no further than Reiter.

SB Restaurant (☎ 22 71; Unterdorf 11; meals €3-7; 🕑 lunch & dinner) This basic, self-service restaurant is the best place for a cheap feed. It serves snacks, soups and salads plus full meals. It's an annexe of the **Zeller Stube** (mains €7-12) above, which has a good vegetarian menu and plenty of fish dishes.

Self-caterers can head to **Billa** (Bahnhofstrasse 5).

Getting There & Away

Normal trains to Mayrhofen (€1.90, 12 minutes) and Jenbach (€4.70, 45 minutes) are cheaper than the steam train. Zell am Ziller is the start of the Gerlos Pass route to the Krimml Falls; postbuses tackle the pass from July to September up to four times daily (€4.70, one to 1½ hours).

Trains to and from Innsbruck (€9.30, 1½ hours, hourly) require a change at Jenbach.

MAYRHOFEN

☎ 05285 / pop 3900

Another 4km further up the valley is the picturesque chalet village of Mayrhofen. It's an excellent base for exploring the four *Gründe* (Alpine valleys), which lead off in a southerly direction.

Orientation & Information

From the train station, Am Marktplatz leads to Durster Strasse, where the **tourist office**

(☎ 67 60; www.mayrhofen.at; Europahaus; 🕑 8am-6pm Mon-Fri, 9am-noon & 2-6pm Sat, 10am-noon Sun Jul & Aug, Christmas, late Jan–mid-Mar & Easter, 8am-6pm Mon-Fri, 9am-noon Sat, 10am-noon Sun rest of year) is located. It basically stocks books of information on the resort; look for the comprehensive *Info von A-Z* for both summer and winter; it's free and written in English. There is also a handy topographic model of the surrounding Alps and outside is an electronic 24-hour accommodation board.

There is also a village **post office** (Einfahrt Mitte 430).

Activities

Mayrhofen offers legion **skiing** and **walking** opportunities and the infrastructure for both is extensive.

Guided walks (free with the *Gästekarte*) are organised by the tourist office on a regular basis. If you'd prefer to go it alone, it produces a helpful list (in English) of the more popular walks heading out of the village. A detailed map of the region is the Kompass *Mayrhofen-Tuxertal-Zillergrund* map (scale 1:25,000), which is a good purchase if you plan to explore the region extensively. From the village itself two cable cars give walkers a great head start; one-way/return fares on both the Ahorn (1965m) and Penken (1800m) are €8.20/12.90 in summer.

Mayrhofen's ski region holds the dubious honour of possessing the steepest piste in Austria; known as the Harikiri, its gradient is a mere 78%. A local ski pass, valid for ski lifts on Ahorn, Penken and Horberg (157km of piste), costs €32 for one day. The resort also provides easy access to year-round skiing on the **Hintertux Glacier**, reaching an altitude of 3250m. In winter a day pass costs €35 and in summer €29. From Christmas till the beginning of May a free bus shuttles skiers from Mayrhofen to the glacier (included in ski pass), but in summer Bundesbuses are the only public transport option (€4, 45 minutes).

Like Zell am Ziller, Mayrhofen is made for **paragliding** or, more accurately, its mountains are made for paragliding. **Action Club Zillertal** (☎ 0664-205 50 11; www.action-club -zillertal.com; Hauptstrasse 458) offers flights for €80 to €160 (10 to 60 minutes). Next door is home of the **Zillertal mountaineering school** (☎ 628 29; www.habeler.com; Hauptstrasse 458), run by the internationally known mountaineer

Peter Habeler; it offers myriad outdoor adventure pursuits.

Cycling does not enjoy as many options as skiing and walking, but there is certainly enough to entertain avid cyclists and the tourist office organises bike tours. Bicycles can be rented from the **train station** (half-/full day €7.20/12), **Hervis Sports** (☎ 640 45; Einfahrt Mitte 433; €7/10) and **BP-Tankstelle Obermair** (☎ 623 08; Am Marktplatz 213; €11/15).

Sleeping

The tourist office can help you scroll through the mountain of accommodation options in the village.

Hotel Kramerwirt (☎ 67 00; www.kramerwirt.at; Am Marienbrunnen 346; s/d €60/120; P ⓡ 🖳) Near the town's church is Kramerwirt, one of the town's top hotels. It's a traditional place with traditionally decorated rooms and plenty of homey touches. The hotel **restaurant** (mains €8-18) is excellent, with Tyrolean and Austrian dishes and a large, covered outdoor seating area. Room prices include breakfast and one other meal.

Ferienwohnungen Central (☎ 623 17; Hauptstrasse 449; apt per person from €40; P) A more central option than this place is hard to find; its rooms are certainly comfortable and modern; some have a balcony.

Landhaus Alpenrose (☎ 622 19; ute.hotter@aon.at; Wiesl 463; apt per person from €50; P) The fully equipped apartments at Alpenrose range in size and have luxuries like a dishwasher and microwave. It occupies a quiet spot near the Penkenbahn cable car.

Campingplatz Kröll (☎ 625 80-51; www.alpenparadies.com - in German; Laubichl 125; camp sites per person/car/tent €6/2.50/2; P ⓡ) This camping ground is rather open and exposed, but enjoys some protection from the pine-clad Zillertal Alps it sidles up to. It's north of the village in the district known as Laubichl, and also has a guesthouse.

Eating

Mayrhofen has a fine range of restaurants, many of which are in the bigger hotels around town.

China-Restaurant Singapore (☎ 639 12; Scheulingstrasse 371; mains €7-12, midday menu €6-7; ☽ lunch & dinner) To find good Asian food in these parts is a rare thing indeed, but Singapore manages to fit the bill. Its midday menu on weekdays is a popular feast.

Cafe Edelweiss (☎ 622 08; Brandberg Strasse 352; mains €7-16, midday menu €8-9; ☽ lunch & dinner) This place offers a complete mix of food, and does most things reasonably well, whether it's snacks, pizzas, Austrian food or grills. It also hosts occasional live music.

Mamma Mia (☎ 67 68; Einfahrt Mitte 432; mains €5-8; ☽ lunch & dinner) Occupying a small rotunda outside the plush Hotel Elisabeth is Mamma Mia, a relaxed place with a menu stacked with Italian cuisine. Inside the hotel you'll find the more upmarket **Wirtshaus zum Griena** (☎ 67 67; mains €7-15; ☽ lunch & dinner Tue-Sun), with mid-price Tyrolean fare.

Supermarkets include a **Billa** (Brandberg Strasse) and **Spar** (Hauptstrasse).

Entertainment

Mo's Eiscafé & Musicroom (☎ 634 35; Hauptstrasse 417; ☽ 11am-late) This American-style bar is a popular hang-out with Mayrhofen's younger crowd, has snack and finger foods and offers free live music on Fridays over summer, more often in winter.

Scotland Yard (☎ 623 39; Scheulingstrasse 372; ☽ 7pm-late) Scotland Yard does a decent job of re-creating a British pub in rural Austria, albeit in an Austrian villa. It's a big place with plenty of outdoor seating and Internet access.

Getting There & Away

By normal train, it's €5.40 each way to Jenbach (55 minutes).

GINZLING
☎ 05286

Arriving in Ginzling, a tiny village another 8km south of Mayrhofen in the Zemmgrundtal Valley, is like travelling back 50 years into Austria's past. Quiet, rural and lacking any obvious tourist infrastructure (including nightlife of any kind), this idyllic village is perfect for those wishing to escape the bold resorts lining the rest of the Zillertal.

The small, helpful **tourist office** (☎ 05286-52 18-3; www.ginzling.at - in German; ☽ 8am-noon & 1-5pm Mon-Fri) is well set up for walking enthusiasts keen on exploring the nearby Hochgebirgs-Naturpark Zillertaler Alpen. The park is basically an untouched Alpine paradise with the only manmade intrusion a handful of huts. Skiing is almost nonexistent; touring for experienced skiers is the only option available.

For a place to stay, **Gasthof Alt-Ginzling** (☎ 05286-52 01; www.altginzling.at; s/d €28/56, for stays under 3 nights extra €3; mains €7-16; **P**) is a great bet; this laid-back chalet with clean, wood-panelled rooms also serves arguably the best trout in the entire Zillertal.

During winter, buses to Mayrhofen are free for those with ski passes; for those without passes (and outside the ski season) it costs €2.80. The road continues on from Ginzling up the valley and eventually ends after a number of hair-pin curves and tunnels at **Stausee Schlegeis** (1782m). This road is controlled by a toll – €10 for visitors to the area, €7.50 for guests staying at Ginzling.

ACHENSEE

Achensee (Lake Achen) is the largest lake in Tyrol, about 9km long and 1km wide. But size isn't everything – its beautiful situation amid forested mountain peaks is what brings in the tourists during summer. The **Achenseebahn** (www.achenseebahn.at; one way/return €17/22), a private cogwheel steam train, makes regular trips to the lake from Jenbach between May and October, connecting with **boat tours** (www.tirol-schiffahrt .at - in German; €12.50) of the lake. Far-reaching views over the lake and the surrounding mountain ranges can be had from Erfurter (1831m), which is easily reached by the **Rofanseilbahn** (☎ 052 43-52 92; www.rofanseilbahn.at - in German; adult/child return €13.50/8; ☼ 8.30am-5pm) from Maurach.

Of the three townships close to the lake, only Pertisau is directly on its shores, but this has also made it the most commercial. The other two, Maurach and Achenkirch, are at the southern and northern ends of the lake respectively; all three have information centres.

KITZBÜHEL

☎ 05356 / pop 8500

Ask an Austrian to name the top two or three ski resorts in the country, and invariably Kitzbühel will be in the list. This small town has a long history in winter sports and is currently one of the premier resorts in the Alps, with plenty of glitz and glamour. But skiing is only a recent inclusion in Kitzbühel's history – it developed as a copper and mining centre centuries ago and its quaint, cobblestone centre still retains a healthy dose of medieval charm.

Orientation & Information

Bahnhof Kitzbühel, the main train station, is 1km north of the resort's hub, which is centred on Vorderstadt and Hinterstadt. You'll find the **tourist office** (☎ 777; www.kitzbue hel.com; Hinterstadt 18; ☼ 8.30am-6pm Mon-Fri, 9am-6pm Sat, 10am-6pm Sun Jul-Sep & Christmas-Easter, 8.30am-12.30pm/2.30-6pm Mon-Fri, 8.30am-noon rest of year) with loads of info in English and an accommodation board and free telephone available 24 hours. Listings in German can be found in *Kitz, Servus* and *Trend Guide* booklets; all are free but heavy on advertising.

Banks and *Bankomats* are everywhere and the **post office** (Josef Pirchl Strasse) is about midway between the train station and the tourist office. Internet access is available at the local video store **Kitz Video** (Schlossergasse 10; per hr €5; ☼ 11am-9pm Mon-Sat, 2-7pm Sun).

Sights

The appealing town centre is dominated not only by picturesque gabled houses but also by the tall steeples of two churches just north of Vorderstadt. **Pfarrkirche St Andreas** (☎ 666 59; Pfarrauweg 2; ☼ daylight hours) is easily the most striking from the outside. This 15th-century church has Gothic features (such as the nave) but, like many in Austria, the subsequent baroque face-lift has obscured most. Above St Andreas is the **Liebfrauenkirche** (Pfarrauweg 4; ☼ daylight hours), with a sturdy square tower and fancy rococo stuccowork inside.

At the far end of the compact centre is **Museum Kitzbühel** (☎ 672 74; Hinterstadt 32; adult/child €4/2; ☼ 10am-6pm mid-Jul–mid-Sep, 10am-1pm & 3-6pm early-Dec–mid-Mar, 10am-1pm Tue-Sat rest of year), the town's major cultural attraction. This museum lovingly displays the history of the town, from its humble beginnings in the Bronze Age right up to the present day, including its connection to winter sports and its most famous son, champion skier Toni Sailer.

On the slopes of Kitzbüheler Horn (1996m) to the northeast of the town is the **Alpine Flower Garden** (admission free; ☼ daylight hours summer), with all manner of Alpine flowers in bloom from June till September. It's best reached by cable car (adult/child €14.50/8), but drivers can also wind their way up to the top of the mountain (road toll per car/motorcycle €4/2, plus €1.50 per person).

Only 3km northwest of the town centre is Kitzbühel's natural swimming hole, the

KITZBÜHEL

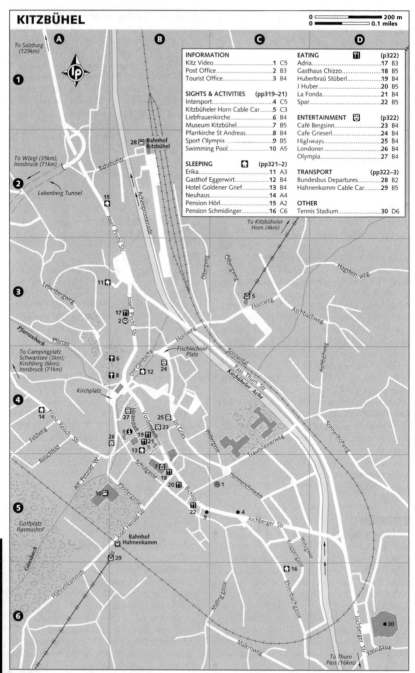

0 ____ 200 m
0 ____ 0.1 miles

INFORMATION	
Kitz Video	1 C5
Post Office	2 B3
Tourist Office	3 B4

SIGHTS & ACTIVITIES	(pp319–21)
Intersport	4 C5
Kitzbüheler Horn Cable Car	5 C3
Liebfrauenkirche	6 B4
Museum Kitzbühel	7 B5
Pfarrkirche St Andreas	8 B4
Sport Olympia	9 D5
Swimming Pool	10 A5

SLEEPING	(pp321–2)
Erika	11 A3
Gasthof Eggerwirt	12 B4
Hotel Goldener Grief	13 B4
Neuhaus	14 A4
Pension Hörl	15 A2
Pension Schmidinger	16 C6

EATING	(p322)
Adria	17 B3
Gasthaus Chizzo	18 B5
Huberbraü Stüberl	19 B4
J Huber	20 B5
La Fonda	21 B4
Spar	22 B5

ENTERTAINMENT	(p322)
Café Bergsinn	23 B4
Cafe Grieserl	24 B4
Higliways	25 B4
Londoner	26 B4
Olympia	27 B4

TRANSPORT	(pp322–3)
Bundesbus Departures	28 B2
Hahnenkamm Cable Car	29 B5

OTHER	
Tennis Stadium	30 D6

To Salzburg
(129km)

To Wörgl (35km);
Innsbruck (71km)

Lebenberg Tunnel

28 Bahnhof
Kitzbühel

To Kitzbüheler
Horn (4km)

To Campingplatz
Schwarzsee (3km);
Kirchberg (6km);
Innsbruck (71km)

Kirchplatz

Golfplatz
Rasmushof

Bahnhof
Hahnenkamm

To Thurn
Pass (16km)

TYROL

scenic **Schwarzsee**. There are two beach complexes, each costing about €3.50 per day.

Activities
Along with the activities listed below, Kitzbühel offers scenic flights, skydiving, paragliding, ballooning, rock climbing, golf, water sports and even bungy jumping.

SKIING
Kitzbühel is suitable for all levels of skiing ability and has plenty of cross-country trails. The ski area extends from 800m to 2000m and offers 145km of pistes accessed by 53 lifts and cable cars, including the most modern ski cable car in the world, opened in 2004. Around 66km of pistes are manicured with snow cannons.

The enormous network of runs and lifts stretches to the northeast and southwest of the town. The **Kitzbüheler Horn**, extending northeast, is mostly criss-crossed with intermediate runs and is favoured by snowboarders. **Hahnenkamm** (1668m) spreads southwest and connects with some black runs in the **Pengelstein** (1938m) area; it can also be approached from Kirchberg (p323) via cable car and chairlift.

Sadly, passes don't come cheap. One-day/two-day and weekly passes in the high season (Christmas to mid-March) cost €35/65/186, at all other times they cost €30/57/161; passes cover all lifts and cable cars as far south as Thurn Pass and include use of ski buses. Everything except a one-day pass allows 50% off the entry fee to the Aquarena swimming pools. For those intending to ski for a week, inquire about the Schneepass before booking accommodation; available from hotels, pensions and private rooms (but not all), it offers seven night's accommodation plus a six-day ski pass at reduced rates.

For real snow enthusiasts, the Kitzbüheler Alpen Skipass is perfect; it encompasses the entire region (including 243 lifts; Kitzbühel, Schneewinkel, Wilder Kaiser-Brixental, Alpbach and Wildschönau) and costs €176 for six consecutive days.

WALKING
Walking is Kitzbühel's main summer activity; zillions of walking trails head off in all directions from the town. The tourist office is well set up to cater to walker's demands too, handing out a comprehensive *Wander-wegeplan* (hiking plan) for free. If you'd prefer some company on the trails, it also organises free guided walks for *Gästekarte* holders (from mid-May to mid-October).

A cable-car pass that also covers Bundesbus connections costs €35 for three days' travel within seven days, or €48 for six days in 10. Individual ascent tickets cost €14.50/8 for adults/children (discounts available with *Gästekarte*) on either Hahnenkamm or Kitzbüheler Horn, and the descent is free with the ascent ticket. Of the two peaks, vista vultures generally consider the view to be superior from Kitzbüheler Horn: the jagged Kaisergebirge range dominates to the north, and beyond the Kitzbüheler Alps, Grossglockner and Grossvenediger are visible in the south.

CYCLING
For those with a thirst for challenging but rewarding cycling and mountain biking there are over 30 cycle paths, in around and over the Kitzbühel and Kirchberg area. All are marked on the *Mountainbiken und Radwandern* map available from the tourist office.

Bikes can be rented from **Intersport** (☎ 625 04; Jochberger Strasse) and **Sport Olympia** (☎ 716 07; Bichlstrasse 26) for around €9 per day and can be transported free of charge on the Hornbahn, Hahnenkammbahn and Fleckalmbahn gondolas.

Festivals & Events
The **Hahnenkamm** professional downhill ski race takes place in January and is a spectacular event.

Late July sees tennis stars compete in the **Austrian Open**, which is held at the tennis stadium just off Jochberger Strasse.

Sleeping
Kitzbühel has its own *Gästekarte*, available from pensions and hotels, which offers various discounts to overnighters. Be aware that a single night surcharge (€2 to €4) may be applied at some accommodation venues and prices are hiked at Christmas, February, July and August (quoted below). Loads of private rooms and homes are also an option; the tourist office can provide you with a list.

Pension Hörl (☎ 631 44; Josef Pirchl Strasse 60; s/d from €22/44; **P**) Clean, simple and pleasant rooms are the order of the day at Hörl, along with friendly service and a good-sized breakfast.

TYROL

Pension Schmidinger (☎ 631 34; www.schmidinger .cc - in German; Ehrenbachgasse 13; s/d €31/62; Ⓟ) Only a short walk from the centre is this fine pension. Rooms are slightly old fashioned but most bathrooms are renovated and each has a balcony.

Gasthof Eggerwirt (☎ 624 55; www.eggerwirt-kitz buehel.at; Gänsbachgasse 12; s/d €58/116; Ⓟ) This atmospheric *Gasthöfe* is extremely central and has attractive rooms with plenty of wood-panelling. Its restaurant is one of the best in town, and serves hefty Austrian and Tyrolean cuisine under heavy wooden beams or in its winter garden.

Neuhaus (☎ 622 00; info@motorradpension.at; Franz Reisch Strasse 23; s/d from €27/54; Ⓟ) Motorbike aficionados shouldn't pass over this place, which has special deals for *Motorrad* riders over summer. It's not only accommodating for lovers of two wheels though; Neuhaus has a relaxed ambiance and pleasant, wood-panelled rooms.

Hotel Goldener Greif (☎ 643 11; www.hotel-gold ener-greif.at; Hinterstadt 24; s/d €106/212; Ⓟ) With its painted façade draped in pot plants and its interior graced with paintings and hunting trophies, the Goldener Greif could almost be classed as a work of folk art. Rooms are suitably large, cosy and full of wood panelling, of which the same could be said of its fine **restaurant** (mains €8-18). Prices in summer drop significantly.

Erika (☎ 648 85; www.erika-kitz.at; Josef Pirchl Strasse 21; s/d €150/300; Ⓟ ⚐) This salmon-coloured villa has all the trappings of a top hotel, including a garden, sauna, steam bath, solarium and massage service. Service is super-friendly and rooms have a noble air. Phone ahead and inquire about the hotel's regular specials.

Campingplatz Schwarzsee (☎ 628 060; www .bruggerhof-camping.at - in German; Reither Strasse 24; camp sites per adult/child €8.10/5.90; Ⓟ) It may be a bit pricy, but Schwarzsee has plenty going for it, including a large kids' playground, peaceful setting, close proximity to the lake and mountains as a backdrop.

Eating

Aside from the restaurants listed below, many of the larger hotels have quality restaurants.

Gasthaus Chizzo (☎ 624 75; Josef Herold Strasse 2; mains €7-17; ☯ lunch & dinner, closed Tue in low season) For Austrian food, Chizzo is certainly a good choice; the menu is packed with classic Austrian and Tyrolean dishes. Aside

from the indoor seating area, there's a small garden and adjoining bar.

La Fonda (☎ 736 73; Hinterstadt 13; mains €6-12; ☯ dinner) This cheap and cheerful restaurant serves up a mixture of Tex-Mex and American fast-food favourites in colourful, upbeat surroundings.

Huberbräu Stüberl (☎ 656 77; Vorderstadt 18; mains €7-14; ☯ 8am-midnight Mon-Sat, 9am-midnight Sun) This convivial and bustling restaurant serves a mix of Tyrolean, Austrian and Italian cuisine and, as the evening wears on, slowly turns into a bar.

Adria (☎ 627 29; Josef Pirchl Strasse 17; mains €6-10; ☯ 10am-11.30pm Sun-Fri, 5-11.30pm Sat) Not far north of the heart of Kitzbühel is this small, simple Italian place with large pizzas and pasta dishes.

J Huber (☎ 624 80; Bichlstrasse 14; mains €4-9; ☯ 8am-1.15pm & 3-6pm Mon-Fri, 8am-noon Sat) This small deli/meat shop has a sit-down section serving inexpensive snacks and hot food.

For self-caterers there's a **Spar supermarket** (Bichlstrasse 22).

Entertainment

With such a large influx of skiers and party-goers over winter, it's no surprise to learn that Kitzbühel has one of the better nightlife scenes of any winter resort in Austria. Fellow English-speakers flock to the **Londoner** (☎ 714 28; Franz Reisch Strasse 4; ☯ from 6pm), while **Café Bergsinn** (☎ 668 18; Vorderstadt 21; ☯ 8am-1am Mon-Fri, 9am-1am Sat, 10am-7pm Sun) attracts those after cocktails. **Cafe Grieserl** (☎ 727 52; Im Gries 6; ☯ nightly) is a more subdued but very cosy bar and **Highways** (☎ 753 50; Im Gries 20; ☯ from 8pm) is a loud, fun establishment with American-themed décor.

Olympia (☎ 721 43; Hinterstadt 6; ☯ from 10pm) is one of the few clubs open year-round.

Getting There & Away

Direct services from Kitzbühel to Innsbruck (€12.20, one hour) run every two hours, while trains to Salzburg normally require a change at Wörgl (€20.80, 2½ hours). Regional trains between Wörgl and Zell am See stop at Kitzbühel Hahnenkamm train station, which is closer to the town centre than Bahnhof Kitzbühel. For Kufstein (€7.40, one hour), change at Wörgl.

Getting to Lienz by train is awkward: one or two changes are required (€12.20, four hours). Bus is a better option as it is direct and only takes two hours (€12.20, twice a day from Monday to Friday, once on weekends). Heading south to Lienz, you pass through some marvellous scenery. Highway 108 (the Felber Tauern Tunnel) and Hwy 107 (the Grossglockner Rd, which is closed in winter) both have toll sections; see p286.

KIRCHBERG
☎ 05357 / pop 5100
Kirchberg, a small town 6km west of Kitzbühel, exudes a more traditional atmosphere than Kitzbühel. It provides access to the same ski slopes as Kitzbühel and is a slightly cheaper base than its famous neighbour – as one skier described it, people wear Swatches, not Rolexes.

The town's **tourist office** (☎ 23 09; www.kirch berg.at; Hauptstrasse 8; ⊗ 8.30am-6pm Mon-Fri year-round, plus 8.30am-noon Sat, 10am-noon Sun winter) can help with accommodation; outside opening hours, consult the accommodation board with a free telephone by its front doors.

Sleeping & Eating
Kirchberg has over 80 hotels and pensions so finding a place to stay in summer should prove no problem; in winter, it's highly advisable to book well ahead.

Of the 10 four-star hotels in the town, **Ferienhotel Elisabeth** (☎ 22 77; www.ferienhotel-elisa beth.at; Aschauer Strasse 75; r from €105; P 🐶) is the largest and has plenty of extras, including a sauna. For something more central and less expensive, try **Gasthof Kirchenwirt** (☎ 28 52; www .kirchenwirt.co.at; Neugasse 14; s/d from €40/80; P).

There are loads of food possibilities in the centre, including two supermarkets on Dorfstrasse and **Ristorante Nabucco** (☎ 350 99; Hauptstrasse 1; mains €6-15; ⊗ lunch & dinner), which has an extensive range of Italian dishes and a sun terrace.

Kirchberg has its share of nightlife, including the obligatory pseudo-English pub-bar **London Pub** (☎ 39 93; Schlossergasse 13; ⊗ 5pm-2am ski season), where English-speakers generally congregate after a day's skiing.

Getting There & Away
Ski buses make the 6km trip from Kitzbühel every 10 or 15 minutes during the day. Bundesbuses run during the summer. From the train station, turn left then bear right for Hauptstrasse (500m). There are various stops, including Hauptstrasse.

Trains depart hourly for Kitzbühel (€1.90, 10 minutes).

KUFSTEIN
☎ 05372 / pop 15,800
Kufstein has a lot going for it; not only is it an attractive town with a large, bulky castle guarding it, but it is surrounded by wonderful nature, including lakes and mountain ranges. It's often full of tourists from Germany, which is only 4km to the north.

Orientation & Information
Kufstein is the northernmost Austrian town in the Inntal. The train station is on the west bank of the Inn River, a three-minute stroll from the core of the town, Stadtplatz, on the east bank. This is where you'll find the **tourist office** (☎ 622 07; www.kufstein.at; Unterer Stadtplatz 8; ⊗ 8.30am-6pm Mon-Fri, 9am-noon Sat summer, 8.30am-5pm Mon-Fri, 9am-noon Sat winter). Staff will hunt down accommodation without charging commission. If you decide to stay overnight, ask for the *Gästekarte*, which has different benefits in summer and winter.

Sights & Activities
Control of the town has been hotly contested by Tyrol and Bavaria through the ages; it changed hands twice before Maximilian I took the town for Tyrol in 1504, was razed to the ground in 1703 during a Bavarian siege, fell under Bavarian control in 1809 during the Napoleonic Wars and finally become Austrian property in 1814. A pivotal point of defence for both sides during these struggles was the **Festung Kufstein** (☎ 602 350; Oberer Stadtplatz 6; adult/concession summer €8/4.40; winter €7/4; ⊗ 9am-5pm summer, 10am-4pm winter), which dates from at least 1205 (when Kufstein was part of Bavaria). The bulky **Kaiserturm** (Emperor's Tower) was added to the fortress in 1522.

Festung Kufstein dominates Kirchberg from its hill overlooking Stadtplatz. Inside is a wide-ranging but not over-large **Heimatmuseum** that includes temporary exhibits on local culture and natural history. Displays are imaginatively presented and incorporate creative lighting and excerpts of suitable music.

Elsewhere in the fortress you can view the **Heldenorgel** (Heroes Organ), below the Kaiserturm. This massive instrument has 4307 pipes, 46 organ stops and a 100m gap between the keyboard and the tip of the pipes; the resultant delay in the sounding of

TYROL

the notes makes playing it a tricky business. Keep an ear out for recitals at noon and, in July and August, 5pm – the music can easily be heard from Stadtplatz and elsewhere, though there's also a special listening auditorium on Stadtplatz by the church.

When the fortress is closed in the evening you can walk up the path (in under 15 minutes) and roam around the castle walls and grounds free of charge. There are fine views of the valley below. During the day a lift up to the fortress/museum will save you some energy, and is included in the admission fee.

Running east of Kufstein is the **Kaisergebirge** range, a rugged landscape soaring to 2300m and extending as far as St Johann in Tirol. It exercises walkers, mountaineers and skiers alike. The Kaisergebirge is actually two ranges, split by the east–west Kaisertal (Kaiserbach Valley). The northern range is the Zahmer Kaiser (Tame Emperor) and the southern is the Wilder Kaiser (Wild Emperor) – no medals for guessing which has the smoother slopes. Before taking the **cable chair** (one way/return €11.60/15.60; ☉ 9am-4pm May-Oct) up to Wilder Kaiser from Kufstein, pick up a free *Wanderkarte* (walking map) from the tourist office.

The **lakes** around Kufstein are an ideal destination for cyclists; bikes can be rented from **Zum Bären** (right; per day €10). Bundesbuses visit some of the lakes; timetables from the tourist office. The smaller, closer lakes are in the wooded area west of the Inn River, where there's a network of walking trails. Hechtsee, 3km to the northwest, and Stimmersee, 2.5km to the southwest, are both attractively situated. Both have swimming areas with entrance fees. Hechtsee is flanked by two other lakes, Egelsee and Längsee. Larger lakes such as the Walchsee, Hintersteinersee and the Thiersee are further afield to the east. A free city bus goes to Hechtsee in summer during fine weather (ask at the tourist office).

Sleeping

Hotel Auracher Löchl (☎ 621 38; www.auracher -loechl.at; Römerhofgasse 3-5; s/d from €42/82) Hotel Auracher is a wonderful hotel that successfully combines old and new; its rooms are bright and modern (those overlooking the Inn River cost a little extra), while the rest of the hotel still retains plenty of medieval charm. Its **restaurant** (mains €7-14), serving up

traditional Tyrolean fare, is one of the better options in town.

Gasthof-Pension Felsenkeller (☎ 627 84; www .felsenkeller.at - in German; Kienbergstrasse 35; s/d from €32/64; ☉ closed Tue; P) In the foothills of the Kaisergebirge east of the city is Gasthof-Pension Felsenkeller, a calm, peaceful oasis hidden among tree-covered rocky crags. Rooms are bright and spacious, and many have a balcony. Its restaurant serves some of the best trout around.

Pension-Café Maier (☎ 622 60; Mitterndorfer Strasse 13; s/d €30/48; P) In a quiet suburb 15 minutes' walk from the centre is this old house with reasonable rooms, grassy garden, friendly atmosphere and small café-restaurant.

Camping Kufstein (☎ 622 29-55; www.hotelbaeren .at; Salurner Strasse 36; camp sites per person/car/tent €4.95/4/3; ☉ May-Oct; P) This shaded camping ground is by the river, 1km south of Stadtplatz. It is run by neighbouring **Zum Bären** (s/d from €49/78), a four-star, chalet-style hotel with plenty of traditional charm.

Eating

There aren't many quality restaurants in and around the heart of Kufstein, but there are enough to satisfy your hunger.

A perfect place to look is highly appealing Römerhofgasse, which is squeezed between the river and the castle. This pedestrianised alley might come as a bit of surprise, with its overhanging arches, painted façades and medieval touches, and while much of it is reproduced for tourists, it still manages to impress. Aside from **Auracher Löchl's** restaurant, the alley is home to **Batzenhäusl** (☎ 624 33; Römerhofgasse 1; mains €7-14; ☉ lunch & dinner), an old-worldly place with plenty of fish dishes and Tyrolean cuisine.

Inn-Café (☎ 645 23; Unterer Stadtplatz 3; snacks & sweets €3-7; ☉ 9am-10pm summer, 9am-8pm winter) For cakes, ice cream and other desserts, don't pass over this fine café, with the best outside terrace in the town, overlooking the river.

For something on the run head for the **Spar** (Unterer Stadtplatz 27) in the centre of the town.

Getting There & Away

The hourly train trip to Kitzbühel (€7.40, one hour) requires a change at Wörgl. The easiest road route is also via Wörgl.

Kufstein is on the main Innsbruck–Salzburg train route; direct trains to Salzburg (€23.50, 1¼ hours) run every two hours; those to Innsbruck (€11.50, 45 to 70 minutes) are half-hourly, as some trains funnel down from Germany (Munich), which is on a direct line a little over an hour away. Postbuses leave from outside the train station.

SÖLL

☎ 05333 / pop 3450

Söll is a well-known ski resort 10km south of Kufstein. Once a favourite of boozy, boisterous visitors in the 1980s, the resort has successfully reinvented itself and is now a quiet, family-orientated place with plenty of outdoor activities in summer and winter.

The helpful staff at the resort's **tourist office** (☎ 52 16; www.soell.com; Dorf 84; ☺ 8am-noon & 1.30-6pm Mon-Fri May-late Dec, plus 3-6pm Sat, 9am-noon Sun late Dec-Apr), in the centre of the village, can provide information on activities in the surrounds and will help you to find accommodation.

The highest skiing area overlooking the resort is Hohe Salve at 1828m, though Söll has also combined with neighbouring resorts Itter, Hopfgarten, Kelchsau, Westendorf and Brixen to form the huge Skiwelt area (www .skiwelt.at) – 250km of pistes, with numerous blue (easy) runs. Passes for the ski region start at €32 for a day's pass in the high season. Cross-country skiing is also a popular pastime in winter, with trails running as far as St Johann in Tirol.

During the summer months walkers take to the nearby hills. Popular destinations are nearby Moorsee and Hintersteiner See, along with **Hohe Salve** (cable car one way/ return €10/13). At the first stage of the cable car climbing Hohe Salve is **Hexenwasser**, a walking trail dotted with fun activities for the whole family. Along the route is a flying fox, water obstacles, a working mill and bakery and playgrounds. Throughout the summer you can see (and sample) bread, schnapps and cheese being made the traditional way.

Getting There & Away

Söll is on Hwy 312 between Wörgl and St Johann in Tirol. It is not on a train line, but there are plenty of buses Monday to Saturday from Kufstein (€4.70, 25 minutes); only three run on Sunday.

WESTERN TYROL

Western Tyrol, stretching from just east of the Ötztal to the border of Vorarlberg (see p329 for information on the Arlberg range), is classic Tyrolean country. High peaks, some of which reach well over 3000m, dominate the skyline of many of the region's long, narrow valleys, and skiing and hiking options abound.

STAMS

☎ 05263 / pop 1300

Stams is an idyllic, rural town visited primarily for its **Zisterzienstift** (Cistercian abbey; ☎ 62 42; Stiftshof 1; tours adult/child €4/3), founded in 1273 by Elizabeth of Bavaria, the mother of Conradin, the last of the Hohenstaufens. The exterior is dominated by two sturdy baroque towers added in the 17th century. The most impressive feature of the church interior is the high altar (1613): the intertwining branches of this version of the 'tree of life' support 84 saintly figures surrounding an image of the Virgin. Near the entrance is the **Rose Grille**, an exquisite iron screen made in 1716.

The abbey can only be visited by guided tour, available 9am to 11am and 1pm to 5pm (afternoon hours are shorter in May and from October to April). Tours leave every hour on the hour except in July and August when they're available every half-hour. Books, clothes, cards and schnapps made on the premises can be bought from the **Kloster shop** (☺ 9am-noon & 1-5pm).

Stams is on the train route between Innsbruck and Landeck, but only (frequent) regional trains stop here (€6.20, 35 minutes). Both the A12/E60 and Hwy 171 pass near the abbey.

THE ÖTZTAL

The Ötztal (Ötz Valley) is the most densely populated of the three river valleys running north from the **Ötztaler Alpen** to drain into the Inn River. The Ötztaler Alpen guard the border to Italy and are home to numerous glaciers that shimmer between soaring peaks, the highest of which is **Wildspitze** (3774m). Mountaineers, walkers and skiers can find plenty to occupy themselves. Most of the small villages lining the valley have a supermarket, bank, camping area and tourist office. The latter can supply you with information on activities and accommodation; room prices are often 30% to 50% lower in summer.

The first village of any size along the narrow valley is **Umhausen**. An enjoyable 40-minute, signposted walk heading southeast from its centre leads to the **Stuibenfall waterfall**, Tyrol's longest waterfall at 150m. About 20 minutes before the waterfall is **Ötzi Dorf** (☎ 05255-500 22; adult/child/family €5.50/2.50/13.50; ⊙ 9.30am-5.30pm May-Oct), an open-air archaeological park that re-creates the world of Ötzi the ice man (below). Exhibitions on other cultures from the Stone Age pop up on a regular basis, and tours of the Dorf are avail-able (€2).

Another 20km down the valley is **Sölden** (1377m), a ski resort basically made up of a string of hotels and pensions. Its **tourist office** (☎ 05254-510-0; www.soelden.com; Rettenbach 466; ⊙ 8am-6pm Mon-Sat, 9am-noon Sun) has Internet access (€6 per hour) and loads of brochures detailing the plethora of walking and skiing opportunities in the area. If you plan to spend a week or more walking in the Ötztal, ask about the Ötztal Card (seven/10 days €47/63), which includes public transport, cable cars and a number of swimming pools in the valley.

From the village, there are two ways to easily reach the surrounding rugged peaks; a chairlift climbs to **Hochsölden** (2090m; one-way/return €5/7), while a cable car rises to **Gaislachkogel** (3058m; €14/19) where there are sweeping views of the entire Ötztaler Alps. In winter, there are **ski pistes** (day/week pass €39/209) for all levels of experience and, in summer, glacial skiing.

Three kilometres south of Sölden is **Zwieselstein**, where the Venter Ache (Venter stream) branches to the southwest. Paths lead up to Wildspitze from the end of this valley.

Further south is the attractive **Obergurgl** (1930m), the highest parish in Austria. It's another well-known ski resort that's popular with families, as pistes are mostly suitable for beginners and intermediates and continue right to the edge of the village. **Hohe Mut** (2659m) is a justly famous lookout, accessible by chairlift year-round. Obergurgl is actually at the head of the valley, but the road doubles back on itself and rises to **Hochgurgl** (2150m). Here the pistes are a little steeper and the views equally impressive. The Ober-

ENTOMBED IN ICE

In September 1991 German hikers in the Ötztaler Alpen came across the body of a man preserved within the Similaun Glacier. Police and forensic scientists were summoned to the scene. The body had been found some 90m within Italy, but was appropriated by the Austrians and taken to Innsbruck University to be studied.

Experts initially decided it was about 500 years old. The ice man, nicknamed 'Ötzi' or 'Frozen Fritz', was thought to have been a soldier serving under Archduke Ferdinand. Carbon dating, however, revealed he was nearly 5400 years old, placing him in the late Stone Age and making him the oldest and best-preserved mummy in the world.

Ötzi became big news, more so because the state of preservation was remarkable; even the pores of the skin were visible. In addition, Ötzi had been found with 70 artefacts, including a copper axe, bow and arrows, charcoal and clothing. Physiologically he was found to be no different from modern humans. His face was reconstructed, right down to his dark hair and blue eyes. X-rays showed he had suffered from arthritis and frostbite, and his ribs had been broken.

For many years debate raged over how the Iceman met his end, but recent analysis has revealed Ötzi was involved in a violent struggle and died while trying to escape. Blood on his weapons and clothes were discovered to be from other persons, and an arrow wound to his back and knife gashes to his arms all pointed to a fight. His copper axe is still a matter of debate however; while copper dating from the age of Ötzi has been found in other parts of Austria, Germany and Switzerland, it predates knowledge of the use of copper in the Ötztal area by 500 years.

Not everybody was worried about the finer points of his heritage, however. Several Austrian and Italian women contacted the university shortly after the discovery and requested that they be impregnated with Ötzi's frozen sperm, but the all-important part of his body was missing.

In 1998 Ötzi was relinquished to the Italians and became the centrepiece of a new museum in Bolzano.

gurgl **tourist office** (☎ 05256-6466; www.obergurgl
.com; Hauptstrasse 108; 🕑 8am-6pm Mon-Fri, 8am-4pm Sat,
9.30am-noon Sun summer, 9am-5.30pm Mon-Sat, 9.30am-
noon Sun winter) cover both resorts, as does one
ski pass (day/week pass €38/183). A gondola allows
easy transfers between Obergurgl's and
Hochgurgl's pistes.

Just beyond Hochgurgl, where the road
makes a sharp right-hand turn, is another
viewing point, the **Windegg Belvedere** (2080m).
The road continues into Italy over the **Timmelsjoch Pass** (2474m; car/motorbike €10/8)
where it joins the course of the Timmelsbach
River.

Getting There & Away

Only buses serve the valley. Coming from
either a westerly or easterly direction by
train, get off at Ötztal Bahnhof, from where
buses head south into the valley. In the summer and winter high seasons buses depart
almost hourly (only every two hours in the
low season) and go as far as Obergurgl (one
way/return €8.60/17.20, 1½ hours). From
approximately mid-July to mid-September
two morning buses continue as far as Timmelsjoch, on the Italian border, but a change
is required at Obergurgl.

If you have your own transport, you should
be able to get at least as far as Hochgurgl all
year, but the road beyond into Italy (via the
Timmelsjoch Pass) is generally blocked by
snow in winter.

IMST
☎ 05412 / pop 9000

Imst is another of Tyrol's historical towns
that is beautifully situated under high
mountain peaks. Its old centre is lined with
eye-catching buildings but the town is better known for its Shrovetide festival, the
Schemenlaufen (ghost dance), which takes
place every four years; the next occurs on
the 15 February 2009. The centrepiece of
this spirited occasion is a colourful procession of 'ghosts' (locals dressed in traditional masks and costumes) through the
town. More can be learnt about the festival
in the **Fasnachthaus** (☎ 69 10; Streleweg 6; admission €4; 🕑 4-6pm Fri), where many of the ghost
masks are on display.

The **tourist office** (☎ 69 10-0; www.imst.at; Jo-
hannesplatz 4; 🕑 9am-6pm Mon-Fri, 9am-noon Sat Sep-
Jun, plus 4-6pm Sat Jul & Aug) is highly informed on
the town and its activities, including the ex-

cellent rafting options on the nearby River
Inn. There's also free Internet access.

The town is slightly to the north of the main
east–west roads (the A12 and Hwy 171), and
is served by frequent Bundesbuses and trains
(from Innsbruck €9.30, one hour).

EHRWALD
☎ 05673 / pop 2550

The crowning glory of the small resort of
Ehrwald is the large **Zugspitze** (2962m), which
marks the border between Austria and Germany and looms mightily over the village. A
modern, fast cable car (summer one way/
return €20.50/32) sails to the top, where
there's a restaurant and a magnificent panorama. All of the main Tyrolean mountain
ranges can be seen, as well as the Bavarian
Alps and Mt Säntis in Switzerland. North
of the Zugspitze is Garmisch-Partenkirchen,
Germany's most popular ski resort, which
also offers access to the mountain summit.

Ehrwald is linked with other resorts in
Austria (including Seefeld) and Germany
(including Garmisch-Partenkirchen) under
the **Happy SkiPass** (adult/child for the minimum 3 days
€83/50). For information on accommoda-
tion and activities, contact the **tourist office**
(☎ 05673-23 95; ehrwald@zugspitze.tirol.at; 🕑 8.30am-
6pm Mon-Fri, 9am-6pm Sat) in the heart of the town.
Staff find rooms free of charge, or there's an
accommodation board with free telephone.

Trains from Seefeld (€8.60, 1¼ hours) and
Innsbruck (€10.70, two hours) to Ehrwald
pass through Germany; you must change at
Garmisch-Partenkirchen. Austrian train tickets are valid for the whole trip.

Ehrwald can also be reached by bus
from Imst (€5.40, one hour), but a change
is required at Nassereith and the service is
infrequent.

LANDECK
☎ 05442 / pop 7500

Landeck is an important transport junction,
guarding the routes to Vorarlberg, Switzerland and Italy. The town has been standing
sentinel for centuries, as demonstrated by
its hillside fortifications, and is now a busy
town more focused on its good burghers
than playing grand host to tourists.

Orientation & Information

The town is rather spread out along the
confluence of the Inn and Sanna Rivers, but

TYROL

most of Landeck's points of interest are in and around the main street, Malserstrasse. Here you'll find the **tourist office** (☎ 656 00; www.tirolwest.at - in German; Malserstrasse; ⏰ 8.30am-noon & 2-6pm Mon-Fri, 8.30am-noon Sat) with an ac-commodation board directly outside.

The train station is 1.5km to the east; walk left on leaving the station and stay on the same side of the river. Local buses also make the trip (one way/return €1.50/3).

Sights & Activities

The **Stadtpfarrkirche** (town parish church; admission free; ⏰ daylight hours), behind the tourist office, was built in 1493 and displays Gothic features such as network vaulting and a winged altar (16th century). On the hill above stands the now quiet and peaceful **Schloss Landeck** (☎ 632 02; Schlossberg; adult/senior/student €4/3/2; ⏰ 10am-5pm Tue-Sun mid-May–Sep, 2-5pm Tue-Sun Oct). Originally built in the 13th century, fire gutted the castle 500 years later and subsequent rebuilding has not stuck to the original form. However, it has been lovingly renovated and inside its whitewashed walls you'll find a small mu-seum of local history, temporary exhibitions and fine views across the town and valley.

Like everywhere in Tyrol, Landeck attracts the odd skier or two, though hikers in the summer are more numerous. The nearby **Venet cable car** (summer one way/return €11.50/5.60) can transport visitors of either type to Krah-berg at 2208m.

Sleeping & Eating

Like most other places in Tyrol, Landeck has a *Gästekarte* for those overnighting in the area, which offers a range of discounts.

Travellers could do worse than find a room in a private house; the tourist office can help you locate one. Herzog Friedrich Strasse, running parallel to Malserstrasse west of the Inn, has a couple of decent places worth trying. **Hotel Sonne** (☎ 625 19; www.hotel-sonne -landeck.at; Malserstrasse 10; s/d from €24/48; **P**) has good rooms (more expensive in winter) and grand views, while **Pension Thialblick** (☎ 622 61; pens.thialblick@utanet.at; Burschlweg 7; s/d €18/36; **P**), at the northern end of the street, is simple and homely.

Gasthof Grief (☎ 622 68; Marktplatz 6; s/d €32/55; **P**) Grief sits on a square above the main street just down from the castle. Its '70s-style rooms are large and accommodating, and its **restaurant** (mains €7-13) serves above-average Tyrolean and Austrian cuisine in-side and out.

Sport Camp Tirol (☎ 646 36; www.sportcamptirol .at; Mühlkanal 1; camp sites per person/tent/car €5.20/3.30/ 3.40; **P**) This camping ground on the north bank of the Sanna River is quite flat, has a scattering of tree cover and is hard up against wooded hills. It also arranges white-knuckle activities such as rafting, kayaking, canyoning and paragliding.

Hotel Schrofenstein (☎ 623 95; Malserstrasse 31; mains €7-20; ⏰ lunch & dinner) Schrofenstein offers the finest dining in town, and has a menu filled with Austrian and Italian dishes, in-cluding seasonal specialities.

Aside from Schrofenstein, there are several places to eat along Malserstrasse, including **Café Wiedmann** (☎ 623 82; Malserstrasse 27; coffee & snacks €3-6; ⏰ 8am-8pm Mon-Fri, 8am-7pm Sat, 10am-7pm Sun). Its popularity is firmly based on good coffee and its huge garden, which is sheltered from the noise of the main street.

Getting There & Away

Landeck is on the east–west InterCity (IC) express train route, 50 minutes from Inns-bruck (€10.70, hourly) and almost two hours from Bregenz (€17.70). Bundesbuses head in all directions, departing from out-side the train station and/or from the bus station in the town centre.

The A12/E60 into Vorarlberg passes by Landeck, burrowing into a tunnel as it ap-proaches the town. Highway 315, the Inntal road, passes through the centre of town and stays on the east side of the river.

THE INNTAL

pop 11,250

The Inntal (Inn Valley) extends for 230km within Tyrol. Its initial stretch, south of Lan-deck, is the only section not shadowed by train tracks. There's little of major interest in this region, though **Pfunds** is picturesque. Many homes here are similar in design to those found in the Engadine, a region in Grau-bünden, Switzerland, further up the Inn Valley.

South of Pfunds, you have the choice of routes; either road offers a corniche sec-tion with fine views. If you continue along the Inn you'll end up in Switzerland (infre-quent buses). Alternatively, if you turn left (south) to Nauders you'll soon reach South Tyrol (Italy) by way of the Reschen Pass

(1508m; open year-round). Six buses daily run from Landeck to Nauders (€6.90, one hour), where it's possible to head on with public transport to Merano in Italy, but at least three changes are required.

THE PAZNAUNTAL
pop 5950

The Paznauntal (Paznaun Valley) runs parallel to the Inntal, but further to the west, and is divided from its more famous neighbour by the Samnaun mountain chain. The main settlement in the valley is **Ischgl**, an attractive resort that is considered one of Austria's best ski areas, despite (or because of) its relative isolation. The **Silvretta ski pass** (winter 2-day pass adult/child €76.50/43.50, summer 3-day pass €31.50/18.50) covers not only Ischgl but also Galtür, Kappl and Samnaun, a duty-free area in Switzerland; its summer equivalent not only covers cable cars and lifts, but also public transport over the Silvretta Pass into Vorarlberg and swimming pools in Ischgl and Galtür. Ischgl's **tourist office** (☎ 05444-52 66-0; www.ischgl.com; ☺ 8am-6pm Mon-Fri, 9am-noon & 4-6pm Sat, 10am-noon Sun) stocks plenty of literature on hiking, biking and skiing in the area.

About 10km on from Ischgl is the tiny settlement of **Galtür**. This Alpine village suffered a major disaster in February 1999 when an avalanche all but swept it away, taking 31 lives with it. A museum documenting the event and explaining the avalanche phenomenon has been built on the spot where the wall of snow came to rest. Inside the **Alpinarium Galtür** (☎ 05443-200 00; www.alpinarium.at - in German; admission €7; ☺ 10am-6pm Tue-Sun) you'll find many poignant reminders the devastation left behind in the shape of photos, newspaper reports and some incredible video footage of an avalanche in action.

Getting There & Away
Only a secondary road (Hwy 188) runs along the valley, crossing into Vorarlberg at Bielerhöhe where there are excellent views. This pass (2036m; toll cars/motorcycles €10.90/10.20) is closed during winter and to caravans at all times and the road rejoins the main highway near Bludenz. Regular Bundesbuses travel along the valley as far as Galtür (€6.20, 70 minutes) from Landeck; only two make the trip daily year-round, with up to five in the summer months, and six over autumn.

ARLBERG REGION

The Arlberg region, shared by Vorarlberg and Tyrol, comprises several linked resorts and is considered to have some of the best skiing in Austria. St Anton am Arlberg is the largest and least elitist of these fashionable chalet resorts but, even here, prices are higher than most resorts in Austria. For the other Arlberg resorts, see p345.

The winter season is long, with snow reliable till about mid-April. Summer is less busy (and cheaper), though still popular with walkers. Even so, some of the restaurants, bars and discos that swing during the ski season are closed. Most others will close between seasons, and open for summer from late June to October. Many guesthouses and some hotels do likewise.

ST ANTON AM ARLBERG
☎ 05446 / pop 2800

St Anton rates among the best ski resorts in Austria, and has a long history in the ski arena; the first ski club in the Alps was founded here in 1901. It enjoys an easygoing atmosphere and vigorous nightlife and is certainly a popular place during the ski season, confirmed by the hundreds of places to stay in and around the town.

Orientation
St Anton is strung out along the northern bank of the Rosanna River. The train station is near the centre (a pedestrian-only zone) and most of the ski lifts. Further east and on the northern side of the train tracks is the area called Nasserein. Further east still is St Jakob, with just one convenient ski lift, a run ending at Nasserein.

Information
The **tourist office** (☎ 226 90; www.stantonamarlberg.com; Arlberg Haus; ☺ 8am-noon & 2-6pm Mon-Fri, 9am-noon Sat & Sun summer, 8.30am-6.30pm Mon-Fri, 9am-6pm Sat, 9am-noon & 2-5pm Sun winter), less than five minutes' walk from the train station, is filled with information on outdoor activities. You can also get with a map of the town and a list of available accommodation, but you'll have to do the phoning. Fortunately, there's an accommodation board and a free telephone directly outside.

ST ANTON AM ARLBERG

0 ————— 500 m
0 ————— 0.3 miles

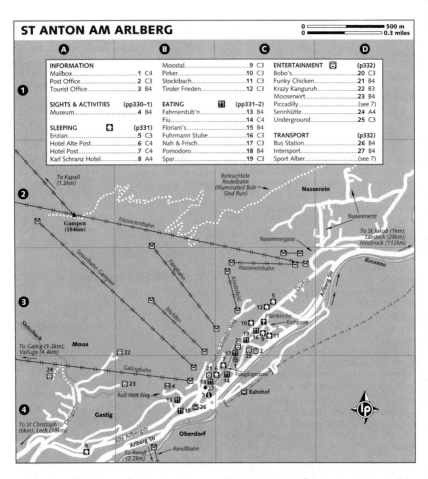

INFORMATION		Moostal	9 C3	ENTERTAINMENT	(p332)
Mailbox	1 C4	Pirker	10 C3	Bobo's	20 C3
Post Office	2 C3	Stockibach	11 C3	Funky Chicken	21 B4
Tourist Office	3 B4	Tiroler Frieden	12 C3	Krazy Kanguruh	22 B3
				Mooserwirt	23 B4
SIGHTS & ACTIVITIES (pp330–1)		EATING (pp331–2)		Piccadilly	(see 7)
Museum	4 B4	Fahrnerstub'n	13 B4	Sennhütte	24 A4
		Fiu	14 C4	Underground	25 C3
SLEEPING (p331)		Floriani's	15 B4		
Enzian	5 C3	Fuhrmann Stube	16 C3	TRANSPORT (p332)	
Hotel Alte Post	6 C4	Nah & Frisch	17 C3	Bus Station	26 B4
Hotel Post	7 C4	Pomodoro	18 B4	Intersport	27 B4
Karl Schranz Hotel	8 A4	Spar	19 C3	Sport Alber	(see 7)

The post office is near the Rosanna River, off the northern end of the pedestrian zone. **Mailbox** (Fussgängerzone 49; per hr €6; ☒ 9am-9pm high season, 11am-7pm low season, closed 1 or 2 days a week) has Internet access.

Sights & Activities

St Anton's only true sight is the small **Ski & Heimat Museum** (☎ 24 75; Rudi Matt Weg; adult/child €3/1; ☒ 11am-5pm Tue-Sun Jul & Aug, 1-5pm Tue-Sun Sep-Jun), which covers the good old days when skis were made of wood and men were as tough as hobnail boots.

The resort offers some of the best **skiing** in Austria for experts, with many difficult runs, both on- and off-piste; it even hosted the World Alpine Skiing Championships in February 2001. In fact, St Anton is one of the best resorts in Austria for off-piste skiing on powder snow. Cable cars go all the way up to Valluga (2811m), from where experts can go off-piste all the way to Lech (with a ski guide only). Galzig (2185m) is along the way to Valluga. There are nursery slopes on Gampen (1850m) and Kapall (2330m), but generally the skiing is not suited to beginners. A single **ski pass** (high season 1-/3-/7-day pass €39/108/230, discounts at other times of the year) covers the whole Arlberg region. It is valid for 83 ski lifts, giving access to 260km of prepared pistes and 180km of high Alpine deep-snow runs.

Walking is by far the most popular activity in summer. During this time, only a handful of **cable cars and lifts** (one way €9-16.50, return €11-19) are in use, but it is still possible to reach all the major peaks. If you plan to do a bit of walking, pick up a detailed walking booklet and map for €6.50 from the tourist office and consider purchasing a **Wanderpass** (7-days €30), which provides unlimited access to all lifts, or a St Anton Card (€45), which offers the same benefits plus entrance to the town's indoor and outdoor swimming pool.

Cyclists are also catered for; the tourist office produces a small booklet (in German only) with a number of suggested trails in the area.

Sleeping

There are some 480 accommodation options in and around St Anton, 80% of which are open during the summer months. Even with all this choice, it can be hard to find somewhere to stay over the winter months without booking ahead (note that short stays of a couple of days will usually incur a surcharge).

There's not a lot of choice between the simpler B&Bs in terms of value for money, and all charge more over winter; prices quoted below are for the winter high season. Many places have five different price levels through the year – two in summer and three in winter – and summer prices can be as low as half those in winter.

Tiroler Frieden (☎ 22 47; tiroler.frieden@st-anton .at; Dorfstrasse 75; s/d €25/50; **P**) This 75-year-old quaint chalet sits slightly above the main road and backs onto the lower ski slopes. Rooms are clean and accommodating, and the place is worth booking ahead during winter.

Enzian (☎ 24 03; haus.enzian@st-anton.at; Dorfstrasse 77; apt €95; **P**) Right next door to Frieden is Enzian, another lovely chalet-type accommodation, but this time offering apartments. Most rooms have a balcony.

Hotel Alte Post (☎ 54 46; www.hotel-alte-post.at; Fussgängerzone 11; s/d €155/310; **P** ⚐ ✕) Right in the heart of St Anton is Alte Post, a hotel of some class. Its rooms are sumptuous, its restaurant and bar lavish while still retaining plenty of rustic Tyrolean charm and the service exemplary.

Hotel Post (☎ 221 30; www.st-anton.co.at; Fussgängerzone 55; s/d €164/306; **P** ⚐ ✕ 🖥) A friendly, four-star hotel slap-bang in the village centre, Hotel Post offers stylish, sizable rooms with added extras such as bottled water and fruit. The bar has a massive selec-

tion of wines, and guests can lounge around in the sauna, Jacuzzi and steam bath.

Pirker (☎ 23 10; www.pirker.com; Dorfstrasse 241; s/d €58/116; **P** 🖥) A little further towards the centre of the village from Enzian is Pirker, with more-modern rooms than many pensions in the town. There's also a sauna and apartments.

Karl Schranz Hotel (☎ 29 77-0; hotel.karl.schranz@ st-anton.at; Alte Arlbergstrasse 76; s/d €128/238; **P** ⚐) This very cosy, Tyrolean-style hotel, owned by the eponymous skier, is good value for a four-star place in town and has a top restaurant to boot. Though it is about 1km uphill from the town centre, a free shuttle takes guests to and fro (call to be picked up from the train station).

Just south of the town church is a grouping of fine accommodation options, including **Stockibach** (☎ 20 72; haus.stockibach@st-anton .at; Kirchgasse 484; s/d €31/62; **P**), which has attractive rooms with wood fittings and often a balcony; and **Moostal** (☎ 28 31; haus.moostal@st -anton.at; Marktstrasse 487; s/d €59/106; **P**), with bright, clean rooms and a sauna.

Generally, the further from the town centre, the cheaper it gets; St Jakob's main street has **Sailer** (☎ 28 14; St Jakober Dorfstrasse 120; s/d €30/60; **P**) and **Schuler** (☎ 31 08; St Jakober Dorfstrasse 106; s/d €22/44; **P**), both simple but good accommodation. The Nasserein area is also slightly cheaper than central St Anton.

Eating

Because of the lopsidedness of St Anton's tourist seasons, many restaurants only open during the high season. There are however a few places open year-round, and some of the bars mentioned in the Entertainment section (p332) also serve food. For a list of places, pick up a copy of *arlbergrevue*, a detailed free magazine in English available from the tourist office.

Brunnenhof (☎ 22 93; St Jakober Dorfstrasse; mains €18-25; ⚐ dinner Thu-Tue Dec-Apr) Outside of town, this restaurant in St Jakob has a deserved reputation as being one of the best in Arlberg. Austrian food, with gourmet flourishes, is served in a 320-year-old farmhouse; reservations are highly recommended.

Fiu (☎ 426 92; Dorfstrasse 38; mains €7-16; ⚐ dinner Dec-Apr) This small and colourful restaurant specialises in Asian cuisine, including sushi. Takeaways are also a possibility here.

TYROL

Fahrnerstub'n (☎ 235 37; Alte Arlbergstrasse 93; mains €8-18; 🕑 dinner Dec-Apr) A small, comfortable place opposite Floriani's and right next to a cold, Alpine stream. This is another in the line of St Anton restaurants that serve up decent Austrian and Tyrolean food.

Fuhrmann Stube (☎ 29 21; Dorfstrasse 456; mains €8-14; 🕑 lunch & dinner) Family-friendly and north of the pedestrian zone, this place has good-value Austrian food and a relaxed air, and is one of the few places open the entire year.

Floriani's (☎ 23 30; Alte Arlbergstrasse 92; mains €6.50-10; 🕑 dinner Tue-Sun) This simple, family-run restaurant has a fine selection of Italian and Austrian cuisine served up in a wood-panelled room.

Pomodoro (☎ 33 33; Fussgängerzone 70; mains about €8; 🕑 dinner Dec-Apr) As the name suggests, this place specialises in Italian cuisine, namely pizza and pasta. The food is not exceptional but the atmosphere is often lively.

Self-caterers have a choice of supermarkets. There's a Nah & Frisch in the Fussgängerzone (pedestrian zone) and a **Spar** (Dorfstrasse 470) supermarket not far northeast. Inside the Spar is the **Murr** (☎ 2202-31) deli counter, which serves hot takeaway lunches Monday to Saturday (€4 to €6) but they must be pre-ordered.

Entertainment

If you come in summer, forget about nightlife, as most places (except Bobo's and Sennhütte) only open from December to April.

On the lower ski slopes, lively aprés-ski bars include **Krazy Kanguruh** (☎ 26 33), **Mooserwirt** (☎ 35 88) and **Sennhütte** (☎ 20 48).

In the town itself, most bars line the Fussgängerzone. **Piccadilly** (☎ 2213-276; Fussgängerzone 55; 🕑 4pm-2am) is an English-style pub with live music, **Funky Chicken** (☎ 30 201; Fussgängerzone 70; 🕑 6pm-2am Wed-Mon) serves up grilled chicken and attracts a younger crowd, while **Bobo's** (☎ 271 4-54; Fussgängerzone; 🕑 5pm-2am) is a Mexican bar-restaurant with good cocktails.

Not far off the Fussgängerzone is **Underground** (☎ 20 00; Im Gries 530; 🕑 4pm-2am), a busy venue with a bar-disco downstairs, bistro on the ground floor and live music.

Getting There & Away

St Anton is the easiest access point to the region. It's on the train route between Bregenz (€14.30, 1½ hours) and Innsbruck (€13.10; 1¼ hours), with fast trains every one or two hours. St Anton and St Christoph are close to the eastern entrance of the Arlberg Tunnel, the toll road connecting Vorarlberg and Tyrol. The tunnel toll is €8.50 for cars and minibuses. You can avoid the toll by taking the B197, but no vehicles with trailers are allowed on this winding road.

Bundesbuses depart from stands southwest of the tourist office.

Getting Around

Free local buses go to outlying parts of the resort (such as St Jakob). Bundesbuses run to Lech and Zürs in Vorarlberg (one way/return €3.40/5.50); they are hourly (till about 6pm) in winter, reducing to four a day in summer. Taking a minibus taxi, which can be shared between up to eight people, is another option: the trip from St Anton to Lech costs €44.

Bicycles can be rented (half-/full day €14/20) from **Sport Alber** (☎ 34 00; Fussgängerzone) and **Intersport Arlberg** (☎ 34 53; Dorfstrasse 1).

Vorarlberg

CONTENTS

Vorarlberg – which literally translates as 'before the Arlberg' – is the country's second-smallest province, and a bit of a mystery to everyone, Austrians included. Occupying the farthest western reaches of Austria, and separated from the rest of the country by the Arlberg massif, it has over the centuries cultivated an individual identity and culture (right down to its language) and still often associates itself with neighbouring Switzerland rather than Vienna.

Its landscapes are its greatest feature: an aesthetically pleasing mix of mountains, hills and valleys. To the east rises the mighty Arlberg range, while creating the international border with Switzerland to the south is the immense Silvretta Alpen (Silvretta Alps). Both gleam bright and white in winter and green and grey in summer, and provide some of the best skiing and walking in the country. Arlberg, in particular, contains ski slopes so esteemed that royalty and the famous are a regular sight carving up the pistes.

Bregenz, Vorarlberg's capital, may not be the biggest city in the province, but it has the most charm. Camped on the shores of Bodensee (Lake Constance), it is a gateway to the lake and the towns lining its shores. The old town, with its peaceful ambience and medieval allure, is a real gem, while the new town boasts rewarding museums and art galleries.

Spread between the capital and the Arlberg range is the Bregenzerwald, a region which seems to pop up out of nowhere. Rolling forested hills, sheer granite crags and sharp peaks are the Bregenzwerwald's most obvious features, but take a closer look and you'll find contemporary architecture, shops full of cheese and a rejuvenating atmosphere.

Lining the Rhine Valley are working towns and villages; Feldkirch, with its pretty medieval heart, shines the most brightly here. Bludenz, a little further to the southeast, is a perfect base for exploring the steep valleys in Vorarlberg's southern region.

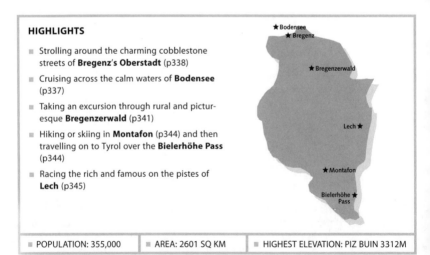

HIGHLIGHTS

- Strolling around the charming cobblestone streets of **Bregenz's Oberstadt** (p338)
- Cruising across the calm waters of **Bodensee** (p337)
- Taking an excursion through rural and picturesque **Bregenzerwald** (p341)
- Hiking or skiing in **Montafon** (p344) and then travelling on to Tyrol over the **Bielerhöhe Pass** (p344)
- Racing the rich and famous on the pistes of **Lech** (p345)

★ Bodensee
★ Bregenz
★ Bregenzerwald
Lech ★
★ Montafon
Bielerhöhe ★ Pass

| ■ POPULATION: 355,000 | ■ AREA: 2601 SQ KM | ■ HIGHEST ELEVATION: PIZ BUIN 3312M |

VORARLBERG

History

Vorarlberg has been inhabited since the early Stone Age but it wasn't until the arrival of the Celts in 400 BC, followed by the Romans around 15 BC, that lasting settlements were maintained. Brigantium, the forerunner of Bregenz, was a stronghold of the Romans until around the 5th and 6th centuries, when the raiding Germanic Alemanni tribes increased their influence and effectively took over.

The province enjoyed a peaceful existence until the early 15th century, when it suffered substantial damage during the Appenzell War with the Swiss Confederation. Relations with its neighbour later improved to such an extent that in 1918 Vorarlberg declared independence from Austria and sought union with Switzerland. The move was blocked by the Allied powers in the post-war reorganisation of Europe; fears that an even-further reduced Austria would be easily assimilated into a recovering Germany were certainly founded. Today, Vorarlberg still looks first towards its westerly neighbours, and then to the Austrian capital, Vienna, 600km to the east.

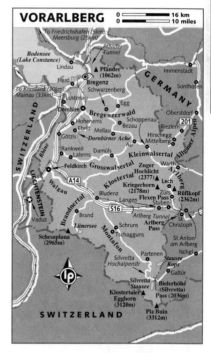

Climate

Vorarlberg is a predominantly mountainous region with an Atlantic climate; plenty of snow in winter and an above average amount of precipitation (around 2000mm per year). Its weather can differ greatly from the east of Austria; quite often it can be sunny and warm in Vorarlberg and miserable in Vienna, or the other way around.

Language

Locals speak an Alemannic dialect of German which is closer to Schwyzertütsch (Swiss-German) than to standard German, a lingering legacy of the Germanic Alemanni tribes who settled in Vorarlberg, Switzerland and parts of southern Germany. This strong dialect is often quite hard for native German speakers to understand; the regional tourist office has even gone so far as to produce a *Voralbergisch für den Urlaub* (Vorarlberg dialect for the holiday) guide which translates common words and phrases into Hoch Deutsch (high German).

Getting There & Away

Vorarlberg has no international airport; the closest is Friedrichshafen in Germany. The province is connected by rail and A14 autobahn to the rest of Austria via the 14km Arlberg tunnel which runs under the Arlberg mountains. To the west, there are plenty of border crossings into Liechtenstein and Switzerland and the main access to Germany is the A14 heading north from Bregenz.

Bodensee ferries (p337) connect Bregenz to various towns and cities in Switzerland and Germany.

Getting Around

Vorarlberg is broken down into *Domino* (individual zones) which are in turn grouped into nine transport regions; a *Regio* travel pass covering one region costs €5.50/€11.70 for one day/week while a *Maximo* pass, costing €12.50/24.20, covers the entire province. Single *Domino* tickets cost €1.10 and a day pass €2.10 – these cover city transport in Bregenz, Dornbirn, Götzis, Feldkirch, Bludenz, Lech and Schruns/Tschagguns.

Children travel for half price and seniors, disabled persons and students receive a 30% discount. Further information, including a handy timetable booklet, is available from the **Verkehrsverbund Vorarlberg** (☎ 05522-835 77, www.vmobil.at - in German; Herrengasse 12, Feldkirch; ☽ 8am-noon & 1-5pm Mon-Fri).

BREGENZ

☎ 05574 / pop 27,000

Bregenz is a small, compact provincial capital with one added advantage over the rest of Austria's provincial centres – the Bodensee (Lake Constance). This large lake not only provides a range of water-sport activities for locals and visitors alike, but also access to Germany and Switzerland. Aside from

the lake, the city's biggest drawcards are the Bregenz Festival and its thoroughly charming *Oberstadt* (upper town).

History

The original settlement of Bregenz gained its name from a Celtic tribe, the Brigantes, who settled the area before the coming of the Romans. It was all but destroyed by the Alemanni tribes in the 5th century but began to rebuild itself again around a monastery established here in 610 by Irish missionary Columban.

Bregenz was first documented as Brigancia in 802 and became the seat of the counts of the area. The city enjoyed a fairly peaceful life through the centuries (apart from being

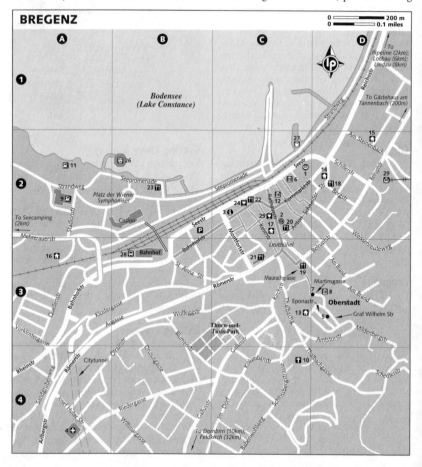

BREGENZ

part of Bavaria during the Napoleonic Wars) and was crowned capital of Vorarlberg in the 20th century.

Orientation
Bregenz is spread out on the eastern shore of Bodensee with the Pfänder hills (1062m) as a backdrop. The *Bahnhof* (train station) is about 10 minutes' walk east of the town centre, the ferry terminal only a couple of minutes' walk north across the railway tracks.

The newer part of the city is down near the waterfront while its historical heart is another 10 minutes' walk further inland.

MAPS
The tourist office hands out a simple, free map of the city.

Information
INTERNET ACCESS
The tourist office and **Rathaus** (town hall; Rathaus 4; 7.30am-5pm Mon-Thu) have free Internet access.

MEDICAL SERVICES
Unfallkrankenhaus (49 01; Josef Huter Strasse 12) Provincial hospital with emergency ward.

MONEY
Bregenz's new centre has a handful of banks and Bankomat machines; the train station also has a Bankomat.

POST
Main post office (49 00-20; Seestrasse)

TOURIST INFORMATION
Tourist office (49 59-0; www.bregenz at - in German; Bahnhofstrasse 14; 9am-7pm Mon-Sat mid-Jul–mid-Aug, 9am-6pm Mon-Fri & 9am-noon Sat mid-Aug–early Sep, 9am-noon & 1-5pm Mon-Fri, 9am-noon Sat early Se –mid-Jun, 9am-noon & 1-6pm Mon-Fri, 9am-noon Sat mid-Jun–mid-Jul) Information on the city and the surrounding area and can

help with accommodation. Outside opening hours, brochures are stacked in front of the office.

Sights & Activities
Everybody who arrives in Bregenz is drawn to the **Bodensee**. It's a major summer holiday destination for Austrians, Swiss and Germans, all of whom take advantage of the many water sports and attractions lining its banks.

A number of companies offer boat services on the lake from April to mid-October, heading to most towns along its northern and southern edges; information and prices on services can be obtained from **ÖBB-Bodenseeschifffahrt Bregenz** (428 68; www.boden seeschifffahrt.at - in German; Seestrasse 4). Services to Konstanz, about two-thirds of the way along the lake, peak at eight departures per day from early July to mid-September (one-way €11.40, 3¾ hours) and normally call in at Lindau, Friedrichshafen, Meersburg and Mainau (among others). Services to towns on the southern side are far less frequent.

Highlights around the Bodensee include the Zeppelin Museum in Friedrichshafen, Meersburg's picturesque half-timbered houses built in classical German style and its two castles, the Cathedral of St Nicholas in Überlingen, the flower island of Mainau and the Gothic cathedral in Konstanz. On the Switzerland side you'll find a 16th-century castle and historical museum at Arbon and a car museum at Rorschach. Possibly the best attraction near the lake is the late-baroque cathedral and adjoining library (a World Heritage listed site) at St Gallen, which is only a short train ride from Rorschach. If you plan to cruise the waters of the lake for a few days, consider purchasing a **Bodensee Pass** (3-/7-/14-day pass €54/67/93), which covers boat tickets and admission to many attractions.

Other activities on the lake include **sailing** and **diving** at Lochau, 5km north of town,

VORARLBERG

and **swimming**. The best place to take a dip is the **Pipeline**, a stretch of beach north of Bregenz so named for the large pipeline running parallel to the lake.

Back on land, the **Oberstadt**, high above the lake, holds almost all of Bregenz's charm. This quarter, with its winding paths, cobblestone streets, quaint homes and overgrown gardens, is more reminiscent of an old English town rather than somewhere in the heart of central Europe. The Oberstadt is still guarded by defensive walls and the sturdy **Martinstor** (St Martin's Gate), above which hangs a suitably grotesque mummified shark. Not far past the gate is the town emblem, the bulbous, baroque **Martinsturm** (St Martin's Tower; ☎ 466 32; Martinsgasse; adult/child €1/0.50; ☯ 9am-6.30pm Tue-Sun Easter–mid-Oct). Built in 1599, it's topped by the largest onion dome in central Europe. On the ground floor there's a church with 14th-century frescoes, and on the upper floors is the small Vorarlberger Militärmuseum (military museum), with the benefit of good views.

Further into the *Oberstadt* you'll find the half-timbered **Altes Rathaus** (old town hall), designed by the baroque architect Michael Kuen and built in 1662. Further to the south, on top of an opposing hill, is the **Stadtpfarrkirche St Gallus** (Thalbachgasse; admission free; ☯ daylight hours); its plain exterior belies a surprisingly light and delicate baroque and rococo interior.

Back in the new centre of Bregenz, the **Vorarlberger Landesmuseum** (☎ 460 50; www.vlm.at - in German; Kornmarktplatz 1; adult/student €2/1; ☯ 9am-noon & 2-5pm Tue-Sun, daily during Bregenz Festival) outlines the region's history, culture and crafts. It begins on the 1st floor with findings from the Stone, Bronze, Iron and Roman ages, and includes a model of the original Roman fort at Bregenz. The 2nd floor delves into more recent arts and crafts from the province; period furniture, musical instruments – including an intricately carved *Tragorgel* (transportable organ) – and traditional dress are all on show. The top floor is given over to religious art, local expressionist painters and works by celebrated Swiss-born artist Angelika Kauffmann (1741–1807).

Nearby, with its back to the lake, is the **Kunsthaus** (☎ 485 94; Karl-Tzian-Platz; adult/concession €6/4.50; ☯ 10am-6pm Tue-Sun, 10am-9pm Thu, 10am-9pm during festival). Built in 1997 to house changing exhibitions of modern art, the architecture (glass and steel exterior, concrete interior) of this cuboid creation is supposed to look like a lamp; the inside is simple, open and perfect for art exhibitions.

The peak of the **Pfänder** (1064m), rising sharply behind the city, offers an impressive view of the lake and beyond to the Allgäuer Alpen range. A **cable car** (☎ 421 60-0; Steinbruchgasse 4; adult/senior/youth 16-19/child under 16 €5.70/5.10/4.50/2.80 one-way, €9.80/8.80/7.80/4.90 return; ☯ 9am-7pm mid-Nov–Oct) climbs to the top of the Pfänder, where a viewing platform and the **Greifvogelflugschau** (bird of prey show; mobile ☎ 0664 9053 040; Pfänder 1; adult/child €4.10/2.10; ☯ 11am & 2.30pm May-Sep), a show by feathered performers of aerial feats, can be found.

Aside from the Pipeline mentioned above, swimmers can enjoy a cool dip in the **bathing complex** (☎ 442 42; Strandweg) just to the northwest of the train station. The complex includes the open-air **Strandbad** (adult/concession €3/2.50; ☯ 9am-8pm mid-May–Sep), with lakeside access, a couple of pools and a self-service restaurant, and the **Seehallenbad** (indoor pool; adult/senior/student/child €3.80/3/2.80/1.90; ☯ 9am-9pm Tue-Fri, 9am-7pm Sat & 10am-6pm Sun year-round).

Festivals & Events

The **Bregenz Festival**, running from late July to late August, is the city's grandiose cultural event. Operas, orchestral works and theatrical productions with international performers are performed on the Seebühne, a vast, open-air floating stage at the edge of the lake, north of the train station. Information and tickets (ranging from €26 to €125) are available from the **ticket center** (☎ 407-6; www.bregenzerfestspiele.com; Postfach 311, A-6901 Bregenz) about nine months before the festival.

Sleeping

On the Austrian monopoly board, two Bregenz streets occupy the most expensive property squares; this is reflected in the price of accommodation. What this means is that some places are not value for money. There are of course exceptions, such as private rooms which are about €20 to €30 per person; the tourist office has a list of such places. Expect prices during the festival to be higher than those quoted here.

Jugendgästehaus (☎ 428 67; www.jgh.at/bregenz; Mehrer Auerstrasse 3-5; dm €17.50; P ⬛) Housed in a former needle factory, this HI hostel is a charismatic place with spacious dorms, a café and restaurant; it's only a few minutes walk west of the train station.

Deuring-Schlössle (☎ 478 00; www.deuring-schloessle .com; Ehregutaplatz 4; s/d €135/210; P) This stunningly renovated castle has the best rooms in Bregenz, all of which retain plenty of medieval charm and elegance. The **restaurant** (mains €20-30) here is the best in Bregenz, with a refined setting and a gourmet menu that changes frequently.

Gästehaus am Tannenbach (☎ 441 74; Im Gehren 1; s/d from €22/44; P) Tannenbach is a homely *Gästehaus* (guesthouse) on a quiet street to the north of the centre; rooms are well cared for and a decent size, as is the colourful flower garden surrounding the house.

Hotel Germania (☎ 427 66-0; www.hotel-germania .at; Am Steinenbach 9; s/d from €75/110; P 🖳) This four-star place particularly tries to attract cyclists, and rents bikes and organises bike tours. It also offers a fitness room and sauna, which are all free for guests, and rooms are suitably comfy. Its upmarket **restaurant** (mains €10-24) compliments its excellent fish dishes with a healthy dose of Austrian classics.

Hotel Bodensee (☎ 423 00; www.hotel-bodensee.at; Kornmarktstrasse 22; s/d from €48/70; P) Hotel Bodensee is another accommodation option more than handy to the city's attractions. Its rooms are clean and tidy, and have an old-fashioned feel.

Pension Sonne (☎ 425 72; www.bbn.at/sonne; Kaiserstrasse 8; s/d from €32/60) This convenient, family-run pension is the most central accommodation around, and has reasonably sized rooms which vary in outlook and décor (many have a homey touch).

Seecamping (☎ 718 95; www.seecamping.at; Bodangasse 7; campsite per person/car/tent €5/5/5; 🕙 mid-May–mid-Sep; P) Seeberger is only a stone's throw from the lake, about 2km west of the Strandbad complex. It's a very flat campsite, with some tree cover and a restaurant.

Eating

Some of the finest dining in Vorarlberg can be found at two of the city's best hotels, Hotel Germania and Deuring-Schössle (see above).

Gasthaus Maurachbund (☎ 440 20; Maurachgasse 11; mains €10-14; 🕙 lunch & dinner Tue-Sat, lunch Sun) A more cosy restaurant than Maurachbund is hard to find in Bregenz; inside you'll find a warm, welcoming atmosphere and a small but selective menu of Austrian dishes.

Pizzeria San Guiseppe (☎ 541 68; Bahnhofstrasse; mains €5-9; 🕙 lunch & dinner) This great little pizzeria packs 'em in most nights with its big pizzas and tasty pasta dishes; on Friday and Saturday nights San Guiseppe doubles as a popular bar.

Gösserbrau Gasthaus (☎ 424 67; Anton Schneider Strasse 1; mains €5-16; 🕙 9am-1am) Gösserbrau offers you two places for the price of one; the comfortable, cultured Gösserstuben, or the rap-sac, with its modern, remodelled, nightclub-esque room and traditional wood-panelled room. Both serve the same food – solid Austrian fare.

Wirtshaus am See (☎ 422 10; Seepromenade; mains €10-20; 🕙 lunch & dinner) On warm summer evenings as the sun sets over the Bodensee, there is no better place to dine than the Wirtshaus am See. Its outdoor patio is hugely popular during this time; over winter the large villa is more favoured. At any time of the year, the fish dishes here are sought after.

China-Restaurant Da-Li (☎ 534 14; Anton Schneider Strasse 34; Sat lunch menu €5, weekday buffet €7, mains €7-14; 🕙 lunch & dinner) Tucked away on a back street in the city centre is this small restaurant, serving standard Chinese fare either indoors or outdoors.

The **GWL** (Römerstrasse 2) shopping centre not only has a Spar supermarket for self-caterers, but also a supremely popular sushi bar, **Tokyo** (☎ 589 78; running sushi €15, sushi sets €7.80-12; 🕙 lunch & dinner) which has a range of sushi sets, tempura and soups and salads.

Drinking

Bregenz's nightlife scene is small and compact, with a handful of bars vying for your attention. Down on Bahnhofstrasse are two ever-popular bars which are packed to the gunnels on weekends; **Wunderbar** (☎ 477 58) is a lively bar frequented by a 20s to 30s crowd and **Cuba** (☎ 470 52) is a fashionably hip place, attracting a well-dressed clientele with its Latin tunes and regular DJs. **Flexibel** (☎ 546 27; Rathausstrasse), a small bar not far away, is more suited to those wishing to see and be seen, and only invites over-18s through the front door.

Getting There & Around

Austrian Airlines fly to Altenrhein in Switzerland, the nearest airport. Friedrichshafen, in Germany, is the nearest major airport served by a couple of no-frill airlines.

VORARLBERG'S ARCHITECTURAL VISION

It's hard to believe that such a traditional province, with its cud-chewing cows, yellow cheese, stark mountains and wooden chalets, is among the most progressive places on the planet when it comes to architecture.

It all started back in the mid-1980s when a group of architects, constrained by the Austrian trade association of architects because of their ideas, split away from the pack and began calling themselves *Baukünstler* (building artists) rather than architects. They managed to gain support from the local authorities and create an environment where anything – as long as it was of high quality and cultivated craftsmanship – was possible.

Much of Vorarlberg's contemporary architecture is denoted by clean lines, sharp angles and plenty of glass and wood. And it's everywhere; private homes, bus stops, supermarkets and kindergartens all compete with hotels, restaurants and office buildings for your undivided attention. Arrive in a non-descript hamlet in the Bregenzerwald and you'll be confronted with not one but half a dozen architecturally sublime houses, or turn a corner in Bregenz or Dornbirn and out pops a building at the cutting edge of design.

Prominent buildings to look out for include Kunsthaus Bregenz (p338), Inatura Dornbirn (below), Dornbirn's Hotel Martinspark, Lauterach's Terminal V, Silvrettahaus (p345) and Lustenau's SIE-Zentrale. For more information, pick up a copy of *architektur land vorarlberg – zeitgenössische baukunst* (modern architecture) from the provincial tourist office; it's in both German and English and has a list of architecturally modern hotels.

Four direct trains daily head for Munich (€54, 2½ hours) via Lindau, while trains for Konstanz (€45, 1½ to two hours) go via the Swiss shore of the lake and may be frequent, but require between one and four changes. There are four daily departures for Zürich (€30, 1¾ hours), all of which call in at St Gallen (€15, 45 minutes).

Nine trains daily depart for Innsbruck (€25.10, 2¼ hours), calling en route at Dornbirn (€2.20, eight minutes), Feldkirch (€4.60, 25 minutes) and Bludenz (€6.80, 45 minutes); there are half-hourly regional trains to the latter three destinations (14, 45 and 70 minutes, respectively).

Boat trips on the Bodensee can take travellers both to and from Germany and Switzerland.

The cable car is the best way to get to Pfänder (p338).

DORNBIRN & AROUND

Bregenz may be the capital, but **Dornbirn** is the largest city in Vorarlberg. This is a place very much for locals; a working city with minimal tourist attractions. Aside from a handful of architecturally intriguing buildings, Dornbirn's biggest drawcard is **Inatura** (☎ 05572-232 35; www.inatura.at; Jahngasse 9; adult/concession/child/family €8/5.50/4/10; ☯ 10am-6pm Fri-Wed, 10am-9pm Thu), a new museum concentrating on nature's splendour. It's a great place

for kids, who can pet (stuffed) foxes and lynx, handle spiders (one day a week), peer into bee and hornet nests, ogle at snakes and fish from behind glass and generally learn something new. There's also a small climbing wall, interactive screens, 3D cinemas and a good restaurant.

Only 4km southeast of Dornbirn lies the **Rappenlochschlucht** (Rappenloch Gorge), a dramatic gorge through which the raging Dornbirner Ache flows; the wooden walkways allow walkers to negotiate the gorge with ease.

Hohenems is another ordinary town 6km south of Dornbirn. In the 17th century it was a haven for Jews, and a fairly large community called it home. Their numbers began to decrease in the 1860s, when Jews were eligible to live anywhere under Habsburg rule. Their legacy is explored in **Jüdisches Museum Hohenems** (☎ 05576-777 93; Schweizer Strasse 5; adult/child €5/3.50; ☯ 10am-5pm Tue-Sun), housed in the Rosenthal villa. The Rosenthals built up a considerable textile business in the town, and part of their wealth – in the likes of gorgeous period furniture – is on show, alongside photos, documents and religious artefacts from the long-defunct Jewish community. Huddled against a tree-lined hill just outside the town on the road to Götzis is the **Jewish cemetery**; get the key from the museum.

Getting There & Away

Dornbirn and Hohenems (from Bregenz: €2.80, 25 minutes) are on the Bregenz–Innsbruck railway line. The Dornbirn–Ebnit Bundesbus passes by the Rappenlochs gorge (€1.50, 22 minutes, six daily).

BREGENZERWALD

Bregenzerwald is the name given to the area between Bregenz and the Arlberg. It's less wooded than the name implies (*Wald* means forest), but that takes nothing away from its beauty; high mountain peaks dominate the region to the east and south while low, wooded hills and sharp rocky outcrops are prominent in the west. Idyllic, rural villages dot the landscape, the clinking of cow bells provide a musical backdrop and a serene atmosphere prevails over the entire place.

The staff at the **Bregenzerwald tourist office** (☎ 05512-2365; www.bregenzerwald.at; Impulszentrum 1135, 6863 Egg) can expound on the attractions of the region, of which skiing (both downhill and cross-country) and walking are the most popular. The **3 Täler Pass** (3-/7-day pass €85/162) covers the skiing regions of Bregenzerwald, Grosses Walsertal and Lechtal. Cheese is a major product here; the tourist office can pass on details of the *Käsestrasse* (cheese road) which winds through the area.

Around 13km east of Dornbirn is the sleepy town of **Schwarzenberg**, which springs to life from the middle of May to the middle of September during the **Schubertiade** summer music festival. This celebration of Schubert's work is hugely popular, so inquire about tickets months in advance. Information is available from **Schubertiade GmbH** (☎ 05576-720 91; www.schubertiade.at; Schweizer Strasse 1; A-6845 Hohenems) and the local **tourist office** (☎ 05512-35 70; ◷ 9am-noon & 2-7pm Mon-Fri, 10am-noon weekends during festival). The town is also home to a small but rewarding **Heimat Museum** (☎ 05512-29 88; adult/child €3/1; ◷ 2-4pm Tue, Thu, Sat & Sun May-Sep, 2-4pm Tue & Sat Oct, 2-4pm during Schubertiade); once home to the mayor, this 300-year-old house now contains traditional arts and crafts from the region and a handful of works by Angelika Kauffmann who had strong ties to the village.

Considering its size, Schwarzenberg has some wonderful places to sleep and eat. **Gasthof Hirschen** (☎ 05512-29 44; www.hirschenschwarzen berg.at - in German; s/d incl breakfast & 5-course dinner from €120/230; P) is a gorgeous alpine chalet with spacious, antique-filled rooms and a gourmet restaurants and **Gasthof Krone** (mains €7-12; ◷ dinner), opposite the town church, serves above-average Austrian cuisine in its romantic, tree-shaded garden.

Another 6km southeast from Schwarzenberg is **Bezau**, the unofficial capital of Bregenzerwald. It makes for an excellent base for exploring the area due to its central position, supermarkets, banks, range of accommodation and rural atmosphere. The **tourist office** (☎ 05514-21 29; bezau.tourismus@aon.at; Platz 39; ◷ 8.30am-12.30pm & 2-6pm Mon-Fri, 9am-noon Sat) in the heart of the town can provide information on walking, paragliding, skiing and accommodation. Further east, **Mellau** has skiing options in winter and walking in summer; a **gondola** (one-way/return summer €6.50/9, day pass winter €29.50) climbs to Alpe Rossstelle (1390m) year-round.

The road continues to head east towards the Arlberg and passes through **Au** and **Schoppernau**, two peaceful villages only a few kilometres apart. About halfway between the two is the **Diedamskopf cable car** (www.diedamskopf.at - in German; one-way/return €10/13.50), which climbs to 2090m. From here paragliders launch themselves into the air and walkers trundle their way back down the side of the mountain. Both places have tourist offices – see www.au-schoppernau.at for more details.

From Au, you have two choices: continue east to fashionable west Arlberg, or turn south and head for Bludenz. Scenically, both are rewarding journeys, passing through rugged alpine country on narrow, winding roads. About 9km along the southern route is the alpine settlement of **Damüls**, a centre for skiing and hiking. Its **tourist office** (☎ 05510-62 00; ◷ 8.30am-noon & 1.30-6pm Mon-Fri, 10am-noon Sat) can help with most enquiries and there's an accommodation board directly outside. While you're here, take time out to climb up to the **Pfarrkircke** (admission free; ◷ daylight hours); its interior is completely Gothic, with beautiful frescoes in fairly good condition considering their age.

Getting There & Away

There are eight direct buses daily to Bezau (€4, one hour) from Bregenz, but for most other destinations a change at Egg is required. A more direct option is from Dornbirn; Schwarzenberg (€2.80, 30 minutes), Bezau (€3.40, 50 minutes), Mellau

(€4, one hour), Au (€5.20, 70 minutes) and Schoppernau (€5.20, 80 minutes) can all be reached a couple of times daily (times vary from season to season). For Damüls (€6.60, 1¼ hours), a change at Au is required.

FELDKIRCH
☎ 05522 / pop 29,300
Of all the towns in Vorarlberg, Feldkirch has the prettiest medieval heart of them all. Its castle also ranks among the finest in the province.

Orientation & Information
The town centre is a few minutes' walk south of the train station (turn left upon exiting); here you'll find the **tourist office** (☎ 734 67; www.feldkirch.at; Schlossergasse 8; ☾ 8.30am-noon & 12.30-5.30pm Mon-Fri, 9am-noon Sat). The post office is opposite the train station.

Sights
The town retains an aura of its medieval past, with old patrician houses lining the squares in the centre, and a couple of towers surviving from the ancient fortifications. Both Neustadt and Marktplatz have arcaded walkways. **Domkirche St Nikolaus** (Cathedral of St Nicholas; admission free; ☾ daylight hours) has a large, forbidding interior which is saved by late Gothic features and vibrantly coloured stained glass. The painting on the side altar to the right of the main altar is by local boy Wolf Huber (1480–1539), a leading member of the Danube school.

The 12th-century **Schloss Schattenburg** dominates the town, and can be reached by stairs or road; extensive views can be enjoyed from its fortifications. Once the seat of the counts of Montfort until 1390, it now houses a small **museum** (☎ 719 82; Burggasse 1; adult/child €2/1; ☾ 9am-noon & 1-5pm Tue-Sun, closed Nov) with displays of religious art and historical artefacts.

Facing the castle across the town is **Ardetzenberg** (631m), a large, heavily forested hill. At its northern end is a **Wildpark** (animal park; admission free), where 200 different species roam.

Festivals & Events
Feldkirch showcases the **Feldkirch Festival**, which is held in the first two weeks of June and features plenty of classical music. Other festivals include a wine festival on the second weekend in July and a **Weihnachtsmarkt** (Christmas market) in December.

Sleeping
Feldkirch doesn't have a huge amount of accommodation options within its centre and most are on the expensive side. Private rooms are an economical option, but there are only a handful and all are outside the centre.

Jugendherberge (☎ 731 81; Reichsstrasse 111; dm €16, heating charge €2 Oct-Apr; P ⊠ ▦) This HI hostel is 1.5km north of the train station (bus No 60 trundles past) in a historic building with plenty of character that formerly served as an infirmary. It has been completely modernised inside and has above-par facilities.

Hotel Central Löwen (☎ 720 70; www.central-hotel-loewen.at; Schlossgraben 13; s/d €78/106; P ⊠) The modern rooms of this centrally located hotel are a good size, and guests can use the sauna and steam bath.

Waldcamping (☎ 743 08; www.waldcamping.at; Stadionstrasse 9, Gisingen; campsites per person/car/tent from €4.40/2.70/3.70; P) This camping ground offers a quiet, forest-fringed location for year-round camping; take bus No 2 from the train station to the last stop (3.5km).

Guesthouses are also worth looking at, including **Gasthof Engel** (☎ 720 56; Liechtensteiner Strasse 106; s/d €28/45; P) which is less than 2km southwest of the centre in Tisis. The tourist office posts a list of available rooms on a board outside its office.

Eating
Schlosswirtschaft Schattenburg (☎ 724 44; Burggasse 1; mains €8-20; ☾ lunch & dinner Tue-Sun) One of the top restaurants in town is this pleasant eatery on the ground floor of the castle. Good Austrian food and local wines are complimented by views of the town below.

Sangam (☎ 735 14; Reichsstrasse 171; mains €8-14; ☾ lunch & dinner) Not far north of the train station is this Indian and Chinese restaurant. On the face of it, the combination of such cuisines seems a little strange, but the tasty dishes soon dispel any doubts. Service is fast and friendly.

Gasthof Lingg (☎ 720 62; Kreuzgasse 10; mains €8-18; ☾ lunch & dinner Tue-Sun) Not far west of the tourist office is this fine restaurant, with a good location overlooking Marktplatz from Kreuzgasse, top-rate Austrian cuisine and an upmarket ambience.

For self-caterers, there is an **Interspar** (St Leonhards Platz) supermarket at the southern end of the town centre.

Getting There & Away

Bundesbuses to destinations around Vorarlberg depart from outside Feldkirch's train station. Trains head north to Bregenz (€4.60, 25 minutes) and Dornbirn (€3.40, 20 minutes), and southeast to Bludenz (€3.40, 15 minutes).

Feldkirch is the gateway to Liechtenstein's capital, Vaduz (€2.20, 40 minutes); a change at Schaans is normally necessary. Liechtenstein has a customs union with Switzerland, so you'll pass through Swiss customs before entering Liechtenstein.

BLUDENZ

☎ 05552 / pop 14,000

Bludenz is a pleasant, unassuming town, standing at the meeting point of five valleys: Klostertal, Montafon, Brandnertal, Grosswalsertal and Walgau. Like Feldkirch, its quaint, cobblestone medieval centre comes as a bit of a surprise; this is the legacy of the

town's heyday as the seat of the Habsburg governors from 1418 to 1806.

Orientation & Information

The town centre is on the northern bank of the Ill River. The **tourist office** (☎ 621 70; tourismus@bludenz.at; Werdenbergerstrasse 42; ☺ 8am-noon & 2-5.30pm Mon-Fri Sep-Jun, 8am-noon & 2-5.30pm Mon-Fri, 10am-noon Sat Jul & Aug) is five minutes' walk from the train station and has free Internet access.

Across the road from the tourist office is the town's **post office** (Werdenbergerstrasse 37), and not far east is a small pedestrian-only shopping area.

Sights & Activities

One of Bludenz's most enjoyable features can't even be seen. Almost anywhere you wander in the centre, the rich, enticing aroma of chocolate will fill your nostrils. The source of such divine smells is the **Suchard chocolate factory**; unfortunately there are no conducted tours but you can stock up on confectionary at its **shop** (☺ 9-11.30am & 1.30-4.30pm Mon-Thu, 9-11.30am & 1.30-4pm Fri). Chocolate also plays an important part in the children's **Milka Chocolate Festival** in mid-July, when 1000kg of the stuff is up for grabs in prizes. There's also music, games and plenty of kids too full of sugar to control.

For other attractions, join one of the free **city tours** organised by the tourist office; they depart from the tourist office at 10am on Thursday from mid-May till October. The most distinctive architectural feature in town is the parish church, **St Laurentiuskirche** (Church of St Lawrence; Mutterstrasse; admission free;

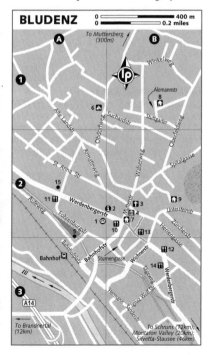

daylight hours), which was built in 1514 and has an unusual octagonal, onion-domed spire. There's also a **Stadtmuseum** (city museum; ☎ 636 21; Kirchgasse 9; admission €1.50; 3-5pm Mon-Sat Jun-early Sep) housing a small display on folk art and prehistoric finds.

About 1km north of the town centre, a **cable car** (☎ 627 52; Hinterplärsch; adult/senior/child one-way €5.60/4.80/3.50, return €9.30/8/5.90; 9am-6pm Sun-Thu, 9am-10pm Fri & Sat May-Oct, 9.30am-5.30pm Sat-Thu, 9.30am-10.30pm Fri Nov-Apr) rises to Muttersberg (1401m). If you don't want to walk it, catch the No 1 bus from in front of the train station to the cable car station.

Bludenz is a good base for exploring the surrounding valleys. There are 15 **skiing** areas within a 30km radius and ski bus transport to/from Bludenz is sometimes included in the price of ski passes. **Walking** and **cycling** are other popular activities; the tourist office has thick booklets on summer and winter outdoor pursuits.

Sleeping

The tourist office can help with accommodation and provide information on the town's *Gästekarte* (guest card). Private rooms are the best value for budget travellers, even though a surcharge of around €2.50 to €3.50 per day usually applies for stays under three days.

Landhaus Muther (☎ 657 04; www.landhaus-muther .at - in German; Alemannstrasse 4; s/d from €29/54; P) This peaceful and quiet small-scale guesthouse has views of the surrounding mountains and an exceptionally friendly welcome. Rooms could do with some renovation, but they are certainly tidy and sizable.

Schlosshotel (☎ 630 16-0; www.schlosshotel.cc; Schlossplatz 5; s/d from €69/105; P) Overlooking the town is this fine hotel, with modern rooms and balconies. Its **restaurant** (mains €8-19) is the best in Bludenz, and serves a token number of regional specialities in amongst a plethora of Austrian dishes; the large terrace is superb during warm summer evenings.

Herzog Friedrich (☎ 627 03-0; Mutterstrasse 6; s/d €37/76; P) Herzog Friedrich is a rather average hotel, but it is extremely central and most rooms are bright and accommodating.

Camping Seeberger (☎ 625 12; Obdorfweg 9; campsites per person/tent €5.35/6.90; P) This small camping ground is about 600m northwest of the centre and is in the heart of suburban Bludenz.

Eating

Nova Bräu (☎ 685 68; Werdenbergerstrasse 53; mains €8-16; 11am-2am Mon-Thu, 11am-4am Fri & Sat, 10am-3am Sun) This large restaurant-bar has many great features, and one bizarre one. It serves up traditional Austrian cuisine in its large indoor area or garden, alongside varieties of local Fohrenburger beer, which is hardly surprising as the brewery is across the road. At night, it becomes a lively meeting place for locals attracted by live music or other events several nights a week. For all intents and purposes, the front bar is an old sailing ship; why a nautical theme in the Alps is anyone's guess!

Remise (☎ 342 82; Am Raiffeisenplatz; mains €6-12; 10am-midnight Mon-Sat, 11am-6pm Sun) Occupying a small villa set back from the road, Remise is a relaxed café with imaginative food and outdoor seating.

Mezzo (☎ 675 42; Postplatz; coffee €3-5; 9am-6pm Mon-Sat) Mezzo is a modern, outdoor café directly outside the post office. On sunny days locals fill tables under big, bright umbrellas.

In the pedestrian-only area in the town centre is the Kronenhaus department store, with a **Spar** (Werdenbergerstrasse 34) supermarket. But for sit-down eating, continue walking west for four minutes to the **Sutterlüty** (Werdenbergerstrasse 5; snacks & meals €3-6; 7.40am-7pm Mon-Fri, 7.40am-5pm Sat) centre which houses a small café.

Getting There & Away

Bludenz is on the east–west InterCity (IC) express rail route, two hours from Innsbruck (€18.50, every two hours) and 45 minutes from Bregenz (€6.80, hourly). By regional train, Bregenz–Bludenz is 70 minutes (every 30 minutes).

The east–west A14 road passes just south of the Ill River and the town centre. Bundesbuses run down all five valleys around Bludenz.

MONTAFON

pop 15,540

Of the valleys accessible from Bludenz, **Montafon** (www.montafon.at) is not only the most developed, but also the most spectacular. The main road (the Silvretta Hochalpenstrasse) shadows the Ill River, winding its way under peaks which rise to well over 2500m, before itself climbing over the 2037m **Bielerhöhe Pass** via a series of tight switchbacks. At the top of the pass is the **Silvretta Stausee** (2030m), an ice-cold alpine lake, across which the snow-capped peaks of Piz Buin (3312m) and Klostertaler Egghorn (3120m) shine brightly on a sunny day. Boats ply the lake in the warmer months and two hotels guard the pass; the architecturally innovative **Silvretta-haus** (☎ 05558-42 46; silvrettahaus@illwerke.at; s/d €32/ 64; P) and homey **Piz Buin** (☎ 05558-42 31-0; www .pizbuin-silvretta.at - in German; s/d from €26/50; P 🖵). Both open from May/June to October.

Walking, cycling and **skiing** are all available along the length of Montafon. During winter, the **Montafon-Card** (3-/7-day pass €94/189) covers public transport and the 65 lifts in the valley; its summer equivalent is the **Montafon-Silvretta-Card** (€31.50/40.50).

The largest resort along the valley is **Schruns**, which has a **tourist office** (☎ 05556-721 66; www.schruns-tschagguns.at; Silvrettastrasse 6; ☺ 8am-6pm Mon-Fri, 9am-noon & 4-6pm Sat, 10.30am-noon Sun mid-Jun–Sep, 8am-5pm Mon-Fri Oct–mid-Jun) and **Hotel Taube** (☎ 05556-723 84; Silvrettastrasse 1; s/d from €24/48; P), a favourite hang-out of Ernest Hemingway in the 1920s. It's a good base from which to explore the area, as is **Tschagguns**, a resort in its own right directly opposite Schruns.

Getting There & Away

There are plenty of daily trains from Bludenz to Schruns (€2.20, 20 minutes), from where up to five buses daily continue onto Partenen (€4.40, 36 minutes) at the base of the Silvretta pass. From mid-July to mid-October, eight buses daily climb from Partenen to the Silvretta Stausee (€2.80, 35 minutes). The pass is controlled by a toll road, which costs €10.90/10.20 for cars/motorcycles.

WESTERN ARLBERG
☎ 05583

The Arlberg area is one of the top destinations for skiing in Austria. Though it straddles Vorarlberg and Tyrol, a general ski pass covers all of its resorts (see p332).

The northernmost and largest village (and also the prettiest) here is Lech (1450m). This upmarket resort is a favourite with royalty, film stars and anybody who likes to pretend to be such from behind dark glasses. Ski runs are mainly medium and easy, with some advanced off-piste possibilities. A cable car goes up Rüfikopf (2362m), but most of the lifts and runs are on the opposite side of the valley, on the Kriegerhorn (2178m)

VORARLBERG'S LITERARY CONNECTION

The small province of Vorarlberg has played host to some big names in literary circles through the years. Most famous of all is Ernest Hemingway, who spent two winters – in 1925 and 1926 – in the ski region of Montafon. While staying at Hotel Taube in Schruns with his wife (his mistress had to find accommodation elsewhere) he worked on the book *Fiesta* and his time here is briefly mentioned in *A Moveable Feast*.

Unable to re-enter Switzerland, seminal author James Joyce was stuck in Feldkirch where, legend has it, part of his epic *Ulysses* was planned. The town is certainly fond of Joyce, naming a street after him. Feldkirch's connection to famous authors doesn't stop with Joyce, though; Sir Arthur Conan Doyle spent years at the town's Jesuit boarding school, Stella Matutina, and Thomas Mann based one of the settings in his novel *Magic Mountain* on the very same school.

---

and Zuger Hochlicht (2377m). Aside from the normal skiing activities, heli-skiing can be arranged through the **Lech skischule** (Lech ski school; ☎ 2355; www.skischule-lech.com; from €280 for 4 persons). Lech's **tourist office** (☎ 2161-0; www. lech-zuers.at; ☺ 8am-noon & 2-6pm Mon-Sat, 8am-noon & 3-5pm Sun), in the centre of the resort, has brochure after brochure on skiing and walking possibilities and an accommodation board. It also organises walks from July to September for €15 (free with the local *Gästekarte*).

Six kilometres to the south lies **Zürs** (1716m), a smaller resort but with its own **tourist office** (☎ 2245; www.lech-zuers.at). There's an obligatory cable car running throughout the year, but in summer the resort has all the character of a dust bowl.

One kilometre south of Zürs is the **Flexen Pass** (1773m), after which the road splits: the western fork leads to **Stuben** (1407m), the eastern one to St Christoph and Tyrol.

Sleeping & Eating

Almost every street in Lech and Zürs is lined with accommodation, but it is still wise to book ahead in winter. The cheapest accommodation options are in private rooms or holiday apartments; all prices quoted here are from the winter high season.

Any of the following are fine bets, but there are over 150 similar places:

Haus Nenning (☎ 2408; haus_nenning@web.de; No 149; s/d €56/100; **P**) Convenient three-star place near the Schlegelkopf lift with wood-panelled rooms.

Pension Brunelle (☎ 2976; No 220; s/d €30/60; **P**) A bargain place near the centre of Lech, on the road towards Stubenbach, with small sun terrace and simple, variable rooms.

Pension Waldesruh (☎ 2402; waldesruh@vol.at; No 144; s/d €60/120; **P**) Chalet-style accommodation away from the main street; rooms neat and tidy, and come with balcony.

Most hotels have a fine, albeit slightly pricy, restaurant so it's easy enough to procure Austrian cuisine. Self-caterers can head to Spar on the main street. The following are all places independent of a hotel and open year-round:

Hûs Nr. 8 (☎ 3322-0; No 8; mains €8-16; ☻ lunch & dinner) Chalet with traditional food, small patio and kids' playground.

Don Enzo Due (☎ 2225; No 163; pizza & pasta €7-14; ☻ lunch & dinner) Good, simple pizzeria/trattoria just below the town's church.

Ambrosius Stüble (☎ 3365; No 229; mains €7-16; ☻ lunch & dinner) Near the Rüflikopf lift, with sunny terrace and regional and Austrian food.

Getting There & Away

There are buses that run between the resorts (see p332). For Bludenz and beyond, a change in Langen is required. Note also that snow has been known to block the Flexen Pass in winter. Lech can also be approached from the north, via the turning at Warth (1494m), but this is only viable in summer.

Directory

CONTENTS

PRACTICALITIES

- The metric system is used in Austria; decimals are indicated with commas and thousands with points (full stops).
- International newspapers are widely available in the larger cities; local big sellers include *Kronen Zeitung*, *Kurier* and *News*.
- Independent broadcaster ÖRF (Österreich-ischer Rundfunk; Austrian Broadcasting Corporation; www.orf.at) runs a total of 13 radio stations and two TV channels, ÖRF1 and ÖRF2. Programmes are generally dubbed rather than subtitled. Radio station FM4 (103.8 FM) has news in English from 6pm to 7pm.
- Film is widely available and reasonably priced; slide film is known as *Dia*.
- Electric sockets have the two small round holes common throughout Central Europe (220V AC, 50Hz). North American (110V) appliances will need a transformer.
- Videos in Austria use the PAL image registration system, as in the UK and Australia, and are not compatible with the NTSC system used in the USA, Canada and Japan.

ACCOMMODATION

Everything from simple mountain huts to five-star hotels fit for kings are offered in Austria. All accommodation is classified and graded in an efficient system, according to the type of establishment and the level of comfort it provides. Tourist offices invariably have extensive information on nearly all available accommodation, including prices and on-site amenities. Often the office will find and book rooms for little or no commission. They tend not to deal with the very cheapest places, but this service could save you a lot of time and effort, especially in popular destinations such as Vienna.

In Austria there has been a general move towards providing higher quality accommodation at higher prices. Rooms where guests have to use *Etagendouche* (shared showers) are gradually being upgraded and fitted with private showers. This makes life more difficult for budget travellers, who will increasingly have to rely on hostels.

It's wise to book ahead at all times, but reservations are definitely recommended in the high season: July and August, at Christmas and Easter and between December and April in ski areas. If the need for a flexible itinerary prevents you from making reservations a long way in advance, a telephone call the day before is better than nothing. However, some places will not accept telephone reservations. Confirmed reservations in writing are

DIRECTORY

binding on either side and compensation may be claimed if you do not take a reserved room or if a reserved room is unavailable.

Breakfast is normally included in hostel, pension and hotel prices. In mountain resorts, high-season prices can be up to double the prices charged in the low season (May and November, which fall between the summer and winter seasons). In towns, the difference may be as little as 10%, or even nothing in budget places.

In some resorts (not so often in cities) a *Gästekarte* (guest card) is issued to people who stay overnight. The card may offer useful discounts on things such as cable cars and admission prices. Check with a tourist office if you're not offered one at your resort accommodation – even campsites and youth hostels should be included in these schemes.

The listings in the accommodation sections of this guidebook are ordered from budget to mid-range to top-end options. The general price range split starts at up to €50 per double for budget options, anything between €50 and €100 per double for mid-range, and top-end is anything above that. As expected, Vienna is an exception to the rule: budget ends at €70, mid-range accommodation falls between €70 and €200, and top-end over and above €200.

Unless otherwise noted, we quote high-season rates throughout this book. Prices are for rooms with bathroom.

Before setting out, consider logging on to the following sites for more information:

www.campsite.at Comprehensive website listing around 70% of campsites in Austria; in a number of languages.

www.austrian-hotelreservation.at Regional listings of hotels, alpine huts and chalets and online booking service; also in English.

www.austria.info Austrian National Tourist Office website, with links to accommodation sites.

www.tiscover.at Hotels, rooms, last-minute deals and holiday packages, alongside general tourist information on Austria.

Alpine Huts

There are over 530 of these in the Austrian Alps that are maintained by the Österreichischer Alpenverein (ÖAV; Austrian Alpine Club; p52). Huts are found at altitudes of between 900m and 2700m and may be used by the general public. Meals or cooking facilities are often available. Bed prices

for non-members are around €24 to €30 in a dorm or €12 to €18 for a mattress on the floor. Members of the ÖAV or affiliated clubs pay half-price and have priority. Contact the ÖAV or a local tourist office for lists of huts and to make bookings.

Camping

Austria has over 400 camping grounds that offer users a range of facilities such as washing machines, electricity connection, onsite shops and, occasionally, cooking facilities. Camping gas canisters are widely available. Campsites are often scenically situated in an out-of-the-way place by a river or lake – fine if you're exploring the countryside but inconvenient if you want to sightsee in a town. For this reason, and because of the extra gear required, camping is more viable if you have your own transport. Prices can be as low as €3 per person or tent and as high as €8.

Some sites are open all year but the majority close in the winter. If demand is low in spring and autumn, some campsites shut, even though their literature says they are open, so telephone ahead to check during these periods. In high season, campsites may be full unless you reserve and higher prices may apply.

Free camping in camper vans is OK in autobahn rest areas and alongside other roads, as long as you're not causing an obstruction (in tents, however, it's illegal). Note that it's prohibited in urban and protected rural areas, and you may not set up camping equipment outside the van.

While in the country, pick up camping guides from the **Österreichischer Camping Club** (Austrian Camping Club; ☎ 01-713 6151; www .campingclub.at; Schubertring 1-3, A-1010 Vienna) and a *Camping Map Austria* from the Österreich Werbung (p359).

Homestays

Rooms in private houses are cheap and widely available. Prices are normally lower than pensions or hotels (anything from €18 to €40 per double), but so is the level of service. However, rooms are invariably homely and comfy, the owners friendly and accommodating and the breakfasts large. Normally every town has a least two or three private rooms available; otherwise look for *Privat Zimmer* (private room) or *Zimmer Frei* (room free) signs.

In rural areas, rooms in *Bauernhof* (farmhouses) are a great accommodation alternative. Facilities differ little from private rooms, apart from the fact that you'll be staying on a working farm. They are becoming increasing popular with both Austrians and foreigners and it's advisable to book in advance for July and August. Many of the regional tourist offices (p359) produce handy booklets with farmhouse listings.

Hostels

Austria is dotted with *Jugendherberge* or *Jugendgästehaus* (hostels), most of which maintain high standards. Facilities are more often than not excellent: four- to six-bed dorms with shower/toilet are the norm, some places have double rooms or family rooms and Internet facilities, and a restaurant or café are commonplace.

Austria has over 100 hostels affiliated with Hostelling International (HI), plus a smattering of privately owned hostels. HI hostels are run by two hostel organisations (either can provide information on all HI hostels):

Österreichischer Jugendherbergsverband (ÖJHV;
☎ 533 53 53; www.oejhv.or.at; 01, Schottenring 28;
🕑 9am-5pm Mon-Thu, 9am-3pm Fri)
Österreichischer Jugendherbergswerk (ÖJHW; ☎ 533 18 33; www.oejhw.at; 01, Helferstorferstrasse 4;
🕑 9.30am-6pm Mon-Fri).

Gästekartes are always required, except in a few private hostels. It's cheaper to become a member in your home country than to join when you get to Austria. Non-members pay a surcharge of €3 per night for a *Gästekarte,* but after six nights the guest card counts as a full membership card. Most hostels accept reservations by telephone or email and some are part of the worldwide computer reservations system. Dorm prices range from €14 to €19 per night.

Cheap dorm-style accommodation is sometimes available in ski resorts even if there is no hostel. Look for *Touristenlager* or *Matratzenlager* (dorm); unfortunately, such accommodation might only be offered to pre-booked groups.

Hotels & Pensions

Pensions and hotels (often known as *Gästehäuse* or *Gasthöfe*) are rated from one to five stars depending on the facilities they offer. However, as the criteria are different you can't assume that a three-star pension is equivalent to a three-star hotel. Pensions tend to be smaller than hotels and usually provide a more personal service, less standardised fixtures and fittings and bigger-sized rooms. Hotels invariably offer more services, including bars, restaurants and garage parking, but if none of that matters to you, stick with the pensions.

With very few exceptions, rooms in hotels and pensions are clean and adequately appointed; expect to pay a minimum of around €25/45 for a single/double room, more in the bigger cities. If business is slow, mid-range and top-end hotels (and to a lesser extent pensions) may be willing to negotiate on prices. It's always worth asking for a special deal as prices can come down quite substantially. Some places will also offer special weekend rates, or two nights for the price of one. Credit cards are rarely accepted by cheaper places.

In low-budget accommodation, a room advertised as having a private shower may mean that it has a shower cubicle rather than a proper en suite bathroom.

Where there is a telephone in the room it's usually direct-dial, but this will still be more expensive than using a public telephone. TVs are almost invariably hooked up to satellite or cable. Higher-quality rooms will usually have the added bonus of a mini-bar.

Usually, meals are available, either for guests only, or more often, in a public restaurant on site. A pension that supplies breakfast only is known as a *Frühstückspension;* the hotel equivalent is *Hotel-Garni.* Other hotels and pensions will offer the option of paying for half board (where breakfast and one main meal is provided) or even full board (where all meals are provided). In budget places, breakfast is basic, usually consisting of only a drink, bread rolls, butter, cheese spread and jam. As you pay more, breakfast gets better: in two-star places it's usually *erweitert* ('extended' to include more choices) and in places with three stars or more it's usually buffet style. A typical buffet will include cereals, juices and a selection of cold meats and cheeses – maybe even (in top places) hot food such as scrambled eggs, sausage and bacon. In five-star hotels breakfast generally costs extra, but may be included in special, lower weekend rates.

Rental Accommodation

Ferienwohnungen (self-catering holiday apartments) are very common in Austrian mountain resorts, though it is often necessary to book these well in advance. The best idea is to contact a local tourist office for lists and prices.

University Accommodation

Studentenheime (student residences) are available to tourists over university summer breaks (from the beginning of July to around the end of September). During university terms the kitchen and dining room on each floor are open, but when they're used as seasonal hotels these useful facilities generally remain locked. Rooms are perfectly OK but nothing fancy; some have a private bathroom. Expect single beds (though beds may be placed together in double rooms), a work desk and a wardrobe. The widest selection is in Vienna, but look for them also in Graz, Salzburg and Innsbruck. Prices per person are likely to range from €20 to €35 and sometimes include breakfast.

ACTIVITIES

See the Outdoor Activities chapter p52 for details on walking, skiing, cycling and other outdoor pursuits in Austria.

BUSINESS HOURS

Offices and government departments generally open from 8am to 3.30pm, 4pm or 5pm Monday to Friday. There are no real restrictions on shop opening hours but most open between 9am and 6pm Monday to Friday and until 1pm Saturday (until 5pm in Vienna).

Banking hours are from 8am or 9am until 3pm Monday to Friday, and there are extended hours to 5.30pm on Thursdays. Many of the smaller branches close from 12.30pm to 1.30pm for lunch. Most post offices open for business from 8am to noon and 2pm to 6pm Monday to Friday; some also open on Saturday from 8am to noon. Restaurants serve lunch between 11am and 3pm and dinner from 6pm to midnight, and often close in between. Cafés tend to open at around 7.30am and shut up shop at about 8pm; pubs and bars close anywhere between midnight and about 4am throughout the week.

CHILDREN

'Seen and not heard' was traditionally the general Austrian attitude towards children, but things have changed over the past few years; it seems that children who experienced such stern discipline have now grown up and are loath to put their own kids through the same treatment. While it hasn't come up roses in every nook and cranny of the country, you shouldn't come across any big hitches travelling with children in Austria; children are welcome at tourist attractions, restaurants and hotels.

Not only has the attitude of parents changed, but so has that of the establishment. Regional tourist offices have attuned part of their focus and now produce brochures aimed directly at families. Museums, parks and theatres often have programs for children over the summer holiday periods and local councils occasionally put on special events and festivals for the little ones.

Log on to www.kinderhotels.at for information on child-friendly hotels throughout the country. For helpful travelling tips, pick up a copy of Lonely Planet's *Travel with Children* by Cathy Lanigan.

Practicalities

Facilities are definitely improving throughout the country but not in all directions. Some restaurants do have children's menus but may not have high chairs or nappy-changing facilities. In general, only mid-range to top-end hotels have cots and can arrange daycare.

In the bigger cities, breast feeding in public draws no stares. Everything you need for babies, such as formula and disposable nappies, is widely available. Rental car companies can arrange safety seats. Newer public transport, such as trams and buses in Vienna, are easily accessible for buggies and prams, but the older models can prove a nightmare. During the summer holidays, children under the age of 15 travel free on Vienna's transport system (children up to the age of six always travel free).

Sights & Activities

With its parks, playgrounds and great outdoors, Austria has plenty to keep the kids entertained. Vienna has two great kids' museums and loads of swimming locations; see p104) for more details. Outside the capital, Graz has the only museum directed at children, FriDa & FreD (p192). Its Schloss-berg Cave Railway (p192) will also enter-tain the little tykes. Closer to the capital, shallow Neusiedler See (p159) is a perfect place to holiday with children. In Linz, Ars Electronica (p171) and the Pöstlingberg (p171) are fine attractions for the kids, as is the Minimundus miniature park (p259) in Klagenfurt. Once the kids are finished with Minimundus, the region's lakes are an enticing destination, as is Die Spur des Einhorns (p268) in Friesach. Austrians love their puppets; look for them at the puppet museums around Villach (p267) or at the Marionettentheater (p248) in Salzburg.

Trips underground also keep the kids amused; the Erzberg mine (p207) in Styria and the salt mines (p217) of Salzkammer-gut are classic examples.

CLIMATE CHARTS

Austria lies within the Central European climatic zone, though the eastern part of the country has what is called a Continen-tal Pannonian climate, characterised by hot summers and mild winters. To the west, the Alps tend to draw the clouds, though the al-pine valleys often escape much of the down-fall. The *Föhn*, a hot, dry wind that sweeps down from the mountains, mainly in early spring and autumn – it can be rather un-comfortable for some people and often has a bad reputation among Austrians.

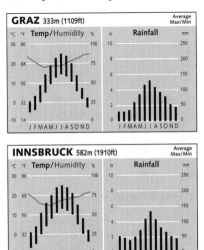

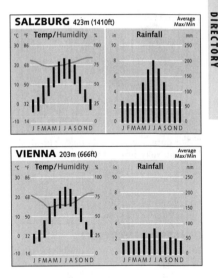

The climate charts show average tem-peratures and rainfall in the larger cities, but these can vary wildly from year to year. For instance, in the summer of 2002 the country was hit by severe flooding, and in 2003 temperatures soared to uncomfort-able levels.

COURSES

Many places offer German courses, includ-ing some of Austria's universities, and they can usually offer the option of accommo-dation for the duration. Two of the better known course providers in Vienna are:
Berlitz (Map pp83–5; ☎ 512 82 86; www.berlitz.at; 01, Graben 13, Vienna; ☺ 8am-8pm Mon-Fri) Offers private, intensive day and evening courses and has four offices in Vienna.
Inlingua Sprachschule (☎ 512 22 25; www.inlingua.at; 01, Neuer Markt 1, Vienna; ☺ 9am-6pm Mon-Fri) Courses run for a minimum of two weeks and can either be taken dur-ing the day or at night. Classes are limited to eight students and individual tuition is also available.

In Innsbruck, try the following:
Innsbruck University (☎ 587 233; ihd@uibk.ac.at; Innrain 52) Intensive courses in July and August.
Inlingua (☎ 562 031; inlingua@tirol.com; Heilig-Geist Strasse 21) Year-round courses, usually in small groups.

Check the *Gelben Seiten* (yellow pages) under *Sprachschulen* for more listings in other towns and cities.

DIRECTORY

CUSTOMS
Theoretically there is no restriction on what you can bring into Austria from other EU states. However, to ensure these remain for personal use, guideline limits are 800 cigarettes, 200 cigars, 1kg tobacco, 10L of spirits, 90L of wine, 110L of beer and 20L of other alcoholic beverages. The same quantity can be taken out of Austria, as long as you are travelling to another EU country.

For duty-free purchases made outside the EU, you may bring into Austria 200 cigarettes or 50 cigars or 250g tobacco, plus 2L of wine and 1L of spirits. Items such as weapons, drugs (both legal and illegal), meat, certain plant materials and animal products are subject to stricter customs control.

DANGERS & ANNOYANCES
Austria is one of the safest countries to travel in and crime rates are low by international standards, but you should always be security conscious. Be wary of leaving valuables in hotel rooms; management will look after expensive items if you ask them, even in hostels. Don't leave valuables in cars, especially overnight. In general, let common sense prevail and don't make it easy for thieves by loosely carrying cameras and jewellery around.

In the event of theft or loss, get a police report – this will be necessary for you to claim on your travel insurance. Your consulate should be able to help replace documents if you're left in a desperate situation.

DISABLED TRAVELLERS
Austria is better than most countries for *Behinderte* (disabled) travellers but it's still not perfect. Hotels over two stars invariably have lifts, but some only from the first floor, and while ramps are reasonably widespread in larger cities, so are awkward cobblestone streets and stairs.

Facilities on public transport are also hit-and-miss; the U-Bahn system in Vienna is well geared for disabled travellers, as are many trams around the country, but buses can prove a nightmare. The more commonly used traffic lights 'bleep' when pedestrians can safely cross. Disabled people may also receive reductions on admission prices and many transport facilities.

Local tourist offices can provide advice and information on hotels and restaurants with disabled access, plus addresses of hospitals, medical equipment shops, parking places, toilets and much more. The detailed pamphlet, *Vienna for Visitors with Disabilities*, from Tourist Info Wien (p89), is available in German or English.

In 2000 the EU issued a standardised Blue Badge granting EU disabled drivers certain parking rights, which in Austria means they can park free in blue zones.

Organisations
There is no national disabled organisation in Austria, but the regional tourist offices or any of the following can be contacted for more information:

Behinderten Selbsthilfe Gruppe (☎ 03332-65 405; www.bsgh.at; Presslgasse 5, 8320 Hartberg)

Bizeps (Map p86; ☎ 523 89 21; www.bizeps.at; 07, Kaiserstrasse 55/3/4a, Vienna)

Upper Austria tourist office (www.oberoesterreich.at /nohandicap) Information (in German) on contacts, guides and wheelchair hire.

DISCOUNT CARDS
There are various discount cards available throughout Austria, covering either a region of a province or an entire province. Some are free and provide discounts at hotels and sights, while others must be purchased but may give you free entry to attractions and include public transport. Contact provincial tourist offices for details.

Examples of such discount cards include the Neusiedler See Gästekarte in Burgenland, which provides free admission to swimming areas and museums, plus free use of public transport, and the Salzburg Card (from €19), which gives free entry to every sight in town and reduced entry to a further 24 attractions plus free public transport for the duration.

Senior Cards
Senior travellers are entitled to many discounts on the cost of such things as public transport and museum admission, provided you show proof of age. The minimum qualifying age for Austrians is 65 for men and 60 for women.

Student & Youth Cards
International Student Identity Cards (ISIC) and Euro26 cards will get you discounts at most museums, galleries and theatres. You may even get a discount on air, bus and train tickets.

EMBASSIES & CONSULATES
Austrian Embassies & Consulates

The Austrian Foreign Ministry website (www
.bmaa.gv.at) has a complete list of embassies
and consulates. It's in German only, but it's
quite easy to navigate.

Australia (☎ 02-6295 1376; www.austriaemb.org.au;
12 Talbot St, Forrest, Canberra, ACT 2603)

Canada (☎ 613-789 1444; www.austro.org; 445 Wilbrod
St, Ottawa, Ontario K1N 6M7)

Czech Republic (☎ 257 09 05 11; www.austria.cz; Viktora
Huga 10, CZ-15115 Prag 5)

France (☎ 01-40 63 30 63; paris-ob@bmaa.gv.at; 6, Rue
Fabert, F-75007 Paris)

Ireland (☎ 715 42 46; vienna@iveagh.irlgov.ie; 01, 5th
floor, Rotenturmstraße 16-18)

Germany (☎ 030-202 87-0; www.oesterreichische
-botschaft.de; Stauffenbergstraße 1, D-10785 Berlin)

Hungary (☎ 01-479 70-10; www.austrian-embassy.hu;
Benczúrutca 16, 1068 Budapest)

Italy (☎ 06-844 01 41; www.austria.it; Via Pergolesi 3,
I-00198 Rom)

New Zealand (consulate only; ☎ 04-499 6393; diessl@
ihug.co.nz; Level 2, Willbank House, 57 Willis St, Wellington)

Slovakia (☎ 02-59 30 15 00; www.embassyaustria.sk;
Venturska 10, SK-81101 Bratislava)

Slovenia (☎ 01-479 07 00; laibach-ob@bmaa.gv.at;
Presernova cesta 23, SI-1000 Ljubljana)

The Netherlands (☎ 070-324 54 70; den-haag-ob@bmaa
.gv.at; van Alkemadelaan 342, 2597 AS Den Haag)

UK (☎ 020-7235 3731; www.austria.org.uk; 18 Belgrave
Mews West, London SW1X 8HU)

USA (☎ 202-895 6700; washington-ob@bmaa.gv.at;
3524 International Court NW, Washington, DC 20008)

Embassies & Consulates in Austria

All the embassies and consulates listed below
are located in Vienna. For a complete listing of embassies and consulates, look in the
Austrian telephone book under *Botschaften*
(embassies) or *Konsulate* (consulates).

Australia (Map pp83-5; ☎ 506 74-0; www.australian
-embassy.at; 04, Mattiellistrasse 2)

Canada (Map pp83–5; ☎ 531 38-3000; www.kanada.at;
01, Laurenzerberg 2)

Czech Republic (☎ 894 321 25; www.mzv.cz/vienna;
14, Penzingerstrasse 11-13)

France (☎ 502 75 200 12; www.consulfrance-vienne.org;
01, Wipplinger Strasse 24-26)

Germany (Map pp83–5; ☎ 711 54-0; www.deubowien
.at; 03, Metternichgasse 3)

Hungary (Map pp83–5; ☎ 537 80-300; kom@huembvie
.at; 01, Bankgasse 4-6)

Ireland (☎ 01-269 4577; dublin-ob@bmaa.gv.at; 15
Ailesbury Court Apartments, 93 Ailesbury Rd, Dublin 4)

Italy (☎ 713 56 71; www.ambitaliavienna.org; 03,
Ungarngasse 43)

New Zealand (Map pp78–9; ☎ 318 85 08; www.nzem
bassy.com; 23, Karl-Tornay-Gasse 34; honourary consulate)

Slovakia (☎ 318 90 55; www.vienna.mfa.sk; 19,
Armbrustergasse 24)

Slovenia (☎ 585 22 40; 01, Nibelungengasse 13)

Switzerland (☎ 795 05-0; www.eda.admin.ch/wien;
03, Prinz Eugen Strasse 7)

The Netherlands (☎ 01-589 39; www.netherlands
-embassy.at; 01, 7th floor, Opernring 5)

UK (Map pp80–2; ☎ 716 13-0; www.britishembassy.at;
03, Jaurèsgasse 12)

USA (Map pp83–5; ☎ 319 39; www.usembassy.at; 4th
floor, Hotel Marriott, 01, Gartenbaupromenade 2-4)

FESTIVALS & EVENTS

Most festivals and cultural events are small-
scale local affairs, so it's worth checking
with local tourist offices or the Österreich
Werbung (Austrian National Tourist Office; ANTO; p359), which compiles a list
of annual and one-off events taking place
in Austria. The cycle of music festivals
throughout the country is almost unceas-
ing, and religious holidays provide an opportunity to stage colourful processions.
Corpus Christi (the second Thursday after
Whitsunday) brings carnivals, including
some held on lakes in the Salzkammergut.
National Day on 26 October inspires various
events, often accompanied by much patriotic flag-waving.

More details of specific events are given
in the text, but here's a selection of annual
highlights throughout the country.

January

New Year concerts (1 January) The new year is welcomed
throughout Austria with classical concerts. The Vienna
Philharmonic's performance in the Staatsoper is the most
celebrated.

Perchtenlaufen (5 to 6 January) Celebrated across much
of western Austria, this festival promotes good fortune and
a prosperous harvest for the forthcoming year. Locals dress
as Perchten (spirits crowned with elaborate headdresses)
and parade through the streets. Salzkammergut's equivalent is Glöckerlaufen.

February

Fasching (Shrovetide Carnival; 11 November to Shrove
Tuesday) Austria's carnival season, which really only gets
going at the end of January/beginning of February, when
people parade around in fancy dress and party till the wee
small hours. Look for *Fasching Krapfen* (a sweet bun filled
with jam) during this time.

March or April
Easter Easter is marked by long-weekend or week-long holidays and family gatherings.

May
Maypole Day (1 May) Colourful, lively countrywide affairs accompanied by maypoles, plenty of alcohol and unabandoned merriment.

June
Midsummer Night (21 June) A celebration of the summer solstice, with hilltop bonfires and partying through the night.

July & August
Music Festivals Classical, jazz and rock festivals take place throughout the country over summer.

October
Cattle Roundup (early October) In the alpine areas the coming of autumn brings the cattle herds down out of the mountains. The event is marked with various festivals.
Wine Harvest (all October) Styria, Burgenland and Lower Austria mark the grape harvest with bottle after bottle of wine and folk music.

November
Allerheiligen (All Saints' Day; 1 November) Austrians flock to cemeteries throughout the country to pay their respects to the dead.
St Martin's Day (11 November) The day of St Martin of Tours is marked with feasts of goose and wine.

December
St Nicholas Day (5 to 6 December) More for the kids, this day sees St Nicholas drift from house to house handing out presents to good children. He is often accompanied by the devil (Krampus), who punishes the bad children (which never happens). In many places, this day is also marked by **Krampuslaufen**: young men dress up as demons in heavy, wood masks and run through the streets, terrorising villagers along the way.
Weihnacht (Christmas; 25 December) A quiet family affair, aside from the *Christkindlmärkte* (Christmas markets), which take place throughout the country from early December till the 24th.

FOOD
A full rundown on local cuisine, drinks, dos and don'ts and when and where to eat can be found in the Food & Drink chapter (p66). As ballpark figures, budget mains are anything up to €8, mid-range up to €12 and top end anything over and above that.

GAY & LESBIAN TRAVELLERS
Vienna is reasonably tolerant towards gays and lesbians, more so than the rest of Austria. The situation is improving all the time; recently, the restricting federal statute 209, which set the consenting age between men at 18 (it is 14 for heterosexuals), was repealed. There is no set age of consent for lesbian sex, apparently because the legislators decided there was no discernible difference between mutual washing of bodily parts and intimate sexual contact. While lesbians welcome the lack of legislation, they see this as a typical (male) denial of female sexuality.

The 'Gay & Lesbian Vienna' boxed text (p106) has specific listings of publications, organisations, hotels and bars for gays and lesbians. Online information (in German) can be found at www.gayboy.at, www.rainbow.or.at, www.gay.at and www.gayguide.at. The Spartacus International Gay Guide, published by Bruno Gmünder (Berlin), is a good international directory of gay entertainment venues worldwide (mainly for men).

HOLIDAYS
Basically everything shuts down on public holidays. The only establishments open are bars, cafés and restaurants and even some of these refuse to open their doors. Museums like to confuse things – some stay closed while others are open and free. The big school break is in July and August. This is a time when most families go on holiday so you'll find some places, like cities, a little quieter and others, such as popular holiday destinations, busier. Avoid ski breaks during much of February; school pupils have a week off during that time and invariably the ski slopes are full to overflowing with kids and parents.

The public holidays in Austria are:
New Year's Day (Neujahr) 1 January
Epiphany (Heilige Drei Könige) 6 January
Easter Monday (Ostermontag)
Labour Day (Tag der Arbeit) 1 May
Whit Monday (Pfingstmontag) 6th Monday after Easter
Ascension Day (Christi Himmelfahrt) 6th Thursday after Easter
Corpus Christi (Fronleichnam) 2nd Thursday after Whitsunday
Assumption (Maria Himmelfahrt) 15 August
National Day (Nationalfeiertag) 26 October

All Saints' Day (Allerheiligen) 1 November
Immaculate Conception (Mariä Empfängnis) 8 December
Christmas Day (Christfest) 25 December
St Stephen's Day (Stephanitag) 26 December

INSURANCE

Organising a travel insurance policy to cover theft, loss and medical problems is an essential part of planning for your trip. There is a wide variety of policies available, so check the small print.

Some policies specifically exclude 'dangerous activities', which can include skiing, motorcycling, rock climbing, canoeing and even hiking. If you're planning on doing any of these activities, be sure to choose a policy that covers you.

You may prefer a policy that pays doctors or hospitals directly rather than having to pay on the spot and claim later. If you have to claim later make sure you keep all documentation. Some policies ask you to call back (reverse charges) to a centre in your home country where an immediate assessment of your problem is made.

Check that the policy covers ambulances or an emergency flight home.

See p374 for more on health insurance. For information on car rental insurance, see p370.

INTERNET ACCESS

All top hotels have plugs for connecting your laptop to the Internet, but as yet it's not possible to organise an ISP in Austria for a short period (minimum contracts run for 12 months) so you'll have to arrange one from home. AOL's access number in Vienna is ☎ 01-585 84 83, Compuserve's ☎ 01-899 33-0 and Eunet's ☎ 180-570 40 70

Public Internet access is well covered across the country; for details of specific Internet cafés see the destination chapters. Prices are generally around €4 to €8 per hour. If there are no cafés in town, its worth checking with the local library; some have computer terminals connected to the Internet which are often free to use. Remember to take some form of ID with you. Otherwise some towns may have a call box with Internet access.

LEGAL MATTERS

Austria offers the level of civil and legal rights you would expect of any industrialised Western nation. If you are arrested, the police must inform you of your rights in a language that you understand.

In Austria, legal offences are divided into two categories: criminal *Gerichtdelikt* (criminal) and *Verwaltungsübertretung* (administrative). If you are suspected of having committed a criminal offence (such as assault or theft) you can be detained for a maximum of 48 hours before you are committed for trial. If you are arrested for a less serious, administrative offence, such as being drunk and disorderly or committing a breach of the peace, you will be released within 24 hours.

Drunken driving is an administrative matter, even if you have an accident. However, if someone is hurt in the accident it becomes a criminal offence. Possession of a controlled drug is usually a criminal offence but if, for example, you have a small amount of dope that is considered to be for personal use only (there's no hard and fast rule on quantity) you may merely be cautioned and released without being charged. Possession of a large amount of dope (around 300g) or dealing (especially to children) could result in a five-year prison term. Prostitution is legal provided prostitutes are registered and have obtained a permit.

If you are arrested, you have the right to make one phone call to 'a person in your confidence' within Austria, and another to inform legal counsel. If you can't afford legal representation, you can apply to the judge in writing for legal aid.

Free advice is given on legal matters in some towns, for example during special sessions at Vienna's *Bezirksgerichte* (district courts). As a foreigner, your best bet when encountering legal problems is to contact your national consulate (see p353).

MAPS

Freytag & Berndt of Vienna offers the most comprehensive coverage of the country. It publishes good town maps (1:10,000 to 1:25,000 scale) and has a *Wanderkarte* series for walkers, mostly on a 1:50,000 scale. Motorists should consider buying its *Österreich Touring* road atlas; this covers Austria (1:150,000) and 48 Austrian towns. If this is too detailed then their *Österreich* road map (1:500,000) will suffice. Extremely detailed walking maps are produced by the ÖAV, on a scale of 1:25,000. Kompass also has a range of excellent walking maps. The most detailed maps, however, are produced by the Bundesamt für Eich- und Vermessungswesen (BEV; Federal Office for Calibration and Measurement); their country-wide and regional maps are available in good bookshops and map stores.

Bikeline maps are recommended for those travelling round the country by bicycle; eight maps (1:100,000 or 1:75,000) cover the most popular areas for cycling and two delve into mountain biking in Carinthia and the Hohe Tauern National Park.

For getting around cities, maps provided by tourist offices, in conjunction with the maps in this book, are generally adequate. These are usually free, but where there's a charge you can probably make do with the hotel map instead.

MONEY

Like other members of the European Monetary Union (EMU), Austria's currency is the euro, which is divided into 100 cents. There are coins for one, two, five, 10, 20 and 50 cents and for €1 and €2. Notes come in denominations of €5, €10, €20, €50, €100, €200 and €500. The Quick Reference page inside the front cover lists exchange rates.

ATMs

In Austria ATMs are known as *Bankomats*. They are extremely common and are accessible 24 hours a day. Even villages should have at least one machine; look for the sign showing blue and green horizontal stripes. ATMs are linked up internationally, have English instructions and are usually limited to daily withdrawals of €400 with credit and debit cards.

Check with your home bank before travelling to see how much the charge is for using a *Bankomat* in Vienna; normally there's no commission to pay at the Austrian end.

Cash

With the plethora of ATMs across the length and breadth of Austria, the practice of carrying large amounts of cash around has become obsolete. It is however worth keeping a small amount in a safe place for emergencies.

Credit Cards

Visa, EuroCard and MasterCard are accepted a little more widely than AmEx and Diners

Club, although a surprising number of shops and restaurants refuse to accept any credit cards at all. Plush shops and restaurants will accept cards, though, and the same applies for hotels. Train tickets can be bought by credit card in main stations. Credit cards allow you to get cash advances at most banks.

For lost or stolen credit cards, call the following:

AmEx	☎ 0800 900 940
Diners Club	☎ 01-501 35 14
MasterCard	☎ 01-717 01 4500
Visa	☎ 01-711 11 770

Moneychangers

Banks are the best places to exchange cash, but it pays to shop around as exchange rates and commission charges can vary a little between them. Normally there is a minimum commission charge of €2 to €3.50, so try to exchange your money in large amounts to save on multiple charges.

Wechselstuben (money-exchange offices) are usually found in the centre of large cities or at train stations. They have the advantage of longer opening hours but quite often their exchange rates are un-competitive and commission charges high. AmEx offices and their representatives charge €7 commission for amounts up to €100, €12 up to €500, €15 up to €1000 and 1.5% for anything over and above €1000.

Taxes & Refunds

Mehrwertsteuer (*MWST*; value-added tax) in Austria is set at 20% for most goods. Prices are always displayed inclusive of all taxes.

All non-EU tourists are entitled to a refund of the MWST on single purchases costing over €75. To claim the tax, a U34 form or tax-free cheque and envelope must be completed by the shop at the time of purchase (show your passport), and then stamped by border officials when you leave the EU. To be eligible for a tax refund, goods must be taken out of the country within three months of the date of purchase. The airports at Vienna, Salzburg, Innsbruck, Linz and Graz have a counter for payment of instant refunds. There are also counters at major border crossings. The refund is best claimed as you leave the EU, otherwise you will have to track down an international refund office or claim by post from your home country.

Before making a purchase, ensure the shop has the required paperwork; some places display a 'Global Refund Tax Free Shopping' sticker. Also confirm the value of the refund; it's usually advertised as 13% (which is the refund of the 20% standard rate of value-added tax after various commissions have been taken), though it may vary for certain categories of goods.

Tipping

Tipping is a part of everyday life in Austria; tips are generally expected at restaurants, bars and cafés and in taxis. It's customary to add a 10% tip, or round up the bill, while taxi drivers will expect around 10% extra. Tips are handed over at the time of payment; add the bill and tip together and pass it over in one lump sum. It also doesn't hurt to tip hairdressers, hotel porters, cloak room attendants, cleaning staff and tour guides one or two euros.

Travellers Cheques

All major travellers cheques are equally widely accepted, though you may want to use AmEx, Visa or Thomas Cook because of their 'instant replacement' policies. A record of the cheque numbers and the initial purchase details is vital when it comes to replacing lost cheques. Without this, you may well find that 'instant' is a very long time indeed. You should also keep a record of which cheques you have cashed. Keep these details separate from the cheques.

There is no commission on changing up to €1000 in AmEx travellers cheques at AmEx offices; for anything over €1000, 0.75% commission is applied. Non-AmEx cheques up to €100 attract €7 commission, up to €500 requires €12 commission. Banks typically charge €7 or more to exchange travellers cheques. Avoid changing a lot of low-value cheques as commission costs will be higher. Big hotels also change money, but rates are invariably poor. Look especially carefully at the commission rates charged by exchange booths; they can be quite reasonable or ridiculously high.

POST

Austria's postal service (www.post.at) is easy to use and reliable. *Postämter* (post offices) are commonplace, as are bright yellow post boxes. Stamps can also be bought at *Tabak*

(tobacconist) shops. Sending letters (up to 20g) within Austria or Europe costs €0.55 and worldwide €1.25. The normal weight limit for *Briefsendung* (letter post) is 2kg; anything over this limit will be sent as a package (from €3.70 to anywhere within Austria, from €11.75 to anywhere else). Up to 20kg can be sent via *Erdwegpakete* (surface mail).

For post restante, address letters *Postlagernde Sendungen* rather than *Postlagernde Briefe* as the former is the preferred term in Austria. Mail can be sent care of any post office and is held for a month; a passport must be shown on collection.

SHOPPING

Austria is a good place to pick up high-quality items, such as jewellery, glassware and crystalware, ceramics, pottery, wood-carvings, wrought-iron work and textiles. There are also many antique shops throughout the country, with a particular concentration in Vienna. Naturally, purchasing these types of gifts doesn't come cheap.

Each large city has its well-known shopping street. Vienna has Kärntner and Mariahilfer Strasse; Graz has Herrengasse and Annenstrasse; Linz has Landstrasse; Salzburg has Getreidegasse and Linzergasse; and Innsbruck has Maria-Theresien-Strasse.

Don't overlook the many markets that flourish throughout the entire country; alongside local produce you may find some local folk-art gems.

For special reductions, look for *Aktion* (sales promotion) signs. Prices are fixed in shops, but it can't hurt to ask for 'a discount for cash' if you're making several purchases. Bargain hard in flea markets. In theory, hotel prices are not negotiable; in practice, you can often haggle for a better rate in the low season or if you're staying more than a few days.

Top Viennese hotels dispense a free booklet called *Shopping in Vienna* that details all sorts of shopping outlets; Graz and Salzburg each have their own version.

SOLO TRAVELLERS

There's no stigma attached to travelling solo in Austria. Many hostels, pensions and hotels have a couple of single rooms available and they're generally a little more than half the price of a double room.

Making contact with the locals is relatively easy in smaller towns and cities if you know

DIRECTORY

a little German; people seem eager to know where you're from and what brought you there. Without German, things are a little harder, but definitely not impossible. Many people speak good English, or at least enough to hold a conversation for an hour or two. In the bigger cities, pseudo-Irish and English pubs are havens for expats and Austrians keen on Guinness and an English chat.

TELEPHONE

Austria's country code is ☎ 0043. **Telekom Austria** (☎ 0800-100 100; www.telekom.at) is Austria's main telecommunications provider and maintains public telephones (particularly inside or outside post offices) throughout the country. These take either coins or phonecards and a minimum of 20 cents is required to make a local call. Every post office has a phone booth where both international and national calls can be made; rates are cheaper from 6pm to 8am Monday to Friday and on weekends. Another option is call centres, which have recently been introduced into the telecommunications arena. They offer competitive rates, especially for long-distance calls.

Free phone numbers start with ☎ 0800 or ☎ 0810 while numbers starting with ☎ 0900 are pay-per-minute. When calling Austria from overseas drop the zero in the area code; ie the number for Vienna's main tourist office is ☎ 0043 1 211 14-555. When calling a number from within the same town or city, that town's code is not

---

TELEPHONE NUMBERS EXPLAINED

Telephone numbers for the same town may not always have the same number of digits: some telephone numbers have an individual line, others a party line, and sometimes numbers are listed with an extension that you can dial direct. This is relevant for reading phone numbers listed in the telephone book. If, for example, you see the number 123 45 67... -0, the 0 signifies that the number has extensions. Whether you dial the 0 at the end or not, you will (with a few exceptions) get through to that subscriber's main telephone reception. If you know the extension number of the person you want to speak to, simply dial that instead of the 0 and you'll get straight through to them.

---

required; however when placing a call to elsewhere in Austria (or from a mobile) the code needs to be used.

Directory assistance for numbers in Austria and the EU is available on ☎ 11 88 77.

International Calls

To direct-dial abroad, first telephone the overseas access code (00), then the appropriate country code, then the relevant area code (minus the initial 0 if there is one), and finally the subscriber number. International directory assistance is available on ☎ 0900 11 88 77.

Tariff for making international calls depends on the zone. To reverse the charges (call collect), you have to call a free phone number to place the call. Some of the numbers are listed below (ask directory assistance for others):

Australia	☎ 0800-200 202
Ireland	☎ 0800-200 213
New Zealand	☎ 0800-200 222
South Africa	☎ 0800-200 230
UK	☎ 0800-200 209
USA (AT&T)	☎ 0800-200 288
USA (Sprint)	☎ 0800-200 236

Mobile Phones

Austria's *Handy* (mobile phone) network works on GSM 1800 and is compatible with GSM 900 phones but generally not with systems from the USA or Japan. *Handy* numbers start with 0699, 0676, 0664 and 0650. The major *Handy* networks – One, A-1 and T-Mobile – sell SIM cards with €10 worth of calls for €39. Telering, a smaller operator, has SIM cards for €30 with €30 worth of calls. Refill cards can be purchased from supermarkets and Trafik for €20 or €40. Before buying an Austrian SIM card, confirm that your phone is unlocked; check with your home network before leaving.

At present, only the A-1 network has a reciprocal agreement with overseas network providers. Vodafone customers can purchase A-1 'pay as you talk' refill cards to credit their phones.

You can rent mobile phones at **Tel-Rent** (☎ 01-700 733 340; rental incl phone & SIM card per day/week €18/90, additional weeks €54), located in the arrivals hall at Schwechat Airport in Vienna. Delivery or pick-up within Vienna is available for €26.

Phonecards

There's a wide range of local and international *Telefon-Wertkarte* (phonecards), which can save you money and let you avoid messing around with change. They are available from post offices, *Tabak* and train stations and come in various denominations (€3.60 & €6.90; calling cards with pin code €10 & €15), some of which give you extra calls for your money.

Lonely Planet's ekit global communication service provides low-cost international calls; for local calls you're usually better off with a local phonecard. Ekit also offers free messaging services, email, travel information and an online Travel Vault, where you can securely store all your important documents. To join online, head to www.ekno.lonelyplanet.com, where you will find the local-access numbers for 24-hour customer service. Once you have joined, always check the ekit website for the latest access numbers for each country and updates on new features.

TIME

See the World Time Zones (p378) for Austria's position.

Note that in German *halb* is used to indicate the half-hour before the hour, hence *halb acht* means 7.30, not 8.30.

TOILETS

Public toilets are found throughout towns and cities and are often marked on tourist office maps: *Damen* means women and *Herren* means men. Toilet cubicles in some places, including many train stations, are attended or coin-operated; either way, expect to pay around 50 cents.

TOURIST INFORMATION
Local Tourist Offices

Any town or village that tourists are likely to visit will have a centrally situated tourist office and at least one of the staff will speak English. They go by various names – *Kurort, Fremdenverkehrsverband, Verkehrsamt, Kurverein, Tourismusbüro* or *Kurverwaltung* – but they can always be identified by a white 'i' on a green background.

Staff can answer a range of inquiries, ranging from where and when to attend religious services for different denominations, to where to find vegetarian food. Most offices will have an accommodation-finding

service, often charging no commission. Maps are always available and usually free.

Some local tourist offices hold brochures on other localities, allowing you to stock up on information in advance. If you're empty-handed and arrive somewhere too late in the day to get to the tourist office, try asking at the railway ticket office, as staff there often have hotel lists or city maps. The tourist office may have a rack of brochures hung outside the door, or there may be an accommodation board you can access even when the office is closed. Top hotels usually have a supply of useful brochures in the foyer.

In addition, each province has its own tourist board (see below), though some of these are geared more to handling written or telephone inquiries than dealing with personal callers.

Österreich Werbung (ANTO; ☎ 0810-10 18 18; www .austria.info) Austria's national tourist office; phone and email enquiries only.

Burgenland Tourismus (☎ 02682-633 84-0; www .burgenland.info; Schloss Esterházy, Eisenstadt; ☼ 9am-5pm Apr-Oct, 9am-2pm Mon-Fri Nov-Mar) A regional tourist office more set up for email and snail-mail information requests, but it does have a number of brochures available for walk-in visitors.

Kärnten Information (☎ 0463-3000; www.kaernten .at; Casinoplatz 1; A-9220 Velden) Carinthia's regional tourist office, with information on the *Kärnten Card*.

Niederösterreich Werbung (Map pp83-5; ☎ 01-536 100; www.niederoesterreich.at; 01, Fischhof 3/3, Vienna; ☼ 8.30am-5pm Mon-Thu, 8.30am-4pm Fri) The official information office for Lower Austria. Ask about the *Niederösterreich karte*, a card that entitles you to discounts throughout the province.

Oberösterreich Tourismus (☎ 070-22 10 22; www .oberoesterreich.at; Schillerstrasse 50, Linz; ☼ 8.30am-noon, 1-4.30pm Mon-Thu, 8.30am-noon Fri) Information office for Upper Austria, with a large selection of brochures.

Salzburger Land Tourismus (☎ 0662-668 8-0; www .salzburgerland.com; Wiener Bundesstrasse 23, A-5300 Hallwang bei Salzburg) Like other regions, Salzburger Land offers a discount card, the *Salzburgerland Card*.

Steirische Tourismus (☎ 0316-400 30; www.steiermark .com; St Peter Hauptstrasse 243, A-8042 Graz) Staff at this Styria information office are happy to send you piles of useful information on the province.

Tirol Info (☎ 0512-72 72; www.tirol.at; Maria-Theresien-Strasse 55, A-6010 Innsbruck) Tyrol's regional tourist office.

Vorarlberg Tourismus (☎ 05574-425 25-0; www .vorarlberg-tourism.at; Bahnstrasse 14, Tourismushaus, A-6901 Bregenz) Information office for Austria's most westerly province.

Tourist Offices Abroad

The Austrian National Tourist Office has branches in many countries. Elsewhere, its functions may be taken care of by the Austrian Trade Commission or the commercial counsellor at the Austrian embassy. ANTO offices abroad include:

Australia (☎ 02-9299 3621; info@antosyd.org.au; 1st fl, 36 Carrington St, Sydney, NSW 2000)

Canada (☎ 0416-96 33 81; anto-tor@sympatico.ca; 2 Bloor Street West, Suite 400, Toronto, Ontario M4W 3E2)

Czech Republic (☎ 2222 12 057; ingrid.sieder@austria .info; Krakovská 7, CZ-12543 Praha 1)

France (☎ 01-53 83 95 30; gerhard.zwettler@austria.info; 6, avenue Pierre 1er de Serbie, F-75116 Paris)

Germany (☎ 030-21 91 48-0; deutschland@austria.info; Klosterstrasse 64; D-101 79 Berlin)

Hungary (☎ 01-41 33 910; budapest@austria.info; Rippl Rónai utca 4, H-1068 Budapest)

Italy (☎ 02-46 75 191; oewmil@autria.info; Via Boccaccio 4, I-20123 Milano)

Japan (☎ 03-358 222 33; oewtyo@austria.info; Kokusai Shin-akasaka Bldg; West Tower 2F, 6-1-20 Akasaka, Minato-ku, Tokyo 107-0052)

Spain (☎ 091-54 78 924; informacion@austria.info; Apartado de Correos 8366, E-28080 Madrid)

Switzerland (☎ 01-457 10 50; zeurich@austria.info; Zurlindenstrasse 60, PO Box, CH-8036, Zürich)

The Netherlands (☎ 020-46 84 791; werner .fritz@austria.info; Wibautstraat 133, Postbus 94285, NL-1097 DN Amsterdam)

UK (☎ 020-7629 0461; info@anto.co.uk; 14 Cork St, London W1N 3NS)

USA (☎ 212-944 6885; travel@austria.info; 120 West 45th St, 9th fl, New York, NY 10036)

There are also tourist offices in Brussels, Rome, Barcelona, Copenhagen, Stockholm, Warsaw, Moscow, Los Angeles, New Delhi and Beijing. Contact the Austrian National Tourist Board for the complete list of addresses.

VISAS

Visas for stays of up to three months are not required for citizens of the EU, the European Economic Area (EEA), much of Eastern Europe, Israel, USA, Canada, the majority of Central and South American nations, Japan, Korea, Malaysia, Singapore, Australia or New Zealand. All other nationalities require a visa; the Ministry of Foreign Affairs website at www.bmaa.gv.at has a list of Austrian embassies where you can apply.

If you wish to stay longer you should simply leave the country and re-enter. For those nationalities that require a visa, extensions cannot be organised within Austria; you'll need to leave and reapply. EU nationals can stay indefinitely but are required by law to register with the local *Magistratisches Bezirksamt* (magistrate's office) if the stay exceeds 60 days.

Austria is part of the Schengen Agreement which includes all EU states (minus Britain and Ireland) and Switzerland. In practical terms this means a visa issued by one Schengen country is good for all the other member countries and a passport is not required to move from one to the other (a national identity card is required, though). Things are a little different for the 10 new EU member states which joined in 2004; a passport is still required to move in and out of these countries, but check with your local embassy for more up-to-date information. Austrians are required to carry personal identification, and you too will need to be able to prove your identify.

Visa and passport requirements are subject to change, so always double-check before travelling. Lonely Planet's website, www .lonelyplanet.com, also has links to up-to-date visa information.

WOMEN TRAVELLERS

In cities, Austrian women enjoy the same status and opportunity as men, though in conservative, rural parts of the country some males still consider that a woman's proper place is in the home.

Female travellers should experience no special problems. Fortunately, physical attacks and verbal harassment are less common than in many other countries. However, normal caution should be exercised when alone or in unfamiliar situations (which obviously occur quite often when you're travelling). Some Austrian trains have a special section for women travelling alone and a growing number of underground car parks have a section near the manned ticketing office designated as a women-only parking space.

Cities usually have a *Frauenzentrum* (women's centre) and/or telephone help-lines. In Vienna, for example, there is the Frauenotruf (☎ 01-71 719), an emergency, 24-hour hotline for reporting rape and sexual violence.

WORK

EU nationals can work in Austria without a work permit or residency permit, though as intending residents they need to register with the police (or the magistrate's office if in Vienna).

Non-EU nationals need both a work permit and a residency permit and will find it pretty hard to get either. Inquire (in German) about job possibilities via local labour offices; look under *Arbeitsmarktservice* in the White Pages for the closest office. Your employer in Austria needs to apply for your work permit. Applications for residency permits must be applied for via the Austrian embassy in your home country. A good website for foreign residents is www.wif.wien.at.

Teaching is a favourite of expats in the bigger cities; look under *Sprachschulen* in the Gelben Seiten for a list of schools. Ski resorts are another good place to look for work; there are often vacancies in snow clearing, chalet cleaning, restaurants and ski equipment shops. Language skills are particularly crucial for any type of work in service industries. Your best chance of finding work is to start writing or asking around early – in summer for winter work and in winter for summer work. Some people do, however, get lucky by arriving right at the beginning of the season and asking around; tourist offices and ski shops should be able to point you in the direction of current vacancies. In October, grape-pickers are usually required in the wine-growing regions.

Useful books for those searching for work abroad include *Working in Ski Resorts – Europe & North America* by Victoria Pybus, *Work Your Way Around the World*, by Susan Griffith, and *The Au Pair and Nanny's Guide to Working Abroad*, by Susan Griffith and Sharon Legg. All are published in the UK by Vacation Work (www.vacationwork.co.uk).

Online jobs are listed on a number of websites, including:

www.austria.info Look under the 'Professionals' section of the official Austria Tourist Board website for a link to jobs around Austria.

www.oeh.jobfinder.at Directed towards professionals; in German only.

www.studentenjob.com Specialises in student jobs; in German only.

www.jobpilot.at Comprehensive site with loads of professional jobs; in German only.

www.ams.or.at/sfa/index.htm Another site aimed at professionals; German only.

Transport

CONTENTS

GETTING THERE & AWAY

Austria is well connected to the rest of the world. Vienna and four of the country's regional capitals are served by no-frills airlines (plus regular airline services), Europe's extensive bus and train networks crisscross the country and there are major highways from Germany and Italy. It's also possible to enter Austria by boat from Hungary, Slovakia and Germany.

ENTERING THE COUNTRY

A valid passport is required when entering Austria. The only exception to this rule occurs when entering from another Schengen country; in this case, only a national identity is required. Procedures at border cross-

---

THINGS CHANGE

The information in this chapter is particularly vulnerable to change. Check directly with the airline or travel agent to make sure you understand how a fare (and ticket you may buy) works and be aware of the security requirements for international travel. Shop carefully. The details given in this chapter should be regarded as pointers and are not a substitute for your own careful, up-to-date research.

---

ings from other EU countries are relatively lax compared with procedures at airports, and provincial capital airports are stricter than those in Vienna. See p360 for more information.

AIR

Vienna is the main transport hub for Austria, but Graz, Linz, Klagenfurt, Salzburg and Innsbruck all receive international flights. Flights to these cities are often a cheaper option than to the capital, as are flights to Bratislava's MR Štefánika Airport, which is only 60km east of Vienna. Bregenz has no airport; your best bet is to fly into Friedrichshafen in Germany or Altenrhein in Switzerland. Austria is a popular destination year-round and while bargain flights do pop up now and then, they often sell out all too soon. No-frills airlines are an exception; booking well in advance will always guarantee value for money.

Seriously consider booking early over the Christmas and New Year period; prices tend to soar at this time.

Airports & Airlines

Austrian Airlines (code OS; ☎ 05 17 89; www.aua.com; 01, Kärntner Strasse 11) is the national carrier and has the most extensive services to Vienna.

The full list of international airports is as follows:

Graz (code GRZ; ☎ 0316-29 02-0; www.flughafen-graz.at - in German)

Innsbruck (code INN; ☎ 0512-225 25-0; www.innsbruck -airport.com - in German)

Klagenfurt (code KLU; ☎ 0463-41 500; www.klagenfurt -airport.com)

Linz (code LNZ; ☎ 07221-600-0; www.flughafen-linz.at)

MR Štefánika Airport (code BTS; ☎ 0421 2 4857 3353; www.airportbratislava.sk) Serves Slovakia's capital Bratislava and has good transport connections to Vienna.

Salzburg (code SZG; ☎ 0662-8580-100; www.salzburg -airport.com - in German)

Vienna (code VIE; ☎ 01-7007 22233; www.viennaair port.com)

Tickets

Except during fare wars, airlines themselves don't usually offer the cheapest tickets (no-frills carriers are one exception). For these

AIRLINES FLYING TO AND FROM AUSTRIA

Aside from Austrian Airlines, the following airlines connect Austria to the rest of the world:

Air Berlin (code AB; www.airberlin.com; ☎ 0810-1025 73 800; hub Köln Bonn Airport; Köln)

Air France (code AF; www.airfrance.fr – in French; ☎ 502 22-240; hub Roissy-Charles De Gaulle Airport, Paris)

Alitalia (code AZ; www.alitalia.com; ☎ 505 17 07; hub Leonardo DaVinci International Airport, Rome)

British Airways (code BA; www.britishairways.com; ☎ 7956 7567; hub Heathrow Airport, London)

Delta Air Lines (code DL; www.delta.com; ☎ 7956 7023; hub Hartsfield-Jackson Airport, Atlanta)

German Wings (code 4U; www.germanwings.com; ☎ 5029 100 70; hub Bonn Airport, Köln)

Flybe (code BE; www.flybe.com; hub Exter International Airport, Exter)

Intersky (code ISK; www.intersky.biz; ☎ 05574-488 00; hub Friedrichshafen Airport)

KLM (code KL; www.klm.at; ☎ 0900-359 556; hub Schiphol Airport, Amsterdam)

Lauda Air (code NG; www.laudaair.com; ☎ 05 17 89; hub Vienna International Airport)

Lufthansa (code LH; www.lufthansa.com; ☎ 0810-1025 80 80; hub Frankfurt Airport, Frankfurt)

Niki (code HG; www.flyniki.com; hub Vienna International Airport)

Ryanair (code FR; www.ryanair.com; ☎ 0900-210 240; hub Stansted Airport, London)

Sky Europe (code 5P; www.skyeurope.com; ☎ 998 555 55; hub MR Štefánika Airport, Bratislava)

Styrian Spirit (code Z2; www.styrianairways.com; ☎ 0508-051 212; hub Graz Airport)

Swissair (code LX; www.swiss.com; ☎ 0810-810 840; hub EuroAirport Schwiez, Basel)

Welcome Air (code 2W; www.welcomeair.com; ☎ 0512-295 296-300; hub Innsbruck Airport)

you must shop around the travel agencies and watch for special offers. A good travel agent can be worth their weight in gold – they have the low-down on special deals, ways to avoid long stopovers and plenty of other useful advice.

Perhaps a more convenient option is booking over the Internet. You can book directly with airlines, or a plethora of web-based companies selling flights; if you search around you can sometimes come up with bargain fares. With any luck, you'll find something that takes your fancy through the following websites:

Airbrokers (www.airbrokers.com) US company specialising in cheap tickets.

Cheap Flights (www.cheapflights.com/www.cheapflights.co.uk) Very informative site with specials, airline information and flight searches, mainly from the US and UK.

Expedia (www.expedia.co.uk) UK-based company listing major airlines; the earlier you book the better.

Flight Centre (www.flightcentre.co.uk) Respected operator handling direct flights, with sites for Australia, New Zealand, the UK, the US and Canada.

Hotwire (www.hotwire.com) Bookings from the US only; some cheap last-minute deals.

Last Minute (www.lastminute.com) One of the better sites for last-minute deals, including hotels.

Price Line (www.priceline.com) Name-your-own-price US site.

Orbitz (www.orbitz.com) Cheap deals when flying from the US.

STA Travel (www.statravel.com) Prominent in international student travel, but you don't necessarily have to be a student to take advantage of bargains; site linked to worldwide STA sites.

Travel (www.travel.com.au/www.travel.co.nz) Reputable Australia and New Zealand online flight bookers.

Travelocity (www.travelocity.com) US site that allows you to search fares (in US dollars) to/from practically anywhere.

Australia & New Zealand

From this side of the globe, it's worth investigating round-the-world (RTW) tickets, as these may not be much more expensive than a straightforward return ticket. Check the travel agencies' advertisements in the Yellow Pages and the Saturday travel sections of the *Sydney Morning Herald*, the *Age* in Melbourne and the New Zealand *Herald*.

From Australia, only Austrian Airlines offers direct flights to Vienna (one daily from Sydney and three times weekly from Melbourne). As with flights coming from North America, there are plenty of connections via London and Frankfurt.

STA Travel (New Zealand ☎ 0800 874 773; www.sta travel.co.nz; Australia ☎ 1300 360 960; www.statravel.com .au) and **Flight Centre** (New Zealand ☎ 0800 243 544; www.flightcentre.co.nz; Australia ☎ 131 600; www .flightcentre.com.au) are good starting points and both have offices throughout New Zealand and Australia.

Continental Europe

Like spokes on a wheel, flights go from Vienna to all parts of Europe. Routes to the east are as well covered as those to the west, with Austrian Airlines flying regularly to Bucharest, Kiev, Moscow, St Petersburg, Vilnius and Warsaw (among other destinations).

Austria's other international airports have connections to Belgium, Croatia, Greece, Germany, Italy, the Netherlands, Switzerland, Sweden, Spain and Turkey.

The following travel agents are recommended:

France OTU Voyages (☎ 0820 817 817; www.otu.fr); Voyageurs du Monde (☎ 01 42 86 16 00; www.vdm.com – in French); Nouvelles Frontiéres (☎ 0825 000 747; www .nouvelles-frontieres.fr - in French)

Germany STA Travel (☎ 01805 456 422; www.statravel.de); Just Travel (☎ 089 747 3330; www.justtravel.de)

Italy CTS Viaggi (☎ 06 462 0431; www.cts.it – in Italian); Viaggi Wasteels (☎ 06 446 6679)

Netherlands Airfair (☎ 020 620 5121; www.airfair.nl); NBBS Reizen (☎ 0900 10 20 300; www.mytravel.nl)

UK & Ireland

Discount air travel is big business in London. In addition to the travel sections of the major Sunday papers, check the travel classifieds in London's weekly *Time Out* and *TNT* entertainment magazines.

Outside London, flights are harder to find, but they do exist. Flybe connects Salzburg with Belfast, Birmingham, Edinburgh, Glasgow, Southampton and Dublin. Austrian Airlines flies direct from Dublin to Vienna, as does Aer Lingus; British Airways has one daily flight to/from Manchester.

The cheapest flights are often offered by obscure bucket shops that don't even appear in the telephone book. Many are honest and solvent, but be careful as some may take your money and disappear, only to reopen elsewhere under a new name.

Some of the more reliable agents in London include:

Bridge the World (☎ 0870 444 7474; www.b-t-w.co.uk)

Flightbookers (☎ 0870 010 7000; www.ebookers.com)

Flight Centre (☎ 0870 890 8099; www.flightcentre.co.uk)

STA Travel (☎ 0870 160 0599; www.statravel.co.uk) Popular travel agency for students or travellers under 26 years.

Trailfinders (☎ 020-7938 3939; www.trailfinders.co.uk)

USA & Canada

The North Atlantic is the world's busiest long-haul air corridor, and various newspapers contain ads placed by consolidators (discount travel agencies). San Francisco is the ticket-consolidator capital of the US, although some good deals can be found in Los Angeles, New York and other big cities.

All direct flights from the US arrive in Vienna. Austrian Airlines has one daily scheduled flight to Washington DC and New York. For all other destinations, you must first pass through either of these cities or a European 'gateway' city such as Frankfurt, London or Paris.

Canadian discount air-ticket sellers are also known as consolidators and their air fares tend to be about 10% higher than those sold in the US. Usually you'll have to fly to Austria via the USA or one of Europe's 'gateway' cities. Exceptions include the direct Toronto–Vienna and Montreal–Vienna services with Austrian Airlines.

Recommended travel agents include:

Travel Avenue (☎ 1-800-333-3335 www.travelavenue .com) Well-established travel agent, based in Chicago.

Travel CUTS (☎ 800-667-2887; www.travelcuts.com) Canada's national student-travel agency.

LAND
Bus

Travelling by bus may not be the most comfortable way to cross Europe, but it is the cheapest. It's easiest to book with **Eurolines** (www .eurolines.com; Vienna Map pp80-2; ☎ 798 29 00; www .eurolines.at; 03, Erdbergstrasse 202; Salzburg ☎ 0662-421 089; Rudolf-Biebl-Strasse 43), a consortium of coach companies with offices all over Europe. Coaches are air conditioned, as fast as the train, and they stop frequently for food and toilet breaks.

While the bulk of Euroline buses pass through Vienna, there are 13 stops in Austria, including Graz, Linz, Salzburg, Klagenfurt and Innsbruck.

Eurolines runs buses to/from London (Victoria coach station) to its bus terminal at Südbahnhof (one way/return €68/72, 23 hours, five or six days per week) on Arsenalstrasse; prices are cheaper if booked 15 days in advance and youth and senior discounts are available on almost all fares and passes. For other destinations see www.euro lines.com.

Austrobus (see Colombus Reisen for contact details) has buses to Prague (one way/return €20/34, six hours, 7am Monday to Saturday, 2pm Sunday), leaving from 01, Rathausplatz 5, Vienna. Buy tickets directly from the driver, or purchase them in advance from **Columbus Reisen** (Map pp83-5; ☎ 534 11-123; 01, Dr Karl Lueger Ring 8; ☺ 9am-5pm Mon-Fri, 9am-noon Sat).

For quick trips around Europe, both Eurolines and the **Busabout** (☎ 020-7950 1661; www .busabout.com), a London-based firm, have bus passes. The **Eurolines Pass** (15/30/60 days UK£195/290/333 Jun–mid-Sep, UK£149/209/265 mid-Sep–May) covers 35 cities across Europe (including Vienna and Salzburg).

Busabout offers two passes for travel around 50 European cities, including Vienna, Salzburg and St Johann in Tyrol. Its Flexi Pass allows so many days travel over a set period; eight days travel within one month costs UK£279, 12 days in two months UK£389. The **Unlimited Pass** (2/4/6 weeks UK£239/389/479) is similar to the Eurolines Pass.

Car & Motorcycle

Getting to Austria by road is simple as there are fast and well-maintained motorways through all surrounding countries.

There are numerous entry points into Austria by road from Germany, the Czech Republic, Slovakia, Hungary, Slovenia, Italy and Switzerland. Liechtenstein is so small that it has just one border crossing point, near Feldkirch in Austria. The presence of the Alps limits options for approaching Tyrol from the south (Switzerland and Italy). All main border-crossing points are open 24 hours; minor crossings are open from around 6am or 8am until 8pm or 10pm.

Proof of ownership of a private vehicle and a driver's licence should always be carried while driving. EU licences are accepted in Austria while all other nationalities require a German translation or an International Driving Permit (IDP). Third-party insurance is a minimum requirement in Europe and you'll need to carry proof of this in the form of a Green Card.

Carrying a warning triangle and first-aid kit in your vehicle is also compulsory in Austria. If you're a member of an automobile association, ask about free reciprocal benefits offered by affiliated organisations in Europe.

A petrol station will typically be lurking just across main border crossings in Austria.

For information on Austria's road rules and regulations, see p370.

Train

Austria benefits from its central location within Europe by having excellent rail connections to all important destinations; 16 express-train routes connect the country to its neighbours. The *Thomas Cook European Timetable* is the trainophile's bible, giving a complete listing of train schedules, supplements and reservations information. It is updated monthly and is available from Thomas Cook outlets.

Express trains can be identified by the symbols EC (EuroCity, serving international routes) or IC (InterCity, serving national routes). The French Train à Grande Vitesse (TGV) and the German InterCityExpress (ICE) trains are even faster. Supplements can apply on fast trains and international trains, and it is a good idea (sometimes obligatory) to make seat reservations for peak times and on certain lines.

Overnight trips usually offer a choice between a *Liegewagen* (couchette) or a more expensive *Schlafwagen* (sleeping car). Long-distance trains have a dining car or snacks available.

Vienna is one of the main rail hubs in Central Europe; for details of the main train stations and the routes they serve, see p124. Elsewhere in Austria, Salzburg has express-train connections in the direction of Munich (€26, 1½ to two hours), Linz towards Prague (€58, five hours) and Regensburg (€40, two hours), Graz towards Budapest (€55, 6¼ hours) and Ljubljana (€34, four hours), Klagenfurt towards Ljubljana (€43, 2½ hours) and Venice (€46, 3½ to five hours); and Innsbruck north to Munich (€32, two hours), south to Verona (€43, 3½ to four hours) and west to Zürich (€46, 3¾ hours). Most of the services listed above depart at least every two to three hours daily.

In the UK, buy tickets through **Rail Europe** (☎ 08705-848 848; www.raileurope.co.uk). A 2nd-class, return ticket from London to Vienna is UK£300 for a 20- to 25-hour trip. Tickets are good for two months and you can break your journey anywhere en route. Other 2nd-class return fares to Vienna include €170 from Paris (15 hours), €300 from Amsterdam (13½ hours) and €70 from Prague (4½ hours).

TRANSPORT

EUROPEAN RAIL PASSES

If you plan to travel widely in Europe, the following special tickets and rail passes may be worth pursuing. Some of these may have different names in different countries. For information on a range of rail passes, visit www.raileurope.com, www.raileurope.co.uk and www.railpassdirect.co.uk.

Eurail Pass

Only available to non-European residents, Eurail passes are valid for 1st-class unlimited travel on national railways and some private lines in much of Western Europe (the UK is not included) and Hungary. Passes come in 15 or 21 day lots (for US$588 or $762) or I, 2 or 3 month lots (for US$946, $1338 or $1654). The Eurail Flexi pass allows 10 or 15 days travel in two months and costs US$694 or $914. Discounts on both are available for people travelling in groups and those under 26.

European East Pass

The European East Pass is only available in the USA and provides unlimited travel in Austria, Slovakia, Czech Republic, Hungary and Poland for any five days within a month. Tickets for 1st-class travel cost US$226, for 2nd-class US$160. Extra days cost US$26 for 1st class, $19 for 2nd.

InterRail Pass

Only available to anyone who has lived in Europe for at least six months, this pass gives travellers unlimited, 2nd-class travel for up to one month on most of the state railways of Western and Central Europe (except in their own country). The 'Zone C' pass for travel in Austria, Switzerland, Germany and Denmark costs UK£223 for 16 days (UK£159 for those under 26). A Global Pass, covering all zones and valid for a month, costs UK£415 (UK£295 for those under 26).

Switzerland 'n Austria Pass

Available only to US citizens, this pass allows four days unlimited travel in Switzerland and Austria within a two month period. Only 1st-class travel is permitted, which costs US$300; extra days cost US$36.

RIVER

The Danube (Donau) is a traffic-free access route for arrivals and departures from Austria. Since the early 1990s the Danube has been connected to the Rhine by the River Main tributary and the Main–Danube canal in southern Germany. The *MS River Queen* does 13-day cruises along this route, from Amsterdam to Vienna, between May and September for around £2000. It departs monthly in each direction.

In Britain bookings can be made through **Noble Caledonia** (☎ 020-7752 0000); it also makes bookings for the *MS Amadeus*, which takes seven days to get from Passau to Budapest. In the USA, you can book through **Uniworld** (☎ 1-800-360 9550; www.uniworld.com). For information on connections to Passau in Germany, see p174.

Heading east, boats travel to Bratislava (hydrofoil one way/return €22/33.50, 1½ hours) once daily from June to early-September, once daily Wednesday to Sun-

day early April to May and early September to October; and Budapest (hydrofoil one way/return €75/99, 5½ hours) twice daily August to early September, once daily April to July and early September to October; and from Vienna April to October. Bookings can be made through **DDSG Blue Danube** (Map pp83-5; ☎ 588 80; www.ddsg-blue-danube.at; 01, Friedrichstrasse 7, Vienna; ⏰ 9am-6pm Mon-Fri); ships dock at 02, Handelskai 265 (Map pp80–2).

GETTING AROUND

Transport systems in Austria are highly developed and generally very efficient, and reliable information is usually available in English. Individual bus and train *Fahrplan* (timetables) are readily available, as are helpful annual timetables.

Austria's main rail provider is the **Österreiche Bundesbahn** (ÖBB; Austrian Federal Railways; www.oebb.at), which has an extensive countrywide rail network. This is supplemented by a handful of private railways. Wherever trains don't run, the public transport system is picked up by **Post.Bus** (www.postbus.at); at times, bus and train services overlap. Timetables and prices for many train and bus connections can be found online at www.oebb.at.

Most provinces have an integrated transport system offering day passes covering regional zones for both bus and train travel. These passes can often save you money compared with buying standard single tickets, so always inquire about this option before you buy. Day passes for city transport often give a one-zone discount on regional travel.

AIR

Austria is not a massive country and the idea of flying from one city to another is a crazy idea for many, if not all, Austrians. There is, however, more than one airline serving the domestic scene.

Note that it may be quicker to fly than take the train, but prices are far more expensive.

Airlines in Austria

Austrian Airlines (p362), and its subsidiaries Tyrolean Airways and Austrian Arrow, maintain a high standard in the airline industry and handle the bulk of domestic flights. They offer several flights daily between Vienna and Graz, Innsbruck, Klagenfurt, Linz and Salzburg, and also flights between Graz and Linz, and Linz and Salzburg.

Welcome Air (p363) has flights from Innsbruck to Graz, along with a handful of international services.

BICYCLE

Cycling is a popular activity in Austria, and most regional tourist boards have brochures on cycling facilities and routes within their region. Separate bike tracks are common, not only in cities, but also in the country. The Danube cycling trail is something of a Holy Grail for cyclists, though there are many other excellent bike routes in the country. Most are close to bodies of water, where there are fewer hills to contend with. For more information on popular cycle routes, see the Outdoor Activities chapter (p52).

It's possible to take bicycles on any train with a bicycle symbol at the top of its timetable; these trains are either regional or *Eilzüge* (medium-fast trains). A transferable bicycle ticket valid on trains costs €2.90 per day, €7.50 per week and €22.50 per month. There is a fixed fare of €12 for transporting a bike as registered luggage on a train (not necessarily the same train as you travel on). This may be the only option on EC and IC trains, though a few do allow you to accompany your bike (€6.80 for a day ticket).

Hire

Bike rental is a common practice in Austria. All large cities have at least one bike shop that doubles as a rental centre. In places where cycling is a popular pastime, such as the Wachau in Lower Austria and the Neusiedler See in Burgenland, almost all small towns have a rental shop and train stations have rental facilities. Rates vary from town to town, but expect to pay around €10 per day; see the destination chapters for specific details on bike hire.

Purchase

It's no problem purchasing a bicycle in Austria (prices are comparable to other Western European countries), but it may prove harder to sell it at the end of you trip. A good way to either sell a bike or pick up a second-hand model is through *Bazar* – the paper for selling and buying anything (available in print or online at www.bazar.co.at) – or at pawn shops in the larger cities.

BOAT

The Danube serves as a thoroughfare between Vienna and Lower and Upper Austria. Services are generally slow, scenic excursions rather than functional means of transport. For more information on boat travel in Vienna, see p124; for Lower Austria see p130; and for Upper Austria p174. Some of the country's larger lakes, such as Bodensee and Wörthersee, have boat services.

BUS

The *Bundesbus* (federal bus) network is best considered a backup to the rail service, more useful for reaching out-of-the-way places and local destinations than for long-distance travel. Rail routes are sometimes duplicated by bus services, but buses really come into their own in the more inaccessible mountainous regions. Buses are clean and punctual, and usually depart

TRANSPORT

from outside train stations. Note that some bus routes are geared to the needs of school children, so if it's not a school day, the frequency of the service greatly diminishes.

For nationwide bus information, call ☎ 01-711 01 between 7am and 8pm, or log on to the websites www.oebb.at or www .postbus.at. Local bus stations or tourist offices usually stock free timetables for specific bus routes.

Costs

Bus fares are comparable to train fares; however you can't buy a long-distance ticket and make stop-offs en route as you can on a train. Prices are listed throughout the destination chapters; here are a few of the more popular fares:

Destination	Cost (€)	Duration (hr)
Vienna–Mariazell	€19.40	3hr
Salzburg–Bad Ischl	€16.60	1½hr
Salzburg–Zell am See	€16.20	2hr
Kitzbühel–Lienz	€30.50	2hr
Graz–Klagenfurt	€27.70	2½hr

Reservations

It's possible to buy tickets in advance on some routes, but on others you can only buy tickets from the drivers. More often than not, though, there is no need to make reservations as most Austrians and tourists use the railway system.

CAR & MOTORCYCLE

Driving in Austria is a pleasure; roads are well maintained, signs are everywhere and rules are usually adhered to. The use of *Personenkraftwagen* (PKW) or *Auto* (cars) is often discouraged in city centres though, and it is a good idea to ditch your trusty chariot and rely on public transport.

The fastest roads round the country are the autobahns, identified on maps by national 'A' numbers or pan-European 'E' numbers (both are usually given in this book). These are subject to a general motorway tax. Their course is often shadowed by *Bundesstrassen* (alternative routes), which are as direct as the terrain will allow, sometimes using tunnels to maintain their straight lines. In the mountains, you can opt instead for smaller, slower

Road Distances (km)

	Bad Ischl	Bregenz	Bruck an der Mur	Eisenstadt	Graz	Innsbruck	Kitzbühel	Klagenfurt	Krems	Kufstein	Landeck	Lienz	Linz	Salzburg	St Pölten	Vienna	Villach	Wiener Neustadt
Bad Ischl	---																	
Bregenz	432	---																
Bruck an der Mur	170	577	---															
Eisenstadt	297	704	127	---														
Graz	193	600	54	175	---													
Innsbruck	239	193	384	511	407	---												
Kitzbühel	191	300	275	469	400	113	---											
Klagenfurt	245	510	145	298	133	322	264	---										
Krems	222	626	175	132	229	433	372	320	---									
Kufstein	161	271	331	460	356	78	37	286	355	---								
Landeck	316	117	461	588	484	77	186	394	510	155	---							
Lienz	232	424	266	393	277	178	94	144	432	142	248	---						
Linz	103	507	190	246	237	314	247	253	145	236	391	359	---					
Salzburg	58	374	228	362	264	181	129	223	257	103	258	180	138	---				
St Pölten	206	610	140	123	194	417	356	285	32	339	494	416	129	241	---			
Vienna	266	670	145	50	191	477	420	316	79	399	554	411	189	301	66	---		
Villach	250	486	178	335	170	287	226	37	353	251	370	109	330	188	318	353	---	
Wiener Neustadt	268	675	98	31	146	482	441	267	137	431	559	364	237	339	114	53	316	---

roads that wind over mountain passes. These can add to your journey but the scenery often makes up for the extra time and kilometres. Some minor passes are blocked by snow from November to May. Carrying snow chains in winter is highly recommended and may be compulsory in some areas.

Cars can be transported by *Autoreisezüge* (motorail trains). Vienna is linked by a daily motorail service to Feldkirch (€75.90, 6½ hours), Innsbruck (€61.90, 4¾ hours), Lienz (€55.90, seven hours), Salzburg (€32.90, 3½ hours) and Villach (€49.90, 4½ hours), as is Graz to Feldkirch (€68.90, eight hours) and Villach to Feldkirch (€61.90, seven hours). Over 200 Austrian train stations offer Park and Ride facilities (free or cheap parking while you continue by train). In rural areas, petrol stations may close on Sunday.

Motorcycling is a popular pastime in Austria, and many mountain passes play host to a multitude of riders over the summer months. Motorcyclists and their passengers must wear a helmet, and dipped lights must be used in daytime. As with cars, motorbikes should also carry a first-aid kit. The National Austrian Tourist Office can provide you with the *Austrian Classic Tour* brochure, which covers 3000km of the best roads for bikers in the country.

Automobile Associations

Two automobile associations serve Austria. Both provide free 24-hour breakdown service to members and have reciprocal agreements with motoring clubs in other countries; check with your local club before leaving. If you're not entitled to free assistance, you'll incur a fee for call-outs which varies, depending on the time of day. The two associations are:

ARBÖ (24-hour emergency assistance ☎ 123, office ☎ 891 21-0; www.arboe.at; 15, Mariahilfer Strasse 180; ⏲ 8am-6pm Mon-Fri, 9am-noon Sat)

ÖAMTC (Map pp83–5; 24-hour emergency assistance ☎ 120, office ☎ 711 99-0; www.oeamtc.at; 01, Schubert-ring 1-3; ⏲ 9am-6pm Mon-Fri, 9am-noon Sat)

Both have offices throughout Austria. It is possible to become a member, but you must join for a year, which costs €62.

Bring Your Own Vehicle

It is no problem to bring your own vehicle into Austria, as long as you have proof of ownership papers and third-party insur-ance. The car must also display a sticker on the rear indicating the country of origin.

Driving Licence

A licence should always be carried; see p365 for more details.

Fuel & Spare Parts

There is no problem finding fuel and car parts in Austria. *Tankstelle* (petrol stations) have diesel, *Benzin* (unleaded; 91 octane), Euro-Super (95 octane) and Super Plus (98 octane). Only a few have liquid gas and leaded petrol is no longer available in the country, but lead additives are available from most petrol stations.

Hire

The minimum age for hiring a car is 19 for small cars and 25 for prestige models, and a valid licence at least a year old is required. If you plan to take the car across the border, especially into Eastern Europe, let the rental company know beforehand and double-check any add-on fees.

For the lowest rates, organise car rental before departure. **Holiday Autos** (www.holidayautos .com) often offers low rates and has offices or representatives in over 20 countries. Shop around to get the best deal; prices between the large multinational companies can vary wildly and local companies often underbid their bigger competitors. Rates normally start at around €60 per day but decrease for longer rentals. Check extra charges before signing an agreement; collision damage waiver (CDW) is an additional charge starting at around €22 per day, theft protection another €7 to €8 and drivers under the age of 25 are often required to pay an additional €4 to €5 per day.

All the multinational rental companies are present in Austria and many have branches in the main cities or at airports. You should be able to make advance reservations online, or arrange something after arriving in Austria through one of the following companies:

Avis (☎ 01-360 277-1543; www.avis.at)
Denzeldrive (☎ 01-740 20-0; www.denzeldrive.at)
Europcar (☎ 01-866 1633; www.europcar.at)
Hertz (☎ 01-795 32; www.hertz.at)
Sixt (☎ 0800-1111 7498; www.sixt.at)

Hitching

Hitching is never entirely safe anywhere in the world and we don't recommend it.

Travellers who decide to hitch should understand that they are taking a small but potentially serious risk. Those who choose to hitch will be safer if they travel in pairs and let someone know where they are planning to go.

If you are still set on hitching across Europe, a worthwhile website to check is www .hitchhikers.org. It provides information on drivers looking for passengers for trips across the continent. Most drivers ask a minimal fee from those catching a lift.

Insurance

Third-party insurance is a minimum requirement in Austria. All companies offer Personal Accident Insurance (PAI) and Collision Damage Waiver (CDW) for an additional charge, although PAI may not be necessary if you or your passengers hold travel insurance.

Motorway Tax & Tunnel Tolls

A *Vignitte* (motorway tax) is imposed on all autobahn; charges for cars below 3.5 tonnes are €7.60 for 10 days, €21.80 for two months and €72.60 for one year. For motorbikes expect to pay €4.30 for 10 days, €10.90 for two months and €29 for one year. *Vignitte* can be purchased from motoring organisations, border crossings, petrol stations, post offices and *Tabak* shops.

Anything above 3.5 tonnes is charged per kilometre. The system uses a GO-Box, available from petrol stations along autobahn for €5, which records the kilometres you travel via an electronic tolling system. A minimum of €45 must be loaded onto the box (payable by credit card). Information on the system and prices can be found online at www .go-maut.at.

A toll is levied on some mountain roads and tunnels (*not* covered by the motorway tax). For a full list of toll roads, consult one of the automobile organisations mentioned on p369.

Road Rules

The minimum driving age is 18, both for Austrians and foreigners. Like the rest of continental Europe, Austrians drive on the right-hand side of the road. Speed limits are 50km/h in built-up areas, 130km/h on autobahns and 100km/h on other roads. In some places speed on country roads is restricted to 70km/h. Priority is given to vehicles coming from the right, and Austrian road signs generally conform to recognised international standards. Wearing a crash helmet is compulsory for motorcyclists, and children under the age of 14 and/or shorter than 1.5m must have a special seat or restraint.

Austrian police have the authority to impose fines for various traffic offences. These can be paid on the spot (ask for a receipt) or within two weeks. The penalty for drink-driving – over 0.05% BAC (blood-alcohol concentration) – is a hefty on-the-spot fine and confiscation of your driving licence. Trams are a common feature in Austrian cities; take care if you've never driven among them before. Trams always have priority and no matter how much you might swear at them, they're never going to deviate from their tracks just to suit you. Vehicles should wait behind while trams slow down and stop for passengers.

Urban Parking

Most town centres have a designated *Kurzparkzone* (short-term parking zone), where on-street parking is limited to a maximum of 1½ or three hours (depending upon the place) between certain specified times. *Parkschein* (parking vouchers) for such zones can be purchased from *Tabak* shops or pavement dispensers and then displayed on the windscreen. Outside the specified time, parking in the *Kurzparkzone* is free.

LOCAL TRANSPORT

Austria's local transport infrastructure is excellent, inexpensive and safe. It runs from about 5am or 6am to midnight, though in smaller towns evening services may be patchy or finish for the night much earlier.

Tickets will generally cover all forms of public transport in a town or city. Passes and multitrip tickets are available in advance from *Tabak* shops, pavement dispensers, and occasionally tourist offices. They usually need to be validated upon first use in the machine on buses or trams. In some towns drivers will sell single tickets, but rarely passes. Single tickets may be valid for one hour, 30 minutes, or a single journey, depending on the place. If you're a senior, attending school in Austria, or travelling as a family, you may be eligible for reduced-price tickets in some towns.

GETTING AROUND •• Train **371**

You can usually buy excellent value one-day or 24-hour tickets which often only cost double the price of a single ticket. Weekly or three-day passes may be available too, as well as multitrip tickets, which will work out cheaper than buying individual tickets for each journey.

Fines for travelling without a valid ticket easily outweigh the price it would have cost to buy one. Depending on the inspector, you could have real problems if you aren't carrying enough cash to pay the fine at the time you're caught.

Bus

Buses are the mainstay of local transport in Austria. Towns that require some form of public transport will at least have a local bus system; it will be well-used, comprehensive and efficient.

Keep alert when you're about to get off a bus: if you haven't pressed the request button and there's nobody waiting at the bus stop, the driver will go right past.

Metro

Vienna is the only city with a metro; see p125 for more details.

Taxi

On the whole, taxis are cheap, ubiquitous and safe. Stands are invariably located outside train stations and large hotels. Fares are metered and consist of two elements: a flat starting fee plus a charge per kilometre. A small tip is expected; add about 10% to the fare. Telephone numbers for taxi companies are given under Getting Around in the destination chapters.

Tram

Many of Austria's larger cities, such as Graz, Linz and Vienna, supplement their bus systems with convenient and environmentally friendly trams. Most towns have an integrated transport system, meaning you can switch between bus and tram routes on the same ticket.

TRAIN

Like much of Europe, Austria's train network is a dense web reaching the country's far-flung corners. The system is fast, efficient, frequent and well used. **ÖBB** (24-hr information ☎ 05 17 17; www.oebb.at) is the main

operator, and is supplemented with a handful of private lines.

The German for train station is *Bahnhof* (abbreviated as *Bf*); the main train station is the *Hauptbahnhof* (abbreviated as *Hbf*). Some small rural stations are unstaffed and tickets cannot be bought there; they're indicated by a rectangle with a diagonal line through the middle on timetables. All reasonably sized stations have facilities for exchanging foreign currency or travellers cheques and make some provision for luggage storage, either at a staffed counter or in 24-hour luggage lockers. Many stations have information centres where the staff speak English. If you can understand some German, pick up the free booklet, *Angebote & Service*, which includes everything about travelling by rail, including information on special tickets, reservations and contact numbers.

Bahnsteig (platforms) at train stations are divided into zones (A, B and sometimes C) and may be used for more than one train; you may find yourself waiting at one end of a platform while your train is leaving from the other. Note that trains occasionally split en route so be sure to sit in the correct carriage. Diagram boards on the platforms show the carriage order (1st or 2nd class, dining car etc) of IC and EC trains. Separate yellow posters in stations list *Ankunft* (arrivals) and *Abfahrt* (departures).

Classes

The type and speed of a train can be identified by its prefix. EuroCity (EC), InterCity (IC) and InterCityExpress (ICE) are all express trains, stopping only at major stations; they usually include a dining car. EuroNight (EN) is an international night train, with sleeping cars and couchettes. D (*Schnellzug*) are fast trains while E (*Eilzug*) are medium-fast trains that stop at some smaller stations. Slow, local trains have no letter prefix and stop everywhere. On small local trains serving relatively isolated routes, there may be a button to press to request the train to stop (as on buses). Trains have smoking and non-smoking compartments, though Vienna's S-Bahn trains are non-smoking only.

Long-distance express trains always provide the choice of travelling in 1st or 2nd class, while overnight trains have the option of a *Schlafwagen* or couchette (*Liegewagen*). Most local services have 2nd-class carriages only.

TRANSPORT

TRANSPORT

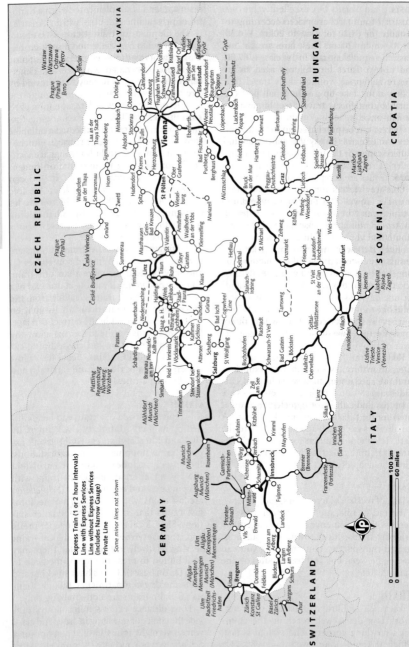

Costs

Austrian train fares are priced according to distance, eg €5.20 for 1km to 20km, €14.30 for 101km to 120km. These fares are for 2nd class; the equivalent rate in 1st class is €7.80 and €24.90. Fares for children aged six to 15 are half price; younger kids travel free if they don't take up a seat. Small pets (in suitable containers) travel free; larger pets go half-price.

Tickets can be purchased on the train but they cost €3 extra (unless you board at an unstaffed station or the ticket machine is out of order). Credit cards, Eurocheque cards and Eurocheques are accepted at all stations.

One-way tickets for journeys of 100km or under are valid for only one day and the journey can't be broken up. For trips of 101km or more, the ticket is valid for one month and you can alight en route, but you should tell the conductor so your ticket can be suitably endorsed. This is worth doing, as longer trips cost less per kilometre. Return tickets of up to 100km each way are also valid for one day; tickets for longer journeys are valid one month, though the initial outward journey must still be completed within three days. A return fare is usually the equivalent price of two one-way tickets.

Reduced rail fares on both national and international routes are sometimes available for those aged under 26; wave your passport and ask.

In this book, the fares quoted are always those for 2nd class.

Reservations

Reserving seats in 2nd class within Austria costs €3 for most express services; in 1st class, it's free. If you haven't reserved a seat, check before you sit whether your intended seat has been reserved by someone else down the line. Reservations are recommended for travel on weekends.

Train Passes

The Vorteilscard is an annual card available to all and sundry. It will probably not be worth the money for the average tourist, but for those sticking around for longer periods, it is a good deal. The Vorteilscard (photo required) entitles you to a 45% reduction on the ÖBB network and most private lines, and costs €99. The Vorteilscard 26 (for people under the age of 26) costs just €19.90 and the Vorteilscard Senior (men over 65, women over 60) costs €26.90; at these prices you can make savings even during a relatively short stay.

The Euro-Domino pass, available to European citizens only, allows three to eight days of unlimited travel within one month in Austria, as well as a reduced fare for those under age 26, and is available in 1st and 2nd class. A 2nd-class three-day pass costs €115 and peaks at €126 for eight days. Outside Europe, US citizens can purchase a similar product, the Austrian Railpass. It provides three days of unlimited travel over 15 days and costs US$109/160 for 2nd/1st-class seats. Extra days cost US$15/20 for 2nd/1st class.

TRANSPORT

Health

CONTENTS

Travel health depends on your predeparture preparations, your health care while travelling and how you handle any medical problems that develop. Major health worries are minimal in Austria; the population is very health-conscious, facilities are excellent, restaurants are highly sanitised and there are no major infectious diseases.

BEFORE YOU GO

Prevention is the key to staying healthy while abroad. A little planning before departure, particularly for pre-existing illnesses, will save trouble later. See your dentist before a long trip, carry a spare pair of contact lenses and glasses, and take your optical prescription with you. Bring medications in their original, clearly labelled, containers. A signed and dated letter from your physician describing your medical conditions and medications, including generic names, is also a good idea. If carrying syringes or needles, be sure to have a physician's letter documenting their medical necessity.

INSURANCE

If you're an EU citizen, an European Health Insurance Card (formerly an E111 form),

It's usually a good idea to consult your government's travel health website before departure, if one is available:

Australia www.dfat.gov.au/travel/
Canada www.travelhealth.gc.ca
UK www.doh.gov.uk/traveladvice/
US www.cdc.gov/travel/

available from health centres, covers you for most medical care. The cards will not cover you for non-emergencies or emergency repatriation home. Citizens from non-EU countries should find out if there is a reciprocal arrangement for free medical care between their country and Austria. If you do need health insurance, make sure you get a policy that covers you for the worst possible scenario, such as an accident requiring an emergency flight home. Find out in advance if your insurance plan will make payments directly to providers or reimburse you later for overseas health expenditures.

RECOMMENDED VACCINATIONS

The World Health Organisation (WHO) recommends that all travellers should be covered for diphtheria, tetanus, measles, mumps, rubella and polio, as well as Hepatitis B, regardless of their destination. Since most vaccines don't produce immunity until at least two weeks after they're given, visit a physician at least six weeks before departure.

ONLINE RESOURCES

The WHO's publication *International Travel and Health* is revised annually and is available online at www.who.int/ith. Other useful websites include www.mdtravelhealth.com (travel health recommendations for every country; updated daily), www.fitfortravel.scot.nhs.uk (general travel advice for the layman), www.ageconcern.org.uk (advice on travel for the elderly) and www.mariestopes.org.uk (information on women's health and contraception).

FURTHER READING

Health Advice for Travellers (currently called the 'T6' leaflet) is an annually updated leaflet by the Department of Health in the UK available free in British post offices. It contains some general information, legally required and recommended vaccines for different countries, reciprocal health agreements and a European Health Insurance Card/E111 application form. Lonely Planet's *Travel with Children* by Cathy Lanigan includes advice on travel health for younger children. Other recommended references include *Traveller's Health* by Dr Richard Dawood (Oxford University Press) and *Traveller's Good Health Guide* by Ted Lankester (Sheldon Press).

IN TRANSIT

DEEP VEIN THROMBOSIS (DVT)

Blood clots may form in the legs during plane flights, chiefly because of prolonged immobility. The longer the flight, the greater the risk. The chief symptom of DVT is swelling or pain of the foot, ankle, or calf, usually but not always on just one side. When a blood clot travels to the lungs, it may cause chest pain and breathing difficulties. Travellers with any of these symptoms should immediately seek medical attention.

To prevent the development of DVT on long flights you should walk about the cabin, contract the leg muscles while sitting, drink plenty of fluids and avoid alcohol and tobacco.

JET LAG & MOTION SICKNESS

To avoid jet lag (common when crossing more than five time zones) try to drink plenty of non-alcoholic fluids and eat light meals. Upon arrival, try to get exposure to natural sunlight and readjust your schedule (for meals, sleep and so on) as soon as possible.

Antihistamines such as dimenhydrinate (Dramamine) and meclizine (Antivert, Bonine) are usually the first choice for treating motion sickness. A herbal alternative is ginger.

IN AUSTRIA

AVAILABILITY & COST OF HEALTHCARE

Good healthcare is readily available and for minor self-limiting illnesses pharmacists can give valuable advice and sell over-the-counter medication. They can also advise when more specialised help is required and point you in the right direction. The standard of dental care is usually good, however it is sensible to have a dental check-up before a long trip. A straightforward, non-urgent appointment with a doctor might cost anything from €40 to €75.

Drugs, with or without prescription, must be paid for. *Apotheke* (pharmacies) handle all drugs, including aspirin.

INFECTIOUS DISEASES

Tickborne encephalitis is spread by tick bites. It is a serious infection of the brain and vaccination is advised for those in risk areas who are unable to avoid tick bites (such as campers, forestry workers and ramblers). Two doses of vaccine will give a year's protection, three doses up to three years'.

ENVIRONMENTAL HAZARDS
Altitude sickness

Lack of oxygen at high altitudes (over 2500m) affects most people to some extent. The effect may be mild or severe and occurs because less oxygen reaches the muscles and the brain at high altitude, requiring the heart and lungs to compensate by working harder. Symptoms of Acute Mountain Sickness (AMS) usually develop during the first 24 hours at altitude but may be delayed up to three weeks. Mild symptoms include headache, lethargy, dizziness, difficulty sleeping and loss of appetite. AMS may become more severe without warning and can be fatal. Severe symptoms include breathlessness, a dry, irritative cough (which may progress to the production of pink, frothy sputum), severe headaches, lack of coordination and balance, confusion, irrational behaviour, vomiting, drowsiness and unconsciousness. There is no hard and fast rule as to what is too high: AMS has been fatal at 3000m, although 3500m to 4500m is the usual range.

Treat mild symptoms by resting at the same altitude until recovery, usually a day or two. Paracetamol or aspirin can be taken for headaches. If symptoms persist or become worse, however, *immediate descent is necessary*; even 500m can help. Drug treatments should never be used to avoid descent or to enable further ascent.

HEALTH

Diamox (acetazolamide) reduces the headache of AMS and helps the body acclimatise to the lack of oxygen. It is only available on prescription and those who are allergic to the sulfonamide antibiotics may also be allergic to Diamox.

To prevent AMS:

- Ascend slowly – have frequent rest days, spending two to three nights at each rise of 1000m. If you reach a high altitude by trekking, acclimatisation takes place gradually and you are less likely to be affected than if you fly directly to high altitude.
- It is always wise to sleep at a lower altitude than the greatest height reached during the day if possible. Also, once above 3000m, care should be taken not to increase the sleeping altitude by more than 300m per day.
- Drink extra fluids. The mountain air is dry and cold and moisture is lost as you breathe. Evaporation of sweat may occur unnoticed and result in dehydration. A practical way to monitor hydration is by ensuring that urine is clear and plentiful.
- Eat light, high-carbohydrate meals for more energy.
- Avoid alcohol as it may increase the risk of dehydration.
- Avoid sedatives.
- Avoid tobacco.

In the UK, fact sheets are available from the **British Mountaineering Council** (177-179 Burton Rd, Manchester, M20 2BB).

Heatstroke

Heat exhaustion occurs following excessive fluid loss with inadequate replacement of fluids and salt. Symptoms include headache, dizziness and tiredness. Dehydration is already happening by the time you feel thirsty – aim to drink sufficient water to produce pale, diluted urine. To treat heat exhaustion, replace fluids with water and/or fruit juice, and cool the body with cold water and fans. Treat salt loss with salty fluids such as soup or Bovril, or add a little more table salt to foods than usual.

Heatstroke is much more serious, resulting in irrational and hyperactive behaviour and eventually loss of consciousness and death. Rapid cooling by spraying the body with water and fanning is ideal. Emergency fluid and electrolyte replacement by intravenous drip is recommended.

Hypothermia

Proper preparation will reduce the risks of getting hypothermia. Even on a hot day in the mountains, the weather can change rapidly; carry waterproof garments, warm layers and inform others of your route.

Acute hypothermia follows a sudden drop of temperature over a short time. Chronic hypothermia is caused by a gradual loss of temperature over hours.

Hypothermia starts with shivering, loss of judgment and clumsiness. Unless rewarming occurs, the sufferer deteriorates into apathy, confusion and coma. Prevent further heat loss by seeking shelter, warm dry clothing, hot sweet drinks and shared bodily warmth.

Frostbite is caused by freezing and subsequent damage to bodily extremities. Seriousness is determined by wind chill, temperature and length of exposure. Frostbite starts as frostnip (white numb areas of skin) from which complete recovery is expected with rewarming. As frostbite develops the skin blisters and then becomes black. The loss of damaged tissue eventually occurs. Adequate clothing, staying dry, keeping well hydrated and ensuring adequate calorie intake best prevent frostbite. Treatment involves rapid rewarming, avoiding refreezing and rubbing the affected areas.

Insect Bites & Stings

Ticks, which are usually found below 1200m in undergrowth at the forest edge or beside walking tracks, can carry encephalitis (see p375). Wearing long trousers tucked into walking boots or socks and using a DEET-based insect repellent is the best prevention against tick bites. If a tick is found attached, press down around the tick's head with tweezers, grab the head and gently pull upwards. (Chemist shops may be able to sell you a special instrument for this purpose.) Avoid pulling the rear of the body as this may squeeze the tick's gut contents through the attached mouth parts into the skin, increasing the risk of infection and disease. Smearing chemicals on the tick will not make it let go and is not recommended.

Mosquitoes are found in Austria, they may not carry malaria but can cause irritation and infected bites. Use a DEET-based insect repellent.

Bees and wasps only cause real problems to those with a severe allergy (anaphylaxis). If you have a severe allergy to bee or wasp stings carry an 'epipen' or similar adrenaline injection.

Bed bugs lead to very itchy lumpy bites. Spraying the mattress with crawling-insect killer after changing bedding will get rid of them.

Scabies are tiny mites that live in the skin, particularly between the fingers. They cause an intensely itchy rash. Scabies is easily treated with lotion from a pharmacy; other members of the household also need treating to avoid spreading scabies between asymptomatic carriers.

Snake Bites

Austria is home to several types of snake, which are more prevalent in the mountains. A couple can deliver a nasty, although not fatal, bite. Avoid getting bitten by wearing boots, socks and long trousers while hiking and do not stick your hand into holes or cracks. Half of those bitten by venomous snakes are not actually injected with poison (envenomed). If bitten by a snake, do not panic. Immobilise the bitten limb with a splint (eg a stick) and apply a bandage over the site with firm pressure, similar to a bandage over a sprain. Do not apply a tourniquet, or cut or suck the bite. Get the victim to medical help as soon as possible so that antivenin can be given if necessary.

TRAVELLING WITH CHILDREN

All travellers with children should know how to treat minor ailments and when to seek medical treatment. Make sure the children are up to date with routine vaccinations, and discuss possible travel vaccines well before departure as some vaccines are not suitable for children under a year old.

In hot, moist climates, any wound or break in the skin is likely to let in infection. The area should be cleaned and kept dry.

Remember to avoid contaminated food and water. If your child has vomiting or diarrhoea, the lost fluid and salts must be replaced. It may be helpful to take rehydration powders for reconstituting with boiled water.

Children should be encouraged to avoid and mistrust any dogs or other mammals because of the risk of rabies and other diseases. Any bite, scratch or lick from a warm-blooded, furry animal should immediately be thoroughly cleaned. If there is any possibility that the animal is infected with rabies, immediate medical assistance should be sought.

WOMEN'S HEALTH

Emotional stress, exhaustion and travelling through different time zones can all contribute to an upset in the menstrual pattern. If using oral contraceptives, remember some antibiotics, diarrhoea and vomiting can stop the pill from working and lead to the risk of pregnancy – remember to take condoms with you just in case. Time zones, gastrointestinal upsets and antibiotics do not affect injectable contraception.

Travelling during pregnancy is usually possible but always consult your doctor before planning your trip. The most risky times for travel are during the first 12 weeks of pregnancy and after 30 weeks.

SEXUAL HEALTH

Emergency contraception is most effective if taken within 24 hours after unprotected sex. The International Planned Parent Federation (www.ippf.org) can advise about the availability of contraception in different countries. If emergency contraception is needed, head to the nearest healthcare centre or consult a doctor.

Condoms are readily available throughout Austria. When buying condoms, look for a European CE mark, which means it has been rigorously tested, and then keep them in a cool dry place or they may crack and perish.

HEALTH

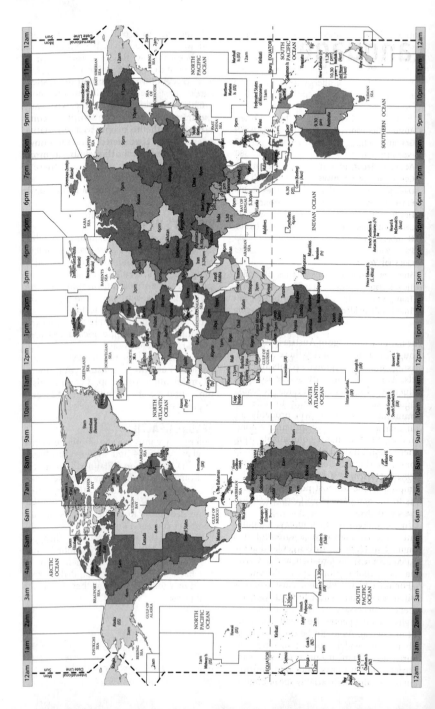

Language

CONTENTS

The national language of Austria is German, though for a small country there are a surprising number of regional accents and dialects. This is due in part to the isolating influence of high mountain ranges, causing language to evolve differently in different communities. Austrians will probably tell you that even they have difficulty understanding the accents of compatriots from other regions; indeed, the dialect spoken in Vorarlberg is much closer to Swiss German (*Schwyzertütsch*) – a language all but incomprehensible to most non-Swiss – than it is to the standard High German (*Hochdeutsch*) dialect.

In some areas of the country, a significant minority may have a different first language to German. In Burgenland about 25,000 people speak Croatian, and in Carinthia about 20,000 people speak Slovene.

Fortunately for visitors, Austrians can switch from their dialect to High German whenever necessary, and many speak some English. Young people are usually quite fluent in English. As might be expected, English is more widely spoken in cities and tourist areas than in out-of-the-way rural districts. Staff at tourist and train information offices almost invariably speak English;

hotel receptionists and restaurant waiters usually do as well, especially in the more upmarket establishments. As with any countries you visit, any attempt to communicate with the people in their native tongue will be appreciated, so some knowledge of German will definitely be an asset.

AUSTRIAN GERMAN

Though the grammar is the same as standard High German, there are also many words and expressions that are used only by Austrians. Some words are used throughout the country, others are only used in particular regions, although they'll probably be understood elsewhere. Most of them would not automatically be understood by non-Austrian German speakers. On the other hand, the 'standard' German equivalents would be understood by all Austrians.

Most of the greetings and farewells that we've included in the list of useful phrases are common only to Austria. *Servus* is an informal greeting, and can also be used when taking your leave. The word has been adopted as a motto by the Austrian national tourist office. *Grüss dich* or *Griassdi* (literally 'greet you') is also a familiar, informal greeting. It's especially used by people who don't want to bring God into the conversation (rather than *Grüss Gott* – 'greet God'). For 'goodbye', *Auf Wiederschauen* is the standard phrase; *Baba*, *Pfiati* or *Ciao* are less formal alternatives.

There are a number of ways to describe your lack of sobriety. If you're tipsy you can say *Ich bin beschwipst* or *Ich habe einen Schwips*. If you're definitely the worse for wear, the Viennese dialect expression is *I'hob an dulliö*. If you're very drunk, you could say *Ich bin zu*, though everyone will probably have figured that out already.

Some useful Austrian words are: *Blunzen* (black pudding); *Erdäpfel* (potato); *Faschiertes* (minced meat); *Gerstl* (money); *Karfiol* (cauliflower); *Maroni* (roasted chestnut); *Maut* (toll charge); *Müch* (milk); *Obers* (cream); *Paradeiser* (tomato); *Scherzl* (crust of bread); and *Stamperl* (glass for Schnapps). For more useful food-related words, see p71.

To request the bill in a restaurant, simply say *Zahlen, bitte* (pay, please).

Words that are more specifically Viennese include:

Beisl	small tavern for food and drink
Bim	tram
Haberer	friend
Stiftl	glass (for wine)
Verdrahn	to sell

The words and phrases included in this language guide should help you through the most common travel situations. Those with the desire to delve further into the language should get a copy of Lonely Planet's *German Phrasebook*.

GRAMMAR

German grammar can be a nightmare for English speakers. Nouns come in three genders: masculine, feminine and neuter (m/f/n). The corresponding forms of the definite article ('the' in English) are *der, die* and *das*, with the universal plural form, *die*. Nouns and articles will alter according to complex grammatical rules relating to the noun's function within a phrase – known as 'case'. In German there are four cases: nominative, accusative, dative and genitive. We haven't allowed for all possible permutations of case in this language guide – it's simply too complex to cover here. However, bad German is better than no German at all, so even if you muddle your cases, you'll find that you'll still be understood – and your efforts will definitely be appreciated regardless.

If you've noticed that written German seems to be full of capital letters, the reason is that German nouns always begin with a capital letter.

PRONUNCIATION

It's not difficult to pronounce German because almost all sounds can be found in English. Follow the pronunciation guide and you'll have no trouble communicating.

Vowels

German	Pronunciation Guide	
a	a	as the 'u' in 'run'
	ah	as the 'a' in 'father'
ei	ai	as as in 'aisle'
ä	air	as in 'air', with no 'r' sound
oo	aw	as in 'saw'
e	ay	as in 'say'
	e	as in 'bed'
ie	ee	as in 'reef'
ö	er	as in 'her', with no 'r' sound
i	i	as in 'bit'
o	o	as in 'pot'
eu/äu	oy	as in 'toy'
u	oo	as in 'moon'
au	ow	as in 'how'
ü	ü	'ee' said with rounded lips
u	u	as in 'put'

Consonants

The only two tricky consonant sounds in German are **ch** and **r**. All other consonants are pronounced much the same as their English counterparts (except **sch**, which is always as the 'sh' in 'shoe').

The **ch** sound is generally like a hiss from the back of the throat, as in Scottish *loch*. When **ch** occurs after the vowels **e** and **i** it's more like a 'sh' sound, produced with the tongue more forward in the mouth. In this book we've simplified things by using the one symbol 'kh' for both sounds.

The **r** sound is different from English, and it isn't rolled like in Italian or Spanish. It's pronounced at the back of the throat, almost like saying a 'g' sound, but with some friction – a bit like gargling.

Word Stress

As a general rule, word stress in German falls mostly on the first syllable. In our pronunciation guides the stressed syllable is shown in italics.

ACCOMMODATION

Where's a ...?

Wo ist ...?	vaw ist ...
bed and breakfast	
eine Pension	*ai*·ne pahng·*zyawn*
camping ground	
ein Campingplatz	ain *kem*·ping·plats
guesthouse	
eine Pension	*ai*·ne pahng·*zyawn*
hotel	
ein Hotel	ain ho·*tel*
inn	
ein Gasthof	ain *gast*·hawf
room in a private home	
ein Privatzimmer	ain pri·*vaht*·tsi·mer
youth hostel	
eine Jugendherberge	*ai*·ne *yoo*·gent·her·ber·ge

MAKING A RESERVATION
(for phone and written requests)

To ...	An ...
From ...	*Von ...*
Date	*Datum*
I'd like to book ...	*Ich möchte ... reservieren.*
	(see the list under 'Accommodation' for bed and room options)
in the name of ...	*auf den Namen ...*
from ... to ... (date)	*Vom ... bis zum ...*
credit card	*Kreditkarte*
number	*Nummer*
expiry date	*gültig bis ...* (valid until)
Please confirm availability and price.	*Bitte bestätigen Sie Verfügbarkeit und Preis.*

What's the address?
Wie ist die Adresse?
vee ist dee a·*dre*·se
I'd like to book a room, please.
Ich möchte bitte ein Zimmer reservieren.
ikh *merkh*·te *bi*·te ain *tsi*·mer re·zer·*vee*·ren
For (three) nights/weeks.
Für (drei) Nächte/Wochen.
für (drai) *nekh*·te/*vo*·khen

Do you have a ... room?
Haben Sie ein ...?   hah·ben zee ain ...
  single
  Einzelzimmer   ain·tsel·tsi·mer
  double
  Doppelzimmer mit   do·pel·tsi·mer mit
  einem Doppelbett   ai·nem do·pel·bet
  twin
  Doppelzimmer mit zwei do·pel·tsi·mer mit tsvai
  Einzelbetten   ain·tsel·be·ten

How much is it per night/person?
Wie viel kostet es   vee feel *kos*·tet es
pro Nacht/Person?   praw nakht/per·*zawn*
May I see it?
Kann ich es sehen?   kan ikh es *zay*·en
Can I get another room?
Kann ich noch ein   kan ikh nokh ain
Zimmer bekommen?   *tsi*·mer be·*ko*·men
It's fine. I'll take it.
Es ist gut, ich nehme es. es ist goot ikh *nay*·me es
I'm leaving now.
Ich reise jetzt ab.   ikh *rai*·ze yetst ap

CONVERSATION & ESSENTIALS

You should be aware that German uses polite and informal forms for 'you' (*Sie* and *du* respectively). When addressing people you don't know well you should always use the polite form (though younger people will be less inclined to expect it). In this language guide we use the polite form unless indicated by 'inf' (for 'informal') in brackets.

If you need to ask for assistance from a stranger, remember to always introduce your request with a simple *Entschuldigung* (Excuse me, ...).

Good day.
  Grüss Gott. (pol)   grüs got
Hello.
  Servus/Grüss Dich/   zer·vus/grüs dikh/
  Griassdi. (inf)   gree·as·dee

Good ...	*Guten ...*	goo·ten ...
day	*Tag*	tahk
morning	*Morgen*	mor·gen
afternoon	*Tag*	tahk
evening	*Abend*	ah·bent

Goodbye.
  Auf Wiedersehen.   owf vee·der·zay·en
  Pfiati/Ciao. (inf)   pfya·tee/chau
See you later.
  Bis später.   bis shpay·ter
Bye.
  Tschüss/Tschau.   chüs/chow
How are you?
  Wie geht es Ihnen? (pol) vee gayt es ee·nen
  Wie geht es dir? (inf)   vee gayt es deer
Fine. And you?
  Danke, gut.   dang·ke goot
... and you?
  Und Ihnen? (pol)   unt ee·nen
  Und dir? (inf)   unt deer
What's your name?
  Wie ist Ihr Name? (pol) vee ist eer nah·me
  Wie heisst du? (inf)   vee haist doo
My name is ...
  Mein Name ist .../   main nah·me ist .../
  Ich heisse ...   ikh hai·se ...

Yes.	*Ja.*	yah
No.	*Nein.*	nain
Please.	*Bitte.*	bi·te
Thank you	*Danke./*	dang·ke/
(very much).	*Vielen Dank.*	fee·len dangk
You're welcome.	*Bitte (sehr).*	bi·te (zair)

LANGUAGE

Sorry.	*Entschuldigung.*	ent·*shul*·di·gung
Excuse me, ...	*Entschuldigung.*	ent·*shul*·di·gung
(before asking for help or directions)		

DIRECTIONS

Could you help me, please?
Können Sie mir bitte helfen?
ker·nen zee meer *bi*·te *hel*·fen

Where's (a bank)?
Wo ist (eine Bank)?
vaw ist (*ai*·ne bangk)

I'm looking for (the cathedral).
Ich suche (den Dom).
ikh *zoo*·khe (dayn dawm)

Which way's (a public toilet)?
In welcher Richtung ist (eine öffentliche toilette)?
in *vel*·kher *rikh*·tung ist (*ai*·ne *er*·fent·li·khe to·a·*le*·te)

How can I get there?
Wie kann ich da hinkommen?
vee kan ikh dah *hin*·ko·men

How far is it?
Wie weit ist es?
vee *vait* ist es

Can you show me (on the map)?
Können Sie es mir (auf der Karte) zeigen?
ker·nen zee es meer (owf dair *kar*·te) *tsai*·gen

SIGNS	
Polizei	Police
Polizeiwache	Police Station
Eingang	Entrance
Ausgang	Exit
Offen	Open
Geschlossen	Closed
Kein Zutritt	No Entry
Rauchen Verboten	No Smoking
Verboten	Prohibited
Toiletten (WC)	Toilets
Herren	Men
Damen	Women

near	*nahe*	*nah*·e
far away	*weit weg*	vait vek
here	*hier*	heer
there	*dort*	dort
on the corner	*an der Ecke*	an dair *e*·ke
straight ahead	*geradeaus*	ge·rah·de·*ows*
opposite ...	*gegenüber ...*	gay·gen·*ü*·ber ...
next to ...	*neben ...*	*nay*·ben ...
behind ...	*hinter ...*	*hin*·ter ...
in front of ...	*vor ...*	fawr ...
north	*Norden*	*nor*·den
south	*Süden*	*zü*·den
east	*Osten*	*os*·ten
west	*Westen*	*ves*·ten

Turn ...
Biegen Sie ... ab.   bee·gen zee ... ap

left/right	*links/rechts*	lingks/rekhts
at the next corner	*an der nächsten Ecke*	an dair *naykhs*·ten *e*·ke
at the traffic lights	*bei der Ampel*	bai dair *am*·pel

EMERGENCIES

Help!
Hilfe!   hil·fe

It's an emergency!
Es ist ein Notfall!   es ist ain *nawt*·fal

Call the police!
Rufen Sie die Polizei!   roo·fen zee dee po·li·*tsai*

Call a doctor!
Rufen Sie einen Arzt!   roo·fen zee *ai*·nen artst

Call an ambulance!
Rufen Sie einen Krankenwagen!   roo·fen zee *ai*·nen *krang*·ken·vah·gen

Leave me alone!
Lassen Sie mich in Ruhe!   la·sen zee mikh in *roo*·e

Go away!
Gehen Sie weg!   gay·en zee vek

I'm lost.
Ich habe mich verirrt.   ikh *hah*·be mikh fer·*irt*

HEALTH

Where's the nearest ...?
Wo ist der/die/das nächste ...? (m/f/n)
vaw ist dair/die/das *naykhs*·te ...

chemist
Apotheke (f)   a·po·*tay*·ke

dentist
Zahnarzt (m)   *tsahn*·artst

doctor
Arzt (m)   artst

hospital
Krankenhaus (n)   *krang*·ken·hows

I need a doctor.
Ich brauche einen Arzt.
ikh *brow*·khe *ai*·nen artst

Is there a (night) chemist nearby?
Gibt es in der Nähe eine (Nacht)Apotheke?
gipt es in dair *nay*·e *ai*·ne (nakht·)a·po·*tay*·ke

I'm sick.
Ich bin krank.
ikh bin krangk

It hurts here.
Es tut hier weh.
es toot heer *vay*
I've been vomiting.
Ich habe mich übergeben.
ikh *hah*·be mikh *ü*·ber·*gay*·ben
I have diarrhoea/fever/headache.
Ich habe Durchfall/Fieber/Kopfschmerzen.
ikh *hah*·be *durkh*·fal/*fee*·ber/*kopf*·shmer·tsen
(I think) I'm pregnant.
(Ich glaube,) Ich bin schwanger.
(ikh *glow*·be) ikh bin *shvang*·er

I'm allergic to ...
Ich bin allergisch gegen ...   ikh bin a·*lair*·gish *gay*·gen ...
  antibiotics
  Antibiotika   ·an·ti·bi·*aw*·ti·ka
  aspirin
  Aspirin   as·pi·*reen*
  penicillin
  Penizillin   pe·ni·tsi·*leen*

LANGUAGE DIFFICULTIES
Do you speak English?
Sprechen Sie Englisch?
shpre·khen zee *eng*·lish
Does anyone here speak English?
Spricht hier jemand Englisch?
shprikht heer *yay*·mant *eng*·lish
Do you understand (me)?
Verstehen Sie (mich)?
fer·*shtay*·en zee (mikh)
I (don't) understand.
Ich verstehe (nicht).
ikh fer·*shtay*·e (nikht)
How do you say ... in German?
Wie sagt man ... auf Deutsch?
vee zagt man ... owf doytsh

Could you please ...?
Könnten Sie ...?   *kern*·ten zee ...
  speak more slowly
  bitte langsamer sprechen *bi*·te *lang*·za·mer *shpre*·khen
  repeat that
  das bitte wiederholen das *bi*·te vee·der·*haw*·len
  write it down
  das bitte aufschreiben das *bi*·te owf·*shrai*·ben

NUMBERS

0	*eins*	aints
1	*ains*	aints
2	*zwei*	tsvai
3	*drei*	drai
4	*vier*	feer
5	*fünf*	fünf
6	*sechs*	zeks
7	*sieben*	zee·ben
8	*acht*	akht
9	*neun*	noyn
10	*zehn*	tsayn
11	*elf*	elf
12	*zwölf*	zverlf
13	*dreizehn*	drai·tsayn
14	*vierzehn*	feer·tsayn
15	*fünfzehn*	fünf·tsayn
16	*sechzehn*	zeks·tsayn
17	*siebzehn*	zeep·tsayn
18	*achtzehn*	akh·tsayn
19	*neunzehn*	noyn·tsayn
20	*zwanzig*	tsvan·tsikh
21	*einundzwanzig*	ain·unt·tsvan·tsikh
22	*zweiundzwanig*	tsvai·unt·tsvan·tsikh
30	*dreizig*	drai·tsikh
31	*einunddreizig*	ain·und·*drai*·tsikh
40	*vierzig*	feer·tsikh
50	*fünfzig*	fünf·tsikh
60	*sechzig*	zekh·tsikh
70	*siebzig*	zeep·tsikh
80	*achtzig*	akh·tsikh
90	*neunzig*	noyn·tsikh
100	*hundert*	hun·dert
1000	*tausend*	tow·sent
2000	*zwei tausend*	tsvai *tow*·sent

PAPERWORK

name	*Name*	*nah*·me
nationality	*Staatsan-gehörigkeit*	shtahts·an·ge·*her*·rikh·kait
date of birth	*Geburtsdatum*	ge·*burts*·dah·tum
place of birth	*Geburtsort*	ge·*burts*·ort
sex/gender	*Sex*	seks
passport	*(Reise)Pass*	(*rai·ze·*)pahs
visa	*Visum*	*vee*·zum

QUESTION WORDS

Who?	*Wer?*	vair
What?	*Was?*	vas
Where?	*Wo?*	vo
When?	*Wann?*	van
How?	*Wie?*	vee
Why?	*Warum?*	va·*rum*
Which?	*Welcher?*	*vel*·kher
How much?	*Wie viel?*	vee feel
How many?	*Wie viele?*	vee *fee*·le

SHOPPING & SERVICES
I'm looking for ...
Ich suche ...
ikh *zoo*·khe ...

Where's the (nearest) ...?
Wo ist der/die/das (nächste) ...? (m/f/n)
vaw ist dair/dee/das (*naykhs*·te) ...
What time does it open/close?
Wann macht er/sie/es auf/zu? (m/f/n)
van makht air/zee/es owf/tsoo
Where can I buy ...?
Wo kann ich ... kaufen?
vaw kan ikh ... *kow*·fen

an ATM	*ein Geldautomat*	ain *gelt*·ow·to·maht
an exchange office	*eine Geldwechsel-stube*	*ai*·ne *gelt*·vek·sel·shtoo·be
a bank	*eine Bank*	*ai*·ne bangk
the ... embassy	*die ... Botschaft*	dee *bot*·shaft
the hospital	*das Krankenhous*	das *krang*·ken·hows
the market	*der Markt*	dair markt
the police	*die Polizei*	dee po·li·*tsai*
the post office	*das Postamt*	das *post*·amt
a public phone	*ein öffentliches Telefon*	ain er·fent·li·khes te·le·*fawn*
a public toilet	*eine öffentliche Toilette*	ain er·fent·li·khe to·a·*le*·te

I'd like to buy ...
Ich möchte ... kaufen.
ikh *merkh*·te ... *kow*·fen
How much (is this)?
Wie viel (kostet das)?
vee feel (*kos*·tet das)
That's too much/expensive.
Das ist zu viel/teuer.
das ist tsoo feel/*toy*·er
Can you lower the price?
Können Sie mit dem Preis heruntergehen?
ker·nen zee mit dem prais he·*run*·ter·gay·en
Do you have something cheaper?
Haben Sie etwas Billigeres?
hah·ben zee *et*·vas *bi*·li·ge·res
I'm just looking.
Ich schaue mich nur um.
ikh *show*·e mikh noor um
Can you write down the price?
Können Sie den Preis aufschreiben?
ker·nen zee dayn prais *owf*·shrai·ben
Do you have any others?
Haben Sie noch andere?
hah·ben zee nokh *an*·de·re
Can I look at (it)?
Können Sie (ihn/sie/es) mir zeigen? (m/f/n)
ker·nen zee (een/zee/es) meer *tsai*·gen

more	*mehr*	mair
less	*weniger*	*vay*·ni·ger
smaller	*kleiner*	*klai*·ner·tee
bigger	*grosser*	*gro*·ser

Do you accept ...?
Nehmen Sie ...? *nay*·men zee ...
  credit cards
  Kreditkarten kre·*deet*·kar·ten
  travellers cheques
  Reiseschecks *rai*·ze·sheks

I'd like to ...
Ich möchte ... ikh *merkh*·te ...
  change money (cash)
  Geld umtauschen gelt *um*·tow·shen
  cash a cheque
  einen Scheck einlösen *ai*·nen shek *ain*·ler·zen
  change some travellers cheques
  Reiseschecks einlösen *rai*·ze·sheks *ain*·ler·zen

I want to buy a phone card.
Ich möchte eine Telefonkarte kaufen.
ikh *merkh*·te *ai*·ne te·le·*fawn*·kar·te *kow*·fen
Where's the local Internet cafe?
Wo ist hier ein Internet-Café?
vaw ist heer ain *in*·ter·net·ka·fay

I'd like to ...
Ich möchte ... ikh *merkh*·te ...
  get Internet access
  Internetzugang haben *in*·ter·net·tsoo·gang *hah*·ben
  check my email
  meine E-Mails checken *mai*·ne *ee*·mayls *che*·ken

TIME & DATES
What time is it?
Wie spät ist es? vee shpayt ist es
It's (one) o'clock.
Es ist (ein) Uhr. es ist (ain) oor
Twenty past one.
Zwanzig nach eins. *tsvan*·tsikh nahkh ains
Half past one.
Halb zwei. ('half two') halp tsvai
Quarter to one.
Viertel vor eins. *fir*·tel fawr ains
am
  morgens/vormittags *mor*·gens/*fawr*·mi·tahks
pm
  nachmittags/abends nahkh·mi·tahks/*ah*·bents

now	*jetzt*	yetst
today	*heute*	*hoy*·te
tonight	*heute Abend*	*hoy*·te *ah*·bent
tomorrow	*morgen*	*mor*·gen
yesterday	*gestern*	*ges*·tern
morning	*Morgen*	*mor*·gen
afternoon	*Nachmittag*	*nahkh*·mi·tahk
evening	*Abend*	*ah*·bent

Monday	Montag	*mawn*·tahk
Tuesday	Dienstag	*deens*·tahk
Wednesday	Mittwoch	*mit*·vokh
Thursday	Donnerstag	*do*·ners·tahk
Friday	Freitag	*frai*·tahk
Saturday	Samstag	*zams*·tahk
Sunday	Sonntag	*zon*·tahk

January	Januar	*yan*·u·ahr
February	Februar	*fay*·bru·ahr
March	März	merts
April	April	a·*pril*
May	Mai	mai
June	Juni	*yoo*·ni
July	Juli	*yoo*·li
August	August	ow·*gust*
September	September	zep·*tem*·ber
October	Oktober	ok·*taw*·ber
November	November	no·*vem*·ber
December	Dezember	de·*tsem*·ber

TRANSPORT
Public Transport
What time does the ... leave?
Wann fährt ... ab?
van fairt ... ap

boat
das Boot — das bawt
bus
der Bus — dair bus
train
der Zug — dair tsook
tram
die Strassenbahn — dee *shtrah*·sen·bahn

What time's the ... bus?
Wann fährt der ... Bus?
van fairt dair ... bus

first
erste — *ers*·te
last
letzte — *lets*·te
next
nächste — *naykhs*·te

Where's the nearest metro station?
Wo ist der nächste U-Bahnhof?
vaw ist dair *naykhs*·te oo·bahn·hawf
Which bus goes to ...?
Welcher Bus fährt ...?
vel·kher bus fairt ...

A ... ticket to (Berlin).
Einen ... nach (Berlin).
ai·nen ... nahkh (ber·*leen*)

one-way
einfache Fahrkarte — *ain*·fa·khe *fahr*·kar·te
return
Rückfahrkarte — *rük*·fahr·kar·te
1st-class
Fahrkarte erster Klasse — *fahr*·kar·te *ers*·ter *kla*·se
2nd-class
Fahrkarte zweiter Klasse — *fahr*·kar·te *tsvai*·ter *kla*·se

The ... is cancelled.
... ist gestrichen. — ... ist ge·*shtri*·khen
The ... is delayed.
... hat Verspätung. — ... hat fer·*shpay*·tung
Is this seat free?
Ist dieser Platz frei? — ist *dee*·zer plats frai
Do I need to change trains?
Muss ich umsteigen? — mus ikh *um*·shtai·gen
Are you free? (taxi)
Sind Sie frei? — zint zee frai
How much is it to ...?
Was kostet es bis ...? — vas *kos*·tet es bis ...
Please take me to (this address).
Bitte bringen Sie mich — *bi*·te *bring*·en zee mikh
zu (dieser Adresse). — tsoo (*dee*·zer a·*dre*·se)

Private Transport
Where can I hire a ...?
Wo kann ich ... mieten?
vaw kan ikh ... *mee*·ten
I'd like to hire a/an ...
Ich möchte ... mieten.
ikh *merkh*·te ... *mee*·ten

automatic
ein Fahrzeug mit — ain *fahr*·tsoyk mit
Automatik — ow·to·*mah*·tik
bicycle
ein Fahrrad — ain *fahr*·raht
car
ein Auto — ain *ow*·to
4WD
ein Allradfahrzeug — ain *al*·raht·fahr·tsoyk
manual
ein Fahrzeug — ain *fahr*·tsoyk
mit Schaltung — mit *shal*·tung
motorbike
ein Motorrad — ain *maw*·tor·raht

How much is it per day/week?
Wie viel kostet es pro Tag/Woche?
vee feel *kos*·tet es praw tahk/*vo*·khe

petrol (gas)	Benzin	ben·*tseen*
diesel	Diesel	*dee*·zel
leaded	verbleites	fer·*blai*·tes
	Benzin	ben·*tseen*

LANGUAGE

ROAD SIGNS

Gefahr	Danger
Einfahrt Verboten	No Entry
Einbahnstrasse	One Way
Einfahrt	Entrance
Ausfahrt	Exit
Ausfahrt Freihalten	Keep Clear
Parkverbot	No Parking
Halteverbot	No Stopping
Mautstelle	Toll
Radweg	Cycle Path
Umleitung	Detour
Überholverbot	No Overtaking

LPG	*Autogas*	ow·to·gahs
regular	*Normalbenzin*	nor·*mahl*·ben·tseen
unleaded	*bleifreies*	blai·frai·es
	Benzin	ben·*tseen*

Where's a petrol station?
Wo ist eine Tankstelle?
vaw ist *ai*·ne *tangk*·shte·le

Does this road go to ...?
Führt diese Strasse nach ...?
fürt *dee*·ze *shtrah*·se nahkh ...

(How long) Can I park here?
(Wie lange) Kann ich hier parken?
(vee *lang*·e) kan ikh heer *par*·ken

Where do I pay?
Wo muss ich bezahlen?
vaw mus ikh be·*tsah*·len

I need a mechanic.
Ich brauche einen Mechaniker.
ikh *brow*·khe *ai*·nen me·*khah*·ni·ker

The car has broken down (at ...)
Ich habe (in ...) eine Panne mit meinem Auto.
ikh *hah*·be (in ...) *ai*·ne *pa*·ne mit *mai*·nem *ow*·to

I had an accident.
Ich hatte einen Unfall.
ikh *ha*·te *ai*·nen *un*·fal

The car/motorbike won't start.
Das Auto/Motorrad springt nicht an.
das *ow*·to/*maw*·tor·raht shpringkt nikht an

I have a flat tyre.
Ich habe eine Reifenpanne.
ikh *hah*·be *ai*·ne *rai*·fen·pa·ne

I've run out of petrol.
Ich habe kein Benzin mehr.
ikh *hah*·be kain ben·*tseen* mair

TRAVEL WITH CHILDREN

I need a/an ...
Ich brauche ... ikh *brow*·khe ...

Is there a/an ...?
Gibt es ...? gipt es ...

baby change room
einen Wickelraum *ai*·nen *vi*·kel·rowm

baby seat
einen Babysitz *ai*·nen *bay*·bi·zits

booster seat
einen Kindersitz *ai*·nen *kin*·der·zits

child-minding service
einen Babysitter-Service *ai*·nen *bay*·bi·si·ter·*ser*·vis

children's menu
eine Kinderkarte *ai*·ne *kin*·der·kar·te

(English-speaking) babysitter
einen (englisch- *ai*·nen (*eng*·lish·
sprachigen) Babysitter shprah·khi·gen) *bay*·bi·si·ter

highchair
einen Kinderstuhl *ai*·nen *kin*·der·shtool

potty
ein Kindertöpfchen ain *kin*·der·terpf·khen

stroller
einen Kinderwagen *ai*·nen *kin*·der·vah·gen

Do you mind if I breastfeed here?
Kann ich meinem Kind hier die Brust geben?
kan ikh *mai*·nem kint heer dee brust *gay*·ben

Are children allowed?
Sind Kinder erlaubt?
zint *kin*·der er·*lowpt*

Also available from Lonely Planet:
German Phrasebook

Glossary

Abfahrt – departure (trains)
Altstadt – old city
Ankunft – arrival (trains)
ANTO – Austrian National Tourist Office
Apotheken – pharmacy
Ausgang – exit
Auto – car
autobahn – motorway

Bad – bath
Bahnhof – train station
Bahnsteig – train station platform
Bankomat – ATM; cash point
Bauernhof – farmhouse
Bauernmarkt – farmer's market
Beisl – small tavern or restaurant
Benzin – unleaded petrol
Berg – hill or mountain
Bergbahn – cable car
Bezirk – district in a town or city
Bibliothek – library
Biedermeier period – 19th-century art movement in Germany and Austria
Botschaft – embassy
Brauerei – brewery
Briefmarken – stamps
Brunnen – fountain
Bundesbus – state bus; run by the railway (Bahnhbus) or the post office (Postbus)
Burg – castle/fortress
Buschenschank (Buschenschenken) – wine tavern(s)

Café Konditorei(en) – coffee house(s)
Christkindlmärkte – Christmas market

Dirndl – women's traditional dress
Donau – Danube
Dorf – village

EC – EuroCity; express train
EEA – European Economic Area; comprises European Union states plus Iceland, Liechtenstein and Norway
EN – EuroNight; international and domestic night train
EU – European Union

Fahrplan – timetable
Feiertag – public holiday
Ferienwohnung(en) – self-catering holiday apartment(s)
Festung – fortress

Fiaker – fiacre; small horse-drawn carriage
Flohmarkt – flea market
Flughafen – airport
Fluss – river
Föhn – hot, dry wind that sweeps down from the mountains, mainly in early spring and autumn
FPÖ – Freedom Party (politics)
Freizeitzentrum – sports and leisure centre
Friedhof – cemetery

Gästehaus – guesthouse; sometimes has a restaurant
Gästekarte – guest card; issued by hostels and resorts, used to obtain discounts
Gasthaus – inn or restaurant without accommodation
Gasthof – inn or restaurant; usually has accommodation
Gemeindeamt – local authority office

Hafen – harbour; port
Handy – mobile phone
Hauptbahnhof – main train station
Hauptpost – main post office
Hauptstadt – capital
Heuriger (Heurigen) – wine tavern(s)

IC – InterCity; express train
Imbiss – snack bar

Jugendherberge/Jugendgästehaus – youth hostel

Kaffeehaus – see *Café Konditorei*
Kapelle – chapel
Kärnten – Carinthia (Austrian province)
Kino – cinema
Kirche – church
Klettern – rock climbing
Konsulat(e) – consulate(s)
Krankenhaus – hospital
Krügerl – glass holding 0.5L
Kunst – art
Kurzparkzone – short-term parking zone

Landesmuseum – provincial museum
Langlauf – cross-country skiing
Lieder – lyrical song
LKW – bus

Mahlzeit – Austrian salutation at the commencement of a meal
Markt – market
Maut – toll (or indicating a toll booth)

Mehrwertsteuer (MWST) – value-added tax
Melange – coffee
Mensa – university cafeteria
Mitfahrzentrale – hitching organisation
Münze – coins

ÖAMTC – national motoring organisation
ÖAV – Austrian Alpine Club
ÖBB – Austrian federal railway
Österreich – Austria
ÖVP – Austrian People's Party (politics)

Parkschein – parking voucher
Pension – B&B
Pfarrkirche – parish church
Pfiff – glass containing 0.125L
PKW – car
Platz – town or village square
Polizei – police
Postamt – post office
Postlagernde Briefe – poste restante
Privat Zimmer – private rooms (accommodation)

Rad – bicycle
radfahren – cycling
Radler – mixture of beer and lemonade
Rathaus – town hall
Reisebüro – travel agency
reiten – horse riding

Saal – hall
S-Bahn – suburban train system
SC – SuperCity; express train
Schloss – palace; castle
Secession movement – early 20th-century movement in Vienna seeking to establish a more functional style in architecture; led by Otto Wagner (1841–1918)
See – lake
sgraffito – mural or decoration in which the top layer is scratched off to reveal the original colour/medium underneath

Silvester – New Year's Eve
skifahren – skiing
Stadt – city
Stadtmuseum – city museum
Stadtpfarrkirch – see *Pfarrkirche*
Steiermark – Styria (Austrian province)
Stift – abbey
Stock – floor, in a multistoried building
Strandbad – designated bathing area on a lake or river; usually has an entry fee
Studentenheime – student residences
surfen – wind surfing

Tabak – tobacconist
Tagesteller/Tagesmenü – the set dish or meal of the day in a restaurant; sometimes abbreviated as 'Menü'
Tal – valley
Telefon-Wertkarte – phonecard
Tirol – Tyrol
Tor – gate
Triebwagen – normal (not steam) train in Tyrol

U-Bahn – urban underground rail system
Urlaub – holiday

Verein – club
Vienna Circle – group of philosophers centred on Vienna University in the 1920s and 1930s
Vienna Group – avant-garde art/literary movement formed in the 1950s

Wald – forest
wandern – walking/hiking
Wein – wine
Wien – Vienna
Wiener Gruppe – see *Vienna Group*
Wiener Kreis – see *Vienna Circle*
Würstel Stand – sausage stand

Zimmer frei – see *Privat Zimmer*
Zug – train

Behind the Scenes

THIS BOOK

This 4th edition of *Austria* was coordinated by Neal Bedford with assistance from coauthor Gemma Pitcher. Lisa Ball wrote the 'Venus of Willendorf' boxed text, and Dr Ed Baxter wrote the 'Viennese Actionism' boxed text. The Health chapter is based on original research by Dr Caroline Evans. The 1st, 2nd and 3rd editions were written by Mark Honan.

THANKS from the Authors

Neal Bedford This book could not have been put together without the help of tourist office staff across the country – many thanks to all those people who answered my (seemingly) endless questions. Special thanks must go to Margot Bachbauer of Steiermark Tourismus, Ulrike Kinz from Kinz Kommunication and Helga Weinhardt of Hall in Tyrol for going that extra distance to provide me with invaluable information. In Graz, a big *Danke* to Carola Hecking for her invaluable help on her beloved city. Viennese residents who had no choice in passing on their extensive national knowledge are next in line for my gratitude. Tom P, Zsuzsa and Tina all went out of their way to help, as did the folks at Schottenfeldgasse: Alice, Barbara, Sandra, Robert, Johannes and the gang at Caramel; more chips and sweets will be supplied. A special thanks to Tiffany for letting me drag her from one castle to the next on my excursions from Vienna. Loads of thanks also goes out to Peter Zulka of the Umweltbundesamt for his invaluable input into the endangered species section of the Environment chapter. Last, but certainly by no means least, thanks to the Kuzaras for everything.

Gemma Pitcher I would like to thank all the helpful Austrians I met along my route, especially the staff of the regional and town tourist offices who made life and research so much easier for me.

CREDITS

Austria 4 was commissioned and developed in Lonely Planet's London office by Judith Bamber, with assistance from Sam Trafford. Cartography for this title was developed by Adrian Persoglia.

The editing of this book was coordinated by Brooke Lyons, with assistance from John Hinman, Simon Sellars, Cinzia Cavallaro, Tasmin McNaughtan, Yvonne Byron, Imogen Bannister, Craig Kilburn and Dan Caleo. Corey Hutchison coordinated the cartography.

Glenn van der Knijff managed the project through production, with assistance from Fabrice Rocher. The book was laid out by Jacqui Saunders. Kristin Guthrie designed the cover, and Jacqui Saunders laid it out. Brooke Lyons prepared the index, with assistance from Tasmin and Dan. The language chapter was compiled by Quentin Frayne. Thanks to Rebecca Lalor and Nick Stebbing for their invaluable technical assistance.

Thanks also to Corrie Waddell for her advice and assistance.

THANKS from Lonely Planet

Many thanks to the following travellers who used the last edition and wrote to us with helpful hints, useful advice and interesting anecdotes.

A Tony Anderson, John Arwe, Derilene Aston **B** Peter Baker, Helmut Bettr, Sam Brkich, Derrick Browne, Stefan Brunnsteiner

THE LONELY PLANET STORY

The story begins with a classic travel adventure: Tony and Maureen Wheeler's 1972 journey across Europe and Asia to Australia. There was no useful information about the overland trail then, so Tony and Maureen published the first Lonely Planet guidebook to meet a growing need.

From a kitchen table, Lonely Planet has grown to become the largest independent travel publisher in the world, with offices in Melbourne (Australia), Oakland (USA) and London (UK). Today Lonely Planet guidebooks cover the globe. We produce an ever-growing list of books and information in a variety of media. Some things haven't changed. Our main aim is still to make it possible for adventurous travellers to get out there – to explore and better understand the world.

At Lonely Planet we believe travellers can make a positive contribution to the countries they visit – if they respect their host communities and spend their money wisely. Every year 5% of company profit is donated to charities around the world.

C Samantha Campbell, Niall Carroll, Polly Cook, Kylie Cox **D** Simon Day, Ron Deacon, Richard Drapes **G** Volkmar Geiblinger, Meahan Grande, Ronalie Green **H** David Haugh, Adrian Hervey, Susanne Hrinkov **I** Irena Irena **J** Chris Jones, Jo Jones, Michl Joos **K** Markus Kaim, Kerry King, Helke Knuetter, Ben Kurrein **L** Anne-Mari Laiho, Clive Langmead, Kathy Lavrila, Michael Lavrila, Ben Li, Anthony Liem **M** Alessandro Maccari, Steve McGrory, Dr J S McLintock, Lin Merry, Craig Mitchell **O** Donal O'Brolchain **P** Peter Preiswerk, Elaine Rati Kochar **R** Lorraine Rees, Ronald Jan Rieger, Miguel Rolo, Anne & Peter Rolston, Nagiller Rudolf, Kathy Ruffing, Sue Rundle **S** Rolf Schlinwein, Richard Scotton, Penelope Seidler, Joanne Shamma, Mel Siew, Eivind Stene, Eva Claire Synkowski **T** Emily Turner-Graham **V** Philippe Voiry, Anne Volmari **W** James Whitson, D S Wyber **Z** Attila Zsunyi

ACKNOWLEDGMENTS

Many thanks to the following for the use of their content:

Globe on back cover © Mountain High Maps 1993 Digital Wisdom, Inc.

SEND US YOUR FEEDBACK

We love to hear from travellers – your comments keep us on our toes and help make our books better. Our well-travelled team reads every word on what you loved or loathed about this book. Although we cannot reply individually to postal submissions, we always guarantee that your feedback goes straight to the appropriate authors, in time for the next edition. Each person who sends us information is thanked in the next edition – and the most useful submissions are rewarded with a free book.

To send us your updates – and find out about Lonely Planet events, newsletters and travel news – visit our award-winning website: **www.lonelyplanet.com/feedback**

Note: We may edit, reproduce and incorporate your comments in Lonely Planet products such as guidebooks, websites and digital products, so let us know if you don't want your comments reproduced or your name acknowledged. For a copy of our privacy policy visit www.lonelyplanet.com/privacy

SEND US YOUR FEEDBACK

Index

INDEX

000 Map pages
000 Location of colour photographs

INDEX

000 Map pages
000 Location of colour photographs

INDEX

INDEX

000 Map pages
000 Location of colour photographs

400

MAP LEGEND

ROUTES

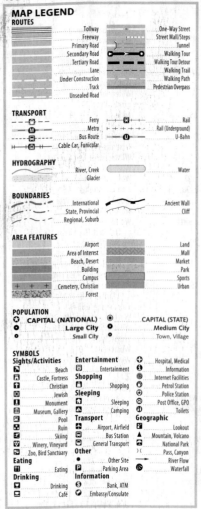

Tollway	One-Way Street
Freeway	Street Mall/Steps
Primary Road	Tunnel
Secondary Road	Walking Tour
Tertiary Road	Walking Tour Detour
Lane	Walking Trail
Under Construction	Walking Path
Track	Pedestrian Overpass
Unsealed Road	

TRANSPORT

Ferry	Rail
Metro	Rail (Underground)
Bus Route	U-Bahn
Cable Car, Funicular	

HYDROGRAPHY

River, Creek	Water
Glacier	

BOUNDARIES

International	Ancient Wall
State, Provincial	Cliff
Regional, Suburb	

AREA FEATURES

Airport	Land
Area of Interest	Mall
Beach, Desert	Market
Building	Park
Campus	Sports
Cemetery, Christian	Urban
Forest	

POPULATION

◎ CAPITAL (NATIONAL)	◉ CAPITAL (STATE)
● Large City	○ Medium City
● Small City	○ Town, Village

SYMBOLS

Sights/Activities
- Beach
- Castle, Fortress
- Christian
- Jewish
- Monument
- Museum, Gallery
- Pool
- Ruin
- Skiing
- Winery, Vineyard
- Zoo, Bird Sanctuary

Eating
- Eating

Drinking
- Drinking
- Café

Entertainment
- Entertainment

Shopping
- Shopping

Sleeping
- Sleeping
- Camping

Transport
- Airport, Airfield
- Bus Station
- General Transport

Other
- Other Site
- Parking Area

Information
- ⓢ Bank, ATM
- ⓔ Embassy/Consulate

- ⊕ Hospital, Medical
- ⓘ Information
- @ Internet Facilities
- Petrol Station
- Police Station
- ⊗ Post Office, GPO
- Toilets

Geographic
- Lookout
- ▲ Mountain, Volcano
- National Park
-)(Pass, Canyon
- → River Flow
- Waterfall

LONELY PLANET OFFICES

Australia
Head Office
Locked Bag 1, Footscray, Victoria 3011
☎ 03 8379 8000, fax 03 8379 8111
talk2us@lonelyplanet.com.au

USA
150 Linden St, Oakland, CA 94607
☎ 510 893 8555, toll free 800 275 8555
fax 510 893 8572, info@lonelyplanet.com

UK
72–82 Rosebery Ave,
Clerkenwell, London EC1R 4RW
☎ 020 7841 9000, fax 020 7841 9001
go@lonelyplanet.co.uk

Published by Lonely Planet Publications Pty Ltd
ABN 36 005 607 983

© Lonely Planet 2005

© photographers as indicated 2005

Cover photographs: Windows, Greg Stott/Masterfile (front); Umbrellas of café, Innsbruck, Tyrol, Chris Mellor/Lonely Planet Images (back). Many of the images in this guide are available for licensing from Lonely Planet Images: www.lonelyplanetimages.com

All rights reserved. No part of this publication may be copied, stored in a retrieval system, or transmitted in any form by any means, electronic, mechanical, recording or otherwise, except brief extracts for the purpose of review, and no part of this publication may be sold or hired, without the written permission of the publisher.

Printed through Colorcraft Ltd, Hong Kong.
Printed in China

Lonely Planet and the Lonely Planet logo are trademarks of Lonely Planet and are registered in the US Patent and Trademark Office and in other countries.

Lonely Planet does not allow its name or logo to be appropriated by commercial establishments, such as retailers, restaurants or hotels. Please let us know of any misuses: www.lonelyplanet.com/ip

Although the authors and Lonely Planet have taken all reasonable care in preparing this book, we make no warranty about the accuracy or completeness of its content and, to the maximum extent permitted, disclaim all liability arising from its use.